Twenty Questions for the Writer

A Rhetoric with Readings

Sixth Edition

Jacqueline Berke
Drew University

Randal Woodland
University of Michigan–Dearborn

Harcourt Brace College Publishers

Fort Worth   Philadelphia   San Diego   New York   Orlando   Austin   San Antonio

Toronto   Montreal   London   Sydney   Tokyo

Publisher	Ted Buchholz
Senior Acquisitions Editor	Stephen T. Jordan
Developmental Editor	Tia Black
Senior Project Editor	Cliff Crouch
Production Manager	Serena Barnett Manning
Art Directors	Vicki Whistler, Priscilla Mingus
Literary Permissions Editor	Cristi Greider
Picture Development Editor	Lili Weiner

Library of Congress Catalog Card Number: 94–76735

International Standard Book Number: 0-15-500857-9

Copyright © 1995, 1990, 1985, 1981, 1976, 1972
by Harcourt Brace & Company

Address for editorial correspondence:
Harcourt Brace College Publishers
301 Commerce Street, Suite 3700
Fort Worth, Texas 76102

Address for orders:
Harcourt Brace, Inc.
6277 Sea Harbor Drive
Orlando, Florida, 32887
Phone:
800/782-4479, or
(*in Florida only*) 800/433-0001

Cover illustration by Michael Crampton, Washington, D.C.

Printed in the United States of America

4 5 6 7 8 9 0 1 2 3   016   9 8 7 6 5 4 3 2 1

Twenty Questions for the Writer
A Rhetoric with Readings

PREFACE

In producing the sixth edition of *Twenty Questions for the Writer: A Rhetoric with Readings,* we have tried to retain those features that users have found most valuable, while updating the book for a new generation of teachers and students.

Those who have used the book before will recognize its familiar organization around the twenty questions that writers most often use in finding and developing their topics. This basic structure has proven remarkably versatile in encompassing new insights into the writing process. Far from a rigid set of modes or a narrowly defined array of prose models, these questions function as critical strategies that help writers to explore their subject actively and in depth, as well as from various angles and perspectives.

Because of its flexible organization, this book can be used in a variety of course plans, whether organized around modes or aims. The Thematic Table of Contents and the Table of Contents by Aims allow teachers to choose readings that will work with a range of course plans. Rather than being mode-driven, this book encourages use of the modes both as strategies for critical thinking and as heuristics for intervention and discovery. Also familiar will be *Twenty Questions'* grounding in classical rhetoric. Even as electronic communication makes possible forms of writing barely imagined even 20 years ago, the works of Aristotle and Quintilian and of such later rhetoricians as Hugh Blair still offer clear and relevant insights to today's student writers. Combined with a discussion of newer rhetorical concepts such as discourse communities, this classical background provides a solid practical basis for student writing. Our book incorporates aims-based writing, but moves beyond it by offering more focused and specific prompts to writing through the questioning strategy.

Many of the readings in the book—almost forty percent—are new. We offer an increased number of essays by women and people of color, making the book more representative of contemporary classrooms and neighborhoods. We have worked to make our book look like America. Students and teachers will be engaged with new readings on chaos theory, AIDS, hip hop music, and the Holocaust. These essays are not only interesting to read, but provide dynamic models of the twenty questions in action.

The Thematic Table of Contents demonstrates that readings in *Twenty Questions for the Writer* are drawn from a range of subject matter, including biology, physics, history, linguistics, sociology, literary study, and political science. In addition, we have given special attention to the kinds of writing situations that students will face in academic settings, focusing on the particular discourse communities they will encounter. Much of the writing students will do in the near future is writing for other college courses. This book gives particular attention to academic writing and writing across the curriculum. We have demonstrated how working with these twenty questions will prepare students for the writing they will be asked to do across the curriculum—in the natural sciences, management, sociology, history, education—even in English classes!

In the sixth edition, we have provided a broader treatment of the writing process, offering extended discussions of prewriting activities and revision strategies. Students are encouraged to try out different approaches to discover which strategies will most help their own particular writing processes.

The new writing opportunities offered by computer use have inspired many changes in this edition. We give fuller attention to the role of computers in the writing process. Library research, too, has been dramatically transformed, and our treatment of the research process offers advice on making the best use of the information available. We encourage students to develop a library search strategy that enables them to plan their research and evaluate the information they find. Two student research papers demonstrate the outcome of such research and provide examples of MLA and APA documentation systems.

Users of *Twenty Questions* will also appreciate the increased number of photographs throughout the book that can be used as prompts to stimulate interesting writing. Chapters contain numerous discussion questions and exercises along with writing assignments geared to the readings.

A reorganized and redesigned "Guide to Effective Language" brings together our treatment of the many writing skills that students will master on the way to becoming accomplished writers. Chapters on writing effective paragraphs and sentences provide guidance for avoiding mistakes and for forging a mature style.

As in previous editions, the twenty questions provide a framework for course design. Though sections are self-contained, they build upon one another. From simple narration and description to complex analysis, chapters engage students with progressively more demanding critical strategies that encourage more sophisticated writing. A cluster of questions leading to summary, evaluation, and analysis provides a focus for discussing means of responding to texts.

We have included much more in this textbook than any single class will cover in a single term. This allows teachers to use their professional judgment in choosing the readings and writing assignments that best meet the needs of individual classes, while keeping class discussions fresh, term after term and year after year. The movement of the twenty questions (toward increasingly demanding analytical writing) ensures that students will continue to receive the challenges and stimulation so necessary for growth.

Our work on this book has been guided by the expert hands of our editors at Harcourt Brace: Stephen T. Jordan, Tia Black, and Clifford Crouch. Their vision and hard work have made this a better book than we could have produced working alone. We are also indebted to teachers across the country who have made comments and suggestions on previous editions:

William Ballard, Becone College; Betty Bolling, Bacon College; Margaret Bretschneider, Lakeland Community College; Richard Costner, Tennessee Temple University; Walter Everett, Indiana State University at Evansville; Joseph Flory, Eastern Kentucky University; Ruth Foreman, South Dakota State University; Loris Galford, McNeese State University; Jennifer Ginn, The University of North Carolina at Chapel Hill; Linda Haskins, Delaware State College; Maureen Houg, Wichita State; Harvey Kasselbaum, Cuyahoga Community College; Susan Betts Landstrom, The University of North Carolina at Chapel Hill; Janet L. Larson, Rutgers University; Roy McAuley, Central Missouri State University; Jayne Menich, University of Wisconsin; George Miller, University of Delaware; Virginia Oram, Southern Methodist University; Peggy Pryzant, Modesto Junior College; Martha Ravits, University of Oregon; Allen Ramsey, Central Missouri State University; Kathy Reuter, University of North Carolina at Chapel Hill; William Sartoris, Camden County Community

College; Louis Spatola, Camden County Community College; Ralph St. Louis, University of Evansville; Jo Koster Tarvers, The University of North Carolina at Chapel Hill; John Teague, The University of North Carolina at Chapel Hill; Jim Vandergriff, Central Missouri State University; Ben Vasta, Camden County Community College; Linda P. Young, University of California, Davis; Sandra Vekasy, Evangel College.

Finally, we also thank the following colleagues for their recommendations for the sixth edition: Maureen Houg, Wichita State University; Peggy Jolly, University of Alabama at Birmingham; David Kann, California Polytechnic State; and Thomas Morgan, Southern University.

CONTENTS IN BRIEF

Part I — **The Writing Process**   1

Chapter   1   Exploring a Subject   2
Chapter   2   Planning a Paper   23
Chapter   3   Drafting a Paper   42
Chapter   4   Revising a Paper   63

Part II — **Writing a Short Paper: Twenty Questions**   88

Question   1   How can X be described?   91
Question   2   How did X happen?   111
Question   3   What kind of person is X?   132
Question   4   What is my memory of X?   159
Question   5   What is my personal response to X?   178
Question   6   What are the facts about X?   192
Question   7   What does X mean?   211
Question   8   What is the essential function of X?   228
Question   9   What are the component parts of X?   243
Question   10   How is X made or done?   259
Question   11   How should X be made or done?   275
Question   12   What are the causes of X?   289
Question   13   What are the consequences of X?   308
Question   14   What are the types of X?   319
Question   15   How does X compare to Y?   334
Question   16   What is the present status of X?   356
Question   17   How can X be summarized?   369
Question   18   How should X be interpreted?   381
Question   19   What is the value of X?   403
Question   20   What case can be made for or against X?   427

Part III — **Beyond the Short Paper**   474

Chapter   5   Generating a Longer Paper   476
Chapter   6   Researching a Longer Paper   505
Chapter   7   Writing a Longer Paper   534

Part IV — **A Guide to Effective Language**   558

Chapter   8   Using Paragraphs Effectively   560
Chapter   9   Using Sentences Effectively   579
Chapter   10   Using Words Effectively   606
Chapter   11   Writing Correct Sentences   618
Chapter   12   Editing and Proofreading   648

CONTENTS

Preface   v
Contents in Brief   ix
Contents by Theme   xxi
Contents by Aim   xxvi
Introduction: Why We Write   xxix

Part I   The Writing Process   1

Chapter 1   Exploring a Subject   2

FINDING A SUBJECT   3
    Listing Possible Subjects   4
    Focusing a Subject   4
    Aristotle's Categories   5
    Asking the Right Questions   6
    Twenty Questions to Ask   7
    From Subject to Writing Topic   9
    Beyond the Twenty Questions   9
DEVELOPING A SUBJECT   10
    Freewriting   11
    Talking to Yourself   13
    Talking to Other People   15
    Brainstorming   15
    Conjuring Up Memories   16
    Keeping a Writer's Journal   18
    Sharpening Powers of Observation   19
    Burke's Pentad   21

Chapter 2   Planning a Paper   23

LOOKING FOR PATTERNS   24
    Clustering   24
UNDERSTANDING THE RHETORICAL SITUATION   28
    Visualizing Your Audience   28
    Establishing a Reader–Writer Relationship   31
ORGANIZING A SUBJECT   34
    Natural Order   35
    Logical Order   35
    Intuitive Order   36
    The Working Plan   38

Chapter 3   Drafting a Paper   42

PARAGRAPH DIVISION   43
THE PARAGRAPH AS A MINIATURE ESSAY   46
PARAGRAPH DEVELOPMENT   47
    Examples   47
    Illustrations   47
    Details   48
    Reasons   49
    Mixed Materials   50
PARAGRAPH UNITY   51
PARAGRAPH COHERENCE   52
    Ordering Principles   53
    Using Transitions   53
    Consistency of Tone   55
THE NEED FOR COHERENCE   55
WRITING SPECIAL PARAGRAPHS   57
    Getting Started   57
    Ending the Paper   61

Chapter 4   Revising a Paper   63
WRITING AND REWRITING   64
    Vision and Revision   65
    Becoming Your Own Editor   66
A PRACTICAL GUIDE TO REVISION   66
    Three Steps in Revision   67
    Five Revision Strategies   68
TWO CASE STUDIES OF REVISION   72
    Case Study 1: A Famous Speech   72
    Case Study 2: Four Successive Student Drafts   79

Part II   Writing a Short Paper: Twenty Questions   88

QUESTION 1 HOW CAN X BE DESCRIBED?   91
EFFECTIVE SELECTION OF DETAIL   92
    Coming to Antigua Jamaica Kincaid   94
EFFECTIVE ARANGEMENT OF DETAILS   98
    The Kingdom of Didd Dr. Seuss   98
    Moonrise over Monument Valley John V. Young   99
    The Earthquake Jonathan Spence   100
DESCRIBING TO INFORM AND DELIGHT   101
    The School at Aké Wole Soyinka   101
DESCRIBING TO CREATE MOOD AND MEANING   104
    Shady Grove, Alabama, July 1936 James Agee   104

QUESTION 2 HOW DID X HAPPEN?   111

STRUCTURE IN NARRATION   112
      A Night in a Calabrian Village Nikos Kazantzakis   112
      An Afternoon in Cleveland Randall Kenan   114
POINT OF VIEW IN NARRATION   116
      Boy Meets Girl, Boy Loses Girl, Man Gets Woman Pete Hamill   117
IMMEDIACY IN NARRATION   120
      When you Gotta Go Truman Capote   120
AUTOBIOGRAPHICAL NARRATION   122
      Not Poor, Just Broke Dick Gregory   122
HISTORICAL NARRATION   124
      Pickett's Charge Shelby Foote   124

QUESTION 3 WHAT KIND OF PERSON IS X?   132
A MEMBER OF THE FAMILY   133
      My Mother Alfred Kazin   133
      The Poets in the Kitchen Paule Marshall   137
      Uncle Bun Maxine Hong Kingston   140
A FAMOUS WOMAN   144
      Sylvia Plath Katinka Matson   144
A MEMORABLE TEACHER   150
      The Prim Mr. Fleagle Russell Baker   150
A TYPE OF PERSON   152
      The Just: The Brave Christians Who Saved Jews from the Nazis
            Elie Wiesel   152

QUESTION 4 WHAT IS MY MEMORY OF X?   159
THE QUALITY OF MEMORY   160
      The Quality of Memory Thomas Wolfe   160
EARLIEST MEMORIES   161
      Everything Has a Name Helen Keller   163
REMEMBERING PLACES   164
      Village Home Subhabrata Bapi Sen   165
REMEMBERING EVENTS   166
      Death of a Pig E. B. White   167
THE PURPOSE OF MEMORY   172
      Sifting Through the Evidence Paul Monette   173

QUESTION 5 WHAT IS MY PERSONAL RESPONSE TO X?   178
THE PERSONAL ESSAY   179
      At the Dam Joan Didion   179
AN APPRECIATION   181
      Crazy about Weather Vanes David M. Schwartz   182
A PERSONAL LETTER   183
      Letter to Sarah Sullivan Ballou   183

A PERSONAL RESPONSE TO A CURRENT ISSUE   184
       Erin Go Brawl Anna Quindlen   185
A PROTEST   186
       Why I Want a Wife Judy Syfers   186

QUESTION 6 WHAT ARE THE FACTS ABOUT X?   192
THE FACTUAL ESSAY   193
RANGE OF PURPOSES   193
       Providing Information   193
       Here Is the Jersey Tomato Deborah A. Boerner   194
       Clearing up Misconceptions   196
       Sweet Truths about Sugar Elizabeth M. Whelan and Frederick J.
           Stare, M.D.   196
       Demystifying the Difficult   198
       The Expanding Universe Stephen Hawking   199
       Making a Social Comment   201
       Inequalities in Education Jonathan Kozol   201
THE FACTUAL FEATURE STORY   202
       All the Facts (Some True) about Gondolas MacDonald Harris   203

QUESTION 7 WHAT DOES X MEAN?   211
EXPLORING A SUBJECT THROUGH DEFINITION   212
       A Definition of Philosophy Bertrand Russell   212
METHODS OF DEVELOPING A DEFINITION   214
       By Citing Different Meanings of X   214
       Three Meanings of Grammar W. Nelson Francis   214
       By Tracing the Historical Development of X   215
       "Universe" and "University" Isaac Asimov   215
       By Restoring the Original Meaning of X   216
       What the Word "Liberal" Used to Mean Ron Brandmayr, Jr.   216
       By Tracing the Development of X as a New Term   216
       What Is Chaos? James Gleick   216
       By Combining Methods   219
       The Limitations of "Holocaust" Michael Berenbaum   219
       By Denoting Formal Definition   220
       By Composing One's Own Definition   220
       What Makes a "Jerk" a Jerk? Sidney Harris   220
       By Describing Experiences   221
       Democracy E.B. White   222
       Mommy, What Does "Nigger" Mean? Gloria Naylor   222

QUESTION 8 WHAT IS THE ESSENTIAL FUNCTION OF X?   228
THE FUNCTION OF A CRITIC   229
       What is the Function of a Critic? W. H. Auden   229

THE FUNCTION OF A WORD 230
>We Are, Like, Poets* Jim Frederick 230
THE FUNCTION OF EDUCATION 231
Another School Year—What For? John Ciardi 231
THE FUNCTION OF SCIENCE 234
The Tucson Zoo Lewis Thomas 234
THE FUNCTION OF HOLIDAYS 236
National Holidays Unite Us Douglas Greenberg 236

QUESTION 9 WHAT ARE THE COMPONENT PARTS OF X? 243
THINKING ANALYTICALLY 244
WRITING ANALYTICALLY 244
Analysis of Education 245
The Skills of Liberal Learning Mike Rose 245
Analysis of a Group 247
A Generation Without a Name Neil Howe and Bill Strauss 247
Analysis of an Institution 250
What Really *Makes a Marriage Work* Francine Klagsbrun 251
Analysis of an Art 254
Five Basic Elements of Music David Randolph 254
Analysis of an Essay 255
The Rhetorical Stance of David Randolph in "Five Basic Elements of Music" 256

QUESTION 10 HOW IS X MADE OR DONE? 259
THE CREATIVE PROCESS 260
Composing a Ballet Agnes DeMille 260
Creating an American Richard Rodriguez 262
PERSONAL PROCESSES 265
How I Learned a New Way to Write Christopher Lee 265
Shootin' the Bull Doug Christian 268
INTELLECTUAL PROCESS 269
Thinking Scientifically T. H. Huxley 269

QUESTION 11 HOW SHOULD X BE MADE OR DONE? 275
QUALITIES OF GOOD "HOW-TO" WRITING 276
Southern Fried Chicken with Country Gravy Bill Neal 276
How to Run for Office in a Very Small Town Shirley Weissenborn 278
VISUALIZING THE "HOW-TO" AUDIENCE 280
How to Lose Weight Sensibly and Successfully and Permanently Norman Kaplan, M.D. 280
Verbs, or, *Put the Pedal to the Metal* Rita Mae Brown 282

QUESTION 12 WHAT ARE THE CAUSES OF X? 289

THE PERENNIAL WHY   290
    On Speaking of Speaking Lewis Thomas   290
    A Small Cause Primo Levi   293
CAUSE AND CONDITION   295
EXPLAINING REASONS   296
    Why College Students Take a Sabbatical Hilary Stout   296
    Why We Dream About the Stars Peggy Noonan   299
PRESENTING PERSONAL REASONS   301
    Remembering Mr. Sweet Alice Walker   302

QUESTION 13 WHAT ARE THE CONSEQUENCES OF X?   308
PREDICTING CONSEQUENCES   309
    Computers and the New Literacy Benjamin Compaine   309
REPORTING CONSEQUENCES   312
    My Wood E. M. Forster   312
IGNORING AND DEPLORING CONSEQUENCES   314
    A Generation Under Curfew Mike Davis   314

QUESTION 14 WHAT ARE THE TYPES OF X?   319
CREATING A CLASSIFICATION   320
    Jung's Psychological Types Frieda Fordham   320
CLASSIFICATION ACCORDING TO PURPOSE   321
    Three Types of Resistance to Oppression The Rev. Martin Luther
        King, Jr.   322
COMPLETENESS OF CLASSIFICATION   324
    Three Kinds of Discipline John Holt   325

QUESTION 15 HOW DOES X COMPARE TO Y?   334
PRINCIPLES OF COMPARISON   335
ORGANIZING A COMPARISON   337
    Grant and Lee: A Study in Contrasts Bruce Catton   337
    Their Amazing Grace Jerry Adler   340
    Comparison of Parts   344
    That Lean and Hungry Look Suzanne Jordan   345
    Similarities and Differences   346
    The Gumbo Battle Peter Feibleman   347
    Comparing Poems   350
    Death Be Not Proud John Donne   350
    Do Not Go Gentle into that Good Night Dylan Thomas   350
    Timor Mortis Conturbat Me R. L. Chapman   351
    Here Paul Monette   351

QUESTION 16 WHAT IS THE PRESENT STATUS OF X?   356
CONCERNING AN HISTORIC MONUMENT   357

No News from Auschwitz A. M. Rosenthal   357
CONCERNING SPORTS—AND WOMEN   359
 The First Girl at Second Base Susan Jacoby   359
CONCERNING TRAVEL   361
 The Latest Fashion in Travel Jan Morris   361
CONCERNING A RECENT EVENT   363
 Giving Voice to Hurt and Betrayal Seth Mydans   363

QUESTION 17 HOW CAN X BE SUMMARIZED?   369
SUMMARIZING IDEAS   370
 Race Matters Cornel West   370
SUMMARIZING PLOT (SYNOPSIS)   376
SUMMARIZING EVENTS   378
 The Paradox of the Sixties James Reston   378

QUESTION 18 HOW SHOULD X BE INTERPRETED?   381
INTERPRETING AN ACTIVITY   382
 Football—The Game of Aggression George Stade   382
INTERPRETING BEHAVIOR   383
 Hallowed Be the Mall Kenneth Cole   384
INTERPRETING A STORY   388
 Clay James Joyce   388
 Interpretation of Joyce's "Clay" Florence L. Walzl   392
INTERPRETING A POEM   394
 anyone lived in a pretty how town e. e. cummings   394
 An Interpretation of cummings' "anyone lived in a pretty how town"
  R. W. Stallman   395
 Additional Poems   397
 Winter Trees Sylvia Plath   397
 Your Departure versus the Hindenburg Richard Brautigan   397
INTERPRETING POPULAR CULTURE   397
 Honky Tonking Molly Ivins   398

QUESTION 19 WHAT IS THE VALUE OF X?   403
EVALUATING A BOOK   404
 Review of A Weave of Women, *by E. M. Broner* John Leonard   405
 Shakespeare's Most Riddling Creation (Review of *Shylock: A Legend and
  Its Legacy,* by John Gross) John Simon   407
EVALUATING A FILM   412
 Predators (Review of Steven Spielberg's *Jurassic Park*) Terrence
  Rafferty   412
 Shakespeare in the Sun (Review of Kenneth Branagh's *Much Ado about
  Nothing*) Anne Barton   415
EVALUATING A TELEVISION SHOW   424

Review of Discover: The World of Science Merrill Panitt   424

QUESTION 20 WHAT CASE CAN BE MADE FOR OR AGAINST X?   427
 THE NATURE OF ARGUMENT   429
    Is and *Ought* Propositions   429
    College Lectures Are Obsolete Allan H. Gilbert   430
 THE STRUCTURE OF ARGUMENT   433
    Shame on Ads that Use Culture to Sell Liquor Nicole Harris   435
 FUNDAMENTALS OF LOGIC   436
    Deduction and Induction   436
 ARGUMENT BY ANALOGY   440
    The Great White Myth Anna Quindlen   441
    Common Logical Fallacies   443
 ARGUING FOR AND AGAINST   445
    Animal Research: An Unnecessary Evil? Ann Squire   446
    On Experimenting with Animals George Bernard Shaw   448
    A Humane and Scientific Necessity Robert J. White   449
 MODERN ARGUMENT: THE EDITORIAL   455
    A Word for the New York Accent Richard Shepard   455
 HUMANIZING ARGUMENT: ROGERIAN STRATEGY   456
    Inaugural Address Bill Clinton   458
 TESTING YOUR ARGUMENT: A CHECKLIST   461
    In Defense of Voluntary Euthanasia Sidney Hook   461
    Communication: Its Blocking and Its Facilitation Carl R. Rogers   469

Part III   Beyond the Short Paper   474

Chapter 5   Generating a Longer Paper   476
 ANSWERING MANY QUESTIONS   477
 TO INFORM   477
    Speaking with a Single Tongue Jared Diamond   477
 TO INTERPRET   485
    Isaac Newton I. Bernard Cohen   486
 TO PERSUADE   490
    Letter from Birmingham Jail The Rev. Martin Luther King, Jr.   491

Chapter 6   Researching a Longer Paper   505
 DETERMINING SUBJECT AND PURPOSE   507
 USING THE LIBRARY   507
    Catalogs   508
    General Reference Books   512
    Subject-specific Reference Books   516
    Periodical Indexes and Abstracts   518

Government Publications   519
DEVELOPING A RESEARCH STRATEGY   520
PLANNING YOUR TIME   520
GATHERING INFORMATION   521
    For a Short Paper   521
    For a Long Paper   523
IDENTIFYING AND EVALUATING SOURCES   525
TAKING NOTES   527
    Direct Quotation   528
    Paraphrase   528
    Summary   530
    Photocopying   532
AVOIDING PLAGIARISM   532

Chapter 7   Writing a Longer Paper   **534**
DRAFTING YOUR PAPER   535
CITING SOURCES   536
    Summary and Paraphrase   536
    Direct Quotation   536
DOCUMENTATION   538
    In-Text Notes   538
    Footnotes and Endnotes   539
    Final Bibliography   539
EXTENDED HISTORICAL PROCESS ANALYSIS   542
    The Molly Maguire Movement Melody Rammel   543
EXTENDED CAUSAL EXPLANATION   549
    Ireland: When Economic and Cultural Agendas Clash
        Matthew Rindfleisch   549

Part IV   A Guide to Effective Language   **558**

Chapter 8   Using Paragraphs Effectively   **560**
PARAGRAPH COHERENCE   561
    Transitional Devices   561
PARAGRAPH PATTERNS   562
    Coordinate Sequence   563
    Subordinate Sequence   565
    Mixed Sequence   568
    Placement of Topic Sentence   571

Chapter 9   Using Sentences Effectively   **579**
COMPOSING SENTENCES   580
    Combining Sentences   580
    Expanding Sentences   582

REVISING FOR AN EFFECTIVE STYLE   585
    Revising for Unity   585
    Revising for Economy   587
    Revising for Emphasis   591
    Revising for Vigor   593
    Revising for Rhythm   595
FORGING A BETTER STYLE   603

Chapter 10   Using Words Effectively   606

WORDS: THE WRITER'S TOOL   607
CHOOSING THE RIGHT WORD   607
    The Natural Word   608
    The Concrete Word   609
    The Accurate Word   609
    The Fresh Word   612
    The Figurative Word   613
    The Connotative Word   615

Chapter 11   Writing Correct Sentences   618

LEARNING GRAMMAR   619
REVIEWING THE GRAMMAR OF THE SENTENCE   621
    Subjects   621
    Predicates   622
    Relationships of Words   627
    Sentence Types   629
REVISING FOR CORRECTNESS   630
    Grammatical Form   630
    Sentence Integrity   638
    Sentence Coherence   641

Chapter 12   Editing and Proofreading   648

PUNCTUATION   649
    Linking Punctuation   650
    Separating Punctuation   652
    Enclosing Punctuation   655
    Punctuation Indicating Omissions   659
MECHANICS   661
    Capitalization   661
    Italics   662
    Abbreviations and Contractions   663
    Numbers   663
SPELLING   664

List of Works Cited   669
Permissions   671
Index   677

CONTENTS BY THEME

Art and Creativity

Katinka Matson — *Sylvia Plath*   144
W. H. Auden — *What Is the Function of a Critic?*   229
David Randolph — *Five Basic Elements of Music*   254
Agnes DeMille — *Composing a Ballet*   260
Jerry Adler — *Their Amazing Grace*   340
Peter Feibleman — *The Gumbo Battle*   347
John Donne — *Death Be Not Proud*   350
Dylan Thomas — *Do Not Go Gentle into That Good Night*   350
R. L. Chapman — *Timor Mortis Conturbat Me*   351
James Joyce — *Clay*   388
Florence L. Wazl — *Interpretation of James Joyce's "Clay"*   392
e. e. cummings — *anyone lived in a pretty how town*   394
R. W. Stallman — *An Interpretation of cummings' "anyone lived in a pretty how town"*   395
Sylvia Plath — *Winter Trees*   397
Richard Brautigan — *Your Departure versus the Hindenburg*   397
Molly Ivins — *Honky-Tonking*   398
John Simon — *Shakespeare's Most Riddling Creation*   407
Terrence Rafferty — *Predators*   412

Culture and Identity

Paule Marshall — *The Poets in the Kitchen*   137
MacDonald Harris — *All the Facts (Some True) About Gondolas*   203
Ron Brandmayr, Jr. — *What the Word "Liberal" Used to Mean*   216
Richard Rodriguez — *Creating an American*   262
Jerry Adler — *Their Amazing Grace*   340
Peter Feibleman — *The Gumbo Battle*   347
Seth Mydans — *Giving Voice to Hurt and Betrayal*   363
Nicole Harris — *Shame on Ads that Use Culture to Sell Liquor*   435
Jared Diamond — *Speaking with a Single Tongue*   477

Life and Death

James Agee — *Shady Grove, Alabama, 1936*   104
Elie Wiesel — *The Just: The Brave Christians Who Saved Jews from the Nazis*   152
Paul Monette — *Sifting Through the Evidence*   173
Sullivan Ballou — *Letter to Sarah*   183

Michael Berenbaum   *The Limitations of "Holocaust"*   219
Primo Levi   *A Small Cause*   293
John Donne   *Death Be Not Proud*   350
Dylan Thomas   *Do Not Go Gentle into That Good Night*   350
R. L. Chapman   *Timor Mortis Conturbat Me*   351
Paul Monette   *Here*   351
A. M. Rosenthal   *No News from Auschwitz*   357
Sidney Hook   *In Defense of Voluntary Euthanasia*   461

Education
Wole Soyinka   *The School at Aké*   101
Paule Marshall   *The Poets in the Kitchen*   137
Russell Baker   *The Prim Mr. Fleagle*   150
Jonathan Kozol   *Inequalities in Education*   201
Bertrand Russell   *A Definition of Philosophy*   212
Isaac Asimov   *"Universe" and "University"*   215
John Ciardi   *Another School Year—What For?*   231
Mike Rose   *The Skills of Liberal Learning*   245
Christopher Lee   *How I Learned a New Way to Write*   265
Hilary Stout   *Why College Students Take
                             a Sabbatical*   296
Benjamin Compaine   *Computers and the New Literacy*   309
John Holt   *Three Kinds of Discipline*   325
Allan H. Gilbert   *College Lectures Are Obsolete*   430

Family
Alfred Kazin   *My Mother*   133
Paule Marshall   *The Poets in the Kitchen*   137
Maxine Hong Kingston   *Uncle Bun*   140
Subhabrata Bapi Sen   *Village Home*   165
Sullivan Ballou   *Letter to Sarah*   183

Gender
Paule Marshall   *The Poets in the Kitchen*   137
Judy Syfers   *Why I Want a Wife*   186
Susan Jacoby   *The First Girl at Second Base*   359
Molly Ivins   *Honky-Tonking*   398
Anne Barton   *Shakespeare in the Sun*   415

Health
Elizabeth Whelan and   *Sweet Truths About Sugar*   196
  Frederick J. Stare, M. D.
Norman Kaplan, M.D.   *How to Lose Weight Sensibly and Successfuly and
                             Permanently*   280

Suzanne Jordan   *That Lean and Hungry Look*   345
Ann Squire   *Animal Research: An Unnecessary Evil?*   446
George Bernard Shaw   *On Experimenting with Animals*   448
Robert J. White   *A Humane and Scientific Necessity*   449

History

Shelby Foote   *Pickett's Charge*   124
Ron Brandmayr, Jr.   *What the Word "Liberal" Used to Mean*   216
Michael Berenbaum   *The Limitations of "Holocaust"*   219
Lewis Thomas   *On Speaking of Speaking*   290
Primo Levi   *A Small Cause*   293
Bruce Catton   *Grant and Lee: A Study in Contrasts*   337
James Reston   *The Paradox of the Sixties*   378

Language and Writing

Theodore Sorenson   *Writing and Rewriting the Inaugural Address*   72
Paule Marshall   *The Poets in the Kitchen*   137
Russell Baker   *The Prim Mr. Fleagle*   150
Helen Keller   *Everything Has a Name*   163
W. Nelson Francis   *Three Meanings of Grammar*   214
Ron Brandmayr, Jr.   *What the Word "Liberal" Used to Mean*   216
Gloria Naylor   *Mommy, What Does "Nigger" Mean?*   222
Jim Frederick   *We Are, Like, Poets*   230
Mike Rose   *The Skills of Liberal Learning*   245
Christopher Lee   *How I Learned a New Way to Write*   265
Rita Mae Brown   *Verbs, or, Put the Pedal to the Metal*   282
Lewis Thomas   *On Speaking of Speaking*   290
Richard Shepard   *A Word for the New York Accent*   455
Jared Diamond   *Speaking with a Single Tongue*   477
Carl Rogers   *Communication: Its Blocking and Facilitation*   469

Leisure

David M. Schwartz   *Crazy About Weather Vanes*   182
Susan Jacoby   *The First Girl at Second Base*   359
Jan Morris   *The Latest Fashion in Travel*   361
George Stade   *Football—The Game of Aggression*   382
Kenneth Cole   *Hallowed Be the Mall*   384

The Natural World

John V. Young   *Moonrise Over Monument Valley*   99
Jonathan Spence   *The Earthquake*   100
E. B. White   *Death of a Pig*   167
Joan Didion   *At the Dam*   179
Stephen Hawking   *The Expanding Universe*   199

Deborah A. Boerner — *Here Is the Jersey Tomato*   194
James Gleick — *What Is Chaos?*   216
Doug Christian — *Shootin' the Bull*   268
E. M. Forster — *My Wood*   312

People and Relationships
Nikos Kazantzakis — *A Night in a Calabrian Village*   112
Pete Hamill — *Boy Meets Girl. . .*   117
Truman Capote — *When You Gotta Go*   120
Alfred Kazin — *My Mother*   133
Maxine Hong Kingston — *Uncle Bun*   140
Katinka Matson — *Sylvia Plath*   144
Thomas Wolfe — *The Quality of Memory*   160
Sullivan Ballou — *Letter to Sarah*   183
Sidney J. Harris — *What Makes a "Jerk" a Jerk?*   220
Francine Klagsbrun — *What Really Makes a Marriage Work*   251
Alice Walker — *Remembering Mr. Sweet*   302
Freida Fordham — *Jung's Psychological Types*   320
Suzanne Jordan — *That Lean and Hungry Look*   345
Richard Brautigan — *Your Departure versus the Hindenburg*   397
Carl Rogers — *Communication: Its Blocking and Facilitation*   469

Race and Ethnicity
Randall Kenan — *An Afternoon in Cleveland*   114
Dick Gregory — *Not Poor, Just Broke*   122
Gloria Naylor — *Mommy, What Does "Nigger" Mean?*   222
Richard Rodriguez — *Creating an American*   262
Mike Davis — *A Generation Under Curfew*   314
Jerry Adler — *Their Amazing Grace*   340
Seth Mydans — *Giving Voice to Hurt and Betrayal*   363
Cornel West — *Race Matters*   370
John Simon — *Shakespeare's Most Riddling Creation*   407
Nicole Harris — *Shame on Ads that Use Culture to Sell Liquor*   435

Science and Technology
James Gleick — *What Is Chaos?*   216
T. H. Huxley — *Thinking Scientifically*   269
Peggy Noonan — *Why We Dream About the Stars*   299
Benjamin Compaine — *Computers and the New Literacy*   309
Terrence Rafferty — *Predators*   412
Merrill Panitt — *Review of* Discover: The World of Science   424
Robert J. White — *A Humane and Scientific Necessity*   449
I. Bernard Cohen — *Isaac Newton*   486

Politics and Society

John F. Kennedy   Inaugural Address   72
Jamaica Kincaid   *Coming to Antigua*   94
James Agee   *Shady Grove, Alabama, 1936*   104
Randall Kenan   *An Afternoon in Cleveland*   114
Dick Gregory   *Not Poor, Just Broke*   122
Ron Brandmayr, Jr.   *What the Word "Liberal" Used to Mean*   216
E. B. White   *Democracy*   222
Douglas Greenberg   *National Holidays Unite Us*   236
Richard Rodriguez   *Creating an American*   262
Shirley Weissenborn   *How to Run for Office in a Very Small Town*   278
Mike Davis   *A Generation Under Curfew*   314
Martin Luther King, Jr.   *Three Types of Resistance to Oppression*   322
Jerry Adler   *Their Amazing Grace*   340
A. M. Rosenthal   *No News from Auschwitz*   357
Bill Clinton   Inaugural Address   458
Martin Luther King, Jr.   *Letter from Birmingham Jail*   491

CONTENTS BY AIM

To Inform

Theodore Sorensen — *Writing and Rewriting the Inaugural Address*   72
John V. Young — *Moonrise over Monument Valley*   99
Jonathan Spence — *The Earthquake*   100
Wole Soyinka — *The School at Aké*   101
Randall Kenan — *An Afternoon in Cleveland*   114
Truman Capote — *When You Gotta Go*   120
Dick Gregory — *Not Poor, Just Broke*   122
Shelby Foote — *Pickett's Charge*   124
Alfred Kazin — *My Mother*   133
Maxine Hong Kingston — *Uncle Bun*   140
Katinka Matson — *Sylvia Plath*   144
Russell Baker — *The Prim Mr. Fleagle*   150
Helen Keller — *Everything Has a Name*   163
Subhabrata Bapi Sen — *Village Home*   165
David M. Schwartz — *Crazy about Weather Vanes*   182
Deborah A. Boerner — *Here Is the Jersey Tomato*   194
Elizabeth Whelan and Frederick J. Stare, M.D. — *Sweet Truths about Sugar*   196
Stephen Hawking — *The Expanding Universe*   199
Bertrand Russell — *A Definition of Philosophy*   212
W. Nelson Francis — *Three Meanings of Grammar*   214
Isaac Asimov — *"Universe" and "University"*   215
James Gleick — *What is Chaos?*   216
Mike Rose — *The Skills of Liberal Learning*   245
Francine Klagsbrun — *What Really Makes a Marriage Work*   251
David Randolph — *Five Basic Elements of Music*   254
Agnes DeMille — *Composing a Ballet*   260
Christopher Lee — *How I Learned a New Way to Write*   265
Doug Christian — *Shootin' the Bull*   268
T. H. Huxley — *Thinking Scientifically*   269
Bill Neal — *Southern Fried Chicken with Country Gravy*   276
Shirley Weissenborn — *How to Run for Office in a Very Small Town*   278
Norman Kaplan, M.D. — *How to Lose Weight Sensibly and Successfully and Permanently*   280
Lewis Thomas — *On Speaking of Speaking*   290
Hilary Stout — *Why College Students Take a Sabbatical*   296
Peggy Noonan — *Why We Dream about the Stars*   299
Benjamin Compaine — *Computers and the New Literacy*   309
Frieda Fordham — *Jung's Psychological Types*   320

John Holt   *Three Kinds of Discipline*   325

Bruce Catton   *Grant and Lee: A Study in Contrasts*   337

Jerry Adler   *Their Amazing Grace*   340

Susan Jacoby   *The First Girl at Second Base*   359

Jan Morris   *The Latest Fashion in Travel*   361

Seth Mydans   *Giving Voice to Hurt and Betrayal*   363

James Reston   *The Paradox of the Sixties*   378

Carl Rogers   *Communication: Its Blocking and Its Facilitation*   469

Jared Diamond   *Speaking with a Single Tongue*   477

I. Bernard Cohen   *Isaac Newton*   486

To Entertain

Dr. Seuss   *The Kingdom of Didd*   98

Nikos Kazantzakis   *A Night in a Calabrian Village*   112

Pete Hamill   *Boy Meets Girl, Boy Loses Girl, Man Gets Woman*   117

E. B. White   *Death of a Pig*   167

MacDonald Harris   *All the Facts (Some True) about Gondolas*   203

Sidney Harris   *What Makes a "Jerk" a Jerk?*   220

Jim Frederick   *We are, Like, Poets*   230

Rita Mae Brown   *Verbs, or, Put the Pedal to the Metal*   282

Suzanne Jordan   *That Lean and Hungry Look*   345

Peter Feibleman   *The Gumbo Battle*   347

James Joyce   *Clay*   388

Molly Ivins   *Honky Tonking*   398

To Express

James Agee   *Shady Grove, Alabama, 1936*   104

Paule Marshall   *The Poets in the Kitchen*   137

Thomas Wolfe   *The Quality of Memory*   160

Joan Didion   *At the Dam*   179

Sullivan Ballou   *Letter to Sarah*   183

Richard Rodriguez   *Creating an American*   262

Primo Levi   *A Small Cause*   293

Alice Walker   *Remembering Mr. Sweet*   302

E. M. Forster   *My Wood*   312

A. M. Rosenthal   *No News from Auschwitz*   357

John Donne   *Death Be Not Proud*   350

Dylan Thomas   *Do Not Go Gentle into that Good Night*   350

R. L. Chapman   *Timor Mortis Conturbat Me*   351

Paul Monette   *Here*   351

e. e. cummings   *anyone lived in a pretty how town*   394

Sylvia Plath   *Winter Trees*   397

Richard Brautigan   *Your Departure versus the Hindenburg*   397

To Argue
John F. Kennedy   Inaugural Address   72
Jamaica Kincaid   *Coming to Antigua*   94
Elie Wiesel   *The Just: The Brave Christians Who Saved Jews
                              from the Nazis*   152
Paul Monette   *Sifting through the Evidence*   173
Judy Syfers   *Why I Want A Wife*   186
Jonathan Kozol   *Inequalities in Education*   201
Ron Brandmayr, Jr.   *What the Word "Liberal" Used to Mean*   216
Michael Berenbaum   *The Limitations of "Holocaust"*   219
E. B. White   *Democracy*   222
Gloria Naylor   *Mommy, What Does "Nigger" Mean?*   222
W. H. Auden   *What is the Function of a Critic?*   229
John Ciardi   *Another School Year—What For?*   231
Lewis Thomas   *The Tucson Zoo*   234
Douglas Greenberg   *National Holidays Unite Us*   236
Neil Howe and Bill Strauss *A Generation Without a Name*   247
Mike Davis   *A Generation Under Curfew*   314
Martin Luther King, Jr.   *Three Types of Resistance to Oppression*   322
Cornel West   *Race Matters*   370
George Stade   *Football—The Game of Aggression*   382
Kenneth Cole   *Hallowed Be the Mall*   384
Florence L. Walzl   *Interpretation of Joyce's "Clay"*   392
R. W. Stallman   *An Interpretation of cummings' "anyone lived in a
                              pretty how town"*   395
John Simon   *Shakespeare's Most Riddling Creation*   407
Terrence Rafferty   *Predators*   412
Ann Barton   *Shakespeare in the Sun*   415
Merrill Panitt   *Review of Discover: The World of Science*   424
Allan H. Gilbert   *College Lectures Are Obsolete*   430
Nicole Harris   *Shame on Ads that Use Culture to Sell Liquor*   435
Anna Quindlen   *The Great White Myth*   441
Ann Squire   *Animal Research: An Unnecessary Evil?*   446
George Bernard Shaw   *On Experimenting with Animals*   448
Robert J. White   *A Humane and Scientific Necessity*   449
Richard Shepard   *A Word for the New York Accent*   455
Bill Clinton   Inaugural Address   458
Sidney Hook   *In Defense of Voluntary Euthanasia*   461
Martin Luther King, Jr.   *Letter from Birmingham Jail*   491

INTRODUCTION: WHY WE WRITE

Writing is a complex human activity comprising a daunting array of skills, abilities, and techniques. Before we begin to examine any particular facet of writing closely, let's ask the question, "Why do we write?" It's easy to get caught up in the work of finding a thesis, crafting an organizational plan, and using effective paragraphs, sentences, and words to get one's idea across—so easy, in fact, that we can lose track of why we sat down to write in the first place. For the next few weeks or months, your answer to the question "Why write?" may be "Because it's the assignment," "To get a good grade," or "To pass the course." Faced with these immediate concerns, you won't have much chance to ponder the larger questions of how writing shapes and reflects the activities of human communities. Considering these questions now may not make finishing your English paper any easier, but at least you'll be able to keep an eye on the larger context.

The simplest answer to the question "Why write?" is that we write to preserve our thoughts and communicate them to others. Perhaps you've awakened in the middle of the night with an idea for an English paper, a great invention, or an Oscar-winning screenplay. You flip on the light, scramble for a pencil and a scrap of paper and scribble some cryptic marks you'll vainly try to decipher in the cold light of morning. People write shopping lists as an aid to accurate memory; we write love letters to give concrete form to a swirl of emotions and desires; we write newspaper articles to convey accurate information to many readers; we write novels to create a world of characters and incidents into which others can enter for years to come. Though papers written for college or university courses may seem to have little to do with shopping lists, love letters, newspapers, or best-selling novels, such academic work often shares the elements of communication, permanence, accuracy, and complexity of those other kinds of writing. To communicate, to preserve, to get it right, to create—these are the *whys* that have led human beings to write across the centuries.

It is only when we view writing from the broadest perspective—as a means by which human beings communicate with one another, transmitting their accumulated culture from one generation to another—that we can see how vital our written language is not only to the life of the individual but to the total life of the community. "Greece and Rome [were] civilized by language," Ezra Pound tells us. The Greeks and Romans approached the art of writing through courses in "rhetoric" that trained young men (and rhetoric courses in those days *were* reserved exclusively for men) to speak effectively—whether to persuade a Greek city–state to levy a grain tax or to convince a court to acquit someone of murder or to marshal an army for a valiant attack on an enemy. The surviving records of such courses form the basis for the modern study of rhetoric.

Many people shy away from the word *rhetoric;* in this book we embrace it. Though *rhetoric* has come to be associated with lying politicians, it has a noble heritage as the art of using language to its best possible effect: to teach, to delight, to move an audience to considered and significant action. This view, that rhetoric issues from shared priciples and common aims is best expressed in Kenneth Burke's deeply moral definition of rhetoric as "the use of language to promote social cooperation in the human jungle." Thus the modern rhetorician—dedicated to the effective and forceful use of language—shuns verbal trickery, sophistry, and all forms of sensationalism and harangue, leaving these to the demagogue, the professional agitator, the propagandist. As citizens in a democracy—and particularly as members of a college community, where our special task is to search out truth—we are expected to make our appeals to reason rather than merely emotion: to inform and explain by indicating precisely how and why; to support, illustrate, demonstrate, amplify, and wherever possible prove our points; to express ourselves clearly and accurately. These qualities are the touchstones of responsible writing.

Only responsible writing makes possible an exchange of views: once you understand what I mean, you can reply to me, and I can then, in turn, reply to you. If both sides treat this exchange with respect and what psychotherapist Carl Rogers calls "empathetic understanding" (understanding *with* and not merely *about* the other person), the resulting dialogue may progress to "mutual communication." Rogers (quoted in Young, *Rhetoric*) says:

> Mutual communication tends to be pointed toward solving a problem rather than toward attacking a person or group. It leads to a situation in which I see how the problem appears to you, as well as to me, and you see how it appears to me, as well as to you. Thus accurately and realistically defined, the problem is almost certain to yield to intelligent attack, or if it is in part insoluble, it will be comfortably accepted as such.

In Question 20, "What case can be made for or against X?," we shall explore how to write such consensus-producing argument; here we may simply say that writing clearly, cogently, and compellingly is imperative. We must build bridges to one another with our written discourse; we must use it to unite and not divide us. Thanks to twentieth-century technology, we live in a global village where electronic media connect even the most remote areas of the world, but we are still tied to the written word as the basic means of human communication and interaction. On a personal and political level we still write to and *for* one another, as the increasing number of newspapers, magazines, and books demonstrates. Even though some social observers suggest that images are playing a greater role in the ways we communicate, we still use words as our primary means of communicating. Machine makers and button pushers follow written instructions. Radio and television programs originate in written proposals, treatments, and scripts. Diplomats and politicians negotiate—endlessly—in formal correspondence, proposals, even casual electronic mail messages. (Witness the huge collections of materials in the presidential libraries.) In short, whether preserved in filing cabinets or stored on computer diskettes, the written record is the vital witness of human endeavor.

BECOMING A MORE EFFECTIVE WRITER

Certainly, then, the ability to write clearly and persuasively is a basic need in our time. Unfortunately, this needs goes largely unfulfilled. Most people write poorly—and thus with great reluctance. As one student complained, pointing first to his head and then to the paper in front of him, "It's all up here; I just can't get it down there." Although he thought this was his unique problem, this student was actually voicing everyone's problem. Writing is the act of transmitting thoughts, feelings, and ideas from "up here" in the head to "down there" on paper. "Putting black on white," as one author described his work, is very exacting and very exciting.

When done well, writing requires many composite skills: (1) *mental*—you must be able to think clearly and to organize your ideas in an orderly, logical sequence; (2) *psychological*—you must feel free and sufficiently relaxed so that ideas will in fact move from head to hand; (3)

rhetorical—you must know the fundamentals of the craft: the various ways you can put sentences together to make a smoothly flowing, readable composition; (4) *critical*—once you have written something, you must be able to judge it, to know whether it is good or bad, and, if it is bad, to improve it.

Students often admit they realize a paper is poor when they turn it in, but they do not know how to improve it. They do not know *specifically* what is weak, or *specifically* how it can be strengthened. Unless we can evaluate our writing in a concrete and constructive way, we cannot hope to write clearly and communicate our ideas effectively. Professional writers who recognize that "hard writing makes easy reading" resign themselves to drudgery. Dorothy Parker complained, "I can't write five words but that I change seven." James Thurber, whose wit seems to have flowed effortlessly from his head to his typewriter, explained his laborious writing process this way:

> There is no writing, only re-writing. The first or second draft of everything I write reads as if it was turned out by a charwoman. For me it's mostly a question of rewriting. . . A story I've been working on—"The Train on Track Six" . . . was rewritten fifteen complete times . . . It's part of a constant attempt on my part to make the finished version smooth, to make it seem effortless.

To make the finished version seem effortless: This is the mark of a supremely good style. Good style is *unobtrusively* good; it does not call attention to itself. In fact, readers are barely aware of *how* the writer has written; they are aware only of *what* has been written; the subject matter alone stands out, not the writing. The writing flows smoothly, like a river moving onward with the current.

Many people who write are simply not aware of what is involved in the writing process. Writing involves thinking, planning, assembling, classifying, organizing—this *prewriting* is necessary for a clear presentation (not to mention the rewriting that comes later). Other people do realize what they need to do but stubbornly refuse to take the necessary pains. Their writing is obscure and hard to read because they will not submit to the discipline that leads to clarity. Unfortunately we sometimes must read the work of such authors: They surround us; sometimes they even write textbooks. Reading their writing means reading and rereading, often to no end, for their prose is an obstacle course through which we wend our uncertain way—as in the following passage:

> In conformity with the preceding point, if all the interacting parties in marriage, in minority–majority groups, in different occupational, religious, political, economic, racial, ethnic, and other interacting groups and persons view the given overly similar (or dissimilar) traits A, S, C, D, N (physical, biological, mental, socio-cultural) as negligible values or as no values at all, as compromising even no similarity (or dissimilarity), such overt similarities–dissimilarities are innocuous in the generation of either solidarity or antagonism (cited in Kiehaber, 129).

If at all possible, of course, the sensible reader refuses to read such gibberish, just as the sensible person refuses to visit a doctor who is careless or a lawyer who is incompetent. To begin with, the writer's thoughts are addled. (We wonder, "Does he know what he is talking about?") One phrase tumbles out after another in no discernible order, and excessive parentheses interrupt the flow of thought. The abstract words, jargon, and perplexing coding (A, B, C, D, N) make the reader's head spin. We can only guess at the writer's meaning. Of course, you cannot hope that a basic writing course—or even a four-year college education—will make you a first-rate writer in control of your craft. But you can expect to gain important insights into the art of writing. You will learn how to analyze a page of prose and to recognize how a piece of writing works. You will understand why some writing communicates and why some only distorts the intended meaning. Most important, you will gain greater control of your own writing; you will learn to find and develop ideas systematically and put them down on paper with greater fluency and flexibility.

THE QUALITIES OF GOOD WRITING

Even before you begin to write, you come prepared by instinct and intuition to make certain judgments about what is good. Take the following familiar sentence, for example: "I know not what course others may take, but as for me, give me liberty or give me death." Do you suppose this thought of Patrick Henry's would have come ringing down through the centuries if he had expressed this sentiment not in one tight rhythmical sentence but as follows?

> It would be difficult, if not impossible, to predict on the basis of my limited information as to the predilections of the public, what the citizenry at large will regard as action commensurate with the present provocation, but after arduous consideration I personally feel so intensely and irrevocably committed to the position of social, political, and economic independence that rather than submit to foreign and despotic control which is anathema to me, I will make the ultimate sacrifice of which humanity is capable—under the aegis of personal honor, ideological conviction, and existential commitment, I will sacrifice my own mortal existence.

How does this rambling, high-flown paraphrase measure up to the bold "Give me liberty or give me death?" Who will deny that something is happening in Patrick Henry's rousing challenge that not only fails to happen in the paraphrase but is actually negated there? Would you bear with this long-winded, pompous speaker to the end? If you were to judge this statement strictly on its rhetoric (its choice and arrangement of words), you might aptly call it more boring than brave. Perhaps a plainer version will work better:

> Liberty is a very important thing for a person to have. Most people—at least the people I've talked to or that other people have told me about—know this and therefore are very anxious to preserve their liberty. Of course I can't be absolutely sure about what other folks are going to do in this present crisis, what with all these threats and everything, but I've made up my mind that I'm going to fight because liberty is really a very important thing to me; at least that's the way I feel about it.

It's not an improvement either, is it? This flat, "homely" prose, weighted down with what French author Gustave Flaubert called "fatty deposits," is grammatical enough. As in the pompous paraphrase, every verb agrees with its subject and every comma is in its proper place; nonetheless it lacks the qualities that make a statement—of one sentence or one hundred pages—pungent, vital, moving, and memorable.

Let us identify these qualities and describe them briefly. (They are described in greater detail at the end of this volume.)

Economy

The first quality of good writing is *economy.* In an appropriately slender volume, *The Elements of Style,* authors William Strunk, Jr., and E. B. White state the case for economy concisely:

> A sentence should contain no unnecessary words, for the same reason that a drawing should have no unnecessary lines and a machine no unnecessary parts. This requires not that the writer make all his sentences short or that he avoid all detail . . . but that every word tell.

In other words, economical writing is *efficient* and *aesthetically satisfying.* While it demands little energy and patience of readers, it returns to them a maximum of sharply compressed meaning. This is one of your basic responsibilities as a writer: to inflict no unnecessary words on your reader—just as a dentist inflicts no unnecessary pain, a lawyer no unnecessary risk. Economical writing avoids strain and at the same time promotes pleasure by producing a sense of form and right proportion, a sense of words that hit the ideas they embody. Economical writing contains no deadwood to dull the reader's attention, not an extra, useless phrase to clog the free flow of ideas, one following swiftly and clearly upon another.

Simplicity

Another basic quality of good writing is *simplicity.* Here again this does not mean that you make all your sentences sound like a second-grade reading book or that you reduce complexities to the bare bones, but rather that you avoid embellishment and embroidery. A natural, unpretentious style is best. It signifies sincerity, for one thing: When people actually say what they mean, they tend to say it with disarming simplicity. But paradoxically, simplicity or naturalness does not come naturally. By the time we are old enough to write, most of us have grown so self-conscious that we stiffen when we are called upon to make a statement in speech or in writing. It is easy to offer the kindly advice "Be Yourself," but many people do not feel like themselves when they take a pencil in hand or sit down at a word processor. During the early days of World War II, when air raids were feared in New York City and blackouts were instituted, an anonymous civil servant produced and distributed the following poster:

Illumination
Is Required
to be
Extinguished
on These Premises
After Nightfall

What this meant, of course, was simply "Lights Out After Dark." But apparently that direct imperative—clear and to the point—did not sound "official" enough, so the writer resorted to long, Latinate words and involved syntax (note the awkward passives "is required" and "to be extinguished") to establish a tone of dignity and authority. In contrast, how beautifully simple are the words of the translators of the King James Version of the Bible, who felt no need for flourish or flamboyance. In their words, the Lord did not proclaim that universal illumination was required to be instantaneously installed. Simply but majestically they tell the story: "God said, Let there be light: and there was light. . . . And God called the light Day, and the darkness He called Night."

Most memorable declarations have been spare and direct. French author Andre Maurois noted that Abraham Lincoln and John F. Kennedy seemed to "speak to each other across the span of a century," for both leaders embodied noble themes in eloquently simple terms. Said Lincoln in his second Inaugural Address, "With malice toward none, with charity for all, with firmness in the right as God gives us to see the right, let us strive on to finish the work we are in. . . ." One hundred years later President Kennedy made this Inaugural dedication: "With a good conscience our only sure reward, with history the final judge of our deeds, let us go forth to lead the land we love. . . ."

Clarity

A third fundamental element of good writing is clarity. Some people question whether it is always possible to be clear. After all, certain ideas are inherently complicated and inescapably difficult. True enough. But the responsible writer recognizes that writing should not add to the complications nor increase the difficulty: It should not set up an additional roadblock to understanding. If writers understand their own ideas and want to convey them to others, they are obliged to render those ideas in clear, orderly, readable, understandable prose—else why bother writing in the first place? Actually, obscure writers are usually confused themselves, uncertain of what they want to say or what they mean; they have not yet completed that process of thinking critically and reasoning into the heart of the subject. Whatever the topic, whatever the occasion, expository writing should be readable, informative, and, whenever possible, engaging. At its best it may even be poetic.

Even in technical writing, where the range of styles is necessarily limited, you must always be aware of the reader over your shoulder. Take topics such as how to follow postal regulations for overseas mail, how to change oil in an engine, or how to produce aspirin from salicylic acid. Readers expect such writing to be clear, dispassionate, and bloodless, but it need not be tedious or confusing. Readers who want to find out about mailing letters, changing oil, or making aspirin should have reasonably easy access to such information. Written instructions should be clear, spare, direct, and, most of all, *human:* No matter how technical the subject, all writing is done for human beings by human beings. Machines may stamp letters, measure oil, and convert acids, but only human beings talk and write about these procedures so that other human beings may better understand them.

Rhetorical Stance

Part of this clarity must stem from your sense of who your readers are. You must understand the rhetorical stance you assume. Indeed this is a fundamental priciple of rhetoric: *Nothing should ever be written in a vacuum.* You should identify your audience—hypothetical or real—so that you may speak to them in an appropriate voice. A student, for example, should never just write without visualizing a definite group of readers—fellow students, perhaps, or the educated community at large (intelligent non-specialists). Without such definite readers in mind, you cannot assume a suitable and appropriate relationship to your material, your purpose, and your audience. To understand your rhetorical stance in a particular situation, examine its elements:

1. Who you are as a writer
2. Who your readers are
3. Why you are addressing them and on what occasion

4. Your relationship to your subject matter
5. How you want your readers to relate to this sbject matter

We will deal with ways to develop your sense of voice, audience, occasion, and purpose in Chapter 2, "Developing a Subject."

A Pleasing Style

In addition to a rhetorical stance, a writer should draw upon those personal and aesthetic effects that enhance a statement without distorting it and that delight—or at least sustain—a reader's attention. "One's case," said Aristotle, "should, in justice, be fought on the strength of the facts alone." This would be ideal: mind speaking to mind. However, people do not react solely on rational grounds, or, to quote Aristotle in a more cynical mood, "External matters do count much, because of the sorry nature of the audience." Facing reality, then, you should try to woo the reader through a kind of courtship. You should try, as Carl Rogers reminds us, to break down the natural barriers and fears that separate people, whether their encounters are face to face or on the printed page. If you personalize your relationship with the reader by using those rhetorical devices, you emerge from the page as a human being, with a distinctive voice and personality.

Rhetoric provides a rich storehouse of devices to enhance the appeal of your writing, and we shall consider these in Part III. For example, the pleasant rhythm of a balanced antithesis is evident in President Kennedy's immortal statement "Ask not what your country can do for you; ask what you can do for your country." The lilting suspense of a periodic sentence (one that suspends its main idea until the end) appears in Edward Gibbon's delightful account of how he came to write his *Decline and Fall of the Roman Empire:*

> It was at Rome, on the 15th of October 1764, as I sat musing amidst the ruins of the Capitol, while the barefooted friars were singing vespers in the temple of Jupiter, that the idea of writing the decline and fall of the city first started to my mind.

Simeon Potter, a modern scholar, has observed that the word picture Gibbon draws, although brief, is "artistically perfect":

> The rhythm is stately and entirely satisfying. The reader is held in suspense to the end. Had he wished, and had he been less of an artist, Gibbon might have said exactly the same things in a different way, arranging them in their logical and grammatical order: "The idea of writing the decline and fall of the city first started to my mind as I sat musing amidst the ruins of the Capitol at Rome on the 15th of October 1764, while the barefooted friars were singing vespers in the temple of Jupiter." What has happened? It is not merely that a periodic sentence has been reexpressed as a loose one. The emphasis is now all wrong and the magnificent cadence of the original is quite marred. All is still grammatically correct, but "proper words" are no longer in "proper places." The passage has quite lost its harmonious rhythm.

In addition, then, to economy, simplicity, and clarity—the foundation of sound, dependable rhetoric—include this marvelous dimension of "harmonious rhythm," of proper words in proper places. If you are sensitive to these strategies, you will delight as well as inform your reader, and in delighting, reinforce your statement.

THE STUDENT WRITER

No small part of the complexity involved in writing is that you must master writing tasks that ask you to assume a range of roles. Understanding the purpose of a piece of writing will help you make choices about voice, style, and rhetorical strategy. Your writing for a particular assignment may be primarily *expository,* aimed at presenting information. When you take an essay examination, for example, you may be repeating information from lectures and readings to demonstrate your mastery of the material. Your aim is to present information when reporting the results of library research or a lab experiment. More common in academic assignments is writing that is *persuasive,* in which you are asked to prove a thesis. Your aim is persuasive if you give a convincing account of your analytical response to a literary work, show which of several theories you find most convincing, or use the results of your original research to prove your own thesis. Some courses, most often creative writing courses, will demand work that is primarily *entertaining* (though as we have said, a pleasing style can ease the way to accomplish almost any writing task). Increasingly, college faculty are assigning writing that is primarily *exploratory,* that is less constrained than writing with other purposes. Such writing may be assigned for a journal or even a formal paper. Perhaps your philosophy professor will ask you to explain your own theory of evil in a paper designed less to test your mastery of the philosophical method and more as a vehicle for exploring your response to course material through the process of writing a paper. Understanding the purpose behind differing writing tasks can make the many choices you face in the course of writing a paper much easier.

Psychologist Erich Fromm has said children "must grow until finally" they "become" their own parents; so we can say to the student writer: You must grow until you become your own teacher, your own critic, and your own editor. Slowly you will cultivate a sensitivity to clear, unpretentious prose. At the same time you will develop an awareness and dislike of diffuse, pompous, or jargon-ridden prose. You will be able to view your own or someone else's writing with a critical eye. You will be able to see what skill has gone into creating it and to judge the finished piece.

Most important, when you have reached maturity as a writer, you will know how to go about the job of writing, no matter what your assignment. Your material will not overwhelm or intimidate you any more than the unworked wood for a desk or a bookcase overwhelms or intimidates a cabinetmaker. You will draw on your raw material and shape it in accordance with your will and plan, much as the cabinetmaker does. You will know what you want to say, just as a cabinetmaker knows before picking up a saw what the final product is to be. You will organize your ideas in a logical, orderly sequence, just as a cabinetmaker assembles the tools and maps out the steps by which he or she transforms raw wood into smooth, polished furniture. Even if you cannot envision every detail of the final product, you will have such confidence in your own strength as a writer to trust what the process of wrestling with words and ideas will produce.

Like the artisan or artist, you will always be in control, and you will experience a sense of creativity. For, in truth, you *will be* creating. Indeed, we should not limit the term *creative writing* to poetry, short stories, and novels as we often do. *All* writing is creative when the writer forges out of his or her raw material (poetic images, anecdotes, statistics, a set of facts) a new whole: a poem, an expository article, an essay, or a term paper. Proficient writers understand language as a medium of expression and shape it in a deliberate and disciplined way to address a chosen audience.

Whether writing fiction or exposition, they work creatively and produce creative writing. You, too, should regard all writing, expository or otherwise, as creative writing. You, too, should regard all writing, expository or otherwise, as a creative challenge; you create out of isolated, separate elements (facts, feelings, memories, ideas, beliefs) a new whole that is, as John Stuart Mill described a chemical compound, "more than the sum of its parts."

PART
I

THE WRITING PROCESS

Chapter 1   Exploring a Subject
Chapter 2   Planning a Paper
Chapter 3   Drafting a Paper
Chapter 4   Revising a Paper

Chapter

1

EXPLORING
A SUBJECT

FINDING A SUBJECT
    LISTING POSSIBLE SUBJECTS
    FOCUSING A SUBJECT
    ARISTOTLE'S CATEGORIES
    ASKING THE RIGHT
        QUESTIONS
    TWENTY QUESTIONS TO ASK
    FROM SUBJECT TO WRITING
        TOPIC
    BEYOND THE TWENTY
        QUESTIONS

DEVELOPING A SUBJECT
    FREEWRITING
    TALKING TO YOURSELF
    TALKING TO OTHER PEOPLE
    BRAINSTORMING
    CONJURING UP MEMORIES
    KEEPING A WRITER'S JOURNAL
    SHARPENING POWERS OF
        OBSERVATION
    BURKE'S PENTAD

FINDING A SUBJECT

Few human activities are so bound up in myth and misconception as the process of writing. When we overdramatize the act of writing, when we think of writers as poets inspired by a divine muse or as essayists whose writing is a simple record of their articulate, opinionated and well-informed mental life, we can easily be discouraged by our own difficult writing process. Yet it is not true that professional writers always have something so vital and compelling to say that it drives them to the typewriter to say it and be *done* until another idea comes along to drive them back to the typewriter. More often, writers are people who have chosen to write because they find writing to be a delight, a disease, or a bit of both. But once they have made this decision, they are not perennially brimming over with subjects or topics to write *about*.

Unlike reporters, who are often given a specific story to cover, student writers and all other writers are periodically faced with a blank page and an equally blank mind. From the "booming buzzing confusion" of the world around you, you must somehow locate and concentrate on one particular, self-contained topic. You must, as Cicero the classical Roman orator and writer, said, "hit upon what to say." Once you have done this, you can go on to "manage and marshal" your materials and finally "to array them in the adornments of style" (Cicero, again). But first—and you cannot get around this—first you *must hit upon what to say*. Sometimes people assume that hitting upon a subject that you want to write about is an uncomplicated matter. Pick a topic. Seek and you shall find. Somehow.

Of course, finding an idea is indeed an inner process, and if you wish to find, you certainly have to seek. But *how* to seek? Where to find? Answering these questions is not easy because in the beginning you don't even know exactly *what* you are seeking—just a good idea. "I wasted the entire week trying to decide what to write about," says a discouraged student. True enough: the student has spent hours at the desk staring at a cursor blinking lonesomely at the upper left corner of a blank screen, blaming fate, moaning, groaning, and chewing erasers off pencils. The finished paper, written between midnight and 4 A.M. and proofread on the way to class, must be submitted on time. On the way to class the student thinks, "I know it's not very good, but at least it's *done. How* I hate to write! If only I could think of things to write about!"

If you've ever had this experience, you'll benefit from exploring what classical Greek and Roman rhetoricians called the art of invention—finding something to write about. The first step in the composition process is an art in itself that you can consciously and conscientiously cultivate. Briefly, invention is the skill of knowing how to "invent" or "discover" (classical rhetoricians used both terms) the subject of a discourse by actively searching out stimulation, the kind of stimulation that will actively generate ideas and produce a specific topic and things to say about the topic.

The two main aspects of invention are finding a subject and developing it. Like every other stage of the composition process, the writer can actively and systematically deal with this first stage of finding something to write about. Even more important, the writer can and must deal with this stage *creatively* because finding an idea and preparing to mold it into a new and original whole is a distinctly creative process.

The aim of this section, then, is to explain how to go about the creative process of invention thoughtfully and purposefully. To help accomplish this aim, we shall draw upon basic principles of rhetoric and concentrate on commonsense techniques like trying to find an idea by *looking* for it and by using simple, easily accessible guides such as the dictionary, a rich source of ideas.

Listing Possible Subjects

In most college courses, the specific subject of your paper is supplied by the subject matter of your course. Even in a first-year English class, your teacher may assign topics based on class readings and discussion. At other times you're on your own. One valuable source for subjects is your own life and your experiences; another is a class you've found interesting. You'll feel more confident if you are writing about a subject on which you can speak with some authority. On the other hand, you're in college to think new thoughts and learn about unfamiliar subjects, and a writing course is as good a place as any to begin.

One way to proceed is to browse through an encyclopedia, a dictionary, or even your college catalog, making a list of subjects that catch your interest. The procedure is simple: Thumb through the pages starting with A and move on through the alphabet, jotting down whatever terms catch your eyes and your interest—whatever you *respond to.* You can be certain that an unconscious as well as conscious process of selection is at work here, guiding you to one or another term that appeals to you and that will therefore provide a good starting point for the invention process. Here are twenty subjects chosen from the dictionary.

1. American Indians	8. Language	15. Prejudice
2. Big Bang	9. Literature	16. Propaganda
3. Books	10. Music	17. Science
4. Creativity	11. Nature	18. Symbols
5. Education	12. Patriotism	19. Women
6. Family	13. Poetry	20. Writing
7. Holocaust	14. Poverty	

Focusing a Subject

Let us begin with the first item on the list—American Indians. Surely we cannot approach this subject as such, for it is as vast and diverse as the Great Plains the Indians once inhabited. Where should we begin? How can we hope to cover the American Indian in less than a volume, or indeed, a whole library full of books? Clearly, the only sensible procedure is to limit *the subject,* to concentrate on one or another of its many aspects. For instance, we could consider one particular tribe in one particular place (Navajos of New Mexico). We could limit the subject still further (Navajos living in New Mexico *at the present time*). The subject is now more manageable in scope, more suitable for the essay form, although we still have not focused sharply on what we will say *about* the Navajos living in New Mexico at the present time. The specific content will come later (as we shall see), when we address a specific question to the limited topic; only then will we arrive at the *real* topic—the thesis, or *point of the piece.*

Let us move to the third item on the subject list—books. Here again, we cannot reasonably expect to write a short, coherent piece about books in general. Why not reduce the subject numerically, then, to *one particular* book? Take education, again much too broad a topic to tackle at once. We might limit ourselves to a specific place (education in Japan), or a specific aspect (mathematics education in elementary schools) or a specific example (general education requirements at your school).

We are not concerned at this point with finding a specific topic, but rather with the preliminary process of narrowing down a subject to some aspect of itself that we can encompass in a single essay of approximately 500 to 750 words (one average weekly paper in a college writing course). This conscious, deliberate narrowing-down process is an imperative first step in invention; without it we are likely to wander over a vast, amorphous field and never get our bearings. Only if we resist such overwhelming subjects as "Science" and consider a limited subject, such as the new scientific field of chaos (consider James Gleick, "The Meaning of Chaos," cited in Question 7, "What Does X Mean?"), can we achieve a unified and coherent unit of discourse. To summarize: In selecting a topic for a paper, we should try to view it in terms of such limiting factors as the following:

1. a specific *kind*   not music in general, but hip-hop music
2. a specific *time*   not music in all periods, but the last decade of twentieth-century music
3. a specific *place*   not music throughout the world, but music in the United States
4. a specific *number*   not all hip-hop musicians, but musicians who represent the range of hip-hop
5. a specific *person*   Speech, the lead singer in the hip-hop group Arrested Development
6. a specific *type*   not all kinds of hip-hop music, but songs that make a comment on social issues
7. a specific *aspect*   not music as a whole, but music as communication
8. a specific *example*   not all hip-hop songs, but Arrested Development's "Mr. Wendel"
9. a specific *experience* the first time you went to a hip-hop concert

Admittedly, we may have times when the normal processes of invention seem to telescope, as if by miracle, into a sudden flash of inspiration ("Ah, this is what I want to say!"), followed by a few hours of pouring forth what we do in fact want to say at a particular moment. This "inspiration" is an exhilarating experience, but we cannot depend on it. We must proceed by plan and regular procedure, as writers did throughout the centuries when rhetoric was taught as a formal discipline.

Aristotle's Categories

Having found and limited our subject, we go on to the second stage of invention: finding something to say *about* our subject and developing it. Let us turn to the classical rhetoricians, for although they were concerned largely with writing speeches to be delivered in public, they recognized that the composition process begins with the mind looking *out* on its subject matter and *in* on itself. The orator read widely and studied conscientiously to "stock" the mind with subject matter. Cicero specified that the ideal orator was a person of vast learning and liberal education, trained in techniques to set the mind in motion: to spur thinking, to stir memory, and to coax imagination. Through these concrete procedures the orator avoided the torments of the blank page, the frustration of just sitting and waiting for a topic to present itself. Aristotle codified the invention procedure by reducing all possible topics to four categories:

1. what is possible or impossible
2. what happened or did not happen
3. what will happen
4. questions of degree (greatness or smallness)

Aristotle's list may seem oversimplified, but notice that these four categories are excellent places to begin thinking about what a writer might want to say about any topic. (Classical teachers of rhetoric called these *topoi,* from the word for "place"; these were places or regions of thinking where an argument might be located and developed). Suppose that you are developing a paper on the subject of AIDS. You might begin with the first *topos*—or, as we now say, topic—**what is possible or impossible:** "Urging teenagers to abstain from sexual activity will not be sufficient to stop the spread of AIDS." The writer asserts that something is possible—a familiar type of proposition. Topic 2 **(what happened or did not happen)** also provides a familiar type of proposition: "The inaction of the federal government in the mid 1980s encouraged the spread of AIDS." Either this *did* or *did not* happen; the writer who asserts either position must prepare an argument. Topic 3 **(what will happen)** characterizes writing from a simple weather forecast to full-scale analyses of future developments in any sphere: why candidate X will win the election, why urban areas are heading for decentralization. For a paper on AIDS, you might argue for or against the proposition that AIDS will increasingly affect poor people, women, and people of color. Finally there is topic 4 **(questions of degree):** "Though AIDS is widely publicized, efforts toward research and prevention have not yet received sufficient funding." The proposition stands as an argument for *more* of something, and, by implication, *less* of something else—ignorance, indifference, apathy.

Aristotle's four basic categories *plus* certain other strategies of thinking recognized by the classical rhetoricians—cause-effect (X causes Y); similarity (X is like Y); dissimilarity (X is unlike Y); example (X illustrates Y); consequence (X is a result of Y)—provided a kind of checklist of mental acts orators might perform when investigating and collecting arguments on a subject. Armed with this checklist, classical orators were never at a loss; they could confidently follow these "discovery procedures" to locate their arguments and line up their proofs.

Asking the Right Questions

Actually, we can sum up this approach in a single phrase: asking the right questions. By using the question as a probing instrument—turned inward to the mind (a repository of dormant ideas) and outward to the subject matter (a source of data and information)—we can make discoveries and ultimately generate a sharply focused idea. In every case, as we shall see, *questions, posed and answered, are at the heart of any piece of discourse*. For what else does the writer do but ask questions and then answer them?

The writer may be telling newspaper readers who robbed which house and what was stolen, explaining in a magazine advertisement why a particular cosmetic cream will prevent "crow's feet" around the eyes, or describing in a controversial book the death of a president or the reasons for violence in American cities. Whatever the subject, whatever the temper and tone of the piece, the writer forever answers questions. "And a writer cannot answer a question," as one journalist pointed out, "unless he has first asked it" (Lobsen, 15). Nor can the writer achieve a sharp focus or a unified thrust in a piece of writing unless he or she is aware of exactly what the question or questions are. The writer must hold firmly to a steady line of development so that the finished piece answers precisely that single question or those several questions.

Like journalists (who apply to all events the five questions: Who? What? When? Where? Why?), writers must always be prepared with the right set of questions if they expect to find a way into a topic, to stimulate thinking, to stake out a special area of interest. They need the right questions to glean enough information about the topic and to make a new whole—a unified piece of writing that has a distinctive identity. A set of questions to guide your exploration of a subject is called a **heuristic**; we'll explore several of these throughout the book—most notably, the twenty questions themselves.

Specifically, what are the right questions? If you flip through the pages of this textbook, you will see that these questions and the many ways they generate and focus a piece of discourse are our central concern. But first we should caution against viewing a modern set of *topoi* with the same complacency Aristotle felt toward the "commonplaces," that is, the common places where one may go in order to invent an argument. The seeming completeness of Aristotle's survey of topics was, as we now know, largely illusory. The number of topics and categories is not fixed; the number is endless. *Discourse is a process; one idea generates another in ongoing, open-ended progression.* As we proceed through this text, you will also proceed through the overlapping and interacting stages of this most complex and challenging of all human activities—writing.

Twenty Questions to Ask

In this cycle of question generating idea, idea generating question, and further questions generating further ideas, we have compiled the following twenty basic questions. Although we have stripped them of all concrete subject reference, their faceless aspect should not put you off: We have referred to the topic as "X" to keep the discussion on an abstract level. These twenty questions present ways of *observing* or thinking *about* a subject. They are "thought starters" to set the wheels of invention turning. As such they apply to any subject matter; as you read them, substitute your subject for X.

Once you've located and begun to limit your subject, you're ready to work with this checklist of questions, each of which can provide the final, focal point of departure for your essay. Each question generates the type of essay listed in the right-hand column. As you move down the list, you also move from more personal questions that draw on your immediate experiences to more abstract questions that draw on your skills of analysis and critical thinking. The column on the right shows the kind of essay each kind of question will generate.

1. How can X be described?	Description
2. How did X happen?	Narration
3. What kind of person is X?	Characterization
4. What is my memory of X?	Reminiscence
5. What is my personal response to X?	Response
6. What are the facts about X?	Information
7. What does X mean?	Definition
8. What is the essential function of X?	Functional definition
9. What are the component parts of X?	Analysis
10. How is X made or done?	Process analysis
11. How should X be made or done?	Process analysis
12. What are the causes of X?	Causal analysis
13. What are the consequences of X?	Causal analysis
14. What are the types of X?	Classification
15. How does X compare to Y?	Comparison
16. What is the present status of X?	Comparison
17. How can X be summarized?	Summary
18. How should X be interpreted?	Interpretation
19. What is the value of X?	Evaluation
20. What case can be made for or against X?	Argumentation

Before we put flesh and bone on X by referring to specific subjects, we should look at a few important points about the questions themselves. First, as you can see, they are not comprehensive. There are more questions you can ask of a subject than we have indicated here. Even the newest discovery procedures do not pretend to cover *all* possible approaches. In this case your imagination can fill in any gaps you may encounter. What's more, you may invent your own questions or frame them differently if that helps you to focus your idea more precisely.

Furthermore, some overlapping occurs within the twenty questions themselves. This is inevitable, whether the list contains principles, rules, regulations, or questions. These questions are only suggestive of the way the mind regularly and automatically goes about its business of thinking and exploring the universe. Like Aristotle's "commonplaces," these questions represent some of the common places the mind naturally travels to when it encounters a person, object, event, or idea in the outside world, or an experience, thought, feeling, or sensation within. What is it?, we wonder. How does it work? Why? We are forever wondering about things and searching for answers and explanations; this is a natural, ongoing process of the human mind. The kind of critical thinking about ideas, experiences and values that these questions engender is at the heart of academic discourse and inquiry. The answers that these questions generate are not only patterns for writing, they are patterns for thinking as well. Such activities as summarizing, comparing, classifying, and analyzing constitute the intellectual building blocks of independent critical thought, as Mike Rose points out.

From Subject to Writing Topic

As we have said, the special job of invention is to start up a specific line of questioning at a given time when the mind may not necessarily be ready to perform; when it may be tired or unconnected to the subject at hand or simply lazy; but when it must, nonetheless, think up something to write about. For by asking a question we find a topic, and by answering the questions about this topic we compose our paper.

The selections reprinted in Part II of this book illustrate answers to the twenty questions. For example, in response to question 1, "How can X be described?" John V. Young produces an essay, "Moonrise Over Monument Valley," that is a narrowed-down, sharply focused presentation of the broad subject area "Nature" (subject 11 on the checklist):

Nature	limited to one type of habitat	*the desert*
	limited to one country	*United States*
	limited to one state	*Arizona*
	limited to one place in that state	*Monument Valley*
	limited to one time	*when the moon rises*

To this narrowed-down aspect of his subject area, Young addresses the question, How can X be described? He gives his answer in the very striking and evocative description of the moon rising over "a limitless expanse of tawny desert."

Beyond the Twenty Questions

Note that Young binds all the descriptive details together with what rhetoricians call a "thesis," a central controlling idea that binds the parts together into a unified whole. What is it *about* the moon rising over Monument Valley that makes it worth an essay in the *New York Times?*

"What's the *story?*" the travel editor may well have asked the reporter when giving the assignment, posing a key twenty-first question to encompass all the others: What single main point do I want to make here? The *story,* as the writer-reporter would discover in the act of writing, is that the moon rising over Monument Valley produces more than a series of separate and spectacular images; it produces an overwhelming total impression: a magical, almost mystical experience.

This perception charges the description with a life of its own, a distinct distinctiveness that is more than the sum of its parts. Without it—without some such central perception or insight or thesis—the essay would lack the "Big Idea" that should activate and animate every piece of writing, giving it a single unifying *point* and a sharply focused *purpose.*

Beyond the twenty questions that generate a topic, then, a writer will profit from exploring a topic still further to discover within it an answer to the additional question: What is the main point of this piece? "What's the story?" as the journalist puts it. Why am I writing this? you might ask yourself; What insight have I gained? What am I trying to tell my readers? What is my Big Idea?

Throughout this textbook, you'll explore different ways to use these questions to explore your subject. Remember, though, that the art of invention itself is not so much a formal technique as it is plain common sense *applied in a deliberate and disciplined manner.* Gaining confidence with the twenty questions will help you fulfill a particular assignment at a particular time and to make you relatively independent of "inspiration"; you will be able to *find* something to write about when you *need* something to write about, not merely when the spirit moves you.

It demeans neither the art of invention nor the question procedure to admit that each is an essentially intuitive process; you have been asking similar questions and inventing topics all your life. The aim of the discovery and development procedure described here is to help you invent and develop topics "on call," with more precision, originality, and ease. Eventually you will come to feel toward this heuristic something of the confidence and assurance that the classical orators felt toward Aristotle's "commonplaces." Eventually the question procedure will serve you in the same efficient and dependable way.

EXERCISES

1. Using a dictionary or any reference work of comparable scope, make up a list of twenty subjects that interest you. They may be fields of study (astronomy, astrology); hobbies (crafts, pets, music); sports (rugby, ice hockey, tennis). Almost any subject area—provided you are interested in it or know something about it—will offer a good starting point for the invention process.

2. Using the list of limiting factors cited on page 5, narrow each of your subjects to one aspect of itself (one specific kind, time, place, or experience).

3. Select five of your twenty subjects and carry them through progressive stages of limitation (as on page 6). Formulate your *real* topic by posing a specific question chosen from the list on page 8 to some aspect of your limited topic. For example: What is my memory of a family vacation? What is the essential function of family vacations? How should a family vacation be planned?

DEVELOPING A SUBJECT

Recent research on the composing process has shown that even after locating a subject, the writer is wise not to approach the subject "cold." Just as a runner limbers up before a race, a writer needs to do a variety of stretching and bending exercises before setting out. These prewriting strategies not only help to make writers more comfortable about the subject but also help to generate new ideas or new perceptions of old ideas.

Professional writers have long been aware of the importance of a prewriting period during which they can probe their own minds and explore feelings and attitudes that may not rise to the surface without conscious and conscientious stirring up. One of the most helpful of these prewriting strategies comes from Peter Elbow, the lively author of *Writing Without Teachers* (Oxford, 1973). As a warming-up exercise he advocates preparatory "self-confrontation." This is especially helpful for students who may be blocked or uptight about their writing, afraid to make the first move. It also helps those who are afraid to make mistakes, the most common fear of beginning writers.

This idea of confronting one's *self* has an almost primal attraction: we've often been told that true knowledge begins with self-knowledge. At the same time, we must acknowledge that our root self is made up of many selves, many identities that we use to face different situations. We act differently among close friends than among strangers, differently around our parents than around people our own age, differently with our best friend than with someone we're involved with romantically. Likewise in our writing, we adopt different voices for different readers and different situations. Freewriting can be a good chance to explore the range of writing voices on which we can call.

Freewriting

Writers can loosen up by trying a form of "freewriting," also called simply "babbling and jabbering exercises." According to Elbow, these should be done at least three times a week:

> The idea is simply to write for ten minutes (later on, perhaps fifteen or twenty). Don't stop for anything. Go quickly without rushing. Never stop to look back, to cross something out, to wonder how to spell something, to wonder what word or thought to use, or to think about what you are doing. If you can't think of a word or a spelling, just use a squiggle or else write, "I can't think of it." Just put down something. The easiest thing is just to put down whatever is in your mind. If you get stuck it's fine to write "I can't think what to say, I can't think what to say" as many times as you want; or repeat the last word you wrote over and over again; or anything else. The only requirement is that you never stop writing.

There are those, says Elbow, who accuse freewriting "of being an invitation to write garbage." Actually freewriting serves an important function by setting the wheels of the mind turning and getting words on paper. As Elbow suggests, the advantage of prewriting is that you always produce something in the assigned time period. This unstructured "free" writing may be only a string of seemingly unrelated sentences, or even fragments or phrases. No matter. Whatever you do is fine. By accepting unconditionally what you are writing, by refusing to pause for spelling or grammar checks or any other correction along the way, you gather momentum, focus on the act of writing itself, and lose yourself in the process. You feel no pressure or concern about grades or future readers because this writing is ungraded and for your eyes alone if you choose. It remains unedited, unrevised—*as is*. Freewriting exists only to put you in closer touch with yourself and with the special rhythm, texture, and tone of your own natural voice. As Elbow points out, and as many professional writers agree, your "natural voice is the main source of power in your writing . . . the force that will make a reader listen to you."

By making regular entries in a freewriting diary, you put yourself on more intimate terms with this natural voice. You get to know what sounds right in your writing and what rings false, even when you are factually correct. Professional writers have long been practitioners of freewriting, turning to their diaries routinely for prewriting warm-ups. Short story writer Katherine Mansfield, for example, described a process that is clearly comparable: "Looking back," she reported, "I imagine I was always writing. Twaddle it was too. But far better write twaddle or anything, anything, than nothing at all."

Still another benefit to be gained from freewriting is that it often provides the seed of an idea that you can later develop further into a full-length finished piece. Take, for example, the following passage of freewriting (or, in this case, "freetyping" on a word processor), this one set off by a suggested topic, Depressing Things:

OK—it's now 11:30 and I'm supposed to write for fifteen minutes—just let my mind wander along paths suggested by this title "depressing things." That's what she told us to do so I'm going to try to see how far I get by free-associating. She said that was a good idea so I'll try that. I never did it before but here goes—depressing/heavy/hot/lead/bread. How did "bread" get in? Well, that's a rhyme. I wonder if that's OK—to rhyme—fine. That's almost a rhyme again: fine/shine/wine/spine/mine. Better get back to depressing words like sadness, death, breath. Gee, I'm rhyming again. Maybe because when I think of death I try to return to life again with breath. Now I'm trying to be a psychologist. Forget it, forget it. Go back to free associating again, back to "depressing." I wonder if I can come up with any more words or ideas that are "depressing." Let's see, let's see: there's a notebook filled with a whole semester's notes left on the train. All that work, exam coming up, no way to get the notebook back. That's not just depressing—that's disgusting, a disaster, panic. Awful, awful, awful. What else can I write about now? I still have more time. Oh yes. I can see where my mind travels with the word "things." I guess that's what I decided to do when I started out—to take up one word at a time, try to get more mileage that way. Not a bad idea, let's see where it takes me. What do I think of that's a "thing." Well, first of all a thing is different from a person, a human being. Things are inanimate objects without sense or feeling. They can't feel pleasure or pain, can they? Of course not. So things in and of themselves can't really be said to be depressing or heartening either. This is a strange assignment then, the two words of the title don't work together sensibly. The more I think about it the more I realize that people can be depressed but things can't. Things can only be associated with something that's depressing and in that way they can create depression in the person doing the associating (things don't associate, either, only people associate one thing with another). I guess I'm saying that depression isn't a quality of a thing, it's not in the thing, that is, only in the person who encounters or experiences the thing and by a process of association becomes depressed by it. Like an old Valentine card from an old boyfriend who now has a new girlfriend. Or something like that. The card becomes a depressing reminder (a reminder that makes you depressed) of happier times. Sniff, sniff, you fool. The point I think I'm making is that the card itself is not depressing. It just <u>is</u>, it exists. But it's a reminder of what might have been—and so it is by a process of association a depressing thing in that it's a thing that can create depression in a person. I said that before. I said that before. I'm beginning to repeat myself, repeat myself, because it isn't time to stop yet, it isn't time to stop yet. Time.

In rereading this passage of "self-confrontation," you discover some interesting things about the way this writer's mind works. She responds playfully to words, for example, letting the rhymes carry her along. Sometimes the writer's feelings drive the flow of words; sometimes her thoughts dominate, as in the analytical distinction she makes between depressing things and depressing people. Having established that things in and of themselves cannot be depressing, the writer points to a phenomenon that could grow into an essay: the way "things," which are inherently neutral, become associated with happy and unhappy circumstances. If the student then sharpens her focus by addressing questions to this observation, she may develop a suitable topic. The kind of internal dialogue that may take place when you follow freewriting with intensive talking to yourself appears in the Talking to Yourself exercise in the assignments. As Thoreau pointed out long ago, "A writer must first speak to himself."

EXERCISES

1. Try a relatively free unfocused freewriting exercise that begins with Peter Elbow's words, "I think I'll write what's on my mind." Give yourself ten minutes.
2. Recall a recent dream. What did you feel afterward? Freewrite for ten minutes.
3. Select one of the following topics, using it as the point of departure for fifteen minutes of freewriting:

marvelous happenings	sound and silence
the occult	solitude
appearance and reality	nature
a personal experience	myself and others
big bangs and black hole	splendid things
the stars	boring things
the sound of a voice	infuriating things
happiness	sad things
somewhere	demanding things

4. Freewrite for fifteen minutes. *Just do it!*

Talking to Yourself

In a sense we talk to ourselves whenever we think. We carry on a conversation with ourselves when we choose between this or that item while shopping in a store and when we try to decide whether to go out to a movie or stay home and watch TV. While you were freewriting you did something very similar. And just as freewriting helped generate useful ideas, so talking to yourself can do the same. But there is an important difference. To get the most out of your self-conversation, it is a good idea to prepare a set of questions beforehand and then write out your answers. In other words, while you did not want to censor or direct the flow of ideas in freewriting, you do want to control the movement of ideas while talking to yourself.

Here is an example of a set of questions and answers. The purpose of this self-examination is to find a topic to write about, but the technique can be used at any stage of the writing process.

Q: Let's begin by thinking about the kinds of activities that give you pleasure. What do you like to do?

A: Well, athletics, of course. I enjoy swimming and getting into a good game of volleyball. I like to take long bike rides. And then there's my computer. If I'm not outside, I'm probably sitting in front of my monitor.

Q: What do you do in front of your computer? Why do you enjoy it?

A: I enjoy doing lots of different things. Sometimes I play games or try to get my life organized. Sometimes I'm learning about one of my hobbies or trying to learn a new computer program that I don't know much about.

Q: What kind of programs?

A: Whatever I can find: spreadsheets, graphics programs, or utilities that make the computer work better.

Q: Where do you get these programs?

A: Sometimes I borrow a copy from a friend, but that's not really legal, you know!

Q: Yeah, I know—but with big companies charging so much, who can afford to buy anything new?

A: That's right—that's why I really like to use shareware I download from bulletin boards.

Q: Hold on! What's "shareware"? What's "downloading"? What's a "bulletin board"?

A: Okay, one at a time. A bulletin board is a system on another computer that you dial up over the phone line and connect your computer to. Once you're connected, you can read messages that other people have left, leave messages of your own, and send and receive E-Mail. (That's electronic mail.) You can also copy programs from that computer to yours over the phone—that's called downloading.

Q: I think I understand. Now what about "shareware"?

A: Most of the software there is shareware, which means that the author of the program wants you to try it out before you buy it. If you don't like it, you can pass it on to someone else, or just erase it from your computer. If you do like it, then you send the author the cost of the program—but it's almost always cheaper than a commercial program.

Q: What's your favorite piece of shareware?

A: Well, there are some games that are well-done and a lot of fun. There's a useful program that archives my compact disks, and another that keeps track of my appointments.

Q: Wow! I didn't realize computers could do so much these days. Maybe you could write about that.

A: That's a paper I'd enjoy writing, I think. But how could I organize it?

Q: Well, you could start with the different ways people use computers, using your life as an example.

A: I bet that would work—but there are so many different things to say.

Q: You could find some general categories. You've told me about using computers for entertainment, to make your life easier, and to get information. That would be a good place to start.

A: That's right. I could talk about my experiences and how they represent the different ways people use computers.

Q: I'd like to read *that* paper. What about a title? How about "Why I Use Computers"?

A: Well, that's a good place to start, but I was hoping for something peppier, like "Do Computers Make Good Pets?" Maybe I'll come up with something better as I go along. I think my next step should be to talk to other people about how they use computers.

Talking to Other People

Although writing is necessarily an independent—even isolated—activity, you can and should collaborate throughout the process. When your idea is still in the germinating stage—before you have begun to write—you might approach other people and ask them to share their knowledge with you and to tell you how they feel and what they have observed. Follow this commonsense principle of listening and learning, confine your side of the conversation to questions, and you will not run the risk of "having your say" too early. You want to save your presentation for your final writing. By listening to what others have to tell you, you open yourself to different points of view and to new and perhaps unexpected insights that might not otherwise occur to you. Interestingly, the most unlikely people may have excellent ideas about your subject, so don't confine your conversations to people you know are knowledgeable. Sometimes the "quiet ones" have more expertise and general background than you suspect. By learning more about the ideas people already hold about your topic, you can more effectively appeal to them as readers when you begin to write.

Here again, prepare a set of questions to serve as a starting point. Avoid conversation stoppers like "Tell me all you know about computers." Just as you yourself need precise probes into a subject, so do the sources you turn to. Be specific whenever possible and always be provocative enough to elicit a response.

Brainstorming

After you talk to yourself and to others, and after you jot down notes for use later on, you may think you are ready to dash off a quick first draft. But before you begin to write, give yourself an opportunity to conjure up other details you may not be aware of. One good method is "brainstorming," a problem-solving procedure originated by business executives. Imaginative breakthroughs using this method have actually saved companies from bankruptcy and put new million-dollar products on the market. The goal of brainstorming, which may be defined as imaginative thinking that goes beyond conventional categories, is to help you to tap deeper levels of imagination and creativity.

Think of brainstorming as another discovery procedure or another path to self-confrontation. To brainstorm, write down a key word and allow this word to lead you to free associate with another, as you do in freewriting. But with brainstorming you don't compose sentences; just let one key word serve as a starting point and allow the others to follow in a free flow. Let's use computers again as an example, and imagine a random string of words: *computer, keyboard, Macintosh, Apple, food, dinner, kitchen.*

You can see that each of the terms easily gives rise to another term that then serves as the point of departure for still other terms, which continue branching off in other directions. Let yourself think wild thoughts—What else can computers help us do? What new experiences can they bring us? How will computers change the way we learn? The way we gather and process information? The way we write? Can a computer ever write an English paper for me? How will computers change the way we accomplish everyday activities like shopping or cooking? A professional freelance writer would instantly spot a potential story here and begin getting ideas. A tentative title might come to mind: "Computers in the Home." or maybe "The Computer in Your Kitchen." Or "The Newest Kitchen Appliance." In trying to come up with a good title, feeling free and uninhibited is especially important. Risk sounding silly and foolish—way off the track—wherever and whatever the track may be. Only when you allow yourself the privilege of making new tracks (six attempts will lead nowhere; the seventh wave will take you where you want to go), only when you persistently demand that your mind yield its hidden potential and that it be active rather than passive, can you get the best from yourself.

Conduct brainstorming sessions routinely and regularly, on your own or with others in small groups. Let your mind supply ideas, some of which will appear on the page as if written by some other hand (the contribution of a deeper level of thinking). As one researcher concluded, all writing begins with some tuning in, by whatever means, to "that great ongoing inner panorama that William James called 'the stream of consciousness' " (Moffett 231).

EXERCISE

Get together with three or four friends or classmates for a brainstorming session, basing it on one of the following topics:

seat belts	hats	tourists
drunk driving	shipwrecks	movie stars
dropouts	hairdryers	voters
God	sex	politicians
marriage	textbooks	justice

Conjuring Up Memories

Novelist Thomas Wolfe could remember with shattering clarity events of his childhood and early youth: they came back to him unsolicited in their minutest, most vivid detail. Because most of us do not have this gift of total recall, we must make a conscious and sustained effort to conjure up the past so that we can reproduce it on paper with a degree of reality and vividness.

Take a memorable event: let us say you once almost drowned. That should provide the ingredients for an exciting narrative account—but maybe not. It depends on how accurately you can recall specific details. If you are a careful writer, you will open your mind to remember the specific sensations and impressions associated with the original experience, then render those experiences in vivid and concrete language: how the water bubbled in your ears as you went down . . . down . . . or the exact way voices sounded in the distance. You know that you can make your experience live again on paper only if you activate those small, telling details that capture its essence. As you spend many hours at various prewriting strategies such as freewriting, brainstorming, and clustering (see Chapter 2), you will recover information from the deepest recesses of memory. You know the facts are all buried there somewhere. If you persist in your digging, you will recover them. Although this is a formidable discipline, you will find it rewarding, for you will recapture your own past.

Interestingly, people who want to prod their memories have worked out many other psychological procedures and even rituals. Two of these are worth mentioning here, for you may adapt them to the writing process. They arise from creativity and "direct experience" workshops conducted by psychotherapist Ira Progoff. These workshops "are designed," says Progoff, "to expand awareness and evoke the unlived creative potential of the individual." But you can apply these methods to retrieving your past experience so that you may recreate it realistically on paper. In his workshop sessions, Progoff tries to help members extend the "time dimensions" of their personalities so that they can feel the movement and direction of their lives "from the outside." Thus at one workshop session Progoff addressed the group as follows:

> Let's put ourselves in adolescence . . . make it early adolescence, pre-sexual awareness. Ask yourself "How did I feel then? Were there any special experiences that stand out in my mind? Funny? Sad? Strange? How did I feel about myself? About life? About my relation to life? What was my image of myself in those days?" Let yourself be carried back . . . relax and think . . . try to remember . . . people . . . images . . . events . . . Just speak out when you *do* remember . . . Tell us what it was like.

You can simulate a creativity workshop by assembling a group of classmates, who systematically set out to evoke memories, their own and one another's. The participants may take turns free associating, letting their minds wander at will and telling their stories as they think of them, or as other people's stories remind them of their own. Or you may structure the session by having one person present a problem, like the following:

> There is an intersection: two roads going in different directions; one road is taken, one is not. Relax and think of yourself on the road, any kind of road that will lead into a crossroad. Get the feeling of being there, walking along, thinking, feeling, coming to the intersection, trying to decide which way to go . . . *which way will it be?* What happens? What is there on the road you finally take? *Why* do you take it? Just speak out as it comes to you on that road . . .

After such a session, spend some time by yourself, writing down the impressions and insights that came to you, perhaps in your journal. Don't worry about shaping them into an essay; just get it down on paper while you can.

Keeping a Writer's Journal

Another way student writers may adapt workshop methods to their own purpose is by keeping a writer's journal, a notebook of significant images or thoughts, flashes of memory, dreams, ideas, feelings, fears. This tangible procedure of reexperiencing one's existence inwardly can be most helpful to you as a writer. Try making daily entries in your notebook; then, after a few days, read the entries at your leisure, ponder their significance, and try to recover those half-forgotten details that are often the key to a whole experience.

Take that most trite of trite topics, for example—"My Summer Vacation." Everyone expects a paper written under this heading to be slapdash and dull, but does it have to be? Is a visit to the Grand Canyon dull if you have truly looked and seen? If you have experienced it genuinely in your own person and remembered not only the familiar outward spectacle but your own inward response as well? When approached in this way—with a sense of the self at the center of the experience ("Let me tell you, reader, what it was like; I have a purpose in writing this piece")—an account of your summer vacation at the Grand Canyon, or anywhere, will not be a bore to yourself or your readers. (For solid proof of this, see "The Latest Fashion in Travel," cited in Question 17.

One last point should be made: Writing an essay that *authentically* recreates one of your own experiences not only gains the instructor's commendation but also, and more importantly, gains for you a portion of your own life seen again from a deeper and more meaningful perspective. In doing this you are, in a sense, extending your life; for it may be that you will see your experiences for the first time in their true shape; it may be that you will recognize for the first time their true and full significance.

SUGGESTED JOURNAL ENTRIES

1. Think about an experience you had in the past week that affected you emotionally. Who was involved? What was the setting? The situation? What was said? Describe the experience in detail. How did you feel? Does the experience remind you of anything similar that happened in the past? Do any images come to mind? Write a one-page journal entry.

2. Choose a twenty-four hour period—beginning tomorrow morning from the moment you awaken. Did you dream during the night? Describe your dream. Describe your morning mood. Enter the events of the entire day in your journal and force yourself to observe and interpret.

3. For one week, try to record your nightly dreams, even if you can recall only fragments. Do not make judgments about the dreams; simply record them. At the end of the week, try to interpret this "script" your subconscious has written. Does it suggest anything to you about the way you feel about your life? hidden attitudes, anxieties, frustrations, or desires? Write a page in your journal.

4. In a one-page paper, try to recall your earliest dream, and explain that dream in the light of the person you are at present.

Sharpening Powers of Observation

Just as you can probe and prod your memory, so you can extend and sharpen your powers of observation by making a conscientious and deliberate effort to gain more than a general impression of something—a place, event, person, object. Anyone can get a general impression merely by being present at an event. But this is not enough for the writer; in fact, merely to look is not enough. Looking must be purposeful; all your senses must be alert to precise details: the exact color, texture, shape, smell, temperature, or tactile sensation of a place or an object; the exact appearance of a person—facial expressions, hand gestures, body movements, tones of voice; the exact event as it occurred and the way people reacted to it and to one another. These raw materials will help you write a vividly realistic account of how something happened, or what someone or something was like. You may not be as gifted as others at observing, but you can at least try to see more than you would ordinarily see if you made no special effort.

Perhaps you have decided to write a piece about a single special place—the campus library. Since you are a regular visitor and pass it daily, you regard this as a relatively simple, straightforward assignment. Are you ready, then, to sit down and start writing? Not at all. Not until you have looked at it with the conscious intention of seeing the library with fresh eyes, as if you had never seen it before. Only then will you discover that in truth you have never seen it before in any richness or sharpness of detail. Chances are that on each previous visit—numerous as they were—you only glossed over its general contour and main features.

In just this way New Yorkers observe their own huge New York Public Library on Fifth Avenue at Forty-second Street. Naturally, everyone notices the stately white columns that frame the entrance and the famous reclining stone lions. But how many observers note that there are precisely six columns and that the lions are angled slightly toward each other? How many of those who look, look still more closely—over the heads of the lions—at the maxim engraved on the building itself: BUT ABOVE ALL THINGS TRUTH BEARETH AWAY THE VICTORY (on the right), and BEAUTY OLD YET EVER NEW, ETERNAL VOICE AND INWARD WORD (on the left). The careful observer will note still another detail: over the revolving doors of the main entrance are three plaques pointing out that this library is in actuality *three separate libraries* housed in one building, a fact that most New Yorkers are unaware of, even though it appears in bold lettering on the face of the building that many thousands of them pass every day.

One famous teacher of the art of observation, Louis Agassiz (the great nineteenth-century naturalist), began his course in zoology by presenting his students with a dead fish, insisting that they look at it. And so they would for an entire morning. Agassiz would then return, asking "Well, what is it like?" As the students recited what they had seen (fringed gill-arches, fleshy lips, lidless eyes), Agassiz's face would reflect disappointment. "Keep looking," he would finally say—and leave them to their observations for the afternoon. One student who had been looking for days and days and days later described the experience as follows:

> I was piqued. I was mortified. Still more of that wretched fish! But now I set myself to my task with a will, and discovered one new thing after another, until I saw how

just the Professor's criticism had been. The afternoon passed quickly; and when, towards its close, the professor inquired:

"Do you see it yet?

"No," I replied, "I am certain I do not, but I see how little I saw before."

"That is next best," said he, earnestly, "but I won't hear you now; put away your fish and go home; perhaps you will be ready with a better answer in the morning."

For eight solid months Agassiz would entreat his pupils to "look at your fish"; he had them compare it with other fish in the same family, note resemblances and differences, detect the orderly arrangement of parts, and finally see the parts in relation to the whole and the whole in relation to an overall principle or law. The lesson in looking ended only after Agassiz had warned his students never to be satisfied with isolated observations, no matter how apt they might be. Agassiz believed that "facts are stupid things until brought into connection with some general law."

In order to see a general law behind a set of particular details, you must carry the process of observation a step further: you must go beyond looking to critical thinking; you must observe and analyze each particular, and then move on through a chain of reasoning to a valid and correct inference about the nature of the whole. To draw an inference, to see one truth as following from another, is still another way of gathering information for a piece of writing. William Blake aspired to see the world in a grain of sand, an essentially poetic insight, to be sure, but also a cerebral one, which he arrived at through rigorous thinking and through a leap (or *inference*) from the facts as observed in a grain of sand to a large truth of nature.

EXERCISES

Make the invisible visible (try to see with the seeing eye) by looking at the things you see around you every day as if you were seeing them for the first time.

Select a place on campus that you know well such as the coffee shop, reading room, or a classroom,

OR

Find a familiar place in town: a store, a landmark, or a park,

OR

Select an object from your pocket or handbag.

Using the prewriting techniques you have learned earlier, write a paragraph in which you answer the following questions:

1. What are its physical characteristics (size, shape, color, composition)?
2. Does it remind you of anything you have seen before?
3. In what ways is it the same?
4. In what ways different?
5. Who produced or constructed it?
6. For what reason?
7. Who uses it?

8. What purpose does it serve?
9. How efficiently does it function?
10. If it were not there or did not exist, would it be missed and why?

Burke's Pentad

Someone once observed that the best questioning procedure "will have all of the elegant simplicity of a profound mathematical formula." Certainly the "Pentad" devised by Kenneth Burke meets that description. According to Burke (xvii) the Pentad reflects the absolute bare and indispensible minimum of any dramatic event. For, as he explains,

> Men may violently disagree about the purposes behind a given act, or about the character of the person who did it, or how he did it, or in what kind of situation he acted; or they may even insist upon totally different words to name the act itself. But be that as it may, any complete statement about motives will offer some kind of answers to these five questions: what was done (act), when or where was it done (scene), who did it (agent), how he did it (agency) and why (purpose).

The Pentad consists of five key questions we can apply to any dramatic event—or any piece of writing we may need to comment on—as we attempt to describe it, analyze motives of characters, action, and so on:

What was done?	*the act,* that which took place in thought or deed
When or where was it done?	*the scene,* the background of the act, the situation in which it occurred; the context—the time and place and the conditions (social, economic, political) of that time and place
Who did it?	*the agent,* the person or kind of person who performed the act
How was it done?	*the agency,* what means or instrument was used
Why was it done?	*the purpose,* the apparent purpose vs. the real purpose

The Pentad is a useful questioning tool for both writer and reader. It can help the writer explore the nuances of a subject, and it can help the reader explore the nuances of a piece of writing. As we shall see in Part III, these five questions can help you as a writer make your way confidently through many of the twenty questions. In particular, the Pentad may be useful with How can X be described? How did X happen? What kind of person is X? What is my memory of X? What are the facts about X? What are the causes of X? What are the consequences of X? What is the value of X?

If the subject you are writing about is itself a piece of writing, the Pentad can be especially helpful. Here's how you might use the Pentad to explore one of the readings in this textbook:

What was done?	*the act,* the piece of writing itself: How can it be summarized?

When or where was it done?	*the scene,* the circumstances of publication: Where and when was the article or essay written? Where was it published?
Who did it?	*the agent,* the author: What kind of person was the author? What kind of background qualifies him or her to write this?
How was it done?	*the agency,* What style and tone does it have? What is the logic used? What genre of writing is it? (for example: memoir, character sketch, news article)?
Why was it done?	*the purpose,* What was the author's motive? What effect was the author trying to have?

EXERCISES

1. Read one or more of the following narrative essays. How has each writer dealt with the five elements of Burke's Pentad? Which of the elements is most prominent? Write a 300–500 word essay presenting the results of your analysis.

Wole Soyinka, "The School at Aké"
Nikos Kazantzakis, "A Night in a Calabrian Village"
E. B. White, "Death of a Pig"
Alice Walker, "Remembering Mr. Sweet"
James Joyce, "Clay"

2. Read one or more of the following essays. Using Burke's Pentad, analyze the rhetorical situation each writer faced. Write a 300–500 word essay presenting the results of your analysis.

Michael Berenbaum, "The Limitations of 'Holocaust' "
Bill Neal, "Southern Fried Chicken with Country Gravy"
Terrence Rafferty, "Predators"
Bill Clinton, Inaugural Address

2

PLANNING
A PAPER

LOOKING FOR PATTERNS
CLUSTERING

UNDERSTANDING THE RHETORICAL SITUATION
VISUALIZING YOUR AUDIENCE
ESTABLISHING A READER-WRITER
RELATIONSHIP

ORGANIZING A SUBJECT
NATURAL ORDER
LOGICAL ORDER
INTUITIVE ORDER
THE WORKING PLAN

LOOKING FOR PATTERNS

Settling on a subject you want to write about and using the techniques of prewriting to generate ideas are important first steps in writing a paper. It can be a real confidence-builder to realize that you have a lot to say, after all. Even though you have a focused topic and a pile of ideas, however, you aren't quite ready to start drafting. You need to decide what comes first, second, and so on; in other words, you need to develop a plan for your writing. Even if this plan changes as you write (and this happens with many writers), gaining a sense of purpose and direction can go a long way toward relieving writer's block. Think of pre-writing as two symbiotic processes: generating and organizing ideas. The ideas themselves suggest certain groupings that can structure your paper; you can also look through the ideas you've generated for patterns of similarity, contrast, or cause-and-effect. Once you've translated those patterns into a logical plan or outline for writing your paper, the plan itself may offer a new perspective that allows you to see and understand your topic more fully.

Clustering

One particularly effective and innovative way of finding the connections between your ideas is a form of brainstorming developed by Gabriele Rico called *clustering*. Like freewriting and other kinds of brainstorming, clustering releases the profusion of ideas and images, language and sound patterns, feelings, observations, and sensations all of us unconsciously respond to. Rico says we must

> begin with the whole, with the fundamental human desire giving shape to experience, for expressiveness, for creating form and structure out of the confusion that constitutes both our inner and outer worlds . . . . Natural writing depends on gaining access to a part of your mind we normally do not associate with skills. (16)

Rico explains that just as certain fruits (such as grapes) and certain flowers (such as lilacs) come in clusters, "thoughts and images, when given free rein, seem to come in clusters of associations" (29). By following these associations, you move through stages of uncertainty until you gradually begin to see the outlines of a pattern or a shape that can then serve as a basis for a piece of writing—an essay, story, character sketch, or editorial.

Where do you begin? As in freewriting or other kinds of brainstorming, you begin the clustering process with a word—any word. Literary critic Northrop Frye originally pointed the way to this approach by observing that any word can become "a storm center of meanings, sounds, and associations radiating out indefinitely like ripples in a pool" (29).

You begin with a word or phrase, using that as a stimulus for setting down—as quickly and spontaneously as possible—all the associations that spring naturally to your mind. Speed is important here in helping you organize ideas into clusters as you set them down on paper. This grouping of ideas and images into "sets" distinguishes clustering from other forms of brainstorming.

Let's see how the clustering process works if you begin with the nucleus word SNOW, as shown in the following illustration. The central term provides the center or nucleus from which branches spread out in all directions. Each can later serve as a separate part or passage of an emerging piece of writing.

The setting down of a cluster design such as that on page 26 should take about five to ten minutes. Given another fifteen to twenty minutes, a writer—using the various cluster-balloons as source and stimulus for a short story or sketch—came up with the following:

It is almost dark along Main Street. It's cold but getting warmer so that the snow, half-melted on the street, makes for slush underfoot. The stores are brightly lit and open late this week for Christmas shoppers, all of them rushing, rushing, clutching gifts wrapped in bright red tissue paper, tied with gold and green ribbons, sealed with Santa stickers; clutching shopping bags filled with Christmas ornaments: bulbs and figurines and long strips of aluminum foil for tossing on the tree where they will hang on branches like snow—silent, silver snow icicles really.

Christmas trees: hundreds are lined up against the high wood fence on the corner in front of the empty lot. The smell of pine is deep and dank and thick, as if the air itself had turned to pine. The world is pine for a little girl of seven, snugly warm in her fleece-lined leather jacket, hurrying home from her Christmas shopping in the local department store. It is getting much too dark; she has never been out alone this late. But she is not frightened, only excited, because she has made her big Christmas purchase, a calendar for her mother, a huge picture calendar showing the seasons of the year. Not one day of this coming year will be equal in pleasure and excitement to this day, this moment of deepening darkness and cold and wetness underfoot and the fragrance of pine everywhere and the spectacle of huge Christmas trees disappearing into the backs of large station wagons, deposited there after long family discussions. This moment as she crosses the street with her own secret purchase under her arm, she thrills to the certainty that no one will ever be able to guess what it is—not until the paper is ripped off—ah, only then will they know!

On Christmas morning she will say to her mother, handing her this mysterious gift: "You'll never guess what I bought you." "Is it a calendar?" her mother will ask.

It is clear that this vignette is more than the sum of its parts, for the writer has forged from the parts a short description-narration that has a unity and coherence and purpose beyond what is contained in the separate clusters. How did this happen? How did the writer create from the scattered balloons one single, self-contained piece?

The aim of the writer should be to achieve "creative interaction" between the two sides of the self: the irrational and spontaneous on one side, the rational and disciplined on the other. As each plays a part in the conduct of human life, so each plays a part in the composing process. In phase one we should try to generate ideas in as free and unrestricted a setting as possible. We should swirl our ideas into freehand circles and clusters of circles and not worry about literal meanings or logical sequences or even about making sense. Later, we enter what Rico calls the "conscious, critical phase, which edits, refines, and revises" what we have conjured up during the previous stage of mental and emotional abandon.

EXERCISES

The following adaptations of Rico's exercises give you a sense of the energy and spontaneous flow of ideas that clustering produces—a toning-up of both sides of the brain, a recognition of the "two persons" writers must confront in themselves.

Remember that surprise is one of the rewards of clustering. As one thought prods another, your mind moves toward a creative burst that usually produces enough material for a good beginning and an equally good ending. Important reminder: work quickly and don't worry about results. You can fit your "sets" together when you write your vignette.

1. Select five of the words below and for each one create a cluster of associations. Let the words and phrases spring from the nucleus word. If you wish, choose comparable words of your own.

star	glitter	fierce
dream	stone	time out
slipper	blessing	pickle
storm	attic	razor
time	echo	whiskers
pain	wired	warm
glove	bottle	water
dark	frost	raid
breaking free	orphan	hardness
leaf	crop	trigger
barefoot	freeway	turnip

Now give yourself twenty to thirty minutes to write a vignette on each of the five words you have clustered.

continued

2. Choose as your nucleus word the name of someone you care for and create a cluster of the things that come to mind about that person: strengths, weaknesses, quirks, sayings, appearance, attitudes—whatever "flows" when you think about the person you choose. Write a vignette (twenty to thirty minutes). You will find a number of unforgettable characterizations in the section about Question 3: What Kind of Person Is X?

3. Select one of the following emotions (or a comparable one of your own) and use it as the basis of a cluster:

joy	anger
fear	tenderness
pain	euphoria
panic	disgust
love	sadness

4. Choose a saying, such as "All that glitters is not gold" or "Marry in haste, repent in leisure," or "Idleness is the Devil's workshop." Write a short explanation of what the saying means. Then cluster it in single words, whole phrases, or both. Be as loose in your clustering as you were tight in your explanation. This exercise brings both sides of the brain into play.

5. Cluster the phrases "I really like . . . " and "I really hate . . . " for about five minutes each and see what you come up with. Avoid the obvious; you may be surprised at what emerges. From each, write a short vignette, allowing yourself twenty to thirty minutes.

6. Quickly cluster the word COLOR and see what happens. Then choose a color you particularly like. Cluster it, setting down as many images as you can. Be open to associations from the past: "Grandma's yellow tablecloth" or "Aunt Jane's brown leather books." Continue until you know where you are going, then in twenty to thirty minutes write a vignette using the images you have conjured up.

UNDERSTANDING THE RHETORICAL SITUATION

A clear understanding of the rhetorical situation you face can also serve as a valuable aid to planning. Understanding who your readers are and what they expect of you will help you decide not only what to include and what to leave out (based on your readers' knowledge of the subject), but also what they will more readily accept and what you should save until the end of your paper, when you have built up some credibility as a writer.

Visualizing Your Audience

As we have seen, writers develop a sense of themselves as writers partly by talking to themselves and to others as they explore a topic. This is an important part of establishing the rhetorical stance described in the Introduction. Another important part of that rhetorical stance, indeed, a critical part, is to understand who your readers are—your audience. Only then can you come to the fullest understanding of your purpose, for the two are inextricably combined. Thus, understanding your audience and purpose, combined with your sense of yourself as a writer and your relationship to the subject matter, can help you speak to your audience appropriately.

Unless your instructor suggests otherwise, the audience you would do best to invent is the educated community at large: intelligent nonspecialists. *Invent* is the accurate term here since many researchers have observed that the writer's audience is always a fiction—and a *necessary* fiction, to borrow a term from the poet Wallace Stevens.

If this seems too general, you could invent a more specific group of readers—your college classmates or more specifically the members of your composition course. If your instructor runs your class as a workshop, as many do, you will periodically present your papers to your fellow writers who are all working to improve their writing.

Of course, members of the class may feel competitive toward your work, but many will also be supportive. In any case, they are there to respond to you and to provide the feedback you need to determine how successfully you have achieved your goals. Have you stated your arguments effectively? (Have you convinced everyone? Anyone?) Are your witty asides in fact witty? (Do people laugh? Or at least smile?) Are your narratives interesting? (Do your listeners listen attentively?) Are your analyses clear and understandable? Study facial expressions, and don't ignore signs of confusion or puzzlement. Without feedback, you can never be certain that you conveyed your intended meaning accurately.

Listeners may send negative responses back to the speaker (shifting in seats, whispering, looking at their wristwatches), or they may give positive reinforcement (smiles, nodding of heads, applause). Because writers receive no such clues, no face-to-face interaction, they must plan ahead more carefully and anticipate their readers' needs. Some writers are more successful at this than others. Writers who try hardest to meet the needs of that collective entity called "the audience" recognize that writing is a human activity (see Introduction); they respect the essential fragility and ambiguity of language itself (see "Using Words Effectively," Chapter 10), and view writing as a way "to serve people rather than impress them." Such writers let good will and common sense guide them.

Good writers will be sensitive to E. B. White's keen observation that whatever their educational level or cultural background, "most readers are in trouble about half of the time." Thus White's compassionate exhortation on behalf of "clarity, clarity, clarity . . . . Even to a writer who is being intentionally obscure or wild of tongue we can say, 'Be obscure clearly! Be wild of tongue in a way we can understand.'" The editor of a large metropolitan daily must have shared White's dedication to clarity, for he posted the following sign in the news room: "Never underestimate the intelligence of your readers, but never overestimate their information."

No one is more sensitive to the requirements of readers than the writer of advertising copy whose very livelihood depends on motivating readers to think, feel, and respond in a given way. Note, for example, what is going on in the advertisement in Figure 2-1.

First, the picture sends its own nonverbal message: an attractive young couple dressed in handsome cable-knit sweaters beam upon their young son (who is drinking apple juice), while the mother cuddles a contented baby (also drinking apple juice, as is the father). Does the writer want to tell you that drinking apple juice will make your family healthy and happy? Well, just look at the picture and then read the text, explicitly addressed to mothers "who care about wholesomeness." (Would any mother claim otherwise?)

Finally, wholesome apple juice from the Farm...Pepperidge Farm.™

Introducing the apple juice made for mothers who care about wholesomeness as well as taste.

Pepperidge Farm guarantees never to use preservatives. Nor water. Nor sugar. Nothing but the pure wood-pressed juice of five kinds of apples. Blended for a rich apple taste that's not too sweet, not too tart.

Your whole family will love it.

Five kinds of apples. One of a kind quality.

Figure 2-1.

The writer provides only two complete sentences in this message; the others are fragments ("Nor water. Nor sugar . . . ."). Such liberties with conventional sentence structure are not usually accepted in formal or academic situations but they serve the copywriter's purpose because they are easy to read, they are emphatic, and they get the reader's attention.

Note the "homey" reassuring tone of the writing; a voice from the past reminds us of how lovingly and painstakingly Grandma pressed juice from five different kinds of apples to make one wonderful drink with a "one of a kind quality." Advertising works by appealing to an unstated shared set of values. What kind of values does this advertisement invoke?

EXERCISES

1. Study the ad in Figure 2-2. Note that this ad presents a very different kind of beverage. To what audience does the advertiser direct this ad? What age group? To what economic group? To men or women—or both? Paraphrase the text: What does it state? What does it imply? What emotions does it try to arouse? Do you consider this ad effective? Explain.

2. Imagine that you are a copy writer. Your agency has just assigned you a new client—a restaurant. You must write an ad for the grand opening. Decide what kind of restaurant it is: fast-food chain, Chinese, vegetarian, a pizza parlor, a steak house, or *haute cuisine*. Then you must decide which customers you want to attract to the restaurant: high school or college students, middle- or upper-income patrons. Present the restaurant, its atmosphere, its cuisine, and its particular appeal in such a way that your readers will storm the doors on opening night.

3. Let's say you want to distribute condoms to a public health clinic. Some people in the town fear that your operation will corrupt the town youth. You want to allay their concern and turn their judgment in your favor, as well as convince the undecided to lend you their support. Write a letter to one of the following groups:

The town council	The school board
The clergy	Parents
Merchants	School students

Establishing a Reader–Writer Relationship

A good way to begin connecting with readers whom you visualize as your chosen audience is by letting them know you are someone they can trust, someone who is on their side. By making this appeal to *ethos* (as classical rhetoricians called it), you can establish a solid and enduring reader–writer relationship. Here again the process begins with self-confrontation.

1. *Your own identity as a writer:* How do you see yourself in relation to the reader and to the subject matter? "Who am I this time?" asks a character in a Kurt Vonnegut short story. He is comfortable only when he is playing a well-defined role that he knows he can handle. As a writer you should ask yourself the same question whenever you undertake a new assignment: *Who am I this time?* What special role is best suited to the needs of this particular piece? How can I most effectively project my "persona?" Am I the calm, confident advocate of civil rights, certain that ultimately "we shall overcome"? Or am I an outraged, up-in-arms opponent? Or am I a dispassionate onlooker, taking no sides, letting the facts I present objectively speak for themselves? Each identity requires its own carefully worked out presentation and its own appropriate voice that you should maintain consistently throughout.

Figure 2-2.

2. *The identity of your readers:* Beyond seeing them as fellow human beings struggling to decipher and make sense of your message, you should try to estimate, as best you can, their specific age group, educational and economic level, cultural context, and special needs. Professional writers submitting an article to a particular publication have received a profile of its average reader (including age group, occupation and profession, and education). Having a good idea, then, of the readers' backgrounds and capabilities, their literacy level, their preferences and special interests, professional writers can speak in an appropriate voice and write in an acceptable style in lively, sophisticated, highly compressed, fast-moving prose for readers of *Time* or *Newsweek;* in a slower, more leisurely style for readers of *Scientific American,* with its more technical, in-depth coverage of specialized scientific subjects. Most specifically, the writer can then make more intelligent and successful choices about words, sentence structure, and style.

A word of caution: Whoever your readers are and however you try to satisfy their distinctive needs and abilities, you should guard against the two futile and offensive extremes of aiming over their heads or talking down to them.

3. *The context or occasion for a given piece of writing:* This third vital consideration is closely related to the readers themselves. Who are they, we ask, and what is the occasion for addressing them? All of us adjust naturally to the occasion when we speak face-to-face. We explain a problem one way to our friends over lunch, another to a formal committee assembled to hear an official report. Audience and occasion are intimately related and can often be checked out together. If you are going to address a student group, for instance, on the occasion of a campus-wide election, you might test your speech on a representative member of your audience, asking for a candid reaction: "Will using slang in this context trivialize or obscure an issue? Might it offend some people?"

Careful study of conventional contexts, such as the Letters to the Editor column in your local newspaper, will give you clues on general usage in that context. You can get a sense of how others writing on the same occasion handled the assignment.

4. *The purpose of a piece of writing:* As obvious as this consideration may sound, many writers never consciously ask before they write—What am I trying to achieve? At the earliest possible time you should decide whether you are trying to entertain or instruct your readers. Do you wish to persuade them to think a certain way? Do you want the reader to take a particular side on a controversial issue and take action in its behalf by voting for or actively supporting a given candidate? Will you shed new light on an old problem?

In order to win assent from your readers—probably the most challenging of all purposes—you must first establish your own credibility; second, you must keep the reader reading. You can achieve both goals by making certain that you present sufficient facts along with convincing supporting data, examples, and lively anecdotes (everyone likes a story). Touches of humor are also helpful and may win the day over a solemnly grim and dull presentation that leaves readers bored and indifferent.

Some rhetoricians say that the writer's purpose is *always* to win assent or agreement from readers (yes, that candidate deserves to win the election; yes, this essay is funny; yes, I understand DNA now; yes, I can now bake a blueberry pie; and so on). Whatever your purpose, you must train yourself to see your subject from the readers' point of view. Why should they see things your way? How do they stand to benefit? What are their expectations to begin with? Are you aware of these and are you fulfilling them? If your purpose is *genuinely* to serve people, and not merely to impress or convince them, then you will make the necessary effort to demonstrate in an orderly and animated manner why your purpose will work in their behalf as well as your own. In fact, you will convince them that you share a single or similar purpose and that you start on common ground.

EXERCISES

Imagine or invent a situation in which you might write on one or more of the following topics. What would be the reader–writer relationship in each of those situations?

1. Hunting black bear with a bow and arrow
2. New treatment for the hyperactive child
3. What's new in stereo equipment
4. Suggestions for getting into the college of your choice
5. Shopping for the perfect retirement home
6. The hidden perils of vitamins
7. Trekking through a rain forest
8. Adjusting to stepparents

In each of these situations, work out the four basic aspects of the reader–writer relationship:

1. What is your identity as a writer?
2. What is the identity of your reader?
3. What is the context or occasion of the piece?
4. What is the purpose of the piece?

   Once you have answered these questions, you will be able to decide on answers to additional questions, such as: What tone should you use? How technical or detailed should your presentation be? How can you best capture and keep your audience? Once you have identified your audience or have some sense of who your readers are, you can begin to explore your subject still further, focusing now on more tangible criteria. What do you know about your subject that would interest your readers? Do you have any special or specific ideas that are particularly suitable? What is the best plan for presenting these ideas to this particular group of readers?

ORGANIZING A SUBJECT

Having developed your topic and asked questions about your rhetorical situation, you face your next—and perhaps most complex—challenge: how to get this material from your mind onto the page. No matter how rich or complex your mental picture of your topic, you must convey it to your readers one idea at a time, one word at a time. This requires thoughtful planning. By looking carefully at the information you've gathered and reflecting on your rhetorical situation, you can *make decisions* about how to sort, select, and classify categories of information; how to isolate main points and weave in supporting details; how to determine what should go where—and why. (You may have accomplished some of this in the clustering process.) Classical rhetoricians referred to this stage of the writing process as "disposition" or "arrangement," the organization of the whole into an orderly sequence of parts. Whether you organize on paper in carefully worked out detail or only roughly in your head, you must plan your paper so that it flows smoothly and logically from one point to another, moving steadily in its intended direction.

These decisions about organizing a paper are not just writing decisions, but occasions for critical thought. Searching for patterns and testing ideas against an analytic framework are some of the cognitive skills you'll need to succeed in other college coursework. Academic thinking searches for the main ideas that connect and illuminate the data of observation and research. In finding the organization that makes individual details relevant, you are, in a sense, *creating meaning* for your readers. Through language, we shape our view of the world so that we can communicate it to others.

Natural Order

Sometimes deciding on an order for your ideas seems simple. Many of the twenty questions that generate topics are, in a sense, self-organizing. A simple analysis, for example, breaks a subject down into its component parts or types, which are then quite naturally listed in a series (part one, part two, and so on). Similarly an analysis of a process (how something is done or made) is inevitably organized chronologically (first this, then this, then this). A description is usually arranged according to space (left to right, north to south), and narration naturally organizes itself according to time (chronological sequence, flashback, and so on). In such cases the materials determine how you should develop them. You need only recognize the structure of your topic and fulfill it; the ideas organize themselves.

Logical Order

This is not always the case, however. In constructing a comparison, for example (Question 15, "How does X compare to Y?"), you must make a conscious decision about its structure: Should you compare X as a whole, then Y as a whole? Should you break X and Y down and systematically examine the parts of each? Should you compare likenesses or contrast differences? The decision rests on how you view your topic and your rhetorical situation: Which ordering principle will exhibit your points in their clearest and sharpest light and best achieve your purpose? There is no single best way to compare two things; different organizational patterns may be better for different audiences.

Presenting a portrait of Isaac Newton (Chapter 5, "Generating a Longer Paper"), the author organizes his materials chronologically, focusing from the beginning on Newton as a "strange, solitary figure" who seemed himself to be an embodiment of the forces of Nature that he would later study and illuminate. Here is an outline of the essay on Newton.

Introduction: The "great powers" of Newton were recognized but their source, like that of the Nile, "had not been discovered."

    I. Childhood
       A. Family background
       B. Political setting
       C. Personality

II. College and Early Career
  A. Trinity College
  B. Seeds of scientific work: the golden 18 months
    1. mathematics
    2. celestial mechanics
    3. physical optics
  C. Public recognition
III. Triumphs and Controversies
  A. Theory of light and colors
  B. Teaching at Cambridge
  C. <u>Principia</u>
IV. Declining Years
  A. Position at Warden
  B. Speculations and hypotheses

Conclusion: Quotation from Pope provides a "cyclical return" to the idea that Newton was himself a force of Nature, his power being to illuminate Nature's Laws (though Newton, curiously, remains mysterious to the end).

In this essay, as in most exposition and argumentation, the author orders parts in a purely logical way. The writer works out his or her own pattern of ideas—establishing causal connections, making inferences, drawing conclusions. If the reasoning process is sound, then the essay seems as inevitably ordered as the steps of a natural process.

Intuitive Order

Still another method of organizing a piece of writing is by intuition, according to an internal voice and rhythm that dictates how to treat a subject. What should come first, second, third? What are the proper points of view, the appropriate tone, the right words? The structure of such a piece follows the contours of the writer's thoughts, which may have their own natural logic. Similarly, the writer establishes the mood not with any pre-meditated plan, but simply by following feelings and setting them down as felt, with no conscious organization. Approached in this way, as critic Herbert Read wrote, an essay is an informal "attempt at the expression of an idea or a mood or feeling lurking unexpressed in the mind . . . an attempt to create a pattern in words which shall correspond with the idea, mood or feeling" (*Modern,* 66).

Read wrote further that this process is comparable to musical improvisation; it is also "the counterpart of the lyric in poetry." The writer's intimate relationship to the subject and his or her desire to explore with readers an essentially "inner experience" make an intuitive ordering of materials not only appropriate but inevitable. In such cases, as in the writing of a poem, it is in the act of writing itself that the writer discovers what he or she wants to say.

Of course, only certain subjects and certain informal types of writing lend themselves to this approach; a term paper, for example, usually does not fall into this category. In a more informal essay, however, this exploratory pattern can be an effective method of letting your readers see your mind at work, as long as you keep a fairly narrow focus. The popular television personality Andy Rooney has pointed out that "our brains have a way of jumping around a lot, thinking of one thing for a few seconds and then flitting off to think of another." Very true. Unless you make a deliberate and determined effort to focus your mind on a given subject and make an orderly exploration of its many aspects, first from one point of view, then from another, you will have trouble moving ahead toward a finished piece.

How apt, then, that Rooney would indicate further that "for me as a writer, it's always been fun to see if I could stop one subject in my head for long enough to take a good look at it." *To stop a subject in one's head in order to take a good look at it:* this is precisely what he does in the following essay. It is characteristic of Rooney, a kind of Everyman to his large TV following, that he has chosen a familiar subject, something we see around us every day. "I was thinking about fences," he says very simply. Note how he proceeds from there, generating ideas as he goes along by answering a series of questions on his announced topic. Though there is a logic to Rooney's writing plan, it is an intuitive logic that unfolds from sentence to sentence.

FENCES

Andy Rooney

What kind of fences are there? How many? What size? What are the differences between fences? What purposes do fences serve? To whom are fences helpful? Any examples? Why are fences built? Where are fences built? Usually? Sometimes? Is it ever hard to tell how a fence is functioning? What is confusing? What do you suspect? What personal response do certain fences elicit? Why? Which fences are most beautiful? What can they be compared to? What makes them beautiful? Which fences are ugliest? What are they made of? Which fences do the best job? What is a "minimal" fence? What message do fences send? How would you define a fence? How does it compare to similar structures such as a wall? A barrier? What adds to the confusion? In what respects are fences like people? What

Our brains have a way of jumping around a lot, thinking of one thing for a few seconds and then flitting off to think of another. For me as a writer, it's always been fun to see if I could stop one subject in my head for long enough to take a good look at it.

For instance, I was thinking about fences. There are as many kinds of fences in this country as there are people. You couldn't *count* all the kinds of fences there are. There are big fences, small fences, teeny-tiny fences.

The biggest difference between one fence and another fence is whether the fence was built to protect what's inside from what's outside or to protect what's outside from what's inside. To protect the people outside, for instance, a mean dog has to be fenced in.

It's a mystery why some fences are ever built at all. Most cemeteries have fences, even though no one outside really wants to get in and no one inside ever tries to get out.

Sometimes you can't tell what a fence is keeping in—or keeping out. You can't tell what a fence is protecting from what. You suspect that sometimes people just put up fences from habit, or as a show of strength or wealth. I hate anyone who has a fence that cost more than my house cost.

The best-looking fences are often the simplest. A simple fence around a beautiful home can be like a frame around a picture. The house isn't hidden; its beauty is enhanced by the frame. But a fence can be a massive, ugly thing, too, made of bricks and mortar. Sometimes the insignificant little fences do their job just as well as the ten-foot walls. Maybe it's only a string stretched between here and there in a field. The message is clear: don't cross here.

There's often a question about whether a barrier is a fence or a wall. Fences, I think, are thinner than walls. And, of course, there are people who confuse us further by building fences on top of walls.

are the types of fences? How do they differ? Do they generate special attitudes or feelings? In what ways? How do people react to fences? What are some of the perils of being a fence? Do fences influence other fences? In what ways? What do people expect of fences? What final response do you have toward fences? What is the future of fences? How do fences influence the world? What would happen if all fences disappeared?

Every fence has its own personality and some don't have much. There are friendly fences. A friendly fence takes kindly to being leaned on. There are friendly fences around playgrounds. And some playground fences are more fun to play on than anything they surround. There are more mean fences than friendly fences overall, though. Some have their own built-in invitation not to be sat upon. Unfriendly fences get it right back sometimes. You seldom see one that hasn't been hit, bashed, bumped or in some way broken or knocked down.

One of the phenomena of fences is their tendency to proliferate. Note, if you will, how often one fence brings on another fence. People often seem to want their own fence, even if it's back to back, cheek by jowl with the neighbor's fence, almost as though the fence was put up to keep the fence out.

The other thing I thought about fences: I thought maybe the world wouldn't be very much changed if tomorrow morning. . . . every fence was gone.

Notice that Rooney has answered primarily the questions, *what* and *how,* but that he has also given some attention to *why, where, when,* and *who.* Journalists, like Rooney, often rely on these questions to jog their thinking processes and, as Rooney says, stop a subject in one's brain to take a good look at it.

The Working Plan

Whatever pattern or organization you decide will be best for your paper, you may find it helpful to take the additional step of committing to paper a specific working plan or working outline. The importance of this practical approach to organization is apparent in such reminders as E. B. White's, "Before beginning to compose something, gauge the nature and extent of the enterprise and work from a suitable design." White's reasoning is simple and convincing:

> Design informs even the simplest structure, whether of brick and steel or of prose. You raise a pup tent from one sort of vision, a cathedral from another. This does not mean that you must sit with a blueprint always in front of you, merely that you had best anticipate what you are getting into. (*Style,* 63)

Journalist John Gunther also believed in anticipating "what you are getting into." Before he had written a single page of his voluminous *Inside Asia,* he had projected thirty-five chapters; he ended up with thirty-six." "It is always a good thing," he suggested, "to have a firm structure in mind." This is helpful advice, for without a structure or goal in mind, the writer resembles the harried gentleman who reportedly jumped on his horse and rode off in all directions.

Of course a writer does not, as some people think, work with a strict outline that establishes once and for all the shape of the final paper. "One's plan is one thing," said Henry James, "and one's result another." Invention is an ongoing process that spills over into the research stage and the organizing and writing stages as well. The writer continues to make discoveries. Writing itself is discovery, and the outline, to cite James again, is but "the early bloom of one's good faith." You must allow for, indeed expect, later blooms as well. In this sense, you should view the outline not as a permanent form but as a working guide, pointing the way in a given direction but open to change when you discover new and better possibilities. Obviously, shorter papers do not need quite as careful planning as longer projects, but many students find that even for an essay exam, when time is of the essence, a few minutes invested in at least a rudimentary plan of attack can pay handsome dividends.

Keeping this in mind, let us see how you could draw up an outline for a representative term paper topic—an extended analysis of hypnosis that includes information on its function, present status, and value. Whether the paper is to be 2,000 or 10,000 words, certain inevitable categories suggest themselves:

definition (What constitutes the hypnotic state?)
history (the phenomenon of hypnosis as observed through the centuries)
hypnotic technique
hypnotic behavior
uses of hypnotism (medicine, dentistry, psychotherapy)
abuses and dangers of hypnotism (unqualified hypnotists)
autohypnosis
individual susceptibility to hypnosis
recent experimental evidence
posthypnotic suggestion
misconceptions about hypnosis
current scientific opinion of hypnosis

Certainly these twelve categories are useful during the note-taking stage when you group your information under specific headings. Later on, however, when you organize your material, you will undoubtedly find twelve categories unwieldy and repetitious.

Yet if these twelve categories pose problems for you as a writer, they would be even more confusing to your future readers. This list of twelve ideas has no structure or pattern that your readers could grasp and offers no clues about how these ideas fit together. It's easy to imagine the unfortunate reader of a paper based on this list finishing her reading and muttering to herself, "What was *that* all about?" *What this paper is all about*—this is another way of talking about your paper's central idea, your main point, your *thesis*. Having a clear thesis is like making a promise to your reader: If you read carefully what I have to say, I will do my best to demonstrate X. A clear understanding of your thesis or central idea will help you make decisions about what to include in your paper and what to leave out; it will also help you identify the main points you need to make.

In the case of the paper on hypnosis, we aren't really planning a strongly persuasive paper (arguing for or against hypnosis, for example). If we condense the categories into three or four main headings under which we list various subheadings, it becomes clearer that we are discussing what hypnosis is and how it is used. Thus the working outline may look something like this:

Tentative titles: "What is Hypnotism?" or "The Continuing Mystery of Hypnosis"
Thesis: Hypnotism, a subject that has intrigued people for centuries and that remains

mysterious despite the probings of modern science, has many uses in modern medicine and psychotherapy

    I. Introduction

       A. Definition of hypnosis

          1. Psychological state

          2. Physiological state

       B. History

          1. Ancient observations, superstitions

          2. Eighteenth and nineteenth centuries: beginning of scientific study

             a. Mesmer

             b. Charcot

   II. What hypnosis is

       A. The hypnotic trance

          1. How induced

             a. Classical techniques (gazing at fixed object)

             b. Drugs (sodium pentothal)

             c. Autohypnosis

          2. How subject reacts (cite examples)

             a. Hypnotic anesthesia (insensitivity to pain)

             b. Hallucinations

             c. Age regression

             d. Unusual muscular strength and rigidity

             e. Organic effects (blisters)

             f. Social effects

          3. Posthypnotic suggestions

       B. Hypnotic subjects

          1. Variations in individual susceptibility

          2. Variations in "how far" people go under hypnosis

             a. Antisocial acts (crime)

             b. Destructive acts

  III. Uses of hypnotism

       A. Positive uses

          1. Medicine (include evidence from recent scientific studies)

          2. Dentistry

          3. Psychotherapy (cite examples)

       B. Abuses and possible dangers (weave in stories to illustrate)

          1. Hypnotism as "entertainment"

          2. Unqualified hypnotists (unable to awaken subject)

Conclusion: Summary of significance of hypnotism; speculation on possible future applications

The actual format of your outline is relatively unimportant. Some people find the traditional outline structure given above to be an aid to logical thinking. Other writers can plan their writing more easily with a more informal approach. Computer programs can also make the planning process easier. Some programs (often called "idea processors") are designed to help you clarify and organize your ideas. The more elaborate word processing programs have outlining components, too, but you don't need such fancy tools to plan your writing.

A word processor can help you develop a working plan. After you've brainstormed a list of ideas, save it, then go over the list and weed out the ideas that seem off the track. Look over what remains, and group similar ideas together, perhaps adding a heading to clarify their relationship. Use the text-movement features of your computer (sometimes called "cut" and "paste") to try out different patterns of organization. Save and print out different organizational plans, then spread them out on your desk and ask yourself which will be the most effective way of getting your ideas across to your readers. (We suggest that you get in the habit not only of saving your work often, but also of saving different versions of it. Sometimes you won't realize until you're in the middle of writing a paper how an idea you discarded early on can be an important part of your argument.)

A working outline helps you to channel your ideas as you write and gives you a chance to check beforehand on their logical progression. Does section three logically follow section two, or should you reverse the order? Should you transfer part of the introduction to the conclusion? Is the first part of the middle section too long in comparison to the second part? And so on. By studying the outline carefully, much as an architect studies a blueprint, you can see whether the structure is likely to hold together: whether you have related the parts clearly and consistently and whether you have developed them soundly and strategically, each in its proper proportion. By checking and improving a paper in the outline stage you can save yourself hours of reworking and rewriting later on.

Chapter 3

DRAFTING A PAPER

PARAGRAPH DIVISION
    STUDYING MUSIC IN INDIA
    RAVI SHANKAR

THE PARAGRAPH AS A MINIATURE ESSAY

PARAGRAPH DEVELOPMENT
    EXAMPLES
    ILLUSTRATIONS
    DETAILS
    REASONS
    MIXED MATERIALS

PARAGRAPH UNITY

PARAGRAPH COHERENCE
    ORDERING PRINCIPLES
    USING TRANSITIONS
    CONSISTENCY OF TONE

THE NEED FOR COHERENCE

WRITING SPECIAL PARAGRAPHS
    GETTING STARTED
    ENDING THE PAPER

When we talk about the experience of writing, we are largely talking about writing in paragraphs. In the actual at-the-desk, word-by-word, sentence-by-sentence drafting situation, you write one paragraph at a time. You are not thinking about rhetorical principles but rather about the rush of ideas whirling about in your mind. How can you commit your ideas to paper, give them shape and form? It is in the paragraph—the major message unit of the piece—that you unfold your ideas, one by one, as your mind dictates and your pen flows.

In this sense we write in paragraphs. True, the writing process proceeds sentence-by-sentence, but we never write a sentence in isolation; we write within the context of the paragraph. Certainly we think in paragraphs, or units of thought that we block out as we write, indenting every so often when it seems "time" to do so. Interestingly, this intuitive approach works well, for studies have shown that most people instinctively begin a new paragraph at the right place; where there is a change or turn of thought, a shift from one phase of the subject to another. In its basic function, the paragraph is both a convenience and a convention. Visually it breaks up a solid mass of print that would otherwise tire readers' eyes and tax their patience.

The paragraph is both a logical, rhetorical unit and a mechanical structure. Marjorie Boulton describes the paragraph as "a small group of thoughts that hang together" (*Prose,* 41). Although they are part of a larger whole, these thoughts generally constitute a self-contained unit that makes sense by itself. Each paragraph marks a stage in the development of the writer's thought. Paragraph indentations, then, help readers by indicating the organization and development of the writer's thought as it moves from one aspect of the subject to another. As you draft your paper, think about each paragraph as a unit of thought to be developed clearly and carefully. Once you master the techniques of effective paragraphing, you're well on your way to becoming a more effective writer.

PARAGRAPH DIVISION

Some paragraph boundaries are fairly obvious, especially if the writer is working from an outline. In a short paper each heading often turns out to be one or two paragraphs; in a longer paper the subheadings frequently constitute or at least suggest paragraph divisions. It is a common and often a wise practice to open a paragraph with a topic sentence that announces the main idea from which the writer constructs the entire paragraph, the idea that determines what belongs and what does not belong in the paragraph. Both writer and reader benefit from topic sentences, for they keep the discourse moving in a single, logical line of development.

In the short essay that follows, note that the first sentence is, in fact, an introductory (topic) paragraph listing the three elements that will make up the whole; the writer then embodies each of these elements in a topic sentence of its own, serving as a base for further amplification and illustration within the paragraph. The essay ends with a fifth paragraph containing a summing-up statement.

STUDYING MUSIC IN INDIA

Ravi Shankar

Guru, vinaya, sadhana—these three words form the heart of the musical tradition of India.

Guru, as many people now know, means master, spiritual teacher, or preceptor. We give a very important place to the *guru,* for we consider him to be the representation of the divine. There is a saying—

> Pani piye chhanke
> Guru banaye janke

—which means that one should drink water only after it has been filtered, and one should take a *guru* only after one feels sure of the decision. The choice of the *guru,* to us, is even more important than choosing a husband or a wife. A potential disciple cannot make a hasty decision to take just any teacher as his *guru,* nor should he break the bond between *guru* and *shishya,* once the *ganda* or *nara* ceremony, the initiation, which symbolically binds the two together for life, has taken place.

Vinaya means humility; it is the complete surrendering of the self on the part of the *shishya* to the *guru.* The ideal disciple feels love, adoration, reverence, and even fear toward his *guru,* and he accepts equally praise or scoldings. Talent, sincerity, and the willingness to practice faithfully are essential qualities of the serious student. The *guru,* as the giver in this relationship, seems to be all-powerful. Often, he may be unreasonable, harsh, or haughty, though the ideal *guru* is none of these. Ideally, he should respond to the efforts of the disciple and love him almost as his own child. In India, a Hindu child, from his earliest years, is taught to feel humble toward anyone older than he or superior in any way. From the simplest gesture of the *namaskar,* or greeting (putting the hands palm to palm in front of the forehead and bowing), or the *pranam* (a respectful greeting consisting of touching the greeted person's feet, then one's own eyes and forehead with the hands held palm to palm) to the practice of *vinaya* or humility tempered with a feeling of love and worship, the Hindu devotee's vanity and pretension are worn away. . . .

The third principal term associated with our music is *sadhana,* which means practice and discipline, eventually leading to self-realization. It means practicing with a fanatic zeal and ardent dedication to the *guru* and the music. If the student is talented, sincere, faithful to his *guru* and devoted in his practicing, and if the *guru* is teaching with utmost dedication and not being miserly with his knowledge, there is a distinct pattern for learning Indian music. The student must begin by acquiring the most basic techniques of the voice or instrument. In vocal music, this skill is achieved by assiduously practicing first one note, trying to produce correct breathing, voice, and pitch control. Students both of vocal and of instrumental music then learn scales and *paltas* (also called *alankars*). *Paltas* are short melodic figures performed in sequential order with a scale and *tala* framework in different tempi. Then, the *sargams* must be learned—the various fixed compositions sung to the note-names. In some fixed compositions *talas* and tempi can be varied, and in others no *tala* is used at all. The student also learns various other fixed compositions called *bandishes,* which include songs in different styles sung to a meaningful text, slow or fast instrumental pieces *(gats),* or some melodic phrases in a variety of melodic motions and tempi *(tans).*

This elementary training, for a talented and persevering student, should last not less than five years, very much like the elementary training for any Western musical discipline. This means the student should practice every day for at least eight hours. . . . Starting from the very beginning, I would estimate that it requires at least twenty years of constant work and practice to reach maturity and a high standard of achievement in our classical music.

Paragraphing does not always correspond so neatly to shifts in thought, for in addition to logic many considerations enter into the division of prose into paragraphs. Indeed, "thought movement itself," as rhetorician Paul C. Rodgers has pointed out, "submits to very flexible partitioning; hence the size of a given logical paragraph frequently reflects secondary influences" (*Composition,* 5). The narrow column format of a newspaper, for example, and readers' demand that they be able to skim the page and get the news almost at a glance, require short, varied paragraphs. Normally, however, you should not fragment your ideas by chopping them up into a series of consistently short paragraph units. We can see immediately that a typewritten page containing four or more paragraphs probably needs reworking: The writer either has not developed his or her ideas sufficiently or has failed to respect their unity and flow.

You may decide to set off a paragraph for a particular purpose: as an introduction, a conclusion, or a transition from one aspect of thought to another. Such paragraphs may contain only one or two sentences, but they nonetheless deserve to stand alone. Finally, we must consider emphasis, rhythm, and tone. A short paragraph, for example, isolates a piece of information and thereby stresses it; it may also contribute to the rhythmic sweep of your essay and the particular tone you hope to establish. A philosophic essay may contain relatively long, detailed paragraphs that reinforce the unity and continuity of your thought. A light essay may embody its scattered and tentative ideas in shorter, less formally structured paragraphs. As always, you must consider not only your subject but your readers as well. Will a demandingly long and bulky paragraph discourage them? If so, you may want to divide a normal unit of thought into two units—that is, to develop one topic sentence over two paragraphs. The writer of the following narrative has done this to increase readability:

In any journey there are three separate and recognizable stages. First there is the setting-out, the more-or-less anxious business of organizing the expedition and getting it off complete and on time. Then there is the journey itself, with its satisfying sense of achievement in each mile travelled. This is the most peaceful stage for the travellers, since we hand ourselves over as so much baggage to be passively transported. Even in a motor-car which we drive ourselves we are only a part of the steering-wheel: we have only to propel the car; and even driving across London in the rush hour is wonderfully soothing, for instance, compared with getting a family off on summer holiday.

The third stage of the journey is less definite and more variable. It begins imperceptibly as we near the end, and we recognize the transition by a growing impatience to arrive. We are no longer travelling, but impatiently covering the distance which still separates us from where we want to be. However it is not the number of miles remaining which decides our impatience: it is their proportion of the whole. On a journey of a hundred miles, at forty-nine we are still placid travellers.

—Nan Fairbrother, *The House in the Country*

THE PARAGRAPH AS A MINIATURE ESSAY

One helpful way to study paragraphs—and to gain practice in writing them—is to view them as miniature essays. Often writers can expand the well-organized paragraph to an essay, just as they can reduce the well organized essay to a paragraph.

Let us take a second, closer look at the Ravi Shankar essay. Its clear organization and neat paragraph divisions enable us to see the expansion-compression process at work. As we have already noted, the introductory paragraph provides a one-sentence summary of the entire piece, a thesis statement, as it is sometimes called:

Guru, vinaya, sadhana—these three words form the heart of the musical tradition of India.

Obviously this introduction gives us the kernel idea, or thesis, which the writer will develop throughout the rest of the essay. Standing alone, for emphasis, this one-sentence paragraph might easily be expanded into a self-contained longer one. Below is this hypothetical paragraph—an expanded form of the introductory sentence and a compressed form of the essay as a whole:

Topic sentence	*Guru, vinaya, sadhana*—these three words form the heart of the musical tradition of India. *Guru,* as many people now know, means master, spiritual teacher, or preceptor. We give a very important place to the *guru,* for we consider him to be
Developing details	the representative of the divine. *Vinaya* means humility; it is the complete surrendering of the self on the part of the disciple or *shishya* to the *guru.* The ideal disciple feels love, adoration, reverence, and even fear toward his *guru.* The third principal term associated with our music is *sadhana,* which means practice and discipline, eventually leading to self-realization. It means practicing with a fanatic zeal and ardent dedication to the *guru* and to the music. Starting from the very
Closing comment	beginning, it requires at least twenty years of constant work and practice to reach maturity and a high standard of achievement in our classical music.

As you can see, the compression of this essay into a paragraph robs it of its rich texture and substance. The paragraph provides only the essential facts about studying music in India; it omits many of the telling details, the nuances, and the overall tone. Such omission is inevitable, however, for the paragraph in its limited space must necessarily serve a limited purpose.

Reread the Shankar essay and you will see how skillfully he developed the skeletal structure of his piece by expanding each section with additional details, examples, and reasons. This expansion procedure is necessarily carried out paragraph by paragraph, for at each stage of exposition the writer must be sure to say enough, that is, to give readers a sense of inclusiveness, a clear well-rounded, and reasonably complete picture of the subject under consideration.

PARAGRAPH DEVELOPMENT

We cannot generalize about how much you should tell your readers at any given stage of exposition. You yourself must decide, paragraph by paragraph, how best to fill out an idea so that you do not leave readers with unanswered questions and gaps in thought. To avoid these problems, provide supporting data that fill in the boundaries of an idea: examples, illustrations, details, reasons, facts, quotations, analogies, anecdotes. These supporting materials of paragraph development may be grouped under five headings:

Examples

Examples support a generalization with concrete information and thereby illuminate it. Nothing is more encouraging to the reader plowing through difficult material than the two words "for example" since the example frequently clarifies the straight exposition that preceded it. In the paragraph below the writer develops the point made in the topic sentence (that many people in Hiroshima were indifferent about the ethics of using the bomb) by citing examples of two "typical" people.

> A surprising number of the people of Hiroshima remained more or less indifferent about the ethics of using the bomb. Possibly they were too terrified by it to want to think about it at all. Not many of them even bothered to find out much about what it was like. Mrs. Nakamura's conception of it—and awe of it—was typical. "The atom bomb," she would say when asked about it, "is the size of a matchbox. The heat of it is six thousand times that of the sun. It exploded in the air. There is some radium in it. I don't know just how it works, but when the radium is put together, it explodes." As for the use of the bomb, she would add, "Shikata ga nai," a Japanese expression as common as, and corresponding to, the Russian word "nicheve": "It can't be helped. Oh, well. Too bad." Dr. Fujii said approximately the same thing about the use of the bomb to Father Kleinsorge one evening, in German: "Da ist Nichts zu machen. There's nothing to be done about it."
>
> —John Hersey, *Hiroshima*

Illustrations

An illustration is a little story, a narrative example or an anecdote that embodies an idea in an action. In illustration, something happens (the distinguishing mark of all narration). The writer may develop his or her point with a one-paragraph illustration or with several shorter ones.

> "Omit needless words!" cries the author on page 17, and into that imperative Will Strunk really put his heart and soul. In the days when I was sitting in his class, he omitted so many needless words, and omitted them so forcibly and with such

eagerness and obvious relish, that he often seemed in the position of having shortchanged himself—a man left with nothing more to say yet with time to fill, a radio prophet who had outdistanced the clock. Will Strunk got out of this predicament by a simple trick: he uttered every sentence three times. When he delivered his oration on brevity to the class, he leaned forward over his desk, grasped his coat lapels in his hands, and, in a husky, conspiratorial voice, said, "Rule Thirteen. Omit needless words! Omit needless words! Omit needless words!"

—William Strunk, Jr., and E. B. White, *Elements of Style*

Never in the history of English letters has there been a more dedicated participant in the literary feuds of his day than the great and cantankerous Dr. Samuel Johnson, who stomped noisily through eighteenth-century London, demolishing arguments and smashing reputations with enormous vigor and gusto. Usually his verbal abuse was enough to smite the unworthy, but sometimes the impatient Doctor resorted to physical violence. ("There is no arguing with Johnson," the novelist, Oliver Goldsmith, said, "for when his pistol misses fire he knocks you down with the butt end of it.") Once, when a waiter used his dirty fingers instead of the proper tongs to drop a lump sugar into the Doctor's tea, Johnson tossed the glass through the window and was about to do the same with the waiter, when a friend appeared and calmed him. On another occasion, the manager had placed a chair on a side stage especially for Dr. Johnson's use. Another man, finding the seat empty, sat in it, and then made the unpardonable error of failing to relinquish it to its rightful holder. Faced with this effrontery, the powerful Dr. Johnson simply picked up the chair, with the man still in it, and threw both chair and occupant into the pit.

—Myrick Land, *The Fine Art of Literary Mayhem*

Details

Details are the component parts that make up a whole—the individual steps in a procedure, the particular aspects of an image or impression. Details include factual data of all kinds: statistics, evidence, direct quotations, analogies. They answer the questions *how* and *what*. In the following description of Ho Chi Minh, the writer supports his judgment that the Vietnamese leader "had altered" by citing specific details of his alteration. Similarly, the writer of the second paragraph below supports his statement—that scientists have learned to supplement the sense of sight in numerous ways—by indicating five specific ways in which this has been done.

He had altered. His eyes had lost a little of the brilliance which used to strike one so forcibly, and his face was no longer ascetically thin. His hair had turned white, of course, and this made his beard look less sparse. The body covered by the sand-colored tunic was as frail as ever; but his cheeks had filled out and taken on a pinkness which gave him a somewhat artificial air. There was still a strong hint of mischief in his expression, however, and his dry laugh supplied the finishing touch—he looked and sounded like some old scholar whose wisdom had led him to discover the virtues of poverty. . . .

—Jean Lacouture, *Ho Chi Minh*

Scientists have learned to supplement the sense of sight in numerous ways. In front of the tiny pupil of the eye they put, on Mount Palomar, a great monocle 200 inches in diameter, and with it see 2000 times farther into the depths of space. Or they look through a small pair of lenses arranged as a microscope into a drop of water or blood, and magnify by as much as 2000 diameters the living creatures there, many of which are among man's most dangerous enemies. Or, if we want to see distant happenings on earth, they use some of the previously wasted electromagnetic waves to carry television images which they re-create as light by whipping tiny crystals on a screen with electrons in a vacuum. Or they can bring happenings of long ago and far away as colored motion pictures, by arranging silver atoms and color-absorbing molecules to force light waves into the patterns of the original reality. Or if we want to see into the center of a steel casting or the chest of an injured child, they send the information on a beam of penetrating short-wave X rays, and then convert it back into images we can see on a screen or photograph. Thus almost every type of electromagnetic radiation yet discovered has been used to extend our sense of sight in some way.

—George R. Harrison, "Faith and the Scientist"

Reasons

Reasons answer the question *why*. Reasons are acceptable and respectable only if the writer bases them on established fact, close observation and experience, or logical analysis. In the following paragraph the writer provides a list of reasons to back up his contention that the life of the student in India is extraordinarily difficult.

The life of a student in India is much more difficult than anything we know in this country. Lack of material resources hampers most of the students at every turn. An overwhelming majority of them live at home, if they have homes, in conditions—by any standards we know—of miserable poverty. Often they have too little to eat, very little to wear, almost never any money to spend on the small things which we take so much for granted in our country. More serious is the fact that they can rarely afford to buy books for study, nor do their libraries have resources remotely comparable with those of our institutions. Beyond this, instruction is frequently anything but inspiring, and study is constrained and limited because the student is required by law to pass an annual examination which puts a high premium on memory work—an examination, set by an outside examining authority, to which each year many more are called than can possibly be chosen. And if a student persists in the face of repeated difficulty and finally in time earns a degree, there is the further debilitating consideration that his chances of finding an appropriate job are frighteningly slim. Yet so great is his inner drive and so bright his hope that the Indian student desires education beyond all else, and perseveres.

—Nathan M. Pusey, *The Age of the Scholar*

Mixed Materials

Not all paragraphs are neatly representative of a type, of course. Writers often mix supporting examples, reasons, and details, as in the following paragraph. In it Norman Podhoretz explains, through a series of vividly recounted details—rendered in anecdotal form—precisely why he finds Norman Mailer "extraordinary."

> The better I got to know Mailer personally—and we became very close friends—the more extraordinary I found him. He was, as the saying goes, a walking bag of contradictions: pugnacious in temperament and yet of a surpassing sweetness of character; foolish beyond belief about people, and yet unbelievably quick to understand the point of what anyone was up to; obsessed with fame, power, and rank, and yet the freest of any man I had ever encountered of snobbishness in any of its forms. Like most famous writers, he was surrounded by courtiers and sycophants, but with this difference: he allowed them into his life not to flatter him but to give his radically egalitarian imagination a constant workout. He had the true novelist's curiosity about people unlike himself—you could see him getting hooked ten times a night by strangers at a party—and his respect for modes of life other than his own was so great that it often led him into romanticizing people and things that might legitimately have been dismissed as uninteresting or mediocre. He would look into the empty eyes of some vapid upper-class girl and announce to her that she could be the madam of a Mexican whorehouse; or he would decide that some broken-down Negro junkie he had met in a Village dive was a battalion-commander at heart. Mailer assumed in the most straightforward way that everyone was out for all the power he could get at every minute of the day, and that from the most casual confrontation between two people, one emerged with a victory and the other with a defeat; he even had a hypochondriacal theory involving the birth and death of cells to cover for the assumption. He himself wanted everything: he would "settle for nothing less" than making a revolution in the consciousness of his time, *and* earning millions of dollars, *and* achieving the very heights of American celebrityhood. He respected the position of celebrityhood precisely as he respected people, sometimes ro-manticizing a particular "office," but never making the more common and worse mistake of underestimating how much it took to get anywhere big in America or pooh-poohing the qualities of mind and character required for staying on top.
>
> —Norman Podhoretz, *Making It*

Similarly, the following paragraph mixes its supporting materials by incorporating into an extended illustration a mass of statistical data that would be dull if presented directly. When included within the frame of a story, however, the facts and figures come alive. It is the concreteness and specificity of the illustrative story—dealing with a family in a specific place, paying a stated amount of money for a prefabricated ranch house (a price that would be considered a run-a-way bargain on today's market)—that demonstrate the truth of the general observation.

Investigating home-buying habits in the Midwest, I found that most home buyers do not compute the burden they are undertaking when a home is offered to them on a long-term mortgage. In Toledo, Ohio, a salesman and his wife proudly showed me their customized pre-fab ranch house which they had just bought for $19,500. Did they have a mortgage? Yes, it was a thirty-year kind for $17,000. How much was their interest rate? The husband said, "Gosh, I don't know . . . $4\frac{1}{2}$ per cent I think." His wife thought it was 6 per cent. Their difference in guesses could make a difference of nearly $6,000 in the total cost. Actually, it turned out, they were paying $5\frac{1}{2}$ per cent interest. The one thing they did know was that their monthly payment was $96.53. We quickly multiplied that figure by the 360 months they had committed themselves to pay it, and added on the $2,500 cash down payment. The result was a figure that plainly dismayed them: $37,250.80. That was the real price of their home, not $19,500.

—Vance Packard, *The Waste Makers*

PARAGRAPH UNITY

A paragraph is unified when it contains only those elements that contribute to the realization of its main idea. No quality is more central to good exposition than *unity*. For only through a series of unified paragraphs, clearly and systematically related to one another, can you produce a good piece of writing—whether a short essay or a long book.

You achieve unity in a paragraph when you recognize and respect the thrust of your own idea, whether it is explicitly stated or only implied. The following passage demonstrates vividly how every detail in a unified paragraph contributes to the total effect—in this case an image of "disgust." Note that the topic sentence is the third sentence of the paragraph; the first two sentences serve as an introduction.

Whoever writes about his childhood must beware of exaggeration and self-pity. I do not want to claim that I was a martyr or that Crossgates was a sort of Dotheboys Hall. But I should be falsifying my own memories if I did not record that they are largely memories of disgust. The overcrowded, underfed, underwashed life that we led was disgusting, as I recall it. If I shut my eyes and say "school," it is of course the physical surroundings that first come back to me: the flat playing-field with its cricket pavilion and the little shed by the rifle range, the draughty dormitories, the dusty splintery passages, the square of asphalt in front of the gymnasium, the raw-looking pinewood chapel at the back. And at almost every point some filthy detail obtrudes itself. For example, there were the pewter bowls out of which we had our porridge. They had overhanging rims, and under the rims there were accumulations of sour porridge, which could be flaked off in long strips. The porridge itself, too, contained more lumps, hairs and unexplained black things than one would have thought possible, unless someone were putting them there on purpose. It was never safe to start on that porridge without investigating it first. And there was the slimy water of the plunge bath—it was twelve or fifteen feet long, the whole school was supposed to go into it every morning, and I doubt whether the water was changed at all frequently—and the always-damp towels with their cheesy smell: and, on occasional visits in the winter, the murky sea-water of the local Baths, which came straight in from the beach and on which I once saw floating a human turd. And the sweaty smell of the changing-room with its greasy basins, and, giving on this, the row of filthy, dilapidated lavatories, which had no fastenings of any kind on the doors, so that whenever you were sitting there someone was sure to come crashing in. It is not easy for me to think of my schooldays without seeming to breathe in a whiff of something cold and evil-smelling—a sort of compound of sweaty stockings, dirty towels, faecal smells blowing along the corridors, forks with old food between the prongs, neck-of-mutton stew, and the banging doors of the lavatories and the echoing chamber-pots in the dormitories.

—George Orwell, *Such, Such Were the Joys*

The most common violation of unity consists of including material in one paragraph that should either appear in a separate paragraph or not be used at all. You should always reread the first draft of each paper to make certain that you have not inadvertently wandered off into an irrelevant side issue or allowed extraneous material to creep in during the writing stage. You must be very critical at this time and examine each point of information and each turn in the development of thought to make sure that they belong where they are and that each point picks up the preceding point and leads to the next in a natural, logical progression. The meticulous development of a single idea through its various stages gives a work its essential unity, the oneness of aim in all its parts.

PARAGRAPH COHERENCE

Coherence literally means "sticking together." Thus a piece of writing is coherent when all its parts stick together, when the writer arranges and connects the individual words, phrases, and sentences so that a clear pattern of thought emerges.

Readers, who are "always in trouble," as E. B. White once noted, have no time or inclination to play games, to reassemble the parts of an essay once they are through; they must accept the writer's composition as they read it. If important pieces are missing so that the elements do not interlock (such as gaps in thought or puzzling jumps from one idea to another), readers cannot see the shape of the writer's thought.

As a conscientious writer, then, you must try to communicate more than the basic raw material of your ideas. You must try to communicate relationships: Why does point three follow point two and not vice versa? Does the example cited at the end of the paragraph illustrate the whole paragraph or only the last point? Is the second point the cause or the effect of the first? And what does reason three have to do with reason two? Are they of equal importance, or is one subordinate to the other?

Don't make your reader guess what these connections could be. Make certain not only that your readers can share the main idea of your paragraph (*unity*), but also that they can follow your particular train of thought from beginning to end (*coherence*).

You can achieve coherence in your writing in three basic ways:

1. By arranging materials according to an appropriate *ordering principle*.

2. By providing *transitions* from one idea to another.
3. By maintaining a *consistent tone* and point of view.

Ordering Principles

Time You can arrange material according to when it happened (past to present, early to late, old to new), or according to a suggested order the reader should follow (first do this, then that, and finally this). Narration, historical accounts, the steps in a process, directions or instructions: all follow an order in which a series of events actually happened—or should happen.

An example of this type of ordering may be seen in this brief but powerful account of the final moments in the life of Mary, Queen of Scots. The writer takes us to the scaffold, allowing us to witness the event moment by moment:

> She laid her crucifix on her chair. The chief executioner took it as a perquisite, but was ordered instantly to lay it down. The lawn veil was lifted carefully off, not to disturb the hair, and was hung upon the rail. The black robe was next removed. Below it was a petticoat of crimson velvet. The black jacket followed, and under the jacket was a body of crimson satin. One of her ladies handed her a pair of crimson sleeves, with which she hastily covered her arms; and thus she stood on the black scaffold with the black figures all around her, blood-red from head to foot.
>
> —Froude, History of England

Chronological order does not necessarily imply an uninterrupted movement forward in time. You may begin with an important or exciting event and weave in background by interrupting the ongoing development of the story to dip into the past for some crucial or illuminating details. You may organize your material in whatever time sequence best suits the subject and purpose of your paragraph (or essay), as long as the presentation proceeds in an orderly manner readers can follow.

Space Just as some material lends itself to a presentation in time, other material calls for a presentation in space. Again no rigid rules prescribe one spatial pattern over another. Writers should visualize the effect they are trying to achieve and then set about achieving that effect in a systematic manner. They should be clear in their own minds where the narrator stands (point of view), and proceed according to a natural or logical principle of progression (left to right, far to near, bottom to top). In the following paragraph from *The Adventures of Huckleberry Finn,* Mark Twain blends a time and space pattern. Huck is a stationary observer, describing what he sees as the day breaks over the water.

> The first thing to see, looking away over the water, was a kind of dull line—that was the woods on t'other side; you couldn't make nothing else out; then a pale place in the sky; then more paleness spreading around; then the river softened up away off, and warn't black any more, but gray; you could see little dark spots drifting along ever so far away—trading-scows, and such things; and long black streaks— rafts; sometimes you could hear a sweep creaking; or jumbled-up voices, it was so still, and sounds come so far; and by and by you could see a streak on the water

which you know by the look of the streak that there's a snag there in a swift current which breaks on it and makes that streak look that way; and you see the mist curl up off the water, and the east reddens up, and the river, and you make out a log cabin in the edge of the woods, away on the bank on t'other side of the river, being a wood-yard, likely, and piled by them cheats so you can throw a dog through it anywheres; then the nice breeze springs up, and comes fanning you from over there, so cool and fresh and sweet to smell on account of the woods and the flowers; but sometimes not that way, because they've left dead fish laying around, gars and such, and they do get pretty rank; and next you've got the full day, and everything smiling in the sun, and the song-birds just going to it!

Importance When presenting a series of ideas, it is best that you arrange them in ascending order of importance or value. This rhetorical advice reflects human nature. We intuitively build to a climax, passing from the least to the most, with the last-mentioned item impressing itself most forcibly on our minds. If a third or fourth item is weak, we say that it is anticlimactic; we have built up to something and then fallen off. For example, you might begin by embedding in your topic sentence a specific kernel, which you then unfold by degrees, working steadily toward a satisfyingly revealing conclusion. Or you might simply move from what your readers expect and find obvious to what they don't and find surprising—as in the following paragraph:

> As Americans are drawn more into overseas travel and service abroad, we are advised to be ready for something called "culture shock." Culture shock, roughly defined, is the total psychological discomfort one feels in foreign situations where every human function is dealt with somewhat differently. Big differences, such as language, are obvious; it is not too hard to make allowances for them and adjust to them. But the many, many tiny differences between life in the United States and life abroad—like the taste of the coffee, the value of time, or the smells—are more insidious. Bit by bit, their effects pile up in the pit of the emotions until they all become too much to be endured. Suddenly, unexpectedly, we have had it.
>
> —Donald Lloyd, "The Quietmouth American"

The building-up order of climax is not always suitable. Sometimes one item is so obvious and all-important that you must state it at the outset—directly after the topic sentence—just as you should present an overwhelmingly strong reason in support of an argument first if you do not want to distract your readers, who may keep wondering why you do not say the obvious. Thus in the following paragraph, the writer quite properly presents his most important explanation first:

> Some people are astonished to find that such primitive transportation as dog traction is still used. Why? Probably the most important reason is economy. A dog team can be assembled without expenditure of too much money. Pups appear in the normal course of events. The team becomes self-supporting since it enables the owner to become a more efficient hunter, especially of seals and caribou. The environment furnishes food for the team and food and clothing for the hunter and

his family. A vehicle such as a weasel, snow-buggy, or motor toboggan requires cash capital for the initial investment and for spare parts, gasoline, and oil. Most Eskimos are relatively wealthy in meat and animal products but desperately poor in money. A recent comparison of motor toboggans and dog teams in the Canadian Arctic showed that, considering weight only of food or fuel needed per mile, the dog teams were more efficient. And—very important—a team can be started in thirty-below-zero weather without preheating, using explosive ether for starting fluid, or "burning" one's hands on the cold steel.

Using Transitions

The word "transition" means, in writing, passing from one subject or idea to another. Thus transitional guides are connectives (symbols, words, phrases; sometimes whole sentences and paragraphs) that make possible a smooth "passing" from one idea to the next. You make transitions by referring to what you have said before, establishing cause-and-effect connections, looking ahead to what you will say, referring to the present, marking time and place, qualifying, comparing, contrasting. For more on transitions, see Chapter 8.

Consistency of Tone

Simply stated, tone embodies your attitude toward your subject and your readers. How do you want them to take your statement: as a formal explanation, a personal impression, an emotional attack, a lament, a joke? Not merely what you say but the *way* that you say it contribute to the total meaning of a piece of writing and either reinforce or violate its coherence.

To maintain a consistent tone, you first decide who is speaking (a first-person *I?* and impersonal *one?* an unbiased *he or she?*) and then consider whether the statement should be made in the present or past tense, the active or passive voice. On a deeper level, you then consider who your readers are; having visualized them, you will know what kind of usage is most appropriate (should you say "conflagration" or "fire"?). On a still deeper level you define the particular effect you are trying to create with your words (should you call a person thin, skinny, or scrawny?) These mechanical and semantic considerations will help you to focus your thinking and ensure that you have a clear idea of how *you* feel about what you are saying and how you want your readers to feel and think.

THE NEED FOR COHERENCE

Though it can be difficult to achieve coherence in your writing, the effort clearly pays off in the final product, as these two examples show. In the first, a disorganized account of New York City, the writer fails to maintain consistency either in tone or point of view (the subject shifts from "I" to "one" to "you"); tenses and voice change throughout; the writer gasps colloquially over a "hunk of engineering" and then comments pompously on what is "therapeutically preferable." There is no discernable pattern of organization, and the writer moves from one idea to another with little attention to the connections between ideas and even less attention to signaling those connections with transitions. The writer has done poorly on many counts, not the least of which is failure to establish and maintain an appropriate tone.

> Although I was born and raised in New York, it still seems to me an enticing city. One can see beautiful sights no matter where you travel, especially up the West Side Highway where I saw the George Washington Bridge eloquently span the Hudson River from New York to New Jersey. What a hunk of engineering! All kinds of recreational activities are offered by New York: at Madison Square Garden you could be a spectator of almost any sport one is interested in: basketball, hockey, boxing. As for participating sports (which are, psychiatrists maintain, therapeutically preferable), I can't imagine any that you wouldn't be able to take up: bowling, tennis, horseback riding, ad infinitum. A veritable cornucopia of cultural activities also awaits the visitor to New York: theatres where thespians from all over the country—nay, the globe—exhibit their talents in plays that rival the splendor of the glorious age of Greek drama; museums which I had the opportunity to visit all my life and were always educational and are also interesting; concerts which are always well-attended by New Yorkers as well as a multitude of outsiders who will be eager to see their favorite artists in the flesh. No kidding, New York is an exciting city.

As a more successful example of tone, examine the following paragraph, also about New York City. That the city works at all is "a miracle," says E. B. White, who then goes on to describe this miracle. Note how skillfully his details are held together by a sustained and pervasive tone of affectionate incredulity.

> It is a miracle that New York works at all. The whole thing is implausible. Every time the residents brush their teeth, millions of gallons of water must be drawn from the Catskills and the hills of Westchester. When a young man in Manhattan writes a letter to his girl in Brooklyn, the love message gets blown to her through a pneumatic tube—pfft—just like that. The subterranean system of telephone cable, power lines, steam pipes, gas mains and sewer pipes is reason enough to abandon the island to the gods and weevils. Every time an incision is made in the pavement, the noisy surgeons expose ganglia that are tangled beyond belief. By rights, New York should have destroyed itself long ago, from panic or fire or rioting or failure of some vital supply line in its circulatory system or from some deep labyrinthine short circuit. Long ago the city should have experienced an insoluble traffic snarl at some impossible bottleneck. It should have perished of hunger when food lines failed for a few days. It should have been wiped out by a plague starting in its slums or carried in by ships' rats. It should have been overwhelmed by the sea that licks at it on every side. The workers in its myriad cells should have succumbed to nerves, from the fearful pall of smoke-fog that drifts over every few days from Jersey, blotting out all light at noon and leaving the high offices suspended, men groping and depressed, and the sense of world's end. It should have been touched in the head by the August heat and gone off its rocker.

No simple or single formula will help you maintain an appropriate tone throughout a unit of writing; your own sensitivity plus a keen awareness of rhetorical stance (your relation to your subject and your audience) must be your guides. However, the tone of modern prose style is, on the whole, natural and informal, for, as mentioned earlier, most expository writers use the rhythms of normal, everyday speech.

Using these principles as a general guide, check for inconsistent or inappropriate tone in the paragraphs of the piece you are writing. If a flippantly irreverent term—unsuited to the context of your subject—slips into a sentence, you should delete it during a later rewriting or revision. So too you should eliminate ponderous or overly elaborate phrases from a light informal piece and tone down strongly emotional outbursts in a serious argument.

Choice of words and phrases, levels of usage, length and rhythm of sentences, juxtaposition of details, and other such rhetorical devices combine to produce the special tone of a piece of writing. You are responsible for forging the tone you feel is appropriate, and, having forged it, you should—in the name of coherence—maintain that tone throughout.

WRITING SPECIAL PARAGRAPHS

Writing is an unnatural act, one might say. To move from communicating through speech and gesture to communicating through ink marks on a page requires both you and your potential reader to adjust your expectations. Likewise, once you have gotten into the rhythms of written language, it can be awkward to switch out of that mode. The inherent awkwardness of these shifts in communication strategy are one reason we often have difficulty writing introductions and conclusions. We want to avoid starting or ending so abruptly that our reader is bewildered, but we also want to avoid introductions that add little to our topic, and conclusions that simply restate what we've just said or introduce an entirely different subject. Sometimes we can rely on formulas that ease the transition, such as the "Dear Sir" and "Very truly yours" that once opened and closed a traditional business letter. The introduction's essential function is to bring the reader from wherever his or her mind is into a position to appreciate what you have to say; the conclusion should ease your reader back into his or her world, the world beyond your text. Even though these paragraphs can be largely formulaic, it's still desirable to enhance the rest of your paper through an effective introduction or conclusion.

Getting Started

Many students complain that getting started is the most difficult job in writing. After you have used the prewriting strategies we have discussed, you will probably have a much easier time. The opening section, however, is least likely to come naturally. This is an important section, though, for here the writer must capture the attention of readers. A provocative introduction that arouses curiosity or establishes the importance of the subject encourages them to read on into the body of the piece. Provided it is not a mere trick to entice readers—provided it creates an honest and appropriate expectation of what will follow—a provocative introduction can be a valuable rhetorical device.

There are many types of introductions. Note that each of the following examples prepares readers for the piece by raising a central issue, making a meaningful observation, creating a mood, or defining a key term.

What promises does each make to the reader? What does each introduction lead you to expect from the rest of the essay?

1. A quotation or meaningful allusion:

"I have traveled a good deal in Concord," said the stationary pilgrim, Henry Thoreau. Today his descendants move from country to country instead, some seeking wisdom, some seeking academic credit, some only fun. Indeed, a latter day Children's Crusade is upon us. No crusaders are sold into slavery, but nobody can say whether any will reach Jerusalem.

—Hans Rosenhaupt, "The New Children's Crusade,
or Going to Jerusalem on a Grant"

William Congreve's opinion that hell has no fury like a woman scorned can fairly be expanded by the alteration of a word. For "woman" read "author"; the cries of exasperation from aggrieved writers come shrieking down the centuries.

—Ivor Brown, "Critics and Creators"

Pascal once remarked that the entire face of the world was changed by the shape of Cleopatra's nose. Almost two thousand years later the entire face of history was nearly changed by the shape of another nose. In the fall of 1831 the twenty-two-year-old divinity student, Charles Darwin, was about to sail as an unpaid naturalist on his Majesty's ship, the *Beagle.* But Captain Fitzroy, who commanded the *Beagle,* hesitated to take Darwin along because he judged, from the shape of Darwin's nose, that the young man had "neither the mentality nor the energy" to become a good scientist.

—Henry Thomas and Dana Lee Thomas, "Charles Robert Darwin"

2. A short narration:

Nine days before his death Immanuel Kant was visited by his physician. Old, ill and nearly blind, he rose from his chair and stood trembling with weakness and muttering unintelligible words. Finally his faithful companion realized that he would not sit down again until the visitor had taken a seat. This he did, and Kant then permitted himself to be helped to his chair and, after having regained some of his strength, said "Das Gefühl für Humanität hat mich noch nicht verlassen"—"The sense of humanity has not yet left me." The two men were moved almost to tears. For though the word *Humanität* had come, in the eighteenth century, to mean little more than politeness or civility, it had, for Kant, a much deeper significance, which the circumstances of the moment served to emphasize: man's proud and tragic consciousness of self-approved and self-imposed principles, contrasting with his utter subjection to illness, decay and all that is implied in the word "mortality."

Historically the word *humanitas* has had two clearly distinguishable meanings. . . .

—Erwin Panofsky, "The History of Art as a Humanistic Discipline"

A young medical student at Pisa was kneeling at the Cathedral. There was silence over the vast auditory save for the annoying rattle of a chain. A sacristan had just filled a hanging oil lamp and had carelessly left it swinging in the air. The tick-tack of the swinging chain interrupted the student's prayer and started him upon a train of thought that was far removed from his devotions.

Suddenly he jumped to his feet, to the amazement of the other worshipers. A flash of light had descended upon him in the rhythm of the swinging lamp. It seemed to him that this rhythm was regular, and that the pendulum of the rattling chain was taking exactly the same time in each of its oscillations although the distance of these oscillations was constantly becoming less and less.

Was this evidence of his senses correct? If so, he had hit upon a miracle. He must rush home and find out immediately whether he had suffered an illusion or discovered one of the great truths of nature.

When he arrived home, he hunted up two threads of the same length and attached them to two pieces of lead of the same weight. He then tied the other ends of the threads to separate nails and was ready for his experiment. He asked his godfather, Muzio Tedaldi, to help him in this experiment. "I want you to count the motions of one of the threads while I count the motions of the other."

The old man shrugged his shoulders. "Another of Galileo's crazy ideas," he mumbled to himself. But he agreed to help.

Galileo took the two pendulums, drew one of them to a distance of four hands' breadth and the other to a distance of two hands' breadth from the perpendicular, and then let them go simultaneously. The two men counted the oscillations of the two threads, and then compared notes. The total was exactly the same—one hundred counts in each case. The two threads, in spite of the great difference in their starting points, had arrived at the same point at the same time.

And thus, in the swinging motion of the cathedral oil lamp, Galileo had discovered the rhythmic principle of nature which today is applied in the counting of the human pulse, the measurement of time on the clock, the eclipses of the sun and the movement of the stars.

> —Henry Thomas and Dana Lee Thomas, "Galileo Galilei"

3. A startling question, observation, or line of dialogue:

The attitude of some citizens is like that of a mother who said to her son, "Why do you want to be a physicist, John? Isn't there enough trouble in the world already?"

> —Joel H. Hildebrand, "The Care and Feeding of Creative Young Minds"

"Now tell me," said the lady, "all about yourself."

> —J. B. Priestley, "All About Ourselves"

4. A definition of a key term:

"Alienation," a term once confined to philosophy, law, psychiatry and advanced literary criticism, has entered the daily vocabulary. Newspaper editorials refer without quotes or elucidation to the alienation of the slum dweller, the drug addict, the vanguard painter; popular fiction writers rely on readers to recognize the symptoms of alienation as a motive for adultery or murder. Alienage, or strangeness, is understood to be not only a condition (as of foreigners) but a process. As they say in the health drives, it can happen to anyone.

—Harold Rosenberg, "It Can Happen to Anyone"

5. A striking contrast:

Not often in the story of mankind does a man arrive on earth who is both steel and velvet, who is as hard as rock and soft as drifting fog, who holds in his heart and mind the paradox of terrible storm and peace unspeakable and perfect.

Here and there across centuries come reports of men alleged to have these contrasts. And the incomparable Abraham Lincoln, born 150 years ago this day, is an approach if not a perfect realization of this character.

—Carl Sandburg, "Lincoln, Man of Steel and Velvet"

6. A direct statement:

Where readers may be assumed to have interest in and some knowledge of the subject, writers may announce their purpose directly, with no preparation or buildup:

The film "Hiroshima, Mon Amour," which is getting a good deal of attention in this country, deserves to be viewed—and reviewed—from a number of perspectives. But I have noticed that reviewers have all tended *not* to explore its moral substance, what the vernacular would call its "message." This is remarkable when a film's message is expressed as urgently as this one's is, and even more remarkable when it is expressed with success *cinematically,* when it is perfectly fused with a web of images and sounds. Here is a film that contradicts the widely-held assumption that messages and good esthetics are incompatible.

—Amitai Etzioni, "Hiroshima in America"

It might well dismay the intelligent reader to be informed at the outset that the years 1600–60 were an age of transition. But while every period in history deserves, and doubtless has received, that illuminating label, there are some periods in which disruptive and creative forces reach maturity and combine to speed up the normal process of change. In the history of England, as in that of Europe at large, the seventeenth century is probably the most conspicuous modern example, unless we except our own age, of such acceleration.

—Douglas Bush, "The Background of the Age"

Critics permit themselves, for this or that purpose, to identify literature with great books, with imaginative writing, with expressiveness in writing, with the non-referential and non-pragmatic, with beauty in language, with order, with myth, with structured and formed discourse—the list of definitions is nearly endless—with verbal play, with uses of language that stress the medium itself, with the expression of an age, with dogma, with the *cri de coeur,* with neurosis. Now of course literature is itself and not another thing, to paraphrase Bishop Butler; yet analogies and classifications have merit. For a short space let us think of literature as sentences.

—Richard Ohmann, "Literature as Sentences"

Ending the Paper

At one point in her adventures in Wonderland, Alice is advised to "begin at the beginning, keep going until you get to the end, and then stop." In some cases you can do exactly the same thing: to stop when you have finished saying what you want to say. Your piece (especially if it is a short paper) ends where your last thought ends, creating its own sense of completeness and finality. However, usually a long paper needs a formal conclusion of some kind: a recapitulation of the main points, a heightened restatement of the thesis or argument (what the classical teachers of rhetoric called a *peroration*), a summing-up question, a reference to an idea or event mentioned earlier. Any one of these devices signals readers that the piece is coming to an end: *Pay close attention; here are my final words on the subject.*

Unquestionably the end is an emphatic position, for the final words impress themselves more forcibly on readers' minds than any others. Similarly, the mood at the end of a piece strongly influences, and may even determine, readers' final feelings about what they read. Though many writers seem content merely to summarize their ideas one final time, more accomplished writers frame that summary within a larger perspective, one that re-establishes the larger context within which their essay has functioned and returns readers to their world. For example, in these two paragraphs, the conclusion to a profile of Karol Wojtyla, Pope John Paul II, the author not only summarizes his subject's personality and career but also casts an eye toward the future.

> Karol Wojtyla, John Paul II, has, perhaps, the most impossible job on earth, and his toughest challenges, his biggest triumphs and failures may still lie ahead. But whatever the inherent contradictions of his office, whatever his apparent short-comings and idosyncracies, he holds together—for better or for worse—the extraordinary demands and resources of all who call themselves Catholics. Despite what they may think of him, they cannot do without him.
>
> What's more, his successor is unlikely to alter the well-established pattern.
> —John Cornwell, "The Infallible Man"

This conclusion to an essay tracing the history of writing instruction in the United States prior to 1900 analyzes this history from the perspective of current theory and practice.

> Perhaps they deserve more credit than they have had. The social and technological changes of the nineteenth century were profound. The new course in English composition, which by the turn of the century was probably the sole common element in American college education, was itself an important invention, an educational "technology" to deal with dramatically changed circumstances and problems. If not giants on whose shoulders we now stand, the current–traditional rhetoricians are nonetheless significant contributors to the tradition of writing

instruction. Seen in the context of the time, their accomplishments are deserving of some attention and respect.

—S. Michael Halloran, "From Composition to Rhetoric"

Since there are no standard endings, you must depend on your own judgment in ending your paper. You must compose a conclusion that is appropriate to the subject and purpose of your piece. One helpful procedure is to set aside, at an early stage of research or writing, some information or a passage of quoted material that might serve as a concluding statement. This ending should not open up a whole new aspect of the subject (it is too late for that), nor should it raise additional questions that you cannot answer. Rather, the ending should tie the paper together so that readers experience a sense of closure, where the unit of discourse has reached a logical conclusion and the end *feels* like the end.

EXERCISES

1. Indicate in outline form the structure of the following essays:

   Bruce Catton, "Grant and Lee" (Question 15)
   A. M. Rosenthal, "No News from Auschwitz" (Question 16)
   George Stade, "Football—the Game of Aggression" (Question 18)
   Allen H. Gilbert, "College Lectures Are Obsolete" (Question 20)
   I. Bernard Cohen, "Isaac Newton" (Chapter 5)

2. Evaluate the opening and closing paragraphs of the above essays. What special devices for opening and closing are used? Are they effective? Can you suggest alternate opening and closing paragraphs that would be equally, or perhaps even more, effective?

REVISING
A PAPER

WRITING AND REWRITING
    VISION AND REVISION
    BECOMING YOUR OWN EDITOR

A PRACTICAL GUIDE TO REVISION
    THREE STEPS IN REVISION
    FIVE REVISION STRATEGIES

TWO CASE STUDIES OF REVISION
    CASE STUDY 1: A FAMOUS
        SPEECH
    INAUGURAL ADDRESS JOHN F.
        KENNEDY
    WRITING AND REWRITING THE
        INAUGURAL ADDRESS
        THEODORE SORENSON
    CASE STUDY 2: FOUR SUCCESSIVE
        STUDENT DRAFTS

As the writer passes through the many states of thinking, prewriting—freewriting, clustering, reading, researching, talking to people and establishing an audience, and then researching and organizing—pressures begin building to get a first draft down on paper, "To get black on white," as Guy de Maupassant put it. According to writer–researcher Donald M. Murray, these pressures act as positive, often urgent "forces for writing." The only force that acts against getting a draft down is the "universal Law of Delay," a force familiar to anyone who has ever sharpened a pencil three times before finally getting down to work.

The four positive forces Murray describes are also well known to experienced writers. The first arises from the increasing information writers collect on their subjects. At some point the "urge to impart" this information, to share it with others, makes itself felt: the writer actually wants to start writing. A second force reinforces the first impulse: you feel increasingly committed to the subject. For the more you know about something, the more interested you become, the more eager you will be to convey it accurately and clearly to those who are not yet informed or committed. Winston Churchill explained that these forces for writing could build to such strength that they could sweep the writer away in the current (Charlton, *Companion*, 37).

And, as you have already learned, the third force moving the writer is the sense of a waiting audience, of readers "out there" who will respond in various ways to the finished piece. That these responses will be largely favorable and sympathetic is, of course, the writer's hope: that readers will smile at amusing passages; that they will glower with indignation or feel appropriate alarm or suitable conviction, as the subject matter and the writer's handling of it dictate. If a good reader becomes one with the writer, as Virginia Woolf advises, then the good writer at this stage must try to become one with the readers, anticipating their support, sparing them possible disappointments.

In place of a large audience, the student can look forward to a single reader—the instructor, plus a group of classmates in a workshop situation. Often this audience will provide sufficient stimulation and challenge. Will the instructor respond as expected and desired? How will the class react? Curiosity itself urges the writer to complete the piece and to find out how the members of the audience will receive it. What will they think?

The final force for writing is the impending deadline, coming closer with each passing day. Would anyone ever complete a piece of writing without benefit of deadline? Possibly not. Only a firm deadline enables the writer to overcome a natural tendency to take more time and still more time—especially when a writing assignment is not moving as smoothly as expected. The deadline sets limits to fuming and fussing and making the kind of last-minute changes that can go on endlessly. What a critic once said of a work of art—that it is never finished but abandoned—applies as well to many kinds of efforts. After doing *just so much,* writers must end the task, even if they are not "finished" in the deepest and most satisfying sense. They must just quit.

WRITING AND REWRITING

The rewriting process includes revising, editing, and proofreading. In one sense rewriting is the final stage in the preparation of a paper, but in another sense writers recognize that they rewrite as they go along. They compose a sentence, for example, in longhand or at a keyboard.

They look at it and perhaps read it aloud so that they can hear it. One word might sound funny, so they substitute another. That may sound better and so may moving an adjective closer to the noun being modified. They may mark in the change immediately. And then they may compose a closing sentence for the paragraph. Somehow the paragraph may sound "up in the air" without it.

Writers revise their work—writing and rewriting at the same time. The process is not strictly linear. Many novelists testify, for example, that they start each writing session with a prewriting warm up. Then they rewrite a passage of the previous day's work. Only then do they begin writing per se, by moving ahead to new pages. To some extent, then, the three stages of prewriting, writing, and rewriting run concurrently, circling back on one another even as they leap ahead from one draft to another and yet another.

Different writers work differently, of course. Some linger over separate sentences, fussing with problems as they arise; others forge ahead, confident that however rough their first draft, they can fix it later. You should follow the procedure that feels most comfortable for you and that proves most productive.

Vision and Revision

In learning how to revise, student writers would do best to follow the lead of professionals who, in turn, follow the lead of editors—people outside the manuscript who read it with a cool, critical eye, maintaining at the same time a concerned and sympathetic attitude. Indisputably, they are on the side of the manuscript, committed to making it better by reinforcing its strengths and reducing, if not eliminating, its weaknesses. They regard revision as just that—a re-vision, a second look—and perhaps a third and fourth look as well! Indeed, revision means not only "to look at" but also "to look over," to note every mechanical and rhetorical detail, every choice of word, every turn of phrase, every sentence construction, paragraph division, and transition from paragraph to paragraph. Do the elements work? Could they work better? If so, how? The good editor is endlessly painstaking in the effort to improve the manuscript: to clarify, simplify, and unify; to sharpen the focus, enliven the style, reduce the verbiage.

Once you have committed the first draft of a piece of writing to paper, you are, of course, entitled to a sense of satisfaction. You have assembled random thoughts and feelings and shaped them into a new whole; you have wrenched words from your mind—from your heart—and organized them into an orderly sequence of sentences; this, in turn, you have organized into a series of paragraphs and finally a series of sections that make up a whole. The worst is over when your first draft is done. But you should remember that the *best still lies ahead.* Every writer must recognize this basic, irrefutable truth, for as one observer has noted, "There is no such thing as good writing, only good re-writing."

A few pages farther on we will see how a medical student moved through four successive revisions of a statement describing his reasons for wanting to be a doctor (pages 79–87). The first draft was a carefree and careless approximation of what he thought and felt. Only on closer examination did he discover that he needed to probe more deeply; he needed to return to his original statement, to reconsider it, and finally to revise it according to what he really *meant* to say. And he had to indicate precisely and strategically what that was, leaving no room for doubt or misunderstanding or unfavorable impression.

Becoming Your Own Editor

Students who are serious about improving their writing must learn to become their own painstaking editors. It is, admittedly, a difficult role to assume because at given points, writer and editor have different points of view. "There it is—at long last—down on paper! It looks so good—*just as it is.*"

"*Not quite good enough,*" must be the editorial reply. Most professional writers have internalized some such insistent voice, however unreasonable and irritating it may initially sound. For it is at this crucial point—after finishing a first draft—that the writer must shift his or her perspective in order to see the finished product not simply as it is (a hard won triumph over chaos) but also as it *could* be and *should* be when it has fulfilled its potential. Visualizing and fulfilling that potential is the job of revision.

Students often ask "Isn't any kind of writing exempt from such rigorous rules?"— referring to deeply personal writing in which they have tried to capture and distill some special inner quality of their experience. What they aspire to is total honesty, sincerity, spontaneity—admirable goals. But not only is personal writing not exempt from the rigors of revision, it is perhaps even more in need of it than any other form of writing. As countless writers have testified, emotional honesty is itself maddeningly elusive. No one hides the truth more zealously from ourselves than we ourselves do.

Spontaneous writing—and this would include freewriting of all kinds—"is a good way to start to learn to write," as poet Donald Hall has pointed out. It is "a good way to uncover material you didn't know was in you." We saw this process at work in clustering and other such spontaneous procedures. But, Hall adds, "we need to revise because spontaneity is never adequate."

> Writing that is merely emotional release for the writer becomes emotional chaos for the reader. Even when we write as quickly as our hand can move, we slide into emotional falsity, into cliché, or other static. And we make leaps by private association that leave our prose unclear. And we often omit steps in thinking, or use a step that we later recognize as bad logic. Sometimes we overexplain something obvious. Or we include irrelevant material. (6)

Hall very sensibly concludes that "First drafts remain first drafts. They are the material that we must shape, a marble block that the critical brain chisels into form."

A PRACTICAL GUIDE TO REVISION

Briefly, we may think of the revision process as consisting of three distinct steps, the last one involving five specific strategies. Given a fair chance, the revision process cannot help but improve your writing. One of the most important strategies for revision is to have a plan. Don't just grab a red pencil and wack away mindlessly at your helpless draft, hoping that whatever results will be better than the rough draft. A plan allows you to work efficiently, so that you don't spend an hour fixing a paragraph that you'll eventually omit entirely. Though we must sometimes forge ahead on instinct, whenever possible ask yourself, What is the problem here? before you start fixing it.

Three Steps in Revision

Step One A<small>SSUME THE</small> N<small>EW</small> I<small>DENTITY OF A</small> R<small>EADER</small>-E<small>DITOR.</small> If you can, wait a day or two between completing the first draft and your rereading for the first time. Try to achieve some degree of detachment. The poet John Ciardi once suggested that bad writers are incapable of being editors because they never see what is on paper but only what is in their heads—that is, they see what they wanted to say rather than what they actually said. They are often passionately subjective, attached to some unworthy feature of their piece—an introductory paragraph, perhaps, that does not effectively introduce the subject (many first paragraphs are mere warm-up and should be deleted in revision).

Thus as a basic first step, you must make a determined effort to stand outside the role of writer, to become—first of all—a reader reading the piece for the first time; and—secondly—an editor who is also a reader but more than that, a person committed to making the piece better than it is.

Step Two A<small>SSESS THE</small> S<small>TRENGTHS AND</small> P<small>ROBLEMS OF THE</small> P<small>APER.</small> Read it through carefully, pencil in hand, making observations, notations, and scribblings in the margin: *good!* where it's good; *no! no!* where you spot such problems as an inaccuracy, a possible contradiction, or a shift in tone; an exclamation mark where you are surprised (favorably or unfavorably); a question mark where you are confused.

If you're writing on a computer, you may find it helpful to print out a paper copy to revise several times in the revision process. This gives you another perspective on your paper, and may make certain kinds of revision easier for you. Studies have suggested, for example, that writers who revise solely on the computer are *more likely* to make revisions of individual sentences or paragraphs, but *less likely* to reorganize larger sections of their papers. By revising both on the screen and on a printed copy, you can benefit from both vantage points. Another reason to revise from a printed copy is equally practical: most of us are still better readers of a text on paper than a text on the computer screen.

Expect to be confused. You may be only one day away from what you've written but now that you are approaching it with fresh eyes and a more critical standard of judgment, you will find that some lines already seem unclear, mystifying, as though someone else had written them.

Hold on to this feeling of detachment; cultivate it. Remember, too, the counsel of E. B. White, who told writers to make sure at the outset that they have said what they intended to say because the chance of their having said it was "only fair." You are now putting your entire paper to the test: Does it accomplish its main purpose and observe its commitments, both stated and implied? Equally important: Is your tone appropriate to the audience you imagine, and do you maintain it consistently throughout? Where you see lapses, note them in the margin.

Let us assume that you now have a reasonable assessment of the paper's strengths and weaknesses. You've done a fair job. Your argument against capital punishment (let's say) has in fact been convincing. Certainly it has not turned out to *support* capital punishment. This reversal of impact can occur in papers if writers lose control because they do not realize—until too late—the full implications of their position or how they really feel about an issue. (We should point out that coming to a better understanding of how you feel about an issue is not necessarily a bad thing, in the end. It does, however, make for a more complex revising task.)

However, in the hypothetical paper we are envisioning here, we'll assume that you have written a competent argument, but that the paper does have some typical problems. Individual points overlap somewhat; one or two need additional supporting detail; others do not lead smoothly to your anticipated climax. Also, the conclusion needs strengthening so that readers can see unmistakably that it follows logically and inevitably from the premises of the argument and the facts as presented. The writing itself seems clear for the most part but needs tightening.

Having taken these two preliminary steps—adopted an objective point of view and assessed the strengths and weaknesses—you are now ready to move ahead to the next important step.

Step Three MAKE A REVISION AGENDA. Before you make up a formal agenda, survey those "problem islands" that need attention, beginning—of course—with the most fundamental and urgent. If your light, supposedly humorous essay is not especially humorous, you had better improve that sagging aspect of the piece first; otherwise you may not have a piece to improve. The logical place to start is with content. Ask yourself whether you have said enough about your subject to satisfy the reader. Remember, you are now the reader; remind yourself to respond as such. If you've encountered disorienting gaps in thought, inadequate development of ideas, or insufficient examples, then clearly your first revision strategy will be to add. Beyond that you may well be required to reorganize, cut, change, and correct. These are the five basic revision strategies.

Five Revision Strategies

Let's consider these strategies one at a time since that is precisely how the revision process must proceed: problem by problem. (Part IV, "A Guide to Effective Language," provides specific guidance on choosing words, revising paragraphs and sentences, and correcting punctuation, mechanics, and spelling. Use the chart inside the back cover to find the appropriate sections.)

Add Addition is obviously a basic task of revision. You may add a one word modifier (a *gray sky*) or enrich a one-sentence example (The grandfather clock, for instance, was worth at least $5,000—*and that was only one item of her inheritance*) or insert a full paragraph of causal explanation. Read through every first draft very carefully with these questions in mind: Have I said enough on the subject? What added details—facts, statistics, research data, reasons, examples, illustrations, quotations, or allusions—would add substance and liveliness and further credibility and authority? Professional writers testify to the value of writing from abundance. Although the first draft will necessarily represent a screening process (since far more information is generally assembled than the writer can incorporate into the finished piece), every writer should make sure that nothing that belongs in the piece—that will enhance it—has been left out.

Since gaps in thought can be a problem in anyone's writing, you should fill them in with needed matter or with suitable transitional devices. Sometimes, in order to make necessary connections, you may have to generate new materials; you may have to think more deeply, or return to the library for further information. You may even find yourself so short of ideas that you go back to pre-writing techniques to generate more supporting detail. As you will see, the medical student cited on pages 79–87 needs to identify a missing link in his thought, for in his first draft he had not realized that his second reason for wanting to be a doctor appeared to contradict his first reason, making him sound either hypocritical or foolishly naive. By adding an explanation, this writer is able to convey more accurately and sympathetically what he had in mind. Only then can the idea intended in his mind be transmitted to the mind of the reader. His purpose, after all, is not merely to express his ideas but to communicate them.

Here are some questions to ask yourself to see whether you need to add material in revision:

Guidelines for Addition

1. Do sentences and paragraphs need additional detail?
2. Are any ideas unclear?
3. Are transitions between ideas awkward or missing?
4. Do any assertions need additional support?

Reorganize Reorganization is closely related to addition as a revising strategy. Just as one entire first reading of the first draft should test its content—what the paper is all about—so another reading should test its organization. Perhaps you should move up *this* sentence (otherwise the reader will have to wait too long for important information); or reverse pages three and four; perhaps an early foreshadowing paragraph tells too much too soon; perhaps the overall organization does not hold up and you need to re-think the whole paper.

You are now reviewing (re-viewing) the outer shape of your paper, studying it closely to determine whether it is a logical, efficient structure. You need to ask such questions as: Is the outer structure compatible with the inner parts? Are the inner parts compatible with one another?

A good place to begin such considerations is with the introduction and conclusion, which frame the piece and serve as anchors. Ask yourself the following questions:

Guidelines for Reorganization

1. Is the introduction interesting? Provocative? Does it prepare the reader accurately for what follows?
2. Does the conclusion serve as an effective wrap up? Does it give a sense of closure and completeness?
3. Have I arranged the materials of the paper in a logical and readable order?
4. Do the parts flow smoothly and coherently into one another—without jarring breaks or unexplained turns of thought? with graceful transitions?
5. Does each paragraph contain material that clearly belongs to that paragraph? or Should I move some passages elsewhere?

6. Does the paragraph sequence accurately reflect the relationship of the paragraphs to one another? Should I combine any paragraphs? or break them up? or reposition them to an earlier or later place?
7. Have I organized the paragraphs coherently within themselves? Do they have clearly stated topic sentences (where appropriate) followed by sentences arranged in logical order?

Cut Once you feel that your organization—or reorganization—is satisfactory, begin to "tighten" at all levels by deleting what you do not need. Whenever possible cut out a solid block of material that does not develop or directly relate to the main thrust of your piece; similarly, cut back on all materials and sentence elements that slow the main action, blur the main point, impede the smooth flow. The importance of economy has been stressed throughout this text. Begin then, by reviewing those sections that deal specifically with the war on wordiness. Recall E. B. White's rousing "call to arms":

> A sentence should contain no unnecessary words, a paragraph no unnecessary sentences, for the same reason that a drawing should have no unnecessary lines and a machine no unnecessary parts. This requires not that the writer make all his sentences short or that he avoid all detail, but that every word tell.

In short, as E.B. White exhorts, *let every word tell.*

As a warm-up to this cycle of revision, review the principles of sentence economy. They will sensitize you to what rhetorician Richard Lanham has called "The Official Style," a kind of wordy, self-important prose that obscures your meaning and frustrates your reader.

Guidelines for Cutting

Find ways to eliminate:
1. unnecessary words
    today's modern world
    Finally, in conclusion
2. useless repetition
    useful and helpful
    brave and courageous
    unnecessary and redundant
3. ineffective intensifiers
    rather
    somewhat
4. mindless introductions
    There is
    It was
    I am of the opinion that
5. noun-heavy replacements for simple verbs
    arrived at a determination that instead of *decided*
    effected the elimination of instead of *eliminated*
    made a choice instead of *chose*

Change Closely related to deletion as a way of tightening your prose is alteration—revising to brighten as well as tighten; to strengthen, clarify, enliven; to render more rhythmic, more graceful, more cogent. An effective writer sees the words on the page as the result of a series of choices. As you revise, ask yourself what other ways you might express a certain idea. Once you've imagined other possibilities, you can use your common sense and your developing skill as a writer to make the best choice.

Guidelines for Changing Sentences

1. Condense long sentences and reduce piled-up prepositional phrases.
2. Establish proper emphasis on important words and ideas.
3. Vary word order, sentence length, and pattern.
4. Use active rather than passive voice wherever possible and appropriate.
5. Invigorate verbs: Avoid weak forms of *to be*.
6. Put the action of the sentence into the verb.
7. Subordinate whenever possible and appropriate.

Guidelines for Changing Words

1. Have I chosen words aptly and accurately, with a sensitivity to connotation?
2. Have I used suitable synonyms to avoid needless repetition? Have I avoided long and pretentious words, preferring the more direct and natural?
3. Have I avoided jargon and clichés?

Correct In checking for correctness, you'll want to give attention to the following areas:

Factual: Check your notes to make sure that you've properly transcribed your facts, accurately reproduced your statistics, and presented in your quotations exactly as in your source. If you're paraphrasing, check that your paraphrase is a fair rendering of what actually was said. You should also check bibliographical items whenever you have a question as to date of publication, page number, and authorship.

Grammatical: To make certain your sentences are grammatically correct, review the section dealing with rules and guidelines at the end of the book. Take the grammar quiz to identify problem areas, then read your paper for the errors you most commonly make. Most importantly, read your sentences aloud—once again—so that your ear can respond to possible lapses. Many times, we can hear a grammatical error more readily than we can see it.

Guidelines for Correcting Grammar and Usage Errors

Watch out for
1. careless sentence fragments
2. comma splice
3. fused sentences
4. unnecessary splits
5. dangling and otherwise misplaced modifiers
6. failure in subject-verb agreement
7. faulty parallelism

8. unnecessary shifts in subject
9. faulty or ambiguous pronoun reference
10. mixed constructions

Mechanical: When we turn our attention to such issues as punctuation, capitalization, abbreviation and contractions, spelling—we are concerned with the copyediting process. Although you have undoubtedly spotted errors all along—during your first rereading of the first draft and even earlier as you read completed sections of the paper—you should now plan on a special run-through devoted solely to checking and standardizing mechanical details.

Move through your paper slowly, line by line, word by word, comma by comma, to make certain that you detect and correct not merely the most blatant errors but *all* errors. Where you are uncertain about a usage (colon or semicolon? capital letter or small case?) consult with the punctuation, spelling, and general mechanics sections of this text.

Check and Proofread As a last step, when the paper is in the final draft, be sure to proofread carefully. It's a good idea to make a list of the errors you commonly make, and check your paper carefully for those specific problems. Read the paper with one single purpose: to make certain everything has been set down as you intended, with no accidental omissions, misspellings, typographical errors, and so on. If possible, get a classmate, roommate, friend, or relative to do another proofreading. It is always helpful to have a second set of eyes look at your paper. By now you are so familiar with what you have written that in your mind you may unconsciously correct errors—adjust misspelling, even fill in a missing line.

TWO CASE STUDIES OF REVISION

Researchers have learned much about the writing process from the case study method: a close examination of the activities a single writer or small group of writers engage in during the course of producing an actual piece of writing. The case study method rewards close observation and the vision to see patterns of behavior that enable certain kinds of writing to be produced. Here we present case studies of two very different writing processes. As you read them, ask yourself what similarities you see to your own process of revision. What would a case study of your revising process reveal?

Case Study 1: A Famous Speech

On January 20, 1961, when John F. Kennedy was sworn in as the thirty-fifth president of the United States, he gave an inaugural address comparable in its impact, economy, and simple but soaring eloquence to Lincoln's inaugural address, delivered a century before. According to Kennedy aide and speechwriter Theodore Sorensen, Kennedy planned this speech with meticulous care, calling upon many of his aides for advice and suggestions, even though he himself knew what he wanted to say and the general tone he wanted to establish. Sorensen tells us:

> He wanted it short. He wanted it focused on foreign policy. He did not want it to
> sound partisan, pessimistic or critical of his predecessor. He wanted neither the
> customary cold war rhetoric about the Communist menace nor any weasel words

that Khrushchev might misinterpret. And he wanted it to set a tone for the era about to begin.

That Kennedy achieved his rhetorical goals is a matter of historical record; how he achieved them is not as well known: namely, through endlessly painstaking effort. "The easily flowing connection of sentence with sentence and paragraph with paragraph has always been won by the sweat of the brow," said nineteenth-century British historian G. M. Trevelyan. "What is easy to read has been difficult to write," he concluded. This brief, simply stated observation is certainly borne out by the case study presented below: an account of the revision process at work in the preparation of John F. Kennedy's famous inaugural address.

Inaugural Address

John F. Kennedy

Vice-President Johnson, Mr. Speaker, Mr. Chief Justice, President Eisenhower, Vice-President Nixon, President Truman, Reverend Clergy, Fellow Citizens:

We observe today not a victory of party but a celebration of freedom—symbolizing an end as well as a beginning—signifying renewal as well as change. For I have sworn before you and Almighty God the same solemn oath our forebears prescribed nearly a century and three-quarters ago.

The world is very different now. For man holds in his mortal hands the power to abolish all forms of human poverty and all forms of human life. And yet the same revolutionary beliefs for which our forebears fought are still at issue around the globe—the belief that the rights of man come not from the generosity of the state but from the hand of God.

We dare not forget today that we are the heirs of that first revolution. Let the word go forth from this time and place, to friend and foe alike, that the torch has been passed to a new generation of Americans—born in this century, tempered by war, disciplined by a hard and bitter peace, proud of our ancient heritage—and unwilling to witness or permit the slow undoing of those human rights to which this nation has always been committed, and to which we are committed today at home and around the world.

Let every nation know, whether it wishes us well or ill, that we shall pay any price, bear any burden, meet any hardship, support any friend, oppose any foe to assure the survival and the success of liberty.

This much we pledge—and more.

To those old allies whose cultural and spiritual origins we share, we pledge the loyalty of faithful friends. United, there is little we cannot do in a host of co-operative ventures. Divided, there is little we can do—for we dare not meet a powerful challenge at odds and split asunder.

To those new states whom we welcome to the ranks of the free, we pledge our word that one form of colonial control shall not have passed away merely to be replaced by a far more iron tyranny. We shall not always expect to find them supporting our view. But we shall always hope to find them strongly supporting their own freedom—and to remember that, in the past, those who foolishly sought power by riding the back of the tiger ended up inside.

To those people in the huts and villages of half the globe struggling to break the bonds of mass misery, we pledge our best efforts to help them help themselves, for whatever period is required—not because the Communists may be doing it, not because we seek their votes, but because it is right. If a free society cannot help the many who are poor, it cannot save the few who are rich.

To our sister republics south of our border, we offer a special pledge—to convert our good words into good deeds—in a new alliance for progress—to assist free men and free governments in casting off the chains of poverty. But this meaningful revolution of hope cannot become the prey of hostile powers. Let all our neighbors know that we shall join with them to oppose aggression or subversion anywhere in the Americas. And let every other power know that this hemisphere intends to remain the master of its own house.

To that world assembly of sovereign states, the United Nations, our last best hope in an age where the instruments of war have far outpaced the instruments of peace, we renew our pledge of support—to prevent it from becoming merely a forum of invective—to strengthen its shield of the new and the weak—and to enlarge the area in which its writ may run.

Finally, to those nations who would make themselves our adversary, we offer not a pledge but a request: that both sides begin anew the quest for peace, before the dark powers of destruction unleashed by science engulf all humanity in planned or accidental self-destruction.

We dare not tempt them with weakness. For only when our arms are sufficient beyond doubt can we be certain beyond doubt that they will never be employed.

But neither can two great and powerful groups of nations take comfort from our present course—both sides overburdened by the cost of modern weapons, both rightly alarmed by the steady spread of the deadly atom, yet both racing to alter that uncertain balance of terror that stays the hand of mankind's final war.

So let us begin anew—remembering on both sides that civility is not a sign of weakness, and sincerity is always subject to proof. Let us never negotiate out of fear. But let us never fear to negotiate.

Let both sides explore what problems unite us instead of belaboring those problems which divide us.

Let both sides, for the first time, formulate serious and precise proposals for the inspection and control of arms—and bring the absolute power to destroy other nations under the absolute control of all nations.

Let both sides seek to invoke the wonders of science instead of its terrors. Together let us explore the stars, conquer the deserts, eradicate disease, tap the ocean depths, and encourage the arts and commerce.

Let both sides unite to heed in all corners of the earth the command of Isaiah—to "undo the heavy burdens . . . [and] let the oppressed go free."

And if a beachhead of co-operation may push back the jungle of suspicion, let both sides join in creating a new endeavor, not a new balance of power, but a new world of law, where the strong are just and the weak secure and the peace preserved.

All this will not be finished in the first one hundred days. Nor will it be finished in the first one thousand days, nor in the life of this administration, nor even perhaps in our lifetime on this planet. But let us begin.

In your hands, my fellow citizens, more than mine, will rest the final success or failure of our course. Since this country was founded, each generation of Americans has been summoned to give testimony to its national loyalty. The graves of young Americans who answered the call to service surround the globe.

Now the trumpet summons us again—not as a call to bear arms, though arms we need—not as a call to battle, though embattled we are—but a call to bear the burden of a long twilight struggle, year in and year out, "rejoicing in hope, patient in tribulation"—a struggle against the common enemies of man: tyranny, poverty, disease, and war itself.

Can we forge against these enemies a grand and global alliance, North and South, East and West, that can assure a more fruitful life for all mankind? Will you join in that historic effort?

In the long history of the world, only a few generations have been granted the role of defending freedom in its hour of maximum danger. I do not shrink from this responsibility—I welcome it. I do not believe that any of us would exchange places with any other people or any other generation. The energy, the faith, the devotion which we bring to this endeavor will light our country and all who serve it—and the glow from that fire can truly light the world.

And so, my fellow Americans: ask not what your country can do for you—ask what you can do for your country.

My fellow citizens of the world: ask not what America will do for you, but what together we can do for the freedom of man.

Finally, whether you are citizens of America or citizens of the world, ask of us here the same high standards of strength and sacrifice which we ask of you. With a good conscience our only sure reward, with history the final judge of our deeds, let us go forth to lead the land we love, asking His blessing and His help, but knowing that here on earth God's work must truly be our own.

WRITING AND REWRITING THE INAUGURAL ADDRESS

Theodore Sorensen

Early in January, with work on his program well under way and his principal nominees named, the President-elect's thoughts turned more and more to his inauguration. He took a lively interest in plans for the Inaugural Concert and five simultaneous Inaugural Balls (all of which he would attend), in plans for the four-hour-long Inaugural Parade (all of which he would watch in twenty-degree temperature), the million-dollar Democratic fund-raising Inaugural Gala (which he greatly enjoyed, despite a two-hour delay due to blizzards) and in all the other festivities. He asked Robert Frost to deliver a poem at the inauguration ceremony. He wanted Marian Anderson to sing "The Star-Spangled Banner." He sought a family Bible on which he could take the oath of office. . . . He indicated that top hats instead of Homburgs would be in order for the official party. And, finally and most importantly, he began to work on his Inaugural Address.

He had first mentioned it to me in November. He wanted suggestions from everyone. He wanted it short. He wanted it focused on foreign policy. He did not want it to sound partisan, pessimistic or critical of his predecessor. He wanted neither the customary cold war rhetoric about the Communist menace nor any weasel words that Khrushchev might misinterpret. And he wanted it to set a tone for the era about to begin.

He asked me to read all the past Inaugural Addresses (which I discovered to be a largely undistinguished lot, with some of the best eloquence emanating from some of our worst Presidents). He asked me to study the secret of Lincoln's Gettysburg Address (my conclusion, which his Inaugural applied, was that Lincoln never used a two- or three-syllable word where a one-syllable word would do, and never used two or three words where one word would do).

Actual drafting did not get under way until the week before it was due. As had been true of his acceptance speech at Los Angeles, pages, paragraphs and complete drafts had poured in, solicited from Kraft, Galbraith, Stevenson, Bowles and others, unsolicited from newsmen, friends and total strangers. From Billy Graham he obtained a list of possible Biblical quotations, and I secured a similar list from the director of Washington's Jewish Community Council, Isaac Franck.

The final text included several phrases, sentences and themes suggested by these sources, as did his address to the Massachusetts legislature. He was, in fact, concerned that the Massachusetts speech had preempted some of his best material and had set a mark that would be hard to top. Credit should also go to other Kennedy advisers who reviewed the early drafts and offered suggestions or encouragement.

But however numerous the assistant artisans, the principal architect of the Inaugural Address was John Fitzgerald Kennedy. Many of its most memorable passages can be traced to earlier Kennedy speeches and writings. For example:

Inaugural Address	*Other Addresses*
For man holds in his mortal hands the power to abolish all forms of human poverty and all forms of human life.	. . . man . . . has taken into his mortal hands the power to exterminate the entire species some seven times over. *—Acceptance speech at Los Angeles*
. . . the torch has been passed to a new generation of Americans. . . .	It is time. In short, for a new generation of Americans. *—Acceptance speech and several campaign speeches*
And so, my fellow Americans, ask not what your country can do for you; ask what you can do for your country.	We do not campaign stressing what our country is going to do for us as a people. We stress what we can do for the country, all of us. *—Televised campaign address from Washington, Sept. 20, 1960*

No Kennedy speech ever underwent so many drafts. Each paragraph was reworded, reworked and reduced. The following table illustrates the attention paid to detailed changes:

First Draft	*Next-to-Last Draft*	*Final Text*
We celebrate today not a victory of party but	We celebrate today not a victory of party but a	We observe today not a victory of party but a

the sacrament of democracy.

Each of us, whether we hold office or not, shares the responsibility for guiding this most difficult of all societies along the path of self-discipline and self-government.

Nor can two great and powerful nations forever continue on this reckless course, both overburdened by the staggering cost of modern weapons . . .

And if the fruits of cooperation prove sweeter than the dregs of suspicion, let both sides join ultimately in creating a true world order—neither a Pax Americana, nor a Pax Russiana, nor even a balance of power—but a community of power.

convention of freedom.

In your hands, my fellow citizens, more than in mine, will be determined the success or failure of our course.

. . . neither can two great and powerful nations long endure their present reckless course, both overburdened by the staggering cost of modern weapons . . .

And if a beachhead of cooperation can be made in the jungles of suspicion, let both sides join some day in creating, not a new balance of power but a new world of law . . . .

celebration of freedom.

In your hands, my fellow citizens, more than mine, will rest the final success or failure of our course.

. . . neither can two great and powerful groups of nations take comfort from our present course—both sides overburdened by the cost of modern weapons . . .

And if a beachhead of cooperation can push back the jungle of suspicion, let both sides join in creating a new endeavor, not a new balance of power, but a new world of law . . . .

Initially, while he worked on his thoughts at Palm Beach, I worked at my home in a Washington suburb with telephoned instructions from the President-elect and the material collected from other sources. Then I flew down, was driven to his father's oceanside home, and gave him my notes for the actual drafting and assembling. We worked through the morning seated on the patio overlooking the Atlantic.

He was dissatisfied with each attempt to outline domestic goals. It sounded partisan, he said, divisive, too much like the campaign. Finally he said, "Let's drop out the domestic stuff altogether. It's too long anyway." He wanted it to be the shortest in the twentieth century, he said. "It's more effective that way and I don't want people to think I'm a windbag." He couldn't beat FDR's abbreviated wartime remarks in 1944, I said—and he settled for the shortest (less than nineteen hundred words) since 1905.

"I'm sick of reading how we're planning another 'hundred days' of miracles," he said, "and I'd like to know who on the staff is talking that up. Let's put in that this won't all be finished in a hundred days or a thousand."

That afternoon, as he was busy with other meetings at the house, I put his notes, changes and additions into a clean draft, working beside the Palm Beach Towers Hotel swimming pool.

The next morning, on the patio in sport clothes, he reworked it further. "Let's eliminate all the "I's," he said. "Just say what 'we' will do. You'll have to leave it in about the oath and the responsibility, but let's cut it everywhere else." The ending, he said, "sounds an awful lot like the ending of the Massachusetts legislature speech, but I guess it's OK." He worked and reworked the "ask not" sentence, with the three campaign speeches containing a similar phrase (Anchorage, Detroit, Washington) spread out on a low glass coffee table beside him.

Later that day—January 17—as we flew back to Washington from Palm Beach, working in his cabin on the *Caroline,* the final phrasing was emerging. A biblical quotation that was later used in his American University speech was deleted. The opening paragraphs were redictated by the President-elect to Evelyn Lincoln en route, and he smilingly placed in the plane's desk drawer his handwritten notes from which he had dictated, saying, "An early draft of Roosevelt's Inaugural was discovered the other day—and brought $200,000 at an auction."

Arriving back in Washington, the work went on at his house and in our Senate offices. Kenneth Galbraith suggested "cooperative ventures" with our allies in place of "joint ventures," which sounded like a mining partnership. Dean Rusk suggested that the other peoples of the world be challenged to ask "what together we can do for freedom" instead of "what you can do for freedom." Walter Lippmann suggested that references to the Communist bloc be changed from "enemy" to "adversary." The President-elect inserted a phrase he had used in a campaign speech on Latin America—"a new alliance for progress." At the last moment, concerned that his emphasis on foreign affairs would be interpreted as an evasion on civil rights, he added to his commitment on human rights the words "at home and around the world."

On January 19, one day before inauguration, it was finished.

DISCUSSION AND EXERCISES

Consider Kennedy's Inaugural Address and Sorensen's analysis of the prewriting, writing, and rewriting process—as Kennedy moved through the various stages.

1. What single sentence in the speech is still widely cited both as a memorable summation of what the speech was all about (its thesis) and as an exhortation worth repeating to later generations? Is it still timely? Discuss.

2. If delivered today, would this address be as appropriate to world conditions as it was over thirty years ago? In what way? What problems still exist? Are specific problems and programs the main feature and "thrust" of this address? If not, what does seem to you to be the essential purpose Kennedy was trying to fulfill?

3. Discuss the several audiences Kennedy addresses in the course of the speech—over and beyond the specific audience he formally addresses—the public officials and "Fellow Citizens" cited at the outset. Discuss Kennedy's tone: does it change as he moves from one audience to another? What underlying features of tone remain consistent? Why was tone especially important in this address?

continued

4. Why did Kennedy want his address "to be the shortest in the twentieth century"? Do you agree with his reasons? Explain. What kind of considerations did he eliminate from the address in order to keep it short? Was he justified, in your opinion?

5. Sorensen tells us that Kennedy "wanted suggestions from everyone" before he began composing his speech. Comment on this and any other features of "prewriting" that Sorensen describes.

6. What is Sorensen referring to when he says that "the principal architect of the Inaugural Address was John Fitzgerald Kennedy"? Why does Sorensen feel it important to make this point?

7. Comment on the three passages Kennedy incorporated from earlier addresses. What made them worth drawing on a second time? How did he change them? What did he achieve by the changes? Are they improvements, in your opinion?

8. Trace the successive versions of the four passages drawn from Kennedy's first, next-to-last, and final drafts. How do the various word changes, additions, and deletions strengthen the passages? Proceed through the speech paragraph by paragraph, noting the rhetorical features that have made it a classic. How do they function? Concentrate especially on the following:

> opening and closing sections
> parallel constructions
> balanced antithesis
> paragraph length
> one-sentence paragraphs
> variety in sentence length and type (note questions, and imperatives, as well as declarative statements)
> long and short sentences
> sentence rhythm
> transitions
> word repetitions
> precise word choice
> alliteration

9. How does the fact that the Inaugural Address was written primarily to be read aloud influence the writing? What specific rhetorical features reflect its form and purpose as a speech rather than an article or position paper?

10. Much has been made of the ways President Kennedy shaped the political goals of Bill Clinton. Read Clinton's Inaugural Address. Do you see any similarity in content? In tone? What are the major differences between the two speeches?

Case Study 2: Four Successive Student Drafts

At the other end of the spectrum from Kennedy and most other experienced writers, there are those—generally less experienced writers—who quit too soon. Consider the following example of a student effort that was clearly all too effortless. Applying to medical school, the student submitted the following reply to the question: What are your reasons for wanting to become a doctor?

> Becoming a doctor is by no means a recent notion, it is a goal which has lingered with me since high school. I am not interested in going into a field of research or teaching, although I am quite aware that without these professions, medicine would not have progressed much from Hippocrates' time. My purpose for obtaining a M.D. is to go into the practice of medicine. To treat patients with the best equipment at my disposal and to establish a personal patient-physician relationship. To me being a doctor is not a five day a week job, one's work is not completed after office hours. A good doctor will be available when he is needed. I want to become a doctor so I can instill a feeling of security and trust in my patients and to convey to them that a doctor can be more than just one who prescibes medication. He can be someone to trust and turn to in time of crisis—a healer in the broadest sense of the word.
>
> A doctor holds an admirable position in today's society and being a physician offers security for the future. There is no worry about having a job for next year or that a bad winter will cause financial difficulties. I am certainly looking forward to having a family some day and expect to send my children through school. As a doctor I would be assured the ability to send my children through school and establish a happy life for my family.

What is wrong with this statement? Since this is a case study, let's trace its history step by step. (Although this essay is much shorter than most of the writing you'll produce, its brevity allows us to see the issues clearly and trace revision through several drafts.)

Background While reviewing the professional school applications of graduating seniors at this college—to make sure all questions had been answered, all necessary information provided—an alert counselor spotted this "embarrassment" as she called it. Turning it over to members of the English Department, she attached the following note: "Putting this student's worst enemy on the Admissions Committee could not do more damage to his chances than this carelessly tossed off essay on why he wants to be a doctor. The student is far from stupid and he does have something to say, no question. But why must he say it so poorly? Couldn't he have taken the time to reread and rewrite so that sentence errors could be corrected, and the ideas developed more fully?"

We agreed that this student's writing did not do justice to his application (to say the least); that it did not reflect his academic ability or his own best thinking; and that his problem, as we saw it, was in submitting hastily scribbled notes on his subject rather than a carefully worked over, properly revised, and polished final draft. Clearly, the statement had potential, which the student could (and ultimately would) fulfill, once he settled down to work. This student was a worker who had earned straight A's in his science courses. "Well," he explained, "I really work at those."

"Fine," a member of the English Department told him. "Now let's see you work at your writing." The instructor began with a quotation from Sinclair Lewis that all students (and many professionals) should tack up on their bulletin boards:

Writing is just work—there's no secret.
If you dictate or use a pen or type or write with your toes—it is still just work.

With a new no-nonsense approach, then, and with the instructor's help, this student finally went to work. Step number one was to review his writing situation. (As we trace the revision process, imagine that you are a peer tutor working with this student to improve his statement. What kind of advice would you give him? How could you most effectively help him to improve?)

Review of the Writing Situation As indicated earlier, every writer needs to consider at the outset the specific context out of which a piece of writing originates. Thus, this student needed to establish a rhetorical stance—that is, to answer for himself the four crucial questions that define every writing situation:

1. *What is my identity as writer?*
   The answer is very clear: He is a graduating college senior aspiring to enter medical school.
2. *Who are my readers?*
   Here again the answer is clear: The readers are members of the medical school Board of Admissions. As respected doctors, they review applications and decide who should be accepted, who rejected.
3. *What is the occasion?*
   Still no ambiguity here: The student is making his case before the board, submitting his credentials, his argument in his own behalf.
4. *What is my purpose?*
   A form of that most common writing purpose—winning assent—guides him; in this case, he wants to convince the medical board to admit him to the medical school.

Critical Analysis With this clear picture of the writing situation—a situation that involved the writer's entire future—the instructor had no difficulty deciding that this student needed to do considerable revision. In preparation, the instructor tried to help him come to a better understanding of what he himself had written, to see more clearly and judge more critically the implications of certain statements he had made. He would have to examine his own ideas more seriously, more attentively.

Under the heading of **Content,** the instructor asked the student to reread and reevaluate the points he had presented: Had he made the best selection? Had he explored his answer, first from one angle, then from another? Most important, had he meant what he said, said what he meant? Had he tapped deep and honest levels of thought and feeling within himself? Had he dealt with these clearly and convincingly? The instructor called attention to certain jarring aspects of his statement, such as the seeming contradiction between idealistic motives (to be a healer) and materialistic motives (security for the future). Did he realize that he had slipped in a self-serving reason at the end? Was it, in fact, a slip? Or had he consciously decided to be completely candid? If so, was such candor appropriate? Was it strategic? Would it help or hinder his purpose?

Organization: Had the student paid careful attention to every detail of organization, the kind of attention to detail required in all aspects of medical study and practice? On the contrary, the student seems to have set down the piece haphazardly—idea following idea, as they flashed into his mind. This procedure, appropriate for prewriting, will not produce a final draft suitable for submission to an official admissions committee. The occasion clearly required a more carefully worked out organization that reflected the writer's ability to shape his materials methodically and to speak in a tone of voice that was neither stiff and formal nor overly familiar.

Specifically, the instructor suggested that the student examine samples of Christensen's "coordinate sequence" as one possible organizational pattern (see Question 12, What are the causes of X?).

Style: A first editing showed that in addition to poor organization, problems included ineffective word choice, broken parallelism, and shifts in tone (see edited copy, which follows). Here again, the problems create a damaging impression of the writer's character and personality since they suggest carelessness, imprecision, and failure to pay attention to details ("Ah, if that's the way he writes, will he diagnose and treat patients in the same nonchalant, offhand manner?")

Concern for **coherence** (sticking together) raises the question of transitions. In this case a graceful transition could not only resolve the seeming contradiction between idealism and materialism within the essay but could also show that both motives are legitimate: To serve others and to serve oneself may be shown as consistent with reason, good will, and human nature. Such a resolution even reflects a healthy attitude toward the profession. For no one today, not even poets, would say that starving in an attic serves any useful or purifying purpose. Thus, the applicant who stressed only the idealistic and altruistic aspects of medicine might be dismissed as patently insincere, too good to be true. What the student has said about promoting his own interests (content) is acceptable; how the student has said it (style) is not acceptable.

Mechanics: To the student's credit, this essay contains no grammatical mistakes or spelling errors (other than the article "a" rather than "an" before "M.D."). Punctuation is a problem, however, as is basic sentence construction.

In summary, you can see that the medical school applicant would have saved himself time and anxiety if he had treated his assignment—from the beginning—in terms of a process, a series of steps, beginning with freewriting and brainstorming to generate ideas and prod his memory. This exploratory and generating stage would have ended in a rough draft that he could have shown to friends or classmates, a trusted instructor, someone competent and interested who could have provided helpful comments and corrections where necessary. On the basis of these responses and continued study of the first draft, a second and third draft might be in order, incorporating the writer's best thoughts and soundest advice. Yes, this is a tedious process, but one that is familiar to all professional writers. In fact, it almost defines the writer, as novelist John Hersey has pointed out: "To be a writer is to throw away a great deal, not to be satisfied, to type again, and then again, and once more, and over and over. . . ."

Since the future career of the medical school applicant depended to a considerable extent on how successfully he projected himself in his written application, he would have been wise to take seriously his role of writer, for his reward was no less that "winning assent" to his application—getting into medical school.

Draft Number One: With corrections and editorial comments[1]

deadwood

Isn't this word
too casual? — Becoming a doctor is by no means
a recent notion, it is a goal that

comma splice has lingered with me since high

gap in
thought here:
a big leap
from one
aspect of
the subject
to another.
school. I am not interested in
going into a field of research or
teaching, although I am quite aware
that without these professions,
medicine would not have progressed
much from Hippocrates' time. My
purpose for obtaining an M.D. is to
go into the practice of medicine.

Is this a
word? Does a
serious goal
"linger" or
does a melody
"linger", a
memory "linger"?

Is this a full
sentence or a
fragment?
To treat patients with the best
equipment at my disposal and to establish a personal patient-physician
relationship. To me being a doctor
is not a five day a week job, one's
work is not completed after office

comma splice:
use ⊙ ⟨⋅⟩ or ⟨∴⟩

hours. A good doctor will be
available when he is needed. I want

wordy,
repetitious—
unnecessary shift
in structure:
broken
parallelism
to become a doctor so I can instill a
feeling of security and trust in
my patients and to convey to them
that a doctor can be more than just
one who prescibes medication. He

transition needed
to bridge gap
between these
two points

can be someone to trust and turn to
in time of crisis—a healer in the

This is not badly
stated, but then
it is dropped!
broadest sense of the word.

A doctor holds an admirable
position in today's society and
being a physician offers security

---

[1]Criticism of content and organization (as described in this draft) was discussed with the student during a private conference.

for the future. There is no worry
about having a job for next year or
that/a bad winter will cause

broken parallelism

financial difficulties. I am certainly
looking forward to having a family
some day and expect to send my
children through school. As a doctor I
would be assured the ability to send my
children through school and establish a
happy life for my family.

diffusely stated; not in tone

--Student application
to medical school

Draft Number Two: An improved version of Draft Number One follows. The organization is now somewhat tighter and no longer slipshod. The statement now lends itself to more intricate editing, deeper analysis of how the student has positioned ideas and how—in the interest of logic and grace—he or she might reposition these ideas more effectively. At this point the instructor could make still other editorial observations about possible redundancies, transitions, and the appropriateness of particular words. Draft Number Two incorporates changes suggested on the first draft. The retyped draft can be edited again and further suggestions made for improvement:

Becoming a doctor is not a new
idea for me; but a dream I have had
since high school. My focus is not
research or teaching (although without those professions, medicine
would not have progressed beyond
Hippocrates) but the actual practice
of medicine.

Is "focus" the word you want?

No - you need "time" or something!

nicely stated

My interest in becoming an M.D.
is twofold. First, I want the
opportunity to treat patients with
the best equipment and knowledge at

Do you treat people with "knowledge"? What you say here shows promise—but have you ordered your statements properly? Think about some reorganizing.

my disposal and [to establish a
personal patient-physician relationship.] To really offer the patient
the best care, I feel that the
practice of medicine is a twenty-four
hour a day job. The dedicated
physician must be available when he
is needed. I want to [instill a
feeling of security and trust in my
patients,] assuring them that my concern goes beyond simply prescribing
medicine. I want to be a healer in
the broadest sense; someone to turn
to in time of crisis; concerned with
the spirit as well as the body.

My second interest is less
idealistic and more practical. Being
a physician offers two attractive
rewards; social prestige and financial
security. A doctor need not worry
about being out of work if the crops
fail or the recession worsens.
Therefore, he can relax in his
ability to provide for his family.

For me, the opportunity to study
medicine is the opportunity to
fulfill my dream of the past and
work toward my dream of the future.

Don't these two points belong together?

Transiton term: "In summary" perhaps?

well said here – a good point

redundant?

Does one relax "in an ability"?

excellent ending

Draft Number Three incorporates the additional suggestions made on Draft Number Two. What emerges here is a much improved version, almost ready to submit except for a few fine points of polishing and still further probing of motives: Has the student resolved his apparent confusion?

For me, becoming a doctor is not
a new idea, but a dream I have had
since high school. Although I respect
research and teaching (for without
those professions there would have
been no progress since the time of Hippocrates) my special interest is in the
actual day-by-day practice of medicine.

Basically I have two goals.
First of all, I want to be a really
dedicated doctor: I want to offer
my patients the best care I can give
them, even if it means working
twenty-four hour a day. I want to
establish the kind of personal
patient-physician relationship that
will instill a feeling of security
and trust in my patients. They will
know that my concern goes beyond
simply prescribing medication. For
I will always endeavor to treat   *try?*
them with the best equipment
available and keep up to date with
medical findings. In essence, I
want to be a healer in the broadest

sense; someone to turn to in time of
crisis; *someone* concerned with the spirit   *parallelism*
as well as the body.

My second goal is less idealistic
and more practical. Being a physician
offers two additional rewards that ap-
peal to me, social position and financial   *Are you*
security. A doctor need not worry   *suggesting that it*
                                                is impractical to
                                                be idealistic? Are
                                                they necessarily

about being out of work if the crops fail   *opposed to one*
another? I'd like
or the recession worsens. Therefore,   *to see you think*
this through still
he ~~can relax and~~ know that he will   *further.*

always be able to provide for his

family, to give his children a good

education and a good life.

    I feel that the opportunity to

study medicine is the opportunity

to fulfill my dream of the past and to

work toward my dream for the future.

Draft Number Four is ready for submission.

    For me, becoming a doctor is not a new idea but a dream I have had since high school. Although I respect research and teaching (without these professions there would have been no progress since the time of Hippocrates), my special interest is the actual day-by-day practice of medicine.

    Basically I have two goals. First, I want to be a really dedicated doctor. I want to offer my patients the best care I can give them, even if it means working twenty-four hours a day. I want to establish the kind of personal patient-physician relationship that will instill a feeling of security and trust in my patients. They will know that my concern goes beyond simply prescribing medicine. For I will always try to treat them with the best equipment available and to keep up-to-date with medical findings. In essence, I want to be a healer in the broadest sense: someone to turn to in times of crisis, someone concerned with the spirit as well as the body.

    My second goal is admittedly more selfish. Being a physician offers two additional rewards that appeal to me: social position and financial security. I feel that doctors earn their social position because it grows out of the respect people have for their many years of training and their medical skills. Financial security—or at least freedom from anxiety about earning a living or holding a job—seems to be an imperative if a doctor is to do good work. Even if the crops fail or the recession worsens, he will go on practicing medicine; he knows he'll also be able to provide for his family, give his children a good education and a good life.

    As I see it, the study of medicine will give me the opportunity to fulfill my dream of the past and to work toward my dream of the future.

EXERCISES

1. In your own words, describe the progression from drafts number one to four. Evaluate the quality of change in each one.
2. Using the prewriting steps you have learned, write a one-page essay of your own in which you explain to a graduate or professional school of your choice why you want to enter a particular discipline or field. Seek editorial response and assistance and incorporate suggestions into successive drafts (as many as you find necessary).

PART II

WRITING A SHORT PAPER: TWENTY QUESTIONS

1. How can X be described?
2. How did X happen?
3. What kind of person is X?
4. What is my memory of X?
5. What is my personal response to X?
6. What are the facts about X?
7. What does X mean?
8. What is the essential function of X?
9. What are the component parts of X?
10. How is X made or done?
11. How should X be made or done?
12. What are the causes of X?

13. What are the consequences of X?
14. What are the types of X?
15. How does X compare to Y?
16. What is the present status of X?
17. How can X be summarized?
18. How should X be interpreted?
19. What is the value of X?
20. What case can be made for or against X?

Question

1

HOW CAN X
BE DESCRIBED?

EFFECTIVE SELECTION OF DETAIL
 COMING TO ANTIGUA, JAMAICA
  KINCAID

EFFECTIVE ARRANGEMENT OF DETAILS
 THE KINGDOM OF DIDD, DR. SEUSS
 MOONRISE OVER MONUMENT VALLEY,
  JOHN V. YOUNG
 THE EARTHQUAKE, JONATHAN SPENCE

DESCRIBING TO INFORM AND DELIGHT
 THE SCHOOL AT AKÉ, WOLE SOYINKA

DESCRIBING TO CREATE MOOD AND MEANING
 SHADY GROVE, ALABAMA, JULY 1936,
  JAMES AGEE

If you've ever thought that, as one student reported, you'd "have to run out and get run over by a truck in order to find something to write about," let us suggest a simpler and safer alternative. You can ask the question, How can I describe it? You can look at some aspect of the environment—a person, place, object or event. You can look at the sky and the stars; look at the school gymnasium or the used-car lot across town (the subject need not be picturesque). You can look up from your desk, look across the room, look at the window, look *out* the window, look out and beyond. Look carefully and purposefully, then answer the question, What does it look like? Describe what you see, hear, smell, feel. Describe your sensations and impressions. Is the night dark and windy (eerie)? Is the day gray and bleak (depressing)? Or is the morning sunny and warm, alive with people and laughter? Whatever is happening out there, take careful note, for, as the poet John Ciardi has said, whatever we look at carefully is worth looking at—and, he might have added, worth writing about as well.

A description may be an essay in itself or part of a longer work (short story, essay, article, novel, biography). Describing is a necessary strategy for all types of writing, because it reconstructs for the reader how something or someone appears. Remember this above all, then, in writing description: You must have a keen eye; in fact, all your senses must be alert if you are to take in the scene and then reproduce it in a verbal picture that will come alive for the reader.

EFFECTIVE SELECTION OF DETAIL

Clearly, a good description must evoke sensory impressions, for only then can the reader begin to respond totally. Although a particular piece of writing may call several senses into play, the visual will usually predominate, since most of us use our eyes as a primary guide and as a check or verifier of our other senses. (Thus Shakespeare, in *A Midsummer Night's Dream*, has Bottom rush into the woods "to see a noise that he heard.") It is not surprising that most descriptions focus on how something or someone looks.

For example, take Henry Fielding's description of Sophia, the lovely heroine of his novel *Tom Jones.*

> Sophia . . . the only daughter of Mr. Western, was a middle-sized woman; but rather inclining to tall. Her shape was not only exact, but extremely delicate; and the nice proportion of her arms promised the truest symmetry in her limbs. Her hair, which was black, was so luxuriant that it reached her middle, before she cut it to comply with the modern fashion; and it was now curled so gracefully in her neck that few could believe it to be her own. If envy could find any part of the face which demanded less commendation than the rest, it might possibly think her forehead might have been higher without prejudice to her. Her eyebrows were full, even, and arched beyond the power of art to imitate. Her black eyes had a lustre in them which all her softness could not extinguish.

Fielding does not give all the details of Sophia's appearance; an overly detailed listing would be tedious and dull. Instead he selects those precise physical characteristics that enable us to see her in our mind's eye: she is tall, with nice proportions (the relationship of the parts of the body); she is delicate (the texture or "aura" of her); her black hair curls gracefully on her neck; she has a relatively low forehead (perhaps a slight imperfection to make her seem more human); she has lovely arched eyebrows and lustrous black eyes (proverbially "the windows of the soul").

Clearly, Fielding had a long list of subquestions in mind when he drew this verbal portrait, questions concerning size, shape, coloring, posture, proportion, expression, style, and manner. For all practical purposes, Sophia stands before us as if in a photograph.

So too does the schoolroom that Dickens describes in *David Copperfield*. Here Dickens selects details with the express purpose of creating a dominant mood or impression. It is a "forlorn and desolate place," we are told in the opening sentence of the paragraph, and the following specific details paint a picture which supports that judgment: the floor is "dirty" and littered (the room looks "forlorn and desolate"); the air itself is "unwholesome" (the room smells "forlorn and desolate").

> I gazed upon the schoolroom into which he took me, as the most forlorn and desolate place I had ever seen. I see it now. A long room, with three long rows of desks, and six of forms, and bristling all around with pegs for hats and slates. Scraps of old copy-books and exercises litter the dirty floor. Some silkworms' houses, made of the same materials, are scattered over the desks. Two miserable little white mice, left behind by their owner, are running up and down in a fusty castle made of pasteboard and wire, looking in all corners with their red eyes for anything to eat. A bird, in a cage very little bigger than himself, makes a mournful rattle now and then in hopping on his perch, two inches high, or dropping from it, but neither sings nor chirps. There is a strange unwholesome smell upon the room, like mildewed corduroys, sweet apples wanting air, and rotten books. There could not well be more ink splashed about it, if it had been roofless from its first construction, and the skies had rained, snowed, hailed, and blown ink through the varying seasons of the year.

Dickens' first impression, that the schoolroom was "the most forlorn and desolate place" he had ever seen, leads him to recreate it for his readers. We see it now, just as he saw it then. He piles detail upon detail in this stirring passage. They appeal to all our senses: we *see* the "long room," the "scraps of old copy-books," the "two miserable little white mice," and the "bird"; we *hear* the bird's "mournful rattle"; we *smell* "mildewed corduroys, sweet apples wanting air, and rotten books." Every detail suggests abandonment and decay—the very opposite of what should happen in the classroom: intellectual and physical growth. It all speaks, as Dickens no doubt intended it to, for a country whose educational system is in a horrifying state of disrepair.

As Dickens well understood, a good verbal description, like a good drawing or painting, rivals the most accurate photograph. In urging students to develop what she called "fresh seeing," artist Emily Carr observed that "we may copy something as faithfully as the camera, but unless we bring to our picture something additional—something creative—something of ourselves—our picture does not live" (*Seeing,* 11). The same is true of verbal pictures: they too must be animated by a creative vision—by "fresh seeing."

In contrast to these writers, Jamaica Kincaid, in the following selection, imagines herself a moving narrator, a tourist in fact, arriving on the island of Antigua for the first time. By imagining a newcomer's response to the place where she grew up, Kincaid gains a fresh point of view on familiar surroundings, though this freshness is balanced by a heavy dose of irony. Read her description several times, identifying the various sensory details she uses to bring the scene alive for the reader.

COMING TO ANTIGUA

Jamaica Kincaid

If you go to Antigua as a tourist, this is what you will see. If you come by aeroplane, you will land at the V. C. Bird International Airport. Vere Cornwall (V. C.) Bird is the Prime Minister of Antigua. You may be the sort of tourist who would wonder why a Prime Minister would want an airport named after him—why not a school, why not a hospital, why not some great public monument? You are a tourist and you have not yet seen a school in Antigua, you have not yet seen the hospital in Antigua, you have not yet seen a public monument in Antigua. As your plane descends to land, you might say, What a beautiful island Antigua is—more beautiful than any of the other islands you have seen, and they were very beautiful, in their way, but they were much too green, much too lush with vegetation, which indicated to you, the tourist, that they got quite a bit of rainfall, and rain is the very thing that you, just now, do not want, for you are thinking of the hard and cold and dark and long days you spent working in North America (or, worse, Europe), earning some money so that you could stay in this place (Antigua) where the sun always shines and where the climate is deliciously hot and dry for the four to ten days you are going to be staying there; and since you are on your holiday, since you are a tourist, the thought of what it might be like for someone who had to live day in, day out in a place that suffers constantly from drought, and so has to watch carefully every drop of fresh water used (while at the same time surrounded by a sea and an ocean—the Caribbean Sea on one side, the Atlantic Ocean on the other), must never cross your mind.

You disembark from your plane. You go through customs. Since you are a tourist, a North American or European—to be frank, white—and not an Antiguan black returning to Antigua from Europe or North America with cardboard boxes of much needed cheap clothes and food for relatives, you move through customs swiftly, you move through customs with ease. Your bags are not searched. You emerge from customs into the hot, clean air: immediately you feel cleansed, immediately you feel blessed (which is to say special); you feel free. You see a man, a taxi driver; you ask him to take you to your destination; he quotes you a price. You immediately think that the price is in the local currency, for you are a tourist and you are familiar with these things (rates of exchange) and you feel even more free, for things seem so cheap, but then your driver ends by saying, "In U.S. currency." You may say, "Hmmmm, do you have a formal sheet that lists official prices and destinations?" Your driver obeys the law and shows you the sheet, and he apologises for the incredible mistake he has made in quoting you a price off the top of his head which is so vastly different (favouring him) from the one listed. You are driven to your hotel by this taxi driver in his taxi, a brand-new Japanese-made vehicle. The road on which you are travelling is a very bad road, very much in need of repair. You are feeling wonderful, so you say, "Oh, what a marvellous change

these bad roads are from the splendid highways I am used to in North America."
(Or, worse, Europe.) Your driver is reckless; he is a dangerous man who drives in
the middle of the road when he thinks no other cars are coming in the opposite
direction, passes other cars on blind curves that run uphill, drives at sixty miles an
hour on narrow, curving roads when the road sign, a rusting, beat-up thing left over
from colonial days, says 40 MPH. This might frighten you (you are on your holiday;
you are a tourist); this might excite you (you are on your holiday; you are a tourist),
though if you are from New York and take taxis you are used to this style of driving:
most of the taxi drivers in New York are from places in the world like this. You are
looking out the window (because you want to get your money's worth); you notice
that all the cars you see are brand-new, or almost brand-new, and that they are all
Japanese-made. There are no American cars in Antigua—no new ones, at any rate;
none that were manufactured in the last ten years. You continue to look at the cars
and you say to yourself, Why, they look brand-new, but they have an awful sound,
like an old car—a very old, dilapidated car. How to account for that? Well, possibly
it's because they use leaded gasoline in these brand-new cars whose engines were
built to use non-leaded gasoline, but you mustn't ask the person driving the car if
this is so, because he or she has never heard of unleaded gasoline. You look closely
at the car; you see that it's a model of a Japanese car that you might hesitate to buy;
it's a model that's very expensive; it's a model that's quite impractical for a person
who has to work as hard as you do and who watches every penny you earn so that
you can afford this holiday you are on. How do they afford such a car? And do they
live in a luxurious house to match such a car? Well, no. You will be surprised, then,
to see that most likely the person driving this brand-new car filled with the wrong
gas lives in a house that, in comparison, is far beneath the status of the car; and if
you were to ask why you would be told that the banks are encouraged by the
government to make loans available for cars, but loans for houses not so easily
available; and if you ask again why, you will be told that the two main car
dealerships in Antigua are owned in part or outright by ministers in government.
Oh, but you are on holiday and the sight of these brand-new cars driven by people
who may or may not have really passed their driving test (there was once a scandal
about driving licences for sale) would not really stir up these thoughts in you. You
pass a building sitting in a sea of dust and you think, It's some latrines for people
just passing by, but when you look again you see the building has written on it
PIGOTT'S SCHOOL. You pass the hospital, the Holberton Hospital, and how wrong you
are not to think about this, for though you are a tourist on your holiday, what if your
heart should miss a few beats? What if a blood vessel in your neck should break?
What if one of those people driving those brand-new cars filled with the wrong gas
fails to pass safely while going uphill on a curve and you are in the car going in the
opposite direction? Will you be comforted to know that the hospital is staffed with
doctors that no actual Antiguan trusts; the Antiguans always say about the doctors,
"I don't want them near me"; that Antiguans refer to them not as doctors but as "the
three men" (there are three of them); that when the Minister of Health himself
doesn't feel well he takes the first plane to New York to see a real doctor; that if any
one of the ministers in government needs medical care he flies to New York to
get it?

It's a good thing that you brought your own books with you, for you couldn't
just go to the library and borrow some. Antigua used to have a splendid library, but

in The Earthquake (everyone talks about it that way—The Earthquake; we Antiguans, for I am one, have a great sense of things, and the more meaningful the thing, the more meaningless we make it) the library building was damaged. This was in 1974, and soon after that a sign was placed on the front of the building saying, THIS BUILDING WAS DAMAGED IN THE EARTHQUAKE OF 1974. REPAIRS ARE PENDING. The sign hangs there, and hangs there more than a decade later, with its unfulfilled promise of repair, and you might see this as a sort of quaintness on the part of these islanders, these people descended from slaves—what a strange, unusual perception of time they have. REPAIRS ARE PENDING, and here it is many years later, but perhaps in a world that is twelve miles long and nine miles wide (the size of Antigua) twelve years and twelve minutes and twelve days are all the same. The library is one of those splendid old buildings from colonial times, and the sign telling of the repairs is a splendid old sign from colonial times. Not very long after The Earthquake, Antigua got its independence from Britain, making Antigua a state in its own right, and Antiguans are so proud of this that each year, to mark the day, they go to church and thank God, a British God, for this. But you should not think of the confusion that must lie in all that and you must not think of the damaged library. You have brought your own books with you, and among them is one of those new books about economic history, one of those books explaining how the West (meaning Europe and North America after its conquest and settlement by Europeans) got rich: the West got rich not from the free (free—in this case meaning got-for-nothing) and then undervalued labour, for generations, of the people like me you see walking around you in Antigua but from the ingenuity of small shopkeepers in Sheffield and Yorkshire and Lancashire, or wherever; and what a great part the invention of the wristwatch played in it, for there was nothing noble-minded men could not do when they discovered they could slap time on their wrists just like that (isn't that the last straw; for not only did we have to suffer the unspeakableness of slavery, but the satisfaction to be had from "We made you bastards rich" is taken away, too), and so you needn't let that slightly funny feeling you have from time to time about exploitation, oppression, domination develop into full-fledged unease, discomfort; you could ruin your holiday. They are not responsible for what you have; you owe them nothing; in fact, you did them a big favour, and you can provide one hundred examples. For here you are now, passing by Government House. And here you are now, passing by the Prime Minister's Office and the Parliament Building, and overlooking these, with a splendid view of St. John's Harbour, the American Embassy. If it were not for you, they would not have Government House, and Prime Minister's Office, and Parliament Building and embassy of powerful country. Now you are passing a mansion, an extraordinary house painted the colour of old cow dung, with more aerials and antennas attached to it than you will see even at the American Embassy. The people who live in this house are a merchant family who came to Antigua from the Middle East less than twenty years ago. When this family first came to Antigua, they sold dry goods door to door from suitcases they carried on their backs. Now they own a lot of Antigua; they regularly lend money to the government, they build enormous (for Antigua), ugly (for Antigua), concrete buildings in Antigua's capital, St. John's, which the government then rents for huge sums of money; a member of their family is the Antiguan Ambassador to Syria; Antiguans hate them. Not far from this mansion is another mansion, the home of a drug smuggler. Everybody knows he's a drug smuggler, and if just as you were driving by he stepped out of his door your driver might point him out to you as the notorious person that he is, for this drug smuggler is so rich people say he buys cars in tens—ten of this one, ten of that one—and that he bought a house (another mansion) near Five Islands, contents included, with cash he carried in a suitcase: three hundred and fifty thousand American dollars, and, to the surprise of the seller of the house, lots of American dollars were left over. Overlooking the drug smuggler's mansion is yet another mansion, and leading up to it is the best paved road in all of Antigua—even better than the road that was paved for the Queen's visit in 1985 (when the Queen came, all the roads that she would travel on were paved anew, so that the Queen might have been left with the impression that riding in a car in Antigua was a pleasant experience). In this mansion lives a woman sophisticated people in Antigua call Evita. She is a notorious woman. She's young and beautiful and the girlfriend of somebody very high up in the government. Evita is notorious because her relationship with this high government official has made her the owner of boutiques and property and given her a say in cabinet meetings, and all sorts of other privileges such a relationship would bring a beautiful young woman.

Oh, but by now you are tired of all this looking, and you want to reach your destination—your hotel, your room. You long to refresh yourself; you long to eat some nice lobster, some nice local food. You take a bath, you brush your teeth. You get dressed again; as you get dressed, you look out the window. That water—have you ever seen anything like it? Far out, to the horizon, the colour of the water is navy-blue; nearer, the water is the colour of the North American sky. From there to the shore, the water is pale, silvery, clear, so clear that you can see its pinkish-white sand bottom. Oh, what beauty! Oh, what beauty! You have never seen anything like this. You are so excited. You breathe shallow. You breathe deep. You see a beautiful boy skimming the water, godlike, on a Windsurfer. You see an incredibly unattractive, fat, pastrylike-fleshed woman enjoying a walk on the beautiful sand, with a man, an incredibly unattractive, fat, pastrylike-fleshed man; you see the pleasure they're taking in their surroundings. Still standing, looking out the window, you see yourself lying on the beach, enjoying the amazing sun (a sun so powerful and yet so beautiful, the way it is always overhead as if on permanent guard, ready to stamp out any cloud that dares to darken and so empty rain on you and ruin your holiday; a sun that is your personal friend). You see yourself taking a walk on that beach, you see yourself meeting new people (only they are new in a very limited way, for they are people just like you). You see yourself eating some delicious, locally grown food. You see yourself, you see yourself . . . You must not wonder what exactly happened to the contents of your lavatory when you flushed it. You must not wonder where your bathwater went when you pulled out the stopper. You must not wonder what happened when you brushed your teeth. Oh, it might all end up in the water you are thinking of taking a swim in; the contents of your lavatory might, just might, graze gently against your ankle as you wade carefree in the water, for you see, in Antigua, there is no proper sewage-disposal system. But the Caribbean Sea is very big and the Atlantic Ocean is even bigger; it would amaze even you to know the number of black slaves this ocean has swallowed up. When you sit down to eat your delicious meal, it's better that you don't know that most of what you are eating came off a plane from Miami. And before it got on a plane in Miami, who knows where it came from? A good guess is that it came from a place like Antigua first, where it was grown dirt-cheap, went to Miami, and came back. There is a world of something in this, but I can't go into it right now.

EFFECTIVE ARRANGEMENT OF DETAILS

As we have just seen, the first basic principle of description is that it should involve the senses or evoke sensory impressions through the selection of details. Maintaining a consistent point of view or arranging details not in random fashion but in an order either inherent in the subject or dictated by the context is the second basic principle. To maintain a consistent point of view, writers describe subjects as they observe them and include only what they can observe. The organization of a descriptive essay or other writing depends on the way in which the writer—and the reader—perceive the subject. For instance, if you are describing a room, you would move from right to left, or from top to bottom (spatial organization). If you were describing an event, you would move from beginning to end (chronological organization). If you were describing a series of related actions, you would move from cause to effect (causal organization). We will examine each of these in turn.

In spatial organization, point of view is especially important because it determines what writers can see, how they see what they do, how what they see makes them feel, and so on. In Kincaid's essay, which is spatially organized, the writer imagines a moving observer, passing from one point in Antigua to another, describing, item by item, what he observes as he goes along. In the selection which follows, a passage from Dr. Seuss's famous children's story *The 500 Hats of Bartholomew Cubbins,* the observer is "fixed"—anchored in one spot. First he looks up; then he looks down, each direction creating not only a different sense of place but a different sense of self in relation to place.

The Kingdom of Didd

Dr. Seuss

The Kingdom of Didd was ruled by King Derwin. His palace stood high on the top of the mountain. From his balcony, he looked down over the houses of all his subjects—first, over the spires of the noblemen's castles, across the broad roofs of the rich men's mansions, then over the little houses of the townsfolk, to the huts of the farmers far off in the fields.

It was a mighty view and it made King Derwin feel mighty important.

Far off in the fields, on the edge of a cranberry bog, stood the hut of the Cubbins family. From the small door Bartholomew looked across the huts of the farmers to the houses of the townsfolk, then to the rich men's mansions and the noblemen's castles, up to the great towering palace of the King. It was exactly the same view that King Derwin saw from his balcony, but Bartholomew saw it backward.

It was a mighty view, but it made Bartholomew Cubbins feel mighty small.

In the following vivid description—also spatially organized—we watch the moon rise over Monument Valley with the writer, John V. Young. We share Young's campsite and, more important, his point of view—facing east "across the limitless expanse of tawny desert." With him, we are turned toward the rising moon, and never—from the opening to the closing paragraph—do we turn away. Our position in relation to the subject is fixed throughout, even when we are momentarily distracted from the scenery by the appearance of "a Navajo girl wearing a long, dark, velvet dress gleaming with silver ornaments."

Actually, the order of this piece is both *chronological* and spatial; it begins "before the sun was fully down" and ends when "the moon had cleared the tops of The Mittens"; the camp faces east, "toward the rising sun and the rising moon." As the scene unfolds, with its sense of the "mysterious and lonely," Young probes beneath the surface of the event to create an underlying mood or atmosphere. The slow passing of time, marked by changes in the natural scenery and the sky, contributes to this effect. So do the many details: We see the colors; we hear the rustle of the night wind; we feel the texture of the surrounding sandstone; we sense in our own muscles the movement of the land upward toward the sky where, soon, the moon will rise.

MOONRISE OVER MONUMENT VALLEY

John V. Young

We were camped here in early spring, by one of those open-faced shelters that the Navajos have provided for tourists in this part of their vast tribal park on the Arizona-Utah border, 25 miles north of Kayenta. It was cool but pleasant, and we were alone, three men in a truck.

We were here for a purpose: to see the full moon rise over this most mysterious and lonely of scenic wonders, where fantastically eroded red and yellow sandstone shapes soar to the sky like a giant's chess pieces and where people—especially white strangers—come quickly to feel like pretty small change indeed.

Because all Navajo dwellings face east, our camp faced east—toward the rising sun and the rising moon and across a limitless expanse of tawny desert, that ancient sea, framed by the towering nearby twin pinnacles called The Mittens. We began to feel the magic even before the sun was fully down. It occurred when a diminutive wraith of a Navajo girl wearing a long, dark, velvet dress gleaming with silver ornaments drifted silently by, herding a flock of ghostly sheep to a waterhole somewhere. A bell on one of the rams tinkled faintly, and then its music was lost in the soft rustle of the night wind, leaving us with an impression that perhaps we had really seen nothing at all.

Just then, a large woolly dog appeared out of the gloom, seeming to materialize on the spot. It sat quietly on the edge of the glow from our camp-fire, its eyes shining like mirrors. It made no sound but when we offered food, it accepted the gift gravely and with much dignity. The dog then vanished again, probably to join the girl and her flock. We were not certain it was not part of the illusion.

As the sun disappeared entirely, the evening afterglow brush tipped all the spires and cliffs with magenta, deepening to purple, and the sand ripples stood out like miniature ocean waves in darkening shades of orange. Off to the east on the edge of the desert, a pale saffron glow told us the moon was about to rise behind a thin layer of clouds, slashed by the white contrail of an invisible jet airplane miles away.

We had our cameras on tripods and were fussing with light meters, making casual bets as to the exact place where the moon would first appear, when it happened—instant enchantment. Precisely between the twin spires of The Mittens, the enormous golden globe loomed suddenly, seeming as big as the sun itself, behind a coppery curtain on the rim of creation.

We were as totally unprepared for the great size of the moon as we were for its flaming color, nor could we have prepared ourselves for the improbable setting. We felt like the wizards of Stonehenge, commanding the planets to send their light through the magic orifices in line at the equinox. Had the Navajo medicine men contrived this for our benefit?

The massive disk of the moon seemed to rise very fast at first, an optical effect magnified by the crystalline air and the flatness of the landscape between us and the distant, ragged skyline. Then it seemed to pause for a moment, as if it were pinioned on one of the pinnacles or impaled on a sharply upthrusting rocky point. Its blazing light made inky shadows all around us, split by the brilliant wedge of the moon's path between the spires. The wind had stopped. There was not a sound anywhere, not even a whisper. If a drum had sounded just then, it would not have been out of place, I suppose, but it would have frightened us half to death.

Before the moon had cleared the tops of The Mittens, the show was over and the magic was gone. A thin veil of clouds spread over the sky, ending the spell as suddenly as it had come upon us. It was as if the gods had decided that we had seen enough for mere mortals on one spring night, and I must confess it was something of a relief to find ourselves back on mundane earth again, with sand in our shoes and a chill in the air.

The causal organization of a piece of descriptive writing occurs most commonly in technical composition. For instance, if the designer of a new piece of equipment wants to describe how its various parts work together, a causal organization would be the most logical. In the following selection, causal combines with a chronological ordering of actions. The parts of an event describe an ongoing process—specifically, an earthquake that strikes in the evening with "the moon just rising." As the writer describes the destructive effects, one leading to another in a deadly causal chain, he makes us painfully conscious that from the first "frightening roar" this ongoing process is irreversible.

THE EARTHQUAKE

Jonathan Spence

The earthquake struck T'an-ch'eng on July 25, 1668. It was evening, the moon just rising. There was no warning, save for a frightening roar that seemed to come from somewhere to the northwest. The buildings in the city began to shake and the trees took up a rhythmical swaying, tossing ever more wildly back and forth until their tips almost touched the ground. Then came one sharp violent jolt that brought down stretches of the city walls and battlements, officials' yamens, temples, and thousands of private homes. Broad fissures opened up across the streets and underneath the houses, jets of water spurted up into the air to a height of twenty feet or more, and streams of water poured down the roads and flooded the irrigation ditches. Those people who tried to remain standing felt as if their feet were round stones spinning out of control, and were brought crashing to the ground.

Some, like Li Hsien-yū, fell into the fissures but were buoyed up on underground streams and able to cling to the edge; others had their houses sheared in half and survived in the living quarters as the storage rooms slid into the earth. Some watched helplessly as their families fell away from them: Kao Te-mou had lived in a household of twenty-nine with his consorts, children, relatives, and servants, but only he, one son, and one daughter survived.

As suddenly as it had come the earthquake departed. The ground was still. The water seeped away, leaving the open fissures edged with mud and fine sand. The ruins rested in layers where they had fallen, like giant sets of steps.

It was, wrote Feng K'o-ts'an, who in 1673 compiled the *Local History of T'an-ch'eng,* as if fate were "throwing rocks upon a man who had already fallen in a well."

DESCRIBING TO INFORM AND DELIGHT

In the following description of his childhood home in Nigeria, the playwright, novelist, and poet, Wole Soyinka, combines descriptive details that will be unfamiliar to most of his readers with information about the Yoruba culture in which he grew up, and its effect on his growing consciousness. Indeed, the sensory details of the village school impress him so much that he demands to be allowed to join his sister at school. Notice how the sounds of the schoolbell and the rhythms of the songs sung by the other children exert a strange attraction for the young boy. The secret rituals of childhood games hold a sense of promise and mystery for him; like his father's books, they represent the promise of a new world of knowledge and experience. Soyinka received the Nobel Prize for Literature in 1986.

THE SCHOOL AT AKÉ

Wole Soyinka

Every morning before I woke up, Tinu was gone. She returned about midday carrying a slate with its marker attached to it. And she was dressed in the same khaki uniform as the hordes of children, of different sizes, who milled around the compound from morning till afternoon, occupied in a hundred ways.

At a set hour in the morning one of the bigger ones seized the chain which dangled from the bell-house, tugged at it with a motion which gave the appearance of a dance and the bell began pealing. Instantly, the various jostling, tumbling, racing and fighting pupils rushed in different directions around the school buildings, the smaller in size towards the schoolroom at the further end of the compound where I could no longer see them. The bigger pupils remained within sight, near the main building. They split into several groups, each group lined up under the watchful eye of a teacher. When all was orderly, I saw father appear from nowhere at the top of the steps. He made a speech to the assembly, then stood aside. One member of the very biggest group stepped forward and raised a song. The others took it up and they marched into the school-building in twos, to the rhythm of the song.

The song changed every day, chosen from the constant group of five or six. That I came to have a favourite among them was because this was the same one which they sang with more zest than others. I noticed that on the days when it was the turn of this tune, they danced rather than marched. Even the teachers seemed affected, they had an indulgent smile on their faces and would even point out a pupil who on a certain charged beat in the tune would dip his shoulders in a most curious way, yet march without breaking the rhythm. It was an unusual song too, since the main song was in English but the chorus was sung in Yoruba; I could only catch the words of the latter:

> B'ina njo ma jẹ'kọ
> B'ole nja, ma jẹ'kọ
> Eni ebi npa, ọmọ wi ti'rẹ*

I never heard any such lively singing from the other school, indeed that group simply vanished from sight, yet this was where my sister went. I never saw her anywhere among the marching group; in any case, there was nobody her size in that section. My curiosity grew every day. She sensed this and played on it, refusing to answer my questions or else throwing off incomplete fragments which only fed my curiosity.

'I am going to school', I announced one day. It became a joke to be passed from mouth to mouth, producing instant guffaws. Mother appeasingly said. 'Wait till you are as old as your sister.'

The hum of voices, once the pupils were within the buildings, took mysterious overtones. Through the open windows of the schoolroom I saw heads in concentration, the majestic figure of a teacher who passed in and out of vision, mumbling incantations over the heads of his attentive audience. Different chants broke out from different parts of each building, sometimes there was even direct singing, accompanied by a harmonium. When the indoor rites were over, they came out in different groups, played games, ran races, they spread over the compound picking up litter, sweeping the paths, clipping lawns and weeding flower-beds. They roamed about with hoes, cutlasses, brooms and sticks, retired into open workshop sheds where they wove baskets, carved bits of wood and bamboo, kneaded clay and transformed them into odd-shaped objects.

Under the anxious eyes of 'Auntie' Lawanle, I played by myself on the pavement of our house and observed these varied activities. The tools of the open air were again transformed into books, exercise books, slates, books under armpits, in little tin or wooden boxes, books in raffia bags, tied together with string and carried on the head, slung over shoulders in cloth pouches. Directly in front of our home was the lawn which was used exclusively by girls from the other school. They formed circles, chased one another in and out of the circles, struggled for a ball and tossed it through an iron hoop stuck on a board. Then they also

---

* If the house is on fire, I must eat
  If the house is being robbed, I must eat
  The child who is hungry, let him speak.

vanished into classrooms, books were produced and they commenced their own observances of the mystery rites.

Tinu became even more smug. My erstwhile playmate had entered a new world and, though we still played together, she now had a new terrain to draw upon. Every morning she was woken earlier than I, scrubbed, fed and led to school by one of the older children of the house. My toys and games soon palled but the laughter still rankled, so I no longer demanded that I join Tinu in school.

Instead, I got up one morning as she was being woken up, demanded my bath at the same time, ate, selected the clothing which I thought came closest to the uniforms I had seen, and insisted on being dressed in them. I had marked down a number of books on father's table but did not yet remove them. I waited in the frontroom. When Tinu passed through with her escort, I let them leave the house, waited a few moments, then seized the books I had earlier selected and followed them. Both parents were still in the dining-room. I followed at a discreet distance, so I was not noticed until we arrived at the infant school. I waited at the door, watched where Tinu was seated, then went and climbed onto the bench beside her.

Only then did Lawanle, Tinu's escort that day, see me. She let out a cry of alarm and asked me what I thought I was doing. I ignored her. The teachers heard the commotion and came into the room. I appeared to be everybody's object of fun. They looked at me, pointed and they held their sides, rocked forwards and backwards with laughter. A man who appeared to be in charge of the infant section next came in, he was also our father's friend and came often to the house. I recognized him, and I was pleased that he was not laughing with the others. Instead he stood in front of me and asked,

'Have you come to keep your sister company?'

'No. I have come to school.'

Then he looked down at the books I had plucked from father's table.

'Aren't these your father's books?'

'Yes. I want to learn them.'

'But you are not old enough, Wole.'

'I am three years old.'

Lawanle cut in, 'Three years old, *wo?* Don't mind him sir, he won't be three until July.'

'I am nearly three. Anyway, I have come to school. I have books.'

He turned to the class-teacher and said, 'Enter his name in the register.' He then turned to me and said, 'Of course you needn't come to school everyday— come only when you feel like it. You may wake up tomorrow morning and feel that you would prefer to play at home. . . .'

I looked at him in some astonishment. Not feel like coming to school! The coloured maps, pictures and other hangings on the walls, the coloured counters, markers, slates, inkwells in neat round holes, crayons and drawing-books, a shelf laden with modelled objects—animals, human beings, implements—raffia and basket-work in various stages of completion, even the blackboards, chalk and duster. . . . I had yet to see a more inviting playroom! In addition, I had made some vague, intuitive connection between school and the piles of books with which my father appeared to commune so religiously in the front room, and which had constantly to be snatched from me as soon as my hands grew long enough to reach them on the table.

'I shall come everyday' I confidently declared.

DESCRIBING TO CREATE MOOD AND MEANING

In its creation of mood and its suggestion of a larger meaning (the meaning of life itself), James Agee's description of Shady Grove, Alabama, is an extraordinary small classic. It combines place (a southern cemetery) and natural event (death); more than that, it provides "data" which are so strange as to be barely believable. Yet we are moved to belief because the painstakingly rendered details and the matter-of-fact tone give the piece a documentary solidity. On the one hand, the description provides objectively verifiable, measurable facts ("The graveyard is about fifty by a hundred yards . . ."); on the other hand, it provides vivid sense impressions rendered in poetic images ("It is heavily silent and fragrant and all the leaves are breathing slowly . . ."). For many reasons, and on many levels, this essay in description will repay your close study.

Shady Grove, Alabama, July 1936

James Agee

The graveyard is about fifty by a hundred yards inside a wire fence. There are almost no trees in it: a lemon verbena and a small magnolia; it is all red clay and very few weeds.

Out at the front of it across the road there is a cornfield and then a field of cotton and then trees.

Most of the headboards are pine, and at the far end of the yard from the church the graves are thinned out and there are many slender and low pine stumps about the height of the headboards. The shadows are all struck sharp lengthwise of the graves, toward the cornfield, by the afternoon sun. There is no one anywhere in sight. It is heavily silent and fragrant and all the leaves are breathing slowly without touching each other.

Some of the graves have real headstones, a few of them so large they must be the graves of landowners. One is a thick limestone log erected by the Woodmen of the World. One or two of the others, besides a headpiece, have a flat of stone as large as the whole grave.

On one of these there is a china dish on whose cover delicate hands lie crossed, cuffs at their wrists, and the nails distinct.

On another a large fluted vase stands full of dead flowers, with an inch of rusty water at the bottom.

On others of these stones, as many as a dozen of them, there is something I have never seen before: by some kind of porcelain reproduction, a photograph of the person who is buried there; the last or the best likeness that had been made, in a small-town studio, or at home with a snapshot camera. I remember one well of a fifteen-year-old boy in Sunday pants and a plaid pull-over sweater, his hair combed, his cap in his hand, sitting against a piece of farm machinery and grinning. His eyes are squinted against the light and his nose makes a deep shadow down one side of his chin. Somebody's arm, with the sleeve rolled up, is against him; somebody who is almost certainly still alive: they could not cut him entirely out of the picture. Another is a studio portrait, close up, in artificial lighting, of a young woman. She is leaned a little forward, smiling, vivaciously, one hand at her cheek. She is not very pretty, but she believed she was; her face is free from strain or fear. She is wearing an evidently new dress, with a mail-order look about it; patterns of beads are sewn over it and have caught the light. Her face is soft with powder and at the wings of her nose lines have been deleted. Her dark blonde hair is newly washed and professionally done up in puffs at the ears which in that time, shortly after the first great war of her century, were called cootie garages. This image of her face is split across and the split has begun to turn brown at its edges.

I think these would be graves of small farmers.

There are others about which there can be no mistake: they are the graves of the poorest of the farmers and of the tenants. Mainly they are the graves with the pine headboards; or without them.

When the grave is still young, it is very sharply distinct, and of a peculiar form. The clay is raised in a long and narrow oval with a sharp ridge, the shape exactly of an inverted boat. A fairly broad board is driven at the head; a narrower one, sometimes only a stob, at the feet. A good many of the headboards have been sawed into the flat simulacrum of an hourglass; in some of these, the top has been roughly rounded off, so that the resemblance is more nearly that of a head and shoulders sunken or risen to the waist in the dirt. On some of these boards names and dates have been written or printed in hesitant letterings, in pencil or in crayon, but most of them appear never to have been touched in this way. The boards at some of the graves have fallen slantwise or down; many graves seem never to have been marked except in their own carefully made shape. These graves are of all sizes between those of giants and of newborn children; and there are a great many, so many they seem shoals of minnows, two feet long and less, lying near one another; and of these smallest graves, very few are marked with any wood at all, and many are already so drawn into the earth that they are scarcely distinguishable. Some of the largest, on the other hand, are of heroic size, seven and eight feet long, and of these more are marked, a few, even, with the smallest and plainest blocks of limestone, and initials, once or twice a full name; but many more of them have never been marked, and many, too, are sunken half down and more and almost entirely into the earth. A great many of these graves, perhaps half to two thirds of those which are still distinct, have been decorated, not only with shrunken flowers in their cracked vases and with bent targets of blasted flowers, but otherwise as well. Some have a line of white clamshells planted along their ridge; of others, the rim as well is garlanded with these shells. On one large grave, which is otherwise completely plain, a blown-out electric bulb is screwed into the clay at the exact center. On another, on the slope of clay just in front of the headboard, its feet next the board, is a horseshoe; and at its center a blown bulb is stood upright. On two or three others there are insulators of bluegreen glass. On several graves, which I presume to be those of women, there is at the center the prettiest or the oldest and most valued piece of china: on one, a blue glass butter dish whose cover is a setting hen; on another, an intricate milk-colored glass basket; on others, ten-cent-store candy dishes and iridescent vases; on one, a pattern of white and colored buttons. On other graves there are small and thick white butter dishes of the sort which are used in lunch-rooms, and by the action of rain these stand free of the grave on slender turrets of clay. On still another grave, laid carefully next the headboard, is a corncob pipe. On the graves of children there are still these pretty pieces of glass and china, but they begin to diminish in size and they verge into the forms of animals and into homuncular symbols of growth; and there are toys: small autos, locomotives and fire engines of red and blue metal; tea sets for dolls, and tin kettles the size of thimbles: little effigies in rubber and glass and china, of cows, lions, bulldogs, squeaking mice, and the characters of comic strips; and . . . what two parents have done here for their little daughter: not only a tea set, and a cocacola bottle, and a milk bottle, ranged on her short grave, but a stone at the head and a stone at the foot, and in the headstone her six month image as she lies sleeping dead in her white dress, the head sunken delicately forward, deeply and delicately gone, the eyes seamed, as that of a dead bird, and on the rear face of this stone the words:

> We can't have all things to please us,
> Our little Daughter, Joe An, has gone to Jesus.

DISCUSSION AND EXERCISES

1. Study the selection and organization of details in the following paragraphs and answer the following questions:
   a. Is there a topic sentence, and if so, how does it function?
   b. Is the observer fixed or moving?
   c. List the individual details in each paragraph and indicate in what ways they are judiciously chosen. Which does the author present with camera-like objectivity and which does he render subjectively and *feelingly?* Which senses does he appeal to (sight or sound)?
   d. Contemplate the spatial pattern of the paragraph; trace its movement from first to last sentence, indicating what point of view and principle of organization govern the arrangement of details. Does the writer move from left to right; from top to bottom; in order of prominence ("the first thing one sees on entering the room . . . ")? Analyze and explain.
   e. Does the paragraph convey a dominant mood or impression? If so, how does the writer create it? Consider such matters as choice of words, sense images, projection of feeling.

   One November evening, in the neighbourhood of Lyndhurst, I saw a flock of geese marching in a long procession, led, as their custom is, by a majestical gander; they were coming home from their feeding-ground in the forest, and when I spied them were approaching their owner's cottage. Arrived at the wooden gate of the garden in front of the cottage, the leading bird drew up square before it, and with repeated loud screams demanded admittance. Pretty soon, in response to the summons, a man came out of the cottage, walked briskly down the garden path and opened the gate, but only wide enough to put his right leg through; then, placing his foot and knee against the leading bird, he thrust him roughly back; as he did so three young geese pressed forward and were allowed to pass in; then the gate was slammed in the face of the gander and the rest of his followers, and the man went back to the cottage. The gander's indignation was fine to see, though he had most probably experienced the same rude treatment on many previous occasions. Drawing up to the gate again he called more loudly than before; then deliberately lifted a leg, and placing his broad webbed foot like an open hand against the gate actually tried to push it open! His strength was not sufficient; but he continued to push and to call until the man returned to open the gate and let the birds go in.

It was an amusing scene, and the behaviour of the bird struck me as characteristic.

—W. H. Hudson, *Birds and Man*

Fog everywhere. Fog up the river, where it flows among green aits and meadows; fog down the river, where it rolls defiled among the tiers of shipping, and the waterside pollutions of a great (and dirty) city. Fog on the Essex marshes, fog on the Kentish heights. Fog creeping into the cabooses of collier-brigs; fog lying out on the yards, and hovering in the rigging of great ships; fog drooping on the gunwales of barges and small boats. Fog in the eyes and throats of ancient Greenwich pensioners, wheezing by the firesides of their wards; fog in the stem and bowl of the afternoon pipe of the wrathful skipper, down in his close cabin; fog cruelly pinching the toes and fingers of his shivering little prentice boy on deck. Chance people on the bridges peeping over the parapets into a nether sky of fog, with fog all round them, as if they were up in a balloon, and hanging in the misty clouds.

—Charles Dickens, *Bleak House*

2. a. Evaluate the effectiveness of the separate images in Kincaid's "Coming to Antigua."
   b. Write a one-paragraph description of the room in which you are now sitting. Begin the paragraph as follows: "As I look around the room, this is what I see." Be sure to follow a principle of organization that best fulfills the purpose you set for yourself. Begin by using prewriting techniques.
3. In a paragraph (150–250 words) describe a *person, place, setting,* or *event* in such a way that you project one of the following moods or atmospheres:

bustling activity	poverty	loneliness
calm and quiet	beauty	despair
sloppiness	luxury	gaiety
cleanliness	fear	ugliness
deprivation	suspicion	

4. In a paragraph (150–250 words), describe a season of the year, an aspect of a season, or a particular mood or emotion associated with a particular month ("April is the cruelest month," wrote T. S. Eliot, "mixing memory and desire"). Try to place your topic sentence at the beginning of the paragraph.
5. As in Andy Rooney's essay on "Fences" there are many subquestions that Johnathan Spence was compelled to ask—consciously or unconsciously—before he could

Continued

write "The Earthquake": When did it happen—day or night? Was it expected? What happened first? From what direction did it originate? What specific objects were involved (buildings, trees, walls)?

    a. What other subquestions can you infer that the writer posed to himself in preparing this description?

    b. How does the writer create a sense of impending catastrophe from which there is no escape (note the adverb "helplessly"; note also imagery depicting forces beyond control such as water spurting and stones spinning, both of which suggest inevitability).

    c. Think about a natural disaster such as Spence's "The Earthquake": a tornado, hurricane, volcanic eruption, flood, violent storm or fire (something you have experienced, seen on television, heard of or read about). Create a cluster around the nucleus word (such as "fire"); then write a 250-word paragraph (one page) drawing on memory and/or imagination.

6. Answer the following questions about Soyinka's "The School at Aké":

    a. Physical description:

    List the physical details Soyinka gives about the school and the village. To which senses does he appeal primarily?

    b. Cultural description:

    What details reveal the most about the Yoruban culture in which Soyinka grew up? Which details differ the most from your early memories? Which are similar?

    c. Subjective description:

    What words does Soyinka use to convey his own emotional response as a young boy to the details he describes? Which words suggest his mature reflection on that childhood experience?

    d. Audience:

    Who would find this description interesting? Who might be interested enough to read more of Soyinka's autobiography, from which this was taken? Do you think he is writing for other Nigerians? For other Africans? For people unfamiliar with his country? For educators? For other writers? How has he chosen and/or excluded certain details to appeal to particular readers?

    e. Using Soyinka's technique, write a description of a scene you remember from your childhood. Resist embellishing your account with the analysis and explanation of your older self and try to capture the simple emotions the scene created in you as a child. Choose one of the following scenes or a similar one:

> your first-grade classroom
> your family dinner table
> breakfast at your grandparents' house
> a birthday party
> Thanksgiving or other holiday
> your backyard
> a picnic
> a church or synagogue

7. Write a one-paragraph (150–250 words) description of a room, a building, a street, a lake, or a mountain, from two different physical points of view: Regard your subject first from a fixed position (as in "Moonrise Over Monument Valley"), and then move through your subject.
8. Evaluate the description of Shady Grove cemetery in the following terms:
   a. 1. Technical elements that give the piece documentary solidness
      2. sensory images, personal impressions, judgments
      3. point of view
      4. selection, arrangement, and significance of details
      5. organization
      6. dominant mood or atmosphere
      7. choice of words and images
      8. tone
      9. aptness of subject (Do you agree with poet John Ciardi that anything looked at carefully is worth looking at?)
   b. Do you think this cemetery is worth looking at? Why?
   c. Write a one-paragraph answer (150–250 words) to the following question: Do you think Agee is making a comment ("thematic statement") on human nature and life in general in this essay? State your position in an opening topic sentence; then support that position with concrete details.

ESSAY SUGGESTIONS

1. Write your own essay version of Jamaica Kincaid's "Coming to Antigua" (500–750 words) depicting a drive through your hometown. Remember, you are a "moving observer"; your essay will reflect your passage from one point to another.
2. In the manner of "Moonrise over Monument Valley," write a descriptive essay (500–750 words) of a natural event as you watch it happen or as you imagine it; organize your material chronologically.
3. Use your cluster of a "disaster" as the basis for an essay of 500–750 words. Try to organize the sequence of events both chronologically and causally, as Spence does in "The Earthquake."

OR

Read John Hersey's account of *Hiroshima*. Using his data, write a 500–750 word essay in which you identify yourself as a surviving witness. Be sure to develop a list of subquestions here can help you to take more detailed and relevant notes on the Hiroshima account.
4. Write a descriptive essay (500–750 words) in which you combine physical data and human interest, as in "Shady Grove, Alabama, July 1936."
5. Describe either the rural or urban landscapes shown on page 110. Use your imagination to add other sensations—sounds, smell, movement. What kinds of emotion does your picture evoke?

Question

2

HOW DID X HAPPEN?

STRUCTURE IN NARRATION
  A NIGHT IN A CALABRIAN VILLAGE,
    NIKOS KAZANTZAKIS
  AN AFTERNOON IN CLEVELAND,
    RANDALL KENAN

POINT OF VIEW IN NARRATION
  *BOY MEETS GIRL, BOY LOSES GIRL,
    MAN GETS WOMAN*, PETE HAMILL

IMMEDIACY IN NARRATION
  WHEN YOU GOTTA GO, TRUMAN CAPOTE

AUTOBIOGRAPHICAL NARRATION
  NOT POOR, JUST BROKE, DICK GREGORY

HISTORICAL NARRATION
  PICKETT'S CHARGE, SHELBY FOOTE

When you ask the question "How Did X Happen?" you are preparing to write narration, a report about how something happened. We shall confine our attention here (as elsewhere in this book) to what *actually did happen.* In narrative there are characters and ongoing action: a series of events unfolding against a specific setting, causally related and moving steadily forward in time and through stages of action. Unlike analysis, which merely *explains* an event, narration attempts to *recreate* it by putting readers into the very flow of the happening so that they may see and hear and feel exactly what it was like; so that they may vicariously *have* the experience, not merely learn about it. To achieve this, the narrator must present the events in the form of a story; there must be both a teller and a tale.

More than that, there must be an outcome: a revelation of character perhaps (as in Kazantzakis's "A Night in a Calabrian Village"); or a demonstration of the effect of social pressures on a group of people (as in Randall Kenan's narrative that we've titled "An Afternoon in Cleveland"); or an illustration of the power of human hope and romantic illusion (as in Hamill's "Boy Meets Girl . . ."). The successful narrative satisfies the reader's expectation that the writer has a point to make—just as Capote's "When You Gotta Go" examines both the rational causes and irrational chance that combine in an episode of violence. Capote adds detail upon detail that forces us to ask what they *add up to,* what they *mean.* A story without a meaning or a point leaves the reader with an uneasy, gnawing sense of "so what?"

STRUCTURE IN NARRATION

A narrative begins at a specifically designated point in time ("Once upon a time" is the best-known fictional opening) and ends at an equally specific time. In the following narrative by Nikos Kazantzakis, the action begins at nightfall and ends the next morning. In between, the author provides us with "markers" indicating where we are located in the progression of the incident ("almost nightfall," "suddenly," "finally," "as soon as"). Note how at the outset Kazantzakis establishes a mood of tension, anxiety, and suspense by describing the deserted streets, bolted doors, and atmosphere of enveloping gloom. The narrator is preparing us for a conflict he fearfully anticipates, and we follow him with mounting suspense as he moves into danger—or *is it* danger? The narrative unfolds quietly toward its gentle climax, revealed in the last line.

A NIGHT IN A CALABRIAN VILLAGE

Nikos Kazantzakis

It was almost nightfall. The whole day: rain, torrents of rain. Drenched to the bone, I arrived in a little Calabrian village. I had to find a hearth where I could dry out, a corner where I could sleep. The streets were deserted, the doors bolted. The dogs were the only ones to scent the stranger's breath; they began to bark from within the courtyards. The peasants in this region are wild and misanthropic, suspicious of strangers. I hesitated at every door, extended my hand, but did not dare to knock.

O for my late grandfather in Crete who took his lantern each evening and made the rounds of the village to see if any stranger had come. He would take him home, feed him, give him a bed for the night, and then in the morning see him off with a cup of wine and a slice of bread. Here in the Calabrian villages there were no such grandfathers.

Suddenly I saw an open door at the edge of the village. Inclining my head, I looked in: a murky corridor with a lighted fire at the far end and an old lady bent over it. She seemed to be cooking. Not a sound, nothing but the burning wood. It was fragrant; it must have been pine. I crossed the threshold and entered, bumping against a long table which stood in the middle of the room. Finally I reached the fire and sat down on a stool which I found in front of the hearth. The old lady was squatting on another stool, stirring the meal with a wooden spoon. I felt that she eyed me rapidly, without turning. But she said nothing. Taking off my jacket, I began to dry it. I sensed happiness rising in me like warmth, from my feet to my shins, my thighs, my breast. Hungrily, avidly, I inhaled the fragrance of the steam rising from the pot. The meal must have been baked beans; the aroma was overwhelming. Once more I realized to what an extent earthly happiness is made to the measure of man. It is not a rare bird which we must pursue at one moment in heaven, at the next in our minds. Happiness is a domestic bird found in our own courtyards.

Rising, the old lady took down two soup plates from a shelf next to her. She filled them, and the whole world smelled of beans. Lighting a lamp, she placed it on the long table. Next she brought two wooden spoons and a loaf of black bread. We sat down opposite each other. She made the sign of the cross, then glanced rapidly at me. I understood. I crossed myself and we began to eat. We were both hungry; we did not breathe a word. I had decided not to speak in order to see what would happen. Could she be a mute, I asked myself—or perhaps she's mad, one of those peaceful, kindly lunatics so much like saints.

As soon as we finished, she prepared a bed for me on a bench to the right of the table. I lay down, and she lay down on the other bench opposite me. Outside the rain was falling by the bucketful. For a considerable time I heard the water cackle on the roof, mixed with the old lady's calm, quiet breathing. She must have been tired, for she fell asleep the moment she inclined her head. Little by little, with the rain and the old lady's rhythmical respiration, I too slipped into sleep. When I awoke, I saw daylight peering through the cracks in the door.

The old lady had already risen and placed a saucepan on the fire to prepare the morning milk. I looked at her now in the sparse daylight. Shriveled and humped, she could fit into the palm of your hand. Her legs were so swollen that she had to stop at every step and catch her breath. But her eyes, only her large, pitch-black eyes, gleamed with youthful, unaging brilliance. How beautiful she must have been in her youth, I thought to myself, cursing man's fate, his inevitable deterioration. Sitting down opposite each other again, we drank the milk. Then I rose and slung my carpetbag over my shoulder, I took out my wallet, but the old lady colored deeply.

"No, no," she murmured, extending her hand.

As I looked at her in astonishment, the whole of her bewrinkled face suddenly gleamed.

"Goodbye, and God bless you," she said, "May the Lord repay you for the good you've done me. Since my husband died I've never slept so well."

Although the action of Kazantzakis' narrative is low-keyed and essentially leisurely, it moves steadily toward its culmination. A basic element of good narration is that the narrative must move steadily forward. It should never slacken or bog down in unessential details or issues not directly related to what it is primarily about. Some beginning writers deliberately try to "draw the story out," on the mistaken idea that this creates suspense. On the contrary, the skillful writer creates suspense—indeed, interest—when the narrative has pace, when it moves without undue interruption toward its climax—the relevation of what happened.

Randall Kenan provides a different kind of story about an encounter in an unfamiliar place—unfamiliar, at least to the members of the rap group Arrested Development, who are in Cleveland for a performance. Novelist Kenan is interviewing the band members for an article in *Spin* magazine when an encounter with local residents transforms their conversation. Notice how Kenan, like Kazantzakis, uses dialogue to supplement the strategies of narration and description.

An Afternoon in Cleveland

Randall Kenan

Without preamble or warning, a large pickup truck speeds by. A white man in the driver's seat yells: "Get off the road, niggers!" Headliner, Arrested Development's DJ, raises an eyebrow and turns around. "Did you hear what he said?"

"He can't have said what I thought he said."

"He said, 'Get off the road, niggers.' Can you believe that?"

"Welcome to Cleveland." Lead vocalist Speech's tone of sarcasm underscores our general feeling, though it does not dispel a sense of disbelief—at least on my part. Though we do not slough off the incident entirely, we do begin to make light of it (as all young black men must learn to do—or pay with ulcers and high blood pressure and jail), transforming being the object of other people's hate and anger and fear, into the absurd, the comic. Our mood begins to resemble, in a short while, something like mirth. Speech tells of incidents he's had back home in certain suburbs of Milwaukee. We talk of racism, of intolerance. Soon we're back on families and the group's success.

Arrested Development's first album, *3 Years, 5 Months and 2 Days in the Life of . . .*, had gone platinum and two singles had reached the Top 10. The great media machine had declared that this new group from Atlanta, Georgia—with its hippiefied look and hyperblack consciousness—supposedly represented a departure from the hard-core gangsta rappers of the past few years. Certainly, a hip hop group mixing four men and two women is indeed something new; and that one member is a 60-year-old "spiritual adviser" is interesting. And though its music—a funky blend of rapping, singing, and sampling, all with live drums—is a fresh sound, could this new wave of positivism replace the old urban anger? Though I had profound doubts about the hype, I was here to see for myself.

We walk and talk along a street in suburban Cleveland. Gingerbread light, Speech (a.k.a. Todd Thomas), wears dreads tucked into an oversize cap, and a commodious black jacket with a huge "X" fashioned from the American flag. The five-foot-six-inch 24-year-old is much gentler and more unassuming than I had assumed, based on my readings of his songs and articles and statements. Speech writes a column called "20th Century African," in the *Milwaukee Community Journal,* which his parents own. An excerpt reads: "Do it your own way, but not Ice Cube's, Quik's, or N.W.A.'s way. |They're| kickin' fantasy and you're the ones making it reality. The joke is on you, brothers. They're getting paid and you're paying the cost! Think about it." The group was so named because, says Speech, "I feel that the development of the world and all that strives from it has been arrested . . . we must free ourselves and develop." Although I had expected a bellicose, self-important, self-styled militant loudmouth with much rhetoric and little gumption, today Speech impresses me as being articulate though soft-spoken; good-humored though quietly guarded.

Headliner (a.k.a. Tim Barnwell), 25, doesn't have a jacket and feels a bit chilly. Speech teases him, "I tried to tell him this is the Midwest, but he wouldn't listen." Headliner is taller than Speech, mocha dark, and his hair is short and neat (he cuts it himself—he was, and is, a barber). Handsome, with a slight gap between his teeth, he seems reserved, thoughtful; he takes his time when he speaks, considering.

Strolling down this street, through a suburb obviously not made for strolls, past well-groomed yards and well-groomed houses, an upper-middle-class chill matching the autumnal air and the turning leaves, we speak of Speech's childhood in Milwaukee and in Ripley, Tennessee. He tells me of how as a boy in summers his grandmother would have them working out in the fields: cotton picking, garden chopping. Headliner, too, knew hard work as a boy in Savannah, Georgia. When he went to visit his grandmother, she would always put him to work.

Headliner's people come from the Geechee or Gullah—the descendents of "salt-water" Africans on the extreme coast and islands of South Carolina and Georgia who have retained and blended a distinct form of African culture—a fact of which he's proud. His family once owned land on Hilton Head Island, South Carolina. But like so many black families in the South, the land was manipulated out of their hands, whether by outrageous taxes or unscrupulous dealings. With great regret he speaks of how the Geechee culture is slowly disappearing; memories of fishing with his father, who still lives on the island, and with other kinfolk, bring a cast of nostalgic delight to his face.

We see a police car and joke that we're under surveillance. Three black men at large. We laugh.

After a few miles, we turn around and head back to the hotel. Speech and Headliner tell me about how they met while students at the Art Institute of Atlanta; how when, with much exuberance and optimism, they said they were going to cut a record deal soon, a female fan dismissively said, "It'll take you three years or more to cut a deal"; and how it did. Three years, five months, and two days to be exact.

Not too far from the hotel, a police car turns into a driveway in front of us. Of course we pay it no mind, deep in conversation about "Fishin' 4 Religion" ("The government is happy with most Baptist churches / Cuz they don't do a damn thing to try to nurture / Brothers and sisters in the revolution / Baptist teaches dying is the only solution"), and how Speech got into a correspondence with his old minister in Milwaukee, asking him to defend what Speech sees as an indifference on the part of the church to the real needs of the people. His minister never answered his letters.

As we pass the driveway, the policeman says something, but we assume he's addressing someone else and continue to walk.

"All right, gentlemen." The policeman approaches us, his hand threateningly near his gun.

Too amazed to be outraged, we stop and turn, dumbfounded.

"What's going on?"

"We're walking," we say in unison.

"You here for a conference or something?"

A conference? Or something? As bewildered as I am angered, I say, "These gentlemen are performers. Musicians. They're appearing tonight at the Front Row Theater." I am about to go on and say these men have had two Top Ten singles and an album about to go double platinum and where the hell do you get off—

But he says, "Oh," and proffers a half-assed smile. "We were just getting calls, that's all." He begins to back away—"Have a good day"—gets into his car, and goes.

I don't remember if we mumbled a response, but I do remember that we looked at one another very hard, desperately in need of a reality check. Anger and disbelief were mingled in Headliner's and in Speech's eyes.

"You know," said Speech as we walked on, "the funny thing is that you first stop and think, 'Did I do anything wrong?' That's how this society affects you. You're walking down the street, minding your own business, you get stopped, not for something you did, but because of who you are, and you first think: Have I done something wrong?"

And people ask us—at this point Speech is getting exercised—"Why did you write 'Revolution'? Why you always talking about revolution this and revolution that. It's because things like this—and worse—still happen. And if you don't speak up about it, it will keep on happening."

POINT OF VIEW IN NARRATION

In narration as in description, you must clearly establish your point of view, the vantage point from which you are narrating. What is your relation to the events? How much do you know? What is your purpose? As a narrator, you may choose from several points of view. You may be an outsider, narrating in the third person and knowing everything that is happening, including what goes on in everybody's head. This is called the *omniscient* point of view, and has generally been used by writers of fiction rather than nonfiction (obviously, since no one is really omniscient). Within the last two decades, however, a group of "new nonfiction" writers such as Tom Wolfe in *The Right Stuff* and Truman Capote in *In Cold Blood* (which he called a "nonfiction novel") have borrowed the techniques of the novelist and short story writer in order to give their reportage a deeper vitality and reality. Thus, they either speculate on what various persons were thinking, or find out (usually through intensive interviews) what they actually were thinking and feeling during the time of a reported happening.

You may also narrate from the viewpoint of one character, seeing and knowing only what that character sees and knows. This is called the *limited* point of view. Or, as we have seen, you may narrate in the first person. Or you may move like a sound camera, recording only what you can see and hear, never delving into anyone's mind or heart—the *objective* or *dramatic* point of view.

In Pete Hamill's lively rendition of a boy-meets-girl plot, we see how effectively the objective point of view allows the facts to speak for themselves. Offering a minimum of explanation as to motives and emotions, Hamill dramatizes the characters; that is, brings them alive through their enactment of themselves—what they say, and even more important, what they do.

Boy Meets Girl, Boy Loses Girl, Man Gets Woman

Pete Hamill

They called her Big Red from the day that she first showed up at the Copa, in the spring of 1944. She was nineteen years old then, with clean, peach-colored skin, legs that started at her rib cage, and a mane of flaming red hair that made grown men walk into lampposts. On that first day, Jules Podell, who ran the place, didn't even rap his pinkie ring against a table when he saw her, or scream from the darkness of the banquettes, or demand an audition. He took one look at the hair and the legs and the skin and he hired her on the spot.

And for a year, Big Red was one of the glories of New York. The waiters loved her; the dishwashers politely bowed their hellos; and Frank Costello, when he came around, always called her Miss Red.

Her secret was a kind of clumsy innocence. Big Red couldn't dance much, although she could kick her legs higher than her chin; her voice was as frail as a sparrow in traffic; she didn't go to acting classes, didn't dream of a niche in the Hollywood solar system. She was just a great big girl who bumped into things—doors, waiters, and other dancers—and was always forgiven because she was so beautiful and so nice. Podell, who usually punished his enemies by screaming them deaf, never raised his voice to her. And the hoodlums protected her. Whenever an armed citizen visiting from Detroit would try to drag her into the Burma Road, a dim purgatory of seats against the back wall, he would be strongly advised to lay off. Big Red was different. Big Red went to grammar school in a convent. Big Red was a nice girl.

"I want the redheaded broad," one underwear buyer shouted one night. "I'd like to give her a boff."

"If ya open ya mout about da red-headed broad again," said a gentleman in an elegant sharkskin suit, "you will never talk for da rest of your life."

A few such choice words usually settled the matter, although it was rumored that several citizens, including the pudgy son of a Caribbean dictator, had to be deposited with force on the cement of East Sixtieth Street before they got the point.

Then Sal came into her life. Sal was from Bensonhurst, and he was only 5 foot 4 and 21 years old. He had clean, perfect features, like a wonderful miniature painting, and he wanted to be a singer. Well, not just a singer. He wanted to be Frank Sinatra.

He came to audition one day and stood next to a piano, held a cigaret in his right hand and loosened the bow tie of his rented tux with his left. He sang "This Love of Mine," "I'll Never Be the Same," "Just One of Those Things" and

"Nancy, with the Laughing Face." He was tender like Frank, and he swaggered like Frank, and he bent the notes the way Frank did, holding the high ones, and reaching down into the lower register when he was hurting the most. Just like Frank.

But in those years, the Copacabana already had one Frank Sinatra. The real one. They didn't need another, particularly one who was only slightly taller than a mailbox. So Jules Podell told the kid to grow six inches and learn to sing like himself, and in the meantime he should try the "Ted Mack Amateur Hour," maybe he could get work at the RKO Prospect in Brooklyn. Sal was destroyed.

He walked out of the frigid darkness of the club into the warm afternoon air, just as Big Red was arriving for a rehearsal. Big Red bumped into him, almost knocking him down, and then realized that tears were streaming down his face.

"Oh, you poor little thing," Big Red said, "You're gonna get your tuxedo wet."

That started it. She put her long arms around him and hugged him, and he leaned into her largeness, and she patted his head, and told him everything was going to be all right—don't you worry, Sal, everything'll be fine. And for a while it was. Three days later, Sal moved into Big Red's place in Chelsea, and when she wasn't working they went everywhere together. She had the money from the Copa; he had his dream.

But as the months went by, Sal started going a little crazy. His pride started to eat away at his brain; would Frank Sinatra let a girl pay the bills? Would Frank let his girl work every night, half-naked in front of a bunch of drunks? Big Red woke up one day about noon and saw Sal looking out the kitchen window into the backyard. His body was shaking as if he couldn't control his laughter. She smiled, tip-toed over to him and leaned down to kiss him on the head, and then realized that he was crying.

It all came pouring out: the bruised pride, the sense of being a leech or worse, his need to make it on his own. And he told her he wanted to go to Vegas, where Bugsy Siegel had built the Flamingo, and where a lot of new joints were opening up. He was sure he could get work there as a singer. He was sure he could get the big break. All he needed was enough money for a car and the trip west. He was sure he could get the money from an uncle on Eighty-sixth Street and Fourteenth Avenue. And he wanted Big Red to go with him.

So Big Red gave her notice, and that was the closest anyone had ever come to seeing Jules Podell cry. He just sat there, like a museum director who had just lost the Mona Lisa. That Saturday night, all the regulars gave Big Red a farewell party after the last show. They gave her phone numbers in Vegas, certain well-connected parties to call. And they gave her a necklace, a set of luggage and a big cake, among other things.

But when she went outside, carrying all the gifts, Sal was not there waiting as he was supposed to be. Sal was in the squad room of a police station in Brooklyn, and two homicide cops were typing up forms charging him with murder. Sal had borrowed a gun and walked into a saloon to get the money for the Vegas trip. There was a fight, the gun had gone off and a bartender was dead. Sal was on his way to Attica.

A few days later, one of the Copa regulars called Big Red. One of the hoodlums. He told her Sal would be gone for a long time. She was welcome to come back to the Copa, but when she said no, that the Copa would only remind her of Sal, this party said that an airline ticket to Vegas would be waiting for her at Idlewild. And a job would be waiting for her when she got there. She cried for two days and then went west. She never heard a word from Sal.

She worked at the Dunes and did the Lido de Paris Show for a couple of years; she married and divorced an Oklahoma oil man, then married a beauty parlor operator who later died in a car crash. Her three children grew up, went to school, married, went away. She settled in Santa Monica in a small house two blocks from the Pacific. She planted a garden, watched TV, talked a lot to her children on the phone and started going to Mass. Every day, to stay in shape, she spent an hour in the ocean.

One morning, she came back from the beach and the phone was ringing. The operator asked her name, and said she had a person-to-person call from New York.

"Okay, that's me. Go ahead, operator."

"I have your party on the line," the operator said, in a metallic voice.

"Oh, great, great, operator, thank you. Thanks."

The voice was familiar.

"It's me, Sal," the voice said, "They just let me out."

She turned around quickly, bumped into the table and knocked the toaster to the floor.

"Sal? That's really you, Sal?"

"Yeah. I have been tryin' for three days to find a number for you. I called everywheres. Vegas. Texas. Jules Podell's dead, you know?"

"Yeah, I heard that, Sal."

"I must of missed it somehow. I didn't know it. New York sure ain't the same, is it?"

"I guess not. That was too bad about Jules."

"Hey, listen. I gotta ask you something."

"Yeah, Sal?"

"Are you married?"

"No."

She could hear him breathe out hard in relief. "Well, I'd like to come out there," he said. "I'd like to get a job out there, start over."

There was a long pause. "I don't look the way I used to look," she said, her voice trembling.

"Neither do I," Sal said, his voice dropping into the lower register.

"I've got grown-up kids and all. I have a garden. I even go to church. I'm really boring."

"So am I."

"Uh, when were you, uh, thinking of coming out?"

"Tonight," he said.

"Tonight?" She turned, tangled in the phone wire, and reached for the toaster. She knocked over a chair. "Uh, well gee, that'd be . . . what flight?"

He gave her the number. She wrote it on the wall beside the phone.

"I'll be there," she said. "I'll be at the gate. I'll be wearing, uh, black slacks and a white blouse. I'll be there, Sal. I'll be there. I'm big, remember? With red hair."

She hung up, stood there for a moment and then kicked a leg higher than her chin.

IMMEDIACY IN NARRATION

Narration clearly enables you to do more than talk about your subject. Through a well-chosen illustration you can embody your points in a dramatic presentation far more meaningful and memorable than simple analysis. The pain and poignancy of the lives of human beings come through powerfully.

In much the same way, Truman Capote in the following narrative makes his point about the banality of evil by simply piling on detail after simple detail. The narrator in this story doesn't make an explicit comment on the events described, but allows them to unfold to their seemingly inevitable conclusion. This brief narrative is taken from *In Cold Blood,* the 1966 book that Capote described as a nonfiction novel. As you read, note how Capote applies a novelist's control of characterization, climax, and simple dialogue to this real-life event.

When You Gotta Go

Truman Capote

It was late afternoon, and the driver of the car, a middle-aged traveling salesman who shall here be known as Mr. Bell, was tired. He longed to stop for a short nap. However, he was only a hundred miles from his destination— Omaha, Nebraska, the headquarters of the large meat packing company for which he worked. A company rule forbade its salesmen to pick up hitchhikers, but Mr. Bell often disobeyed it, particularly if he was bored and drowsy, so when he saw the two young men standing by the side of the road, he immediately braked his car.

They looked to him like "O.K. boys." The taller of the two, a wiry type with dirty-blond, crew-cut hair, had an engaging grin and a polite manner, and his partner, the "runty" one, holding a harmonica in his right hand and, in his left, a swollen straw suitcase, seemed "nice enough," shy but amiable. In any event, Mr. Bell, entirely unaware of his guests' intentions, which included throttling him with a belt and leaving him, robbed of his car, his money, and his life, concealed in a prairie grave, was glad to have company, somebody to talk to and keep him awake until he arrived at Omaha.

He introduced himself, then asked them their names. The affable young man with whom he was sharing the front seat said his name was Dick. "And that's Perry," he said, winking at Perry, who was seated directly behind the driver.

"I can ride you boys as far as Omaha."

Dick said, "Thank you, sir. Omaha's where we were headed. Hoped we might find some work."

What kind of work were they hunting? The salesman thought perhaps he could help.

Dick said, "I'm a first-class car painter. Mechanic, too. I'm used to making real money. My buddy and me, we just been down in Old Mexico. Our idea was, we wanted to live there. But hell, they don't pay any wages. Nothing a white man could live off."

Ah, Mexico. Mr. Bell explained that he had honeymooned in Cuernavaca. "We always wanted to go back. But it's hard to move around when you've got five kids."

Perry, as he later recalled, thought, Five kids—well, too bad. And listening to Dick's conceited chatter, hearing him start to describe his Mexican "amorous conquests," he thought how "queer" it was, "egomaniacal." Imagine going all out to impress a man you were going to kill, a man who wouldn't be alive ten minutes from now—not if the plan he and Dick had devised went smoothly. And why shouldn't it? The setup was ideal—exactly what they had been looking for during the three days it had taken them to hitchhike from California to Nevada and across Nevada and Wyoming into Nebraska. Until now, however, a suitable victim had eluded them. Mr. Bell was the first prosperous-seeming solitary traveler to offer them a lift. Their other hosts had been either truck drivers or soldiers—and, once, a pair of Negro prizefighters driving a lavender Cadillac. But Mr. Bell was perfect. Perry felt inside a pocket of the leather windbreaker he was wearing. The pocket bulged with a bottle of Bayer aspirin and with a jagged, fist-sized rock wrapped in a yellow cotton cowboy handkerchief. He unfastened his belt, a Navajo belt, silver-buckled and studded with turquoise beads; he took it off, flexed it, placed it across his knees. He waited. He watched the Nebraska prairie rolling by, and fooled with his harmonica—made up a tune and played it and waited for Dick to pronounce the agreed-upon signal: "Hey, Perry, pass me a match." Whereupon Dick was supposed to seize the steering wheel, while Perry, wielding his handkerchief-wrapped rock, belabored the salesman's head—"opened it up." Later, along some quiet side road, use would be made of the belt with the sky-blue beads.

Meanwhile, Dick and the condemned man were trading dirty jokes. Their laughter irritated Perry; he especially disliked Mr. Bell's outburst—hearty barks that sounded very much like the laughter of Tex John Smith, Perry's father. The memory of his father's laughter increased his tension; his head hurt, his knees ached. He chewed three aspirin and swallowed them dry. Jesus! He thought he might vomit, or faint; he felt certain he would if Dick delayed "the party" much longer. The light was dimming, the road was straight, with neither house nor human being in view—nothing but land winter-stripped and as somber as sheet iron. Now was the time. Now. He stared at Dick, as though to communicate this realization, and a few small signs—a twitching eyelid, a mustache of sweat drops—told him that Dick had already reached the same conclusion.

And yet when Dick next spoke, it was only to launch another joke. "Here's a riddle. The riddle is: What's the similarity between a trip to the bathroom and a trip to the cemetery?" He grinned. "Give up?"

"Give up."

"When you gotta go, you gotta go!"

Mr. Bell barked.

"Hey Perry, pass me a match."

But just as Perry raised his hand, and the rock was on the verge of descent, something extraordinary occurred—what Perry later called "a goddam miracle." The miracle was the sudden appearance of a third hitchhiker, a Negro soldier, for whom the charitable salesman stopped. "Say that's pretty cute," he said as his savior ran toward the car. "When you gotta go, you gotta go."

AUTOBIOGRAPHICAL NARRATION

In the following selection Dick Gregory, comedian and civil rights activist, tells how hate and shame entered his life. Note how this effective narrative flows smoothly and easily—as if the events were taking place at the very moment of telling—and how the conversational dialogue rings true: the easy, speech of the narrator, the cold, unbending tones of the teacher, the flustered repetitions of the child.

Not Poor, Just Broke

Dick Gregory

I have never learned hate at home, or shame. I had to go to school for that. I was about seven years old when I got my first big lesson. I was in love with a little girl named Helene Tucker, a light-complected little girl with pigtails and nice manners. She was always clean and she was smart in school. I think I went to school then mostly to look at her. I brushed my hair and even got me a little old handkerchief. It was a lady's handkerchief, but I didn't want Helene to see me wipe my nose on my hand. The pipes were frozen again, there was no water in the house, but I washed my socks and shirt every night. I'd get a pot, and go over to Mister Ben's grocery store, and stick my pot down into his soda machine. Scoop out some chopped ice. By evening the ice melted to water for washing. I got sick a lot that winter because the fire would go out at night before the clothes were dry. In the morning I'd put them on, wet or dry, because they were the only clothes I had.

Everybody's got a Helene Tucker, a symbol of everything you want. I loved her for her goodness, her cleanness, her popularity. She'd walk down my street and my brothers and sisters would yell, "Here comes Helene," and I'd rub my tennis sneakers on the back of my pants and wish my hair wasn't so nappy and the white folks' shirt fit me better. I'd run out on the street. If I knew my place and didn't come too close, she'd wink at me and say hello. That was a good feeling. Sometimes I'd follow her all the way home, and shovel the snow off her walk and try to make friends with her Momma and her aunts. I'd drop money on her stoop late at night on my way back from shining shoes in the taverns. And she had a Daddy, and he had a good job. He was a paper hanger.

I guess I would have gotten over Helene by summertime, but something happened in that classroom that made her face hang in front of me for the next twenty-two years. When I played the drums in high school it was for Helene and when I broke track records in college it was for Helene and when I started standing behind microphones and heard applause I wished Helene could hear it, too. It wasn't until I was twenty-nine years old and married and making money that I finally got her out of my system. Helene was sitting in that classroom when I learned to be ashamed of myself.

It was on a Thursday. I was sitting in the back of the room, in a seat with a chalk circle drawn around it. The idiot's seat, the troublemaker's seat.

The teacher thought I was stupid. Couldn't spell, couldn't read, couldn't do arithmetic. Just stupid. Teachers were never interested in finding out that you couldn't concentrate because you were so hungry, because you hadn't had any breakfast. All you could think about was noontime, would it ever come? Maybe you could sneak into the cloakroom and steal a bite of some kid's lunch out of a coat pocket. A bite of something. Paste. You can't really make a meal of paste, or put it on bread for a sandwich, but sometimes I'd scoop a few spoonfuls out of the paste jar in the back of the room. Pregnant people get strange tastes. I was pregnant with poverty. Pregnant with dirt and pregnant with smells that made people turn away, pregnant with cold and pregnant with shoes that were never bought for me, pregnant with five other people in my bed and no Daddy in the next room, and pregnant with hunger. Paste doesn't taste too bad when you're hungry.

The teacher thought I was a troublemaker. All she saw from the front of the room was a little black boy who squirmed in his idiot's seat and made noises and poked the kids around him. I guess she couldn't see a kid who made noises because he wanted someone to know he was there.

It was on a Thursday, the day before the Negro payday. The eagle always flew on Friday. The teacher was asking each student how much his father would give to the Community Chest. On Friday night, each kid would get the money from his father, and on Monday he would bring it to school. I decided I was going to buy me a Daddy right then. I had money in my pocket from shining shoes and selling papers, and whatever Helene Tucker pledged for her Daddy I was going to top it. And I'd hand the money right in. I wasn't going to wait until Monday to buy me a Daddy.

I was shaking, scared to death. The teacher opened her book and started calling out names aphabetically.

"Helene Tucker?"

"My Daddy said he'd give two dollars and fifty cents."

"That's very nice, Helene. Very, very nice indeed."

That made me feel pretty good. It wouldn't take too much to top that. I had almost three dollars in dimes and quarters in my pocket. I stuck my hand in my pocket and held onto the money, waiting for her to call my name. But the teacher closed her book after she called everybody else in the class.

I stood up and raised my hand.

"What is it now?"

"You forgot me."

She turned toward the blackboard. "I don't have time to be playing with you, Richard."

"My Daddy said he'd . . ."

"Sit down, Richard, you're disturbing the class."

"My Daddy said he'd give . . . fifteen dollars."

She turned around and looked mad. "We are collecting this money for you and your kind, Richard Gregory. If your Daddy can give fifteen dollars you have no business being on relief."

"I got it right now, I got it right now, my Daddy gave it to me to turn in today, my Daddy said . . ."

"And furthermore," she said, looking right at me, her nostrils getting big and her lips getting thin and her eyes opening wide, "we know you don't have a Daddy."

Helene Tucker turned around, her eyes full of tears. She felt sorry for me. Then I couldn't see her too well because I was crying, too.

"Sit down, Richard."

And I always thought the teacher kind of liked me. She always picked me to wash the blackboard on Friday, after school. That was a big thrill, it made me feel important. If I didn't wash it, come Monday the school might not function right.

"Where are you going, Richard?"

I walked out of school that day, and for a long time I didn't go back very often. There was shame there.

Now there was shame everywhere. It seemed like the whole world had been inside that classroom, everyone had heard what the teacher had said, everyone had turned around and felt sorry for me. There was shame in going to the Worthy Boys Annual Christmas Dinner for you and your kind, because everybody knew what a worthy boy was: Why couldn't they just call it the Boys Annual Dinner, why'd they have to give it a name? There was shame in wearing the brown and orange and white plaid mackinaw the welfare gave to 3,000 boys. Why'd it have to be the same for everybody so when you walked down the street the people could see you were on relief? It was a nice warm mackinaw and it had a hood, and my Momma beat me and called me a little rat when she found out I stuffed it in the bottom of a pail full of garbage way over on Cottage Street. There was shame in running over to Mister Ben's at the end of the day and asking for his rotten peaches, there was shame in asking Mr. Simmons for a spoonful of sugar, there was shame in running out to meet the relief truck. I hated that truck, full of food for you and your kind. I ran into the house and hid when it came. And then I started to sneak through alleys, to take the long way home so the people going into White's Eat Stop wouldn't see me. Yeah, the whole world heard the teacher that day, we all know you don't have a Daddy.

HISTORICAL NARRATION

All historical accounts are, in a sense, answers to the question "How did it happen?" But only some historical accounts can be called "narrative." Only relatively few writers present history not merely as a record of the past (wars, treaties, dates) but also as an unfolding drama, a direct presentation of human experience. A recent master of historical narration is novelist and historian Shelby Foote, who is familiar to many people from his appearance in Ken Burns' epic documentary *The Civil War.* Foote's three-volume history of the American Civil War has been praised by many readers for its almost novelistic treatment of detail and action. Foote reveals the craft of the story-teller in this excerpt from his description of the Battle of Gettysburg. The particular incident he describes, known as Pickett's Charge, typifies both the gallant courage of soldiers on both sides and the brutal bloodshed that resulted. In this dramatic turning point of the war, the Army of Northern Virginia, under the command of Robert E. Lee, mounted a sweeping attack against Union forces on the high ground. Notice how Foote creates memorable characters with a few well-chosen words, how he suggests the sweep of battle with careful selection of incident, and how he paces his narrative to create an almost palpable feeling of tension.

Pickett's Charge

Shelby Foote

Pickett by then had already acted on the first of the two dispatches. Glad to receive anything that might end the strain of waiting, he mounted his horse and rode at once to Longstreet, whom he found sitting on a snake rail fence out front, observing the bombardment. Dismounting, he handed him the note. Old Peter read it deliberately, but said nothing. "General, shall I advance?" Pickett asked eagerly. Longstreet, who later explained: "My feelings had so overcome me that I could not speak, for fear of betraying my want of confidence," responded with a silent nod. That was enough for the jaunty long-haired Virginian. "I am going to move forward, sir," he said. Then he saluted, remounted, and rode back to join his men.

Front and center of his division, he delivered from horseback what one of his officers called "a brief, animated address" which only those soldiers nearest him could hear but which ended on a ringing note: "Up, men, and to your posts! Don't forget today that you are from old Virginia!" There was, however, no disconcerting haste as the troops were placed in attack formation. For the most part, they simply rose to their feet and began to dress their regimental lines while their colonels passed among them repeating the instructions received from above: "Advance slowly, with arms at will. No cheering, no firing, no breaking from common to quick step. Dress on the center." In at least one outfit, a survivor would recall, one of the captains led in the singing of a hymn and a white-haired chaplain offered prayer. Nor was the step-off itself unduly precipitate. Pettigrew gave the signal on the left to the new leader of his old brigade: "Now, Colonel, for the honor of the good Old North State, forward!" The advance was somewhat ragged at first, as if the Virginians, Mississippians, Alabamians, and Tennesseans of his division supposed that the spoken order only applied to the Carolinians, but the laggard brigades soon restored the alignment by double-timing to catch up. Meanwhile, in the wooded swale to the south, others had taken up the cry. Armistead, whose brigade comprised the supporting line on the right, as Trimble's two did on the left, did not neglect the opportunity afforded for another display of determination. "Sergeant, are you going to plant those colors on the enemy works today?" he asked a nearby colorbearer, and when the sergeant gave the staunch expected answer, "I will try, sir, and if mortal man can do it, it shall be done," the general removed his wide-brimmed black felt hat, placed it on the point of his sword, and raised it high for all to see, shouting in a voice that carried from flank to flank of his brigade: "Attention, 2d Battalion, the battalion of direction! Forward, guide centerrr, *march!*" and led the way.

By now—some twenty or thirty minutes after the Union guns stopped firing, and consequently about half that long since Alexander followed suit—much of the smoke had been diffused or had drifted off, so that for the attackers, many of whom had stepped at a stride from the dense shade of their wooded assembly areas into the brilliant sunlight that dappled the floor of the valley, the result was not only dazzling to their eyes but also added to their feeling of elation and release. "Before us lay bright fields and fair landscape," one among them would recall.

It was not until the effect of this began to wear off, coincidental with the contraction of their pupils, that they saw at last the enormity of what was being required of them, and by then, although the vista afforded absolute confirmation of their direst apprehensions, the pattern of exhilaration had been set. Under the double influence of secondary inertia and terrific deliberation, the long gray lines came on, three brigades to the south under Pickett and six to the north under Pettigrew and Trimble, with a quarter-mile gap between the interior flanks of the two formations, the former composed of fifteen and the latter of twenty-seven regiments, all with their colors flying at more or less regular intervals along the rows of nearly 11,000 striding men. Harvey Hill was to say of the individual Confederate, as he had observed him in offensive action: "Of shoulder-to-shoulder courage, spirit of drill and discipline, he knew nothing and cared less. Hence, on the battlefield, he was more of a free-lance than a machine. Whoever saw a Confederate line advancing that was not crooked as a ram's horn? Each ragged rebel yelling on his own hook and aligning on himself." But Hill, though he was to see about as much combat as any general on either side before the war was over, was not at Gettysburg. If he had been, he would have had to cite it as the exception. Forbidden to step up the cadence or fire their rifles or even give the high-pitched yell that served at once to steady their own nerves and jangle their opponents', the marchers concentrated instead on maintaining their alignment, as if this in itself might serve to awe the waiting bluecoats and frighten them into retreat. And in point of fact, according to one among the watchers on the ridge across the way—a colonel commanding a brigade adjacent to the little clump of trees—it did at least produce the lesser of these two reactions. For him, the advancing graybacks had "the appearance of being fearfully irresistible," while a foreign observer, whose point of vantage was on the near side of the valley, used the same adjective to communicate the impression the attackers made on him: "They seemed impelled by some irresistible force." Out front with the rebel skirmishers, a captain had a closer view of the troops as they strode down the slope toward where he crouched, and he remembered ever afterwards the "glittering forest of bayonets," the two half-mile-wide formations bearing down "in superb alignment," the "murmur and jingle" of trouser-legs and equipment, and the "rustle of thousands of feet amid the stubble," which stirred up dust and chaff beneath and before them "like the dash of spray at the prow of a vessel."

They came on at a steady rate of about one hundred yards a minute, and before they had been three minutes in the open—barely clear of the line of friendly guns, whose cannoneers raised their hats in salute and wished them luck as they passed through—the Union batteries, as if in quick recovery from the shock of seeing them appear thus, massed for slaughter, began to roar. The gray lines dribbled rag-doll shapes, each of which left a gap where it had been while still in motion. Flags plunged with sudden flutters in the windless air, only to be taken up at once as the fallen colorbearers were replaced. This happened especially often in the regiments on the flanks, which came under galling long-range fire delivered in enfilade from the two heights, Cemetery Hill on the left and Little Round Top on the right. Pettigrew's troops had farther to go, since they had begun their march from Seminary Ridge itself, but this had been foreseen and allowed for; Pickett had been charged with closing the quarter-mile interval between the two formations, which would lengthen the distance his three brigades would have to cover in the course of their advance. Accordingly, once they were clear of the line of guns, in plain view of the little clump of trees just over half a mile ahead, he gave his troops the order, "Left oblique!" They obeyed it neatly, executing in midstride a half-face to the north, which, at every full step of their own, brought them half a step closer to the flank of the undeviating marchers on their left. All this time, both groups were taking losses, a more or less steady leakage of killed and wounded, who lay motionless where they fell or turned and hobbled painfully up the slope they had descended. Coming presently to a slight dip, about midway of the valley—a swale not deep enough to hide them from the enemy gunners, but conveniently parallel to the ridge that was their objective—Pickett's men received their second order, which was to halt, close up the gaps their casualties had left, and dress the line. They did so, once more with the deliberate precision of the drill field, but with the difference that such gaps continued to appear at an even more alarming rate as the Union gunners, delighted with this sudden transformation of a moving into a stationary target, stepped up their rate of fire. The result was the first evidence of confusion in the Confederate ranks. A soldier would look toward the comrade on his right, feeling meanwhile with his extended hand for the shoulder of the comrade on his left, and there would be a constant sidling motion in the latter direction, as men continued to fall all down the line, leaving additional gaps that had to be closed. This might have gone on indefinitely, or at any rate until there were no survivors left to dress or dress on, but at last the order came for them to continue the advance, still on the oblique.

This they did, to the considerable relief of most of the bluecoats on the ridge ahead, whose reaction to the maneuver was one of outrage, as if they had been exposed to a blatant indecency, such as the thumbing of a nose, though for others the feeling of revulsion was tempered by awe and incredulity. "My God, they're dressing the line!" some among the waiting infantry exclaimed, more by way of protest than applause. In the course of the ten- or fifteen-minute lull allowed by the enemy guns before the attackers first appeared on the far side of the valley, the defenders had improved the time by repairing what little damage had been done to their improvised earthworks by the rebel cannonade. Now there was nothing left to do but wait, and in some ways that was the hardest thing of all.

DISCUSSIONS AND EXERCISES

1. Evaluate Dick Gregory's "Not Poor, Just Broke."
   a. Why does Gregory use this title? Does "Broke" have more than one meaning here?
   b. How do the two opening sentences function in the story?
   c. Does Gregory draw the characters convincingly? Quote specific details.
   d. Outline the "plot." What is the central conflict? What additional conflicts does the author imply in the story?
   e. How does the writer establish and maintain an element of suspense?
   f. How does the third paragraph function? What rhetorical device unifies the second sentence? What rhetorical device unifies the second sentence? What rhetorical purpose does it serve?
   g. List descriptive details that seem to you especially well-selected and evocative in helping you to see, hear, feel, and understand what is going on.
   h. Does the crucial event or climax of the story have sufficient impact? Explain.
   i. Where and how does the mood of the story change? Is there a reversal?

Continued

2. We can easily see how the narration in Kazantzakis's "A Night in a Calabrian Village" fits into the context of Burke's Pentad:

1. What do the characters do?	The main "act" consists of an encounter in which two people exchange warmth and trust.
2. Where does the action take place?	The "scene" or setting is a little village in Italy—Calabria.
3. Who does it?	A traveler and an old lady are the main "agents."
4. How do they accomplish it?	The "agency" is a chance meeting and wordless communication.
5. Why do they do it?	His "purpose": to find shelter. Her "purpose": to assuage loneliness.

Apply the Pentad to other narratives in this section, showing how each of them applies—and replies—to Burke's five basic questions.

Compare the Kenan and Kazantzakis narratives on the basis of the following:

a. point of view (voice, tone, rhetorical stance)
b. setting (locale, atmosphere)
c. characters (compare their respective moods at the beginning and end of the narrative)
d. action (sequence and development of events, climax)
e. theme (suggestions about human nature, economic values, and the impact of chance encounters)
f. style (sentence structure, choice of words, images)

3. Consider Pete Hamill's "Boy Meets Girl, Boy Loses Girl, Man Gets Woman."
   a. Indicate in what ways the following passages contribute to the development of character, plot, and the main action of the story:
      1. He took one look at the hair and the legs and the skin and he hired her on the spot.
      2. Her secret was a kind of clumsy innocence.
      3. Podell . . . never raised his voice to her. And the hoodlums protected her.
      4. He had clean, perfect features, like some wonderful miniature painting, and he wanted to be a singer. Well, not just a singer. He wanted to be Frank Sinatra.
      5. She had the money from the Copa; he had his dream.
      6. Sal was on his way to Attica.
      7. She cried for two days and then went west.
      8. "I've got grown-up kids and all. I have a garden. I even go to church. I'm really boring."
      9. She . . . stood there for a moment and then kicked a leg higher than her chin.
   b. How are Big Red and Sal like one another? In what ways are they different? What is their appeal for each other?
   c. Although Hamill does not delve into the mind and heart of his characters, the reader comes to *know* what they are thinking and feeling. Indicate specific places where the dramatic point of view makes this deeper understanding possible.

d. Approximately twenty years are telescoped in one paragraph. In what sense is this a fair proportion? What is the writer saying about these twenty years—beyond the recounting of events?

e. Can you project ahead and imagine what happens to the characters in the next twenty years of their lives?

4. a. Show how the following images from "When You Gotta Go" contribute to the overall effect of the piece:

1. "When he saw the two young men standing by the side of the road, he immediately braked the car."

2. "The taller of the two, a wiry type with dirty-blond, crew-cut hair, had an engaging grin and a polite manner."

3. "Perry, as he later recalled, thought, *Five kids—well, too bad.*"

4. "The pocket bulged with a bottle of Bayer aspirin and with a jagged fist-sized rock wrapped in a yellow cotton cowboy handkerchief."

5. "The light was dimming, the road was straight, with neither house nor human being in view—nothing but land winter-stripped and as somber as sheet iron."

b. What is the effect of having so little information given about the three characters in the story? How would it affect your reading to know more about Mr. Bell, Dick, or Perry?

c. What kinds of feelings does this narrative evoke in you? How did you feel after the plot twist in the last paragraph?

5. Study the Pulitzer prize–winning photograph on page 130 and compose a short narrative (150–250 words) explaining what happened.

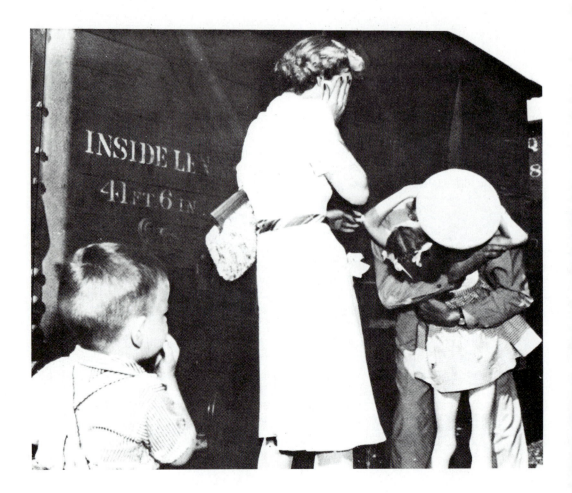

ESSAY SUGGESTIONS

1. Write a narrative essay (750–1,000 words) in which you describe how some dimension of feeling or understanding entered your life (as in Dick Gregory's "Not Poor, Just Broke"). Make certain your description is cast within the frame of a narrative in which there is a specific setting, characters (let them speak in normal, natural tones), and action. You may wish to follow the general structure of Gregory's essay:

   Introduction
   Background situation described (conflict)
   Crucial incident (climax)
   Long-term effect (resolution)

   Be sure to choose an appropriate tone for your narrative and use a prewriting plan.

2. Write an essay (750–1,000 words) in which you tell the story of your encounter with another person, describing how it affected you, for either good or ill (as in the Kazantzakis and Kenan narratives).

3. Write a journalistic narrative in the manner of Pete Hamill's "Boy Meets Girl . . ." (500–750 words). Try to invent a switch on the old boy-meets-girl formula.

4. Write a dramatization (750–1,000 words) of an event you have witnessed in which you suggest rather than explicitly state your judgement of its meaning and moral significance (as in "When You Gotta Go").

5. Write a narrative essay (750–1,000 words) in which you describe an historical event, using the panoramic point of view as Shelby Foote does in "Pickett's Charge." He sweeps across the battlefield, moving from one event to another, closing in briefly here and there for a close-up, then moving on again.

   a. Historic incidents:

> Boston Tea Party
> Chicago Fire
> Signing of the Declaration of Independence
> Pocahontas saves John Smith (fact and fiction)
> Francis Scott Key composes the "Star-Spangled Banner"
> The first humans walk on the moon
> Charlemagne is crowned emperor of the Holy Roman Empire
> Napolean dies
> Balboa views the Pacific Ocean
> Fulton takes his steamboat up the Hudson River
> The Wright brothers fly at Kitty Hawk

   b. Battles:

> Hastings   Crecy   Bunker Hill
> Bull Run   Poitiers   Themopylae
> Shiloh   Waterloo   Dunkirk

6. Write a full-length essay (500–750 words) based on a photograph such as "Coming Home," reprinted above. Or write on "Coming Home" itself.

Question

3

WHAT KIND OF PERSON IS X?

A MEMBER OF THE FAMILY
  MY MOTHER, ALRED KAZIN
  THE POETS IN THE KITCHEN,
    PAULE MARSHALL
  UNCLE BUN, MAXINE HONG KINGSTON

A FAMOUS WOMAN
  SYLVIA PLATH, KATINKA MATSON

A MEMORABLE TEACHER
  THE PRIM MR. FLEAGLE, RUSSELL BAKER

A TYPE OF PERSON
  THE JUST, ELIE WIESEL

Many artists can create the "sense" of a person by simply setting down on their sketch pads a few swift, well-placed lines that answer the question, What kind of person is X? So it is with writers. By concentrating on a few well-selected, representative characteristics of their subject—a few broad brush strokes—they give a character sketch, a word-picture, of what those persons essentially are from the writers' point of view.

As Boswell told us, the aim of the biographer is to present the person so that readers can ". . . see him live, and 'live o'er each scene with him, as he actually advanced through the several stages of his life.'" Clearly, essayists cannot do as much, although they must obviously try to bring the subject to life on the page. The character essay can merely point to the thread that runs through a life and that thereby defines it, or to the single quality that seems to sum it up—to what Mary McCarthy calls (in reference to her fictional characters) the "key" that turns the lock.

A MEMBER OF THE FAMILY

Detachment is rarely possible when writing about close relatives, for in viewing them the writer sees and feels the edges of his or her own life. That emotional tie, though, can often be used to good advantage in writing, as we see in Alfred Kazin's "My Mother." Here the renowned literary critic conjures up the kitchen of his Brooklyn childhood and in the process paints a touching portrait of his mother.

Kazin approaches his portrait obliquely, describing the kitchen (with its bare light bulb hanging from the ceiling) and explaining his mother's talent for dressmaking. The importance of the kitchen becomes clear in the opening sentence of the second paragraph: "The kitchen held our lives together." He soon explains why: "The kitchen gave a special character to our lives; my mother's character." He then describes this remarkable woman as a whirlwind of energy: ceaselessly sewing, cooking, shopping, welcoming neighbors, kibitzing, more sewing, more pedaling of the machine, more fitting of dresses. As his mother moves, she fills the room with meaning.

My Mother

Alfred Kazin

In Brownsville tenements the kitchen is always the largest room and the center of the household. As a child I felt that we lived in a kitchen to which four other rooms were annexed. My mother, a "home" dressmaker, had her workshop in the kitchen. She told me once that she had begun dressmaking in Poland at thirteen; as far back as I can remember, she was always making dresses for the local women. She had an innate sense of design, a quick eye for all the subtleties in the latest fashions, even when she despised them, and great boldness. For three or four dollars she would study the fashion magazines with a customer, go with the customer to the remnants store on Belmont Avenue to pick out the material, argue the owner down—all remnants stores, for some reason, were supposed to be shady, as if the owners dealt in stolen goods—and then for days would patiently fit and baste and sew and fit again. Our apartment was always full of women in their housedresses sitting around the kitchen table waiting for a fitting. My little bedroom next to the kitchen was the fitting room. The sewing machine, an old nut-brown Singer with golden scrolls painted along the black arm and engraved along the two tiers of little drawers massed with needles and thread on each side of the treadle, stood next to the window and the great coal-black stove which up to my last year in college was our main source of heat. By December the two outer bedrooms were closed off, and used to chill bottles of milk and cream, cold borscht and jellied calves' feet.

The kitchen held our lives together. My mother worked in it all day long, we ate in it almost all meals except the Passover *seder,* I did my homework and first writing at the kitchen table, and in winter I often had a bed made up for me on the three kitchen chairs near the stove. On the wall just over the table hung a long horizontal mirror that sloped to a ship's prow at each end and was lined in cherry wood. It took up the whole wall, and drew every object in the kitchen to itself. The walls were a fiercely stippled whitewash, so often rewhitened by my father in slack seasons that the paint looked as if it had been squeezed and cracked into the walls. A large electric bulb hung down the center of the kitchen at the end of a chain that had been hooked into the ceiling; the old gas ring and key still jutted out of the wall like antlers. In the corner next to the toilet was the sink at which we washed, and the square tub in which my mother did our clothes. Above it, tacked to the shelf on which were pleasantly ranged square, blue-bordered white sugar and spice jars, hung calendars from the Public National Bank on Pitkin Avenue and the Minsker Progressive Branch of the Workman's Circle; receipts for the payment of insurance premiums, and household bills on a spindle; two little boxes engraved with Hebrew letters. One of these was for the poor, the other to buy back the Land of Israel. Each spring a bearded little man would suddenly appear in our kitchen, salute us with a hurried Hebrew blessing, empty the boxes (sometimes with a sidelong look of disdain if they were not full), hurriedly bless us again for remembering our less fortunate Jewish brothers and sisters, and so take his departure until the next spring, after vainly trying to persuade my mother to take still another box. We did occasionally remember to drop coins in the boxes, but this was usually only on the dreaded morning of "midterms" and final examinations, because my mother thought it would bring me luck. She was extremely superstitious, but embarrassed about it, and always laughed at herself whenever, on the morning of an examination, she counseled me to leave the house on my right foot. "I know it's silly," her smile seemed to say, "but what harm can it do? It may calm God down."

The kitchen gave a special character to our lives; my mother's character. All my memories of that kitchen are dominated by the nearness of my mother sitting all day long at her sewing machine, by the clacking of the treadle against the linoleum floor, by the patient twist of her right shoulder as she automatically pushed at the wheel with one hand or lifted the foot to free the needle where it had got stuck in a thick piece of material. The kitchen was her life. Year by year, as I began to take in her fantastic capacity for labor and her anxious zeal, I realized it was ourselves she kept stitched together. I can never remember a time when she was not working. She worked because the law of her life was work, work, and anxiety; she worked because she would have found life meaningless without work. She read almost no English; she could read the Yiddish paper, but never felt she had time to. We were always talking of a time when I would teach her how to read, but somehow there was never time. When I awoke in the morning she was already at her machine, or in the great morning crowd of housewives at the grocery getting fresh rolls for breakfast. When I returned from school she was at her machine, or conferring over *McCall's* with some neighborhood woman who had come in pointing hopefully to an illustration—"Mrs. Kazin! Mrs. Kazin! Make me a dress like it shows here in the picture!" When my father came home from work she had somehow mysteriously interrupted herself to make supper for us, and the dishes cleared and washed, was back at her machine. When I went to bed at night, often she was still there, pounding away at the treadle, hunched over the wheel, her hands steering a piece of gauze under the needle with a finesse that always contrasted sharply with her swollen hands and broken nails. Her left hand had been pierced through when as a girl she had worked in the infamous Triangle Shirtwaist Factory on the East Side. A needle had gone straight through the palm, severing a large vein. They had sewn it up for her so clumsily that a tuft of flesh always lay folded over the palm.

The kitchen was the great machine that set our lives running; it whirred down a little only on Saturdays and holy days. From my mother's kitchen I gained my first picture of life as a white, overheated, starkly lit workshop redolent with Jewish cooking, crowded with women in housedresses, strewn with fashion magazines, patterns, dress material, spools of thread—and at whose center, so lashed to her machine that bolts of energy seemed to dance out of her hands and feet as she worked, my mother stamped the treadle hard against the floor, hard, hard, and silently, grimly at war, beat out the first rhythm of the world for me.

Every sound from the street roared and trembled at our windows—a mother feeding her child on the doorstep, the screech of the trolley cars on Rockaway Avenue, the eternal smash of a handball against the wall of our house, the clatter of *"der Italyéner's"* cart packed with watermelons, the sing-song of the old-clothes men walking Chester Street, the cries *"Árbes! Árbes! Kinder! Kinder! Heyse gute árbes!"* All day long people streamed into our apartment as a matter of course—"customers," upstairs neighbors, downstairs neighbors, women who would stop in for a half-hour's talk, salesmen, relatives, insurance agents. Usually they came in without ringing the bell—everyone knew my mother was always at home. I would hear the front door opening, the wind whistling through our front hall, and then some familiar face would appear in our kitchen with the same bland, matter-of-fact inquiring look: no need to stand on ceremony: my mother and her kitchen were available to everyone all day long.

At night the kitchen contracted around the blaze of light on the cloth, the patterns, the ironing board where the iron had burned a black border around the tear in the muslin cover; the finished dresses looked so frilly as they jostled on their wire hangers after all the work my mother had put into them. And then I would get that strangely ominous smell of tension from the dress fabrics and the burn in the cover of the ironing board—as if each piece of cloth and paper crushed with light under the naked bulb might suddenly go up in flames. Whenever I pass some small tailoring shop still lit up at night and see the owner hunched over his steam press; whenever in some poorer neighborhood of the city I see through a window some small crowded kitchen naked under the harsh light glittering in the ceiling, I still smell that fiery breath, that warning of imminent fire. I was always holding my breath. What I must have felt most about ourselves, I see now, was that we ourselves were like kindling—that all the hard-pressed pieces of ourselves and all the hard-used objects in that kitchen were like so many slivers of wood that might go up in flames if we came too near the white-blazing filaments in that naked bulb. Our tension itself was fire, we ourselves were forever burning—to live, to get down the foreboding in our souls, to make good.

Twice a year, on the anniversaries of her parents' deaths, my mother placed on top of the ice-box an ordinary kitchen glass packed with wax, the *yortsayt,* and lit the candle in it. Sitting at the kitchen table over my homework, I would look across the threshold to that mourning-glass, and sense that for my mother the distance from our kitchen to *der heym,* from life to death, was only a flame's length away. Poor as we were, it was not poverty that drove my mother so hard; it was loneliness—some endless bitter brooding over all those left behind, dead or dying or soon to die; a loneliness locked up in her kitchen that dwelt every day on the hazardousness of life and the nearness of death, but still kept struggling in the lock, trying to get us through by endless labor.

With us, life started up again only on the last shore. There seemed to be no middle ground between despair and the fury of our ambition. Whenever my mother spoke of her hopes for us, it was with such unbelievingness that the likes of us would ever come to anything, such abashed hope and readiness for pain, that I finally came to see in the flame burning on top of the ice-box death itself burning away the bones of poor Jews, burning out in us everything but courage, the blind resolution to live. In the light of that mourning-candle, there were ranged around me how many dead and dying—how many eras of pain, of exile, of dispersion, of cringing before the powers of this world!

It was always at dusk that my mother's loneliness came home most to me. Painfully alert to every shift in the light at her window, she would suddenly confess her fatigue by removing her pince-nez, and then wearily pushing aside the great mound of fabrics on her machine, would stare at the street as if to warm herself in the last of the sun. "How sad it is!" I once heard her say. "It grips me! It grips me!" Twilight was the bottommost part of the day, the chillest and loneliest time for her. Always so near to her moods, I knew she was fighting some deep inner dread, struggling against the returning tide of darkness along the streets that invariably assailed her heart with the same foreboding—Where? Where now? Where is the day taking us now?

Yet one good look at the street would revive her. I see her now, perched against the windowsill, with her face against the glass, her eyes almost asleep in enjoyment, just as she starts up with the guilty cry—"What foolishness is this in me!"—and goes to the stove to prepare supper for us: a moment, only a moment, watching the evening crowd of women gathering at the grocery for fresh bread and milk. But between my mother's pent-up face at the window and the winter sun dying in the fabrics—"Alfred, see how beautiful!"—she has drawn for me one single line of sentience.

In the following essay, author Paule Marshall remembers a family member in a different kitchen. Marshall recalls the kitchen conversations of her mother and her mother's friends who, through their talk, "were able to overcome the humiliations of the work-day." Like Kazin, she demonstrates the influence of adults in shaping the values and personality of a child.

THE POETS IN THE KITCHEN

Paule Marshall

I grew up among poets. Now they didn't look like poets—whatever that breed is supposed to look like. Nothing about them suggested that poetry was their calling. They were just a group of ordinary housewives and mothers, my mother included, who dressed in a way (shapeless housedresses, dowdy felt hats and long, dark, solemn coats) that made it impossible for me to imagine they had ever been young.

Nor did they do what poets were supposed to do—spend their days in an attic room writing verses. They never put pen to paper except to write occasionally to their relatives in Barbados. "I take my pen in hand hoping these few lines will find you in health as they leave me fair for the time being," was the way their letters invariably began. Rather, their day was spent "scrubbing floor," as they described the work they did.

Several mornings a week these unknown bards would put an apron and a pair of old house shoes in a shopping bag and take the train or streetcar from our section of Brooklyn out to Flatbush. There, those who didn't have steady jobs would wait on certain designated corners for the white housewives in the neighborhood to come along and bargain with them over pay for a day's work cleaning their houses. This was the ritual even in the winter.

Later, armed with the few dollars they had earned, which in their vocabulary became "a few raw-mouth pennies," they made their way back to our neighborhood, where they would sometimes stop off to have a cup of tea or cocoa together before going home to cook dinner for their husbands and children.

The basement kitchen of the brownstone house where my family lived was the usual gathering place. Once inside the warm safety of its walls the women threw off the drab coats and hats, seated themselves at the large center table, drank their cups of tea or cocoa, and talked. While my sister and I sat at a smaller table over in a corner doing our homework, they talked—endlessly, passionately, poetically, and with impressive range. No subject was beyond them. True, they would indulge in the usual gossip: whose husband was running with whom, whose daughter looked slightly "in the way" (pregnant) under her bridal gown as she walked down the aisle. That sort of thing. But they also tackled the great issues of the time. They were always, for example, discussing the state of the economy. It was the mid and late 30's then, and the aftershock of the Depression, with its soup lines and suicides on Wall Street, was still being felt.

Some people, they declared, didn't know how to deal with adversity. They didn't know that you had to "tie up your belly" (hold in the pain, that is) when things got rough and go on with life. They took their image from the bellyband that is tied around the stomach of a newborn baby to keep the navel pressed in.

They talked politics. Roosevelt was their hero. He had come along and rescued the country with relief and jobs, and in gratitude they christened their sons Franklin and Delano and hoped they would live up to the names.

If F.D.R. was their hero, Marcus Garvey was their God. The name of the fiery, Jamaican-born black nationalist of the 20s was constantly invoked around the table. For he had been their leader when they first came to the United States from the West Indies shortly after World War I. They had contributed to his organization, the United Negro Improvement Association (UNIA), out of their meager salaries, bought shares in his ill-fated Black Star Shipping Line, and at the height of the movement they had marched as members of his "nurses' brigade" in their white uniforms up Seventh Avenue in Harlem during the great Garvey Day parades. Garvey: He lived on through the power of their memories.

And their talk was of war and rumors of wars. They raged against World War II when it broke out in Europe, blaming it on the politicians. "It's these politicians. They're the ones always starting up all this lot of war. But what they care? It's the poor people got to suffer and mothers with their sons." If it was *their* sons, they swore they would keep them out of the Army by giving them soap to eat each day to make their hearts sound defective. Hitler? He was for them "the devil incarnate."

Then there was home. They reminisced often and at length about home. The old country. Barbados—or Bimshire, as they affectionately called it. The little Caribbean island in the sun they loved but had to leave. "Poor—poor but sweet" was the way they remembered it.

And naturally they discussed their adopted home. America came in for both good and bad marks. They lashed out at it for the racism they encountered. They took to task some of the people they worked for, especially those who gave them only a hard-boiled egg and a few spoonfuls of cottage cheese for lunch. "As if anybody can scrub floor on an egg and some cheese that don't have no taste to it!"

Yet although they caught H in "this man country," as they called America, it was nonetheless a place where "you could at least see your way to make a dollar." That much they acknowledged. They might even one day accumulate enough dollars, with both them and their husbands working, to buy the brownstone houses which, like my family, they were only leasing at that period. This was their consuming ambition: to "buy house" and to see the children through.

There was no way for me to understand it at the time, but the talk that filled the kitchen those afternoons was highly functional. It served as therapy, the cheapest kind available to my mother and her friends. Not only did it help them recover from the long wait on the corner that morning and the bargaining over their labor, it restored them to a sense of themselves and reaffirmed their self-worth. Through language they were able to overcome the humiliations of the work-day.

But more than therapy, that freewheeling, wide-ranging, exuberant talk functioned as an outlet for the tremendous creative energy they possessed. They were women in whom the need for self-expression was strong, and since language was the only vehicle readily available to them they made of it an art form that—in keeping with the African tradition in which art and life are one—was an integral part of their lives.

And their talk was a refuge. They never really ceased being baffled and overwhelmed by America—its vastness, complexity and power. Its strange customs and laws. At a level beyond words they remained fearful and in awe. Their uneasiness and fear were even reflected in their attitude toward the children they had given birth to in this country. They referred to those like myself, the little Brooklyn-born Bajans (Barbadians), as "these New York children" and complained that they couldn't discipline us properly because of the laws here. "You can't beat these children as you would like, you know, because the authorities in this place will dash you in jail for them. After all, these is New York children." Not only were we different, American, we had, as they saw it, escaped their ultimate authority.

Confronted therefore by a world they could not encompass, which even limited their rights as parents, and at the same time finding themselves permanently separated from the world they had known, they took refuge in language. "Language is the only homeland," Czeslaw Milosz, the emigré Polish writer and Nobel Laureate, has said. This is what it became for the women at the kitchen table.

It served another purpose also, I suspect. My mother and her friends were after all the female counterpart of [novelist] Ralph Ellison's *Invisible Man*. Indeed, you might say they suffered a triple invisibility, being black, female and foreigners. They really didn't count in American society except as a source of cheap labor. But given the kind of women they were, they couldn't tolerate the fact of their invisibility, their powerlessness. And they fought back, using the only weapon at their command: the spoken word.

Those late afternoon conversations on a wide range of topics were a way for them to feel they exercised some measure of control over their lives and the events that shaped them. "Soully-gal, talk yuh talk!" they were always exhorting each other. "In this man world you got to take yuh mouth and make a gun!" They were in control, if only verbally and if only for the two hours or so that they remained in our house.

For me, sitting over in the corner, being seen but not heard, which was the rule for children in those days, it wasn't only what the women talked about—the content—but the way they put things—their style. The insight, irony, wit and humor they brought to their stories and discussions, and their poet's inventiveness and daring with language—which of course I could only sense but not define back then.

They had taken the standard English taught them in the primary schools of Barbados and transformed it into an idiom, an instrument that more adequately described them—changing around the syntax and imposing their own rhythm and accent so that the sentences were more pleasing to their ears. They added the few African sounds and words that had survived, such as the derisive suck-teeth sound and the word "yam," meaning to eat. And to make it more vivid, more in keeping with their expressive quality, they brought to bear a raft of metaphors, parables, Biblical quotations, sayings and the like:

"The sea ain't got no back door," they would say, meaning that it wasn't like a house where if there was a fire you could run out the back. Meaning that it was not to be trifled with. And meaning perhaps in a larger sense that man should treat all of nature with caution and respect.

"I has read hell by heart and called every generation blessed!" They sometimes went in for hyperbole.

A woman expecting a baby was never said to be pregnant. They never used that word. Rather, she was "in the way" or, better yet, "tumbling big." "Guess who I butt up on in the market the other day tumbling big again!"

And a woman with a reputation of being too free with her sexual favors was known in their book as a "thoroughfare"—the sense of men like a steady stream of cars moving up and down the road of her life. Or she might be dubbed "a free-bee," which was my favorite of the two. I liked the image it conjured up of a woman scandalous perhaps but independent, who flitted from one flower to another in a garden of male beauties, sampling their nectar, taking her pleasure at will, the roles reversed.

And nothing, no matter how beautiful, was ever described as simply beautiful. It was always "beautiful-ugly": the beautiful-ugly dress, the beautiful-ugly house, the beautiful-ugly car. Why the word "ugly," I used to wonder, when the thing they were referring to was beautiful, and they knew it. Why the antonym, the contradiction, the linking of opposites? It used to puzzle me greatly as a child.

There is the theory in linguistics which states that the idiom of a people, the way they use language, reflects not only the most fundamental views they hold of themselves and the world but their very conception of reality. Perhaps in using the term "beautiful-ugly" to describe nearly everything, my mother and her friends were expressing what they believed to be a fundamental dualism in life: the idea that a thing is at the same time its opposite, and that these opposites, these contradictions make up the whole. But theirs was not a Manichean brand of dualism that sees matter, flesh, the body, as inherently evil, because they constantly addressed each other as "soully-gal"—soul: spirit; gal: the body, flesh, the visible self. And it was clear from their tone that they gave one as much weight and importance as the other. They had never heard of the mind/body split.

As for God, they summed up His essential attitude in a phrase. "God," they would say, "don' love ugly and He ain't stuck on pretty."

Using everyday speech, the simple commonplace words—but always with imagination and skill—they gave voice to the most complex ideas. Flannery O'Connor would have approved of how they made ordinary language work, as she put it, "double-time," stretching, shading, deepening its meaning. Like Joseph Conrad they were always trying to infuse new life in the "old old words worn thin . . . by . . . careless usage." And the goals of their oral art were the same as his: "to make you hear, to make you feel . . . to make you *see*." This was their guiding esthetic.

No more vivid character can be imagined than the "round and bald," compulsively talkative "Uncle Bun," vividly evoked in Maxine Hong Kingston's *China Men*. "He's crazy," Kingston's mother says of this frequent, uninvited guest at the family laundry where he regales the children—and any adult who will listen—with long speeches on food phobias and his paranoid conviction that some nameless enemy is trying to poison him. Something about Uncle Bun was obviously unforgettable to Kingston, for after many years she could still see him clearly in her mind's eye, still hear his long ramblings and wild imaginings.

Uncle Bun

Maxine Hong Kingston

We had an uncle, a second or third cousin maybe, who went back to China to be a Communist. We called him Uncle Bun, which might have been his name, but could also be a pun, Uncle Stupid. He was a blood relative and not just a villager. He was very talkative. In fact, he hardly ever stopped talking, and we kids watched the spit foam at the corners of his mouth. He came to the laundry and sat, or if it was very hot, he stood near the door to talk and talk. It was more like a lecture than a conversation. He repeated himself so often that some of what he said seeped into the ears. He talked about wheat germ. "You ought to eat wheat germ," he said, "because wheat germ is the most potent food in the world. Eat it and you'll stay young for a long time; you'll never get sick. You'll be beautiful and tall and strong, also intelligent. The reason for so much unhappiness and strife is that people have been eating wrong. Meat turns them into animals. Wheat germ, which we can digest easier, can help us evolve into better people. Wheat germ is full of vitamins (*why-huh-ming*), and it is very cheap. A, C, thiamine, riboflavin, niacin, calcium, carbohydrates, fats, iron (*eye-yun*)." He was a scientific and up-to-date man who used English scientific terms. In two weighty syllables, both equally accented, a spondee, he said "Wheat Germ." Wheat germ would fatten up my father and also fatten up all the skinny children. Unlike the rest of the men in the family, who were thin and had white hair, this uncle was round and bald with black hair above his ears and around the back of his head. He wore a pearl gray three-piece suit and a necktie with a gold tiepin, the gold chain of his pocket watch linking one vest pocket to the other, the last button of his vest open over his prosperous paunch. He opened his eyes wide to see everything through his round gold-framed eyeglasses.

"Wheat germ—you can put it into any food," he said. "Sprinkle it on the rice and strew it on all the accompaniments. Stir it into milk and juices. Drink it in soups and beverages; it melts right in. Mix it with ice cream and strawberries. Combine it with flour. Combine it with rice. Beat it into cakes and pancakes. Scatter it on fried eggs for a crunchy texture. You can eat it by itself. Eat it by the handful, cooked or raw. Add it to cold food or hot food, sauces and gravies. Rain it on vegetables. Coat fish, meat, and fowl with it. Use it as a binder in meatballs and fishcakes. It goes with anything." Wheat germ. I could not imagine this miracle food, whether it was sweet or salty, what size it was, what it was, what color, whether it tasted good. Was it a liquid or a solid? Was *germ* the same germ as in bacteria? "Wheat germ is golden brown," he said, "though the color blends with whatever you're cooking. A pinch of it changes regular food into a medicine." It sounded like a fairy-tale elixir, fairy food. "You cannot taste or detect its presence in other foods," he said, "Yet you can eat it by itself like cornflakes," which he also pronounced spondaically in his accent, *Coon Flex*. "Wheat germ is the heart of the wheat," he said, "the heart of bread and wheat, which is more nutritious in the first place than rice. It repairs broken parts and tissues.

"Hum," said my father and mother.

"We ought to buy some, don't you think?" I asked my parents, hating to ask them to spend more money, but we might be wasting away from the lack of a vital food.

"He's crazy," my mother said. "Anything that necessary has to have been invented long ago."

He brought us some sample wheat germ, which tasted like raw peas or raw oats.

Although he was about my father's age, Uncle Bun, like many of the old men, did not appear to have a job and was able to afford entire mornings, afternoons, days and evenings sitting and chatting while we worked. Maybe his sons sent money from Chicago. My father did join him talking politics, a man's topic as gray as newspapers . . . .

"We have to examine the causes of poverty," said Uncle Bun, "The world has never experimented to find out if it is rich enough and big enough to support all its people. It probably is. Look at all the rich people who own too much, and you can see there's extra food, land, and money. And certainly, there's always work enough. Only the distribution is wrong; we have to divide up the goods evenly." We kids divided every five-cent candy bar and all the chores. "Who really owns the land?" he asked. "The man who farms it with his sweat and piss or the man whose name is on the paper? And shouldn't the worker on the assembly line own his labor and the results of his labor?

"Actually these aren't dreams or plans," Uncle Bun said. "I'm making predictions about ineluctabilities. This Beautiful Nation, this Gold Mountain, this America will end as we know it. There will be one nation, and it will be a world nation. A united planet. Not just Russian Communism. Not just Chinese Communism. World Communism."

He said, "When we don't need to break our bodies earning our daily living any more, and we have time to think, we'll write poems, sing songs, develop religions, invent customs, build statues, plant gardens, and make a perfect world." He paused to contemplate the wonders.

"Isn't that great?" I said after he left.

"Don't get brainwashed," said my mother. "He's going to get in trouble for talking like that. He's going to get us in trouble; the barbarians think that Communists and Chinese are the same."

Even when the uncles were killed during the Revolution and the aunts tortured, Uncle Bun did not change his mind about Communism. "We have to weigh the death of a few against the lives of millions of poor workers and the coming generations," he said.

"A fermentation of dreams," said my father. Uncle Bun should not have said such Communist things against our dead relatives . . . .

"Ah, sad, sad America, which does not respect the poor," he said, "The poor are important. And look, even if we distribute everything, and it's spread so thin that we're all poor—that's good. Consider the culture we poor have invented—vegetarianism and fasting, pencil sketches, pottery, singing without instruments, mending, saving and reusing things, quilting, patchwork, the poetry written on leaves, rocks and walls, acrobatics, dancing, and kung fu, which doesn't require expensive sports equipment. Oh, let's value the poor, who in a way are all of us. Even with money, the rich can't buy good food. They eat white bread and poisoned food. What they ought to do is eat wheat germ."

Amazing! His two big ideas—wheat germ and Communism—connected . . . .

"He's gone crazy," my mother diagnosed. "He's getting crazier. When he comes to the house, and we're at the laundry, you kids don't let him in." . . .

He did come to our house one day when neither of our parents were home. Unfortunately, the front door was wide open, so we couldn't hide and pretend we were out. It would be embarrassing to tell him why he couldn't come in. Being the oldest, I decided that we children would go outside and talk to him on the porch. It was pleasant out there under the grapevines. We stood between him and the red door and asked him questions to distract him. He usually walked right in. "What exactly is wheat germ?" we asked, but he seemed not as interested in wheat germ as before. "How's shopping at the new grocery store?" "Fine. Fine," he said, "May I have a drink of water?" he asked. "We'll get it," we said, some of us blocking his way while one ran inside, very rude, a guest having to ask for refreshments. He drank the entire glassful quickly. "You must finish all your water," he advised us. "When you have milk, finish all of it. Finish you food. Eat everything. Don't leave scraps. Scraps turn into garbage. Food one moment, garbage the next. Same with paper. Don't blotch it, and if you do, save it for scratch paper. Cross out the mistakes rather than crumple the paper. Make every page count." He did not go berserk, did not break into the house and throw himself against the sofa like a padded cell, did not act like a maniac at all. He sounded like other adults, advising this, advising that, advising to eat.

At the laundry, where it would be dangerous to run amok among the hot machines, he announced: "*They* are not *only* hiding the poison in my food. I am on the verge of discovering the *real* plot. Have you noticed—oh, surely, you must have been alarmed by it—you must have seen how many garbage demons there are in this country?" "Yes, there are," said my mother. "Do you see," he asked, "how the white demons are very careful with garbage? And how much garbage there is?" . . .

A few days later he again came running into the laundry. He was highly excited and frightened, as if he were being chased. "I've discovered what they do with the garbage." He was sweating. "They're collecting it for me. They're going to feed it to me. They'll capture me and tie me down and shovel it into my mouth. They're going to make me eat it. All of it. It's all for me. You must see what a big plot it is. Everybody is manufacturing garbage constantly, some knowing the purpose and some just because everyone else is doing it. It all ties in with the poisoning, don't you see? The newspapers and radios are in on it too, telling them to buy, buy, and then they turn everything they buy into garbage as fast as they can. They're preparing and saving for the day when they'll shovel it into my mouth. They've been collecting for years, and I didn't see the plot till now. That day is coming soon. They'll make me eat it."

"Why should they do that to you?" asked my mother.

"Because of my talk about Communism," he said.

"The garbage is not for you," said my father. "The garbage isn't that important. You're not that important. Forget the garbage."

"You should go to a mind doctor," said my mother.

He got offended and left. "You'll be sorry when the day arrives, and you see it all come true. Feeding day."

His stomach got thinner. He refused most food; he ate only greens and browns, leaving not a scrap, not contributing to the garbage that "they" would feed him later. "Paper garbage too," he said, "Paper cups, paper plates, paper napkins, Kleenex, gum and gum wrappers."

At last he said, "I'm going back to China. I've outsmarted them. I know which day the feeding will be on, and I'll leave before then. It was not like this in China. Remember? In fact, they couldn't poison your milk and bread because we didn't drink milk; only babies drank milk. And we didn't eat much bread. We used everything thoroughly in China. Remember? There was hardly any garbage. We ate all the food. Remember how we could see with our own eyes that the hogs ate the peelings? If the human beings didn't eat rinds, the animals did, and the fish bones got plowed into the fields. Remember how paper gatherers collected paper that had writing on it and burned it in wood furnaces? Remember we saved the bags and boxes? Why, this—" he picked up a cornflakes box—"we would have treasured a pretty box like this, such bright colors, such sturdy cardboard. We would have opened the flaps carefully and used it to store valuable and useful things in. We'd have taken good care of it, made it last, handed it down. I'm going back to New Society Village." . . .

From that decision on, he acted saner and saner, happier, and stopped talking about the garbage except to say, "I'm returning to China before feeding day," "Returning" is not to say that he necessarily had ever been there before . . . .

The day he left, he spoke to my youngest sister, who was about three years old. He bent over so that she could hear and see him very well. "Don't forget me, will you?" he asked. "Remember I used to play with you. Remember I'm the man who sang songs to you and gave you dimes. What's my name?" She laughed that he would ask her such a silly, easy question. Of course, she knew his name. He coaxed her to say it several times for him. "You won't forget? Tell me you won't forget."

"I won't forget," she said. He seemed satisfied to leave, and we never saw him or heard from him again.

For a while I reminded my sister, "Do you remember Uncle Bun, the bald fat man who talked a lot? Do you remember him asking you not to forget him?"

"Oh, yes, the funny man. I remember."

I reminded her periodically. But one day, I noticed that I had not asked her for some time. "Do you remember the funny man who talked a lot, the one who smuggled himself into Red China?"

"Who?" she asked.

"Uncle Bun. Remember?"

"No," she said.

A FAMOUS WOMAN

The following essay on Sylvia Plath draws on biographical and other material for background information. Carefully researched and documented, this essay provides a brief overview for the reader who knows little or nothing about the life and work of Sylvia Plath. By supplementing the vital passages from her poems, her letters, and her posthumous novel, the writer adds an emotional dimension to her portrait, a poignant sense of the young woman whose ordeals were finally too overwhelming to struggle against.

Sylvia Plath: A Short Life

Katinka Matson

Dying
Is an art, like everything else,
I do it exceptionally well.

I do it so it feels like hell.
I do it so it feels real.
I guess you could say I've a call.

       ("Lady Lazarus," *Ariel*)

Sylvia Plath. American poet. She was a pretty, all-American girl with bright red lips and a pageboy haircut. After her suicide, a manuscript of poems was discovered and published. Critics called the book, *Ariel,* terrifying, visionary, terrible and strange. Sylvia Plath attained cult status. She became a priestess of poetry, a category unto herself.

    I saw that my body had all sorts of little tricks, such as making my hands go limp at the crucial second, which would save it, time and again, whereas if I had the whole say, I would be dead in a flash.
    I would simply have to ambush it with whatever sense I had left or it would trap me in its stupid cage for fifty years without any sense at all.

       (*The Bell Jar*)

Sylvia Plath was born in Boston, Massachusetts, on 27 October 1932. Her father, Otto Emil Plath, was a German emigré and professor of entomology at Boston University; his specialty was bumble-bees. He was twenty-one years older than Plath's mother, Aurelia Schober, a woman of Austrian parentage whom he met in one of his German classes. Sylvia was their first child. Her brother, Warren, was born exactly two and a half years later. When Plath was eight years old her father died.

Daddy, I have had to kill you.
You died before I had time—
Marble-heavy, a bag full of God,
Ghastly statue with one grey toe
Big as a Frisco seal

And a head in the freakish Atlantic
Where it pours bean green over blue
In the waters off beautiful Nauset.
I used to pray to recover you.
Ach, du.

       ("Daddy," *Ariel*)

Aurelia Plath went to work teaching secretarial skills at Boston University. The children were left in the care of her parents, who moved into their home in Winthrop. Soon after, the entire family moved to Wellesley, an upper-middle-class college town with good schools for the children.

    Aurelia made a "tireless effort to see that her children had all the advantages given their much-better-off contemporaries. These included summer camps, Scouting, sailing, piano and viola lessons, dance 'assemblies,' painting and watercolour lessons, and numerous other, frequently expensive, extracurricular activities" (Blutscher, *Sylvia Plath: Method and Madness*).

> Mother, you sent me to piano lessons
> And praised my arabesques and trills
> Although each teacher found my touch
> Oddly wooden in spite of scales
> And the hours of practising, my ear
> Tone-deaf and yes, unteachable.
> I learned, I learned, I learned elsewhere
> From muses unhired by you, dear mother.
> ("The Disquieting Muses," *The Colossus*)

A model student with a "genius" IQ, Plath's high-school years were highlighted by rows of straight As, honour roll, special awards and achievement certificates (even one for punctuality). She had a story published in *Seventeen* magazine and a poem in the *Christian Science Monitor*. She was editor of the yearbook in her senior year and wrote a column for the town paper. She was also growing up tall and slender, with long brown hair, and a lovely smile.

> *To Aurelia Plath:*
> It was one of those cartoon and personality write-ups titled "Teen Triumphs." There was a sketch of a girl s'posed to be me—writing, also a cow. It said, and I quote: "BORN TO WRITE! Sylvia Plath, seventeen, really works at writing. To get atmosphere for a story about a farm she took a job as a farmhand. Now she's working on a sea story." Then there's another sketch of me saying, "and I get a job on a boat." Not only that. "A national magazine had published two of her brain children, the real test of being a writer."
> (Aurelia Schober Plath, *Letters Home*)

At Smith College, where Plath had a partial scholarship, she continued to excel. In her sophomore year she won a $1,500 *Mademoiselle* prize for college fiction. In her junior year she won a guest editorship to the same magazine, and headed for New York City.

> I knew something was wrong with me that summer, because all I could think about was the Rosenbergs and how stupid I'd been to buy all those uncomfortable, expensive clothes, hanging limp as a fish in my closet, and how all the little successes I'd totted up so happily fizzled to nothing outside the slick marble and plate-glass fronts along Madison Avenue.
> I felt very still and very empty, the way the eye of a tornado must feel, moving dully along in the middle of the surrounding hullabaloo.
> (*The Bell Jar*)

Plath returned to Wellesley after her month in New York to learn that she had not been accepted for Frank O'Connor's summer writing course at Harvard. She had been counting on the class to occupy her during the long summer and had no alternative plans. Suddenly, she was at loose ends. She became insomniac and was unable even to read. Obviously disturbed, Plath saw a psychiatrist and was given shock treatments. She refused to return to him. On 24 August her mother found a note from her daughter: "Have gone for a long walk. Will be home tomorrow" (Aurelia Schober Plath, *Letters Home*). She was discovered three days later lying in a crawlspace under the house—her brother had heard her faint cries.

> The second time I meant
> To last it out and not come back at all.
> I rocked shut
>
> As a sea shell.
> They had to call and call
> And pick the worms off me like sticky pearls.
>   ("Lady Lazarus," *Ariel*)

Plath spent six months at McLean Hospital in Belmont, Massachusetts, an expensive psychiatric institution, where she underwent insulin therapy and shock treatments. She was pronounced 'cured' in time to return to Smith for the second semester. She bleached her hair blonde and pursued a social life with her old determination to succeed, seeing many different men and experimenting with sex. She began to write poetry again, and won a scholarship for her final year at Smith.

> *Gordon Lamayer (friend):*
> Life was always full to the brim for Sylvia at Smith in those days and cresting over the brim, "overflowing." If she had been a Marlovian heroine, she would have been an "over-reacher," because she could not stick by the golden mean, nothing too much, but was always anxious to experiment *in extremis,* with Blake, to find out what "enough" was by indulging herself "too much." Her letters were filled with purple passages. In retrospect, I would say that at times she was whistling Dixie, telling herself she was extremely happy in an effort to mask her anxiety.
>   (Butscher, *Sylvia Plath: The Woman and the Work*)

In 1955, her last year at Smith, she dyed her hair back to its natural brown, and deliberately subdued her "healthy bohemianism" to concentrate on her studies, her writing, and the ever-present question of her future. Ever striving, she made a clean sweep of the poetry prizes, graduated summa cum laude, and won a Fulbright scholarship to study at Cambridge.

> If only England would by some miracle come through, I would be forced shivering into a new, unfamiliar world, where I had to forge anew friends and a home for myself, and although such experiences are painful and awkward at first, I know, intellectually, that they are the best things to make one grow—always biting off just a slight bit more than you chewed before.
>
>   (Aurelia Schober Plath, *Letters Home*)

At Cambridge, Plath continued to succeed, both academically and socially. In March she met Ted Hughes at a party and fell in love with the "brilliant ex-Cambridge poet . . . the only man I've met yet here who'd be strong enough to be equal with" (*Letters Home*). Hughes was a tall, lanky, handsome man, the son of a Yorkshire carpenter, a "large, hulking, healthy Adam" (*Letters Home*). Most important, Hughes was a serious and dedicated poet. Since it was against the rules for Plath to be married while a student at Cambridge, she and Ted were married secretly in London in June, her mother in attendance.

> The last thing I wanted was infinite security and to be the place an arrow shoots off from. I wanted change and excitement and to shoot off in all directions myself, like the coloured arrows from a Fourth of July rocket.
>
> (*The Bell Jar*)

Plath and Ted spent the summer in a rented house in Spain, rising at seven each morning to write. Besides doing her own work, she typed Ted's poems for submission to magazines. To her mother, she described her newly wedded life with Ted in ecstatic, glowing terms. Her life was now perfect and it had a purpose. She could not remember what her life had been like without Ted.

> I felt myself melting into the shadows like the negative of a person I'd never seen before in my life.
>
> (*The Bell Jar*)

Back in Cambridge in the fall, Plath went back to her studies while she and Ted continued writing and submitting poems and stories. They received many rejections, but also some acceptances. In February 1957, Ted's volume of poems entitled *Hawk in the Rain* won the Poetry Centre First Publication Award and was accepted for publication by Harper's in the US and Faber in England.

> I'm so happy *his* book is accepted *first*. It will make it so much easier for me when mine is accepted—if not by the Yale Series, then by some other place. I can rejoice then, much more, knowing Ted is ahead of me. There is no question of rivalry, but only mutual joy and a sense of us doubling our prize-winning and creative output.
>
> (Aurelia Schober Plath, *Letters Home*)

In the summer of 1957, she and Ted returned to the United States and rented an apartment in Northampton: Plath had a job teaching English at Smith. She soon discovered, however, that the amount of labour involved in teaching was "death to writing." She was frustrated and unhappy in the airless campus life. After the first year, she quit and they moved again, this time to an apartment on the "slummy side" of Beacon Hill, and she worked part-time for Massachusetts General Hospital. During this period she met poet Anne Sexton in Robert Lowell's poetry course.

> *Anne Sexton:*
> Often, very often, Sylvia and I would talk at length about our first suicides, at length, in detail, in depth . . . Suicide is, after all, the opposite of the poem.
>
> (Sexton, *A Self-Portrait in Letters*)

By October 1959, she was pregnant. She and Ted decided to return to London to live. They moved into a small, inexpensive flat in Chalcot Square. In February, Plath signed a contract with Heinemann to publish her first book of poems, *The Colossus,* some of which had been written during the previous fall at Yaddo, an artists' colony in Saratoga, New York. The dedication read: "For Ted." In March, a daughter, Frieda Rebecca, was born at home.

> I also remembered Buddy Willard saying in a sinister, knowing way that after I had children I would feel differently, I wouldn't want to write poems any more. So I began to think maybe it was true that when you were married and had children it was like being brainwashed, and afterwards you went about numb as a slave in some private, totalitarian state.
>
> *(The Bell Jar)*

In January 1961, Plath became pregnant again; she miscarried a month later. The *New Yorker* offered her a "first reading" contract in March which she accepted. In May, Alfred Knopf announced it would publish an American edition of her book of poetry entitled *The Colossus*. In September, pregnant once more, she moved into a cottage in Devon with Ted and Frieda. Nicholas, a son, was born in the new year.

> I do not stir.
> The frost makes a flower,
> The dew makes a star,
>
> The dead bell,
> The dead bell.
>
> Somebody's done for.
> ("Death & Co," *Ariel*)

The bubble burst: the world of the tall handsome "writing Hugheses" with their two beautiful babies in their cottage in Devon ended when Ted Hughes became seriously involved with another woman. Plath was stunned, heartbroken, and finally outraged. By August 1962, Ted had departed. Plath tried to manage in the country but it was difficult, and, above all, isolated.

> Everything is breaking—my dinner set cracking in half, the health inspector says the cottage should be demolished—there is no hope for it . . . Even my beloved bees set upon me today when I numbly knocked aside their sugar feeder, and I am all over stings.
>
> (Aurelia Schober Plath, *Letters Home*)

Plath moved herself and the children back to London, to a flat in "Yeats's house!" arriving just in time for one of the worst winters in the city's history. Severe bouts with flu for her and the babies, blackouts, frozen pipes, the inescapable cold, and no outside help contributed to her emotional and physical exhaustion. At first she managed to sustain herself, writing poem after poem each morning in the dawn hours before the children awoke and needed her.

> If I've killed one man, I've killed two—
> The vampire who said he was you
> And drank my blood for a year,
> Seven years, if you want to know.
> Daddy, you can lie back now.
> ("Daddy," *Ariel*)

On a cold Monday morning, 11 February 1963, Sylvia Plath, her two children asleep, went downstairs to the kitchen, turned on the gas jets, and put her head in the oven. Her body was discovered several hours later by a nurse who had been sent over by her physician to help out with the children. Plath was thirty years old.

> The woman is perfected.
> Her dead
>
> Body wears the smile of accomplishment,
> The illusion of a Greek necessity
>
> Flows in the scrolls of her toga,
> Her bare
>
> Feet seem to be saying:
> We have come so far, it is over.
>
> ("Edge," *Ariel*)

Sources

Aird, Eileen. *Sylvia Plath: Her Life and Work.* Edinburgh: Oliver & Boyd, 1973.
Butscher, Edward. *Sylvia Plath: Method and Madness.* New York: Pocket Books, 1977.
————. *Sylvia Plath: The Woman and the Work.* London: Faber & Faber, 1968.
Plath, Aurelia Schober, ed. *Letters Home by Sylvia Plath, 1950–63.* New York: Bantam, 1977.
Plath, Sylvia. *Ariel.* New York: Harper & Row, 1966.
————. *The Bell Jar.* London: Faber & Faber, 1963.
————. *The Colossus.* London: Faber & Faber, 1972.

A MEMORABLE TEACHER

Many people have a well-loved teacher in their past who opened their eyes to new possibilities in the world around them or who alerted them to new possibilities in themselves. Few teachers have been more fondly and amusingly depicted than Russell Baker's third-year English teacher, the prim Mr. Fleagle, "notorious among City students for dullness and inability to inspire." No wonder Baker anticipated "a listless unfruitful year." What a happy reversal, then, of expectations! We learn about it ("don't you see?" as Mr. Fleagle would put it) in the following essay, which combines description and narration to produce a picture of the quintessentially good teacher lurking beneath the reputed "comic antique" the students laughed at.

The Prim Mr. Fleagle

Russell Baker

When our class was assigned to Mr. Fleagle for third-year English I anticipated another grim year in that dreariest of subjects. Mr. Fleagle was notorious among City students for dullness and inability to inspire. He was said to be stuffy, dull, and hopelessly out of date. To me he looked to be sixty or seventy and prim to a fault. He wore primly severe eyeglasses, his wavy hair was primly cut and primly combed. He wore prim vested suits with neckties blocked primly against the collar buttons of his primly starched white shirts. He had a primly pointed jaw, a primly straight nose, and a prim manner of speaking that was so correct, so gentlemanly, that he seemed a comic antique.

I anticipated a listless, unfruitful year with Mr. Fleagle and for a long time was not disappointed. We read *Macbeth*. Mr. Fleagle loved *Macbeth* and wanted us to love it too, but he lacked the gift of infecting others with his own passion. He tried to convey the murderous ferocity of Lady Macbeth one day by reading aloud the passage that concludes

> . . . I have given suck, and know
> How tender 'tis to love the babe that milks me.
> I would, while it was smiling in my face,
> Have plucked my nipple from his boneless gums. . . .

The idea of prim Mr. Fleagle plucking his nipple from boneless gums was too much for the class. We burst into gasps of irrepressible snickering. Mr. Fleagle stopped.

"There is nothing funny, boys, about giving suck to a babe. It is the—the very essence of motherhood, don't you see."

He constantly sprinkled his sentences with "don't you see." It wasn't a question but an exclamation of mild surprise at our ignorance. "Your pronoun needs an antecedent, don't you see," he would say, very primly. "The purpose of the Porter's scene, boys, is to provide comic relief from the horror, don't you see."

Late in the year we tackled the informal essay. "The essay, don't you see, is the . . . " My mind went numb. Of all forms of writing, none seemed so boring as the essay. Naturally we would have to write informal essays. Mr. Fleagle distributed a homework sheet offering us a choice of topics. None was quite so simpleminded as "What I Did on My Summer Vacation," but most seemed to be almost as dull. I took the list home and dawdled until the night before the essay was due. Sprawled on the sofa, I finally faced up to the grim task, took the list out of my notebook, and scanned it. The topic on which my eye stopped was "The Art of Eating Spaghetti."

This title produced an extraordinary sequence of mental images. Surging up out of the depths of memory came a vivid recollection of a night in Belleville when all of us were seated around the supper table—Uncle Allen, my mother, Uncle Charlie, Doris, Uncle Hal—and Aunt Pat served spaghetti for supper. Spaghetti was an exotic treat in those days. Neither Doris nor I had ever eaten spaghetti, and none of the adults had enough experience to be good at it. All the good humor of Uncle Allen's house reawoke in my mind as I recalled the laughing arguments we had that night about the socially respectable method for moving spaghetti from plate to mouth.

Suddenly I wanted to write about that, about the warmth and good feeling of it, but I wanted to put it down simply for my own joy, not for Mr. Fleagle. It was a moment I wanted to recapture and hold for myself. I wanted to relive the pleasure of an evening at New Street. To write it as I wanted, however, would violate all the rules of formal composition I'd learned in school, and Mr. Fleagle would surely give it a failing grade. Never mind. I would write something else for Mr. Fleagle after I had written this thing for myself.

When I finished it the night was half gone and there was no time left to compose a proper, respectable essay for Mr. Fleagle. There was no choice next morning but to turn in my private reminiscence of Belleville. Two days passed before Mr. Fleagle returned the graded papers, and he returned everyone's but mine. I was bracing myself for a command to report to Mr. Fleagle immediately after school for discipline when I saw him lift my paper from his desk and rap for the class's attention.

"Now, boys," he said, "I want to read you an essay. This is titled 'The Art of Eating Spaghetti.' "

And he started to read. My words! He was reading *my words* out loud to the entire class. What's more, the entire class was listening. Listening attentively. Then somebody laughed, then the entire class was laughing, and not in contempt and ridicule, but with openhearted enjoyment. Even Mr. Fleagle stopped two or three times to repress a small prim smile.

I did my best to avoid showing pleasure, but what I was feeling was pure ecstasy at this startling demonstration that my words had the power to make people laugh. In the eleventh grade, at the eleventh hour as it were, I had discovered a calling. It was the happiest moment of my entire school career. When Mr. Fleagle finished he put the final seal on my happiness by saying, "Now that, boys, is an essay, don't you see. It's—don't you see—it's of the very essence of the essay, don't you see. Congratulations, Mr. Baker."

For the first time, light shone on a possibility. It wasn't a very heartening possibility, to be sure. Writing couldn't lead to a job after high school, and it was hardly honest work, but Mr. Fleagle had opened a door for me. After that I ranked Mr. Fleagle among the finest teachers in the school.

A TYPE OF PERSON

Elie Wiesel, in the following essay, puts the rhetorical strategy of characterization to a different use, describing not a specific person, but a group of people he calls "The Just," those "Righteous Gentiles" who risked their lives and freedom to save Jews threatened by the Nazis during World War II. Who were the Just?, asks Wiesel; What compelled these people to act as they did? These questions lead on to others. Wiesel's essay ponders deeper questions of the nature of good and evil. By describing the lives and actions of individuals, Wiesel outlines a larger category of human character. Such descriptions of "a type" of person can help us understand the patterns of human behavior that underlie ordinary and extraordinary actions.

The Just: The Brave Christians Who Saved Jews from the Nazis

Elie Wiesel
Translated by Richard Howard

A few flashes of light in the darkness . . .

They are called "the Just among nations": the Righteous Gentiles. We know their names—most of them are inscribed on the honor roll at Yad Vashem, the Israeli Holocaust Memorial in Jerusalem, where trees forming a unique, deeply moving avenue have been planted in their memory. Walk there and you recover your faith—sad though it may be, uneasy though it may be—in humanity.

I confess that their stories do not overlap with mine. None of the Just crossed my path during the war. None of our Christian neighbors in my small village of Sighet, in Romania, risked his life to take in, to hide, to rescue a Jewish friend or a Jewish child (I can never forget our last walk to the station, to the cattle cars: the town, in spring sunshine, seemed surreally peaceful. Not sad at all to see us leaving, setting out toward the unknown.)

But the Just existed. If not in Sighet, then elsewhere. In Holland. In Poland. In France and Italy. Even as the evil expanded through occupied Europe, something inspired certain individuals to resist, to help the victims being handed over to the enemy and to death.

Anton Schmidt, an Austrian corporal, paid with his life for helping the Jews of the Vilna ghetto. Joop Westerweel, a Dutch teacher, sacrificed his while helping the Jewish children of Holland. Ingebjorg Fostyedt Sletten, a member of the Norwegian Resistance, saved Jewish families in Oslo—including that of the chief rabbi. And others—Leopold Ros of Belgium, Enzio Giogetti of Italy, Maria Cholova of Greece, Col. Imre Revicky of Hungary. With each name came a heroic, humane story, stories that the Jewish people, loyal to those who helped, continue to cite as examples. In Germany, Oskar Schindler was virtually unknown. In Israel, he was welcomed as a hero. This is true of the majority of Righteous Gentiles: forgotten in their own countries, they remain legendary to the Jews.

The most famous, of course, is Raoul Wallenberg. This young Swedish diplomat, a member of one of that nation's most illustrious families, left the security of a neutral capital to save thousands of Jews in Budapest.

Here again I must tell the truth: his fate did not intersect with mine. With regard to the provincial Jewish communities, especially those of Transylvania, Raoul Wallenberg came too late to keep Adolf Eichmann from operating the death mills at Auschwitz. But there still were Jews in Budapest, and it was Eichmann to whom Heinrich Himmler entrusted the job of eradicating them. By the time Wallenberg arrived in Budapest in July 1944, just over a quarter of a million terrified Jews remained trapped in the city. Through Wallenberg's efforts, thousands—too few given their numbers—escaped.

In point of fact, Wallenberg was not the only one in Budapest to put himself between Jewish victims and German exterminators. The Swiss consul, Charles Lutz, the Spanish consul, Don Angel Sans-Briz, the Papal nuncio, the Red Cross, and the clandestine Zionist resistance all have their part in the story, too. But it was Wallenberg, by his courage, imagination and nerve, who showed the way.

Elsewhere, there were other collective efforts. The case of Denmark will forever remain one glorious example, Bulgaria another. We know the former well: the Danish King astounded the Nazis by announcing his intention to wear a yellow star as a sign of solidarity with his Jewish subjects. Then, in 1943, alerted by a German officer, the Danish Resistance, in an admirable gesture of collective heroism, managed to save almost all the country's Jews by evacuating them to Sweden.

The Bulgarians protected the Jewish population, too. Inspired by a brave intellectual, Dimo Kazasov, they, with the exception of a few Nazi collaborators, foiled German plans for the deportation of Jews to the death camps. The questions, of course, are simple, simple to ask and hard to answer: how do we account for these human acts? To what can we attribute the boldness, compassion and generosity of some, whereas others—often the majority—opted for collaboration, complicity, indifference, or simply for their own comfort and safety? Are Danes better human beings than Poles? Are they more humane? More heroic? Are Bulgarians more concerned with ethical imperatives than Ukranians? How do we explain the courage of Father Rufino Niccacci, a Franciscan monk who, in the heart of Fascist Italy, managed to hide 300 Jews in Assisi? How do we understand selflessness on the part of a few individuals when the society surrounding them was dominated and poisoned by terror, cowardice and hate?

Studying their stories, one is amazed to discover that the choice they made—the choice of life—was both easier and more difficult than we supposed. A strange dichotomy? Let me explain.

More difficult: of course. We must not forget two things: the occupier's cruel and bloody power, and the loneliness, the isolation, of those who opposed it. In some places the Germans punished any attempt to shelter fugitive Jews by imprisonment or death. There was no lack of informers. Denunciations of neighbors were frequent and frequently well rewarded. So taking in a Jewish family or even a Jewish child involved grave risks, especially since there was no way of telling how long those risks would last. A week? A year? A lifetime?

I know a young Jewish woman from a Polish village who lived through the whole ordeal in a tiny, lightless attic. And a man who hid crouching in a wardrobe for months. And a little boy who was shut up in a stable. And newlyweds who lost their youth in an underground hideout.

How could the owners of these refuges be sure that their attics, cellars, stables, would not be inspected? Or that some neighbor would not notice odd, suspicious noises? Like the victims, the Just lived alone, always on the lookout. They could not rely on their environment, or on any clandestine resistance movement. Siding with the victims, they themselves came under the same pressures; came to know fear and trembling. But they also came to know the dignity of accepted sacrifice.

That having been said, it should also be noted that the choice to side with humanity was relatively easy. You didn't have to be either heroic or insane to take pity on an abandoned child. It was enough to open a door, to offer a piece of paper, or bread. It was enough to look, to listen, to shudder at the sight of so much misery, so much pain.

Indeed, in order to be "Just" in those days, in order to attain the pinnacle of humanity in those days, it was enough simply to *remain human*.

Who were the Just? Ordinary people for the most part: priests and nuns, farmers and workers, doctors and storekeepers, artisans and schoolteachers. Not many celebrities among them—in fact, none at all. And all the Just have insisted they didn't regard themselves as heroes. To hear them tell it, they merely acted like decent men and women who, to paraphrase De Gaulle, had a "certain idea" about humanity. "The law against the Bulgarian Jews would have endangered the Bulgarian people itself," Dimo Kazasov wrote to his prime minister in 1940.

"I have seen," Anton Schmidt wrote in his last letter to his family, "how 200–300 Jews were shot. I have seen how children were massacred . . . . By helping the Jews, I have simply acted as a human being who wished no one any harm."

If the Just were mostly common folk, what does this tell us about the elite? One answer can be found by examining the files of the famous "Plot of the Generals" to assassinate Hitler in July 1944. In reading over the papers, one discovers—not without a certain sadness—that the conspirators discussed strategy, politics and philosophy, but never the crimes their government and their army were committing against the Jews—crimes they could not have helped but know about. But these were generals. Anton Schmidt was only a corporal.

At Yad Vashem there are approximately 4500 names of the Just. Is this a great number? For so many countries? For six million victims?

Let us try to avoid extremes. Still, if these few Righteous Gentiles justify our faith in humanity, they should also, on another level, justify our suspicion of society. For one Oskar Schindler, how many collaborators were there? For one Anton Schmidt, how many volunteered for the S.S. brigades? For each charitable soul, how many "Smalcovniks"—those vile hooligans who scoured the streets of occupied cities looking for Jews with forged Aryan papers? For one Raoul Wallenberg, how many indifferent onlookers?

Are a few flashes of light enough to illuminate the darkness? Are a few courageous men and women enough to redeem a murderous universe? Where is the balance and what are the scales?

The mystery of Good certainly equals the mystery of Evil. The question is: are we talking about the same mystery?

DISCUSSION AND EXERCISES

1. Consider Alfred Kazin's "My Mother."
   a. Study Kazin's various descriptions of the light in the family kitchen and suggest how each image of light contributes to the mood in that section of the essay and to the effect of the light described in the final two paragraphs.
   b. If Kazin's actual topic is his mother, why do you think he begins with a mention of the kitchen and spends so much of the first two paragraphs focusing on objects in the room?
   c. What are the chief characteristics of Kazin's mother? Is the order in which he presents them important?
   d. How would you characterize the speaker in this essay?
   e. What purpose do the following items serve in the essay: Yiddish words and phrases, the collection boxes with Hebrew letters, the collection man, and the mourning?
   f. Study the last sentence of the essay: in saying "Alfred, see how beautiful!" what has Kazin's mother actually "drawn" for her son?
2. Consider Marshall's "The Poets in the Kitchen."
   a. Why do the women Marshall describes gather in the kitchen every day?
   b. What is the nature of the conversations the women have?
   c. How did these conversations shape Marshall's attitude toward language and her growth as an author?
   d. Try a freewriting exercise. Begin by completing this sentence: "I grew up among. . . ."

Continued

3. Consider "Uncle Bun" by Maxine Hong Kingston.
   a. Describe what was likeable about Uncle Bun. What was not likeable?
   b. What did he bring of value to the Hong family? What harm did he do?
   c. Can you identify Kingston's feelings about her uncle from the tone of the piece? Explain.
   d. Make a list of Uncle Bun's physical characteristics.
   e. Make a list of his opinions.
   f. How did the children's attitudes toward Uncle Bun differ from their parents' attitudes? How were they the same?
   g. In your opinion, is someone like Uncle Bun worth listening to? Why or why not?
   h. How do you feel about Uncle Bun by the end of the piece? About the parents? Were they justified in rejecting him? Did they have cause for alarm? Explain.
   i. "We never saw him or heard from him again," Kingston tells us. What might have happened to Uncle Bun in China?
   j. In what way does the short epilogue between Kingston and her sister enhance the narrative which frames this portrait?

4. Consider the portrait, "Sylvia Plath: A Short Life."
   a. How does Katinka Matson weave together the facts of Plath's life and Plath's emotional responses to the facts?
   b. In what ways is this technique of allowing Plath essentially to "speak for herself" effective?
   c. What contrasts do you note between Plath's outward appearance and her inner turmoil?
   d. Why was she called "a category unto herself"?
   e. Characterize her feelings about her father. Love and/or hate? What evidence that reveals her feelings do you find in her poems? What was her attitude toward her mother? Do you note signs of affection? Resentment? What evidence does the author give us in the essay?
   f. When did Plath begin to feel "something was wrong"? Discuss points of contrast between what she was doing and what she was feeling.
   g. What metaphors does Plath use to describe happiness and unhappiness?
   h. What evidence does Matson provide for Sylvia Plath's progression toward suicide? Documented facts? Poems? Letters? Other?

5. Consider Russell Baker's Mr. Fleagle.
   a. How does the word "prim" work in describing him? Does the repetition of this word detract from or enhance the description? What is Baker's tone? Does it tend to make the reader dismiss Mr. Fleagle or become more interested in him? What does the expression "don't you see?" reveal of Mr. Prim's character?
   b. What words convey Baker's boredom with English and the writing of essays? What words convey his excitement upon discovering a topic that stimulated him? For whom did he write his essay? Why was the writing of it so important to him? What feelings did it bring back? What memories? Why was he willing to take a chance on violating the rules of formal composition?

   c. Compare Baker's feelings before and after the reading of his essay aloud in class. What had he expected from Fleagle when he turned in the paper? What were his feelings when his words were read? What was the class's response? What was Mr. Fleagle's response? What power did Baker find in the words he had written? What difference did it make in his life? What caused him to rank Mr. Fleagle among "the finest teachers in the school"?

   d. List the subquestions you see "at work" in this portrait.

6. Look carefully at the portrait below, noting such details as the posture of the woman, her quizzical (possibly mischievous) expression, the position of her hands, her wine glass, and other details. Who is she? What is she up to? Write a short character sketch.

7. Consider Elie Wiesel's "The Just."

   a. What is the effect of the sentence with which Wiesel begins his essay?

   b. Which of the vignettes that Wiesel provides do you find most memorable? What about that vignette makes it memorable to you?

   c. Why did the Just act as they did, according to Wiesel?

Continued

ESSAY SUGGESTIONS

1. Write an essay (750–1,000 words) in which you draw a portrait of a particular friend or relative. Try in prewriting to focus on one dominant quality that in your view characterizes the person (as "obsessiveness" characterizes Uncle Bun). Present your character in action, as Kazin does: i.e., set your character sketch within the frame of the narration.

2. Katinka Matson's anthology of "Short Lives: Portraits of Writers, Painters, Poets, Actors, Musicians, and Performers in Pursuit of Death" includes the following prominent people who died young:

> F. Scott Fitzgerald
> Jack Kerouac
> Marilyn Monroe
> Vincent Van Gogh
> Anne Sexton
> Billie Holiday
> Montgomery Clift
> James Dean
> Janis Joplin
> Edgar Allan Poe
> Simone Weil

Select one of the above (or a comparable character of your own choosing) and compose a "portrait" of 750–1,000 words, using documented facts and quotes drawn from outside sources. This is an opportunity to practice incorporating research notes into a finished piece.

3. Write an essay (750–1,000 words) about a teacher who influenced you in some positive way and possibly changed the direction of your life—or a teacher whose influence was memorable but *negative*.

4. Choose one of the "types" listed below and write an essay (750–1,000 words) that "interprets" the type—as Goodman interprets, as well as describes, the company man.

> the genius
> the generous soul
> the hypocrite
> the rebel
> the devil-may-care person
> the perfect angel
> the complainer
> the hero/heroine
> the flirt
> the loner
> the reliable hand

5. Expand the character sketch (based on the photo on page 157) into a 500–750 word portrait.

Question

4

WHAT IS MY
MEMORY OF X?

THE QUALITY OF MEMORY
    THE QUALITY OF MEMORY, THOMAS WOLFE

EARLIEST MEMORIES
    EVERYTHING HAS A NAME, HELEN KELLER

REMEMBERING PLACE
    VILLAGE HOME, SUBHABRATA BAPI SEN

REMEMBERING EVENTS
    DEATH OF A PIG, E. B. WHITE

THE PURPOSE OF MEMORY
    SIFTING THROUGH THE EVIDENCE,
    PAUL MONETTE

"It is necessary to remember and necessary to forget, but it is better for a writer to remember." So said William Saroyan in a truism worth repeating, for it points to a large body of literature built upon "remembrance of things past."

THE QUALITY OF MEMORY

No writer had a more prodigious memory than Thomas Wolfe (1900–1938), whose novels are distinguished by his genius for conjuring up sense impressions from the past: sounds, sights, odors, colors, shapes—the very texture of experience reexperienced in memory. In a remarkable and revealing account of his creative process, Wolfe described the compulsive memory which, with its shattering intensity, drove him "night and day."

The Quality of Memory

Thomas Wolfe

The quality of my memory is characterized, I believe, in a more than ordinary degree by the intensity of its sense impressions, its power to evoke and bring back the odors, sounds, colors, shapes, and feel of things with concrete vividness. Now [during a summer in Paris] my memory was at work night and day, in a way that I could at first neither check nor control and that swarmed unbidden in a stream of blazing pageantry across my mind, with the million forms and substances of the life that I had left, which was my own, America. I would be sitting, for example, on the terrace of a cafe watching the flash and play of life before me on the Avenue de l'Opéra and suddenly I would remember the iron railing that goes along the boardwalk at Atlantic City. I could see it instantly just the way it was, the heavy iron pipe; its raw galvanized look; the way the joints were fitted together. It was all so vivid and concrete that I could feel my hand upon it and know the exact dimensions, its size and weight and shape. And suddenly I would realize that I had never seen any railing that looked like this in Europe. And this utterly familiar, common thing would suddenly be revealed to me with all the wonder with which we discover a thing which we have seen all our life and yet have never known before. Or again, it would be a bridge, the look of an old iron bridge across an American river, the sound the train makes as it goes across it; the spoke-and-hollow rumble of the ties below; the look of the muddy banks; the slow, thick, yellow wash of an American river; an old flat-bottomed boat half filled with water stogged in the muddy bank; or it would be, most lonely and haunting of all the sounds I know, the sound of a milk wagon as it entered an American street just at the first gray of the morning, the slow and lonely clopping of the hoof upon the street, the jink of bottles, the sudden rattle of a battered old milk can, the swift and hurried footsteps of the milkman, and again the jink of bottles, a low word spoken to his horse, and then the great, slow clopping hoof receding into silence, and then quietness and a bird song rising in the street again. Or it would be a little wooden shed out in the country two miles from my home town where people waited for the street car, and I could see and feel again the dull and rusty color of the old green paint and see and feel all of the initials that had been carved out with jackknives on the planks and benches within the shed, and smell the warm and sultry smell so resinous and so thrilling, so filled with a strange and nameless excitement of unknown joy, a coming prophecy, and hear the street car as it came to a stop, the moment of brooding, drowzing silence; a hot thrum and drowsy stitch at three o'clock; the smell of grass and hot sweet clover; and then the sudden sense of absence, loneliness and departure when the street car had gone and there was nothing but the hot and drowsy stitch at three o'clock again.

Or again, it would be an American street with all its jumble of a thousand ugly architectures. It would be Montague Street or Fulton Street in Brooklyn, or Eleventh Street in New York, or other streets where I had lived; and suddenly I would see the gaunt and savage webbing of the elevated structure along Fulton Street, and how the light swarmed through in dusty, broken bars, and I could remember the old, familiar rusty color, that incomparable rusty color that gets into so many things here in America.

Wolfe's memory was, of course, a phenomenon. He is quoted here simply to indicate the extent of an ability that all of us possess to some degree. Most of us can *remember*, in other words, but only vaguely and in snatches. Images do not ordinarily loom up on their own, "in a stream of blazing pageantry." If we ask ourselves the question, What is my memory of X? we must make a conscious and sustained effort to recover the past. It is not waiting on the surface of the mind, ready to be recalled in all its original concreteness and intensity.

Even so, those of us with a less natural endowment than Wolfe's can, by probing and pondering and digging beneath the surface layers of consciousness, recapture scattered episodes and experiences from the past. For they are still *there,* fixed in the memory and capable of being conjured up through such prewriting strategies as freewriting, brainstorming, and clustering.

EARLIEST MEMORIES

In this justifiably famous passage from her autobiography, Helen Keller captures that singular moment in her childhood when she discovered the power of language. Nearly seven years old at the time—blind, deaf, and mute—Keller would never forget that awesome marvel. Nor can we, after reading her account, written in her later years when she had become a noted author, educator, and lecturer. By describing a series of sensations—the warmth of sun on her face, the texture of familiar leaves, the bustle in the house, and her anxiety at someone's approach—she draws us into her account, makes us feel we are there with her, startled as she is by her isolation and vulnerability.

The arrival of teacher Ann Mansfield Sullivan changes her life, for as Keller tells us, Sullivan came "to reveal all things to me, and, more than all things else, to love me." Had Keller not felt love before? We can only wonder. Perhaps she simply needed a word for love before she could know she was feeling it.

Not until Keller feels the chill of bubbling water on her hand—while Sullivan signs w-a-t-e-r on her other hand—does Keller discover the power of language to name phenomena and, as she puts, to unleash her "soul." With that revelation, Keller grasps the capacity of language to make "the world blossom" for: "each new name gave birth to a new thought."

Everything Has a Name

Helen Keller

The most important day I remember in all my life is the one on which my teacher, Anne Mansfield Sullivan, came to me. I am filled with wonder when I consider the immeasurable contrast between the two lives which it connects. It was the third of March, 1887, three months before I was seven years old.

On the afternoon of that eventful day, I stood on the porch, dumb, expectant. I guessed vaguely from my mother's signs and from the hurrying to and fro in the house that something unusual was about to happen, so I went to the door and waited on the steps. The afternoon sun penetrated the mass of honeysuckle that covered the porch, and fell on my upturned face. My fingers lingered almost unconsciously on the familiar leaves and blossoms which had just come forth to greet the sweet southern spring. I did not know what the future held of marvel or surprise for me. Anger and bitterness had preyed upon me continually for weeks and a deep languor had succeeded this passionate struggle.

Have you ever been at sea in a dense fog, when it seemed as if a tangible white darkness shut you in, and the great ship, tense and anxious, groped her way toward the shore with plummet and sounding-line, and you waited with beating heart for something to happen? I was like that ship before my education began, only I was without compass or sounding-line and had no way of knowing how near the harbour was. "Light! give light!" was the wordless cry of my soul, and the light of love shone on me in that very hour.

I felt approaching footsteps. I stretched out my hand as I supposed to my mother. Some one took it, and I was caught up and held close in the arms of her who had come to reveal all things to me, and, more than all things else, to love me.

The morning after my teacher came she led me into her room and gave me a doll. The little blind children at the Perkins Institution had sent it and Laura Bridgman [the first deaf and blind person to be educated in the United States] had dressed it; but I did not know this until afterward. When I had played with it a little while, Miss Sullivan slowly spelled into my hand the word "d-o-l-l." I was at once interested in this finger play and tried to imitate it. When I finally succeeded in making the letters correctly I was flushed with childish pleasure and pride. Running downstairs to my mother I held up my hand and made the letters for doll. I did not know that I was spelling a word or even that words existed; I was simply making my fingers go in monkey-like imitation. In the days that followed I learned to spell in this uncomprehending way a great many words, among them *pin, hat, cup,* and a few verbs like *sit, stand* and *walk.* But my teacher had been with me several weeks before I understood that everything has a name.

One day, while I was playing with my new doll, Miss Sullivan put my big rag doll into my lap also, spelled "d-o-l-l" and tried to make me understand that "d-o-l-l" applied to both. Earlier in the day we had had a tussle over the words "m-u-g" and "w-a-t-e-r." Miss Sullivan had tried to impress it upon me that "m-u-g" is *mug* and that "w-a-t-e-r" is *water,* but I persisted in confounding the two. In despair she had dropped the subject for the time, only to renew it at the first opportunity. I became impatient at her repeated attempts and, seizing the new doll, I dashed it upon the floor. I was keenly delighted when I felt the fragments of the broken doll at my feet. Neither sorrow nor regret followed my passionate outburst. I had not loved the doll. In the still, dark world in which I lived there was no strong sentiment or tenderness. I felt my teacher sweep the fragments to one side of the hearth, and I had a sense of satisfaction that the cause of my discomfort was removed. She brought me my hat, and I knew I was going out into the warm sunshine. This thought, if a wordless sensation may be called a thought, made me hop and skip with pleasure.

We walked down the path to the well-house, attracted by the fragrance of the honeysuckle with which it was covered. Someone was drawing water and my teacher placed my hand under the spout. As the cool stream gushed over one hand she spelled into the other the word *water*, first slowly, then rapidly. I stood still, my whole attention fixed upon the motions of her fingers. Suddenly I felt a misty consciousness as of something forgotten—a thrill of returning thought; and somehow the mystery of language was revealed to me. I knew then that "w-a-t-e-r" meant the wonderful cool something that was flowing over my hand. That living word awakened my soul, gave it light, hope, joy, set it free! There were barriers still, it is true, but barriers that could in time be swept away.

I left the well-house eager to learn. Everything had a name, and each name gave birth to a new thought. As we returned to the house every object which I touched seemed to quiver with life. That was because I saw everything with the strange, new sight that had come to me. On entering the door I remembered the doll I had broken. I felt my way to the hearth and picked up the pieces. I tried vainly to put them together. Then my eyes filled with tears; for I realized what I had done, and for the first time I felt repentance and sorrow.

I learned a great many new words that day. I do not remember what they all were; but I do know that *mother, father, sister, teacher* were among them—words that were to make the world blossom for me, "like Aaron's rod, with flowers." It would have been difficult to find a happier child than I was as I lay in my crib at the close of that eventful day and lived over the joys it had brought me, and for the first time longed for a new day to come.

REMEMBERING PLACES

Next to people, places generally fix themselves most firmly in the mind, especially in the child's mind. Is there anyone, for example, who does not have clear memories associated with that most impressionable period of life, that central experience of childhood—going to school? Note that in the essay that follows, Subhabrata Sen—like Helen Keller—chooses a judicious, yet ample array, of details to convey his memory of a childhood vacation spot in India. In this essay, written for a university composition course, Sen organizes details from several summers into a chronological account of a typical week with his father and brothers in the village of Gaighata. Though we are probably safe in assuming that no single summer vacation week contained all of these memories, by creating this memory of a typical week, Sen conveys the truth of these weeks more accurately than any newspaper or diary could. Notice how Sen weaves together immediate details from his memory with reflective comments drawn from the perspective of his older self.

Village Home

Subhabrata Bapi Sen

The most memorable times of my boyhood years were spent in a small village, usually for a week every summer. This village, called Gaighata, was situated about sixty miles (not much of a distance for modern roadways and fast cars) outside of my home town, Calcutta, the capital city of West Bengal. During my early years, there were no highways in West Bengal and the cost of cars, especially gasoline, was out of most peoples' reach; therefore, we relied entirely on public transportation for going there. In fact, the charm of this place started with the process of getting there, a journey filled with five hours of excitement.

At first we took a local train, which went initially through a densely populated suburb of Calcutta (physically ugly but a curious experience for someone with a relatively affluent life style), then slowly moved on through the green paddy fields, stopping at uncountable small stations, and finally after two hours arrived at a big railway-junction station named Habra. At Habra we promptly went for lunch in my father's favorite sweet shop, which was reputed to be the best cottage cheese–sweet maker in the entire West Bengal. After a sumptuous lunch, we stocked up for the week, as always, to compensate for the make-shift cook who was more interested in the stories of the city boys than in his culinary activities.

The highlight of the trip was the last nine miles, Habra to Gaighata, which we covered using two bicycle-pulled rikshas, I and my brother Bani occupying one, typically, and my father and youngest brother occupying the other. We always had a race going between our two rikshas in which we cheered the riksha drivers who pedaled harder and harder, even against gusty winds, propelling the three-wheelers to a speed that could not have been checked even if the need arose. Suffice it to say that my father did not like this racing, though he did not dampen our excitement; however, he worried, especially when the rikshas had to move to the shoulder as huge overloaded buses, with people literally hanging out, stormed by us. However, for us brothers, this was the climax of our adventure. After two hours of racing on this narrow Grand Tank (GT) road, built around 800 A.D., we would arrive at our tiny cottage with the thatched roof, surrounded by a huge garden—a welcome departure from our home in Calcutta.

The caretaker always had the cottage (usually locked up for most of the year) ready and meticulously cleaned, and always welcomed us to this idyllic, slow moving, friendly and warm village setting. My father used this place as an outlet for his idealistic dreams: He started a secondary school for the local boys and a free clinic for the poor. He built a small mill so that farmers could mill the rice from their paddies, and flour from their crops of wheat. He cultivated varieties of fruit trees extending an already-existing large collection of mango trees; and he experimented with high-yield rice cultivation using Japanese techniques. The ventures were a drain on our family income, so much so that my mother disliked this place and never even came to this childhood oasis of mine.

Our property was a charming piece of land, long and narrow, with the GT road that connected Calcutta to a major trading post in East Pakistan (now Bangladesh) in the front and a winding river at the back. Besides the small cottage, there was an office building with a big grain-storage facility; a mill house with a corrugated-tin sheet roof by the river where villagers came by boat to mill their crops, and quite often obliged us with short rides; a gigantic concrete open floor for drying the boiled paddies (we found to be an excellent place for playing cricket); and finally a very mysterious big tomb in a remote corner (the burial tomb of the previous owner's wife), which always aroused our curiosity, however, unknown fear (I cannot fathom even today) prevented us from going near there.

As my father got busy with his employees on various projects, the three of us could essentially direct our own daily activities. We would have our early morning refreshing juice (usually fermented into a country liquor if not consumed or thickened by the evening) directly from the earthen pitcher that the gardener had hung from the date tree (a type of palm) the previous day. Both our breakfast and lunch consisted of different types of mangoes, eaten while obtaining them from the high branches of various trees. Around noon, we always spent a long time swimming in the river, racing with the local boys, which sometimes put us in the middle of an undercurrent, an experience that is hard to forget. In the afternoon, we would go to the nearby school that my father helped restart to chat with a few teachers who were working on a special project during summer. Before dusk, we sometimes played with the local soccer team in their field, directly on the other side of the road from our house.

With darkness, life got a bit boring since there was no electricity, no variety in the dinner despite our cook's best effort, and no mother. However, we managed to distract our attention by playing games using the light from the lantern, and always went to bed early so we could start our adventure at the crack of dawn.

Only on Wednesday, you could shop in this village when farmers, poultry and dairy owners, artisans, and everyone who had something to sell, from far and near, displayed their goods in a field that usually lay empty all week. To my dismay, the little village almost turned into a city, though some of the produce, sweets, and especially the handmade toys were quite different from what we would find in Calcutta.

The day of return was always with mixed feelings. It was not easy to leave behind unlimited freedom and the constant opportunities for exploring the wide open fields, climbing the most complicated set of tree branches, riding a boat, or swimming the river full of undercurrents. At the same time, I was looking forward to a structured life, homey comforts, and especially to seeing my mother. We packed our things, including a big basket full of mangoes. And this time we went straight away by a bus that stopped in front of the cottage and brought us back to Calcutta.

REMEMBERING EVENTS

In "Death of a Pig," E. B. White proves that other people's memories can haunt us. Here White confronts—at times lightly, at times ruefully—the change in the very feel of life when a time-honored ritual unexpectedly and unaccountably goes awry. The "classical pattern of the tragedy"—in this case the annual purchase of a pig in springtime, its fattening in summer and fall, and its butchering in early winter—dissolves into slapstick and even farce as White meticulously, almost compulsively cares for the stricken animal.

One of White's chief rhetorical tools here is his "voice," a seemingly casual mixture of humor and self-deprecation. The humor is easy to detect in social observations ("there is in hostesses a special power of divination . . . they deliberately arrange dinners to coincide with pig failure"), hyperbole (his dachshund "would be bedridden if he could find anyone willing to serve him meals on a tray"); and situational comedy (the local operator's interruptions during a telephone call to the veterinarian and White's administering of an enema to the pig). Interestingly, both the comic relief and the tragic implications in this reminiscence stem from White's implicit comparison between his own malaise and the pig's. As White remembers with astonishing clarity, he was obviously overcome with the feeling that "the pig's lot and mine were inextricably bound." So it is that we too become involved in this pig's death, for the rich details White conjures up draw us inexorably into every scene of the unfolding event.

DEATH OF A PIG

E. B. White

I spent several days and nights in mid-September with an ailing pig and I feel driven to account for this stretch of time, more particularly since the pig died at last, and I lived, and things might easily have gone the other way round and none left to do the accounting. Even now, so close to the event, I cannot recall the hours sharply and am not ready to say whether death came on the third night or the fourth night. This uncertainty afflicts me with a sense of personal deterioration; if I were in decent health I would know how many nights I had sat up with a pig.

The scheme of buying a spring pig in blossomtime, feeding it through summer and fall, and butchering it when the solid cold weather arrives, is a familiar scheme to me and follows an antique pattern. It is a tragedy enacted on most farms with perfect fidelity to the original script. The murder, being premeditated, is in the first degree but is quick and skillful, and the smoked bacon and ham provide a ceremonial ending whose fitness is seldom questioned.

Once in a while something slips—one of the actors goes up in his lines and the whole performance stumbles and halts. My pig simply failed to show up for a meal. The alarm spread rapidly. The classic outline of the tragedy was lost. I found myself cast suddenly in the role of pig's friend and physician—a farcical character with an enema bag for a prop. I had a presentiment, the very first afternoon, that the play would never regain its balance and that my sympathies were now wholly with the pig. This was slapstick—the sort of dramatic treatment that instantly appealed to my old dachshund, Fred, who joined the vigil, held the bag, and, when all was over, presided at the interment. When we slid the body into the grave, we both were shaken to the core. The loss we felt was not the loss of ham but the loss of pig. He had evidently become precious to me, not that he represented a distant nourishment in a hungry time, but that he had suffered in a suffering world. But I'm running ahead of my story and shall have to go back.

My pigpen is at the bottom of an old orchard below the house. The pigs I have raised have lived in a faded building that once was an icehouse. There is a pleasant yard to move about in, shaded by an apple tree that overhangs the low rail fence. A pig couldn't ask for anything better—or none has, at any rate. The sawdust in the icehouse makes a comfortable bottom in which to root, and a warm bed. This sawdust, however, came under suspicion when the pig took sick. One of my neighbors said he thought the pig would have done better on new ground—the same principle that applies in planting potatoes. He said there might be something unhealthy about that sawdust, that he never thought well of sawdust.

It was about four o'clock in the afternoon when I first noticed that there was something wrong with the pig. He failed to appear at the trough for his supper, and when a pig (or a child) refuses supper a chill wave of fear runs through any household, or ice-household. After examining my pig, who was stretched out in the sawdust inside the building, I went to the phone and cranked it four times. Mr. Dameron answered. "What's good for a sick pig?" I asked. (There is never any identification needed on a country phone; the person on the other end knows who is talking by the sound of the voice and by the character of the question.)

"I don't know, I never had a sick pig," said Mr. Dameron, "but I can find out quick enough. You hang up and I'll call Henry."

Mr. Dameron was back on the line again in five minutes. "Henry says roll him over on his back and give him two ounces of castor oil or sweet oil, and if that doesn't do the trick give him an injection of soapy water. He says he's almost sure the pig's plugged up, and even if he's wrong, it can't do any harm."

I thanked Mr. Dameron. I didn't go right down to the pig, though. I sank into a chair and sat still for a few minutes to think about my troubles, and then I got up and went to the barn, catching up on some odds and ends that needed tending to. Unconsciously I held off, for an hour, the deed by which I would officially recognize the collapse of the performance of raising a pig; I wanted no interruption in the regularity of feeding, the steadiness of growth, the even succession of days. I wanted no interruption, wanted no oil, no deviation. I just wanted to keep on raising a pig, full meal after full meal, spring into summer into fall. I didn't even know whether there were two ounces of castor oil on the place.

Shortly after five o'clock I remembered that we had been invited out to dinner that night and realized that if I were to dose a pig there was no time to lose. The dinner date seemed a familiar conflict: I move in a desultory society and often a week or two will roll by without my going to anybody's house to dinner or anyone's coming to mine, but when an occasion does arise, and I am summoned, something usually turns up (an hour or two in advance) to make all human intercourse seem vastly inappropriate. I have come to believe that there is in hostesses a special power of divination, and that they deliberately arrange dinners to coincide with pig failure or some other sort of failure. At any rate, it was after five o'clock and I knew I could put off no longer the evil hour.

When my son and I arrived at the pigyard, armed with a small bottle of castor oil and a length of clothesline, the pig had emerged from his house and was standing in the middle of his yard, listlessly. He gave us a slim greeting. I could see that he felt uncomfortable and uncertain. I had brought the clothesline thinking I'd have to tie him (the pig weighed more than a hundred pounds) but we never used it. My son reached down, grabbed both front legs, upset him quickly, and when he opened his mouth to scream I turned the oil into this throat—a pink, corrugated area I had never seen before. I had just time to read the label while the neck of the bottle was in his mouth. It said Puretest. The screams, slightly muffled by oil, were pitched in the hysterically high range of pig-sound, as though torture were being carried out, but they didn't last long: it was all over rather suddenly, and his legs released, the pig righted himself.

In the upset position the corners of his mouth had been turned down, giving him a frowning expression. Back on his feet again, he regained the set smile that a pig wears even in sickness. He stood his ground, sucking slightly at the residue of oil; a few drops leaked out of his lips while his wicked eyes, shaded by their coy little lashes, turned on me in disgust and hatred. I scratched him gently with oily fingers and he remained quiet, as though trying to recall the satisfaction of being scratched when in health, and seeming to rehearse in his mind the indignity to which he had just been subjected. I noticed, as I stood there, four or five small dark spots on his back near the tail end, reddish brown in color, each about the size of a housefly. I could not make out what they were. They did not look troublesome but at the same time they did not look like mere surface bruises or chafe marks. Rather they seemed blemishes of internal origin. His stiff white bristles almost completely hid them and I had to part the bristles with my fingers to get a good look.

Several hours later, a few minutes before midnight, having dined well and at someone else's expense, I returned to the pighouse with a flashlight. The patient was asleep. Kneeling, I felt his ears (as you might put your hand on the forehead of a child) and they seemed cool, and then with the light made a careful examination of the yard and the house for sign that the oil had worked. I found none and went to bed.

We had been having an unseasonable spell of weather—hot, close days, with the fog shutting in every night, scaling for a few hours in midday, then creeping back again at dark, drifting in first over the trees on the point, then suddenly blowing across the fields, blotting out the world and taking possession of houses, men, and animals. Everyone kept hoping for a break, but the break failed to come. Next day was another hot one. I visited the pig before breakfast and tried to tempt him with a little milk in his trough. He just stared at it, while I made a sucking sound through my teeth to remind him of past pleasures of the feast. With very small, timid pigs, weanlings, this ruse is often quite successful and will encourage them to eat; but with a large, sick pig the ruse is senseless and the sound I made must have made him feel, if anything, more miserable. He not only did not crave food, he felt a positive revulsion to it. I found a place under the apple tree where he had vomited in the night.

At this point, although a depression had settled over me, I didn't suppose that I was going to lose my pig. From the lustiness of a healthy pig a man derives a feeling of personal lustiness; the stuff that goes into the trough and is received with such enthusiasm is an earnest of some later feast of his own, and when this suddenly comes to an end and the food lies stale and untouched, souring in the sun, the pig's imbalance becomes the man's, vicariously, and life seems insecure, displaced, transitory.

As my own spirits declined, along with the pig's, the spirits of my vile old dachshund rose. The frequency of our trips down the footpath through the orchard to the pigyard delighted him, although he suffers greatly from arthritis, moves with difficulty, and would be bedridden if he could find anyone willing to serve him meals on a tray.

He never missed a chance to visit the pig with me, and he made many professional calls on his own. You could see him down there at all hours, his white face parting the grass along the fence as he wobbled and stumbled about, his stethoscope dangling—a happy quack, writing his villainous prescriptions and grinning his corrosive grin. When the enema bag appeared, and the bucket of warm suds, his happiness was complete, and he managed to squeeze his enormous body between the two lowest rails of the yard and then assumed full charge of the irrigation. Once, when I lowered the bag to check the flow, he reached in and hurriedly drank a few mouthfuls of the suds to test their potency. I have noticed that Fred will feverishly consume any substance that is associated with trouble—the bitter flavor is to his liking. When the bag was above reach, he concentrated on the pig and was everywhere at once, a tower of strength and inconvenience. The pig, curiously enough, stood rather quietly through this colonic carnival, and the enema, though ineffective, was not as difficult as I had anticipated.

I discovered, though, that once having given a pig an enema there is no turning back, no chance of resuming one of life's more stereotyped roles. The pig's lot and mine were inextricably bound now, as though the rubber tube were the silver cord. From then until the time of his death I held the pig steadily in the bowl of my mind, the task of trying to deliver him from his misery became a strong obsession. His suffering soon became the embodiment of all earthly wretchedness. Along toward the end of the afternoon, defeated in physicking, I phoned the veterinary twenty miles away and placed the case formally in his hands. He was full of questions, and when I casually mentioned the dark spots on the pig's back, his voice changed its tone.

"I don't want to scare you," he said, "but when there are spots erysipelas has to be considered."

Together we considered erysipelas, with frequent interruption from the telephone operator, who wasn't sure the connection had been established.

"If a pig has erysipelas can he give it to a person?" I asked.

"Yes, he can," replied the vet.

"Have they answered?" asked the operator.

"Yes, they have," I said. Then I addressed the vet again. "You better come over here and examine this pig right away."

"I can't come myself," said the vet, "but McFarland can come this evening if that's all right. Mac knows more about pigs than I do anyway. You needn't worry too much about the spots. To indicate erysipelas they would have to be deep hemorrhagic infarcts."

"Deep hemorrhagic what?" I asked.

"Infarcts," said the vet.

"Have they answered?" asked the operator.

"Well," I said, "I don't know what you'd call these spots, except they're about the size of a housefly. If the pig has erysipelas I guess I have it, too, by this time, because we've been very close lately."

"McFarland will be over," said the vet.

I hung up. My throat felt dry and I went to the cupboard and got a bottle of whiskey. Deep hemorrhagic infarcts—the phrase began fastening its hooks in my head. I had assumed that there could be nothing much wrong with a pig during the months it was being groomed for murder; my confidence in the essential health and endurance of pigs had been strong and deep, particularly in the health of pigs that belonged to me and that were part of my proud scheme. The awakening had been violent and I minded it all the more because I knew that what could be true of my pig could be true also of the rest of my tidy world. I tried to put this distasteful idea from me, but it kept recurring. I took a short drink of the whiskey and then, although I wanted to go down to the yard and look for fresh signs, I was scared to. I was certain I had erysipelas.

It was long after dark and the supper dishes had been put away when a car drove in and McFarland got out. He had a girl with him. I could just make her out in the darkness—she seemed young and pretty. "This is Miss Owen," he said "We've been having a picnic supper on the shore, that's why I'm late."

McFarland stood in the driveway and stripped off his jacket, then his shirt. His stocky arms and capable hands showed up in my flashlight's gleam as I helped him find his coverall and get zipped up. The rear seat of his car contained an astonishing amount of paraphernalia, which he soon overhauled, selecting a chain, a syringe, a bottle of oil, a rubber tube, and some other things I couldn't identify. Miss Owen said she'd go along with us and see the pig. I led the way down the warm slope of the orchard, my light picking out the path for them, and we all three climbed the fence, entered the pighouse, and squatted by the pig while McFarland took a rectal reading. My flashlight picked up the glitter of an engagement ring on the girl's hand.

"No elevation," said McFarland, twisting the thermometer in the light. "You needn't worry about erysipelas." He ran his hand slowly over the pig's stomach and at one point the pig cried out in pain.

"Poor piggledy-wiggledy!" said Miss Owen.

The treatment I had been giving the pig for two days was then repeated, somewhat more expertly, by the doctor, Miss Owen and I handing him things as he needed them—holding the chain that he had looped around the pig's upper jaw, holding the syringe, holding the bottle stopper, the end of the tube, all of us working in darkness and in comfort, working with the instinctive teamwork induced by emergency conditions, the pig unprotesting, the house shadowy, protecting, intimate. I went to bed tired but with a feeling of relief that I had turned over part of the responsibility of the case to a licensed doctor. I was beginning to think, though, that the pig was not going to live.

He died twenty-four hours later, or it might have been forty-eight—there is a blur in time here, and I may have lost or picked up a day in the telling and the pig one in the dying. At intervals during the last day I took cool fresh water down to him and at such times as he found the strength to get to his feet he would stand with head in the pail and snuffle his snout around. He drank a few sips but no more; yet it seemed to comfort him to dip his nose in water and bobble it about, sucking in and blowing out through his teeth. Much of the time, now, he lay indoors half buried in sawdust. Once, near the last, while I was attending him I saw him try to make a bed for himself but he lacked the strength, and when he set his snout into the dust he was unable to plow even the little furrow he needed to lie down in.

He came out of the house to die. When I went down, before going to bed, he lay stretched in the yard a few feet from the door. I knelt, saw that he was dead, and left him there: his face had a mild look, expressive neither of deep peace nor of deep suffering, although I think he had suffered a good deal. I went back up the house and to bed, and cried internally—deep hemorrhagic tears. I didn't wake till nearly eight the next morning, and when I looked out the open window the grave was already being dug, down beyond the dump under a wild apple. I could hear the spade strike against the small rocks that blocked the way. Never send to know for whom the grave is dug, I said to myself, it's dug for thee. Fred, I well knew, was supervising the work of digging, so I ate breakfast slowly.

It was a Saturday morning. The thicket in which I found the gravediggers at work was dark and warm, the sky overcast. Here, among alders and young hackmatacks, at the foot of the apple tree, Lennie had dug a beautiful hole, five feet long, three feet wide, three feet deep. He was standing in it, removing the last spadefuls of earth while Fred patrolled the brink in simple but impressive circles, disturbing the loose earth of the mound so that it trickled back in. There had been no rain in weeks and the soil, even three feet down, was dry and powdery. As I stood and stared, an enormous earthworm which had been partially exposed by the spade at the bottom dug itself deeper and made a slow withdrawal, seeking even remoter moistures at even lonelier depths. And just as Lennie stepped out and rested his spade against the tree and lit a cigarette, a small green apple separated itself from a branch overhead and fell into the hole. Everything about this last scene seemed overwritten—the dismal sky, the shabby woods, the imminence of rain, the worm (legendary bedfellow of the dead), the apple (conventional garnish of a pig).

But even so, there was a directness and dispatch about animal burial, I thought, that made it a more decent affair than human burial: there was no stopover in the undertaker's foul parlor, no wreath nor spray; and when we hitched a line to the pig's hind legs and dragged him swiftly from his yard, throwing our weight into the harness and leaving a wake of crushed grass and smoothed rubble over the dump, ours was a businesslike procession, with Fred, the dishonorable pallbearer, staggering along in the rear, his perverse bereavement showing in every seam in his face; and the post-mortem performed handily and swiftly right at the edge of the grave, so that the innards that had caused the pig's death preceded him into the ground and he lay at last resting squarely on the cause of his own undoing.

I threw in the first shovelful, and then we worked rapidly and without talk, until the job was complete. I picked up the rope, made it fast to Fred's collar (he is a notorious ghoul), and we all three filed back up the path to the house, Fred bringing up the rear and holding back every inch of the way, feigning unusual stiffness. I noticed that although he weighed far less than the pig, he was harder to drag, being possessed of the vital spark.

The news of the death of my pig traveled fast and far, and I received many expressions of sympathy from friends and neighbors, for no one took the event lightly and the premature expiration of a pig is, I soon discovered, a departure which the community marks solemnly on its calendar, a sorrow in which it feels fully involved. I have written this account in penitence and in grief, as a man who failed to raise his pig, and to explain my deviation from the classic course of so many raised pigs. The grave in the woods is unmarked, but Fred can direct the mourner to it unerringly and with immense good will, and I know he and I shall often revisit it, singly and together, in seasons of reflection and despair, on flagless memorial days of our own choosing.

THE PURPOSE OF MEMORY

In this selection from the first part of his autobiography *Becoming a Man,* Paul Monette examines the purpose of memory. More specifically, he explains what his memories give him and why he feels they must be preserved. His reasons may surprise you, or even shock you. Faced with his own approaching death, Monette examines the memories of his life, looking for patterns of meaning, for right and wrong. Before he dies, he must get down his story so that others may recognize themselves: "But every memoir now is a kind of manifesto, as we piece together the tale of the tribe." The stories he will tell are important not just to his own identity, but to the identity of others who have shared some of his experiences.

What reasons would compel you to make such a record of your memories? Why does Monette feel it important that readers understand his reasons before going further into his autobiography?

SIFTING THROUGH THE EVIDENCE

Paul Monette

Everybody else had a childhood, for one thing—where they were coaxed and coached and taught all the shorthand. Or that's how it always seemed to me, eavesdropping my way through twenty-five years, filling in the stories of straight men's lives. First they had their shining boyhood, which made them strong and psyched them up for the leap across the chasm to adolescence, where the real rites of manhood began. I grilled them about it whenever I could, slipping the casual question in while I did their Latin homework for them, sprawled on the lawn at Andover under the reeling elms.

And every year they leaped further ahead, leaving me in the dust with all my doors closed, and each with a new and better deadbolt. Until I was twenty-five, I was the only man I knew who had no story at all. I'd long since accepted the fact that nothing had ever happened to me and nothing ever would. That's how the closet feels, once you've made your nest in it and learned to call it home. Self-pity becomes your oxygen.

I speak for no one else here, if only because I don't want to saddle the women and men of my tribe with the lead weight of my self-hatred, the particular doorless room of my internal exile. Yet I've come to learn that all our stories add up to the same imprisonment. The self-delusion of uniqueness. The festering pretense that we are the same as they are. The gutting of all our passions till we are a bunch of eunuchs, our zones of pleasure in enemy hands. Most of all, the ventriloquism, the learning how to pass for straight. Such obedient slaves we make, with such very tidy rooms.

Forty-six now and dying by inches, I finally see how our lives align at the core, if not in the sorry details. I still shiver with a kind of astonished delight when a gay brother or sister tells of that narrow escape from the coffin world of the closet. *Yes yes yes,* goes a voice in my head, *it was just like that for me.* When we laugh together then and dance in the giddy circle of freedom, we are children for real at last, because we have finally grown up. And every time we dance, our enemies writhe like the Witch in *Oz,* melting, melting—the Nazi Popes and all their brocaded minions, the rat-brain politicians, the wacko fundamentalists and their Book of Lies.

We may not win in the end, of course. Genocide is still the national sport of straight men, especially in this century of nightmares. And death by AIDS is everywhere around me, seething through the streets of this broken land. Last

September I buried another lover, Stephen Kolzak—died of homophobia, murdered by barbaric priests and petty bureaucrats. So whether or not I was ever a child is a matter of very small moment. But every memoir now is a kind of manifesto, as we piece together the tale of the tribe. Our stories have died with us long enough. We mean to leave behind some map, some key, for the gay and lesbian people who follow—that they may not drown in the lies, in the hate that pools and foams like pus on the carcass of America.

I don't come from the past, I come from now, here in the cauldron of plague. When the doors to the camps were finally beaten down, the Jews of Europe no longer came from Poland and Holland and France. They came from Auschwitz and Buchenwald. But I will never understand how the straights could have let us die like this—year after year after year, collaborating by indifference—except by sifting through the evidence of my queer journey.

Why do they hate us? Why do they fear us? Why do they want us invisible?

I don't trust my own answers anymore. I'm too twisted up with rage, too hooked on the millennium. But I find myself combing the past these days, dreaming dreams without sleep, puzzling over my guys, the gay and the straight and the in-between. Somewhere in there is a horror of love, and to try to kill the beast in them, they take it out on us. Which is not to say I don't chastise myself for halving the world into *us* and *them*. I know that the good guys aren't all gay, or the bad all straight. That is what I am sifting for, to know what a man is finally, no matter the tribe or gender.

Put it this way. A month after Stevie died, running from grief, I drove three days through Normandy. In the crystalline October light I walked the beach at Omaha, scoped the landing from a German bunker, then headed up the pasture bluff to the white field of American crosses. American soil in fact, this ocean graveyard, unpolluted even by the SS visit of Reagan in '84, who couldn't tell the difference between the dead here and the dead at Bitburg. You can't do Normandy without D-Day. After Omaha, the carnage and heroism shimmer across the pastureland, ghosts of the soldiers who freed the world of evil for a while.

Two days later I fetched up in Caen, where they've built a Museum of Peace on the site of an eighty-day battle fought by three million men. Newsreel footage and camp uniforms, ration books, code breakers, yellow star and pink triangle. You watch it all happen like a slow bomb, from the end of World War I, the dementia of power, till the smithereens are in smithereens. You walk numbly from year to year, country to country, helpless as a Jew or a Gypsy or a queer.

And in the belly of the place there's this extraordinary room lined with pictures on either side. On the right are the collaborators, men—all men, of course—who ran the puppet governments for the Nazis. Vichy and Belgium and Denmark, the whole of Europe ruled by fawning men with dead eyes and fat ties, grins that show the gristle between their teeth. On the left wall, opposite, are the leaders of the Resistance—several women here—and they're lean and defiant and *alive*. Europe is in prison and the world is imploding, and these people are smiling because they can't lose.

So that is what I am doing in the past, figuring out who goes on the left wall and who on the right. For that is the choice, it seems to me: collaborate or resist. The left wall is not all gay and lesbian, and not everyone is out of the closet. I can't judge the world of my first twenty years by the laws of freedom that followed

Stonewall. No man was the same after that. And I understand that every ethics—the gods I don't believe in and the wise men I do—tells me to forgive. But if that is what I have to do, I will have to learn not to forget first; to let in the light on the last attic room, the bones of a buried life.

It isn't all mine anyway—neither the lost years nor the victory—this tale of a boy who made it out of the woods. For I am the final gleam of Roger and Stephen as well, the two men I am surest of, who willed their stories to me. We couldn't have met each other anywhere but out in the open. As to whether being in the closet puts you on the wrong wall, with the collaborators, that is for men and women to judge themselves. I can't conceive the hidden life anymore, don't think of it as life. When you finally come out, there's a pain that stops, and you know it will never hurt like that again, no matter how much you lose or how bad you die. This I know: Those who are still in the closet will get the tale wrong, however I tell it.

DISCUSSION AND EXERCISES

1. Consider Thomas Wolfe's "The Quality of Memory."
   a. Identify and comment on the sense impressions Wolfe describes.
   b. Evaluate the choice of words (nouns, verbs, adjectives).
   c. What special rhetorical devices (alliteration, repetition) contribute to the rhythm and momentum of Wolfe's sentences?

2. Review Helen Keller's "Everything Has a Name."
   a. Is Keller's simile of a fog-bound ship appropriate to the writing of a blind person?
   b. How do you account for its presence in the essay?
   c. How does Keller suggest the difference between knowing words and understanding language? Is the distinction important? Explain.
   d. What can we gather about the personality of Keller's teacher, Ann Sullivan? What details substantiate your portrait of her?
   e. In likening her now-blossoming world to "Aaron's rod," Keller refers to the Old Testament Pentateuch story of Moses and his brother. How is the comparison apt?
   f. Compare the second paragraph to the last two paragraphs. Do you see any similarities? Any differences? If so, what are they and how might they serve Keller's purpose?

3. Pair off with a friend or classmate and go on a "trust walk." Blindfold yourself carefully and have your friend lead you around an area either on campus or not far from where you live. Continue the walk for 20 minutes before returning to your starting place and removing your blindfold. Then write three paragraphs in which you recall the sensory details of your walk, how you felt, and what you learned from the experience.

4. Write a paragraph (150–250 words) describing a vivid memory of some past experience. Be sure to include concrete sensual detail (colors, shapes, sounds) so that you do not merely recount but evoke the experience. Be sure to begin prewriting with a cluster using "an early memory" as your nucleus words.

Continued

5. Examine the different paragraphs of Sen's "Village Home." What is the dominant image in each paragraph? What techniques does he use to create such images? Why does he order the paragraphs as he does? Try rearranging the paragraphs: what is lost? what is gained?

6. Try to simulate a creativity workshop with three or four other people, either in class (if the instructor suggests) or outside of class. Work together to trigger memories and excite recollections; write your impressions in a cluster or list them, whichever is more comfortable. Your cluster should begin like the one below and continue to radiate outward.

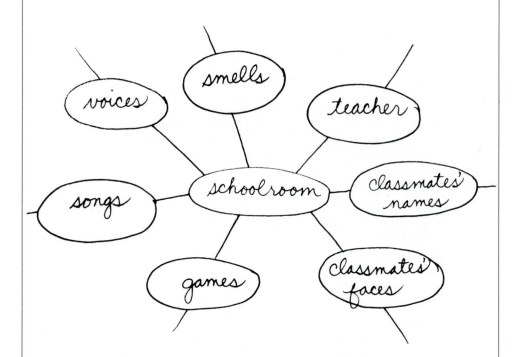

7. Study E.B. White's "Death of a Pig."
   a. What does the essay's opening sentence suggest about White's reasons for recounting this memory?
   b. White refers to "classic tragedy" and alludes throughout to other forms of drama. Find all the verbs, nouns, and adjectives that echo this metaphor. Why do you think White employed it?
   c. Speculate about White's reasons for mentioning his dachshund's condition and behavior. Indeed, what does Fred contribute to the essay?
   d. Cite specific incidents in which White follows that perennial piece of writer's wisdom, "show, don't tell." What does White thereby accomplish?

8. Consider Paul Monette's "Sifting Through the Evidence."
   a. What are the dominant images and memories that Monette provides here? Why do you think he chose them to use in this way?
   b. Why does Monette say that sharing stories makes gay people "children for real at last, because we have finally grown up"?
   c. What passages in the essay have the strongest sense of emotion? How does Monette create such a striking tone? How do you respond to that emotion?
   d. What is Monette's reason for writing his memoirs?
   e. Whom do you think Monette imagines as his audience? Is his intended audience primarily gay and lesbian? Can you identify passages that seem to envision a particular group of readers?

ESSAY SUGGESTIONS

1. Using Keller's "Everything Has a Name" as an example of an important early memory, describe an important memory of your own, one that generated some new awareness or perception. Start with a cluster or a freewriting exercise to develop a list of details; then write an essay (750–1,000 words) based on the exercise.

2. Write an essay (750–1,000 words) based on your "schoolroom" cluster.

3. Think about, E.B. White's "Death of a Pig"; then, write an essay (750–1,000 words) in commemoration of an animal that played an important role in your life.

4. Read Dylan Thomas's "A Child's Christmas in Wales" and write an essay (750–1,000 words) describing any holiday as you remember your family celebrating it. Be sure to begin prewriting with a cluster that uses the holiday as the nucleus term.

Question

5

WHAT IS MY PERSONAL RESPONSE TO X?

THE PERSONAL ESSAY
   AT THE DAM, JOAN DIDION

AN APPRECIATION
   CRAZY ABOUT WEATHER VANES,
      DAVID M. SCHWARTZ

A PERSONAL LETTER
   LETTER TO SARAH, SULLIVAN BALLOU

A PERSONAL RESPONSE TO A CURRENT ISSUE
   ERIN GO BRAWL, ANNA QUINDLEN

A PROTEST
   WHY I WANT A WIFE, JUDY SYFERS

One of the most common and popular types of writing is the personal essay, an informal, discursive piece in which you describe your response to some aspect of your surroundings: an object, situation, or event; a fleeting thought or observation; an emotional opinion or reaction. This type of essay is friendly, often intimate in tone. The writer, rather than the subject of the essay, is the main source of interest. Indeed, the success of your personal essay will depend primarily on your personality and the quality of your imagination. Are you sensitive and perceptive? Do you see things with a fresh eye and clear spirit? Do you respond in a recognizably human way? Can readers feel for you—and with you?

A good personal essay requires the writer to draw upon a composite of writing skills centered mainly on the ability to render experiences through vivid description and narration, believable characterization, and sharply evoked memory. The personal or "familiar" essay, as it was once called (for it places writer and reader on close or familiar terms) is not easy to write, but it is generally rewarding and may even be therapeutic. People need to "talk," to tell their secrets within the frame of a literary form. Here, then, is another human use of writing: through the personal essay people share experiences and thereby come to see the many ways in which they are both different and alike.

The personal essayist talks to us, then, as a friend, with no need to stand on ceremony. The essay itself is likely to be relaxed and loosely organized, usually brief and tentative in tone, for it is searching for answers, not giving them. The writer is sharing his or her thoughts with us; they may not even be rational thoughts—and the writer will freely admit this—as Joan Didion does in the following personal essay.

THE PERSONAL ESSAY

Joan Didion's essay, "At the Dam," draws heavily on description and memory to produce a highly personal response to a feature of the landscape that is—as Didion herself acknowledges—hardly worth reflecting on: "Dams, after all, are commonplace: we have all seen one." But this particular dam—Hoover Dam—has such a haunting quality that "its image," Didion says, "has never been entirely absent from my inner eye."

What is it about this dam, we wonder, that sets off such an intense response? We must turn to the essayist herself to find out.

At the Dam

Joan Didion

Since the afternoon in 1967 when I first saw Hoover Dam, its image has never been entirely absent from my inner eye. I will be talking to someone in Los Angeles, say, or New York, and suddenly the dam will materialize, its pristine concave face gleaming white against the harsh rusts and taupes and mauves of that rock canyon hundreds or thousands of miles from where I am. I will be driving down Sunset Boulevard, or about to enter a freeway, and abruptly those power transmission towers will appear before me, canted vertiginously over the tailrace. Sometimes I am confronted by the intakes and sometimes by the shadow of the heavy cable that spans the canyon and sometimes by the ominous outlets to unused spillways, black in the lunar clarity of the desert light. Quite often I hear the turbines.

Frequently I wonder what is happening at the dam this instant, at this precise intersection of time and space, how much water is being released to fill downstream orders and what lights are flashing and which generators are in full use and which just spinning free.

I used to wonder what it was about the dam that made me think of it at times and in places where I once thought of the Mindanao Trench, or of the stars wheeling in their courses, or of the words *As it was in the beginning, is now and ever shall be, world without end, amen.* Dams, after all, are commonplace: we have all seen one. This particular dam had existed as an idea in the world's mind for almost forty years before I saw it. Hoover Dam, showpiece of the Boulder Canyon project, the several million tons of concrete that made the Southwest plausible, the *fait accompli* that was to convey, in the innocent time of its construction, the notion that mankind's brightest promise lay in American engineering.

Of course the dam derives some of its emotional effect from precisely that aspect, that sense of being a monument to a faith since misplaced. "They died to make the desert bloom," reads a plaque dedicated to the 96 men who died building this first of the great high dams, and in context the worn phrase touches, suggests all of that trust in harnessing resources, in the meliorative power of the dynamo, so central to the early Thirties. Boulder City, built in 1931 as the construction town for the dam, retains the ambience of a model city, a new town, a toy triangular grid of green lawns and trim bungalows, all fanning out from the Reclamation building. The bronze sculptures at the dam itself evoke muscular citizens of a tomorrow that never came, sheaves of wheat clutched heavenward, thunderbolts defied. Winged Victories guard the flagpole. The flag whips in the canyon wind. An empty Pepsi-Cola can clatters across the terrazzo. The place is perfectly frozen in time.

But history does not explain it all, does not entirely suggest what makes that dam so affecting. Nor, even, does energy, the massive involvement with power and pressure and the transparent sexual overtones to that involvement. Once when I revisited the dam I walked through it with a man from the Bureau of Reclamation. For a while we trailed behind a guided tour, and then we went on, went into parts of the dam where visitors do not generally go. Once in a while he would explain something, usually in that recondite language having to do with "peaking power," with "outages" and "dewatering," but on the whole we spent the afternoon in a world so alien, so complete and so beautiful unto itself that it was scarcely necessary to speak at all. We saw almost no one. Cranes moved above us as if under their own violition. Generators roared. Transformers hummed. The gratings on which we stood vibrated. We watched a hundred-ton steel shaft plunging down to that place where the water was. And finally we got down to that place where the water was, where the water sucked out of Lake Mead roared through thirty-foot penstocks and then into thirteen-foot penstocks and finally into the turbines themselves. "Touch it," the Reclamation man said, and I did, and for a long time I just stood there with my hands on the turbine. It was a peculiar moment, but so explicit as to suggest nothing beyond itself.

There was something beyond all that, something beyond energy, beyond history, something I could not fix in my mind. When I came up from the dam that day the wind was blowing harder, through the canyon and all across the Mojave. Later, toward Henderson and Las Vegas, there would be dust blowing, blowing past the Country-Western Casino FRI & SAT NITES and blowing past the Shrine of Our Lady of Safe Journey STOP & PRAY, but out at the dam there was no dust, only the rock and the dam and a little greasewood and a few garbage cans, their tops chained, banging against a fence. I walked across the marble star map that traces a sidereal revolution of the equinox and fixes forever, the Reclamation man had told me, for all time and for all people who can read the stars, the date the dam was dedicated. The star map was, he had said, for when we were all gone and the dam was left. I had not thought much of it when he said it, but I thought of it then, with the wind whining and the sun dropping behind a mesa with the finality of a sunset in space. Of course that was the image I had seen always, seen it without quite realizing what I saw, a dynamo finally free of man, splendid at last in its absolute isolation, transmitting power and releasing water to a world where no one is.

AN APPRECIATION

Writing for a travel magazine, David Schwartz admits that punning friends tease him about being a "vane man" and about his "vane love affair." The light tone of his essay on weather vanes, which generates warmth and easy familiarity, issues partly from alliterative phrasing ("life list," "roof-top rotators," "personal pilgrimage") and partly from breezy commentary ("Now *there* was a man who liked to know which way the wind blew!").

Schwartz's summary of the history of weather vanes, the origin of the weather cock, and the evolution of various shapes gives us the factual aspects of the hobby (see Question 6: What Are the Facts about X?). His esoteric details link the shape of vanes to local geography or to the occupations or idiosyncrasies of their owners. The pleasures of the hobby are evident in Schwartz's description of such "worthy weather vanes" as the owl watching over Sterling Library on the Yale campus or such whimsical vanes as the stork delivering a baby, tennis players, or the three bears with their porridge bowls. By directing our attention to unusual

and enigmatic weather vanes, Schwartz suggests that weather vanes may have a deeper purpose than simply "to point to the wind." What that purpose may be is left to our imagination.

CRAZY ABOUT WEATHER VANES

David M. Schwartz

Some people return from vacation with a tally of exciting museums or sporting events or birds that they have seen. My boast is more apt to go something like this: two pigs, one leaping deer, a Viking ship, a single-prop plane and the Statue of Liberty. My close friends understand that I'm talking about weather vanes. I've been called a "vane man" and teased about having a "vane love affair," but no amount of banter will dissuade me from focusing on those lofty subjects. For me, the risks of driving with one eye on the road and the other cocked out the side windows at a 30-degree angle are justified by the pleasure of adding another weather vane to my life list.

Sometimes, the main reason for my trip is the pursuit of these rooftop rotators. Last year, for instance, I drove to Albany, New York, not to tour the State Capitol but to take a gander at America's oldest rooftop rooster. Still proud after more than 325 years, this weathercock is on display inside The First Church in Albany—a replica waves outside. Like Plymouth Rock, the vane itself is unimpressive, but its history made the trip a personal pilgrimage. In Boston, the famous copper grasshopper that has crowned Faneuil Hall since 1749 beckons me to adjacent Quincy Marketplace even more irresistibly than the wonderful food I can purchase there.

My most vivid memories of Mount Vernon and Monticello are of what's above the roof, not under it. George Washington's wind indicator is a dove of peace bearing an olive branch. Down at Monticello, Thomas Jefferson's simple banneret weather vane is a less compelling design, but it is rigged to an indoor dial that shows where it's pointing. Now *there* was a man who liked to know which way the wind blew!

On city streets and rural roads all over the country, the weather vane is waiting to be appreciated, as it has for centuries. Other than roosters (which date to a 10th-century papal decree intended to remind the faithful of Peter's treachery at cockcrow), most early weather vanes were heraldic flags or swallow-tailed banners cut from sheets of iron or copper. After the American Revolution, patriotic eagles took to the rooftops. Since an eagle in silhouette looks about as patriotic as a squashed pigeon, techniques for making outsize, three-dimensional vanes proliferated.

By the late 19th century, several companies specialized in the crafting of gold-leafed copper weather vanes that boldly depicted the achievements, pursuits and fantasies of the American people. Fire engines complete with crew and trailing dogs, locomotives belching smoke, steamboats, farm machinery, quill pens and flagpole acrobats are just a few of the popular ones. Tradesmen flew appropriate symbols on their places of business—an arm and hammer for a mechanic, an anvil above a blacksmith's shop, or a cleaver on a butcher's roof. And every conceivable creature on four legs, from horses to flame-spitting dragons, made an appearance against the sky.

Many of these old vanes still wave, and they are the ones usually responsible for my erratic driving when they appear unexpectedly at a bend in the road. As far as I'm concerned, no trip through the countryside can be considered memorable unless I score a fine fat ram or boar, or perhaps a trotter and sulky driven by whip-wielding jockey. Near the seacoast, I look for spouting whales and three-masted schooners, along with codfish, lobsters and breaching marlin.

On visits to ivy-covered campuses, I note not the number of books in the library, but the density of worthy weather vanes. Yale stands cap and tassel above the rest of the Ivy League. An elegant owl watches over the Sterling Library where, presumably, it imparts its wisdom to those who enter; a wrought-iron bishop's mitre swings atop Berkeley College in honor of Bishop Berkeley, for whom the college is named, and a sleek scull is rowed through the waves on a spire above the boathouse.

Impressive as the old vanes are, my favorites are the newer, more whimsical roof-toppers that have been designed to announce their owner's field or fancy. I have seen a stork delivering a baby on the roof of an obstetrician's residence and a backpacker leaning on his staff to advertise an outfitter's shop. A tennis player in full stretch and a smartly dressed lady with golf clubs leave little question as to their owner's pastimes.

But I can only wonder why the family occupying a certain farmhouse I once passed in Wisconsin decided to put up a vane showing the three bears holding their bowls of porridge. Or what possessed a Delaware resident to install a grinning man in the moon. When I see weather vanes like those, or magnificent works of art like the butterfly with stained-glass wings that perches proudly on a cupola in Middlebury, Connecticut, I have a hard time remembering that the purpose of these rotating devices was once solely to point into the wind.

A PERSONAL LETTER

Extreme circumstances—illness, physical suffering, war—can sometimes reduce our view of human life to its essential elements and help us sort out the things that are truly important to us. The following letter, written by Civil War soldier Sullivan Ballou to his wife Sarah, offers his personal response to an impending battle. Rather than give a list of recent troop movements or speculate on military strategy or complain about the rigors of army life, Ballou speaks from the heart about his fears and hopes for the future.

Letter to Sarah

Sullivan Ballou

July 14, 1861
Camp Clark, Washington

My very dear Sarah:

The indications are very strong that we shall move in a few days—perhaps tomorrow. Lest I should not be able to write again, I feel impelled to write a few lines that may fall under your eye when I shall be no more. . . .

I have no misgivings about, or lack of confidence in the cause in which I am engaged, and my courage does not halt or falter. I know how strongly American Civilization now leans on the triumph of the Government, and how great a debt we owe to those who went before us through the blood and sufferings of the Revolution. And I am willing—perfectly willing—to lay down all my joys in this life, to help maintain this Government, and to pay that debt. . . .

Sarah my love for you is deathless, it seems to bind me with mighty cables that nothing but Omnipotence could break; and yet my love of Country comes over me like a strong wind and bears me unresistibly on with all these chains to the battle field.

The memories of the blissful moments I have spent with you come creeping over me, and I feel most gratified to God and to you that I have enjoyed them so long. And hard it is for me to give them up and burn to ashes the hopes of future years, when, God willing, we might still have lived and loved together, and seen our sons grown up to honorable manhood, around us. I have, I know, but few and small claims upon Divine Providence, but something whispers to me—perhaps it is the wafted prayer of my little Edgar, that I shall return to my loved ones unharmed. If I do not my dear Sarah, never forget how much I love you, and when my last breath escapes me on the battle field, it will whisper your name. Forgive my many faults, and the many pains I have caused you. How thoughtless and foolish I have often times been! How gladly would I wash out with my tears every little spot upon your happiness. . . .

But, O Sarah! if the dead can come back to this earth and flit unseen around those they loved, I shall always be near you; in the gladdest days and in the darkest nights . . . *always, always,* and if there be a soft breeze upon your cheek, it shall be my breath, as the cool air fans your throbbing temple, it shall be my spirit passing by. Sarah do not mourn me dead; think I am gone and wait for thee, for we shall meet again. . . .

Like many historical documents, this one has a coda from real life: Sullivan Ballou was killed in the first battle of Bull Run.

A PERSONAL RESPONSE TO A CURRENT ISSUE

Newspaper columnists, such as Anna Quindlen of the *New York Times,* have as their task to reflect on and analyze the news of the day. They are expected to put their own personal spin on current events—that's what makes them (one hopes) interesting and readable. In writing about the controversy over a gay and lesbian club marching in New York's annual St. Patrick's Day parade, Quindlen responds personally—both as a supporter of gay rights and as a person proud of her Irish heritage.

It's tempting to dismiss an essay such as this by saying, "Well, it's only her opinion," and then adding, "And she's entitled to her opinion." The problem with this kind of response is that if we are each content to rest in the pool of our own indifference, we will never challenge or be challenged, never grow, never learn. A columnist like Anna Quindlen respects both the right to her opinion and the responsibility to defend it.

Erin Go Brawl

Anna Quindlen

I never felt entirely at home at St. Patrick's Day parades. As constituted by the Ancient Order of Hibernians—emphasis on the Ancient—they reminded me until recently of two perceptions of the Irish: as silver-haired civil servants redolent of Old Spice, and as intoxicated teenagers throwing up into the hedges of Central Park.

Neither of those is me, and I am Irish and proud of it. But then, both of those stereotypes have their limits. A woman was grand marshal of the parade not long ago, and the ranks are now filled with black and Latino children who attend the city's parochial schools. The parade has changed.

But not enough.

Ethnic stereotypes are misshapen pearls, sometimes with a sandy grain of truth at their center. It is true that my forebears were the folks for whom the paddy wagon was named, because of the number of them taken away drunk and disorderly on long-ago Saturday nights. The words Tammany Hall speak for themselves. We are storytellers, accomplished mourners, devout Catholics.

And we are none of these. Because all of them are stereotypes.

And now we are stereotyped as antediluvian bigots, because the Ancient Order of Hibernians—still Ancient—decided to deny the Irish Lesbian and Gay Organization permission to march in the parade. First the organization was told there was no room, which is a familiar line to anyone who has read the Christmas story.

Then, after the mayor said that room could be made, the addition to the parade was judged "impractical," which is familiar to anyone who has dealt with a bureaucracy and is a fancy way of saying "we don't want to."

Finally, the gay group was told that its members could march if they melted into other groups and did not carry their banner, which is a familiar request to all who have ever been forced to deny what they are, closeted by the will of the majority.

Ethnic stereotypes are sometimes based on observed behavior, but they ignore complexity, change, and individuality. My earliest perception of my countrymen was of people shaped by blighted potatoes and empty stomachs, people who held fast to what they had and so sometimes had a closed fist. Like many immigrant groups, they found contempt and hatred everywhere, and so they drew together, in neighborhoods, churches, fraternal organizations.

Some characteristics of the Irish I know and love have always seemed to me contradictory. Hail fellows well met, without being met at all. The unknowable extroverts. It is no accident that some have taken to professions that give the illusion of being among the people while remaining essentially separate. Newspapermen, who are of events but outside them. Politicos, who always stand apart in the crowd. Priests.

Stereotypes, of course. If you see it differently, I understand.

But understand that the stereotypes about gay people grow not from small knowledge inflated but from ignorance writ large. "No queers in the parade," people on Staten Island shouted at the mayor. These are the cries of those who don't know any gay people—or, more accurately, don't know they know any—and so create the bogeyman. Pederasts, drag queens, instead of the reality: the man at the next desk, the girl you went to high school with. Ordinary people who are gay. And Irish. And proud.

I can't imagine why those people want to march after what has happened. The A.O.H. has made a mess of this. When it barred gay people, there was the suspicion that it was reflecting the faith of its fathers, which considers homosexual acts sinful. But when it also barred a group of kids in wheelchairs—kids! in wheelchairs!—it appeared that it had forgotten that faith entirely. Hope those guys never get a chance to run Lourdes.

This is a parade that should belong to everyone. But they turned it into something that belongs to none of us, or at least none of us who have been stung by stereotype, none of us who were raised on the memory of the signs that said NO IRISH because all employers were sure the Irish were lazy and unreliable.

The members of the Ancient Order of Hibernians should remember those signs. They tried to hang a variation on Fifth Avenue this year. And in doing so they tarnished not the gay community but their own. Everything they've done stinks of stereotype, of the small-minded Irishman. For all of us who know that stereotypes exist to reduce understanding, not to enlarge it, I say they should be ashamed of themselves.

A PROTEST

The personal essay may also be a protest—a "sounding off" at something one finds objectionable. The following essay, now a classic, appeared first in the introductory issue of *Ms.* magazine. The writer, contemplating the countless duties and responsibilities of the "ideal" wife, decides ironically that—of course—she too would like a wife. Who wouldn't? Where else can anyone get so many multi-purpose services performed? By framing her personal essay in the form of casual analysis—a deadpan listing of the reasons *why* she'd like a wife—the writer transforms a seeming explanation into a subtle attack.

Why I Want a Wife

Judy Syfers

I belong to that classification of people known as wives. I am A Wife. And, not altogether incidentally, I am a mother.

Not too long ago a male friend of mine appeared on the scene fresh from a recent divorce. He had one child, who is, of course, with his ex-wife. He is looking for another wife. As I thought about him while I was ironing one evening, it suddenly occurred to me that I, too, would like to have a wife. Why do I want a wife?

I would like to go back to school so that I can become economically independent, support myself, and, if need be, support those dependent upon me. I want a wife who will work and send me to school. And while I am going to school I want a wife to take care of my children. I want a wife to keep track of the children's doctor and dentist appointments. And to keep track of mine, too. I want a wife to make sure my children eat properly and are kept clean. I want a wife who will wash the children's clothes and keep them mended. I want a wife who is a good nurturant attendant to my children, who arranges for their schooling, makes sure that they have an adequate social life with their peers, takes them to the park, the zoo, etc. I want a wife who takes care of the children when they are sick, a wife who arranges to be around when the children need special care, because, of course, I cannot miss classes at school. My wife must arrange to lose time at work and not lose the job. It may mean a small cut in my wife's income from time to time, but I guess I can tolerate that. Needless to say, my wife will arrange and pay for the care of the children while my wife is working.

I want a wife who will take care of *my* physical needs. I want a wife who will keep my house clean. A wife who will pick up after my children, a wife who will pick up after me. I want a wife who will keep my clothes clean, ironed, mended, replaced when need be, and who will see to it that my personal things are kept in their proper place so that I can find what I need the minute I need it. I want a wife who cooks the meals, a wife who is a *good* cook. I want a wife who will plan the menus, do the necessary grocery shopping, prepare the meals, serve them pleasantly, and then do the cleaning up while I do my studying. I want a wife who will care for me when I am sick and sympathize with my pain and loss of time from school. I want a wife to go along when our family takes a vacation so that someone can continue to care for me and my children when I need a rest and change of scene.

I want a wife who will not bother me with rambling complaints about a wife's duties. But I want a wife who will listen to me when I feel the need to explain a rather difficult point I have come across in my course of studies. And I want a wife who will type my papers for me when I have written them.

I want a wife who will take care of details of my social life. When my wife and I are invited out by my friends, I want a wife who will take care of the babysitting arrangements. When I meet people at school that I like and want to entertain, I want a wife who will have the house clean, will prepare a special meal, serve it to me and my friends, and not interrupt when I talk about things that interest me and my friends. I want a wife who will have arranged that the children are fed and ready for bed before my guests arrive so that the children do not bother us. I want a wife who takes care of the needs of my guests so that they feel comfortable, who makes sure that they have an ashtray, that they are passed the hors d'oeuvres, that they are offered a second helping of the food, that their wine glasses are replenished when necessary, that their coffee is served to them as they like it. And I want a wife who knows that sometimes I need a night out by myself.

I want a wife who is sensitive to my sexual needs, a wife who makes love passionately and eagerly when I feel like it, a wife who makes sure that I am satisfied. And, of course, I want a wife who will not demand sexual attention when I am not in the mood for it. I want a wife who assumes the complete responsibility for birth control, because I do not want more children. I want a wife who will remain sexually faithful to me so that I do not have to clutter up my intellectual life with jealousies. And I want a wife who understands that *my* sexual needs may entail more than strict adherence to monogamy. I must, after all, be able to relate to people as fully as possible.

If, by chance, I find another person more suitable as a wife than the wife I already have, I want the liberty to replace my present wife with another one. Naturally, I will expect a fresh, new life; my wife will take the children and be solely responsible for them so that I am left free.

When I am through with school and have a job, I want my wife to quit working and remain at home so that my wife can more fully and completely take care of a wife's duties.

My God, who *wouldn't* want a wife?

DISCUSSION AND EXERCISES

1. The effectiveness of a personal essay depends on the authenticity of the writer's voice. Does that voice speak in a natural rhythm that you can hear? Is it distinctively and recognizably the writer's own? Is a suitable tone established and maintained throughout the essay? How do you derive from this tone a sense of how the writer feels about his or her subject and how he or she wants you to feel? These are the questions you address in the personal essay. Since the writer is the unifying thread running through the piece, it is important that he or she play a clear and consistent role. Before attempting to write your own personal essays, it will be helpful to analyze those in this chapter so that you can see exactly how these writers have achieved those special effects that make their essays effective.

   a. In a sentence or two summarize the substance and what you believe to be the writer's purpose in each essay.

   b. In a sentence tell why you think the writer has or has not succeeded in achieving his or her purpose.

   c. In terms of the following rhetorical features, show how the writer establishes and maintains an attitude and tone of voice appropriate to the purpose of the essay.

      1. words

precision of nouns, verbs, adjectives	connotation
concreteness	repetition
levels of usage	sound

      2. sentences

         construction (word order, economy, emphasis, main and subordinate ideas)
         length
         variety
         rhythm and balance (use of parallelism, balanced antithesis)
         texture
         opening and closing sentences

      3. choice of examples and illustrations
      4. citing of authorities
      5. use of images
      6. use of figurative language
      7. use of irony
      8. use of allusions
      9. smoothness of transitions

2. William Hazlitt (1778–1830), an early master of the personal essay, recorded and defined its style as follows:

> It is not easy to write a familiar style. Many people mistake a familiar for a vulgar style, and suppose that to write without affectation is to write at random. On the contrary, there is nothing that requires more precision, and, if I may so say, purity of expression, than the style I am speaking of. It utterly rejects not only all unmeaning pomp, but all low, cant phrases, and loose, unconnected slipshod allusions. It is not to take the first word that offers, but the best word in common use; it is not to throw words together in any combinations we please, but to follow and avail ourselves of the true idiom of the language. To write a genuine familiar or truly English style, is to write as any one would speak in common conversation, who had a thorough command and choice of words, or who could discourse with ease, force and perspicuity, setting aside all pedantic and oratorical flourishes.

Comment on Hazlitt's description of the familiar style, explaining what is meant by the following terms:

a. familiar versus vulgar
b. unmeaning pomp
c. low, cant phrases
d. slipshod allusions
e. the true idiom of our language
f. ease, force, and perspicuity
g. pedantic and oratorical flourishes

3. Write a personal response (150-250 words) to a painting such as Edward Munch's "The Scream" or the picture of the Angel Gabriel weathervane.

4. Think of a place that has affected you deeply—as the Hoover Dam affected Joan Didion—and create a cluster using the name of the place as your nucleus word or phrase.

5. Look again at David Schwartz's "Crazy About Weather Vanes."
   a. When Schwartz likens America's oldest weathercock to Plymouth Rock and calls both "unimpressive," what is he saying about the nature of the two historic artifacts and the reasons for pilgrimages to see them?
   b. What purpose does Schwartz's digression into the history of weather vanes serve in paragraphs four and five?
   c. What accounts for Schwartz's greater pleasure with the newer vanes?
   d. Study Schwartz's first two sentences. How do they draw the reader into the essay?
   e. Study the structure of the following four sentences:

   (paragraph 2) "I drove to Albany, New York, not to tour the State Capitol but to gander at America's oldest rooftop rooster."

   (paragraph 3) "My most vivid memories of Mount Vernon and Monticello are of what's above the roof, not under it."

   (paragraph 7) "On visits to ivy-covered campuses, I note not the number of books in the library, but the density of worthy weather vanes."

Continued

(paragraph 8) "Impressive as the old vanes are, my favorites are the newer, more whimsical roof-toppers that have been designed to announce their owner's field or fancy."

What do the sentences have in common?

6. Refer again to Sullivan Ballou's "Letter to Sarah." What is your reaction to the following phrases? How do they affect your response to the letter as a whole?
   a. "My courage does not halt or falter"
   b. "my love of Country comes over me like a strong wind"
   c. "our sons grown up to honorable manhood"
   d. "when my last breath escapes me on the battle field it will whisper your name"
   e. "if there be a soft breeze upon your cheek, it shall be my breath"
   f. "Sarah, do not mourn me dead"

7. Consider Anna Quindlen's "Erin Go Brawl":
   a. What is the effect of Quindlen's description of common images of the Irish in the first paragraph?
   b. What does Quindlen mean by calling stereotypes "misshapen pearls, sometimes with a sandy grain of truth at their center"?
   c. How many times in the essay does Quindlen refer to her own Irish identity? Why do you suppose she does that?

ESSAY SUGGESTIONS

1. Using a cluster as the basis for an essay (750–1,000 words), describe your personal response to a place that haunts you—as Hoover Dam haunted Joan Didion.

2. Remembering David Schwartz's attitude to weather vanes, write an essay (750–1,000 words) describing your feelings about a favorite object or collectible (stamps, for example).

3. Imagine that you are writing a letter to a loved one on the eve of a significant historical event in which you will participate. As Sullivan Ballou did in his letter, describe your personal reaction to an event.

4. Choose a current news event that has some connection to some aspect of your own identity. Write a personal essay modeled on Anna Quindlen's in which you acknowledge how your identity shapes your response to the event.

5. As Judy Syfer protests the traditional role of a wife, address yourself to some current social arrangements that you find irritating (500–750 words). If you prefer, describe instead your negative response to some innovation in our culture.

6. During his lifetime Hazlitt wrote essays on the subjects listed below, most of them collected in his *Table Talk: Opinions on Books, Men and Things*. Choose one topic as the basis for a personal essay of your own (500–750 words).

   On Disagreeable People
   On the Want of Money
   On Reading New Books

On Persons One Would Wish to Have Seen
On Going on a Journey
On the Pleasure of Painting
On the Ignorance of the Learned
On the Fear of Death
On Sitting for One's Picture
On Fashion
On Nicknames
On Public Opinion
On Personal Identity
The Qualifications Necessary to Success in Life
Envy
Egotism
Hot and Cold
The Pleasure of Hating

7. Look carefully at the photograph below of the young Navaho girl. (Or choose one of the other photographs in the book.) Do some freewriting about your personal reaction to the photograph. Review your freewriting, pick out several of the ideas from it, and use these as the basis of another freewriting. Don't worry if you begin to stray from the apparent subject of the photograph. After you've done several sessions of freewriting, combine your insights into a brief account (300–500 words) of your personal reaction to the photograph.

Question

6

WHAT ARE THE FACTS
ABOUT X?

THE FACTUAL ESSAY

RANGE OF PURPOSES
    PROVIDING INFORMATION
    HERE IS THE JERSEY TOMATO, DEBORAH A.
        BOERNER
    CLEARING UP MISCONCEPTIONS
    SWEET TRUTHS ABOUT SUGAR, ELIZABETH M.
        WHELAN AND FREDERICK J. STARE, M.D.
    DEMYSTIFYING THE DIFFICULT
    THE EXPANDING UNIVERSE, STEPHEN HAWKING
    MAKING A SOCIAL COMMENT
    INEQUALITIES IN EDUCATION, JONATHAN KOZOL

THE FACTUAL FEATURE STORY
    ALL THE FACTS (SOME TRUE) ABOUT GONDOLAS
        MACDONALD HARRIS

THE FACTUAL ESSAY

"*I* try to report facts as I see them," said journalist John Gunther, whose massive compilations of fact resulted in such famous books as *Inside USA* and *Inside Europe*. Gunther was commenting on the difficulty of being completely objective in reporting facts, for it is almost impossible to separate our "view" of the facts from the actual "facts" themselves. As Gunther pointedly added: "A reporter with no bias at all would be a vegetable." More than that, it is our biases that determine the facts we see and often the way in which we see them. The central question in a piece of factual writing is: how do we know what *really* happened?

For a reporter, facts are the data that emerge from research, study, investigation, and corroboration by authority or reliable witnesses. Scientists, of course, apply an even more rigorous standard to matters of fact, regarding them merely as hypotheses until they have been verified by experiment or demonstration. Not as exacting as the scientist, nor as dogged as the reporter, conscientious student writers should begin early on to address themselves to the facts of a given subject or situation. In doing so, they will come to recognize that there are countless sources for a factual or informative essay ranging from matters of historical significance to the timely and newsworthy to the seemingly trivial. The obvious prerequisite of a good fact piece is knowing how to track down the facts (see Gathering Information). Equally important is getting the facts straight; accuracy is a prime virtue in reportorial writing. So are genuine interest and enthusiasm for, as one wise observer remarked, "There are no boring subjects, only boring writers." Writers, then, must play to their own strengths, relying on subject matter that they know something about or would like to know something about. An informed essay on bowling by someone who bowls and enjoys the sport has infinitely more merit than a listlessly written survey of a so-called important topic of social significance.

RANGE OF PURPOSES

When writing factual essays, writers must also know how to select facts judiciously. Since writers cannot tell everything, they include only those details that promote a particular purpose. The purpose determines what specific facts writers present and how they present them (seriously, satirically, calmly, angrily). Since the purpose of the fact essay gives it its distinctive shape and tone, we will review certain recurrent purposes that impel writers to approach a subject with this question in mind: What are the facts about X?

Providing Information

The purpose of a fact piece may be simply to provide interesting information and to satisfy what Aristotle called "natural curiosity."

A basic fact of nature is that—given a certain fruit or vegetable—some soils produce better or more notable crops than others. Thus we have Florida oranges, Maine potatoes, California avocados, and so on. In the following article, a New Jersey writer presents us with the Jersey tomato, making clear that it is both beautiful to behold and delicious to eat. What else would you like to know about this unique strain of a popular vegetable? The writer has provided a view of the subject from every possible angle including who grows it, how it grows, where and when it grows, why it is grown, and how it came into being. Note the first five subquestions indicated in the margin; see how many additional questions you can observe "at work" in the piece (almost thirty more).

Here Is the Jersey Tomato

Deborah A. Boerner

How would you characterize a Jersey tomato?

Who grows them?

How long is the growing season?

What is New Jersey's rank among tomato producers?

Why is the term "Jersey tomato" a misnomer?

Anyone who has ever tasted a "Jersey tomato" does not need to be told of its unique flavor and quality. For those who haven't, it's impossible to describe. New Jersey tomato lovers suffer all winter long, tolerating expensive yet bland-tasting tomatoes sold in the supermarket. But when summer comes, farmers and backyard gardeners throughout the state grow a tomato that knocks the "imports" right off the market produce counters.

In fact, the tomatoes grown during New Jersey's three-month growing season are enough to make this state the fourth-ranked producer of fresh market tomatoes in the nation. The three states which exceed New Jersey—Florida, California, and South Carolina—are all states where the growing season is much longer. If production was tabulated by the month, New Jersey would undoubtably rank much higher in the production of tomatoes for the fresh market.

"The term 'Jersey tomato' is really a misnomer," says W. Bradford Johnson, Extension Specialist for Vegetable Crops at Rutgers University. There's no particular variety the term refers to, but it's a term used for any large-size tomato grown in New Jersey. Although it's not known what makes the tomatoes grown in this state so special, an important factor is the soil. Farmers who retire to Florida often send for seed but are disappointed when they find the product is just not the same, Johnson said.

The latest figures (1980—from New Jersey Agricultural Statistics 1981) indicate New Jersey farmers produce more than 500,000 cwt. (hundred-weight) of fresh tomatoes each summer. Year after year, tomatoes rank first in value over all other vegetable crops grown in the state. In 1980, tomatoes accounted for 21 percent of the value of all major vegetables. Fresh market varieties were valued close to $9.7 million while the value of processing tomatoes was $4.6 million.

Even though production of tomatoes for processing is only half as valuable as fresh-variety production in the state, tomato processing is an important industry. It is especially important in the southern counties of Salem, Gloucester, and Cumberland, where 85 percent of the processing crop is grown. Unfortunately, five major processing plants have closed down in recent years, resulting in hard economic times for some South Jersey communities. However, six canneries are still operating in the state and New Jersey has been able to retain its rank among the top five states in the country producing processed tomatoes. Another indication tomato processing will not become a dying industry here is the fact that much of the tomato research being done in New Jersey today is geared towards the processing varieties.

The fact that tomato production is any kind of business at all in New Jersey is somewhat ironic, considering how unpopular the vegetable was just a few generations ago. The South Jersey community of Salem boasts of a legend which explains how the tomato was finally accepted there. Colonel Robert Gibbon Johnson, who later became the town's first mayor, is said to have stood on the county courthouse steps in 1820 and eaten a tomato. A crowd which had gathered to watch him gasped in disbelief. Quite a feat it was, for tomatoes, or "love apples" as they were called then, were thought to be poisonous. When the crowd saw that Johnson suffered no ill effects, others tried eating them and so began the tomato's popularity.

It is not known why tomatoes were believed to be poisonous. Most likely, it had something to do with the nightshade plant family, which is a group of plants that includes some very toxic plants as well as the non-toxic tomato. Whatever the reason, these mistaken fears persisted even into this century and definitely stunted the tomato's improvement and its migration between continents.

Because all parts of the tomato plant are perishable, it's difficult to trace its origin through archeological records. The genus to which the tomato belongs is native to South Africa. It is believed a wild, tiny, red-fruited tomato of Peruvian origin was carried northward to Mexico by prehistoric Indians. There it was domesticated in Pre-Columbian times. Introduction of the Mexican cultivars to the Mediterranean region probably did not occur until the 16th century. Even after the tomato reached Europe, migration to northern Europe was slow. It was first grown there as a curiosity or for decoration, possibly because of its poisonous mystique.

There is no evidence the American Indian knew of the tomato. It was reintroduced to the New World via the colonists in the 1700s. Here, too, it was initially grown in flower gardens. In 1781, Thomas Jefferson was one of the first in the country to grow the tomato for its food value. It was brought to the Philadelphia area in 1798 but was not sold in the market until 1829.

The first real attempts to breed improved varieties, since the tomato's domestication in Mexico, occurred after the Civil War. Until the tomato gained popularity as a food which could be eaten, breeding was done mainly by selecting plants within European stocks. More recently, primitive cultivars and the native wild species have proven useful for breeding resistance to wilt diseases and nematodes, two major problems with tomatoes today.

New Jersey has played a dominant role in improving its most valued vegetable crop, the tomato. In 1934, L. G. Schermerhorn, working at Rutgers University, developed a tomato which was popular well into the 1950s, longer than any variety since then. Dubbed the "Rutgers" tomato, it was excellent for both processing and fresh sales; it was particularly noted for producing a flavorful, red-colored tomato juice. Grown flat or on stakes, the Rutgers tomato was widely adapted in the southern states, too.

When a tomato more resistant to wilt diseases was needed, Ramapo, another variety developed at Rutgers, replaced the Rutgers variety on the fresh market. Many varieties for canning and the fresh market have been developed since that time, as the research at Rutgers, the Agricultural Experiment Station, and research plots throughout the state continues. As mentioned before, much of the research today is geared not towards finding a bigger tomato but towards developing a smaller, more crack-resistant tomato that will ripen fast and withstand more punishment from mechanical harvesters when picked for processing.

For fresh market and home gardeners, however, the biggest is still the best. For the past five years, the New Jersey Championship Tomato Weigh-In has been held with that theme in mind. Last year, a 3.905-pound Super Steak tomato earned its grower, John Malyar, Sr., a $1000 check. Drawing local winners from all over the state, the idea of the contest is to "further popularize the already popular Jersey tomato," according to Joseph Heimbold, originator of the contest. Heimbold's goal is to have a tomato grown in New Jersey which will triumph over the current 6.5-pound World Champion from Wisconsin. He believes it will happen and predicts the "champ" will not be grown by a farmer; only one of the past five winning tomatoes was farm-grown.

The tomato has certainly come a long way to become a summer tradition and to affect so many facets of life in New Jersey. If the legend of Colonel Johnson eating a tomato at the Salem County Courthouse is true, there are many people who would gladly thank him. New Jersey farmers would thank him for bringing the most valued crop they grow out of the flower garden. The processing plants and people they employ would have him to thank for making possible a million-dollar industry in catsup, tomato juice, and spaghetti sauce. Backyard gardeners would thank him for giving them something to brag about, whether they win a contest for their tomatoes or just show them off to friends and neighbors. But best of all, tomato lovers have a summertime treat they'd find it difficult to live without.

Clearing Up Misconceptions

In recent years the public has grown increasingly concerned about the relationship of food to health and disease. Which foods that we eat are nutritionally sound? Which ones contribute to physical fitness and longevity? Which should be shunned as bad for our health and mental outlook? After all, "You are what you eat," as most nutritionists point out.

Sugar is one food that has had a consistently bad press in that it has been accused of "causing everything from obesity to learning disabilities." Does sugar deserve its bad reputation? Is it, *in fact,* "one of the world's most fearsome scourges"? Not if you look at the facts as presented by two health authorities who have recently published a book with the tongue-twisting title *The One-Hundred Percent Natural, Purely Organic, Cholesterol-Free Megavitamin, Low Carbohydrate Nutrition Hoax.* According to these experts, many of the charges against sugar are "devoid of solid scientific support." The short article that follows presents the "facts" in condensed form:

Sᴡᴇᴇᴛ Tʀᴜᴛʜs Aʙᴏᴜᴛ Sᴜɢᴀʀ

Elizabeth M. Whelan and Frederick J. Stare, M.D.

In recent years sugar has increasingly been pronounced one of the world's most fearsome scourges—right up there with the Black Plague. We are told that sugar causes everything from obesity to learning disabilities. No one, from infant to centenarian, seems immune to its deadly attack.

The U.S. government itself has stood ready to further this belief. Soon after the Senate Select Committee on Nutrition and Human Needs dubbed sugar an unnecessary evil in its 1977 report, the Federal Trade Commission proposed banning the advertising of sugary products from children's television shows. (The proposal was later dropped.) Even food processors jumped on the bandwagon:

"Low in Sugar" scream their TV commercials. People brag that they no longer use the substance, as though that by itself was a virtue.

Much of this apprehension is based on two popular misconceptions: that Americans are consuming more table sugar than ever before; that sugar consumption contributes to poor health.

In fact, government statistics reveal that consumption of table sugar (sucrose) in the United States is now about the same as it was 70 years ago, while the use of other sweeteners—especially the corn syrups in processed foods—*has* greatly increased. But the figures for sweeteners include those in products such as ketchup and salad dressings, as well as those in soft drinks and desserts, and therefore estimates of the amount that people actually consume vary widely.

Just what *is* sugar? Chemically, there are many compounds called sugars, but only a few are found naturally in the foods we eat. Among sweeteners that are added the most common are sucrose—refined from cane or beet sugar—and corn syrups. Naturally occurring sugars include lactose, found in milk, and glucose and fructose, both common in fruits and vegetables. In order to be used by the body, all sugars must be converted to glucose—the sugar found in our blood. The human body cares little where its supplies originate.

Health faddists maintain that refined white sugar is dangerous, and that natural sweeteners are fine. But a molecule of sugar, refined or not, is a molecule of sugar. While it is true that sugar contains no vitamins, minerals or protein, the amounts of nutrients in less-refined sugars such as raw or brown sugar or in honey, for example—are too small to be important. If you prefer the taste of brown sugar or honey to table sugar, use them. But don't think that you are swallowing anything nutritionally superior.

Of course, popular misconceptions about sugar extend far beyond a vague, "It's not good for you." Let's look at some of the specific charges laid at sugar's door:

Obesity. Excess calories, regardless of where they come from, are fattening. No one kind of calorie is more fattening than any other. Fat, however, contains more than twice as many calories per ounce as carbohydrates (including sugar) or proteins. Thus, a pat of butter on a slice of toast is more than twice as fattening as an equal weight of jelly. Clearly, then, it makes no sense to attempt a sugar-free reducing diet if you replace the sugar with gravies, french fries and other fatty foods.

Diabetes. Insulin, a hormone produced by the pancreas, is necessary for metabolizing glucose in the blood. In diabetes, the pancreas either fails to produce enough insulin or the insulin it does produce is unable to function properly. Diabetics, therefore, are subject to excessive blood-sugar levels, especially after ingesting sugar. Eating sugary foods, however, has *not* been shown to cause the disease.

Hypoglycemia. The opposite of diabetes occurs when the pancreas produces too much insulin, resulting in blood-sugar levels that are abnormally low. True hypoglycemia is an extremely rare condition, with symptoms that display a remarkable parallel to those of anxiety neurosis. This condition is tailor-made for some hypochondriacs who insist that a vague collection of symptoms be tagged with a name.

Low blood-sugar levels in those few genuine hypoglycemics can be caused by pancreatic tumors. However, popular "wisdom" has decreed that too much sugar in the diet (particularly refined sugar) stimulates the pancreas to produce too much insulin, thus leading to lowered blood sugar. This is unadulterated hogwash.

Tooth decay. Although sugar can indeed contribute to cavities, don't think that dental problems can be avoided simply by replacing table sugar with good old "natural" honey or dried fruits. *Exposure time* is what we need to be concerned with. The stickier the sweet, the longer it will remain in contact with the tooth, the more damage will be done. The only way to cut down on exposure time is to eliminate sticky sweets between meals—and to clean your teeth more often. The bacteria in the mouth that cause cavities aren't the least bit particular about the type of sugar they feed on. In fact, some "health" foods, such as raisins, can nestle among the teeth all day, providing hours of tasty fare for bacteria.

Heart disease. In 1964 an English physician, John Yudkin, made the widely publicized charge that sugar is a causative factor in heart disease. Yudkin had arrived at his theory by comparing the sugar intake of 45 heart patients with 13 hospitalized accident victims and 12 men residing in the area. His study found that the heart patients consumed substantially more sugar. Thus he concluded, and the press duly reported, that sugar is bad for the heart.

When other scientists repeated his study in four hospitals—using as a control only people outside the hospital—they found that heart patients consumed the same amount of sugar as did their controls. But this attracted nowhere near the publicity of Yudkin's original statements.

A quick look at some simple statistics illustrates why the sugar-heart-disease theory makes so little sense. If the relationship were positive, countries with high sugar consumption should have a higher rate of heart disease. In fact, some—such as Venezuela, Cuba, Brazil and Costa Rica—have a rather low incidence.

Learning disabilities. In this case there aren't even any scientific studies to refute. We hear a great deal about sugar creating learning difficulties, but what is being circulated is a combination of uncontrolled studies, testimonials, opinion and conjecture. Also unsubstantiated is the contention that sugar and sugar products cause deviant behavior. After killing the mayor and a supervisor of San Francisco in 1978, former supervisor Dan White included as part of his legal defense testimony that he had eaten a lot of junk food shortly before the murder. (This was the so-called Twinkie Defense.) One health-food advocate even claimed that the infamous Manson "family" who murdered Sharon Tate had subsisted mainly on candy bars. "Where the diet is good," she declared, "there is no crime." These and similar hypotheses are still devoid of solid scientific support.

"Empty" calories. The charge that sugar is full of "empty" calories is plain silly. All calories are full calories—i.e., full of energy. If sugar products are consumed in place of other needed nutrients, dietary deficiencies can occur. But as long as the Recommended Dietary Allowance is being met for all nutrients, there is no harm whatever in using snack foods to fulfill additional calorie requirements.

So, the evidence is clear: sugar is sweet. But that *doesn't* mean it's bad for you.

Demystifying the Difficult

Though the informational papers you write are likely to cover some small, easily definable area of knowledge, the following reading covers an extraordinarily broad subject—the universe itself. Famed astrophysicist Stephen Hawking, in his book *A Brief History of Time* (from which this selection is taken), explains with startling clarity what scientists have discovered about the universe, its history and its future. By relating unimaginable stretches of time and space to our own human experience, Hawking makes the incomprehensible understandable and the complex plain. Among the most notable marks of his style is a personal quality that conveys his own fascination with what he is telling us. Most of us have had the experience of being taught by a teacher with little interest in his or her subject. Make sure that your own writing has that vital spark of liveliness and commitment that Hawking displays here.

THE EXPANDING UNIVERSE

Stephen Hawking

If one looks at the sky on a clear, moonless night, the brightest objects one sees are likely to be the planets Venus, Mars, Jupiter, and Saturn. There will also be a very large number of stars, which are just like our own sun but much farther from us. Some of these fixed stars do, in fact, appear to change very slightly their positions relative to each other as the earth orbits around the sun: they are not really fixed at all! This is because they are comparatively near to us. As the earth goes round the sun, we see them from different positions against the background of more distant stars. This is fortunate, because it enables us to measure directly the distance of these stars from us: the nearer they are, the more they appear to move. The nearest star, called Proxima Centauri, is found to be about four light-years away (the light from it takes about four years to reach Earth), or about twenty-three million million miles. Most of the other stars that are visible to the naked eye lie within a few hundred light-years of us. Our sun, for comparison, is a mere eight light-minutes away! The visible stars appear spread all over the night sky, but are particularly concentrated in one band, which we call the Milky Way. As long ago as 1750, some astronomers were suggesting that the appearance of the Milky Way could be explained if most of the visible stars lie in a single disklike configuration, one example of what we now call a spiral galaxy. Only a few decades later, the astronomer, Sir William Herschel, confirmed his idea by painstakingly cataloging the positions and distances of vast numbers of stars. Even so, the idea gained complete acceptance only early this century.

Our modern picture of the universe dates back to only 1924, when the American astronomer Edwin Hubble demonstrated that ours was not the only galaxy. There were in fact many others, with vast tracts of empty space between them. In order to prove this, he needed to determine the distances to these other galaxies, which are so far away that, unlike nearby stars, they really do appear fixed. Hubble was forced, therefore, to use indirect methods to measure the distances. Now, the apparent brightness of a star depends on two factors: how much light it radiates (its luminosity), and how far it is from us. For nearby stars, we can measure their apparent brightness and their distance, and so we can work out their luminosity. Conversely, if we knew the luminosity of stars in other galaxies, we could work out their distance by measuring their apparent brightness. Hubble noted that certain types of stars always have the same luminosity when they are near enough for us to measure; therefore, he argued, if we found such stars in another galaxy, we could assume that they had the same luminosity—and so calculate the distance to that galaxy. If we could do this for a number of stars in the same galaxy, and our calculations always gave the same distance, we could be fairly confident of our estimate.

In this way, Edwin Hubble worked out the distances to nine different galaxies. We now know that our galaxy is only one of some hundred thousand million that can be seen using modern telescopes, each galaxy itself containing some hundred thousand million stars. . . . We live in a galaxy that is about one hundred thousand light-years across and is slowly rotating; the stars in its spiral arms orbit around its center about once every several hundred million years. Our sun is just an ordinary, average-sized, yellow star, near the inner edge of one of the spiral arms. We have certainly come a long way since Aristotle and Ptolemy, when we thought that the earth was the center of the universe!

Stars are so far away that they appear to us to be just pinpoints of light. We cannot see their size or shape. So how can we tell different types of stars apart? For the vast majority of stars, there is only one characteristic feature that we can observe—the color of their light. Newton discovered that if light from the sun passes through a triangular-shaped piece of glass, called a prism, it breaks up into its component colors (its spectrum) as in a rainbow. By focusing a telescope on an individual star or galaxy, one can similarly observe the spectrum of the light from that star or galaxy. Different stars have different spectra, but the relative brightness of the different colors is always exactly what one would expect to find in the light emitted by an object that is glowing red hot. (In fact, the light emitted by any opaque object that is glowing red hot has a characteristic spectrum that depends only on its temperature—a thermal spectrum. This means that we can tell a star's temperature from the spectrum of its light.) Moreover, we find that certain very specific colors are missing from stars' spectra, and these missing colors may vary from star to star. Since we know that each chemical element absorbs a characteristic set of very specific colors, by matching these to those that are missing from a star's spectrum, we can determine exactly which elements are present in the star's atmosphere.

In the 1920s, when astronomers began to look at the spectra of stars in other galaxies, they found something most peculiar: there were the same characteristic sets of missing colors as for stars in our own galaxy, but they were all shifted by the same relative amount toward the red end of the spectrum. To understand the implications of this, we must first understand the Doppler effect. As we have seen, visible light consists of fluctuations, or waves, in the electromagnetic field. The frequency (or number of waves per second) of light is extremely high, ranging from four to seven hundred million million waves per second. The different frequencies of light are what the human eye sees as different colors, with the lowest frequencies appearing at the red end of the spectrum and the highest frequencies at the blue end. Now imagine a source of light at a constant distance from us, such as a star, emitting waves of light at a constant frequency. Obviously the frequency of the waves we receive will be the same as the frequency at which they are emitted (the gravitational field of the galaxy will not be large enough to have a significant effect). Suppose now that the source starts moving toward us. When the source emits the next wave crest it will be nearer to us, so the time that wave crest takes to reach us will be less than when the star was stationary. This means that the time between the two wave crests reaching us is smaller, and therefore the number of waves we receive each second (i.e., the frequency) is higher than when the star was stationary. Correspondingly, if the source is moving away from us, the frequency of the waves we receive will be lower. In the case of light, therefore, this means that stars moving away from us will have their spectra shifted toward the red end of the spectrum (red-shifted) and those moving toward us will have their spectra blue-shifted. This relationship between frequency and speed, which is called the Doppler effect, is an everyday experience. Listen to a car passing on the road: as the car is approaching, its engine sounds at a higher pitch (corresponding to a higher frequency of sound waves), and when it passes and goes away, it sounds at a lower pitch. The behavior of light or radio waves is similar. Indeed, the police make use of the Doppler effect to measure the speed of cars by measuring the frequency of pulses of radio waves reflected off them.

In the years following his proof of the existence of other galaxies, Hubble spent his time cataloging their distances and observing their spectra. At that time most people expected the galaxies to be moving around quite randomly, and so expected to find as many blue-shifted spectra as red-shifted ones. It was quite a surprise, therefore, to find that most galaxies appeared red-shifted: nearly all were moving away from us! More surprising still was the finding that Hubble published in 1929: even the size of a galaxy's red shift is not random, but is directly proportional to the galaxy's distance from us. Or, in other words, the farther a galaxy is, the faster it is moving away! And that meant that the universe could not be static, as everyone previously had thought, but is in fact expanding; the distance between the different galaxies is growing all the time.

Making a Social Comment

Frequently, informative essays do more than simply inform. Woven into the facts is a social commentary, an aside to the reader (only partly explicit) that asks, What do you think of this state of affairs? In the following excerpt from his book *Savage Inequalities,* Jonathan Kozol transforms what could be a dry recitation of facts and budget figures into an indictment of our educational system.

INEQUALITIES IN EDUCATION

Jonathan Kozol

The city of Detroit has had a black administration for close to two decades. But the city is poor and mainly black and its school system, which is 89 percent black, is so poorly funded that three classes have to share a single set of books in elementary schools. "It's not until the sixth grade," the Detroit *Free Press* reports, "that every student has a textbook. . . ." At MacKenzie High School in Detroit, courses in word processing are taught without word processors. "We teach the keyboard . . . so, if they ever get on a word processor, they'd know what to do," a high school teacher says. Students ask, "When are we going to get to use computers?" But, their teacher says, the school cannot afford them. Of an entering ninth grade class of 20,000 students in Detroit, only 7,000 graduate from high school, and, of these, only 500 have the preparation to go on to college. Educators in Detroit, the *New York Times* reports, say that "the financial pressures have reached the point of desperation."

In 1988, according to a survey by the *Free Press,* the city spent some $3,600 yearly on each child's education. The suburban town of Grosse Pointe spent some $5,700 on each child. Bloomfield Hills spent even more: $6,250 for each pupil. Birmingham, at $6,400 per pupil, spent the most of any district in the area.

"Kids have no choice about where they're born or where they live," says the superintendent of another district, which has even less to spend per pupil than Detroit. "If they're fortunate [enough] to [have been] born in . . . Birmingham, that's well and good." Their opportunities, he says, are very different if they're born in a poor district.

His words, according to the *Free Press,* echo mounting criticism of a funding scheme "that has created an educational caste system." But equalizing plans that might address the problem, says the paper, have been bitterly opposed by wealthy districts, some of which deride these plans as "Robin Hood" solutions. "It would take money out and send it to Detroit . . . ," a teacher in one of the wealthy districts says.

Former Michigan Governor James Blanchard's educational adviser says that higher funding levels do not "necessarily" improve a public school.

As the *Free Press* notes, however, many educators have opposed a funding shift because they fear that "it would benefit large urban districts" like Detroit.

Thus, as in New Jersey, equal funding is opposed for opposite reasons: either because it won't improve or benefit the poorer schools—not "necessarily," the governor's assistant says—or because it would improve and benefit those schools but would be subtracting something from the other districts, and the other districts view this as unjust.

Race appears to play a role in this as well, according to the Speaker of the Michigan House of Representatives. People in affluent Farmington, he says, "are not going to vote for more taxes so the poor black kids in Ypsilanti can get . . . better reading programs."

A rural superintendent seems to justify the Speaker's explanation. "I'm concerned," he says, that, if the funding of the schools is changed, "you'll get most of the money going to Saginaw, Flint, Detroit"—all three being cities where the public schools are heavily nonwhite. The racial point, however, isn't generally expressed.

THE FACTUAL FEATURE STORY

It is not surprising that the feature story, a popular journalistic form that provides entertainment and relief from the grim news-of-the-day, is often solidly factual. Journalists, after all, are occupationally committed to fact. Indeed, they are—in their own way—professional interrogators trained to answer all five of the basic news questions (who? what? when? where? why?) either in the very first sentence or—at most—first paragraph of their stories.

When offered a more leisurely feature spot—as opposed to a straight news account—the reporter may shape the feature as a narrative in which the usual "objective" tone of the journalist is replaced by the more informal, even intimate voice of the personal essayist.

So it is in the story reprinted below: "All the Facts (Some True) About Gondolas" provides a narrative frame for a considerably detailed, delightfully rambling exploration of gondolas.

Confiding that his original reason for coming to Venice was to write a novel about the fabled city, the writer—MacDonald Harris—goes on (in the same disarmingly confiding spirit) to explain his fascination with the "motoscafo." As he watched this small motor bus scooting about the canals of Venice, he found himself led, in turn, to a more compelling fascination with the gondola, the highly efficient Venice equivalent of the city taxi-cab. *What made the gondola move through water in a straight line rather than in circles since the gondolier rowed on only one side?* Even more mystifying, as Harris points out, the gondolier could also "make turns to the right or left, he could stop it, back it up and start out again in a straight line, all with nothing but the long oar sticking out over the water to the right." Harris was so tantalized by the mystery of the gondola that he suspended work on his novel until he could figure it out, calculating that "either the gondoliers were enchanters who had learned how to trangress the laws of physics, or they were doing something with the oar I couldn't grasp."

As a first step toward gathering the facts, Harris made friends with Alvise, a gondolier, a man who, as you shall see, resolved some of the perplexities—but in doing so created others.

All the Facts (Some True) About Gondolas

MacDonald Harris

We have Venetian friends who live in a 16th-century palazzo near Campo San Cassan, in a quiet part of the city out of the ordinary tourist track. We have borrowed their apartment occasionally and have lived in it for two long stays. In

this way I have had the opportunity to become familiar with the more remote parts of the city, have struck up friendships with all kinds of ordinary people and have even learned a few words of the Venetian dialect, which in some ways is more like Spanish than Italian. A street is a *calle,* pronounced exactly like the Spanish, and a small canal is a *rio.* A number of words from Venetian have passed into English—ghetto, lagoon, canal and arsenal, for example. And of course gondola.

Like practically every other writer who has lived in Venice, I was eventually seized with the idea of writing a book about it. As I imagined it, it was to be a historical novel set in 1797, at the time of the fall of the Venetian Republic to the Bonapartist armies. The climax of the novel was to take place in the Arsenal—but the trouble was that the Arsenal was still being used by the Italian navy and was a military reservation off limits to all civilians, especially foreigners.

I soon made what seemed to me a remarkable discovery. A certain motoscafo—one of the small water-buses that ply around through the canals, like buses in any other city—went directly down a rio through the center of the Arsenal, exposing all of its military secrets, such as the huge covered bays in which war-galleys were constructed in the 16th century. It is as though, for some unexplained reason, an American bus line went directly through the center of Fort Knox. Anyone can take this motoscafo; it is line No. 5, called Circolare Sinistra because it circles around the city to the left, and you can board it at San Zaccaria near San Marco.

I went through the Arsenal countless times on No. 5 and took a lot of photos. I liked the idea of doing my work on a floating bus. Venice, entrancing for anyone, is all the more so if you love water, and if you love ships and boats, as I do. In Venice everything that is done by trucks and motor vehicles in other cities is done by boats. Refrigerators, grand pianos and stage sets for the opera at the Fenice are delivered in boats and criminals are taken to jail in floating Black Marias. The hearses that carry the dead to the cemetary at San Michele are boats. And for taxis, there are gondolas.

—

I was fascinated by the gondola the first time I ever saw one. Like the Micronesian prua, the clipper ship and the Indian birchbark canoe, the gondola is one of the great naval designs of all time. Its lines are perfect and its proportions are graceful. It is exactly suited to its function, and in addition to this—or perhaps because of this—it is exquisitely beautiful. The secret of its design—but I anticipate.

Since the research on my novel was going rather slowly, I decided that first I should perhaps write a small non-fiction book about gondolas, with pictures and technical details. I started off on this job full of confidence. I was certainly qualified; I knew Venice, I understood boats and I knew how to write. I discovered that, although a great deal has been written about gondolas, there was almost nothing about their technical aspects, including their design and construction. The thing that intrigued me—the thing that would intrigue anyone who took the slightest interest in boats—was the secret of how the gondolier made the thing go straight even though he rowed only on one side. He could make turns to the right or left, he could stop it, back it up and start out again in a straight line, all with nothing but the long oar sticking out over the water to the right. There was a mystery here that I was determined to clear up. Either the gondoliers were enchanters who had learned how to transgress the laws of physics, or they were doing something with the oar I couldn't grasp. I made friends with a gondolier.

His name was Alvise, which is simply the Venetian form of Louis, and he was a very helpful and friendly young man. The trouble was that much of his explanation involved Venetian terms, such as *stalì* and *premi,* and my Venetian was still imperfect. I did gather that there was a sort of feathering motion at the end of the stroke, the sort of thing you do when paddling a canoe on one side. The trick couldn't be explained by analogies from canoes, however. (For one thing, in a canoe you paddle close to the hull and you don't have a long unwieldy oar sticking out 10 feet over the water on the right-hand side.)

—

I examined Alvise's gondola a little more carefully and learned the names of some of its parts. It was out of season and he had nothing much to do but chatter to me about these matters. The most curious and beautiful part of the gondola, it seemed to me, was the elaborately carved hardwood oarlock or wooded post against which the oar was set to make the stroke. It had all sorts of notches and convexities in it to hold the oar for different maneuvers. It was called the *forcola.* When I got the idea of buying one to take home as a souvenir, Alvise offered to sell me his own for a million lire, about $1,600. I was beginning to see that he had a nice sense of humor. Later, prowling about the various antique shops in the city, I found you could get one a good deal cheaper; they ranged from $500 to $300. In fact, I found a shop near Campo Santo Stefano where workmen could be seen making *forcole* in the rear, amid a mounting pile of chips on the floor. A kindly antiquarian explained to me that scores of these were manufactured every day to sell to tourists. They never got near a gondola. A real *forcola,* he told me, was carved from a natural crook of a tree, and no two were the same; gondolas were custom-made for their owners and each gondolier had a slightly different notion of where the notches and convexities were to go. He had an authentic *forcola,* from a real gondola, which he offered to sell me. The price was a million lire.

Back to the nomenclature—the elaborately worked iron halberd at the bow of the gondola was called the *ferro,* which was straightforward enough; it simply means "iron." Alvise had several explanations, all of them contradictory, as to why there were six projecting blades on the *ferro* plus a broader one at the top. The best story was that the small blades represented the six precincts or *sestieri* of Venice, and the large one represented the whole city. As to why the *ferro* was on the bow of the gondola at all, there were also several stories. Perhaps it was so that the patricians in the old days—sharpening their halberds—could warn other craft out of their path. Perhaps it was to catch weeds in case the gondola went out into the marshes. Or perhaps it was on account of the *felze.*

Felze? The *felze,* Alvise explained, was the cabin that fitted over the passengers in cold weather. All gondolas used to have them *poco fa,* a while back. (I discovered later that he meant in the 18th century.) The *ferro,* you see, Sior Capitan (since I knew so much about boats he had decided by this time I was a captain), is just the same height as the *felze.* So, if you want to go under a low bridge, if the *ferro* will go through, then the *felze* will go through too. Like a cat's whiskers, the *ferro* was a feeler for testing small openings.

So far so good. In order to see what a *felze* really looked like, I went to inspect an authentic 18th-century gondola in the museum of the Ca' Rezzonico. As far as I could tell, it was exactly like the gondolas in use today, except for the *felze*. The *felze* looked something like one of those removable hard-tops you can get for your Mercedes Benz or other sports car, except that it was taller in its proportions and it was black. When I examined it more closely, however, I found out finally what a Venetian blind was. This was something that had puzzled me for years. There are no Venetian blinds in Venice, just as there is no French toast in France. The high windows of the older palazzi are closed with solid wooden shutters, and you must remember to latch them when there is a thunderstorm, or they will swing around wildly like loose cannons on a warship and smash the windows. Most Venetian houses are so close together that the sun never comes in anyhow, so there is no need for Venetian blinds. But there, on the *felze* of the gondola in Ca' Rezzonico, I saw them—thin black narrow slats, hinged at the ends and held together with another slat you could push to open and shut them. Some ingenious American, no doubt, who saw them on his travels, was caught by the idea and went back to his own country to found the first Venetian blind factory. I was really pleased with this discovery.

———

There was another mystery I had been pondering over for years, and it was a rather delicate one. How did people manage to carry out these—romances—in gondolas that we were always reading about in stories? The largest of the three seats, black like everything else, was a kind of double armchair called the *poltrona,* and the back of it was bolt upright. With my limited knowledge of anatomy, and of romance, I didn't see how it could be done. But, impending this antique gondola more carefully, I found a cunning latch at the rear of the seat, where a hand could reach around and feel for it. Turn the latch and the back of the *poltrona* fell flat. The gondolier, presumably, was a discreet fellow, and besides he couldn't see anything through the *felze*. Of course gondolas didn't have *felzi* anymore. It was true, I thought, that the quality of life had declined in the 20th century.

Well, all of these discoveries, proper and improper, had still not explained how you made a gondola go straight by rowing only on one side. I asked Alvise if he would give me a lesson. *Certo,* he said, mentioning an astronomical price, which I agreed to pay. When we got out on the water, however, I discovered that he had no intention whatsoever of letting me stand up there on the stern and take hold of the oar. What he had in mind was a demonstration. It *was* probably only a problem in translation. Very well, I would pay the astronomical price for a demonstration. It was all research, and perhaps the gondola book would make some money. He demonstrated several different oar-strokes. It was something like paddling a canoe—*premi* meant a stroke with a little outward swish at the end that corrected the tendency to curve to the left, and *stali* was a stroke in which you held water at the end, in order to—well, I still didn't quite understand it.

———

I crawled far out on the end of the gondola, past the place where Alvise was standing, in order to photograph the swirls of water around the oar-blade as it went through its various strokes. I thought that if I studied the photos later I could figure out how the various strokes differed and how they made the gondola turn to left or right. This was successful; the trouble was that when I leaned out for the last shot I fell off the gondola into the lagoon. Perhaps "fell off" is too violent a term. What happened was simply that I lost my balance on the stern, found that I had nothing to hang onto and slid limb by limb, with as much dignity as I could muster, into the lagoon. I had plenty of time to hand my Pentax to Alvise.

Alvise, who was really a friendly fellow, didn't jeer at me at all on account of this mishap. Instead he advised me to go for information to the local office of the gondoliers' guild, which is called the Cooperativa Daniele Manin fra Gondolieri di Venezia. There I found another friendly person, the director of the guild, Commendatore Ugo Palmarin. When I explained to him what I wanted—I had dry clothes on by this time and was very plausible, casually dropping terms like *forcola* and *premi*—Commendatore Palmarin was quite helpful. He not only provided me with a photocopy of the hull-lines of a typical gondola—exactly what I had been looking for—but he gave me a note to the proprietor of the *squero,* or gondola boatyard, in San Trovaso, an out-of-the-way corner of Venice seldom visited by tourists, even though it is not far from the Accademia. I should have gone to him in the first place.

With the help of Commendatore Palmarin's plans and explanations—he demonstrated for me, using a teaspoon as an oar and an ashtray as a gondola—and what I learned by visiting the *squero,* I soon felt that I had solved the mysteries about gondolas and their design. At the *squero* a dozen or more of them were hauled out, upside down or on their sides, in various stages of repair. The chief secret was that the bottom of the gondola was not straight. One side of the hull was more deeply curved and the other was flatter, like a bow and its bowstring. An empty gondola, therefore, set into the water and given a push, would describe a long and gentle curve to the right—thus counteracting the tendency to turn to the left caused by rowing on only one side. And that wasn't all. The flat bottom of the craft was tilted, so that as it sat in the water empty it heeled to one side. When the gondolier stepped onto it, he stood with his weight on one side, so that he brought it level again. This forced the asymmetrical hull farther down into the water, and increased the built-in tendency of the hull to curve to the right. The gondolier could steer the craft, I now saw, simply by moving his weight a few inches to the right or left on the piece of rug where he stood behind the passengers. This incidentally solved another mystery—why gondoliers are so particular about exactly where the passengers sit and how they distribute their weight.

I took some pictures at the *squero* and shook hands with everybody, including the workmen whose hands were covered with pitch—I saw now how they made the lightly-built wooded boat watertight. But, for one reason or another, I never did write the technical book about gondolas. Perhaps I was so awed by the mysteries I had solved that I foresaw, or feared, there would be many more—too many for any mere foreigner to grasp. Why, for example, are all gondolas painted black? I had never thought about that.

I did, however, write my novel; *Pandora's Galley* was published a couple of years later. Coming back to Venice after the book was published, I took a trip through the Arsenal on motoscafo No. 5 just for old time's sake. As soon as I saw the gondolas in the rio, I got excited again and thought that perhaps I could do the gondola book after all. I knew all about rowing them, which nobody else did. If there were other mysteries, I would get to the bottom of them. What if they *were* painted black! I could ask Alvise why it was; he would give me some explanation or other, even though it might not be the right one.

I got off the motoscafo at San Zaccaria and soon found him near the Molo. He was maneuvering his gondola to get it in between the big mooring stakes stuck into the mud along the quay, and in some way he was making it go sideways. There is absolutely no way that you can make a gondola go sideways by doing anything whatsoever with an oar while standing far back on the narrow stern of the thing. He pretended not to recognize me and stopped making the gondola go sideways as soon as he saw I had noticed what he was doing.

DISCUSSION AND EXERCISES

1. "Anyone who has ever tasted a 'Jersey Tomato' does not need to be told of its unique flavor and quality," says Deborah A. Boerner in "Here's the Jersey Tomato." How many subquestions were you able to identify as underlying the data gathered for this piece. Discuss. How do the voluminous data of this short article give you a sense of the unique character and quality of the Jersey tomato? Discuss.

2. Consider the article on "Sweet Truths About Sugar," written by two physicians:
   a. What are some popular beliefs about the dangers of sugar?
   b. What sources of information do Whelan and Stare cite in their article?
   c. How do they define sugar?
   d. What are the "specific charges" laid at sugar's door?
   e. How do statistics debunk the sugar–heart disease theory?
   f. Upon concluding the article, are you convinced that sugar is acceptable? Why? Why not?

3. Consider Hawking's "The Expanding Universe."
   a. Notice how Hawking begins his description with an experience common to us all: looking up at the sky. How does he use that beginning to begin to teach us and change our preconceptions about what we are seeing?
   b. Examine Hawking's description of the work of Edwin Hubble. What techniques does Hawking use to make these complex calculations simple enough for a layperson to understand?
   c. Re-read the paragraph beginning "Stars are so far away." How many everyday objects and experiences does Hawking refer to to make his ideas clear to us. Re-write the paragraph omitting these comparisons. How many people do you think would understand that version?
   d. Make an outline of the ideas in Hawking's essay. How does he move—in the course of only six paragraphs—from the very ordinary experience of looking at the night sky to the cosmic conclusion that the universe must be expanding?

ESSAY SUGGESTIONS

In preparing these assignments, follow the procedures described in Gathering Information.

1. Write a brochure (750–1,000 words) on one of the following subjects:

cosmic rays	digestion	fire	giants
inertia	coral reefs	haunted houses	gypsies
gravity	opera	tobacco	clowns
mirages	pigeons	hara-kiri	astrology
cyclotrons	drought	sea serpents	sundials
glaciers	buried treasure	falling stars	ice fishing

2. In Boerner's article "Here Is the Jersey Tomato," we are given the "facts" about this well-known item of produce. Consider other fruits and vegetables that are associated with specific states, use prewriting techniques, and write an essay (750–1,000 words) giving comparable facts about Hawaiian pineapples, Georgia peaches, or Michigan apples. You might want to compare and contrast such competing items as Idaho and Maine potatoes, or California and Florida oranges. (See Question 16, How does X compare to Y?) In gathering information on your subject, begin with your own experience and observations and move on to library research, consulting such reliable sources as the United States Department of Agriculture or local Chambers of Commerce.

3. Write a fact piece on one of the following (500–750 words) designed to entertain or inform:

cosmic rays	Arctic Ocean	buried treasure	fire
gravity	wind	giants	haunted houses
mirages	cavemen	gypsies	tobacco
cylcotrons	cavewomen	dwarfs and midgets	hara-kiri
glaciers	chromosomes	magic	sea serpents
earthquakes	digestion	voodoo	falling stars

4. Select one of the following controversial foods:

chocolate	coffee	herb tea	cheeses
beef	fried foods	milk	bacon
frozen foods	canned foods	salt	eggs

Write an essay (750–1,000 words) entitled "The Truth About . . ." Here again you should look into various government publications such as those published by the U.S. Department of Agriculture, or the Food and Drug Administration. Pertinent articles in such reliable publications as *Science* and *Scientific American* are listed in *Reader's Guide,* as are popular articles in *Newsweek* and *Time.* Many of these articles give helpful leads and cite medical and nutritional sources and authorities which you can investigate as follow-up.

Continued

5. Write an essay (500–750 words) on one of the following widely misunderstood topics:

hypnotism	Zen	chemical welfare
group therapy	pollution	parochial schools
missionaries	homosexuality	sex education
conscientious objectors	conservation	pesticides
alcoholism	capital punishment	smoking
drug addiction	abortion	

6. Write an updated version of the 1982 gondolas piece (750–1,000 words). Suggested title: "Gondolas: The Truth, The Whole Truth and Nothing But The Truth." Create your own setting and circumstance (you might even use Harris's feature story itself as point of departure, indicating that it piqued your curiosity, inspired you to further research for possible resolution of "mysteries."

7. Write a feature story (750–1,000 words) on some aspect of the world around you that you find fascinating, perhaps astounding: for example, a vehicle such as the gondola (which somehow functions beyond its seeming potential); the space shuttle, or some comparably intricate and ingenious man-made vehicle, instrument, or machine that you have encountered, (either directly or indirectly) and that confounds or astounds you. Weave your compilation of facts into a narrative frame; adopt a relaxed, personal tone of voice.

Question 7

WHAT DOES
X MEAN?

EXPLORING A SUBJECT THROUGH DEFINITION
   A DEFINITION OF PHILOSOPHY, BERTRAND RUSSELL

METHODS OF DEVELOPING A DEFINITION
   BY CITING DIFFERENT MEANINGS OF X
   THREE MEANINGS OF GRAMMAR,
      W. NELSON FRANCIS
   BY TRACING THE HISTORICAL DEVELOPMENT OF X
   "UNIVERSE" AND "UNIVERSITY," ISAAC ASIMOV
   BY RESTORING THE ORIGINAL MEANING OF X
   WHAT THE WORD "LIBERAL" USED TO MEAN,
      RON BRANDMAYR, JR.
   BY TRACING THE DEVELOPMENT OF X AS A NEW TERM
   WHAT IS CHAOS? JAMES GLEICK
   BY COMBINING METHODS
   THE LIMITATIONS OF "HOLOCAUST,"
      MICHAEL BERENBAUM
   BY DENOTING FORMAL DEFINITION
   BY COMPOSING ONE'S OWN DEFINITION
   WHAT MAKES A "JERK" A JERK? SIDNEY HARRIS
   BY DESCRIBING EXPERIENCES
   DEMOCRACY, E. B. WHITE
   MOMMY, WHAT DOES "NIGGER" MEAN?
      GLORIA NAYLOR

EXPLORING A SUBJECT THROUGH DEFINITION

The Roman rhetorician Cicero said that every discourse should begin with a definition in order to make clear what the subject under consideration *is*. True enough. A definition helps to clarify the issue in an essay, whether its purpose is informative or persuasive. Definition, then, assures that writer and readers stand on the common ground of shared meanings. Thus many essays, articles, and books begin with the author's explanation of how she or he intends to use a given word or words.

In his introduction to a *History of Western Philosophy,* for example, Bertrand Russell states that since the term "philosophy" is used in many different ways, he will explain what *he* means by it:

A Definition of Philosophy

Bertrand Russell

"Philosophy" is a word which has been used in many ways, some wider, some narrower. I propose to use it in a very wide sense, which I will now try to explain.

Philosophy, as I shall understand the word, is something intermediate between theology and science. Like theology, it consists of speculations on matters as to which definite knowledge has, so far, been unascertainable; but like science, it appeals to human reason rather than to authority, whether that of tradition or that of revelation. All *definite* knowledge—so I should contend—belongs to science; all *dogma* as to what surpasses definite knowledge belongs to theology. But between theology and science there is a No Man's Land, exposed to attack from both sides; this No Man's Land is philosophy. Almost all the questions of most interest to speculative minds are such as science cannot answer, and the confident answers of theologians no longer seem too convincing as they did in former centuries. Is the world divided into mind and matter, and, if so, what is mind and what is matter? Is mind subject to matter, or is it possessed of independent powers? Has the universe any unity or purpose? Is it evolving towards some goal? Are there really laws of nature, or do we believe in them only because of our innate love of order? Is man what he seems to the astronomer, a tiny lump of impure carbon and water impotently crawling on a small and unimportant planet? Or is he what he appears to Hamlet? Is he perhaps both at once? Is there a way of living that is noble and another that is base, or are all ways of living merely futile? If there is a way of living that is noble, in what does it consist, and how shall we achieve it? Must the good be eternal in order to deserve to be valued, or is it worth seeking even if the universe is inexorably moving towards death? Is there such a thing as wisdom, or is what seems such merely the ultimate refinement of folly? To such questions no answer can be found in the laboratory. Theologies have professed to give answers, all too definite; but their very definiteness causes modern minds to view them with suspicion. The study of these questions, if not the answering of them, is the business of philosophy.

Russell has done more than look up the word *philosophy* in the dictionary, that repository of all accepted, conventional meanings of words. Instead, Russell sets forth the *one* meaning he likes best and finds most useful. In a sense, Russell has gone beyond conventional meaning in this definition; certainly he has particularized and elaborated on the conventional meaning in a way that is both inventive and illuminating. Thus, we do not receive from Russell any of the routine dictionary definitions:

1. Philosophy is the love or pursuit of wisdom.
2. Philosophy is the search for underlying causes.
3. Philosophy is a critical examination of fundamental beliefs.
4. Philosophy is the study of the principles of human nature and conduct.

Instead, Russell begins by locating the word with almost geographical precision: "Philosophy . . . is something intermediate between theology and science." We can almost *see* it:

$$\text{Theology} \longleftrightarrow \text{Philosophy} \longleftrightarrow \text{Science}$$

This diagram suggests the original meaning of "definition," a word derived from the Latin *definare:* to put boundaries around. In defining a word, we set up boundaries or limits that separate it from other words, just as a fence separates one piece of land from another. This agricultural metaphor is appropriate since the definer does stake out a special territory of meaning for his or her term. Under the "No Man's Land" of philosophy, for example, Russell has very skillfully included all the traditional concerns of the discipline: questions relating to the nature of reality ("Is the world divided into mind and matter?"); the problem of good and evil ("Is there a way of living that is noble and another that is base?"); and the possibility of knowledge ("Is there such a thing as wisdom?"). Russell concludes his definition by further restricting the domain of the discipline by indicating that it is the *studying* of these questions rather than the *answering* of them that is "the business of philosophy."

Like Russell's definition, many definitions are really introductions to larger essays, ranging in length from one paragraph to several pages. At the same time, the definition can exist as an independent form—an essay in definition.

Whatever its form or length, however, definition offers vast possibilities to the writer, for you can hit upon a topic simply by asking, What does it mean? or, What *should* it mean? about any term that seems uncertain, mystifying, curious, provocative, troublesome, or simply in need of a closer look. As we shall see, many abstract and ambiguous words in our language mean different things to different people: a word like "excellence," for example, about which John Gardner said, "It is a little like those ink blots that psychologists use to interpret personality. As the individual contemplates the word "excellence" he reads into it his own aspirations, his own conceptions of high standards, his hopes for a better world." (*Excellence,* xii–xiii) The same is true of words such as "honor," "loyalty," "liberty," "progress," "courage," "justice," "democracy," "capitalism," and "communism" (any *-ism*). They are all "ink blots" and as such create an opportunity for an essay that may establish common criteria of meaning or offer a personal meaning, as E. B. White does in his brief but vivid definition-description, "Democracy."

In addition to ambiguous terms, you may analyze terms that are, in your opinion, not well understood either because their meaning has changed or because they have acquired connotations. Linguists have shown that language grows organically, moved by its own inner forces. No external pressure—not even the most determined efforts of the strictest purists—can dictate its destiny. This does not imply, however, that the users of language may not concern themselves with the way specific words are faring. Since meanings often blur, it is appropriate that periodically someone reappraise a word by recognizing and redefining its boundaries. It may even happen, as in the case of the word "grammar," that in the course of its development, a word will radiate so widely from its original sense that it will come to mean several different things and require several different definitions. The essay "Three Meanings of Grammar" by W. Nelson Francis illustrates this point.

METHODS OF DEVELOPING A DEFINITION

You can develop a definition in many ways. Bertrand Russell, as we have seen, lists the questions that in his view constitute the subject matter or "business" of philosophy. These writers have established boundaries for their subjects. The essays that follow illustrate various methods writers may use to set boundaries and thereby answer the question, What does X mean?

By Citing Different Meanings of X

THREE MEANINGS OF GRAMMAR

W. Nelson Francis

Need for definition stated

A curious paradox exists in regard to grammar. On the one hand it is felt to be the dullest and driest of academic subjects, fit only for those in whose veins the red blood of life has long since turned to ink. On the other, it is a subject upon which people who would scorn to be professional grammarians hold very dogmatic opinions, which they will defend with considerable emotion. Much of this prejudice stems from the usual sources of prejudice—ignorance and confusion. Even highly educated people seldom have a clear idea of what grammarians do, and there is an unfortunate confusion about the meaning of the term "grammar" itself.

Current uses are confusing

Hence it would be well to begin with definitions. What do people mean when they use the word "grammar"? Actually the word is used to refer to three different things, and much of the emotional thinking about matters grammatical arises from confusion among these different meanings.

Three meanings isolated

The first thing we mean by "grammar" is "the set of formal patterns in which the words of a language are arranged in order to convey larger meanings." It is not necessary that we be able to discuss these patterns self-consciously in order to be able to use them. In fact, all speakers of a language above the age of five or six know how to use its complex forms of organization with considerable skill; in this sense of the word—call it "Grammar 1"—they are thoroughly familiar with its grammar.

The second meaning of "grammar"—call it "Grammar 2"—is "the branch of linguistic science which is concerned with the description, analysis, and formularization of formal language patterns." Just as gravity was in full operation before Newton's apple fell, so grammar in the first sense was in full operation before anyone formulated the first rule that began the history of grammar as a study.

The third sense in which people use the word "grammar" is "linguistic etiquette." This we may call "Grammar 3." The word in this sense is often coupled with a derogatory adjective: we say that the expression "he ain't here" is "bad grammar." What we mean is that such an expression is bad linguistic manners in certain circles. From the point of view of Grammar 1 it is faultless; it conforms just as completely to the structural patterns of English as does "he isn't here." The trouble with it is like the trouble with Prince Hal in Shakespeare's play—it is "bad," not in itself, but in the company it keeps.

Why the new three-part definition is better (it unravels confusion)

As has already been suggested, much confusion arises from mixing these meanings. One hears a good deal of criticism of teachers of English couched in such terms as "they don't teach grammar any more." Criticism of this sort is based on the wholly unproved assumption that teaching Grammar 2 will increase the student's proficiency in Grammar 1 or improve his manners in Grammar 3. Actually the form of Grammar 2 which is usually taught is a very inaccurate and misleading analysis of the facts of Grammar 1; and it therefore is of highly questionable value in improving a person's ability to handle the structural patterns of his language. It is hardly reasonable to expect that teaching a person some inaccurate grammatical analysis will either improve the effectiveness of his assertions or teach him what expressions are acceptable to use in a given social context.

Summary/ Conclusion

These, then, are the three meanings of "grammar": Grammar 1, a form of behavior; Grammar 2, a field of study, a science, and Grammar 3, a branch of etiquette.

By Tracing the Historical Development of X

"Universe" and "University"

Isaac Asimov

Origin of word

A group of individuals acting, in combination, toward a single goal under a single direction, behaves as though it were one person. In the Middle Ages, such a group was called a "universitas," from the Latin "unum" (one) and "vertere" (to turn); a group, in other words, had "turned into one" person. In the most general sense, this came to mean the group of everything in existence considered as a unit; that is, the *universe.*

Historical context

It also came to be used in a more restricted sense. In the early Middle Ages, for instance, a school of higher learning was called a "studium," from the Latin "stud-ere," meaning "to be zealous" or "to strive after." From this, come our words *study* and *student.* The Italian version of "studium" is *studio,* which has come into English as a place where the fine arts, particularly, are studied or practiced (a memorial to the fact that in Renaissance times, Italy was the center of the world of fine art).

New definition

A group of students at such a school would refer to themselves (with the usual good opinion of themselves that students always have) as "universitas magistrorum et scholarium"—a "group of masters and scholars." They were a "universitas," you see, because they were all pursuing the single goal of learning. And gradually the name of the group became, in shortened form, the name of the schools which, around 1300, began to be known as *universities.*

Origin of parallel term New definition of parallel term

Meanwhile, within the university, groups of students following a particular specialty, as, for instance, law, would band together for mutual aid. They were a group of *colleagues* (Latin, "collegae") from the Latin "com-" (together) and "ligare" (to bind). They were bound together for a common purpose. Such a group of colleagues formed a *college* (Latin, "collegium"), a word now used to denote a particular school within a university.

Continuity of original sense

The older meaning as simply "a group of colleagues" persists today in the College of Cardinals of the Roman Catholic Church, and in America's own electoral college which meets every four years to elect a president.

By Restoring the Original Meaning of X

WHAT THE WORD "LIBERAL" USED TO MEAN

Ron Brandmayr, Jr.

An acquaintance recently told me she was proud to be a liberal, because the founding fathers were liberals. At that, I heard a chorus of moans from the Beyond.

The word "liberal" has undergone a grotesque transformation since Tom Jefferson's day. It used to mean the belief in individual freedom and limited government, but modern liberalism is exactly what Jefferson and Madison tried to protect the nation from.

Liberals invoke Jefferson's name with reverence, then denigrate everything he stood for. President Clinton's visit to Monticello back in January was a good example of this Orwellian antic. Here's a guy who has built his career expanding the size and power of government, praising a man who made history admonishing against it. Either Clinton is an historical know-nothing or he assumes everyone else is.

Today's liberals are suspicious of individual liberty and see voters as a threat to their orthodoxy. This is why they oppose initiative and referendum, for example. They want to keep social issues out of the hands of voters as much as possible and in the hands of elitist judges, who think like they do.

Liberals say they are "pro-choice," but this is clearly not true. They don't trust taxpayers to choose how to invest their own money. They oppose the right of parents to choose what schools their children will attend. They seek to limit the rights of employers to choose who will work for them, and to some extent, don't even trust them to run their own companies. Now they're attempting to take away the choices Americans have taken for granted in matters of their health.

If they really believed in "choice" on abortion, they wouldn't want to force moral objectors to pay for them, but of course they do.

When conservatives insist that the Constitution should be interpreted as the ratifiers intended, liberals accuse them of "turning back the clock." The political clock ought to be turned back—about 200 years, when being called a liberal was actually something to be proud of.

By Tracing the Development of X as a New Term

WHAT IS CHAOS?

James Gleick

Where chaos begins, classical science stops. For as long as the world has had physicists inquiring into the laws of nature, it has suffered a special ignorance about disorder in the atmosphere, in the turbulent sea, in the fluctuations of wildlife populations, in the oscillations of the heart and the brain. The irregular side of nature, the discontinuous and erratic side—these have been puzzles to science, or worse, monstrosities.

But in the 1970s a few scientists in the United States and Europe began to find a way through disorder. They were mathematicians, physicists, biologists, chemists, all seeking connections between different kinds of irregularity. Physiologists found a surprising order in the chaos that develops in the human heart, the prime cause of sudden, unexplained death. Ecologists explored the rise and fall of gypsy moth populations. Economists dug out old stock price data and tried a new kind of analysis. The insights that emerged led directly into the natural world—the shapes of clouds, the paths of lightning, the microscopic intertwining of blood vessels, the galactic clustering of stars.

When Mitchell Feigenbaum began thinking about chaos at Los Alamos, he was one of a handful of scattered scientists, mostly unknown to one another. A mathematician in Berkeley, California, had formed a small group dedicated to creating a new study of "dynamical systems." A population biologist at Princeton University was about to publish an impassioned plea that all scientists should look at the surprisingly complex behavior lurking in some simple models. A geometer working for IBM was looking for a new word to describe a family of shapes—jagged, tangled, splintered, twisted, fractured—that he considered an organizing principle in nature. A French mathematical physicist had just made the disputatious claim that turbulence in fluids might have something to do with a bizarre, infinitely tangled abstraction that he called a strange attractor.

A decade later, chaos has become a shorthand name for a fast-growing movement that is reshaping the fabric of the scientific establishment. Chaos conferences and chaos journals abound. Government program managers in charge of research money for the military, the Central Intelligence Agency, and the Department of Energy have put ever greater sums into chaos research and set up special bureaucracies to handle the financing. At every major university and every major corporate research center, some theorists ally themselves first with chaos and only second with their nominal specialties. At Los Alamos, a Center for Nonlinear Studies was established to coordinate work on chaos and related problems; similar institutions have appeared on university campuses across the country.

Chaos has created special techniques of using computers and special kinds of graphic images, pictures that capture a fantastic and delicate structure underlying complexity. The new science has spawned its own language, an elegant shop talk of *fractals* and *bifurcations, intermittencies* and *periodicities, folded-towel diffeomorphisms* and *smooth noodle maps.* These are the new elements of motion, just as, in traditional physics, quarks and gluons are the new elements of matter. To some physicists chaos is a science of process rather than state, of becoming rather than being.

Now that science is looking, chaos seems to be everywhere. A rising column of cigarette smoke breaks into wild swirls. A flag snaps back and forth in the wind. A dripping faucet goes from a steady pattern to a random one. Chaos appears in the behavior of the weather, the behavior of an airplane in flight, the

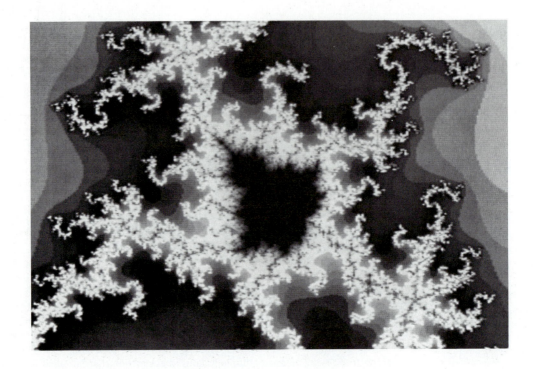

behavior of cars clustering on an expressway, the behavior of oil flowing in underground pipes. No matter what the medium, the behavior obeys the same newly discovered laws. That realization has begun to change the way business executives make decisions about insurance, the way astronomers look at the solar system, the way political theorists talk about the stresses leading to armed conflict.

Chaos breaks across the lines that separate scientific disciplines. Because it is a science of the global nature of systems, it has brought together thinkers from fields that had been widely separated. "Fifteen years ago, science was heading for a crisis of increasing specialization," a Navy official in charge of scientific financing remarked to an audience of mathematicians, biologists, physicists, and medical doctors. "Dramatically, that specialization has reversed because of chaos." Chaos poses problems that defy accepted ways of working in science. It makes strong claims about the universal behavior of complexity. The first chaos theorists, the scientists who set the discipline in motion, shared certain sensibilities. They had an eye for pattern, especially pattern that appeared on different scales at the same time. They had a taste for randomness and complexity, for jagged edges and sudden leaps. Believers in chaos—and they sometimes call themselves believers, or converts, or evangelists—speculate about determinism and free will, about evolution, about the nature of conscious intelligence. They feel that they are turning back a trend in science toward reductionism, the analysis of systems in terms of their constituent parts: quarks, chromosomes, or neurons. They believe that they are looking for the whole.

By Combining Methods

This essay, by the Director of the Holocaust Memorial Museum in Washington, D.C., is part of the introduction to a book that traces the history of the Holocaust through the resources of the museum. Michael Berenbaum combines several of the methods of defining words we have seen in other definitions—looking at a word's history, tracing its emergence with a new meaning, constrasting it to other words.

THE LIMITATIONS OF "HOLOCAUST"

Michael Berenbaum

We have used one word again and again in this book, as we have in the museum. It is the accepted word by which historians and scholars, poets and writers, presidents and ordinary men and women refer to the cataclysmic events of 1933–1945. But despite its widespread usage, the word is inappropriate. That word is, of course, *Holocaust.* The word is Greek in origin. The Septuagint, the Greek translation of the Hebrew Bible, translates the Hebrew word *olah* as *holokauston.* The Hebrew literally means that which is offered up; it signifies a burnt offering offered whole unto the Lord. The word itself softens and falsifies the event by giving it a religious significance.

The Nazis called the murder of the Jews "The Final Solution to the Jewish Problem." It was their way of speaking euphemistically. Defining Jews as a problem or a question demands a resolution. The word *final* was only too accurate. Their intention was total—to end Jewish history, to eliminate all Jewish blood. The murder of the Jews was filled with apocalyptic meaning. It was, in the eyes of the Nazi perpetrators, essential to the salvation of the German people.

Yiddish-speaking Jews used the word *churban,* destruction, to signify the Holocaust. It is also the word that ancient Jews used to speak of the destruction of the first and second Temples and their exile from Jerusalem. In the years following World War II, Israelis spoke of *Shoah ve'gevurah*—Holocaust and heroism—as if the two were synonymous, which they are not. More recently, *Shoah* has been used alone, to signify a whirlwind of destruction. Raul Hilberg, the pre-eminent Holocaust scholar of this generation, called his major book *The Destruction of the European Jews,* an apt description. The Jews were murdered systematically. In Eastern Europe only a remnant remains—an aging group of men and women, heirs of a long past with no future. Cities that once were vibrant with Jewish life are without Jews. Historian Lucy Dawidowicz called the Holocaust *The War Against the Jews,* and perhaps she is right. In these pages, you will read of the second battlefront of World War II. The planned destruction of an entire people was a war the Nazis came close to winning. Had Allied policymakers recognized the double nature of the war that occurred during 1939–1945, they might have been more responsive to the victims of the Holocaust and not restricted attention to battlefields, weapons, and armies.

Still, the word *Holocaust* has come to signify the event, and despite its limitations it will be used. We will, however, resist at all points treating the victims as an offering to the Lord of History. This would be unworthy of God—and of us.

By Denoting Formal Definition

If you examine the above definitions carefully, you will note that a three-part *formal* or *logical* definition (so-called by rhetoricians) is at the core of most of them. According to this pattern, place a term to be defined in a larger category or class; then distinguish it from other members of the class by noting "differentiae." The following illustrates this process:

Term	Class (or genus)	Differentiae (distinguishing characteristics)
philosophy	is a field of study	that speculates on matters for which there is no definite knowledge and that appeals to reason rather than authority.
grammar 1	is a set of formal patterns	whereby the words of a language are arranged to convey a larger meaning
grammar 2	is a branch of linguistic science	concerned with the description, analysis, and formularization of formal language patterns
grammar 3	is a branch of language study	concerned with etiquette
a symbol	is any "thing"	that stands for something else
universitas	is a group of individuals	acting, in combination, toward a single goal.

Unlike the logician, the writer is not obliged to follow the logical formula *exactly.* Yet most good expository definitions have the three-part formal pattern, even if it is implicit rather than explicit. And most rhetorical definitions satisfy the basic *logical* prerequisites of a good definition: that the "differentiae" (distinguishing characteristics) be neither too broad nor too narrow and that the definition be the equivalent of the term defined.

In any case, both the writer and reader should search out and apply the basic logical pattern of a term to the rhetorical definition, for nothing marks off an area of meaning with greater precision than the formal one-sentence definition. It often provides a foundation and thesis for the entire piece that the writer may then extend by a number of methods, as we have seen in the preceding illustrations and as we see in the following.

By Composing One's Own Definition

What Makes a "Jerk" a Jerk?

Sidney J. Harris

Background

I don't know whether history repeats itself, but biography certainly does. The other day, Michael came in and asked me what a "jerk" was—the same question Carolyn put to me a dozen years ago.

At that time, I fluffed her off with some inane answer, such as "A jerk isn't a very nice person," but both of us knew it was an unsatisfactory reply. When she went to bed, I began trying to work up a suitable definition.

Need for definition

It is a marvelously apt word, of course. Until it was coined, not more than twenty-five years ago, there was really no single word in English to describe the kind of person who is a jerk—"boob" and "simp" were too old hat, and besides they really didn't fit, for they could be lovable, and a jerk never is.

Preliminary definition   Thinking it over, I decided that a jerk is basically a person without insight. He is not necessarily a fool or a dope, because some extremely clever persons can be jerks. In fact, it has little to do with intelligence as we commonly think of it; it is, rather, a kind of subtle but pervasive aroma emanating from the inner part of the personality.

Example of use   I know a college president who can be described only as a jerk. He is not an unintelligent man, nor unlearned, nor even unschooled in the social amenities. Yet he is a jerk *cum laude,* because of a fatal flaw in his nature—he is totally incapable of looking into the mirror of his soul and shuddering at what he sees there.

Definition of word   A jerk, then, is a man (or woman) who is utterly unable to see himself as he appears to others. He has no grace, he is tactless without meaning to be, he is a bore even to his best friends, he is an egotist without charm. All of us are egotists to some extent, but most of us—unlike the jerk—are perfectly and horribly aware of it when we make asses of ourselves. The jerk never knows.

By Describing Experiences

Formal definition is not always possible. Some words are too inextricably tied to an individual vantage point: too subjective, too relative, too experimental. One such word, as Abraham Lincoln pointed out, is "liberty":

> The world has never had a good definition of the word liberty. . . . We all declare for liberty, but using the same word we do not mean the same thing. With some, the word liberty may mean for each man to do as he pleases with himself and the product of his labor; while with others the same word may mean for some men and the product of other men's labor. . . .
>
> The shepherd drives the wolf from the sheep's throat, for which the sheep thanks the shepherd as his liberator, while the wolf denounces him for the same act. . . . Plainly the sheep and the wolf are not agreed upon a definition of liberty.
>
> —Abraham Lincoln, "Definition of Liberty"

What should writers do, then, with such subjective words? They can write essays containing *not* formal definitions, worked out against fixed, objective standards, but rather personal definitions worked out on the basis of their own beliefs, feelings, and experiences. Thus the eloquent judge Learned Hand had this to say about the spirit of liberty:

> What then is the spirit of liberty? I cannot define it; I can only tell you my own faith. The spirit of liberty is the spirit which is not too sure that it is right; the spirit of liberty is the spirit which seeks to understand the minds of other men and women; the spirit of liberty is the spirit which weighs their interests alongside its own without bias; the spirit of liberty remembers that not even a sparrow falls to earth unheeded; the spirit of liberty is the spirit of Him who, near two thousand years ago, taught mankind that lesson it has never learned, but has never quite forgotten: that there may be a kingdom where the least shall be heard and considered side by side with the greatest.
>
> Learned Hand, "The Spirit of Liberty"

Similarly, E. B. White was moved, during the Second World War, to define "democracy" *not* by following formal procedures, but by exploring his own experiences and associations.

DEMOCRACY

E. B. White

We received a letter from the Writers' War Board the other day asking for a statement on "The Meaning of Democracy." It presumably is our duty to comply with such a request, and it is certainly our pleasure.

Surely the Board knows what democracy is. It is the line that forms on the right. It is the *don't* in *don't shove*. It is the hole in the stuffed shirt through which the sawdust slowly trickles; it is the dent in the high hat. Democracy is the recurrent suspicion that more than half of the people are right more than half of the time. It is the feeling of privacy in the voting booths, the feeling of communion in the libraries, the feeling of vitality everywhere. Democracy is a letter to the editor. Democracy is the score at the beginning of the ninth. It is an idea that hasn't been disproved yet, a song the words of which have not gone bad. It's the mustard on the hot dog and the cream in the rationed coffee. Democracy is a request from a War Board, in the middle of a morning in the middle of a war, wanting to know what democracy is.

According to political scientist Anatol Rapoport, the personal definition is no less valuable than the formal; in fact, it is sometimes the best, perhaps the *only* way to formulate certain definitions—by indicating the feelings, experiences, and ideas associated with the term in question. What *happens* in connection with it? What is done? What is thought, felt? In Rapoport's view the question "What do you mean?" is essentially a request to share the experiences associated with the words you are using.

In the following response to a child's question about a racial slur, novelist Gloria Naylor reminds us of the social dimension of language and of the ways our definitions of words can have a dramatic impact on our lives. Students are often tempted to begin a definition by citing the dictionary's definition. Naylor reminds us that it is the way words are used that should be our starting point.

MOMMY, WHAT DOES "NIGGER" MEAN?

Gloria Naylor

Language is the subject. It is the written form with which I've managed to keep the wolf away from the door and, in diaries, to keep my sanity. In spite of this, I consider the written word inferior to the spoken, and much of the frustration experienced by novelists is the awareness that whatever we manage to capture in even the most transcendent passages falls far short of the richness of life. Dialogue achieves its power in the dynamics of a fleeting moment of sight, sound, smell and touch.

I'm not going to enter the debate here about whether it is language that shapes reality or vice versa. That battle is doomed to be waged whenever we seek intermittent reprieve from the chicken and egg dispute. I will simply take the position that the spoken word, like the written word, amounts to a nonsensical arrangement of sounds or letters without a consensus that assigns "meaning." And building from the meanings of what we hear, we order reality. Words themselves are innocuous; it is the consensus that gives them true power.

I remember the first time I heard the word *nigger*. In my third-grade class, our math tests were being passed down the rows, and as I handed the papers to a little boy in back of me, I remarked that once again he had received a much lower mark than I did. He snatched his test from me and spit out that word. Had he called me a nymphomaniac or a necrophiliac, I couldn't have been more puzzled. I didn't know what a nigger was, but I knew that whatever it meant, it was something he shouldn't have called me. This was verified when I raised my hand, and in a loud voice repeated what he had said and watched the teacher scold him for using a "bad" word. I was later to go home and ask the inevitable question that every black parent must face—"Mommy, what does 'nigger' mean?"

And what exactly did it mean? Thinking back, I realize that this could not have been the first time the word was used in my presence. I was part of a large extended family that had migrated from the rural South after World War II and formed a close-knit network that gravitated around my maternal grandparents. Their ground-floor apartment in one of the buildings they owned in Harlem was a weekend mecca for my immediate family, along with countless aunts, uncles and cousins who brought along assorted friends. It was a bustling and open house with assorted neighbors and tenants popping in and out to exchange bits of gossip, pick up an old quarrel or referee the ongoing checkers game in which my grandmother cheated shamelessly. They were all there to let down their hair and put up their feet after a week of labor in the factories, laundries and shipyards of New York.

Amid the clamor, which could reach deafening proportions—two or three conversations going on simultaneously, punctuated by the sound of a baby's crying somewhere in the back rooms or out on the street—there was still a rigid set of rules about what was said and how. Older children were sent out of the living room when it was time to get into the juicy details about "you-know-who" up on the third floor who had gone and gotten herself "p-r-e-g-n-a-n-t!" But my parents, knowing that I could spell well beyond my years, always demanded that I follow the others out to play. Beyond sexual misconduct and death, everything else was considered harmless for our young ears. And so among the anecdotes of the triumphs and disappointments in the various workings of their lives, the word *nigger* was used in my presence, but it was set within contexts and inflections that caused it to register in my mind as something else.

In the singular, the word was always applied to a man who had distinguished himself in some situation that brought their approval for his strength, intelligence or drive:

"Did Johnny *really* do that?"

"I'm telling you, that nigger pulled in $6,000 of overtime last year. Said he got enough for a down payment on a house."

When used with a possessive adjective by a woman—"my nigger"—it became a term of endearment for husband or boyfriend. But it could be more than just a term applied to a man. In their mouths it became the pure essence of manhood—a disembodied force that channeled their past history of struggle and present survival against the odds into a victorious statement of being: "Yeah, that old foreman found out quick enough—you don't mess with a nigger."

In the plural, it became a description of some group within the community that had overstepped the bounds of decency as my family defined it: Parents who neglected their children, a drunken couple who fought in public, people who simply refused to look for work, those with excessively dirty mouths or unkempt households were all "trifling niggers." This particular circle could forgive hard times, unemployment, the occasional bout of depression—they had gone through all of that themselves—but the unforgivable sin was a lack of self-respect.

A woman could never be a *nigger* in the singular, with its connotation of confirming worth. The noun *girl* was its closest equivalent in that sense, but only when used in direct address and regardless of the gender doing the addressing. "Girl" was a token of respect for a woman. The one-syllable word was drawn out to sound like three in recognition of the extra ounce of wit, nerve or daring that the woman had shown in the situation under discussion.

"G-i-r-l, stop. You mean you said that to his face?"

But if the word was used in a third-person reference or shortened so that it almost snapped out of the mouth, it always involved some element of communal disapproval. And age became an important factor in these exchanges. It was only between individuals of the same generation, or from an older person to a younger (but never the other way around), that girl would be considered a compliment.

I don't agree with the argument that use of the word *nigger* at this social stratum of the black community was an internalization of racism. The dynamics were the exact opposite: the people in my grandmother's living room took a word that whites used to signify worthlessness or degradation and rendered it impotent. Gathering there together, they transformed *nigger* to signify the varied and complex human beings they knew themselves to be. If the word was to disappear totally from the mouths of even the most liberal of white society, no one in that room was naïve enough to believe it would disappear from white minds. Meeting the word head-on, they proved it had absolutely nothing to do with the way they were determined to live their lives.

So there must have been dozens of times that the word *nigger* was spoken in front of me before I reached the third grade. But I didn't "hear" it until it was said by a small pair of lips that had already learned it could be a way to humiliate me. That was the word I went home and asked my mother about. And since she knew that I had to grow up in America, she took me in her lap and explained.

DISCUSSION AND EXERCISES

Reminder: A definition, as has been pointed out, never occurs in a vacuum but always within a specific rhetorical stance, within a given context established by the writer to meet the needs of a given occasion. Consequently, before you begin an assignment in definition you should visualize or *invent* the occasion that calls it forth, keeping in mind a particular problem or situation, a specific audience, a fixed point of view.

1. Read the following definition of an intellectual and evaluate its structure, stated purpose, and the degree of success with which it fulfills that purpose.

> In certain ways the word "intellectual" is not a happy choice in America, for it seems to set aside the individual falling within this category from the rest of society. But no substitute can be found for the term. We use "intellectual" here in a functional sense, as seems to be the common practice in this country. Thus Merle Curti uses it to include all who "are dedicated to the pursuit of truth in some special field or to the advancement of learning in general." This would include scholars, teachers, and perhaps others such as editorial writers, columnists, and serious journalists who are concerned with the advancement of learning. More specifically, Peter Viereck tells us: "I define intellectuals as all who are full-time servants of the Word or of the word. This means educators in the broadest sense: philosophers, clergymen, artists, professors, poets, and also such undreamy and uncloudy professions as editors and the more serious interpreters of news." In an attempt to separate the true intellectual from his pseudo counterpart or the "egghead"—from the blind specialist, who knows nothing but his specialty, and from the dilettante, who purveys what he does not really understand—Professor Charles Frankel describes the intellectual thus: "He has, in fact, become increasingly rare. He is the man who has made himself master of some definite intellectual skill or field of learning, and who knows from his own first-hand experience what the difference is between solid thinking and empty vaporizing. But while he cultivates his own private garden, he is also a man who looks beyond its walls occasionally and comments on the public world as it looks from his angle of vision." This definition excludes many scholars who are obviously engaged in intellectual activity but do not possess the broadness of view that Frankel would like all those deserving the term "intellectual" to have.
>
> Let us accept as a functional definition of the term "intellectual" one who is engaged professionally in the pursuit or the propagation of the truth. This includes those who may be mistaken in their view of the truth as long as they believe they are pursuing or propagating the truth in their professional capacity. Just as the incompetent or dishonest physician does not discredit medicine as a profession, nor can it be denied that he is a physician, neither does the incompetent or dishonest intellectual discredit intellectuals as a class or intellectual activity as a profession.
>
> —Thomas P. Neill

Continued

2. Write a one-sentence formal or logical definition of each of the following terms. Compare your definitions with those of classmates, noting relative merits of each.

lawyer	idiot	navy	photosynthesis
doctor	imbecile	marines	fireplace
rhetoric	needle	psychotic	radar
biology	pencil	neurotic	book
botany	rock	jet	
archeology	rock music	star	

3. Expand one of your definitions into a paragraph of 100–150 words, using the definition as your topic sentence. Cite examples wherever possible.

4. In a paragraph (150–250 words) trace recent changes in the meaning of one of the following words:

survey	affluent	computer
recession	retarded	beat
stoned	cool	tough
center	liquidate	loophole

5. About the spirit of liberty, Judge Learned Hand said "I cannot define it; I can only tell you my own faith." In a paragraph (150–300 words) tell your "own faith" in the spirit of one of the following words:

justice	honor	brotherhood
courage	sportsmanship	democracy
love	loyalty	idealism
freedom	charity	neighborliness

ESSAY SUGGESTIONS

1. In a form comparable to that of Russell's definition of "philosophy," write a definition essay (500–750 words) of one of the following disciplines:

literature	chemistry	sociology
music	physics	anthropology
economics	geology	political science

2. Write a definition essay (500–750 words) of one of the following general terms, using the one-sentence, formal definition (explicitly stated or implicit) as a base or thesis:

patriotism	public opinion	mass media
plagiarism	libel	isolationist
atheism	heresy	internationalist
communism	reactionary	myth
(any) -ism	liberal	jazz
censorship	radical	temperance
poverty	religion	nature

3. In an essay (500–750 words) restore one of the following words to respectability by stripping it of negative connotations and redefining it in a more respectable light:

gang	exploit	censorship
politician	charity	slang
bookworm	cliché	militarist
shrewd	informer	welfare
manipulator	gossip	intellectual

4. In the manner of Isaac Asimov's essay "'Universe' and 'University'" write an essay (500–750 words) tracing the history of one of the following words:

romance	grammar	hussy	serious
tragedy	citizen	pride	undertaker
comedy	boor	science	scruple
epic	boycott	atomic	lynch
gossip	affair	bunk	corporation
logic	cad	scissors	rifle
rhetoric			

5. Compose your own definition of a "jerk" or other character type (500–750 words) by combining different methods of development (examples, contrast, and so forth).

6. Choose a word that interests you and write an essay (500–1,000 words) defining that word. Remember that in defining a word you are in effect setting the boundaries for the legitimate use of that word. Use the following outline as a guide in writing your essay:
   a. State the need for a definition.
   b. Review past or current usage and show how or in what way it is inadequate, inappropriate, or confusing.
   c. Offer your own definition (which can be a restatement of diversely held opinions of the word) and show how it can be applied to the situation that prompted the need for definition.

Question

8

WHAT IS THE ESSENTIAL
FUNCTION OF X?

The Function of a Critic
>   *What Is the Function of a Critic?*
>   W. H. Auden

The Function of a Word
>   *We Are, Like, Poets*, Jim Frederick

The Function of Education
>   *Another School Year—What For?*
>   John Ciardi

The Function of Science
>   *The Tucson Zoo*, Lewis Thomas

The Function of Holidays
>   *National Holidays Unite Us*
>   Douglas Greenberg

If defining terms is an appropriate first step in discourse, a second step may well be explaining functions. In each case the writer attempts to reach the heart of a subject. What does the subject mean? What is it for? What—by its very nature—is it supposed to do? How does it fit into a larger field of other objects and other functions? How can it best meet and fulfill that function for which it is most suited?

A writer might begin by asking such questions about a particular profession. What is the function of a teacher, a lawyer, a doctor, a philosopher, or a clergyperson? What role or roles do they serve in society? What human needs do they meet? The function of other professions may not be quite as clear without some further research. What is the function of the producer of a film or a play? Of a financier? Of an image consultant? Of a public health worker? What are their special roles, their main business, their responsibilities? Essays that answer the question *What is the function of X?* can themselves have different functions: They can explain the function of X to an audience unfamiliar with the subject area, or they can propose a new and previously unrealized function of a familiar subject.

THE FUNCTION OF A CRITIC

Poet W. H. Auden addressed the question of function to the somewhat mystifying, frequently misunderstood profession of the critic. How does this person "whose knowledge is extensive" serve the rest of us whose knowledge is not nearly so extensive? As tutor? Teacher? Guide? Tastemaker?

Auden organizes his answer in the form of a simple listing, a series of verbs. The function of the critic, he tells us, is to *introduce . . . , convince . . . , show . . . , give . . . , throw light on . . . .* Following the listing Auden goes on to offer two paragraphs of explanation: the first three services "demand scholarship," he tells us: the last three "demand . . . insight." In a final paragraph, Auden specifies what function the critic should *not* serve: he should "not . . . lay down the law."

What Is the Function of a Critic?

W. H. Auden

What is the function of a critic? So far as I am concerned, he can do me one or more of the following services:

1. Introduce me to authors or works of which I was hitherto unaware.
2. Convince me that I have undervalued an author or a work because I had not read them carefully enough.
3. Show me relations between works of different ages and cultures which I could never have seen for myself because I do not know enough and never shall.
4. Give a "reading" of a work which increases my understanding of it.
5. Throw light upon the process of artistic "Making."
6. Throw light upon the relation of art to life, to science, economics, ethics, religion, etc.

The first three of these services demand scholarship. A scholar is not merely someone whose knowledge is extensive; the knowledge must be of value to others. One would not call a man who knew the Manhattan Telephone Directory by heart a scholar, because one cannot imagine circumstances in which he would acquire a pupil. Since scholarship implies a relation between one who knows more and one who knows less, it may be temporary; in relation to the public, every reviewer is, temporarily, a scholar, because he has read the book he is reviewing and the public has not. Though the knowledge a scholar possesses must be potentially valuable, it is not necessary that he recognize its value himself; it is always possible that the pupil to whom he imparts his knowledge has a better sense of its value than he. In general, when reading a scholarly critic, one profits more from his quotations than from his comments.

The last three services demand, not superior knowledge, but superior insight. A critic shows superior insight if the questions he raises are fresh and important, however much one may disagree with his answers to them. Few readers, probably, find themselves able to accept Tolstoi's conclusions in "What is Art?" but, once one has read the book, one can never again ignore the questions Tolstoi raises.

The one thing I most emphatically do not ask of a critic is that he tell me what I "ought" to approve of or condemn. I have no objection to his telling me what works and authors he likes and dislikes; indeed, it is useful to know this for, from his expressed preferences about works which I have read, I learn how likely I am to agree or disagree with his verdicts on works which I have not. But let him not dare to lay down the law to me. The responsibility for what I choose to read is mine, and nobody else on earth can do it for me.

THE FUNCTION OF A WORD

In this lighthearted essay, Jim Frederick examines the function of a common feature of oral language—the use of "like" to fill in and extend a sentence. Though some observers criticize this habit of language as a sign of sloppy thought and the decline of the English language, Frederick suggests another view.

WE ARE, LIKE, POETS

Jim Frederick

Our elders would have us believe that we—the twenty-something generation, Generation X, the MTV generation—are doomed to fail, not in the least by our supposed grammatical ineptness. Paramount to our problems, they claim, is a tendency to pepper our dialogue with the word "like" as if it were a verbal tic, demonstrating our abysmal vocabularies and utter lack of neurological activity.

Don't believe it. Much more than the random misfire of a stunted mind, "like" is actually a rhetorical device that demonstrates the speaker's heightened sensibility and offers the listener added levels of color, nuance and meaning.

Take the sentence, "I can't drive you to the mall because, like, my mom took the car to get her hair frosted." Here, "like" is a crucial phonic punctuation mark that indicates: "Important information ahead!" In our frenetic society, where silence is no longer powerful but completely alien, the dramatic pause doesn't carry much rhetorical clout. We employ "like" to replace that now obsolete device.

Or consider: "The human tongue is, like, totally gross." The use of "like" acknowledges that the tongue is not *exactly* totally gross but something *similar* to totally gross. It shows awareness that an indictment this harsh needs tempering. We repeatedly display such linguistic savvy in everyday observances: "My dad is, like, an anal-retentive psycho." Both acknowledge that the concept of direct correspondence between word and meaning has been, since Wittgenstein and Saussure, little more than a deluded fantasy.

In a new, ingenious usage, the word "like" becomes a verb form employed to recount an earlier conversation. Consider, "And she was like, 'You told us all to meet in *front* of the Burger King.' And I was like, '*Whatever,* you liar. Why would I when I knew it was going to snow?'" The difficulty here in determining what was actually said is not a limitation, but rather the strength of "like" as a dialogical indicator. It allows us to present the complete experience of a conversation, not just one of its component parts. "Like" is more than a shabby substitute for "said" (as is commonly supposed), but a near equivalent of the word "meant."

Also, "like" is often a broker of diplomacy. In the sentence, "Tiffany, you, like, still owe me that $10, you know," the skillful inclusion of "like" eases a potentially confrontational statement. The British do this sort of thing all the time with words like "rather," "quite" and "actually," and no one complains.

Our generation is not nearly as bad off as we have been told. Hardly a generation of jacked-in, zoned-out illiterates, we the bike couriers, the paralegals, the skate punks and the mall rats are actually a generation of poets. With a sublime sensibility to the power of "like," we view our lives, indeed human existence itself, as a grand, eternal and ever-changing metaphor.

THE FUNCTION OF EDUCATION

Let us take subject five on the checklist of subjects of this book—Education—narrow this down to College Education, and ask, What is its essential function? In other words, what main purpose does—and should—a college serve, particularly a liberal arts college? Addressing himself to an incoming freshman class, poet-educator John Ciardi develops his "enrichment of life" principle through a long and lively illustration, observing along the way that "the business of the college is not only to train you, but to put you in touch with what the best human minds have thought."

ANOTHER SCHOOL YEAR—WHAT FOR?

John Ciardi

Let me tell you one of the earliest disasters in my career as a teacher. It was January of 1940 and I was fresh out of graduate school starting my first semester at the University of Kansas City. Part of the reading for the freshmen English course was *Hamlet*. Part of the student body was a beanpole with hair on top who came into my class, sat down, folded his arms, and looked at me as if to say: "All right, damn you, teach me something." Two weeks later we started *Hamlet*. Three weeks later he came into my office with his hands on his hips. It is easy to put your hands on your hips if you are not carrying books, and this one was an unburdened soul. "Look," he said, "I came here to be a pharmacist. Why do I have to read this stuff?" And not having a book of his own to point to, he pointed at mine which was lying on the desk.

New as I was to the faculty, I could have told this specimen a number of things. I could have pointed out that he had enrolled, not in a drugstore-mechanics school, but in a college, and that at the end of his course he meant to reach for a scroll that read Bachelor of Science. It would not read: Qualified Pill-Grinding Technician. It would certify that he had specialized in pharmacy and had attained a certain minimum qualification, but it would further certify that he had been exposed to some of the ideas mankind has generated within its history. That is to say, he had not entered a technical training school but a university, and that in universities students enroll for both training and education.

I could have told him all this, but it was fairly obvious he wasn't going to be around long enough for it to matter: at the rate he was going, the first marking period might reasonably he expected to blow him toward the employment agency.

Nevertheless, I was young and I had a high sense of duty and I tried to put it this way: "For the rest of your life," I said, "your days are going to average out to about twenty-four hours. They will be a little shorter when you are in love, and a little longer when you are out of love, but the average will tend to hold. For eight of these hours, more or less, you will be asleep, and I assume you need neither education nor training to manage to get through that third of your life.

"Then for about eight hours of each working day you will, I hope, be usefully employed. Assume you have gone through pharmacy school—or engineering, or aggie, or law school, or whatever—during those eight hours you will be using your professional skills. You will see to it during this third of your life that the cyanide stays out of the aspirin, that the bull doesn't jump the fence, or that your client doesn't go to the electric chair as a result of your incompetence. These are all useful pursuits, they involve skills every man must respect, and they can all bring you good basic satisfactions. Along with everything else, they will probably be what sets your table, supports your wife, and rears your children. They will be your income, and may it always suffice.

"But having finished the day's work what do you do with those other eight hours—with the other third of your life? Let's say you go home to your family. What sort of family are you raising? Will the children ever be exposed to a reasonably penetrating idea at home? We all think of ourselves as citizens of a great democracy. Democracies can exist, however, only as long as they remain intellectually alive. Will you be presiding over a family that maintains some basic contact with the great continuity of democratic intellect? Or is your family life going to be strictly penny-ante and beer on ice? Will there be a book in the house? Will there be a painting a reasonably sensitive man can look at without shuddering? Will your family be able to speak English and to talk about an idea? Will the kids ever get to hear Bach?"

That is about what I said, but this particular pest was not interested. "Look," he said, "you professors raise your kids your way; I'll take care of my own. Me, I'm out to make money."

"I hope you make a lot of it," I told him, "because you're going to be badly stuck for something to do when you're not signing checks."

Fourteen years later, I am still teaching, and I am here to tell you that the business of the college is not only to train you, but to put you in touch with what the best human minds have thought. If you have no time for Shakespeare, for a basic look at philosophy, for the continuity of the fine arts, for that lesson of man's development we call history—then you have no business being in college. You are on your way to being that new species of mechanized savage, the Push-button Neanderthal. Our colleges inevitably graduate a number of such life-forms, but it cannot be said that they went to college; rather the college went through them—without making contact.

No one gets to be a human being unaided. There is not time enough in a single lifetime to invent for oneself everything one needs to know in order to be a civilized human.

Assume, for example, that you want to be a physicist. You pass the great stone halls of, say, M.I.T., and there cut into the stone are the names of the master scientists. The chances are that few if any of you will leave your names to be cut into those stones. Yet any one of you who managed to stay awake through part of a high school course in physics, knows more about physics than did many of those great makers of the past. You know more because they left you what they knew. The first course in any science is essentially a history course. You have to begin by learning what the past learned for you. Except as a man has entered the past of the race he has no function in civilization.

And as this is true of the techniques of mankind, so is it true of mankind's spiritual resources. Most of these resources, both technical and spiritual, are stored in books. Books, the arts, and the techniques of science, are man's peculiar accomplishment. When you have read a book, you have added to your human experience. Read Homer and your mind includes a piece of Homer's mind. Through books you can acquire at least fragments of the mind and experience of Virgil, Dante, Shakespeare—the list is endless. For a great book is necessarily a gift: it offers you a life you have not time to live yourself, and it takes you into a world you have not time to travel in literal time. A civilized human mind is, in essence, one that contains many such lives and many such worlds. If you are too much in a hurry, or too arrogantly proud of your own limitations, to accept as a gift to your humanity some pieces of the minds of Sophocles, of Aristotle, of Chaucer—and right down the scale and down the ages to Yeats, Einstein, E. B. White, and Ogden Nash—then you may be protected by the laws governing manslaughter, and you may be a voting entity, but you are neither a developed human being nor a useful citizen of a democracy.

I think it was La Rochefoucauld who said that most people would never fall in love if they hadn't read about it. He might have said that no one would ever manage to become human if he hadn't read about it.

I speak, I am sure, for the faculty of the liberal arts college and for the faculties of the specialized schools as well, when I say that a university has no real existence and no real purpose except as it succeeds in putting you in touch, both as specialists and as humans, with those human minds *your* human mind needs to include. The faculty, by its very existence, says implicity: "We have been aided by many people, and by many books, and by the arts, in our attempt to make ourselves some sort of storehouse of human experience. We are here to make available to you, as best we can, that experience."

THE FUNCTION OF SCIENCE

In the following essay the question *What is the function of X?* is more subtly, although just as surely, at work. Is it the proper function of science to be reductionist—"exploring the details, then the details of the details, until the smallest bits of the structure, or the smallest parts of the mechanism, are laid out for counting and scrutiny."

Thomas suggests that this "endless, obsessive preoccupation with the parts" may not be the true or appropriate function of science. Perhaps science should provide us with a broader perspective. Thomas's personal experience at the zoo points to a most provocative answer that involves a view not only of the essential function of science but of mankind itself.

THE TUCSON ZOO

Lewis Thomas

Science gets most of its information by the process of reductionism, exploring the details, then the details of the details, until all the smallest bits of the structure, or the smallest parts of the mechanism, are laid out for counting and scrutiny. Only when this is done can the investigation be extended to encompass the whole organism or the entire system. So we say.

Sometimes it seems that we take a loss, working this way. Much of today's public anxiety about science is the apprehension that we may forever be overlooking the whole by an endless, obsessive preoccupation with the parts. I had a brief, personal experience of this misgiving one afternoon in Tucson, where I had time on my hands and visited the zoo, just outside the city. The designers there have cut a deep pathway between two small artificial ponds, walled by clear glass, so when you stand in the center of the path you can look into the depths of each pool, and at the same time you can regard the surface. In one pool, on the right side of the path, is a family of otters; on the other side, a family of beavers. Within just a few feet from your face, on either side, beavers and otters are at play, underwater and on the surface, swimming toward your face and then away, more filled with life than any creatures I have ever seen before, in all my days. Except for the glass, you could reach across and touch them.

I was transfixed. As I now recall it, there was only one sensation in my head: pure elation mixed with amazement at such perfection. Swept off my feet, I floated from one side to the other, swiveling my brain, staring astounded at the beavers, then at the otters. I could hear shouts across my corpus callosum, from one hemisphere to the other. I remember thinking, with what was left in charge of my consciousness, that I wanted no part of the science of beavers and otters; I wanted never to know how they performed their marvels; I wished for no news about the physiology of their breathing, the coordination of their muscles, their vision, their endocrine systems, their digestive tracts. I hoped never to have to think of them as collections of cells. All I asked for was the full hairy complexity, then in front of my eyes, of whole, intact beavers and otters in motion.

It lasted, I regret to say, for only a few minutes, and then I was back in the late twentieth century, reductionist as ever, wondering about the details by force of habit, but not, this time, the details of otters and beavers. Instead, me. Something worth remembering had happened in my mind. I was certain of that; I would have put it somewhere in the brain stem; maybe this was my limbic system at work. I became a behavioral scientist, an experimental psychologist, an ethologist, and in the instant I lost all the wonder and the sense of being overwhelmed. I was flattened.

But I came away from the zoo with something, a piece of news about myself: I am coded, somehow, for otters and beavers. I exhibit instinctive behavior in their presence, when they are displayed close at hand behind glass, simultaneously below water and at the surface. I have receptors for this display. Beaver and otters possess a "releaser" for me, in the terminology of ethology, and the releasing was my experience. What was released? Behavior. What behavior? Standing, swiveling flabbergasted, feeling exultation and a rush of friendship. I could not, as the result of the transaction, tell you anything more about beavers and otters than you already know. I learned nothing new about them. Only about me, and I suspect also about you, maybe our reaction to each other as well. We are stamped with stereotyped, unalterable patterns of response, ready to be released. And the behavior released in us, by such confrontations, is, essentially, a surprised affection. It is compulsory behavior and we can avoid it only by straining with the full power of our conscious minds, making up conscious excuses all the way. Left to ourselves, mechanistic and autonomic, we hanker for friends.

Everyone says, stay away from ants. They have no lessons for us; they are crazy little instruments, inhuman, incapable of controlling themselves, lacking manners, lacking souls. When they are massed together, all touching, exchanging bits of information held in their jaws like memoranda, they become a single animal. Look out for that. It is a debasement, a loss of individuality, a violation of human nature, an unnatural act.

Sometimes people argue this point of view seriously and with deep thought. Be individuals, solitary and selfish, is the message. Altruism, a jargon word for what used to be called love, is worse than weakness, it is sin, a violation of nature. Be separate. Do not be a social animal. But this is a hard argument to make convincingly when you have to depend on language to make it. You have to print up leaflets or publish books and get them bought and sent around, you have to turn up on television and catch the attention of millions of other human beings all at once, and then you have to say to all of them, all at once, all collected and paying attention: be solitary; do not depend on each other. You can't do this and keep a straight face.

Maybe altruism is our most primitive attribute, out of reach, beyond our control. Or perhaps it is immediately at hand, waiting to be released, disguised now, in our kind of civilization, as affection of friendship or attachment. I don't see why it should be unreasonable for all human beings to have strands of DNA coiled up in chromosomes, coding out instincts for usefulness and helpfulness. Usefulness may turn out to be the hardest test of fitness for survival, more important than aggression, more effective, in the long run, than grabbiness. If this is the sort of information biological science holds for the future, applying to us as well as to ants, then I am all for science.

One thing I'd like to know most of all: when those ants have made the Hill, and are all there, touching and exchanging, and the whole mass begins to behave like a single huge creature, and *thinks,* what on earth is that thought? And while you're at it, I'd like to know a second thing: when it happens, does any single ant know about it? Does his hair stand on end?

THE FUNCTION OF HOLIDAYS

History professor Douglas Greenberg addresses the function of national holidays by focusing on the history of our Thanksgiving celebrations and the evolution of Independence Day. In its own way each holiday is "an opportunity for the whole nation to renew itself, for people to confirm their allegiance to one another and to their shared values." While religious holidays and thanksgiving days in times of tragedy and destruction have historically led us to "seek the forgiveness of God" and "to restore threatened social ties," national holidays also define "the special and distinctive character" of our values and our way of life.

Greenberg's essay, which appeared early in 1986, was in part a reply to protests by public officials and some private citizens over a projected holiday to celebrate the Reverend Martin Luther King, Jr.'s, birthday. In his last several paragraphs Greenberg isolates the distinctive American values inherent in a celebration of the slain civil-rights leader and his legacy. We celebrate King's birthday not just because he was a great man, for, as Greenberg concedes, "There have been . . . other great Americans whose birthdays we do not celebrate." We have added King's birthday because he led the "Second American Revolution" and spoke for a uniquely American vision that stretches back to our colonial period.

National Holidays Unite Us

Douglas Greenberg

What is it that makes the whole country pause to recall an event, to honor a person? We've been doing it for a long time—in fact, since before the nation began. There must be some powerful forces at work, deep needs that these holidays meet.

Virginians may give their Massachusetts friends an argument about where the first Thanksgiving actually took place, but no one disputes the mythic power of the story of the Pilgrims and the "first" Thanksgiving. And Americans, almost without exception, feel and respond to its pull.

Why should this be so? Partly because the story itself is so gripping and dramatic. But also because we instinctively grasp the meaning of that event in the life of a new and struggling colony.

We can leave it to historians to decide about the truth of the details as they have been handed down and to determine the exact site of the "first" Thanksgiving. But, true or not, the story reveals some of the roles of celebration in a community that is beset by trouble and that is seeking to establish an identity for itself.

Indeed, for much of the colonial period, the drama of the Plymouth legend was enacted frequently on smaller, less remembered stages throughout the colonies. When an epidemic passed through a town without taking many lives, the town would declare a communal day of thanks. If the king's troops had won a great victory or a town had enjoyed an especially bountiful harvest, the members of the community would come together not only to offer thanks but to reaffirm their shared beliefs and their connection to one another.

When Boston was beset by earthquakes in the 1720s and 1730s, authorities declared communal days of fasting to beseech the mercy of an angry God. In fact, if tragedy of any kind struck, the community would spend a day together in prayer and fasting, not only to seek the forgiveness of God but also to restore threatened social ties.

There was yet another level of meaning in these early shared traditions. When society was still deeply agrarian and therefore still very much at the mercy of the natural world, such days—whether of fasting or of feasting—were times for members of communities to reaffirm their reliance not just upon their God but also upon one another. These customs were part of the British heritage of the colonists who dominated early American social and religious life.

Even after the American Revolution, when new celebrations came to exert an equally powerful influence upon the national and communal imagination, these older observances continued. And gradually they took on important secular as well as religious functions.

In ceremonies repeated in community after community, colonists came together to celebrate good fortune and to mourn the bad. Their purpose was to define, by their participation in these ceremonies, the special and distinctive character of their values and their way of life.

When the American Revolution transformed the cultural life of the American people, they imbued a new, truly national holiday with similar social significance. The former colonists easily integrated Independence Day into the older ceremonial tradition—a tradition that had already strayed somewhat from its religious origins into a more secular mode.

Independence Day was a holiday with a new layer of meaning, however. Though it did embody the religious faith of the founders, it focused not upon the terrifying power of the natural world but upon the power of human will and agency in society and politics.

This new holiday exalted the men who had pledged their "lives," their "fortunes" and their "sacred honor" in a struggle for liberty, during the hot Philadelphia summer of 1776.

More than that, Independence Day defined the nation's values by memorializing the Declaration of Independence as an almost sacred text. In that remarkably succinct statement of political philosophy and grievances, Americans discovered the distinctive character of their values and way of life.

The celebration of Independence Day was an opportunity for the whole nation to renew itself, for people to confirm their allegiance to one another and to their shared values, much as individual communities and colonies had long been doing by means of the thanksgivings and fasts of the older tradition.

After the revolution, those older traditions faded into insignificance. Both had a brief resurgence during and after the Civil War, then withered into disuse until Franklin D. Roosevelt revived Thanksgiving in the 1930s.

July 4, on the other hand, gained in importance with every passing year. In the 19th century particularly, this holiday assumed a central role in defining for successive generations of Americans the values and aspirations that had inspired the revolution and informed the founding of the nation. The Fourth of July oration functioned much as the Thanksgiving and Fast Day sermons had for earlier generations.

In addition, the deaths of both Thomas Jefferson and John Adams on July 4, 1826—the fiftieth anniversary of the Declaration of Independence—did not go unremarked. Symbolizing, as it did, the passing of the revolutionary generation into history, this extraordinary fitting, almost poetic coincidence cemented the significance of July 4 in the national consciousness.

Critics have occasionally suggested that the nation's real birthday ought to be celebrated on September 21, Constitution Day; the coming bicentennial of the Constitution may prompt renewed lobbying in that direction. It is unlikely, however, that even the most vigorous efforts will dislodge Independence Day from what continues to be its special and distinctive role in American life. Apart from the abandoned holidays of Washington's and Lincoln's birthdays, no other holiday speaks so directly or so profoundly of those values of liberty and equality that we hold most dear. Other societies have harvest celebrations (like Thanksgiving) or holidays honoring their war dead (like Memorial Day), and some have celebrations to honor workers (like Labor Day). No other nation celebrates July 4, for Independence Day and the way we celebrate it represent a peculiarly American point of view and set of values.

None of our national holidays has as continuous a history as Independence Day. Thanksgiving, though earlier in its beginnings, was pretty much a state and local holiday until it was revived as a national celebration in the 1930s. Memorial Day—originally called Decoration Day—began only at the close of World War I. And Labor Day came into being as the result of a campaign undertaken by organized labor in the late 19th century.

Even Lincoln's and Washington's birthdays had interrupted histories. And, needless to say, Lincoln's birthday was never accepted in many parts of the South.

These discontinuous histories stem, in all likelihood, from the fact that the celebrations do not embody values that speak directly to our life as a nation. Nor do they articulate the central ideas and principles for which the nation stands. July 4 does.

Our celebrations on that day focus directly upon our national history and purpose as a nation. The traditional July 4 orations, the reading on courthouse steps of the Declaration of Independence, even the "bombs bursting in air" of fireworks displays constitute an annual acknowledgement of the heritage that has shaped us as a people.

Such holidays have enormous value to us as a society. They provide occasions for communal and, indeed, for national expressions of faith in our system of government and a determination to maintain the liberties it protects.

Holidays and communal rituals gave early Americans strength in times of adversity and bound them together in purposeful communities. So, too, July 4 strengthens our sense and our understanding of a national commitment, first conceived in the 18th century, to liberty and equality for all people.

How fitting, then, that our newest national holiday should commemorate the Second American Revolution. The Civil Rights Movement, of which Dr. King was the preeminent leader, was the 20th-century embodiment of the ideals first set forth in the Declaration of Independence.

Thus, the reason for a holiday honoring Dr. King is not just that he was a great man. There have been, after all, other great Americans whose birthdays we do not celebrate.

Dr. King was different because he spoke for a dream, for a vision of the world that was and is uniquely American. The ideals he articulated could only have emerged in the United States. Indeed, at the intellectual and emotional center of Dr. King's vision was his hope, his absolute insistence that his country live up to the standards set by the Declaration of Independence. The celebration of King's birthday as a national holiday therefore fits a long tradition of celebration in this country.

DISCUSSION AND EXERCISES

1. Consider the Auden essay on the function of a critic.
   a. Do you agree with the six basic services of the critic as Auden states them? Explain.
   b. Comment on Auden's statement: "But let him [the critic] not dare to lay down the law to me."

2. Compose a paragraph (150–250 words) using the following topic sentence. "So far as I am concerned, . . . a doctor, lawyer, teacher or clergyman (choose one such designation) can do me one or more of the following services." Be sure to follow Auden's listing pattern; also be sure your sentences are grammatically parallel (in Christensen's words, "like things in like ways").

3. Evaluate Ciardi's essay in terms of the following:
   a. general readability, tone, style
   b. organization (do you like the story that introduces the piece?)
   c. paragraphs (locate topic sentences)
   d. sentence construction
   e. choice of words, level of usage (for example, how do you respond to the phrase "this particular pest"?)

4. Summarize Ciardi's description of the function of education in a one-paragraph coordinate sequence, using the following topic sentence: "Ciardi's essay describes the several ways that a liberal arts education enriches life." (See question, How can X be summarized?) According to a Christensen schematization, your paragraphs will look like this:

   > 1 (topic sentence)
   >   2—function one
   >   3—comment on function one
   >   2—function two
   >   3—comment on function two
   >   2—function three
   >   3—comment on function three

Continued

5. Consider the various audiences for which Ciardi might have prepared his statement on the function of education (children, faculty colleagues, college administrators, general public, senior citizens). In what ways would the address have needed changing to meet the special needs of each audience?

6. Consider the Thomas essay, "The Tucson Zoo."
   a. Describe the organization of the essay; is it effective?
   b. Describe the theme of the essay as Thomas expresses it in the following sentence: "Maybe altruism is our most primitive attribute, out of reach, beyond our control."
   c. Comment on the effectiveness of the last sentence about the single ant who together with other ants "made the Hill": "Does his hair stand on end?"
   d. What audience do you think Thomas is addressing: general public? scientists?

7. Compose a paragraph (150–250 words) using the following topic sentence, drawn from Thomas's essay: "Left to ourselves . . . we hanker for friends." Again, write a coordinate sentence and then rewrite the paragraph as a subordinate sentence.

8. Review Douglas Greenberg's "National Holidays Unite Us" and answer these questions:
   a. What sort of Thanksgiving celebrations occurred in Boston during the 1720s and 1730s?
   b. How did the celebration of Independence Day differ from previous thanksgiving rituals? How did Independence Day retain the sacred aspects of previous holidays?
   c. What did the deaths of John Adams and Thomas Jefferson add to Independence Day?
   d. According to Greenberg, what does the discontinuous history of some holidays signify?
   e. Given Greenberg's emphasis on Martin Luther King, Jr.'s, birthday only at the very end of the essay, speculate on the rhetorical reasons Greenberg focuses so much attention on Independence Day.
   f. Outline the four major functions of national holidays as Greenberg presents them.
   g. Greenberg's essay appeared in a special issue of magazine commemorating Martin Luther King, Jr.'s, birthday. Why would Greenberg have spent so much of the article discussing American celebrations of Thanksgiving and Independence Day and only the last few paragraphs on the recently added Martin Luther King, Jr.'s, Day?
   h. Observe the consistently short paragraphs in this piece, originally published in a magazine format, laid out in narrow columns. Discuss the influence of format on paragraph length.

ESSAY SUGGESTIONS

1. Using Auden's description of the function of the critic as a model, write an essay (500–750 words) in which you describe the function of one of the following professionals:

scientist	minister, rabbi, priest, or nun
artist	police officer
musician	lawyer
writer	doctor
teacher	philosopher
athlete	

   Follow Auden's organization:
   Introduction: A listing of five or six "services" or functions
       I. What special qualifications the first two or three services demand
       II. What special qualifications the rest of the services demand
       III. What services or functions should *not* be performed
   Conclusion (optional)

2. In an essay (700–1,000 words) describe the main function of higher education as you view it, drawing on the essay reprinted here and on any other sources you wish to consult.

3. As Greenberg describes the function of national holidays in general, describe (in an essay of 750–1,000 words) the functions of any single national holiday or a secular or religious holiday.

4. In an essay (750–1,000 words) describe the functions of any of these institutions, paying attention to the historical evolution of their functions:

local government	religion
the free press	progressive taxation
fraternal organizations	social customs and manners
the legal system	national pride
aesthetic principles	tourism

5. Write an essay (750–1,000 words) in which you explain the essential function, as you view it, of any aspect of your life or environment: a hobby, sport, or recreation; a person or place; an object. If you are scientifically inclined, you might consider, in a less personal manner, the essential function of some element of nature, such as the moon or sun; or of some part of the body, such as the heart or brain; or of some social ritual, such as courtship or the cocktail party.

6. Examine the photograph on page 242 of a smiling family. What function do you suppose that photograph served in that family? Look over some of the photographs of your family. Write an essay (500–750 words) explaining the essential function of family photographs.

Question

9

WHAT ARE THE COMPONENT PARTS OF X?

THINKING ANALYTICALLY

WRITING ANALYTICALLY
    ANALYSIS OF EDUCATION
        THE SKILLS OF LIBERAL LEARNING,
        MIKE ROSE
    ANALYSIS OF A GROUP
        A GENERATION WITHOUT A NAME,
        NEIL HOWE AND BILL STRAUSS
    ANALYSIS OF AN INSTITUTION
        *WHAT REALLY MAKES A MARRIAGE
        WORK*, FRANCINE KLAGSBRUN
    ANALYSIS OF AN ART
        FIVE BASIC ELEMENTS OF MUSIC,
        DAVID RANDOLPH
    ANALYSIS OF AN ESSAY
        *THE RHETORICAL STANCE OF DAVID
        RANDOLPH IN "FIVE BASIC ELEMENTS
        OF MUSIC"*

THINKING ANALYTICALLY

To ask about the component parts of something, to find out what they are and how they are related to one another—this is *analysis*. We are, of course, forever analyzing things, simply because the only way to understand a person, an object, an idea, an event, a process, or an organization is to take it apart in a systematic manner to try to see what makes it tick, what made it happen, why it is as it is. Thus, analysis is a natural function of the human mind, going on all the time as we explore the world around us in order to understand it better. Thinking, itself, is impossible without analysis; every subject we contemplate with any seriousness— whether we write or talk about it—is necessarily analyzed.

All the questions in this book, but particularly the next ten, deal with analysis in that they attempt to break down a total subject into its parts. Logicians call this process *division;* it is a necessary first step in problem-solving and in writing as well. Before we can deal with a subject we must see its internal divisions.

WRITING ANALYTICALLY

Analysis is a challenging and demanding form of thinking and writing that requires systematic and rigorously logical thinking conducted in the light of clear and consistent principles. We cannot concern ourselves here with formal logic, but neither can we ignore three basic logical principles that are fundamental to all analysis, whether performed by a logician or by a writer:

1. Analysis (or division) must take place according to the structure of the thing being observed. In logical terms, to smash a glass is not to divide it, because a glass is not composed of fragments of glass. A chemical analysis is necessary to determine the component parts of a glass.
2. The interest of the analyzer determines the kind of structure being analyzed. Thus, you can analyze English literature as a chronological structure into old, middle, modern, or you can analyze it by separating it into various genres—poetry, drama, essays, and so on. Whatever structure you choose to work with, you must be consistent to achieve the primary purpose of analysis: to keep component parts clear and distinct. Thus, you cannot analyze literature by separating it into old, middle, and poetry; such an analysis shifts its basis of division from chronology to genre.
3. Analysis should also be complete—that is, you should divide X into *all* its component parts, not just some of them. In scientific or technical analysis this is mandatory; in a general essay on a nonscientific subject, however, you need not be quite as strict. You may choose to deal with only the main part or selected aspects of your subject. In that case you should indicate that the analysis is partial and incomplete, letting the reader know you have not inadvertently overlooked the elements you have not mentioned. One simple device for completing a division is to include the category "others" or "miscellaneous." In analyzing the body of an author's works, you might divide the works into novels, plays, short stories, and "miscellaneous writings." In this way you leave nothing out.

Analysis of Education

Analysis is but one of the skills required of students in a college or university. Students are often bewildered by the range of new skills expected of them. Mike Rose, a teacher of writing, felt this same confusion when he was an undergraduate, and remembered it when he became a teacher. In this passage from his book *Lives on the Boundary,* Rose explains what happened when he began to teach a group of Viet Nam veterans who were having a great deal of difficulty dealing with the writing demands of college. Rather than throw up his hands in frustration, Rose took the effort to analyze the components of undergraduate education, to break it down into its component parts.

This selection contains both Rose's account of how he went about doing his analysis and the results of that analysis. It's important to understand *why* Rose analyzed undergraduate education the way he did. There are many other ways we can—and do—analyze the undergraduate curriculum. You probably think of your education in terms of the requirements for your major; from your perspective, that is the most useful analysis. The administration of your school probably thinks of its curriculum most often in terms of departments: *that* determines where the money goes, where faculty are housed, how books are ordered for the library, and so forth. No one of these particular analyses is necessarily truer than any other one. Each reveals part of the truth as it obscures others; that is the nature of an analytical perspective.

THE SKILLS OF LIBERAL LEARNING

Mike Rose

The veterans' encounter with college led me to reflect on my education in a way I hadn't done before. More than I realized, I had learned a lot in El Monte about developing a curriculum: I approached learning carefully, step by step, systematically. I found that I knew what questions to ask. What had I really learned from studying history and psychology and philosophy and literature? I thought a lot about my best teachers, about Jack MacFarland at Mercy High, about Dr. Carothers and Ted Erlandson and the others at Loyola. I browsed through the books that had mattered and thought about those courses that had opened up ways of considering the world. What intellectual orientations persisted? I went back to UCLA and sat in on a few lectures in the humanities and the social sciences, listening, this time, with a different ear. I talked with other teachers. And this is how I started to think about the curriculum I would fashion.

Given the nature of these men's needs and given the limited time I would have with them, could I perhaps orient them to some of the kinds of reading and writing and ways of thinking that seem essential to a liberal course of study, some of the habits of mind that Jack MacFarland and the many that followed him had helped me develop? If I could do this in some systematic and manageable way, then I would be enhancing the veterans' chances of participating in the institutions they would soon be entering. And while I wanted to be pragmatic—college preparation was the name of this game—I also wanted to go beyond utility. I was looking for a methodical way to get my students to think about thinking. Thinking. Not a fussbudget course, but a course about thought. I finally decided to build a writing curriculum on four of the intellectual strategies my education had helped me develop—some of which, I would later discover, were as old as Aristotle—strategies that kept emerging as I reflected on the life of the undergraduate: summarizing, classifying, comparing, and analyzing.

Liberal studies had really sharpened my ability to find the central notion in an argument or the core of a piece of fiction. Thinking back on it, I couldn't imagine a more crucial skill than summarizing; we can't manage information, make crisp connections, or rebut arguments without it. The great syntheses and refutations are built on it. The veterans would have to have practice summarizing various kinds of academic materials. It would give them a nice sense of mastery if they could determine and express the gist of readings that might, at first glance, seem opaque as medieval texts.

Classifying. You could almost define the undergraduate's life as the acquisition of the ways Western scholars have classified their knowledge. The very departments in which I took my classes represented one way to classify inquiry, and I encountered classification schemes in every course I took: taxonomies in biology, genres and periods in literature and the arts, the catalogs of motive and behavior in psychology and sociology. I wanted the veterans to become familiar with academic classification schemes, to sharpen their own abilities to systematize what they study, and to develop a critical awareness of the limitations of the classification schemes that will surround them. I thought up some simple exercises: Bring to class twenty copies of paintings of the human body. Have the paintings represent a wide range of styles, from Florentine humanism to cubist geometrics, but have all information on artist and period removed. It would be the students' job to classify this collection of paintings by any system they could develop. They would probably begin with a simple binary scheme: some of the paintings look like people and some don't. But through my questions as well as through the observations rising from their interaction, they would be encouraged to elaborate and revise until they'd agreed that they could go no further. I would then ask them to discuss what they felt was gained and what was lost as they classified paintings and moved from one scheme to another.

Another thing that became clear to me was how much knowledge in the arts and sciences is gained by methodically examining one object or event or theory in relation to another. What comes into focus when a student places *A Farewell to Arms* alongside a piece of journalism? What understanding is gained by listing the features of French schooling next to a description of American education? Entire disciplines—comparative politics to comparative anatomy—are built on this intellectual strategy. Simply by virtue of their humanity, the men in the Veteran's Program continually made comparisons, but I wanted to give them the chance to develop confidence and facility in comparing points of view and explanations and works of art.

The further along I got in college, the more I was asked to "analyze" an artistic product, a physical phenomenon, a social event, *to analyze* meaning, to break something down to its constituent elements so as to better understand its nature. But that wasn't the whole story. There was a kind of implied directive to the request to analyze, and it took me quite a while before I realized it. Students are not usually told that such analytic investigation is always carried out with a set of assumptions, and these assumptions are crucial determinants of how you proceed in your examination, what you find, and how you explain your discovery to others. I figured that developing the ability to probe the assumptions beneath an analysis or explanation would be exciting and empowering for the veterans, a little insight into how to pick the academic lock. They would be able to read with a critical eye and thus speak and write with more authority. While I could probably develop this critical awareness by modeling it for the class and by questioning them on their reading, I thought they might also benefit by engaging in a kind of intellectual role-playing that would highlight the assumptive base of analysis. I could, for example, present them with a newspaper story about a man who commits an apparently senseless murder. Next would come an account of how Freud would explain violent behavior. It would be the student's job to slip into that perspective and discuss the story as though they were psychoanalysts. This passage would be followed by one written by a more existentially oriented social critic. The class would then discuss the crime with that perspective, discussing as well what happens to their analysis as they shift assumptions about human nature. How did the frameworks they used affect what they saw?

Analysis of a Group

Social observers love to categorize people, to define a group of people who share common interests and life experiences. One such group was Baby Boomers, people born in the fifteen or twenty years following World War II. In the last few years, writers for newspapers and magazines have turned their attention to the latest generation of Americans to come of age. Though there is no commonly agreed upon name for this generation (one of the most popular is "Generation X," from Douglas Coupland's book of the same name), social analysts seem to have reached some agreement about the component features of this group. The selection below is from *13th Gen,* a popular book by sociologists Neil Howe and Bill Strauss, based on their research into generational groupings in America. What follows is both analysis and definition: In outlining the disparate groups and common features of people born since 1961, the authors argue for the identifiable unity of such a group. Most of you reading this textbook fall into this grouping: How accurate do you find this analysis?

A GENERATION WITHOUT A NAME

Neil Howe and Bill Strauss

Imagine arriving at a beach at the end of a long summer of wild goings-on. The beach crowd is exhausted, the sand shopworn, hot, and full of debris—no place for walking barefoot. You step on a bottle, and some cop yells at you for littering. The sun is directly overhead and leaves no patch of shade that hasn't already been taken. You feel the glare beating down on a barren landscape devoid of secrets or innocence. You look around at the disapproving faces and can't help but sense that, somehow, the entire universe is gearing up to punish you.

This is how today's young people feel as members of what 30-year-old writer Nancy Smith calls "the generation after. Born after 1960, after you, after it all happened." After Boomers. And before the Babies-on-Board of the 1980s, those cuddly tykes deemed too cute and fragile to be left *Home Alone.* Who does that leave stuck in the middle? Eighty million young men and women, ranging in age from

11 to 31. They make up the biggest generation in American history (yes, bigger than the Boom); the most diverse generation—ethnically, culturally, economically, and in family structure, the only generation born since the Civil War to come of age unlikely to match their parents' economic fortunes; and the only one born this century to grow up personifying (to others) not the advance, but the decline of their society's greatness.

As they shield their eyes with Ray-Ban Wayfarer sunglasses, and their ears with their Model TCD-D3 Sony Walkmen ($229.99 suggested retail), today's teens and twenties tone-setters look shocking on the outside, unknowable on the inside. To older eyes, they present a splintered image of brassy sights and smooth manner. Families aside, what the older crowd knows of them comes mostly from a mix of film cuts, celebrity blurbs, sports reports, and crime files.

Over-30 moviegoers see them as hard-to-like kids, kids who deserve not a break but a kick, a pink slip, maybe even jail time. They are *The Breakfast Club's* "brat pack," enduring pointless punishments at the hands of befuddled adults. Hard Harry trying to *Pump Up the Volume* for his "why bother generation." Bill and Ted having adventures that could only seem "excellent" to somebody as terminally stupid as them. Tom Cruise proving he's a *Top Gun* only by breaking a few rules. A *Heathers* wilderness of teen suicides. Death-dosed *Boyz n the Hood.* Rob Lowe's *Bad Influence.* An evil teenage *Hand That Rocks the Cradle* for a baby far more precious than she ever was. Here and there, screenwriters lighten up a little—for example, when Ferris Bueller combs for pleasure in a world gone mad, or when *Edward Scissorhands* becomes an artist with the aid of his deformity, or when Wayne emerges from his parents' basement to find a "Way" in a "No Way" world. But, mostly, the impression is of kids growing up too hard to be cute.

The shortened scripts of TV sitcoms and the quick bites of ads and music videos leave an even brassier image of affluent wise guys and sassy girls more comfortable shopping than working or studying. Ads target them as beasts of pleasure and pain who have trouble understanding words longer than one syllable, sentences longer than three words. Pop music on their ever-declining number of Top 40 stations—the heavy metal, alternative rock, New Wave, rap—strikes many an older ear as a rock 'n' roll endgame of harsh sounds, goin'-nowhere melodies, and poetry that ranges from the clumsy to the foul or racist. There's other stuff—a capella "voicestras," acoustic revival—but not many aging classic rockers ever hear much of it.

News clips document a young-adult wasteland of academic non-performance, disease-ridden sex, date-rape trials, wilding, and hate crimes. Today's youngish sports figures often look to elders like American Gladiators, athletically proficient but uncerebral, uncivic, lacking nuance. To older eyes, the Neon Deions differ from the Namaths and Aarons partly in their size, speed, and muscularity, but also in their in-your-face slam dunks, end-zone boogies, and weak team loyalties. Those who, like Mary Lou Retton, do succeed in capturing our hearts invariably set off to "rettonize" themselves and capture our product endorsements. Team logos, once sources of local pride, now mark territory for inner-city gangs. But the Ickey Shuffle, Shark jacket, and Air Jordan high-top aren't the only sporting icons new to this generation: There's also one-armed Jim Abbott pitching in the major leagues, America's world-champion women soccer players, and second-generation black student-athletes like Duke's basketball star Grant Hill (the son of Yale and Dallas Cowboy football star Calvin Hill).

Yes, this is a generation with a PR problem. Its collective reputation comes from young celebrities and criminals, from the biggest stories of success and failure. Yet most in their teens and twenties are quick to insist that *People* cover stories and police blotters tell little about them personally, about their circles of friends, about their lives in school or on the job, about what it means to come of age in 1990s America. And, they insist, their generation will remain a mystery until elders take the trouble to block out the iconography and look more discerningly at the young men and women in daily American life.

In polyglot American cities—New York and Los Angeles especially—we see them as the reckless bicycle messengers (who, like *Bicycle Days* author John Schwartz, like to "live a little faster"), the rollerblading commuters, the pizza and package-delivery drivers, the young Koreans helping their fathers at grocery stores, the local-access cable TV producers, the deal making wannabees whom trader-turned-writer Michael Lewis says "age like dogs" before making their fortunes—or going broke trying. Other times, we notice them as the directionless college "slackers," the non-voters, the wandering nomads of the temp world, the store clerks whose every declaration sounds like it ends with a question mark, the women in tennis shoes lunching at the gym, the computer jockeys loading games onto their office PCs when the boss isn't looking.

In the inner city, they're the unmarried teen mothers and the unconcerned teen fathers. They're the lethal gangsters, the Crips and Bloods—and the innocent hiphoppers who have no illusions about why older white guys cross the street to avoid them. Across the landscape of urban youth, we see more millionaires and more hopelessly poor, more immigrants and more nativist skinheads, more social fractures and cultural fissures than today's 40-, 60-, or 80-year-olds could possibly remember from their own younger days.

In 'burb and town life, they are kids at the mall. Kids buying family groceries for busy moms and dads. Kids doing the wave at the ballpark. Kids of divorce. (Omigosh, it's Saturday, and I'm supposed to be with Dad, and I have, like, *so* much homework this weekend.) Kids battling back against drugs and alcohol. Kids in mutual-protection circles of friends, girding against an adolescent world far more dangerous than anything their parents knew. Kids struggling to unlink sex from date-rape, disease, and death.

In school, the diversity of student bodies has never been greater—not just in ethnicity, but also in attitude, performance, and rewards. Asian-Americans (and immigrant children generally) are achieving at a tremendous clip, and black and Hispanic aptitude test scores are rising, while Anglo aptitude test scores remain below levels seen one, even two, generations ago. On campus, women outperform men and soar into graduate programs, while collegians of both sexes struggle with a faculty-fueled debate over how to undo their various alleged insensitivities. Their handbills are more likely to promote products than ideologies, their protests more against the immediate scourges of their world—hikes in tuition, cuts in library hours, the hiring of teaching assistants who can't speak English—than against injustice in the world beyond. Most of them support global causes but don't have the money or time to contribute. Besides, they figure, what difference could they possibly make?

As college alumni, these are the grads with the big loans who were supposed to graduate into jobs and move out of the house, but didn't. They had more bucks in their pockets (and more employers in tow) before college than after. Whatever their schooling, these young adults seem to get poorer the longer they've been away from home,—unlike their parents at that age, who seemed to get richer. In the workplace, they lower their sights and take jobs as yardworkers, Walmart shelf-stockers, Blockbuster checkers, health care trainees, and as the miscellaneous scavengers and nomads in the low-wage/low-benefit service economy. In unions and corporations, they face career ladders where the bottom rungs have been cut off.

Overseas, the dressed-down kids of '70s-era Amsterdam have been replaced by dressed-up kids of '90s-era Prague: get-it-done whizzes, exporters of U.S. culture, entrepreneurial globalites who know how to make bucks out of social chaos, experts at exploring the sprawling world frontiers of capitalism. If they're on the skids at home, what they're good at doing is in demand elsewhere—whether as conquering warriors of Panama and Kuwait, as McDonald's-Moscow managers in Adam Smith ties, or as multilingual aides to the Tokyo or London financiers busy gobbling up American assets.

With each passing year, these young men and women are gradually but surely making their mark on the national character. In them lies much of the doubt, distress, and endangered dream of late twentieth-century America. In them also lies a reason for hope. As a group, they aren't what older people wish they were, but rather what they themselves know they need to be: street-smart survivalists clued into the game of life the way it really gets played, searching for simple things that work in a cumbersome society that offers little to them.

When they look into the future, they see a much bleaker vision than any of today's older generations ever saw in their own youth. Then the hard-pressed youths of the Great Depression saw a path (albeit difficult) to a bright future, under the guidance of wise and determined older adults. But today's teens and twenties aren't singing about any "over the rainbow" reward and see precious little wisdom and determination up the age ladder. They have trouble identifying the path that does not lead to decline for them and their nation. Instead, they sense that they're the clean-up crew, that their role in history could be sacrificial—that, whatever comeuppance America has to face, they'll bear more than their share of the burden. It's a new twist, and not a happy one, on the American Dream.

Are they a "generation"? Yes, with a personality that reaches across the board—rich and poor, black and white, Hispanic and Asian, male and female, celebrity and everyman. Whatever a 15- or 25-year-old's individual circumstances, he or she can sense a composite personality, a generational core. It's something each individual can help define, "slack" within, or fight against—but cannot easily ignore. The simple fact of ethnic and socioeconomic diversity (in contrast to the far greater homogeneity found in older generations) is an essential part of this persona.

Analysis of an Institution

Research and a subtle reading of the evidence are important for analyzing institutions, as Francine Klagsbrun proves in "What *Really* Makes a Marriage Work." Klagsbrun's research (nearly 90 interviews with couples married more than 15 years) led her to discover not one single elusive secret of marriage but—rather—eight common elements in marriages that endure. "Marriage is too complex a matter to be reduced to one secret," she cautions, offering insights into those skills and attitudes partners need to nurture if they want their marriage to succeed. She reminds us that we need to ask the right question: "Don't we have more to learn from focusing on the positives, on why marriages succeed rather than why they fail?" Her eight factors underscore the importance of attitude in marriage, suggesting that in this age of divorce, couples have unfortunately asked only, "Why do marriages fail?" The right question is also important for cultural observers studying the institution: if they ask pessimistic questions, they will receive pessimistic answers.

Note that the separate features of the good marriage are listed in parallel construction and that Klagsbrun quotes liberally from her interviews to provide a human voice addressing itself to the problems and joys of marriage. "Sex isn't everything in a marriage—but it's a lot!" "Tony likes to relax on vacations and I like to be on the run." "He loved to spend; she watched every cent." Klagsbrun's balanced treatment of the positions of husbands and wives plus her sensible advice suggests that there need not be impassible gulfs between partners. As the essay progresses, Klagsbrun increasingly de-emphasizes individual traits and differences in favor of shared values, shared trust, shared history, and shared attitudes that keep couples together.

What *Really* Makes a Marriage Work

Francine Klagsbrun

"How have you managed to stay married for so long?" a woman in her late 20s asked me, referring to my marriage of almost 30 years.

Her question puzzled me. I had thought that marriage was fashionable again, and "commitment" a favored word. But as I pursued the matter further, I realized that while *getting* married has made a comeback, *staying* married is still suspect. I have heard long-married couples accused not only of cowardice—fear of striking out on their own—but of complacency, inertia and lack of imagination.

I suppose our high divorce rate has made a lasting marriage seem an almost impossible dream to some. Yet, if almost one of every two marriages now ends in divorce, more than one of every two still remains intact. While some of these marriages may be troubled, most would not have lasted unless they were working. Don't we have more to learn from focusing on the positives, on why marriages succeed rather than why they fail?

It was from this perspective that I set out to interview couples whose marriages had lasted 15 years or more. (Fifteen seemed a logical base line because most marital splits take place earlier. A marriage that has lasted 15 years is more likely to continue.) After screening, I interviewed 87 couples intensively. Some spoke about struggles and problems that I wondered how I could have handled. But most had found emotional riches as well as difficulties. In general, these were ordinary people who chose to stay married not because they felt they had to, but because the marriage was important to them.

It would be nice to say I found *the* secret of lasting marriages, but marriage is too complex a matter to be reduced to one secret. Rather, I found, there are certain abilities and outlooks that couples in strong marriages share a good part of the time. They fall, it seems to me, into eight categories.

1. Enjoyment of each other. Wives and husbands in satisfying marriages enjoy being together and talking to each other. Though they may spend some evenings in comfortable silence, mostly they do talk. And they listen. I watched the faces of people I interviewed, and while they might argue or interrupt, they were engaged. They laughed at each other's jokes. They held hands, they touched.

I could sense a sexual electricity between some partners. The couples I met all considered sex a major part of marriage, but nobody regarded it as the core of marriage, its reason for being. As one husband put it, "Sex isn't everything in a marriage—but it's a lot."

These couples also find each other interesting. But they do not necessarily have the same interests, and that was a surprise to me. Typical was this comment made by a wife: "Tony likes to relax on vacations and I like to be on the run. So one summer we travel a lot, and the next summer we rent a house and look at the view."

But if sharing interests is not important, sharing *values* is. Those who valued religion, for example, considered it the strongest bond in their lives. One couple said their biggest arguments were about money. He loved to spend; she watched every cent. Yet they had an instant meeting of minds when it came to buying a cello for their musically gifted daughter. They bought the best they could afford, because they both valued education above anything else money could buy.

2. An ability to change. Change is inevitable in marriage—children are born, leave home; spouses grow old, get sick—and it can bring anxieties. Even good changes can upset equilibrium. "As he went up the corporate ladder," said one woman, "I didn't like the person he became."

Yet, in the strongest marriages, each partner is able to make "strategic midcourse corrections," as one psychiatrist put it. Couples who stay together in spite of changes are, in effect, making constant decisions to be remarried.

One man married 29 years talked about a midlife crisis—his wife's: "I had a very simple view of marriage when we began, I worked as many hours as I wanted to, then relaxed playing golf and tennis. Pamela took care of me and the children. Nine years ago, my world toppled. Pamela had an affair. She told me she hated my selfishness and disinterest in her and the kids, and she was ready to leave me.

"My family was the most important thing in life to me, so I decided to win back my wife by changing myself. I put Pamela first, and my work last. I soon came to enjoy the things we did together and to regret the wasted years. Now I have my family back, and that change is the thing I feel proudest of in my life."

Today, couples whose marriages have lasted 15 years or more have lived through some of the most rapid social change in history. New emphases on a woman's rights outside her home, and on a man's responsibilities inside his, have brought tension to many marriages. Other couples, however, have had the flexibility to pick up what was useful to them and incorporate new ideals in their marriage.

People who stay happily married see themselves not as victims of fate, but as free agents who make choices. They willingly choose to change themselves when necessary to keep their marriages alive and vital.

3. An ability to live with the unchangeable. Many happily married people said they didn't expect perfection. They accepted qualities in their partners that they didn't necessarily like. As one woman said, "We've been so bombarded with advice about 'improving' marriage that we forget it is also possible just to let things be."

A number of long-married couples acknowledge that they have unresolved conflicts—about personality differences, say, or styles of dealing with things. But they stop fighting about those issues and go about their lives. They focus on the strengths of the marriage, on compatibilities rather than dissonances. As a shopkeeper, married 38 years, put it, "You have to know when to holler and when to look away."

4. An assumption of permanence. Most marriages begin with the expectation that they will last "forever." In marriages that do last, "forever" is not only a hope but an ongoing philosophy. The partners simply do not think seriously about divorce as a viable option. This attitude that a marriage will last, *must* last, tempers their approach to conflicts and imperfections.

These people are committed to the marriage as well as to each other. They know that love needs time to take root and then expand; that in an enduring marriage time is on your side. Time allows you the security of "taking each other for granted," in the best sense of the term, without having constantly to impress or to prove yourself.

5. Trusting each other. Love may wax and wane in a good marriage, but trust is a constant. Trust not only allows for the sense of security and comfort that marks satisfying unions but also makes possible the freedom marriage provides— the "right," in the words of psychiatrist Aaron Stein, "people have to be themselves." Each partner trusts that his or her core self will not be ridiculed or violated, that it will be nurtured and safe. And in that safety lies a special kind of freedom.

Trust forms the basis for marital intimacy, and intimacy is probably the quality most longed for in marriage—closeness and affection as well as sexual intimacy. "Sex is richer and deeper for us," said one woman, "because we trust each other and we're not ashamed to get pleasure."

Trust is the reason invariably given for a commitment to monogamy, for trust in marriage presupposes exclusivity. One reason the "open marriage" movement of the 1970s faded fast is because it disregarded the need for exclusivity in marriage, for being the most important person in the other's life.

6. A balance of dependencies. In the best marriages, partners are mutually dependent. When they speak of needing each other, they are not talking about weaknesses, but strengths.

One person I interviewed was a widow who had held public office at a time when few other women had. Her husband of 30 years, an attorney, had helped and encouraged her, opening her eyes to new ideas, giving her pointers on new Supreme Court decisions, for example. "I didn't lose part of myself by depending on him for this thinking," she said. "You have just so much time, energy and intellect, and it's good to be able to depend on your spouse to fill in the gaps. Our dependencies enriched both our lives."

7. A shared and cherished history. Building a history together, chapter by chapter, every couple creates a "story," and couples in long marriages respect their own stories—about how they met, their private jokes, their code words and rituals, even the sadnesses they shared. Theirs is not mere nostalgia, but an attachment to the significance of their past and of the time spent together.

Educators complain that young people today have little sense of history; they live in the present, without memory. This amnesia adds to their rootlessness, and I believe it contributes to their high divorce rate. People in long marriages, by contrast, value their history together. When the present gets raggedy, they look to the past to find the good they have shared.

Humor is the universal salve, easing tensions and marriage fatigue. "If you can laugh about it," everyone said, "you know it will be all right."

8. The ability to be lucky. Even with trust and flexibility, people need a little bit of luck to keep a marriage going. You need luck, first of all, in choosing a partner who has the capacity to trust and to change, someone who will mature and grow as you mature. Then, too, you need a little luck with life. A gang-up of illnesses, job losses, family feuds or personal failures can push a marriage off-course, when it might otherwise have succeeded.

But the good thing about luck is that it is not entirely out of our control. Luck in marriage is as much attitude as chance. Couples who regard themselves as lucky are not blind to the soft spots of their marriages—they just consider the positives more important. These people grab luck by the tail.

Marriage has its faults, heaven knows. It has its pains and tediums, its rages and despair. However, when it works, it has its moments: of adventure and passion, of calm contentment, of companionship and profound love. The married people I spoke to think that nothing can compare with those moments.

Analysis of an Art

Skillfully written analysis can reveal the essence of a seemingly difficult or esoteric subject. Take music, for example, which many people enjoy but relatively few understand. Hoping to increase enjoyment by promoting understanding, musicologist David Randolph wrote the following analysis in which he considers the totality of "music" from his chosen point of view: what the listener responds to. The analysis is strictly logical in that Randolph sticks scrupulously throughout to the special ground on which the analysis rests. He never shifts to types of music, individual instruments, and so on. He also leaves no question as to whether it is complete. There are five and only five important elements to respond to in music. Even "if we wanted to be rigid about definitions," Randolph assures us, "we could say that music consists of nothing but the manipulation of the five elements."

Five Basic Elements of Music

David Randolph

Let us see what it is that you respond to in music.

Do you find something appealing about the famous tune from Schubert's Unfinished Symphony? If so, then you are responding to one of the most important elements of music—*melody*.

Do you find that you feel like tapping your foot during the march movement of Tchaikovsky's Pathétique Symphony? If so, then you are responding to another extremely important element—*rhythm*.

Yet observe that rhythm is present in the melody of Schubert's Unfinished (just tap out the melody on a table with your finger, without singing, and you will isolate the rhythm), and that melody is present in even the most rhythmic portion of the Tchaikovsky march. Therefore, in the process of merely "liking" one of these works, you are actually appreciating two musical elements at once. While this example may not impress you by its profundity, the *principle*—being aware of what it is that you respond to—is at the root of all genuine music appreciation.

Now imagine how much less satisfying Schubert's melody would be if it were buzzed through a tissue-papered comb, instead of being played by the entire cello section of an orchestra. The melody and the rhythm would still be present as before; the difference would lie only in the quality of the sound that reached your ears. Therefore, when you enjoy the richness of the sound of the massed cellos playing the melody, you are responding to another of the basic elements—*tone color*. Your appreciation, then, really involves *three* elements.

Now, let us suppose that a pianist is playing one of your favorite songs—the melody in the right hand, the accompanying chords in the left. Suppose that his finger slips as he plays one of the chords, causing him to play a sour note. Your immediate awareness of the wrong note comes from your response to another of the basic elements—*harmony*.

Let us briefly consider the more positive implications of harmony. Whether you are attracted by barbershop-quartet singing, or by an atmospheric work by Debussy, or by the powerful, forthright ending of Beethoven's Fifth Symphony, *part* of your reaction stems from your response to the harmony, which may be defined as the simultaneous sounding of two or more notes (usually more than two, as in these three examples). Thus we have found a *fourth* element in your appreciation.

Do you have a sense of completeness at the conclusion of a performance of (we will use only one of countless possible examples) Beethoven's Ninth Symphony? Are you left with a feeling of satisfaction as well as elation? If so, part of that sense of satisfaction—of completion—comes from your feeling for *form*, which is the last of the five basic elements of music. . . .

If we wanted to be rigid about definitions, we could say that music consists of nothing but the manipulation of the five elements. The statement is correct in that there is no music in the world, regardless of the time or place of its origin, that can be based upon anything other than some combination of these five elements. Thus, to offer the most extreme contrast possible, what we may imagine as the ritual stamping on the ground by the savage appealing to his god partakes of some of the same basic elements as does Bach's *Passion According to St. Matthew*, notably rhythm and tone color, and certainly, to a degree, form.

Analysis of an Essay

In Part One, The Writing Process, we examined aspects of a writer's "rhetorical stance"—a term used by rhetoricians to describe a writer's view of his or her (1) purpose, (2) audience,

(3) occasion or context, and (4) reader-writer relationship (see Visualizing Your Audience and Establishing a Reader-Writer Relationship).

From the vantage point of rhetorical stance, we might analyze any essay in this text (or elsewhere), in order to see or infer how the writer envisioned it—such as its projected purpose and readers. We might look at how well the writer carried out his or her projections. Because such analyses can benefit those who wish to improve their writing, it will be helpful to do a sample analysis of the preceding essay.

THE RHETORICAL STANCE OF DAVID RANDOLPH IN "FIVE BASIC ELEMENTS OF MUSIC"

Assessing the rhetorical stance of David Randolph in his short, helpful essay describing the basic features that all of us respond to when we listen to music is not difficult, for we may infer whatever his words and style omit. Let us consider the four aspects of rhetorical stance, each in its turn:

Purpose:	Clearly Randolph's purpose is to help readers understand what is going on when they listen to music, what they are *responding* to, whether in a pop tune or Bach's *Passion According to St. Matthew.* The title of the book—*This is Music: A Guide to the Pleasures of Listening*—from which this essay was excerpted, provides a further clue to Randolph's purpose. The author is trying to help people increase their listening pleasure by increasing their information and deepening their sensitivity.
Audience:	Is Randolph visualizing an audience of peers, his fellow musicologists? A special age, education, or interest group? Or is he addressing the general public? Clearly Randolph is addressing people interested in music who are not musicians (if they were professionals, they would already know what Randolph is telling them). Seeking to know more about music, presumably so that they can enjoy it more, they are implicitly asking Randolph, "Can you help me?"
Occasion or Context:	His readers have bought his book or borrowed it from the public library. Randolph is meeting with them, although not in a lecture hall where he can talk to them, face to face. On this occasion, however, at this moment of reading (the moment when readers open the book, eager to find answers to their questions), Randolph will try to answer them—as if he were face to face with them "telling" them what they need to know.
Reader-Writer Relationship:	"Let us see what it is that you respond to in music." With these words of direct address Randolph opens his "conversation." "Let *us*," he says—meaning *you* (in the library or in your easy chair at home) and *I* (here at my typewriter) "take a look together at how *you* respond." The writer asks the reader questions: "Do you find . . .? Do you have a sense that . . .?" In this "simulated" personal encounter, the reader silently replies, nodding in agreement or shaking the head in disagreement. "Observe this . . .," Randolph suggests (note low-key imperative verb); "Now imagine . . ." (another imperative). The reader-writer relationship here is clearly like that of teacher and student, lecturer and audience, specialist and nonspecialist. The elements of tone, diction, level of usage, and voice indicate that this was the relationship Randolph envisioned and, as we can judge, the one he successfully established.

DISCUSSION AND EXERCISES

1. Using the above analysis of Randolph's "Five Basic Elements of Music" as a guide, explain the rhetorical stance assumed by the writers of the following essays:

   > Rose: "The Skills of Liberal Learning"
   > Howe and Strauss: "A Generation Without a Name"
   > Ciardi: "Another School Year—What For?" (Question 8).

2. In the same essays, evaluate paragraph structure according to where "breaks" occur. Indicate how they do or do not coincide with steps in the unfolding and development of the ideas in each essay. Are the paragraphs themselves unified? Are they internally consistent? Reconstruct what you perceive to have been the writer's working outline.

3. Write a paragraph (100–250 words) in which you break down one of the following into three or more component parts. Be prepared to describe your rhetorical stance.

   > the spirit of modern art
   > the spirit of the new morality
   > the spirit of dissent
   > the spirit of revolution
   > the spirit of liberal education

   Instead of devoting a paragraph or two to each part, devote only two sentences, the first naming the part and the second adding specific details or examples. In Christensen's terms this paragraph will be a three-level, coordinate sequence.

   > 1 Topic sentence
   >   2 Naming of first part
   >   3 Specific detail of first part
   >   2 Naming of second part
   >   3 Specific detail of second part
   >   2 Naming of third part
   >   3 Specific detail of third part

ESSAY SUGGESTIONS

1. Expand the paragraph in Exercise 3 above into a full-length essay (750–1,000 words).

2. Write an essay (500–750 words) in which you analyze the component parts of a physical or physiological structure.

3. Assuming a rhetorical stance similar to Randolph's and using the informal direct "you" address to the reader, write an essay (500–750 words) in which you isolate the elements of one of the following:

Arts	*Sports*
ballet	baseball
painting	soccer
architecture	tennis
photography	golf
literature	skiing

4. Following the example of "What *Really* Makes a Marriage Work," write an essay (750–1,000 words) analyzing the components of any one of the following:

the successful chief executive	the spirit of modern religion
the well-made machine	the proper funeral
a functioning neighborhood	patriotism
a romantic evening	a mature outlook
the ideal teacher	proper child-rearing

5. In an essay (750–1,000 words) analyze the rhetorical stance of Lincoln's Gettysburg Address or his Second Inaugural Address; Winston Churchill's "blood, sweat, and tears" speech; or John F. Kennedy's Inaugural Address.

Question

10

HOW IS X
MADE OR DONE?

THE CREATIVE PROCESS
   COMPOSING A BALLET, AGNES DEMILLE
   CREATING AN AMERICAN, RICHARD RODRIGUEZ

PERSONAL PROCESSES
   HOW I LEARNED A NEW WAY TO WRITE,
      CHRISTOPHER LEE
   SHOOTIN' THE BULL, DOUG CHRISTIAN

INTELLECTUAL PROCESS
   THINKING SCIENTIFICALLY, T. H. HUXLEY

If you were to ask how to make or do something, you would be entering into a special form of analysis that rhetoricians call *process analysis*. Here, instead of dividing a given subject into its component parts, you divide a process into its successive stages.

An essay of this kind presents an orderly, step-by-step, chronologically arranged description of how a process of some kind takes place: how a poet writes a poem (a creative process); how we think (an intellectual process); how a clock keeps time (a mechanical process); how plants make chlorophyll (a natural process); how a baker makes bread (a manufacturing process); how women won the vote (a social process); how the Russian Revolution began (an historical process). An essay in process analysis is likely to be readable and lively, for by its very nature it keeps moving from stage one to stage two to stage three, and so on.

THE CREATIVE PROCESS

Suppose, for example, you address the question *How is X made or done?* to one aspect of creativity (subject four in the checklist): the creative art of choreography. In this case you might write an essay like the following vividly descriptive analysis by choreographer Agnes DeMille of how she composes a ballet.

COMPOSING A BALLET

Agnes DeMille

To make up a dance, I still need . . . a pot of tea, walking space, privacy and an idea. . . .

When I first visualize the dance, I see the characters moving in color and costume. Before I go into rehearsal, I know what costumes the people wear and generally what color and texture. I also, to a large extent, hear the orchestral effects. Since I can have ideas only under the stress of emotion, I must create artificially an atmosphere which will induce this excitement. I shut myself in a studio and play gramophone music, Bach, Mozart, Smetana, or almost any folk music in interesting arrangements. At this point I avoid using the score because it could easily become threadbare.

I start sitting with my feet up and drinking pots of strong tea, but as I am taken into the subject I begin to move and before I know it I am walking the length of the studio and acting full out the gestures and scenes. The key dramatic scenes come this way. I never forget a single nuance of them afterwards; I do usually forget dance sequences.

The next step is to find the style of gesture. This is done standing and moving, again behind locked doors and again with a gramophone. Before I find how a character dances, I must know how he walks and stands. If I can discover the basic rhythms of his natural gesture, I will know how to expand them into dance movements.

It takes hours daily of blind instinctive moving and fumbling to find the revealing gesture, and the process goes on for weeks before I am ready to start composing. Nor can I think any of this out sitting down. My body does it for me.

It happens. That is why the choreographic process is exhausting. It happens on one's feet after hours of work, and the energy required is roughly the equivalent of writing a novel and winning a tennis match simultaneously. This is the kernel, the nucleus of the dance. All the design develops from this.

Having established a scenario and discovered the style and key steps, I then sit down at my desk and work out the pattern of the dances. If the score is already composed, the dance pattern is naturally suggested by and derived from the pattern of the music. If it remains to be composed as it does in all musical comedies, the choreographer goes it alone. This, of course, is harder. Music has an enormous suggestive power and the design of the composer offers a helpful blueprint. . . .

Through practice I have learned to project a whole composition in rough outline mentally and to know exactly how the dancers will look at any given moment moving in counterpoint in as many as five groups. As an aid in concentration, I make detailed diagrams and notes of my own arbitrary invention, intelligible only to me and only for about a week, but they are not comparable in exactness to music notation.

At this point, I am ready, God help me, to enter the rehearsal hall.

Organizing an essay in process analysis is not difficult because it generally organizes itself in a time sequence. What *can be* difficult is dividing the process into logical sequential stages and making certain that you describe each stage accurately, for if the chain has one weak link the entire explanation can collapse, leaving the reader in confusion.

Notice how carefully DeMille has divided the choreographic act into its stages—the six successive steps through which it is carried out:

Step one: getting the ideas (and the conditions for developing them; a pot of tea, walking space)

    Step two: visualizing the dancers "moving" in color and costume and "hearing" the music

        Step three: establishing key dramatic scenes

Step four: discovering the basic gestures, rhythms, and style of character ("My body does it for me.")

Step five: writing down the pattern of the dances (detailed diagrams and notes)

Step six: entering the rehearsal hall (with God's help!)

Notice also that the six steps *flow* into one another. At no point do you wonder what stage you are at, for "time" words (plus "place" words, pronouns that refer to earlier nouns, repetition of key words) keep you oriented and moving steadily *ahead:*

When I first visualize the dance . . .
Before I go into rehearsal . . .
At this point I avoid using the score . . .
I *begin* to move and *before* I know it . . .
I never forget a single nuance . . . *afterwards* . . .
The *next* step is to find the style . . .
. . . *again* behind locked doors and *again* with a gramophone . . .
Before I find how a character dances . . .

. . . the process *goes on for weeks* . . .
. . . *after* hours of work . . .
I *then* sit down at my desk . . .
At this point, I am ready . . . .

After reading a clearly written process-analysis essay, you often feel as though you know exactly how a particular action or event occurs. The author identifies the important steps and shows how one leads to another. Sometimes, though, such a step-by-step analysis can oversimplify the process being described. It's like being told that the steps in beginning to write a paper are (1) find a topic; (2) make an outline; (3) write a thesis. That all may be important, but such a description hardly conveys the complexities of thought and action involved in writing. In trying to give the reader an understanding of a complex process, particularly one involving human experience and its variables, an author may choose other strategies to suggest the various ways such a process may occur.

In the following selection, author Richard Rodriguez describes the changes that affect children born to immigrants in the United States. In a sense, he is answering the question, How does assimilation happen? As you read, ask yourself why he chose not to give a step-by-step account of this process. See how many different stages of the process you can identify in this passage.

CREATING AN AMERICAN

Richard Rodriguez

For the child of immigrant parents the knowledge comes like a slap: America exists.

America exists everywhere in the city—on billboards; frankly in the smell of burgers and French fries. America exists in the slouch of the crowd, the pacing of traffic lights, the assertions of neon, the cry of freedom overriding the nineteenth-century melodic line.

Grasp the implications of American democracy in a handshake or in a stranger's Jeffersonian "hi." America is irresistible. Nothing to do with choosing.

Our parents came to America for the choices America offers. What the child of immigrant parents knows is that here is inevitability.

A Chinese boy says his high-school teacher is always after him to stand up, speak up, look up. Yeah, but then his father puts him down at home: "Since when have you started looking your father in the eye?"

I'd like you to meet Jimmy Lamm. Mr. Lamm was an architect in Saigon. Now he is a cabbie in San Francisco. Stalled in traffic in San Francisco, Jimmy tells me about the refugee camp in Guam where, for nearly two years, he and his family were quartered before their flight to America. A teenager surfs by on a skateboard, his hair cresting in purple spikes like an iron crown, his freedom as apparent, as deplorable, as Huck Finn's.

Damn kid. Honk. Honk.

The damn kid howls with pleasure. Flips us the bird.

Do you worry that your children will end up with purple hair?

Silence.

Then Jimmy says his children have too much respect for the struggle he and his wife endured. His children would never betray him so.

On the floor of Jimmy Lamm's apartment, next to the television, is a bowl of fruit and a burning wand of joss.

He means: his children would never *choose* to betray him.

Immigrant parents re-create a homeland in the parlor, tacking up postcards or calendars of some impossible blue—lake or sea or sky.

The child of immigrant parents is supposed to perch on a hyphen, taking only the dose of America he needs to advance in America.

At the family picnic, the child wanders away from the spiced food and faceless stories to watch some boys playing baseball in the distance.

—

My Mexican father still regards America with skepticism from the high window of his morning paper. "Too much freedom," he says. Though he has spent most of his life in this country, my father yet doubts such a place as the United States of America exists. He cannot discern boundaries. How else to describe a country?

My father admires a flower bed on a busy pedestrian street in Zurich—he holds up the *National Geographic* to show me. "You couldn't have that in America," my father says.

When I was twelve years old, my father said he wished his children had Chinese friends—so polite, so serious are Chinese children in my father's estimation. The Spanish word he used was *formal*.

I didn't have any Chinese friends. My father did. Seventh and J Street was my father's Orient. My father made false teeth for several Chinese dentists downtown. When a Chinese family tried to move in a few blocks away from our house, I heard a friend's father boast that the neighbors had banded together to "keep out the Japs."

Many years pass.

In college, I was reading *The Merchant of Venice*—Shylock urging his daughter to avoid the temptation of the frivolous Christians on the lido. Come away from the window, Shylock commands. I heard my father's voice:

Hear you me, Jessica.
Lock up my doors, and when you hear the drum
And the vile squealing of the wry-necked fife,
Clamber not you up to the casements then,
Nor thrust your head into the public street
To gaze on Christian fools with varnished faces,
But stop my house's ears, I mean my casements.
Let not the sound of shallow foppery enter
My sober house.

—

I interview the mother on Evergreen Street for the *Los Angeles Times*. The mother says they came from Mexico ten years ago, and—look—already they have this nice house. Each year the kitchen takes on a new appliance.

Outside the door is Los Angeles; in the distance, the perpetual orbit of traffic. Here old women walk slowly under paper parasols, past the Vietnam vet who pushes his tinkling ice-cream cart past little green lawns, little green lawns, little green lawns. (Here teenagers have black scorpions tattooed into their biceps.)

Children here are fed and grow tall. They love Christmas. They laugh at cartoons. They go off to school with children from Vietnam, from Burbank, from Hong Kong. They get into fights. They come home and they say dirty words. Aw, Ma, they say. Gimme a break, they say.

The mother says she does not want American children. It is the thing about Los Angeles she fears, the season of adolescence, of Huck Finn and Daisy Miller.

Foolish mother. She should have thought of that before she came. She will live to see that America takes its meaning from adolescence. She will have American children.

—

The best metaphor of America remains the dreadful metaphor—the Melting Pot. Fall into the Melting Pot, ease into the Melting Pot, or jump into the Melting Pot—it makes no difference—you will find yourself a stranger to your parents, a stranger to your own memory of yourself.

A Chinese girl walks to the front of the classroom, unfolds several ruled pages, and begins to read her essay to a trio of judges (I am one of her judges).

The voice of the essay is the voice of an immigrant. Stammer and elision approximate naïveté (the judges squirm in their chairs). The narrator remembers her night-long journey to the United States aboard a Pan Am jet. The moon. Stars. Then a memory within a memory: in the darkened cabin of the plane, sitting next to her sleeping father, the little girl remembers bright China.

Many years pass.

The narrator's voice hardens into an American voice; her diction takes on rock and chrome. There is an ashtray on the table. The narrator is sitting at a sidewalk café in San Francisco. She is sixteen years old. She is with friends. The narrator notices a Chinese girl passing on the sidewalk. The narrator remembers bright China. The passing girl's face turns toward hers. The narrator recognizes herself in the passing girl—herself less assimilated. Their connective glance lasts only seconds. The narrator is embarrassed by her double—she remembers the cabin of the plane, her sleeping father, the moon, stars. The stranger disappears.

End of essay.

The room is silent as the Chinese student raises her eyes from the text.

One judge breaks the silence. Do you think your story is a sad story?

No, she replies. It is a true story.

What is the difference?

(Slowly, then.)

When you hear a sad story you cry, she says. When you hear a true story you cry even more.

—

The U.S. Army took your darling boy, didn't they? With all his allergies and his moles and his favorite flavors. And when they gave him back, the crystals of his eyes had cracked. You weren't sure if this was the right baby. The only other institution as unsentimental and as subversive of American individuality has been the classroom.

PERSONAL PROCESSES

Another kind of process analysis comes into play when a person describes a change in his or her own life. In such a case the author is clearly in a very good position to understand the process and may decide to tell readers about that experience for a variety of reasons (See Question 2, How did X happen? and Question 4, What is my memory of X?) In the reading that follows, Christopher Lee, a student at the University of Florida describes that process by which he learned to write. More specifically, he is describing how he learned to write in a new way. Classified as learning disabled, Lee had to learn new ways to connect meanings to words on the page. He has come to adopt the term "different learner" for people who share his condition, a term that emphasizes not limitations but possibilities. As you read, ask yourself who his audience is. How does he choose details and organize stages of the process in order to make his experience clear to his readers? Why is it important to him that his readers do understand his experience?

How I Learned a New Way to Write

Christopher Lee

My first memory of learning to write was in the second grade when we started learning to write in cursive. I know I must have struggled through learning to print because I still have trouble keeping my *b*'s and *d*'s and *n*'s and *u*'s straight. However, like many other difficult or embarrassing things in my life, I have managed to bury those memories too deep to recall. I feel that it is important to try to describe what writing is like for me because writing is one of my biggest handicaps.

It is important to remember that all learning disabilities are different and that other people with learning disabilities may have difficulty writing for entirely different reasons. My unique learning abilities affect my ability to both see and hear the letters correctly, and my language disabilities affect my ability to express my thoughts.

Thoughts of writing give me a very uneasy feeling. When I am writing, everything is uncertain. I never know if anything I'm writing is correct; stopping and starting, I am constantly trying to figure out how to form the next letter or to decide what the next letter should be. Certain words are particularly difficult. For instance, I can never spell "girl" right. I go back and forth—is it "girl" or "gril"? Neither looks right. I see everything as being jagged. The rules of punctuation and spelling have never made sense. Words never seem to be spelled the way I hear them, and they never look the same way twice.

It is difficult to explain what goes on in my head when I am trying to write because language itself is an obstacle for me. When I am trying to spell a word, it's as if there are twenty-six letters spinning around in my head, each letter having its own box. The boxes contain sounds. The letters are trying to find their boxes by finding their sounds. I don't really see them but I feel like they're up there looking for a place to settle. Only a few of the letters in my head have dropped out of the flurry into their proper boxes. For instance, the letter *b* has come to be easier to understand then other letters; therefore, I assume I have found the box containing the sound for *b*. There are times when I still have trouble forming the letter because I confuse it with *d,* but the sound-symbol connection has been made. I am aware that I have found this box because without hesitation, I can name some words that start with *b.* I cannot do this with many letters.

The boxes in my head are not in any kind of order. The letters are flying above the boxes searching for some sort of order. All these boxes are screaming out sounds, and I cannot pull the letters down to match the sounds. I have been trying to match these boxes with their sounds for almost twenty years. It becomes very frustrating when communication depends so much on knowing these twenty-six little letters.

When I am writing I try to match the sounds with the letters the best I can. Even if I have all the time in the world I never seem to be able to match enough letters with sounds to write a word. After concentrating so hard on trying to match the letters to the boxes, I eventually force the letters into a word. The end result is that I am never sure if I have written the word correctly. After so many years of forcing the fit, the boxes are all out of shape, making it easier to place the wrong letters within. At the same time, I have to concentrate on what the final spelling looks like so I can store it in my memory. I have to remember *my* spelling so I will know the word when I come back to it. Concentration is the key here. I am concentrating so much on just finding the correct letters and figuring out how to form the letter so that I will recognize it later, that to put my ideas into some kind of coherent order is almost impossible. I feel very lucky when I have a teacher who is organized enough to put important notes on the board during a lecture. Then I simply have to worry about transferring the letters correctly onto my paper; I worry about trying to decipher what they say another time.

I did not learn how to write until I learned how to use a computer . . . This sounds ironic, but in my past, writing was spelling, and since I could not spell, I could not write. When I discovered a word-processing system with a spelling check, I finally understood that writing involved putting thoughts and ideas into some kind of written form. Knowing that the computer would catch my spelling errors, I began to ignore my spelling. Then I began to look at writing as content. This did not happen until I was a freshman in college. Before learning to use a computer, I saw writing as a bunch of spelling words that I had to reproduce in horizontal fashion. Writing was simply a horizontal spelling test.

The computer helped me to discover that there was more to writing than just spelling. First of all, the computer was something new and different and was a relief from pencil and paper. All my life pencil and paper had been a nightmare. When I picked up a pencil and paper to write, my stomach would automatically tighten, and my nightmare would begin. The computer helped me view writing in a different way. It helped me to shed my fear of the pencil and paper. Sitting down in front of a computer was not nearly as frightening to me as sitting down with a pencil and paper. For this reason, I immediately saw the computer as a sign of hope. I had never been able to put down the right words with a pencil, but sitting at a keyboard seemed to free my mind. A pencil was like a piece of dead wood in my hands, and trying to make this stick form letters always seemed awkward and difficult. When using a keyboard, however, the letters seemed to come out through my fingertips. The writing seemed to be closer to my brain.

Not only did the computer allow me to view writing with a sense of excitement, it also allowed me to see the written symbols in a neat, organized fashion. For years I had trained my handwriting to be messy and as unreadable as possible so I could hide all my mistakes. This was a con job. When my teachers selected papers to read in class, I was sure they wouldn't read mine because they couldn't. Using a computer forced the letters out in such a neat manner that I actually started to look at the words. Before, I was afraid to look at the words. Now, instead of looking at a scribbled blurb on a page, I looked at a crisp, black-and-white image. To quote a friend of mine, it "made the words stand still." Being able to see a clear image helped me to focus on the words. I have now learned to tell when a word is wrong. I may not always be able to correct it, but the spelling check can do that for me. I have found myself trying to spell the words correctly before I put the paper through the spelling check in the word processor. Once the spelling check has checked the words, I pay attention to the change, thus reinforcing the correct spelling.

Writing in cursive is a very messy, undefined type of writing. Cursive is also an easy way out of spelling. It allows the student to compact letters together. Because of its easy flow, it does not allow the student to see how the words are actually formed. To me, it's a lazy type of writing. Before the computer, I always printed when I needed to do something right because this helped me see all the letters in the word. Even today, when I don't know a word and I don't have access to my computer, I find myself writing in cursive because it's an easy way to hide. Words I feel comfortable with, I find that I print, but words that I am not sure of, I scribble out. I believe that teachers who stress cursive writing are giving students with creative learning abilities a way out. They are allowing the student to reinforce bad habits . . .

Much of this chapter so far has dwelled on the subject of spelling, just as much of a person's writing education is often spent on learning to spell. If I make one point in this chapter, it is that spending so much time on trying to teach someone with a learning disability to spell might be detrimental to that person's ability to ever learn to write. I have spoken to several groups of teachers, and I am aware of how uneasy this statement makes teachers feel. However, the purpose of this book is to show what goes on in the mind of a creative learner in an attempt to explain why we have such trouble learning certain things. I cannot spell today, and it is certainly not because teachers did not try year after agonizing year to teach me. They spent so much time trying to teach me to spell that no one ever got around to teaching me how to write. To me it is an outrage that I reached college before I understood that writing is putting thoughts on paper.

A good process analysis often includes explanations of why key procedures are followed. The next essay, Doug Christian's "Shootin' the Bull," illustrates the effectiveness of citing such specific details.

Before we learn its true topic, Christian's essay (submitted for a college writing assignment) catches us off-guard with his disarmingly slangy title, for it suggests that the essay will tell us how to "pull the wool over someone's eyes" by boasting, bragging, or

"B.S.ing," as it's popularly known. But no, this is an essay *literally* about *shooting a bull*—Christian's experience of shooting, gutting, skinning, and butchering a bull on his family's farm. The grisly details, which leave little to the imagination, create an unmistakable air of authenticity: we know this young man has done exactly what he describes. Christian's almost clinical report of the entire process nevertheless suggests that, despite his expertise, he had ambivalent feelings about the job; that he had to steel himself to relive this exhausting and draining experience.

Shootin' the Bull

Doug Christian

Making money was my goal when I headed home in early December. My finances were running extremely low, so when my dad told me he would pay $100 for some easy work I naturally accepted.

The job, I was told, was to butcher our Scottish Highlander bull, which we kept along with about thirty cattle in our pasture over the summer. The Scottish bull was a huge fellow, weighing about 1,400 pounds, with long blond hair that curled around his head and neck, which itself was about as thick as a 100-year-old tree stump. But the most outstanding feature on this bull was his huge horns. Those horns curled slightly up and forward and measured a good three-and-a-half to four feet from tip to tip.

The horns were the main reason my dad wanted to be rid of the bull. Transporting cattle requires driving them up a chute and loading them into a truck. To load that bull into the truck we had to turn his head to make the horns fit while we pushed him up the chute. So dad decided it would be less hassle to pay me $100 to shoot and quarter him in the pasture.

On a cold December afternoon I set out in our truck with a log chain, two bales of hay, four knives, a chain saw, and a 30.06 rifle. I spread the hay about 15 yards from the truck. When the cattle came to feed, I hopped in the back of the truck with my rifle, and when I had a clear shot, I hit him in the head just behind the ear. His legs collapsed and after kicking for a while he remained still.

I had never skinned a cow or bull before but had performed the operation on many a deer, antelope, and small-game animal. I approached him with my knife, grasped his thick neck, cut through his skin, and pulled out his windpipe to let the blood drain out to prevent spoilage of the meat. After letting him bleed, I hooked the log chain around his horns and pulled him away from the puddle of blood so I would not have to kneel in it while working on him. I made a long cut through the skin of his belly, from his neck where I had pulled out the windpipe all the way back to his tail. In two hours I went through four knives in the process of cutting and peeling off his skin. Next I cut open his gut and pulled out his organs. I practically had to crawl into the beast to cut out his huge green stomach. It did not help matters when a slip of the blade cut open his intestine, spraying half-digested alfalfa all over me.

After completely gutting him, I picked up the chain saw. I buzzed off all his legs up to the second joint and cut his head off with a stroke through his neck. Next I cut straight down his back along the vertebral column, then across his back between the fourth and fifth ribs to separate the meat into quarters. It took three of us to lift each hindquarter into the truck.

The whole process took me eight and a half hours. Before I returned to school my dad paid me the $100 and gave me the skull with the horns and the large blond hide, which I had made into a rug.

INTELLECTUAL PROCESS

When you try to present a train of thought or a line of reasoning—in order to explain your views, or to argue a case for or against something—you are attempting to describe an intellectual or logical process based on the laws of reasoning. T. H. Huxley has created an eminently readable analysis of the act of thinking itself: how we use the inductive and deductive modes in our everyday lives.

THINKING SCIENTIFICALLY

T. H. Huxley

There is a well-known incident in one of Molière's plays, where the author makes the hero express unbounded delight on being told that he had been talking prose during the whole of his life. In the same way, I trust, that you will take comfort, and be delighted with yourselves, on the discovery that you have been acting on the principles of inductive and deductive philosophy during the same period. Probably there is not one here who has not in the course of the day had occasion to set in motion a complex train of reasoning, of the very same kind, though differing of course in degree, as that which a scientific man goes through in tracing the causes of natural phenomena.

A very trivial circumstance will serve to exemplify this. Suppose you go into a fruiterer's shop, wanting an apple,—you take up one, and, on biting it, you find it sour; you look at it, and see that it is hard and green. You take up another one, and that too is hard, green, and sour. The shopman offers you a third; but, before biting it, you examine it, and find that it is hard and green, and you immediately say that you will not have it, as it must be sour, like those that you have already tried.

Nothing can be more simple than that, you think; but if you will take the trouble to analyse and trace out into its logical elements what has been done by the mind, you will be greatly surprised. In the first place you have performed the operation of induction. You found that, in two experiences, hardness and greenness in apples went together with sourness. It was so the the first case, and it was confirmed by the second. True, it is a very small basis, but still it is enough to make an induction from; you generalise the facts, and you expect to find sourness in apples where you get hardness and greenness. You found upon that a general law, that all hard and green apples are sour; and that, so far as it goes, is a perfect induction. Well, having got your natural law in this way, when you are offered another apple which you find is hard and green, you say, "All hard and green apples are sour; this apple is hard and green, therefore this apple is sour." That train of reasoning is what logicians call a syllogism, and has all its various parts and terms,—its major premiss, its minor premiss, and its conclusion. And, by the help of further reasoning, which if drawn out, would have to be exhibited in two or three other syllogisms, you arrive at your final determination. "I will not have that apple." So that, you see, you have, in the first place, established a law by induction, and upon that you have founded a deduction, and reasoned out the special conclusion of the particular case. Well now, suppose, having got your law, that at some time afterwards, you are discussing the qualities of apples with a friend: you will say to him, "It is a very curious thing,—but I find that all hard and green apples are sour!" Your friend says to you, "But how do you know that?" You at once reply, "Oh, because I have tried them over and over again, and have always found them to be so." Well, if we were talking science instead of common sense, we should call that an experimental verification. And if still opposed, you go further, and say, "I have heard from the people in Somersetshire and Devonshire, where a larger number of apples are grown, that they have observed the same thing. It is also found to be the case in Normandy, and in North America. In short, I find it to be the universal experience of mankind wherever attention has been directed to the subject." Whereupon, your friend, unless he is a very unreasonable man, agrees with you, and is convinced that you are quite right in the conclusion you have drawn. He believes, although perhaps he does not know he believes it, that the more extensive verifications are,—that the more frequently experiments have been made, and results of the same kind arrived at,—that the more varied the conditions under which the same results are attained, the more certain is the ultimate conclusion, and he disputes the question no further. He sees that the experiment has been tried under all sorts of conditions, as to time, place and people, with the same result: and he says with you, therefore, that the law you have laid down must be a good one, and he must believe it.

In science we do the same thing;—the philosopher exercises precisely the same faculties, though in a much more delicate manner. In scientific inquiry it becomes a matter of duty to expose a supposed law to every possible kind of verification, and take care, moreover, that this is done intentionally, and not left to a mere accident, as in the case of the apples. And in science, as in common life, our confidence in a law is in exact proportion to the absence of variation in the result of our experimental verifications. For instance, if you let go your grasp of an article you may have in your hand, it will immediately fall to the ground. That is a very common verification of one of the best established laws of nature—that of gravitation. The method by which men of science establish the existence of that law is exactly the same as that by which we have established the trivial proposition about the sourness of hard and green apples. But we believe it in such an extensive, thorough, and unhesitating manner because the universal experience of mankind verifies it, and we can verify it ourselves at any time; and that is the strongest possible foundation on which any natural law can rest.

DISCUSSION AND EXERCISES

1. Answer these questions about the Rodriguez essay:
   a. If Rodriguez had organized his essay as a list of the steps people go through in adjusting to American culture, what would those steps be?
   b. How would you describe the tone of this essay? What particular sentences have a distinctive tone?
   c. What does each of the following images contribute to Rodriguez' overall purpose?
      1. "frankly in the smell of burgers and French fries"
      2. "On the floor of Jimmy Lamm's apartment, next to the television, is a bowl of fruit and a burning wand of joss."
      3. "the Viet Nam vet who pushes his tinkling ice-cream cart past little green lawns, little green lawns, little green lawns"
      4. "her diction takes on rock and chrome"
   d. Why does Rodriguez refer to Huck Finn and Daisy Miller, characters in novels by American authors Mark Twain and Henry James?
   e. Why do you think Rodriguez chose to develop his ideas as a series of narratives rather than as a step-by-step account?

2. For the following questions and exercises, refer to Doug Christian's "Shootin' the Bull":
   a. In the fifth and sixth paragraphs, circle all transitional words and phrases; then study each to determine how it contributes to the flow of events.
   b. Christian's pay for "shootin' the bull" is mentioned three times: why is that fact important?
   c. What information about the butchering do you think is missing from this essay? Are questions about this process left unanswered?
   d. Why do the bull's skull and horns represent an appropriate bonus for Christian's work?
   e. Beyond his title Christian employs slang and other colloquial usages: describe their effectiveness.
   f. Note Christian's precise list of tools. Why is he so thorough in presenting them?
   g. How does Christian convey the idea of his physical exhaustion at the end of this process?

3. Consider Huxley's examples of scientific thinking in everyday life.
   a. Write a paragraph (150–250 words) called, Thinking Scientifically, in which you illustrate your own everyday use of inductive and deductive reasoning.
   b. Write another paragraph of equal length supporting Dr. Samuel Johnson's counterobservation that "most men think indistinctly." Cite examples of the illogical, the irrational, the impulsive, the half-thought-through. Suggested title: Thinking Unscientifically.

ESSAY SUGGESTIONS

1. Creative Process

    The creative process, as it has been described by many scientists and artists, falls roughly into four stages: *preparation*—the stage of deliberate and conscious planning, training, and effort; *incubation*—the stage in which you are not consciously dwelling on a problem but are nonetheless mulling it over on a subconscious level; *illumination*—the "flash" wherein you see the solution to the problem; and finally *verification*—the stage in which you test your newly discovered hypothesis, reviewing and possibly revising it. Knowing these stages of the creative process may help you to organize an essay around one of the following: (Notice how similar these stages are to prewriting techniques.)

    a. Write an essay (500–750 words) describing, as Agnes DeMille does, a creative experience you have had—the composition of a poem, story, or piece of music; the painting of a picture; the design of a room or a piece of furniture.

    or

    b. Describe in an essay (500–750 words) the process of learning how to do something. Any accomplishment will provide a suitable topic: how you learned to swim, ski, speak French, play bridge—maybe even how you learned "to think," that is, to think *rigorously*.

2. Historical-Social Process

    Write an essay (500–750 words) on one of the following topics, chosen from one of the following groups: (Be sure to use prewriting techniques after you have done your preliminary research.)

    a. Discoveries and Inventions

    How Schliemann discovered Troy
    How Columbus discovered America
    How Salk discovered the polio vaccine
    How Pasteur discovered the pasteurization process
    How the Curies discovered radium
    How Bell invented the telephone
    How Edison invented the electric light
    How Fleming discovered penicillin

    b. General Historical Events

    Beginnings:

    How Alaska became a state
    How the Great Wall of China was built
    How the Third Reich rose
    How World War II started
    How the U.S. "got involved" in Vietnam
    How Glasnost and Perestroika evolved

Endings:

    How the French Revolution ended
    How the Roman Empire fell
    How Germany was defeated in World War II
    How Hitler died

c. Social and Political Process

    How Congress conducts investigations
    How a U.S. president is elected
    How women won the vote
    How Prohibition was repealed

d. General Enterprises

    How a newspaper or magazine is "put to bed"
    How the paper is delivered (from press to doorstep)
    How a class is conducted
    How a party is organized
    How a trip is planned
    How traffic is regulated
    How a university (or any part thereof) is run

3. Technical-Natural Processes
   a. Write an essay (500–750 words) on one of the following complex processes.

    How explosives are manufactured
    How glass is blown
    How skyscraper windows are washed
    How paintings are restored
    How tobacco is cured

   b. Write an essay (500–750 words) explaining one of the following natural processes:
      1. Physiology (how X is done)

    How we see
    How we hear
    How we maintain balance
    How we breathe
    How we digest food
    How we think
    How we remember
    How we fall asleep

Continued

2. Botany (how X is made)

> How plants manufacture food
> How plants reproduce
> How plants evolve
> How trees develop rings

c. Write an essay (500–750 words) describing an unusual process with which you have had personal experience, as Christian did in "Shootin' the Bull." Be certain to pay attention to transitions and to the specific details of the process. Decide whether including your reactions to each stage is appropriate and explain the reasons for key actions.

d. Write an essay (500–750 words) about any of the following:

> How computer programs work
> How xerox copying machines work
> How a hot-air balloon is inflated and launched
> How a brick wall is laid
> How a moving van is packed
> How a road is built or repaired

4. Intellectual Process

Using Huxley's discussion of induction, write an essay (500–750 words) in which you show how you use the inductive mode of thinking in your daily life.

5. Write an essay (500–700 words) explaining the stages of a common human experience. Use one or two narratives as Rodriguez did to develop your essay. Possible experiences:

> | | |
> |---|---|
> | falling in love | deciding on a career |
> | moving to a new place | dealing with loss |
> | learning a new skill | reaching a decision |

Question

11

HOW SHOULD X BE MADE OR DONE?

QUALITIES OF GOOD
  "HOW-TO" WRITING
    *SOUTHERN FRIED CHICKEN WITH COUNTRY
      GRAVY,* BILL NEAL
    *HOW TO RUN FOR OFFICE IN A VERY SMALL
      TOWN,* SHIRLEY WEISSENBORN

VISUALIZING THE "HOW-TO"
  AUDIENCE
    *HOW TO LOSE WEIGHT SENSIBLY AND
      SUCCESSFULLY AND PERMANENTLY,*
      NORMAN KAPLAN, M.D.
    VERBS, OR, *PUT THE PEDAL TO THE METAL,*
      RITA MAE BROWN

QUALITIES OF GOOD "HOW-TO" WRITING

With this question we come to the most practical type of writing: the how-to piece, a form of process analysis that tells readers not only how a particular process *is* made or done, but how it *should be* made or done. This analysis becomes a set of directions from you to your readers, telling them precisely how to move through a series of steps toward a given goal. All recipes are instances of the how-to form, as are all inside-the-package instructions. We conduct much of the business of the world by means of this kind of writing.

How-to or directional writing automatically puts you in the authoritative position of instructor, telling your less informed readers-students exactly what to do and how to do it. With the sense of self-importance that inevitably accompanies the use of imperative voice, you should feel an equal sense of responsibility, for in assuming the role of teacher and counselor, you must make certain you are teaching well and counseling wisely.

Your first responsibility, of course, is to be accurate and clear. If, for example, you are instructing readers in the art of winning at bridge, you should be absolutely certain first that you have your facts right, and second that you explain them clearly, not leaving out a single step or important detail, taking nothing for granted, and allowing for no uncertainties or ambiguities as to what you mean. The cardinal virtues of directional writing are accuracy, clarity, and conciseness. No extra words should clog the free flow of information. You should write instructions in a systematic, lucid, and readable manner.

How-to pieces present no serious organizational problems since directions must follow a strict chronological order (first do this, then do that, and so on), and the mode of address, as we have seen, is invariably imperative. The how-to form clearly lends itself to an extraordinarily wide range of readers and of subject matter, plus an equally wide variety of tones. In general, the writer and reader come together in close contact (direct address from *me* to *you*), thereby establishing a situation in which the deeper humanistic purposes of writing can be fulfilled: increasing understanding among people, sharing knowledge and skills, and helping one another.

Obviously the first step must be to win the reader's trust. This requires that the reader hear a trustworthy voice, a writer's voice that demonstrates knowledge, honesty, and directness.

Writing a good recipe is more difficult than it seems. Though the steps and ingredients may be easily organized, much of what makes a good cook can't be boiled down into a simple series of events. In the following recipe, from a volume on the cooking of the American South, Bill Neal divides his recipe into two parts—a discussion of what a good cook knows about frying chicken and a more traditional recipe. Both parts are needed to show how fried chicken with country gravy should be made. Notice Neal's supportive and helpful tone. Do you get the sense that he is a trustworthy teacher?

Southern Fried Chicken with Country Gravy

Bill Neal

Southern fried chicken is the center of more controversies than perhaps any other item of food. Some people will tell you to remove the skin before battering, some swear by a double-dip. There is chicken fried in oil, in butter, in shortening, in lard, and in bacon grease. Some poor birds are saturated with all sorts of foreign elements, from Worcestershire to soy sauce. Now, what makes southern fried chicken a classic is its perfect combination of raw material and technique. You want chicken that tastes like chicken, with a crust that snaps and breaks with fragility—a contrast to the tender, moist meat. No detail can be overlooked without spoiling the integrity of your bird, so be patient and careful. Scrutinize every aspect of the job, and a perfectly fried chicken will unfold itself. No new tricks or magic seasonings can improve its beautiful simplicity.

First, the bird: only a whole, fresh chicken will do. (Frozen chicken tastes bloody and turns dark at the bone when fried. If you find yourself in the possession of one, stew it or bury it.) Wash it well under running cold water and let it dry. Then, and always, cut the bird into nine pieces, that is, with a wishbone—southerners call it the "pulley-bone." Fried chicken without a wishbone is like a life without a childhood, so resign yourself to a little butcher work.

To find this amuletic morsel, press firmly with your fingertips the meat at the neck end of the breasts. The wishbone connects these two muscles, rising from a base on each side near the wing joint to a small but protruding knob. Cut behind the knob with a sharp pointed boning knife down to the base on either side, with plenty of meat attached. (Take care to preserve the magic and avoid cracking the bones.) Disjoint the remaining carcass so you have two wings, two thighs, and two legs. In all these separations, find the actual joints and work the knife between them. Do not cut, hack, or splinter any bones or you might as well buy packaged parts. Detach the whole breast from the backbone by running through the fragile ribs, and snapping it at the neck end. Then split the breasts as cleanly as possible through the septum.

Second, the pan: A heavy cast-iron skillet is the only *authentic* implement (an enameled cast-iron skillet is an acceptable substitute). Go to a good, old-fashioned hardware store and buy one if you don't already have it. Gourmet and cooking stores do not generally carry them. To fry a whole chicken in one batch, buy one 12 inches (30 cm) in diameter with a lid to match. Take it home and wash it, for this *one time only,* in hot water, *no* soap. Dry it immediately and place it on a burner. Pour in ½ inch (1 cm) of vegetable oil and turn the burner to a low heat. Season the pan for 40 minutes, periodically oiling the inside walls with a natural bristle pastry brush. Discard the oil and cool the pan, wiping it well with paper towels. Never wash this pan again—over the years it will blacken with use, and, if necessary, can be scoured with a small amount of salt. Soaps, detergents, and metal pads will destroy the patina you want to nurture. Now that you have a pan and the know-how to butcher your bird, get ready to cook.

Yields 4 servings

1 chicken weighing 3 to 3½ pounds	*1 teaspoon salt*
(1350–1575 g), cut into 9 pieces	*½ teaspoon black pepper*
1 cup (235 ml) buttermilk	*1 cup (225 g) lard*
1 cup (235 ml) all-purpose flour	*1½ cups (355 ml) peanut oil*

Recommended equipment: A boning knife, medium mixing bowl, 12-inch (30 cm) cast-iron skillet with cover (see introduction above), frying thermometer, two paper bags, wooden whisk.

Put the chicken pieces in a glass or stainless steel bowl and toss with the buttermilk. Let marinate for at least 2 hours. Combine the flour, salt, and pepper in a large paper bag and preheat the lard and peanut oil in the skillet to medium high (375° F or 190° C). Drop the chicken pieces into the paper bag, shaking well to coat them evenly with the seasoned flour. Add the dark pieces to the fat first, skin side down, followed by the white pieces. Reduce heat to medium, cover, and fry 15 minutes. Remove cover, turn each piece, and fry another 10 to 15 minutes uncovered. Remove chicken to the second paper bag to drain and prepare the gravy.

2 tablespoons fat plus drippings from the pan	*2 tablespoons of the seasoned flour*
½ cup (100g) raw country ham cut in julienne strips	*2 cups (475 ml) whole milk or buttermilk*

Slowly pour all but 2 tablespoons of cooking fat from the skillet, being careful to leave behind all of the browned flour drippings in the bottom of the pan. Over moderate heat stir in the country ham and cook for 3 minutes. Add flour and stir constantly with a whisk until the flour is well browned—do not scorch. Gradually add the milk or buttermilk, stirring all the while, and bring to a gentle boil for 5 minutes. Serve over rice or biscuits, but not over the chicken.

In the following piece, a former candidate for political office shows us "the ropes" of campaigning; her purpose is to take the reader behind the scenes and reveal the comic, sometimes absurd side of campaigning. By preparing the reader for the realities of the elective process she is also pointing out the pitfalls. Candidates must maintain a delicate balance and plan their strategy carefully. For example, they must wage appropriately aggressive campaigns, but at the same time avoid alienating their opponents.

How to Run For Office in a Very Small Town

Shirley Weissenborn

If you feel stirred to serve your community or to revamp the system, or perhaps—simply to "be in charge," you may someday decide to run for political office. If you do, and you live in a very small town (10,000 or less) here are some basic rules to follow.

Find out who is on your side. To enter a political race, you must present a petition signed by a designated number of registered voters composed of your family, friends, neighbors and people who owe you money. Your petition may or may not be greeted with hurrahs, depending upon whether the party leaders have you labeled as a winner or loser. Next, call on your supporters to serve as Campaign Manager, Activities Chairman, Publicity Chairman, Treasurer and Ego Chairman. Ego Chairman's job is to call you every morning during the campaign to tell you that you are a shoo-in and the whole town reveres you.

Define your issues. Deciding what you stand for in a small town is a difficult task, for the basic issues have probably remained static for the past 20 years. You may get lucky with a public frenzy over the possible grand opening of a massage parlor in the center of town. Failing that, you may find a safe issue in a heated denouncement of rising taxes. Because incumbents find high taxes difficult to defend, they are frequently placed on the defensive. You, on the other hand, as a non-incumbent, have a simpler time. You are free to attack, sneer, and point with scorn at the many mistakes of those already in office.

Present a news release each week to your local newspaper. Each release must contain a different issue or a new version of an old one. Finding new issues is very difficult. The subject matter must be innocuous enough to offend no one and yet present you as a dedicated, innovative public servant and a wonderful human being. Accompany your article with a photograph of yourself starting with tight-lipped disapproval at some object of public concern, such as a pot hole in the middle of Main Street.

Learn to give speeches with confidence and flair. You will be called upon during your months of campaigning to speak to many groups. The most terrifying of these is the League of Women Voters. They have done their homework and will challenge a candidate fearlessly. Be ready to back up your statements. Know what you are talking about. Salt the audience with friends and provide them with questions that you can answer effectively. Panic is a speaker's greatest hazard. It causes one's mouth to become dry and the upper lip to stick to one's teeth, making speech unintelligible. Fortunately, if one cannot be understood, one cannot be disagreed with.

Ring every doorbell in town. Get to know the people. They are more likely to give you their vote if they have had some personal contact. And don't worry about snubs: most people are friendly and pleased to meet you; it is their dogs that have a bad attitude. You are advised to wear high stout boots to protect your legs from painful bites and "anointing" as surrogate fire hydrants.

Attend everything. Your Activities Chairman will arrange coffees, teas, sherry parties, desserts, and brunches in order for you to meet and talk to as many people as possible. Try to attend all the public meetings the town provides. Make every effort to stand and contribute to the proceedings. Be sure your comments are intelligent and pertinent. A public statement might get your name in the paper or at least bring you to the attention of others attending the meeting. Of course, your opponents will be making themselves heard too. Often the clamor of candidates drowns out the business at hand.

Avoid dirty tricks. In a small town, your opponents are almost always people you know well and you will still be neighbors after the election is over. Beware the snide tracts slipped under doors at the dawning of Election Day, accusing opponents of unspeakable closet activities. Do not resort to spreading rumors through the town gossip that your opponent has been transferred and will be moving to Indianapolis shortly after the election. If you are the victim of dirty tricks, rise above it. Pray for a backlash of public opinion that will turn the voters against your worthy opponents and make them look like the bums they are.

Embarking on a political campaign is like a ride on the roller coaster. There are peaks and valleys, thrills and frights, and no way off until you roll to a complete stop. That stop is called Election Day. If you win, you have the privilege of serving your community. If you lose, you will have gained experience and self-knowledge. But win or lose, the chances are you will be back in line someday, ticket in hand, ready to take another ride.

VISUALIZING THE "HOW-TO" AUDIENCE

No "how-to" today wins a larger audience than how to lose weight. Thus we see this "how-to" everywhere—in newspapers and magazines, in best-selling books, on television: how not to ruin your body, endanger your health, jeopardize your love life, or die young. Most of these how-to-lose-weight guides are geared to a huge audience.

The writer of the following article has the most impressive credentials, a medical degree certifying that he understands the processes of the human body as well as the essentials of nutrition. His credentials give his readers reason to trust him. Note how he adjusts his rhetorical stance to this central fact: He is talking to plain people, not medical colleagues, and he gets directly to the point, avoiding technical terms or explanations. He speaks in a calm, reassuring voice, gently but firmly describing how we can "win at the losing game" (as one diet center advertises). Confidently and authoritatively, he issues simple imperatives: "Eat three meals a day"; "Go slow"; "Set sensible goals."

Although he cites ample supporting facts and figures, he is careful not to inundate or overwhelm his audience: One good statistic can stun readers into awareness: "Ten billion dollars a year spent on weight losing methods." And finally, note the formal organization of the piece. Each paragraph is numbered, representing a separate step of the process. Following instructions is much easier when the writer presents them in this graphic 1–2–3 fashion.

How to Lose Weight Sensibly and Successfully and Permanently

Norman Kaplan, M.D.

For most persons wanting to lose weight, the problem of both calorie intake and calorie expenditure must be attacked. . . . Here are some sensible guidelines for successful weight loss.

1. Set sensible short-term goals for yourself. If you're 75 pounds overweight, the idea of shedding all of that in a short period of time is so overwhelming that most people give up in desperation. Go after 5 or 10 pounds at a time and feel good when you've managed that.

2. Recognize that the tendency to be overweight is an incurable but controllable condition, in many ways like hypertension. You've got to establish a new set of eating habits.

3. Go slow and be thankful for small blessings. It doesn't seem you're accomplishing much if you lose 1 pound a week, but remember, that's 52 pounds in a year! Since it took you 5 or maybe 10 years to gain that much, try to accept a gradual but steady weight loss as a reasonable goal.

4. Weigh in only once a week so as not to become frustrated by a slow weight loss. If you accomplish your short-term goal, reward yourself with a nonfattening treat. You may want to go on a "maintenance" diet for a few weeks before taking on another 5 to 10 pounds, or you may be flushed by victory as to want to go right on.

5. Use various techniques to modify your eating behavior: Prepare only enough food for the meal; put the food on the plate (a small one) without having extra portions at the table: eat without distractions, never in front of the TV set; eat slowly; realize that it is not a sin to leave food on your plate—the starving Armenians will not find out.

6. If your willpower fails and you give in to temptation, try to be satisfied with the first few bites of "forbidden" foods. And when you do give in, recognize that you're only human. Falling off the wagon temporarily needn't mean that you have to lose the whole wagon and the horse as well.

7. Eat three meals a day and always have low-calorie snacks available. You never know when the urge will strike, and you must be ready with carrots, cauliflower or other ammunition.

8. Don't look for magic from pills or spas. They may provide temporary help, but it still gets down to cutting calories—roughly 500 a day less than what you burn in order to lose a pound a week, since there are 3,500 calories in a pound of fat.

9. Exercise as much as you can, starting slowly and gradually building up your capacity. Be sensible about the form of exercise you perform. Few people will stick with jogging a mile every day. But everyone can walk an extra mile a day, particularly if it's six blocks to the office or shopping center. Make this part of your regular routine and not a time-consuming extra effort that quickly becomes such a burden that you quit. A mile of brisk walking a day burns about 90 calories, enough to shed 7 pounds in a year.

10. Remember that both beer and booze have several hundred calories each. Lower-calorie beer and wine are available. Nevertheless, a six-pack of lite beer is still almost 600 calories.

You need to reduce your caloric intake below your caloric expenditure by 500 calories per day to lose 3,500 calories or one pound of fat a week. To lose two pounds of weight per week, a daily deficit of 1,000 calories is needed. That should be accomplished by a combination of decreased intake by a diet and, to a lesser degree, increased expenditure by exercise.

There are many sources of complete diet programs, but you really may not need to do much more than cut out some high-calorie sweets, desserts, breads and dressings and substitute lower-calorie foods for very caloric ones.

Obesity is common, and we've not been very successful up to this point in overcoming it. Despite spending more than $10 billion a year on weight-losing methods and ideas, millions of Americans continue on their seemingly hopeless quest for a size-six figure or a 34-inch waist.

Much more likely to succeed is a program of prevention. Infant feeding habits can be altered to provide adequate nutrition without increasing the child's risk for later obesity or hypertension. The renewed interest in breast-feeding is a good sign. In Stanford, California, children in the fourth and fifth grades of school were given an effective instructional program and altered their own eating behavior, increased their level of physical activity and influenced their family's eating patterns as well. If we can reach parents and children early enough, healthy eating habits should be easy to adopt and easier to maintain.

Some kinds of advice are not so easily organized into a series of steps. The craft of writing, for example, can be taught, but it's not a process that's the same for everyone—or even the same every time for the same writer. The advice given here by novelist Rita Mae Brown relies on a wealth of specific detail and the author's own force of personality. By focusing on one aspect of writing—the use of verbs—she makes her advice come alive.

VERBS, *or* PUT THE PEDAL TO THE METAL

Rita Mae Brown

Verbs blast you down the highway. If you want to get your black belt in boredom, load your sentences with variations of the verb *to be*. Granted, sometimes you can't help using them, especially with nonfiction, but at every opportunity knock out *is, are, was,* etc., and insert something hot.

Strong verbs are always hot. A strong verb changes forms inside the word itself. The sound alters. *Drink, drank, drunk* is a strong verb. *Love, loved, loved* is a weak verb. Strong verbs, memorized from childhood, spill off our tongues. Imagine how difficult it is for a non-English-speaking person to learn the language. We create past tense in two ways. The first way—as in *drink, drank, drunk*—and the second way—by adding "ed" to the ending—must drive the poor souls to evangelists or bourbon. If you're a native speaker you are hardly aware of this peculiarity. But you hear strong verbs differently from the way you hear weak verbs. As a writer you've got to hear them like separate notes on a scale.

I'm not saying that weak verbs lack punch—it depends on the sentence—but I am saying that the "to be" family falls flat on its face with overuse.

English is the international language of pilots. The language conveys maximum information in the minimum amount of time. Verbs help our ability to condense and transmit information and so does our sentence structure.

If you've studied Latin you know it's an inflected language. Endings, like earrings, hang on to words; they tell you the tense of the verb, whether a noun is a subject or direct object. In English, we've dispensed with inflection and we rely on word order. While our language is remarkably flexible, on this one plane English is rigid, immobile, unalterable. I can say "Man bites dog" in terms of word order in Latin and it still means the dog bites the man. *Virum morderet canis* or *Canis morderet virum*. It doesn't matter how I shift the words around, because *um* in *virum* means the man is the direct object of the dog's teeth. If I used *vir* then man would not be the direct object but the subject of the sentence.

An English speaker says, "The dog bites the man," and that's the end of it. While this locks us into structure it does give us speed. We know where our verb will appear. It's between the subject and the object. Yes, sometimes it can be at the beginning of the sentence when we command someone: "Come here." The subject, "You," is understood. And sometimes, for poetry's sake, it can appear at the end of the sentence but this is uncommon. Our verbs hinge our thoughts. It's literary architecture.

I studied Attic Greek in college. It nearly wiped me out. The sentences are built like onions. You peel away layer after layer, adjectives, modifiers, and so forth. So an adjective can be on the left side of the verb modifying a noun resting to the right of the verb. Finally, buried in the heart of this Godawful mess, is the verb. By the time I found it I was too exhausted to look at the ending and identify the tense. Furthermore, I no longer cared. To hell with Thuycidides. I reached for the crib. This complicated structure gives Greek a facility with intellectual material that shimmers. The language dazzles but you've got to be patient. English speakers are not patient people.

You and I have only to stick our verb where it belongs and all is well. There are no surprises.

This quickness of our language forces us to choose words carefully. We need the exact right word to make up for our lack of inflection. No wonder we've got the largest vocabulary of the world's languages.

Therefore the verb is the key to writing. You know that your sentences can be slowed down with subordinate clauses. You can drop anchor by using passive voice—and if you aren't careful you'll drag your entire sentence down with that voice. You don't want to write at the same speed. You need to vary it and the way you do that is with your verbs.

Any action verb will accelerate a sentence. Run, jump, shoot, ride, and so on. However, if you've got characters sitting in a formal dining room, your verbs better reflect some inner motion or the reader will be bored by the characters' physical inactivity. So you might have a character steaming, seething, writhing.

My point is not that you hurtle the reader forward at every opportunity but that you be technically aware of how verbs control the movement of your prose. It's as easy to write a peaceful, light paragraph as it is to write a torrent. You choose when and where. Don't let the verbs choose for you.

Aside from providing the energy in a sentence, every verb is a clock. Coded into the word itself is the time of the action. So, present tense is exactly that. Unfortunately, a rash of novels in the last decade have been written in the present tense. It's a fad and it won't last. There are good reasons for writing in the past tense.

The first is familiarity. Every story we've read since *The Iliad* has been written in past tense. Don't argue with thousands of years of success.

The second reason is that the reader needs and wants distance and protection from the story. This safety zone, provided by the past tense, allows the reader eventually to open up for the emotional impact of the story. You've got to vault your reader's defenses. The reader doesn't want to get hurt, yet you want that reader to identify with your characters and that means to feel their pain and their joy. I feel strongly about this. Anyone who buys your book has plenty of problems in his or her life. You have no moral right to disturb them unless you also entertain them. Art is moral passion married to entertainment. Moral passion without entertainment is propaganda, and entertainment without moral passion is television. By using the past tense (except in your dialogue, of course) you enable your reader to come to you.

The third reason to use past tense is technical. Do you want the reader to focus on the story or focus on your participles and gerunds? Don't distract a reader with your style. That's you showing off. A great style is one that appears effortless and one that is individual. Your voice should not sound like Faulkner's.

The fourth reason to use the past tense and not the present tense is: Why would anyone want to read a novel that sounds like a screenplay? Screenplays are in the present tense. They have to be. You're giving the director his marching orders. Fiction is not a screenplay. A screenplay can be a work of towering imagination but it will never be a novel. The two functions are unrelated. . . . I'm not disparaging screenplays. I've written seven of them and hope to write many more. I'm saying don't mix your mediums. It's trendy and you'll get attention for a while and then boom, it'll be over.

There is one good reason to write in the present tense and that is to gain immediacy. My feeling is you can capture immediacy through your dialogue. The sacrifices of tradition, reader identification, and technical smoothness don't justify the use of present tense.

Past tense is one thing. Past perfect is quite another. Why load auxiliary verbs? You're freighting down your sentence, and also, the cadence gets predictable and soon tedious. What's the purpose of *had* and *have* jammed in front of otherwise healthy verbs? Are they anemic? Are they lonesome? Do they need to feel that old familiar "to be" verb snuggled up against them? Get rid of that stuff. I use past perfect only to indicate a long passage of time. For instance. Simple past—"I was walking the dog" or "I walked the dog" (see, already you've got a choice; English forces you to make choices)—means you performed this function recently. If you say "I had walked the dog" or "I have been walking the dog," the time frame is different. You should be able to feel this difference. Time is a tool. You don't want to confuse your reader by confusing your time frames within your sentences. You might wish to check a grammar book. Sometimes by dropping the past perfect you will be committing a grammatical error. However, you will still be picking up reading "speed." It's a difficult choice. Unless something happened at a distinct point in the past or you wish to call attention to the event, consider laying off the past perfect. Then when you do use it, it will have impact. Your reader isn't going to be technically aware of what you've done but s/he'll sense the result. Never, ever underestimate your readers. Everything you do registers.

English is in a constant process of both simplifying itself and enriching itself. Since the past perfect means one more word to stack up, one more beat to slow one down, there is a possibility it will be used less in time.

So I'm trying to anticipate the future. This is tricky. First I excoriate authors who use the present tense but then I state my willingness to bend a tradition—nay, not a tradition, a grammatical law—to gain "cleanness."

I am aware of the contradiction . . . and I'm willing to brave it.

The last thing I have to say is that ice is the past tense of water. I've always wanted to write that sentence and now I have.

DISCUSSION AND EXERCISES

1. To what extent do each of the how-to essays in this section fulfill the following principles of writing?
    a. accuracy (Are the facts correct? Indicate in what ways the writer may have oversimplified or overcomplicated a process.)
    b. clarity (Are the steps clearly presented?)
    c. economy (Are there any unnecessary words? Any irrelevant information?)
    d. rhetorical stance (To whom is the piece addressed? What is the writer's point of view? Tone? Purpose in writing the piece?)
    e. What special aspects of style such as the use of imperative voice and short sentences are especially useful in how-to's?

2. Consider Weissenborn's "How to Run for Office in a Very Small Town":
    a. How does the writer convey the impression of having first-hand knowledge of her subject?
    b. What is the effect of short sentences and the use of imperatives in the piece?
    c. Indicate touches of humor. What effect do they have?
    d. To what audience does the author direct this piece? What is the tone?

e. Using a comparable tone, write a short set of instructions (200-250 words) for some simple process like how to iron a shirt, whittle a stick, apply mascara, serve a volleyball. Remember: each step should be cast in parallel imperatives (as in Weissenborn's progression: *find out, define, present, learn.*)

3. Read the following paragraph written by Benjamin Franklin, describing a technical process for which he was famous:

> Secure to the big end of the rod a strong eye or a ring half an inch in diameter. Fix the rod upright to the chimney or the highest part of a house. It should be fixed with some sort of staples or special nails to keep it steady. The pointed end should extend upward, and should rise three or four feet above the chimney or building to which the rod is fixed. Drive into the ground an iron rod about one inch in diameter, and ten or twelve feet long. This rod should also have an eye or ring fixed to its upper end. It is best to place the iron rod some distance from the foundation of the house. Ten feet away is a good distance, if the size of the property permits. Then take as much length of iron rod of a smaller diameter as will be necessary to reach from the eye on the rod above to the eye of the rod below. Fasten this securely to the fixed rods by passing it through the eyes and bending the ends to form rings too. Then close all the joints with lead. This is easily done by making a small bag of strong paper around the joints, tying it tight below, and then pouring in the molten lead. It is useful to have these joints treated in this way so that there will be a considerable area of contact between each piece. To prevent the wind from shaking this long rod, it may be fastened to the building by several staples. If the building is especially large or long, extending more than one hundred feet for example, it is wise to erect a rod at each end. If there is a well sufficiently near to the building to permit placing the iron rod in the water, this is even better than the use of the iron rod in the ground. It may also be wise to paint the iron to prevent it from rusting. A building so protected will not be damaged by lightning.

a. In what ways has Franklin made each step clear and distinct?

b. Comment on Franklin's choice of verbs, transitional devices, qualifications, and explanations.

c. Write a paragraph (150-250 words) comparable to Franklin's in which you explain to a friend how to make something. Suggestions:

a loudspeaker	a ceramic bowl
a bookcase	a decal
a tray	a blanket
a lamp	a basket
an omelet	a bracelet
a sweater	a string of beads
a slipcover	a leather belt
a potholder	a blouse or shirt

continued

4. Write a short self-help piece (150-250 words) in which you:
   a. Offer concrete suggestions on how to treat the following physical ills:

high fever	hangover
cold	first-degree burn
frostbite	bee sting
poison ivy	dog bite
acne	muscle strain

   b. Offer concrete, sensible, and restrained suggestions on how to deal with the following psychological problems:

attempts to stop smoking	depression
insomnia	anxiety
hysteria	fatigue
shock	anger

   c. Offer sweepingly oversimplified advice on the problems listed above.
   d. Give yourself ten minutes to "cluster" around the nucleus phrase "Let me tell you how to . . ."

5. Visualizing your how-to audience (see Part One, Visualizing Your Audience, pages 28–30), write three paragraphs (250 words each) on a subject in which you have some level of expertise such as how to design a computer program, write a poem, prepare a quiche, restore a vintage Ford, or win at tennis (be sure to use prewriting techniques):
   a. Address your first paragraph to your peers—people who speak your language, or share your enthusiasm. Since you are at one with your audience, feel free to use terms and jokes outsiders would not understand.
   b. Address a second paragraph to a general audience of readers who may know little or nothing about your subject. Your purpose here is to get them interested and involved if possible. In this paragraph avoid technical terms and in-jokes. Take nothing for granted. The cautionary approach to your audience bears repeating here: Never underestimate the intelligence of your readers, but never overestimate their intelligence.
   c. Finally, in a third paragraph, speak to an audience of preschoolers, instructing them in language they can readily understand—in simple, basic terms, free of jargon, technicalities, embellishment. Avoid being patronizing or simplistic, however. As critic Northrop Frye (among others) has pointed out, the ability to explain your subject to a young child is a test of your own grasp of the subject.

ESSAY SUGGESTIONS

1. Following the example of Weissenborn's "How to Run for Office" or Kaplan's "How to Lose Weight," write an essay (750-1,000 words) in which you present basic instructions for one of the following:

bird watching	planning a campus campaign
folk dancing	diving
tightrope walking	hiking
hunting an alligator	pitching horseshoes
bicycle riding	mountain climbing
serving a tennis ball	kite flying
playing billiards	fishing
planning a political rally	planning a picnic

   Where you think it will be helpful, clarify the process by using an appropriate typography. Use separate paragraphs for each step; first lines of each paragraph indented five spaces and numbered. Remember that typographical devices do not take the place of careful analysis—they merely clarify it; further clarification is achieved by maintaining parallel structures at each stage in the series: *fix, drive, fasten,* and *close* as Franklin tells us in his directions on making lightning rods. Use prewriting techniques to prepare for actual writing.

2. Write a set of instructions (750-1,000 words) for improving any skill, craft, art, or sport in which you are proficient.

3. Read the following list of "Six Ways to Win Over Your New Staff" from a magazine for executives.

   > Unless you're planning a complete turn-over, you can't afford to be so cold and distant that you alienate your staff early on. Here are some things you can do to create confidence in your leadership:
   >
   > —**Be visible.** Walk the halls, let yourself be seen.
   > —**Be available.** Make time for appointments with people who work for you. Listen to questions they have. Be quick to respond, because it's likely they're upset at the change.
   > —**Be sensitive of feelings** of fear, grief or anger.
   > —**Be clear and firm** in the way you set up your new goals and procedures.
   > —**Be appreciative of their efforts.** At the earliest opportunity, once you've completed staff evaluations, express confidence in their abilities. Offer challenges and opportunities to grow. Give them a place in your new scheme of things.
   > —**Be human.** Sometimes the small daily courtesies and attentions—sharing a joke over coffee in the morning, discussing weekend plans or family

   continued

activities—have the biggest impact on building good staff morale after a transition. Being human also means understanding the limitations of those who work for you.

—Jane Ciabattari, *Working Woman*

Note the parallel construction and the consistent use of the imperative mood in the instructions. Notice as well that the writer instructs the reader how to *be*, not what to *do*. Now use a prewriting period to create six appropriate points for one of the topics below and write a "how-to" essay (500-750 words) based on those points.

how to hit it off with a new roommate
how to make friends in a new town
how to get along with your parents (siblings, children)
how to shop for holiday and birthday gifts
how to be romantic
how to deal with peer pressure
how to help support a friend in trouble
how to survive your parents' divorce
how to prevent your house from being burglarized

Question

12

WHAT ARE THE
CAUSES OF X?

THE PERENNIAL WHY
> *ON SPEAKING OF SPEAKING*, LEWIS THOMAS
> *A SMALL CAUSE*, PRIMO LEVI

CAUSE AND CONDITION

EXPLAINING REASONS
> *WHY COLLEGE STUDENTS TAKE*
> *A SABBATICAL*, HILARY STOUT
> *WHY WE DREAM ABOUT THE STARS*,
> PEGGY NOONAN

PRESENTING PERSONAL REASONS
> *REMEMBERING MR. SWEET*,
> ALICE WALKER

THE PERENNIAL WHY

Surely there is no more provocative question than the simple *why*. Why is the sky dark at night? Why are we more or less intelligent? Why do we choose one way of life over another?

When asking why, the writer is preparing to write a causal analysis—that is, seeking to locate and explain the causes for a given act, idea, feeling, condition, or event. As Aristotle pointed out, human beings are naturally curious, almost as soon as we begin to think, we begin to wonder why. As early as the fifth century B.C. the Greek philosopher Leucippus said: "Nothing happens without a ground but everything through a cause and of necessity." Here, then, is the principle of universal causation, believed to run through all things, confirming us in our impulse to ask why.

One of the most interesting, and at times frustrating, aspects of understanding and explaining causes is the almost infinite regression of causes and effects. Once we have determined that X is caused by Y and Z, the natural follow-up question is What are the causes of Y and Z? Soon we can become lost in a tangle of partial causes and multiple effects that frustrates our attempts to find a unifying principle. Yet a careful and logical examination of the evidence can reveal one cause without which none of the effects would have happened—*a necessary cause,* to use the term assigned to this single important cause by logicians. In the following explanation of what causes language to change, the biologist Lewis Thomas examines several possible explanations for linguistic evolution before settling on a biological explanation. There are two points to be made about Thomas's conclusion: The first is that the necessary cause he identifies at the end of his essay does not invalidate the other causes he has described; they are contributory causes that also have an effect on the outcome. The second point relates to the perspective from which Thomas pursues his analysis; it is not surprising that this noted biologist identifies a biological cause, since causal analysis, like any other kind of analysis, is often given shape by the perspective taken by the author.

On Speaking of Speaking

Lewis Thomas

There is nothing at all wrong with the English language, so far as I can see, but that may only be because I cannot see ahead. If I were placed in charge of it, as chairman, say, of a National Academy for the Improvement of Language, I would not lay a finger on English. It suits every need that I can think of: flexibility, clarity, subtlety of metaphor, ambiguity wherever ambiguity is needed (which is more often than is generally acknowledged), and most of all changeability. I like the notion of a changing language. As a meliorist, I am convinced that all past changes were for the better; I have no doubt that today's English is a considerable improvement over Elizabethan or Chaucerian talk, and miles ahead of Old English. By now the language has reached its stage of ultimate perfection, and I'll be satisfied to have it this way forever.

But I know I'm wrong about this. English is shifting and changing before our eyes and ears, beyond the control of all individuals, committees, academies, and governments. The speakers of earlier versions undoubtedly felt the same satisfaction with their speech in their time. Chaucer's generation, and all the generations before, could not have been aware of any need to change or improve. Montaigne was entirely content with sixteenth-century French and obviously delighted by what he could do with it. Long, long ago, the furthermost ancestors of English speech must have got along nicely in Proto-Indo-European without a notion that their language would one day vanish.

"Vanish" is the wrong word anyway for what happened. The roots of several thousand Indo-European words are still alive and active, tucked up neatly like symbionts inside other words in Greek, Latin, and all the Germanic tongues, including English. Much of what we say to each other today, in English, could be interpreted as Greek with an Indo-European accent. Three or four centuries from now, it is probable that today's English will be largely incomprehensible to everyone except the linguistic scholars and historians.

The ancient meanings of the Indo-European roots are sometimes twisted around, even distorted beyond recognition, but they are still there, resonating inside, reminding. The old root *gheue,* meaning simply to call, became *gudam* in Germanic and then "God" in English. *Meug* was a root signifying something damp and slippery, and thousands of years later it turned into "meek" in proper English and "mooch" in slang, also "schmuck." *Bha* was the Indo-European word for speaking, becoming *phanai* in Greek with the same meaning, then used much later for our most fundamental word indicating the inability to speak: "infancy." *Ster* was a root meaning to stiffen; it became *sterban* in Germanic and *steorfan* in Old English, meaning to die, and then turned into "starve" in our speech.

The changes in language will continue forever, but no one knows for sure who does the changing. One possibility is that children are responsible. Derek Bickerton, professor of linguistics at the University of Hawaii, explores this in his book *Roots of Language.* Sometime around 1880, a language catastrophe occurred in Hawaii when thousands of immigrant workers were brought to the islands to work for the new sugar industry. These people, speaking Chinese, Japanese, Korean, Portuguese, and various Spanish dialects, were unable to communicate with one another or with the native Hawaiians or the dominant English-speaking owners of the plantations, and they first did what such mixed-language populations have always done: they spoke Pidgin English (a corruption of "business English"). A pidgin is not really a language at all, more like a set of verbal signals used to name objects but lacking the grammatical rules needed for expressing thought and ideas. And then, within a single generation, the whole mass of mixed peoples began speaking a totally new tongue: Hawaiian Creole. The new speech contained ready-made words borrowed from all the original tongues, but bore little or no resemblance to the predecessors in the rules used for stringing the words together. Although generally regarded as a "primitive" language, Hawaiian Creole was constructed with a highly sophisticated grammar. Professor Bickerton's great discovery is that this brand-new speech could have been made only by the children. There wasn't time enough to allow for any other explanation. Soon after the influx of workers in 1880 the speech was Hawaiian Pidgin, and within the next twenty-five or thirty years the accepted language was Creole. The first immigrants, the parents who spoke Pidgin, could not have made the new language and then taught it to the children. They could not themselves understand Creole when it appeared. Nor could the adult English speakers in charge of the place either speak or comprehend Creole. According to Bickerton's research, it simply had to have been the work of children, crowded together, jabbering away at each other, playing.

Bickerton cites this historic phenomenon as evidence, incontrovertible in his view, for the theory that language is a biological, innate, genetically determined property of human beings, driven by a center or centers in the brain that code out grammar and syntax. His term for the gift of speech is "bioprogram." The idea confirms and extends the proposal put forward by Noam Chomsky, almost three decades ago, that human beings are unique in their possession of brains equipped for generating grammar. But the most fascinating aspect of the new work is its evidence that children—and probably very young children at that—are able to construct a whole language, working at it together, or more likely *playing* at it together.

It should make you take a different view of children, eliciting something like awe. We have always known that childhood is the period in which new languages as well as one's own can be picked up quickly and easily. The facility disappears in most people around the time of adolescence, and from then on the acquisition of a new language is hard, slogging labor. Children are gifted at it, of course. But it requires a different order of respect to take in the possibility that children make up languages, change languages, perhaps have been carrying the responsibility for evolving language from the first human communication to twentieth-century speech. If it were not for the children and their special gift we might all be speaking Indo-European or Hittite, but here we all are, speaking several thousand different languages and dialects, most of which would be incomprehensible to the human beings on earth just a few centuries back.

Perhaps we should be paying serious attention to the possible role played by children in the origin of speech itself. It is of course not known when language first appeared in our species, and it is pure guesswork as to how it happened. One popular guess is that at a certain stage in the evolution of the human skull, and of the brain therein, speech became a possibility in a few mutant individuals. Thereafter, these intellectual people and their genes outcompeted all their speechless cousins, and natural selection resulted in *Homo sapiens*. This notion would require the recurrence of the same mutation in many different, isolated communities all around the globe, or else one would have to assume that a lucky few speakers managed to travel with remarkable agility everywhere on earth, leaving their novel genes behind.

Another possibility, raised by the new view of children and speech, is that human language did not pop up as a special mutation, but came into existence as a latent property of all human brains at some point in the evolution of the whole species. The environment required for expression of the brain centers involved in the process was simply children, enough children crowded together in circumstances where they could spend a lot of time playing together. A critical mass of children in a sufficiently stable society could have been achieved whenever large enough numbers of families settled down to live in close quarters, as may have happened long ago in the tribal life of hunters and gatherers or in the earliest agricultural communities.

It makes an interesting scenario. The adults and wise elders of the tribe, sitting around a fire speaking a small-talk pidgin, pointing at one thing or another and muttering isolated words. No syntax, no strings of words, no real ideas, no metaphors. Somewhere nearby, that critical mass of noisy young children, gabbling and shouting at each other, their voices rising in the exultation of discovery, talking, talking, and forever thereafter never stopping.

The analysis of causes is not merely the province of physical scientists, of course. In fact, understanding the causes of human behavior might be seen as a primary task facing almost any social or behavioral scientist. Their research into the factors that determine how people act can be very useful in understanding human behavior on a large scale. The events of an individual's life, however, are often shaped by causes much more unexpected and capricious than those explained by psychologists or sociologists. In this chapter from his autobiography, Primo Levi—an Italian scientist who survived the Nazi concentration camp at Auschwitz— explains the totally unexpected consequences of an everyday action and in so doing offers us a memorable insight into the workings of fate.

A Small Cause

Primo Levi

Forty years ago I was a prisoner in Auschwitz, working in a chemical laboratory. I was hungry and on the lookout for something small and unusual (and therefore of high commercial value) to steal and exchange for bread. After various attempts (some successful, some not), I found a drawer full of pipettes. Pipettes are small glass tubes, precisely graduated, which are used to transfer exact amounts of liquid from one container to another. Nowadays more hygienic methods are employed, but at the time this was done by sucking up the liquid so that it rose exactly to the desired marking, then letting it descend by its own weight. There were a lot of pipettes. I slipped a dozen into a hidden pocket I had sewed inside my jacket, and took them back to the Camp. They are graceful, delicate objects, and on the way back several of them broke. Anyway, as soon as roll call was over and before the distribution of the evening soup began, I ran to the infirmary and offered the unbroken ones to a Polish male nurse whom I knew and who worked in the Contagious Ward, explaining that they could be used for clinical analyses.

The Pole looked at my booty with little interest and then told me that for that day it was too late; he no longer had any bread. All he could offer me was a bit of soup. He was a shrewd bargainer and knew that I had no choice. To carry those obviously stolen goods around in the Camp was dangerous, and there was nobody else I could offer them to. He enjoyed a monopoly and took advantage of it.

I accepted the proposed payment; the Pole disappeared among the patients of his ward and came back shortly with a bowl half full of soup, but half full in a curious way: vertically. It was very cold, the soup had frozen, and someone had removed half of it with a spoon, like someone eating half a cake. Who could have left half a bowl of soup in that reign of hunger? Almost certainly someone who had died halfway through the meal, and, given the sort of place this was, someone sick with a contagious disease. In the last weeks, diphtheria and scarlet fever had broken out in the Camp in epidemic proportions.

But at Auschwitz we didn't observe precautions of this kind. First came hunger, then all the rest; leaving something edible uneaten was not what is commonly called "a shame," it was unthinkable, indeed physically impossible. That same evening, my alter ego, Alberto, and I shared the suspect soup. Alberto was my age, had the same build, temperament, and profession as I, and we slept in the same bunk. We even looked somewhat alike; the foreign comrades and the Kapo considered it superfluous to distinguish between us. They constantly confused us, and demanded that whether they called "Alberto" or "Primo," whichever one of us happened to be closest should answer.

We were interchangeable, so to speak, and anyone would have predicted for us two the same fate: we would both go under or both survive. But it was just at this point that the switch-pointer came into play, the small cause with the determining effects: Alberto had had scarlet fever as a child and was immune; I was not.

I realized the consequences of our rashness a few days later. At reveille, while Alberto felt perfectly all right, I had a bad sore throat, I had trouble swallowing and had a high fever, but "reporting" sick in the morning was not allowed, so I went to the lab as I did every day. I felt deathly sick but on that day of all days I was given an unusual task. In that lab, half a dozen girls, German, Polish, and Ukrainian, worked, or pretended to work. The head of the lab called me aside and told me I must teach Fräulein Drechsel an analytical method which I myself had learned only a few weeks before. Fräulein Drechsel was a chubby German adolescent, clumsy, sullen, and dumb. Most of the time she avoided looking at us three slave-chemists. When she did, her dull eyes expressed a vague hostility, made up of mistrust, embarrassment, revulsion, and fear. She had never addressed a word to me. I found her disagreeable and distrusted her as well, because on preceding days I had seen her slink off with the very young SS man who watched over that department. And besides, she alone wore a swastika badge pinned to her shirt. She might have been a Hitler Youth squadron-leader.

She was a very bad pupil because of her stupidity, and I was a very bad teacher because I didn't feel well, didn't speak German well, and above all because I wasn't motivated; if anything, I was countermotivated. Why in the world should I have to teach that creature anything? The normal teacher-pupil relationship, which is a descending one, came into conflict with ascending relationships: I was Jewish and she was Aryan, I was dirty and sick, she was clean and healthy.

I believe it was the only time I have deliberately done someone wrong. The analytical method I was supposed to teach her involved the use of a pipette: a sister of those to which I owed the illness coursing through my veins. I took one from the drawer and showed Fräulein Drechsel how to use it, inserting it between my feverish lips, then held it out to her and invited her to do the same. In short, I did all I could to infect her.

A few days later, while I was in the infirmary, the Camp broke up under the tragic circumstances that have been described many times. Alberto was a victim of the small cause, of the scarlet fever from which he had recovered as a child. He came to say goodbye, then went into the night and the snow together with sixty thousand other unfortunates, on that deadly march from which few returned alive. I was saved in the most unpredictable way by that business of the stolen pipettes, which gave me a providential sickness exactly at the moment when, paradoxically, not being able to walk was a godsend. In fact, for reasons never clarified, at Auschwitz the fleeing Nazis abstained from carrying out explicit orders from

Berlin: Leave no witnesses behind. They left the Camp in a hurry, and abandoned us who were sick to our fate.

As for Fräulein Drechsel, I know nothing about what happened to her. Since it may be that she was guilty of nothing more than a few Nazi kisses, I hope that my deed, the small cause set in motion by me, did not bring her grievous harm. At seventeen scarlet fever is cured quickly and leaves no serious aftereffects. In any case, I feel no remorse for my private attempt at bacteriological warfare. Later on, reading books on the subject, I learned that other people in other Camps had taken better-aimed and more systematic action. In places ravaged by exanthematic typhus—often fatal, and transmitted by lice in clothing—the prisoners who washed and ironed the SS uniforms would search for comrades who had died of typhus, pick lice off the corpses, and slip them under the collars of the ironed and spruced-up military jackets. Lice are not very attractive animals, but they do not have racial prejudices.

In establishing causal connections, the writer must think carefully and rigorously, recognizing that it is easy to fall into such common fallacies as *post hoc ergo propter hoc* (after this, therefore because of this). Only to the simple mind (or the mind intent on deceiving) is any event that follows another necessarily the *result* of it. Thus, as Mark Twain once pointed out in a humorous *post hoc* application: "I joined the Confederacy for two weeks. Then I deserted. The Confederacy fell."

Most superstitions grow out of this fallacy: "A black cat crossed my path. Later that day I twisted my ankle. The black cat *caused* my twisted ankle. Black cats are therefore unlucky." And: "John eats a lot of fish. John is smart. Eating fish is good for the brain." The writer who wishes to be taken seriously must guard against superstitious, oversimplified cause-and-effect connections. Thus the second question a critical mind addresses to an assertion of causal relationship should be: Was the supposed cause *sufficient* to produce the given effect? Obviously a black cat cannot be sufficient cause for a twisted ankle, fish does not demonstrably stimulate the brain, nor a four-leaf clover demonstrably bring luck. In each case the stated cause, however colorful, is *insufficient* to produce the given effect.

CAUSE AND CONDITION

As a careful thinker and writer, you must make certain that you consider *all* possible causes for any given event. You must recognize not only that there *can* be more than one cause behind any given situation (war, recession, racial unrest), but that there usually is, that the world of events is rarely characterized by

$$\text{single cause} \rightarrow \text{single effect}$$

More than that, you must be aware that for every individual effect, you must also take into account countless conditions if your causal explanation is to be reasonably accurate and complete. Let us say that the direct cause of your answering the telephone is that it rings:

$$\text{cause} \longrightarrow \text{effect}$$

(telephone ringing)   (you answer the telephone)

You could view this event in this linear manner; It is accurate, but only roughly. In actual fact, countless conditions enter into this situation that enable it to occur: The telephone is in good repair (each small part is working); your ears are "attuned" (here again, each small part is working); you are within hearing distance (you might have stepped outside for a moment). And so on. If any one of these numerous small conditions had not held to its exact course at the precise moment the telephone rang, you would not have answered it: The given effect would *not* have followed the supposed cause.

With this in mind, we can look back to Bliven's essay on nighttime darkness and note that many conditions had to remain equal and constant in order for the law of causation to operate in its ordinary manner. Of course the sun rises each morning, as he states—but only if no untoward occurrences take place in the solar system that throw the entire causal chain out of gear.

The careful thinker and writer, then, will take into account not only the basic *causes* of a given effect, but the surrounding *conditions* as well.

EXPLAINING REASONS

The writer of the following article was a junior at Brown University when he wrote this causal explanation of why students "stop out" (rather than "drop out") for a year or two during their college careers. Although he himself did not take a sabbatical, he did investigate thoroughly the reasons why many of his classmates chose to do so: to travel, to work, to think, to—in effect—restore their souls.

The organization of this article rests on categories of evidence the writer obtained from such sources as personal interviews with students, deans of colleges, administrators, and "job banks." He has succeeded in weaving many strands of information and explanation into a clear, coherent whole, an article with an obvious purpose: to explain a common practice on the contemporary college scene.

WHY COLLEGE STUDENTS TAKE A SABBATICAL

Hilary Stout

Salil Mehta, an undergraduate at Brown University, doesn't know whether he wants to be a doctor or a lawyer, so for the last two years he has sampled courses in political science and biology. This fall he is in Washington, interning for a Congressman and doing volunteer work for a public defender; next spring he plans to be somewhere else, working in a hospital, after which he expects to be sitting in Brown classrooms again—this time with a major and a goal.

Kevin White, a junior at the University of Pennsylvania's Wharton School, is having a hard time meeting Penn's $12,000 yearly cost. Next January, while continuing to live in his fraternity at school, he will stop taking classes for a semester and get a job. And because of advanced credits awarded when he entered college, he will still graduate with his class next June.

One day last September, Stuart Handlesman was sitting in the University of Vermont's Bailey-Howe Library feeling restless, confused and bored. "This is ridiculous," he said to himself and withdrew from school to travel and work for a year. This September he was back in the library with a new sense of purpose, he said, studying political science and art history.

According to administrators and students throughout the country, taking a leave from college to work, think and pursue something other than academics has become a common practice. The students have even coined a name for it— "stopping out"—to distinguish it from dropping out.

Half of all Stanford undergraduates "stop out" during their college careers, making the average period for degree completion five years. The assistant director of career services at Wesleyan University, Suzanne Kiar-Tuttle, said that 30 to 40 percent of the student body took a leave at some point, and Haverford's president of student services and administration, David Potter, estimated that a quarter to a third of all Haverford students did so.

"The nature of the times makes stopping out more likely," said George Clever, a dean and student adviser at Stanford.

Had Mr. Mehta, Mr. White and Mr. Handlesman been students 15 to 20 years ago, they probably would have plodded through college in four years like the rest of their classmates. Fear of the draft kept young men in school; lower tuition and abundant Government grants minimized financial hardship; a stable job market made career concerns less pressing, and when students left college it was generally assumed they wouldn't come back.

"Today's leave-takers are very different students," said Katherine Hall, associate dean of the college at Brown. "They don't drop out." According to a report prepared by deans at Brown, only 70 percent of recent classes graduated in four years. An average of 95 percent of all stop-outs return to school.

"I knew there was no way I was going to walk out of this place without a degree," said Dean Rapoza, who is now completing his senior year at Brown after having spent a year working at several part-time hospital jobs.

Uncertainty about a major or a career, academic exhaustion and general malaise are the reasons most often cited by students for stopping out. "I experienced senior panic a year early," said Jacquelyn Clymore, a student at Vassar who spent last semester as a writer for a New York City advertising agency. "It wasn't academic burnout. I just wasn't sure where I was going to go and what I was going to do after college."

And Peggy Willens, a senior at Wesleyan who worked for six weeks in a health-food store last winter, then spent the rest of her semester off teaching fifth-graders about nature and the environment, explained, "It was the big old question: 'What am I doing here?'"

Stanford's Dean Clever said that sometimes athletes and musicians took a leave from school to develop their talents. Others, he said, take time off to pursue cultural interests, such as returning to the country of their origin.

Few of today's leave-takers, however, seem to be wandering aimlessly in the manner of the 1960s. "The leave to surf is almost nonexistent," said Stanford's Dean Clever. "Most students who decide to stop out have thought about it very thoroughly." In fact, the advice most often given by former stop-outs seems to be: "Know what you want to do with your time."

What most are doing is working—at jobs, in internships or in volunteer positions. A stack of "Re-admit Surveys" of 1981-82 stop-outs at Brown shows students working as anything from waitresses, mother's helpers and department-store clerks to surgeon's technicians, staff members in political campaigns and counselors for emotionally disturbed children.

"The majority do go out and work—to earn money, and gain practical experience," said Jeff Ashby, adviser in the division of undergraduate studies at Pennsylvania State University.

Dean Clever believes the opportunities for undergraduates stopping out are growing. "The number of internships available is expanding," he said. "A lot of people are seriously working to provide undergraduates with opportunities for experience."

Both Miss Clymore and Miss Willens found their jobs through the College Venture Program, founded in 1974 for the purpose of placing students on leave in jobs or internships. About 200 students at the 10 colleges that make up the College Venture consortium—Bates, Brown, Colby, the University of Chicago, Oberlin, Skidmore, Wesleyan, Northwestern, William and Mary, and Vassar—obtain employment through the organization each year, according to Susan Stroud, the director.

More than 400 annually consult Venture's "job bank," which lists a vast array of temporary jobs including teaching posts in Zimbabwe, apprenticeships to graphic designers and positions with the National Coalition to Ban Handguns. "We will work with students with any interest at trying to develop any job," Miss Stroud said.

In general, colleges are supportive of stop-outs these days. Several departments at Penn State strongly encourage students to take a break from studies to gain related experience. Brown holds a party at the start of each academic year to welcome returning stop-outs. Nearly every college offers a period, usually between one and three years, during which a student can leave school and be accepted back automatically.

Stopping out "is a perfectly normal and reasonable part of some students' development," said Haverford's Dean Potter. And Mrs. Hall of Brown added: "It is a very positive experience. I have never seen a person harmed by a year away."

According to Mrs. Hall, parents are also more accepting than they used to be to proposals by their son or daughter that he or she leave school for a time. "The more it is done, the less anxiety you see from parents," she said.

Students' verdicts on stopping out are overwhelmingly positive. Preliminary findings of a survey of stop-outs from the schools in the Venture consortium show that 29 percent think their leaves exceeded their highest hopes, and 62 percent say their time off was fully justified.

"It was a phenomenal year," said one student who worked for Ralph Nader. "Now I'm definitely a lot calmer about going out into the world."

Miss Claymore, who wrote copy for the advertising agency, said that as a result, "I'm hoping to go into advertising." And Miss Willens, who worked in the health-food store and taught children about nature, declared: "I have a better idea now of why I'm at Wesleyan."

Some students and administrators fear that the hard financial times and uncertain job market will begin to have the opposite effect on students considering leaves. "The pressure to get through and get a job may be increasing," said Miss Stroud. And with tuition rising 10 to 15 percent each year, Mrs. Hall predicts, "Students will feel they can't afford to stop out." But for now, students still seem to be following the advice so often given by former stop-outs in Brown's Re-admit Survey: "Do it!"

Even without interviews and research, writers sometimes seek to explain causes by applying some fresh insight or angle of observation. In the following essay, for example, former presidential speechwriter Peggy Noonan brings the special perspective of a White House staffer to her causal analysis of "Why We Dream about the Stars."

Noonan's "lead" captures the reader's attention with the moon rock, apt image for all our sense of wonder and awe at space exploration. Although the rock has rested in Washington, D.C., for twenty years, it still captivates our imagination, drawing countless Americans to make a special pilgrimage, just to see it. Noonan's image thereby unerringly seizes and holds the reader's attention, the task of every lead. Her essay also demonstrates how a causal essay may share traits with the personal essay (see Question 5, What Is My Personal Response to X?) and with the analytical essay (see Question 9, What Are the Component Parts of X?). Her nine reasons for why we dream about space (all cast in parallel construction) combine her analysis of American history ("We respond to a good goosing") with reactions she would have heard while working for President Reagan ("We breed heroes," "We speak American") and with what she herself observed of American character from her vantage point ("We are generous," "We are guided by spirit"). The essential impetus for rocketing into space— curiosity and adventure—belongs to the entire human race.

Why We Dream about the Stars

Peggy Noonan

At the Smithsonian Institution's Air and Space Museum in Washington, D.C., it's not hard to find the moon rock: Just follow the crowds. The rock's been there for sixteen years, but there are still people waiting in line to see it and touch it. Why? It's from *out there.*

Upstairs you'll find Alan Shepard's space suit, the one he wore on America's first manned space flight. There's something surprising about that suit: It looks small and old-fashioned. In fact, it looks downright antique. And in a way it is. There are almost as many years between Lindbergh's flight and Shepard's flight as there will be between Shepard's orbit and the next lift-off of the space shuttle. Space is both our future and our past, it lives both in our museums and in our research labs. We're on our way in a journey that shows no signs of ending. We're still pioneers.

There's something intrinsically American about this quest. It's true that ours is the blood of pioneers who crossed an ocean, tamed a continent, invented a nation, and then thought: What next? But the quest for space also reflects the way we are now. It is an expression of our current character.

And it can be captured, perhaps in nine details—nine things that are very American about America in space.

1. We respond to a good goosing. The launching in 1957 of *Sputnik,* the first artificial satellite, provided a thanks-I-needed-that slap for the U.S. space program. News of the Soviet triumph broke at night in this country, and a radio reporter in

New York called Cape Canaveral for reaction. The fellow who answered the phone said. "Gosh, we're all asleep here!" That said it all. The reporter raced to put those words on the air; they were picked up all across the country and, finally, around the world. Cape Canaveral was mightily embarrassed and soon woke up. This is an early and prime example of a free press sticking it to complacent bureaucrats to good effect and for a good cause.

2. We are generous. The day we landed on the moon, the *New York Times* headline said MAN WALKS ON MOON. Not American, not Yank—man. This was an expression of the American attitude toward our space triumphs: Share them. That goes for our tragedies, too. When the shuttle exploded, it was our shared disaster, our grief, available on videotape for all the world to see.

3. We always knew we'd get there. Cars are machines that float along the highways. They resist gravity. America is a country where everyone has a car. Mass production produced a populace that was at home with the idea of progress from the start, and that saw the defeat of gravity by machines as not only achievable but probable. When the first Model T got to the top of the first hill, that's when the space age began.

4. We like guts. One of the casualties of the *Challenger* explosion was the illusion that all this space business is completely safe. It was never safe. We almost lost John Glenn, we almost lost *Apollo 13*. Michael Collins, who piloted the orbiter in the first moon landing, calculated his chances of a safe return at fifty-fifty. What happened to the *Challenger* crew will no more stop space exploration than what happened at the Donner Pass stopped the settlement of the West.

5. We breed heroes. Jack Swigart was a studious, earnest man who loved to fly. He commanded Apollo 13, in many ways the most harrowing of the space missions. They were on their way to the moon and everything was fine until an oxygen tank blew up. It was Swigart who coolly reported, "Houston, we've got a problem." They aborted the flight and it was touch and go as they made their way back in the lifeboat mode. A few years later, Swigart ran for the Senate in Colorado, but he lost his party's nomination to Bill Armstrong. His astronaut training helped Swigart not to hate the man he was competing against; he joined in Armstrong's campaign during the general election. A few years later, it was Armstrong helping Swigart, who had just been elected to Congress and who was suddenly dying of cancer. Fate wasn't kind to Swigart, zigging him toward service and then zagging him away at the last minute. But he wasn't bitter and he wasn't afraid. Later Armstrong said, "Jack never panicked. He talked about his sickness with the interest of a scientist. It was 'Houston, we've got a problem.'"

6. We speak American. The language of the space program has a poetry all its own. "All systems go" and "T minus twenty," "A-OK" and "We have lift-off." Space gives new power to those of plain speech.

The best words spoken in space: the transmission that had all the natural clipped rhythm of genuine drama, "Mission Control, Tranquility Base here. The Eagle has landed." Those are words to make the skin constrict. Compare them to the tell-me-about-the-rabbits-George clunkiness of "That's one small step for a man . . ." and draw the inescapable lesson: Never rehearse joy.

7. Our children are ready. The future resides in the imaginations of our children, and have you seen the cartoons they've been watching? Space is real to

them; it lives in the most creative parts of their little brains. You can explain the idea of a strategic defence shield to nine-year-olds and they will (a) immediately understand and (b) know it's a good idea. This is because when it comes to the possibilities of space, they *get* it in a way that those sad souls whose most sophisticated weekly entertainment program was *Sky King* do not and cannot.

8. We love excitement. The future promises space stations, space settlements, space colonies like floating supertankers. We're going to use lasers and particle beams to build a strategic defense system against nuclear weapons; we're going to build massive solar-powered satellites; we're going to mine the moon for metals. We're going to learn to live up there. Your great-great-grandchildren may well visit Earth on vacation the way we visit the cathedrals of Europe: to see and touch the splendid past.

9. We're guided by spirit. In December of 1968, *Apollo 8* was on a very exciting trip. It was the first time we had entered the moon's gravity and curved into lunar orbit, preparing us for a moon landing to come. No one knew if we could do it. At the Cape, scientists aimed and pushed the buttons. Three days later, Anders, Borman, and Lovell began their orbit. It was Christmas Eve. As they circled, they marked that most modern of moments by reaching back to an earlier dawn. As the Earth rose in the blackness beyond, they read from Genesis: 'In the beginning God created the heaven and the earth. And the earth was without form, and void; and darkness was upon the face of the deep. And the Spirit of God moved upon the face of the waters. And God said, Let there be light: and there was light. . . ."

It was *the* moment of the space program, the moment that said we're really going to the moon, the moment that contained within it the dry footfalls of inevitability—and that suggested the mystery at the heart of the endeavor: We would go into space because it was the next, inevitable step in the life of man on Earth. It was in some way a continuation. It still is.

PRESENTING PERSONAL REASONS

In a still more subjective type of causal analysis the writer tries to explain why he or she has felt or acted a certain way. In this case the causes are *personal* and therefore cannot be evaluated objectively as accurate or inaccurate but rather as sincere or insincere, convincing or unconvincing, logically consistent or inconsistent, and reasonable or unreasonable in terms of themselves. Thus in Alice Walker's "Remembering Mr. Sweet" (and to a lesser degree in the Noonan essay above)—the standards of uniformity, necessity, sufficiency, and accuracy clearly give way to concerns for sincerity, logical consistency, credibility, and tone. The author of *The Color Purple* here tells us what factors led to the writing of her first published short story. Under the guise of recalling a drunken guitar player from her impoverished Georgia childhood (note the link with Question 4, What Is My Memory of X?), Walker dredges up the source of a despondency that gripped her in college, driving her to the brink of suicide. The memory of Mr. Sweet (*"He continued to sing"* despite his agony) rescued Walker, impelling her to produce the irreverently titled "To Hell with Dying," recently reissued with illustrations as a children's book.

Remembering Mr. Sweet

Alice Walker

There was in my rural, farming, middle-Georgia childhood, in the late 40s and early 50s, an old guitar player called Mr. Sweet. If people had used his family name, he would have been called Mr. Little; obviously nobody agreed that this was accurate. Sweet was. The only distinct memory I have is of him playing his guitar while sitting in an ancient, homemade (by my grandfather) oak-bottomed chair in my grandmother's cozy kitchen while she baked biscuits and a smothered chicken. He called the guitar his "box." I must have been 8 or 9 at the time.

He was an extremely soulful player and singer, and his position there by the warm stove in the good-smelling kitchen, "picking his box" and singing his own blues, while we sat around him silent and entranced, seemed inevitable and right. Although this is the only memory I have, and it is hazy, I know that Mr. Sweet was a fixture, a rare and honored presence in our family, and we were taught to respect him—no matter that he dranked, loved to gamble and shoot off his gun, and went "crazy" several times a year. He was an artist. He went deep into his own pain and brought out words and music that made us happy, made us feel empathy for anyone in trouble, made us think. We were taught to be thankful that anyone would assume this risk. That he was offered the platter of chicken and biscuits first (as if he were the preacher and even if he was tipsy) seemed only just.

Mr. Sweet died in the '60s, while I was a student at Sarah Lawrence College in Westchester, in an environment so different from the one in which he and my parents lived, and in which I had been brought up, that it might have existed on another planet. There were only three or four other black people there, and no poor people at all as far as the eye could see. For reasons not perhaps unrelated to this discrepancy, I was thinking of dying myself at the very time I got the news of his death. But something of my memory of Mr. Sweet stopped me: I remembered the magnitude of his problems—problems I was just beginning to truly understand—as a black man and as an artist, growing up poor, forced to endure the racist terrorism of the American South. He was unlucky in love, and no prince as a parent. *Irregardless,* as the old people said, and Mr. Sweet himself liked to say, not only had he lived to a ripe old age (I don't doubt that killing himself never entered his head, however, since I think alcoholism was, in his case, a slow method of suicide), but he had continued to share all his troubles and his insights with anyone who would listen, taking special care to craft them for the necessary effect. *He continued to sing.*

This was obviously my legacy, as someone who also wanted to be an artist and who was not only black and poor, but a woman besides, if only I had the guts to accept it.

Turning my back on the razor blade, I went to a friend's house for the Christmas holidays (I was too poor even to consider making the trip home, a distance of about a thousand miles), and on the day of Mr. Sweet's burial I wrote "To Hell With Dying." If in my poverty I had no other freedom—not even to say goodbye to him in death—I still had the freedom to love him and the means to express it, if only to myself. I wrote the story with tears pouring down my cheeks. I was grief-stricken, I was crazed, I was fighting for my own life. I was 21.

—

It was the first short story I ever published, though it was not the first one I wrote. The first one I wrote, before my memory of Mr. Sweet saved me, was entitled "The Suicide of an American Girl."

The poet Muriel Rukeyser was my don (primary teacher) and friend at Sarah Lawrence. So was Jane Cooper, in whose writing course I wrote the story. Between them they warmly affirmed the life of Mr. Sweet and the vitality of my art, which, I was beginning to see, merged in unexpected ways, very healing and effective ways, with my life. I was still hanging by a thread, so their enthusiasm was important. Without my knowledge, Muriel sent the story to the greatest of the old black singer poets, Langston Hughes, who was able to publish it two years after he read it.

When I met Langston Hughes I was amazed. He was another Mr. Sweet! Aging and battered, full of pain, but writing poetry, and laughing, too, and always making other people feel better. It was as if my love for one great old man down in the poor and beautiful and simple South had magically, in the new world of college and literature and poets and publishing and New York, led me to another.

DISCUSSION AND EXERCISES

1. Consider Hilary Stout's article, "Why College Students Take a Sabbatical"; then answer the following questions:
   a. If you were to "stop out" at some future date, how would you spend your time away from school?
   b. Do you feel that "stopping out" is a valuable practice? Why or why not? How does it differ from "dropping out"?
   c. Why was "stopping out" virtually unheard of fifteen to twenty years ago?
   d. What reasons do students give for stopping out today?
   e. How does your college regard stop-outs?

2. Answer the following questions about Peggy Noonan's "Why We Dream about the Stars."
   a. Why does Noonan claim that Alan Shepard's spacesuit looks antique? Is it, in fact, the passage of time (as she suggests) or some other implied reason?
   b. Using Christensen's method of diagramming paragraphs, chart the structure of each of Noonan's nine reasons. Are the paragraphs primarily coordinate or subordinate in structure?
   c. Note how each of Noonan's reasons begins with the pronoun *we*. What effect does she gain with this parallelism?
   d. Speculate on Noonan's reason for juxtaposing her fourth reason—"We like guts"—and her fifth reason—"We breed heroes."

Continued

e. What is it in Jack Swigart's character that Noonan finds emblematic of our spacemen and women?

f. With phrases such as "lunar excursion module" and "extra-vehicular activity," test Noonan's thesis that the "language of the space program has a poetry all its own." Even if Noonan may stretch her point, what is she trying to say about the language of the space program?

g. Using Noonan's last paragraph, explain how flying into space can be "the next, inevitable step in the life of man on earth."

3. Answer the following questions about Alice Walker's "Remembering Mr. Sweet."

a. Given the marvelous emotional details Walker provides about Mr. Sweet, which ones might she have identified with most as a young writer? Why is it important for Walker to present those traits early in her piece?

b. What was crucial about Walker's situation and location when she heard of Mr. Sweet's death?

c. What effect is produced by Walker's use of words and phrases such as "box," "smothered chicken," "went 'crazy' several times a year," and "irregardless"?

d. What freedom does Walker claim was hers in writing "To Hell with Dying"?

e. Walker closes this explanation by associating poet Langston Hughes with Mr. Sweet. What is appropriate about that connection? Chart the similarities between the two figures, as Walker sees them.

f. At several points in the essay, Walker follows a series of lilting, sometimes lengthy sentences with a short one. Look at "Sweet was." (paragraph one), "He was an artist." (paragraph two), *"He continued to sing."* (paragraph three), and "I was 21." (paragraph five). What purpose do these sentences serve in Walker's account?

g. What does the sentence structure in the first and last paragraphs tell you about Walker's feelings toward Mr. Sweet and the poet Langston Hughes?

4. Study Edvard Munch's *The Scream* (on the opposite page) and try to imagine or infer the causes of the cry. Write a one-paragraph explanation (150–200 words) in coordinate sequence.

ESSAY SUGGESTIONS

1. Write an essay (750-1,000 words) indicating the main causes for any one of the following: (Be sure to use the prewriting techniques described earlier.)

a. Natural phenomena

green grass
rain
blue sky
white clouds
appearance of stars at night
revolution of the earth around the sun

Edvard Munch, *The Scream* (1895).
National Gallery of Art, Washington, D.C.
Rosenwald collection.

sunrise
sunset
movement of the tides

b. Biological-psychological conditions

Disorders

headaches	hay fever
arteriosclerosis	AIDS
high blood pressure	schizophrenia
diabetes	suicide
cirrhosis	aphasia
epilepsy	amnesia
pneumonia	stuttering

Accidents

automobile accidents
home accidents
fires
airplane crashes
nuclear plant accidents

c. Architecture

the construction of one of the Seven Wonders of the World
the construction of cathedrals (or one particular cathedral) in the Middle Ages
the popularity of prefabricated houses
the evolution of the skyscraper in the United States
the belief that Frank Lloyd Wright was a great architect.

2. Write an essay (500–750 words) correcting the causal fallacies at the root of the medical superstitions listed below; in other words, cite the *facts* behind the superstition:

Night air is unhealthy.
Fish is brain food.
Insanity is inherited.
Green apples cause a stomachache.
Children born of cousins will be defective or deformed.
Frogs and toads cause warts.
Feed a cold, starve a fever.

3. Write an essay (500–750 words) in which you explain the causal implications in arguing for or against one of the following:

a. Law

the death penalty	present divorce laws
civil rights legislation	alimony

the jury system	inheritance tax
immigration quotas	executive privilege
the presumption of innocence	prostitution as a crime
diplomatic immunity	drug abuse as a crime
present income tax laws	conscientious objectors.

b. Religion

religion *per se*	Day of Judgment
God as "giver"	original sin
churchgoing	free will
the Bible as literature	doctrine of the elect
immortality	agnosticism
heaven and hell	atheism
missionaries	reincarnation
salvation	jihad

4. Write an essay (750–1,000 words) based on Stout's essay "Why College Students Take a Sabbatical," focusing on a student or group of students on campus who have either stopped-out or are considering it. Interview as many students as you can, using quotes, facts, and statistics.
5. Write a speculative, personal essay (750–1,000 words)—as in "Why We Dream about the Stars"—filling in the blank as you choose: "Why We Dream About _____."
6. Write a causal analysis (750–1,000 words) explaining why you feel or behave in a given way (e.g., Why I Fly a Kite).
7. Using Alice Walker's "Remembering Mr. Sweet" as a guide, write an essay (750–1,000 words) about your personal reasons for an act of which you are proud, that required great courage, or that you accomplished at great emotional expense.

Question

13

WHAT ARE THE CONSEQUENCES OF X?

PREDICTING CONSEQUENCES
  COMPUTERS AND THE NEW LITERACY,
  BENJAMIN COMPAINE

REPORTING CONSEQUENCES
  MY WOOD, E. M. FORSTER

IGNORING AND DEPLORING CONSEQUENCES
  A GENERATION UNDER CURFEW,
  MIKE DAVIS

PREDICTING CONSEQUENCES

Just as we are naturally curious about the causes of various ideas, acts, or events, so are we naturally curious about consequences—what follows from various ideas, acts, or events. Thus while the previous question, *What are the causes of X?*, started with effects and traced them *back* to causes ("I failed the exam. I wonder why."), the present question, *What are the consequences of X?*, reverses the direction. It starts with a given or hypothetical condition and projects *ahead* to what naturally or necessarily follows. (If I don't study, I will—as a consequence—fail the exam.) In predicting consequences, as in tracing causes, it is essential that you be rigorously logical.

You may also need to draw on the past to establish a casual explanation envisioning consequences. In the following article, for example, "Computers and the New Literacy," Benjamin Compaine, executive director of the Harvard Information Bureau Resource Policy program, gives us a glimpse of the future, basing his prediction of what *will happen* upon his observation of what *has happened* in the past. Combining his historical analysis with facts and figures drawn from present studies and statistical data, he takes a leap into the future: The developing Computer Age will surely revolutionize and redefine our patterns of literacy, he tells us, while pointing to a long list of trends.

Note that this article is a model of clear, logical organization. (Marginal notes indicate the main structural units.) Note also how skillfully the writer has generated supporting materials by addressing multiple questions to his topic:

> Question 6, What are the facts about X? (produces data and hard evidence)
>
> Question 7, What does X mean? (produces a definition of "literacy")
>
> Question 10, How is X made or done (produces an historical account of how concepts of literacy have changed through the ages)
>
> Question 16, What is the present status of X? (produces the observation that today we seem to be entering the stage at which the masses can use [the computer] without having to understand how it works)

As for the specific question we are concerned with here, we can see that the question that represents the main thrust of this piece—*What are the consequences of X?*—has shaped the article as a whole: the consequences of our present entrance into the computer age should "be neither saluted nor feared."

COMPUTERS AND THE NEW LITERACY

Benjamin Compaine

Introduction: Youngsters today are "fluent in the language of the future"; their elders are not

After last year's World Future Society assembly on telecommunications, a 16-year-old suggested that youngsters already fluent in the language of the future are amused by their elders' tentative, tortured attempts to make contact: "I think the message was clear that it's really our world. I was kind of laughing at the people here. This technology, all they talked about, they really couldn't grasp. This belongs to us."

Thesis: The new literacy of the future will require familiarity with computers

Some people are going to have trouble grasping the fact that we are on the verge of an era in which the ability to read and write may not be sufficient to define what it is to be literate. Literacy may soon mean being able to access, manipulate and store information in a computer.

Note development here in terms of historic process: how concepts of literacy changed through the ages

Each generation tends to assume its definition of literacy is the ultimate; literacy is, however, a dynamic construct, a bundle of culturally relevant skills that change over time. Before the written word was widely used, the oral tradition predominated. In twelfth-century England, for example, literacy meant the ability to compose and recite in Latin. To "make a record" of something meant to bear oral witness, not produce a document for others to read. Eventually, English replaced Latin as the language for discourse. But even then, because of the difficulty of using a quill on parchment or a stylus on wax, writing in the Middle Ages was considered a special skill that was not automatically coupled with the ability to read. The most common way of committing words to writing was by dictating to a scribe, not himself necessarily able to compose. Thus, reading and dictating, rather than reading and writing, were typically paired.

With the development of the printing press in the fifteenth century, the basic skills of modern literacy—reading and writing—became relatively widespread. Still, the definition of literacy did not remain static. By the mid-nineteenth century, the English literati stiffened the requirements for admission to their ranks. Not merely the ability to read, they said, but the reading of the "right" materials separated the truly literate from the great unwashed. "How, if at all, they asked, did the spread of the printed word contribute to the spiritual enrichment and intellectual enlightenment of the nation?" wrote Altick in *The English Common Reader.*

Even an institution as sacrosanct as the library has not always been held in high regard by the literary elite. Free libraries for the English common man were viciously criticized by those who felt that, instead of encouraging study and self-improvement, they inflamed the popular passion for the wanton reading of fiction. Indeed, one librarian told a meeting in 1879 that "school-boys or students who took to novel reading to any great extent never made much progress in after [later] life." The irony of attitudes such as this may be instructive to critics of video games, who decry them as a corrupting influence on today's schoolchildren.

Historically, literacy developed in a series of identifiable stages. It starts in the hands of specialists, then begins to have a wider impact on institutions as it becomes the preferred medium of business, culture and politics. Finally, it becomes so pervasive that even the masses are considered handicapped without it. We can trace modern notions of literacy from their beginnings in twelfth-century England—with its movement away from reliance on the spoken word and toward written records—to their first plateau, which appeared with the introduction of the printing press. The development culminated in newspapers and mass-market books, along with popular education, in the nineteenth century.

History also suggests that one does not have to be fully literate to participate in literacy. One measure of changing literacy in thirteenth-century England was the possession of a seal. Earlier, only the king possessed a seal; it was used to authenticate documents. In the reign of Edward I, however, the Statute of Exeter required even unlettered serfs to have one.

Looking back over the 35 or so years since the development of modern computers, we can spot trends similar to the much slower advance of traditional literacy. At first, computers were strictly for a "priestly" class that could read and write the *lingua electronica*. All computer users were dependent upon this group of plugged-in clergy. As computers became more widespread and their application more pervasive, however, they began to have a greater impact on business and social institutions. The languages (COBOL, FORTRAN, BASIC, etc.) evolved into something closer to the vernacular, and more people were able to use them.

Today, we seem to be entering the stage at which the computer is becoming so simple and inexpensive that the masses can use it without having to understand how it works. They can thus participate in computer literacy without necessarily being part of the electronic elite themselves. It may be no more necessary for the mass of people to understand how a computer works than it is to understand the mechanics of the internal combustion engine in order to drive a car.

Last year, about $2 billion was spent, worldwide, on cartridges for home video games. And well over 22 billion quarters were dropped into arcade video games. Meanwhile, about 7 million people—from stockbrokers to travel agents—use VDTs, video display terminals, as part of their everyday work. In ever greater numbers, secretaries are writing the boss's letters and memos on word processors. And the executives themselves are likely to be getting information for their decisions via a desktop computer.

The kids playing video games and the adults working with VDTs have one thing in common. To an increasing degree, they are using a computer for storing and manipulating data. They are using computers directly and they are using them in place of older information and entertainment processes, most notably ink and paper. By the time today's 10-year-olds graduate from college, they may be using computers as readily as an older generation uses books.

The video game craze, even if it turns out to be a passing fad, may hold considerable cultural significance. For the first time, the video tube is something more than a medium for passive masses. Without becoming computer experts, the kids and others who play the games may be intuitively learning the strengths and limitations of computer logic. They are certainly learning how to manipulate a computer (whether with a keyboard, joy stick or some other mechanism). The U.S. Army, which must train large numbers of youngsters just removed from the video game parlors, is experimenting with training exercises that use video-game-like lessons played on microcomputers. The schools are not far behind. Microcom- *Looking into the* puters are showing up in classrooms all over the country; surprisingly, it's the kids *future* and their parents, not the educational establishment, who are pushing for the change. PTAs are holding bake sales to raise money not for library books but for desktop computers. According to Mary Alice White, chief of the Electronic Learning Laboratory at Columbia University's Teachers College, today's youth spend more time using electronic devices (like television and video games) to learn with than they spend with print.

Some of these changes are already showing up on the job market. A study shows that jobs in the help wanted ads in the *New York Times* that required some form of computer literacy doubled between 1977 and 1982. None of the listings for travel agents in 1977 mentioned the need for any computer-related skills, for example, but five years later, 71 percent required the ability to operate computer-based reservations systems. Secretary-typist jobs that demanded word-processing skills went from zero to 15 percent.

To speculate on the long-term societal impacts that may grow out of the trends identified here would be foolish. Indeed, most of the predictions being made today about the new information technologies are reminiscent of Victorian warnings. There was once speculation that the pneumatic tire would lead to the demise of books because the family out riding bicycles would forever shun the tradition of fireside reading.

While the evidence points to another step in the evolution of literacy, it is unlikely that the older skills will die. Neither the printing press nor the telephone resulted in the elimination of handwriting or postal services. The electronic calculator has not replaced the need to *understand* mathematics. The new literacy is likely to involve a greater emphasis on graphics and the spoken word, continuing a trend that reflects improvements in photography, printing, recordings and television. Above all, the new literacy need be neither saluted nor feared. Whatever evolves will take place in stages, giving society a chance to adjust.

REPORTING CONSEQUENCES

Writers need not speculate on consequences; they may simply report them. E. M. Forster, for example, builds an entire essay around the consequences of owning property. What happens, he asks, when you "own things"? Forster cites an example from his own life. He bought himself "a wood" with a check he received for writing a book about the difficulties of the English in India. Although it was not "a large wood," the consequences of owning it—as he vividly describes them—were considerable.

My Wood

E. M. Forster

A few years ago I wrote a book which dealt in part with the difficulties of the English in India. Feeling that they would have had no difficulties in India themselves, the Americans read the book freely. The more they read it the better it made them feel, and a check to the author was the result. I bought a wood with the check. It is not a large wood—it contains scarcely any trees, and it is intersected, blast it, by a public footpath. Still, it is the first property that I have owned, so it is right that other people should participate in my shame, and should ask themselves, in accents that will vary in horror, this very important question: What is the effect of property upon the character? Don't let's touch economics; the effect of private ownership upon the community as a whole is another question—a more important question, perhaps, but another one. Let's keep to psychology. If you own things, what's their effect on you? What's the effect on me of my wood?

In the first place, it makes me feel heavy. Property does have this effect. Property produces men of weight, and it was a man of weight who failed to get into the Kingdom of Heaven. He was not wicked, that unfortunate millionaire in the parable, he was only stout; he stuck out in front, not to mention behind, and as he wedged himself this way and that in the crystalline entrance and bruised his well-fed flanks, he saw beneath him a comparatively slim camel passing through the eye of a needle and being woven into the robe of God. The Gospels all through couple stoutness and slowness. They point out what is perfectly obvious, yet seldom realized: that if you have a lot of things you cannot move about a lot, that furniture requires dusting, dusters require servants, servants require insurance stamps, and the whole tangle of them makes you think twice before you accept an invitation to dinner or go for a bathe in the Jordan. Sometimes the Gospels proceed further and say with Tolstoy that property is sinful; they approach the difficult ground of asceticism here, where I cannot follow them. But as to the immediate effects of property on people, they just show straightforward logic. It produces men of weight. Men of weight cannot, by definition, move like the lightning from the East unto the West, and the ascent of a fourteen-stone bishop into a pulpit is thus the exact antithesis of the coming of the Son of Man. My wood makes me feel heavy.

In the second place, it makes me feel it ought to be larger.

The other day I heard a twig snap in it. I was annoyed at first, for I thought that someone was blackberrying, and depreciating the value of the undergrowth. On coming nearer, I saw it was not a man who had trodden on the twig and snapped it, but a bird, and I felt pleased. My bird. The bird was not equally pleased. Ignoring the relation between us, it took fright as soon as it saw the shape of my face, and flew straight over the boundary hedge into a field, the property of Mrs. Henessy, where it sat down with a loud squawk. It had become Mrs. Henessy's bird. Something seemed grossly amiss here, something that would not have occurred had the wood been larger. I could not afford to buy Mrs. Henessy out, I dared not murder her, and limitations of this sort beset me on every side. Ahab did not want that vineyard—he only needed it to round off his property, preparatory to plotting a new curve—and all the land around my wood has become necessary to me in order to round off the wood. A boundary protects. But—poor little thing—the boundary ought in its turn to be protected. Noises on the edge of it. Children throw stones. A little more, and then a little more, until we reach the sea. Happy Canute! Happier Alexander! And after all, why should even the world be the limit of possession? A rocket containing a Union Jack, will, it is hoped, be shortly fired at the moon. Mars. Sirius. Beyond which . . . But these immensities ended by saddening me. I could not suppose that my wood was the destined nucleus of universal dominion—it is so small and contains no mineral wealth beyond the blackberries. Nor was I comforted when Mrs. Henessy's bird took alarm for the second time and flew clean away from us all, under the belief that it belonged to itself.

In the third place, property makes its owner feel that he ought to do something to it. Yet he isn't sure what. A restlessness comes over him, a vague sense that he has a personality to express—the same sense which, without any vagueness, leads the artist to an act of creation. Sometimes I think I will cut down such trees as remain in the wood, at other times I want to fill up the gaps between them with new trees. Both impulses are pretentious and empty. They are not honest movements towards moneymaking or beauty. They spring from a foolish desire to express myself and from an inability to enjoy what I have got. Creation, property, enjoyment form a sinister trinity in the human mind. Creation and enjoyment are both very very good, yet they are often unattainable without a material basis, and at such moments property pushes itself in as a substitute, saying, "Accept me instead—I'm good enough for all three." It is not enough. It is, as Shakespeare said of lust, "The expense of spirit in a waste of shame": it is "Before, a joy proposed; behind, a dream." Yet we don't know how to shun it. It is forced on us by our economic system as the alternative to starvation. It is also forced on us by an internal defect in the soul, by the feeling that in property may lie the germs of self-development and of exquisite or heroic deeds. Our life on earth is, and ought to be, material and carnal. But we have not yet learned to manage our materialism and carnality properly; they are still entangled with the desire for ownership, where (in the words of Dante) "Possession is one with loss."

And this brings us to our fourth and final point: the blackberries.

Blackberries are not plentiful in this meagre grove, but they are easily seen from the public footpath which traverses it, and all too easily gathered. Foxgloves, too—people will pull up the foxgloves, and ladies of an educational tendency even grub for toadstools to show them on the Monday in class. Other ladies, less educated, roll down the bracken in the arms of their gentlemen friends. There is paper, there are tins. Pray, does my wood belong to me or doesn't it? And, if it does, should I not own it best by allowing no one else to walk there? There is a wood near Lyme Regis, also cursed by a public footpath, where the owner has not hesitated on this point. He has built high stone walls each side of the path, and has spanned it by bridges, so that the public circulate like termites while he gorges on the blackberries unseen. He really does own his wood, this able chap. Dives in Hell did pretty well, but the gulf dividing him from Lazarus could be traversed by vision, and nothing traverses it here. And perhaps I shall come to this in time. I shall wall in and fence out until I really taste the sweets of property. Enormously stout, endlessly avaricious, pseudo-creative, intensely selfish, I shall weave upon my forehead the quadruple crown of possession until those nasty Bolshies come and take it off again and thrust me aside into the outer darkness.

IGNORING AND DEPLORING CONSEQUENCES

In the following excerpt from his *City of Quartz,* Mike Davis traces the recent social history of Los Angeles and the region surrounding it. As crime rates sky-rocket and voters, spurred on by the media, urge that more drastic measures be taken, the escalating war on drugs may be having unintended consequences in the lives of young people, Davis argues. In his view, by imposing curfews on neighborhoods that are predominantly African-American and Latino, politicians and the police force are criminalizing an entire generation.

A Generation under Curfew

Mike Davis

> I think people believe that the only strategy we have is to put a lot of police officers on the street and harass people and make arrests for inconsequential kinds of things. Well, that's part of the strategy, no question about it.
>
> —Chief Gates

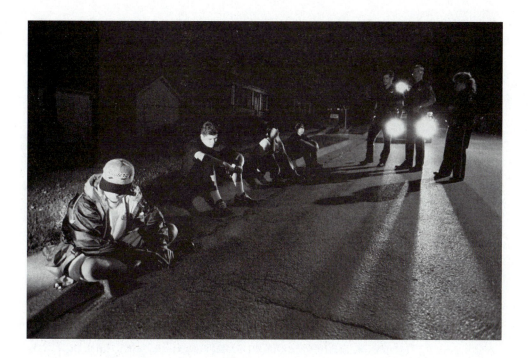

As a result of the war on drugs every non-Anglo teenager in Southern California is now a prisoner of gang paranoia and associated demonology. Vast stretches of the region's sumptuous playgrounds, beaches and entertainment centers have become virtual no-go areas for young Blacks or Chicanos. After the Westwood gang shooting, for example, Don Jackson, an off-duty Black policeman from Hawthorne, precisely in order to make a point about de facto apartheid, led some ghetto kids into the Village. They carefully observed the law, yet, predictably, they were stopped, forced to kiss concrete, and searched. Jackson, despite police identification, was arrested for "disturbing the peace." Afterwards at a press conference, Chief Gates excoriated him for "provocations" and a "cheap publicity stunt," descriptions more aptly applied to the LAPD. Similarly, a few weeks later, a busload of well-dressed Black members of Youth for Christ were humiliatingly surrounded by security guards and frisked for "drugs and weapons" at the popular Magic Mountain amusement park. Park managers adamantly defended their right to search "suspicious" (i.e., Black) youth as a matter of policy. More recently twenty-four Black and Latino kids out to play baseball at Will Rogers State Park were arrested for violating some white cops' personal Jim Crow law. The *Times* reported the kids' account of how they "spent 90 terrifying minutes held face down on the polo field . . . while a group of LAPD taunted and brutalized them. . . . One officer was quoted as having told them that the scenic park in Pacific Palisades was 'for rich white people' only." (The NAACP and the Mexican American Political Association have jointly filed suit against the LAPD for this incident.). . . .

Curfews have become essential weapons in the LAPD's campaign against the subversive crowd. Residential curfews are deployed selectively and almost exclusively against Black and Chicano neighborhoods. As a consequence, thousands of youth in Southcentral acquire minor records for behavior that would be legal or inoffensive on the Westside. During daylight hours, moreover, the post-Bird California Supreme Court has given police *carte blanche* to stop and search any youthful person for suspicion of truancy. As with the random drunk-driver checkpoints that the Lucas court has also authorized, or the random car weapons searches that the legislature has enacted as part of anti-gang legislation—the "probable cause" safeguard against capricious stop-and-search is rendered practically extinct. Police now have virtually unlimited discretion, day or night, to target "undesirables," especially youth.

One of the most disturbing instances of such police "targeting" has been the LAPD Ramparts Division's relentless campaign against Salvadorean youth in the MacArthur Park district just west of Downtown. Community workers in this poor and overcrowded neighborhood, the home of tens of thousands of refugees from US-financed state terrorism in Central America, tell bitter tales of police brutality. Ramparts cops were particularly incensed by church efforts to work with members of *Mara Savatrucha* (MS) (liberally translated: "cool Salvadorean dudes," but also known as "Crazy Riders"), a vast, loosely organized gang grouping. When the Joffrey Ballet in 1988 offered some free seats to Salvadorean youngsters studying dance at a local church center, Ramparts Division warned the Ballet that the kids were the most "ruthlessly violent in the city" and that the church was basically a gang hangout. The terrified Ballet withdrew the tickets. Meanwhile, coincident with the HAMMER sweeps in Southcentral, the LAPD's CRASH (Community Resources Against Street Hoodlums) program launched a new offensive to "decimate" the leadership of MS. Howard Ezell, Western regional commissioner for the INS . . . assigned eight teams of federal immigration agents to work with the LAPD identifying and deporting gang members. As the leader of the INS agents explained, gang *membership,* not necessarily criminal activity, was the qualification for deportation. "If a gang member is out on the street and the police can't make a charge, we will go out and deport them for being here illegally if they fit that criterion." Fifty-six of the 175 youth deported were returned to El Salvador, to uncertain fates at the hands of the military and death squads.

But the growing authoritarian reach of police control is nowhere as disturbingly evident as in Los Angeles schools. Another of Chief Gates's publicity-generating "body count" projects is the so-called "School Buy" program. As ACLU attorney Joan Howarth describes it, "Up to high school, kids are taught to look on cops as friends; after the eighth grade, School Buy cops are trying to entrap them into drug deals." Youthful undercover cops, in fact, infiltrate high schools, enticing students to sell them drugs. Howarth particularly denounces "the exploitation of peer pressure to create narcotic offenses; in many cases the undercover police (male and female) exploit sexuality and attractiveness. For this reason, 'special education' [educationally handicapped] students, approached for possibly the first time in their life by an attractive member of the opposite sex, are especially likely to become entrapped. The program is a complete fraud." With little impact on the actual volume of drug sales and negligible success in capturing adult suppliers, the School Buy program is primarily a cheap source of the felony arrests that make the Chief look heroic in the media.

Thanks partially to such police "vigilance," juvenile crime in Los Angeles County is increasing at 12 per cent annually. One out of twelve kids in Los Angeles, aged eleven to seventeen, will be arrested, half for serious felonies. For older juveniles tried as adults, moreover, conviction rates have soared ominously over the last decade as prosecutors routinely overcharge suspects, threatening them with long sentences, in order to force them to "cop pleas" to lesser charges. Public defenders and civil libertarians alike have denounced this practice of railroading thousands of poor and frightened teenagers into undeserved criminal convictions.

At the same time, the new punitive increments that STEP and federal and state anti-drug laws have added to sentencing expose a terrible class and racial bias. As the *Times* points out:

> Under new federal statutes, defendants convicted of selling 5 grams or more of crack cocaine, worth perhaps $125, receive a mandatory minimum of five years in prison. However, it takes 500 grams of the powdered drug, nearly $50,000 worth of "yuppie cocaine," to receive an equivalent sentence. Consequently, someone caught in a drug bust with a relatively small amount of cocaine can receive a sentence that is two to three years longer than a person convicted of selling nearly 100 times that amount.

A few illustrations of this new, Kafkaesque class justice: In Southcentral L.A. a young Black three-time loser, never charged with violent crime, but holding a weapon, was sentenced to life imprisonment *without possibility of parole* for the possession of 5.5 grams of crack. A 20-year-old Chinese man received *two* life terms (parole in forty years) for being accessory to the murder of federal agents even though he was not at the scene, did not know that the murders would occur, and was described by the judge as playing "only a minor role." Meanwhile, a 21-year-old Baldwin Park Chicano, high on PCP, who ran into the back of a truck and killed his passenger, was charged with murder because he was a suspected gang member. Finally, an elite LAPD stake-out team that the *Times* had exposed as a virtual police death squad, ambushed four young Latinos who had just robbed a MacDonalds in Sunland with a pellet gun. Three of the Latinos were killed by the cops, while the fourth, seriously wounded, was charged with murder, for the deaths of his companions!

Processed by such "justice" (which since 1974 has arrested *two-thirds* of all younger Black males in California), a flood of captives, four-fifths of whom are substance addicted and less than half of whom have committed violent crimes, overwhelm the state prisons—84,000 inmates in a system with room for 48,000. With the prison population expected to continue to soar, as a result of the "victories" of the war on drugs and gangs, to 145,000 by 1995, California is creating a time-bomb of multiple-Attica potential. Lacking minimal educational, job-training or drug-treatment resources, the prisons of today have all but abandoned the pretense of "rehabilitation." Some are merely minimum security warehouses, where the inmate populations are turned over to endless television gameshow viewing; others, especially designed to accommodate the hardcore gangsters from Los Angeles's ghettoes and barrios, are Orwellian hells.

The ultimate destination for a damned generation is an Antarctica of solitude moored to the picturesque Redwood Coast, just south of the Oregon border. The prison's name, "Pelican Bay," evokes a nature reserve or peaceful sanctuary, but this is only a cruel joke in face of the incredible social isolation and sensory deprivation contained inside. As journalist Miles Corwin describes it:

> Pelican Bay is entirely automated and designed so that inmates have virtually no face-to-face contact with guards or other inmates. For twenty-two and a half hours a day, inmates are confined to their windowless cells, built of solid blocks of concrete and stainless steel so that they won't have access to materials they could fashion into weapons. They don't work in prison industries; they don't have access to recreation; they don't mingle with other inmates. They aren't allowed to smoke because matches are considered a security risk.

The justification for this kind of isolation—"unprecedented in modern prisons" according to one authority whom Corwin interviewed—is simply that "these inmates are the worst of the worst." As a prison officer elaborates:

> Prisons are representative of what's going on in the streets. . . . You've got more gangs and violence on the streets, so you've got more gangs and violence in the prisons. You need a place to put these people . . . that's why a place like Pelican Bay is necessary.

Question

14

WHAT ARE THE
TYPES OF X?

CREATING A CLASSIFICATION
    JUNG'S PSYCHOLOGICAL TYPES,
    FRIEDA FORDHAM

CLASSIFICATION ACCORDING TO PURPOSE
    THREE TYPES OF RESISTANCE TO OPPRESSION,
    THE REV. MARTIN LUTHER KING, JR.

COMPLETENESS OF CLASSIFICATION
    THREE KINDS OF DISCIPLINE, JOHN HOLT

CREATING A CLASSIFICATION

Classification is a highly methodical form of analysis and an indispensable condition of systematic thought, for it involves a sorting process that groups elements into categories based on similar characteristics. We see this process at work in the story of Adam bringing order out of chaos by naming the creatures around him. We can reconstruct the procedure in our imagination: As the multitude of creatures was paraded before him, Adam began a sorting process in his own mind. Noting at the outset that some creatures were of the field, he called them "beasts"; noting that others were of the air, he called them "fowl" or "birds." We can imagine that within these two large categories, Adam classified further. Some of the beasts—or animals—were large and lumbering, with extraordinarily long noses: these he named "elephants." Others with long sleek bodies and stripes he called "tigers"; still others with spots, "leopards"; and so on. Adam continued the classification and naming procedure until all the birds and beasts had been grouped together into appropriate identifying categories.

Since earliest times, then, human beings have been classifying things, arranging them in order to see their similarities and differences more clearly, and in that way to learn more about them.

We frequently use classification in our daily living; for example, we may sort our daily mail into three categories: bills, junk mail, and personal letters (an incomplete but still useful system of classification). We put the bills to one side, throw away the junk mail unopened, and give our time to the letters.

You can see that an essay concerned with "the types of X" presents no serious problem in organization, because the organization is more or less given: the three or four (or however many) designated types generally make up the three or four sections of the piece.

This organization underlies Carl Jung's classic division of people into two personality types (extravert and introvert). Note that in this essay the author does not regard the types as mutually exclusive, with discernibly fixed personalities (an imperative of the scientific or technical classification), but rather as poles on the scale of personality (people are predominantly one or the other; no one is purely extravert or introvert). Thus in this essay, as in all rhetorical rather than strictly logical classifications, the categories may overlap to some extent.

Jung's Psychological Types

Frieda Fordham

Introduction   Jung's contribution to the psychology of the conscious mind is largely embodied in his work on psychological types. The attempt to classify human beings according to type has a long history; it is nearly two thousand years since the Greek physician, Galen, tried to distinguish four fundamental temperamental differences in men, and his descriptive terms (though psychologically naive)— the sanguine, the phlegmatic, the choleric, and the melancholic—have passed into common speech. There have been various attempts which, taking modern knowledge into account, aim at a more precise formulation—for instance,

Kretschmer's—and [Carl] Jung's division of people into extraverts and introverts has already come to be widely known, if not fully understood. Jung distinguishes two differing attitudes to life, two modes of reacting to circumstances which he finds sufficiently marked and widespread to describe as typical.

> There is a whole class of men [he says] who at the moment of reaction to a given situation at first draw back a little as if with an unvoiced no, and only after that are able to react; and there is another class who, in the same situation, come forward with an immediate reaction, apparently confident that their behavior is obviously right. The former class would therefore be characterized by a certain negative relation to the object, and the latter by a positive one . . . the former class corresponds to the introverted and the second to the extraverted attitude.

Type one   The extraverted attitude is characterized by an outward flowing of libido, an interest in events, in people and things, a relationship with them, and a dependence on them; when this attitude is habitual to anyone, Jung describes him or her as an *extraverted type*. This type is motivated by outside factors and greatly influenced by the environment. The extraverted type is sociable and confident in unfamiliar surroundings. He or she is generally on good terms with the world, and even when disagreeing with it can still be described as related to it, for instead of withdrawing (as the opposite type tends to do) they prefer to argue and quarrel, or try to reshape it according to their own pattern.

Type two   The introverted attitude, in contrast, is one of withdrawal; the libido flows inward and is concentrated upon subjective factors, and the predominating influence is "inner necessity." When this attitude is habitual, Jung speaks of an "introverted type." This type lacks confidence in relation to people and things, tends to be unsociable, and prefers reflection to activity. Each type undervalues the other, seeing the negative rather than the positive qualities of the opposite attitude, a fact which has led to endless misunderstanding, and even in the course of time, to the formulation of antagonistic philosophies.

Conclusion   In the West we prefer the extraverted attitude, describing it in such favourable terms as outgoing, well-adjusted, &c., while on the other hand, in the East, at least until recent times, the introverted attitude has been the prevailing one. On this basis one may explain the material and technical development of the Western Hemisphere as contrasted with the material poverty but greater spiritual development of the East.

CLASSIFICATION ACCORDING TO PURPOSE

What characteristics you use as the basis of a classification depend on your own interests and purpose. You can classify people politically, socially, economically, or even by the color of their eyes, depending on what special point you want to make.

You are, of course, free to choose whatever basis of classification best suits your purpose, but once you have chosen you must not switch midway to a different ground. If you do, you will be committing the logical error of cross-ranking, that is, producing overlapping rather than mutually exclusive categories. Someone who classifies the types of houses in a town as

Victorian, colonial, ranch, and two-story is guilty of cross-ranking because Victorian and colonial style houses can have an upstairs and a downstairs.

Classification is an extraordinarily useful method of inventing an essay, for there is always a "story" in the designation of types—as you choose to depict them. And the choice will depend on *why* you are making the classification in the first place, and on what new insights or refinements of understanding you hope to provide by analyzing your subject in terms of a given set of categories.

In the essay below, Martin Luther King, Jr., presents three ways of resisting oppression to demonstrate to his followers the futility of two of the ways; only the third way should be pursued.

THREE TYPES OF RESISTANCE TO OPPRESSION

Martin Luther King, Jr.

Oppressed people deal with their oppression in three characteristic ways. One way is acquiescence: the oppressed resign themselves to their doom. They tacitly adjust themselves to oppression, and thereby become conditioned to it. In every movement toward freedom some of the oppressed prefer to remain oppressed. Almost 2800 years ago Moses set out to lead the children of Israel from the slavery of Egypt to the freedom of the promised land. He soon discovered that slaves do not always welcome their deliverers. They become accustomed to being slaves. They would rather bear those ills they have, as Shakespeare pointed out, than flee to others that they know not of. They prefer the "fleshpots of Egypt" to the ordeals of emancipation.

There is such a thing as the freedom of exhaustion. Some people are so worn down by the yoke of oppression that they give up. A few years ago in the slum areas of Atlanta, a Negro guitarist used to sing almost daily: "Been down so long that down don't bother me." This is the type of negative freedom and resignation that often engulfs the life of the oppressed.

But this is not the way out. To accept passively an unjust system is to cooperate with that system; thereby the oppressed become as evil as the oppressor. Noncooperation with evil is as much a moral obligation as is cooperation with good. The oppressed must never allow the conscience of the oppressor to slumber. Religion reminds every man that he is his brother's keeper. To accept injustice or segregation passively is to say to the oppressor that his actions are morally right. It is a way of allowing his conscience to fall asleep. At this moment the oppressed fails to be his brother's keeper. So acquiescence—while often the easier way—is not the moral way. It is the way of the coward. The Negro cannot win the respect of his oppressor by acquiescing; he merely increases the oppressor's arrogance and contempt. Acquiescence is interpreted as proof of the Negro's inferiority. The Negro cannot win the respect of the white people of the South or the peoples of the world if he is willing to sell the future of his children for his personal and immediate comfort and safety.

A second way that oppressed people sometimes deal with oppression is to resort to physical violence and corroding hatred. Violence often brings about momentary results. Nations have frequently won their independence in battle. But in spite of temporary victories, violence never brings permanent peace. It solves no social problem; it merely creates new and more complicated ones.

Violence as a way of achieving racial justice is both impractical and immoral. It is impractical because it is a descending spiral ending in destruction for all. The old law of an eye for an eye leaves everybody blind. It is immoral because it seeks to humiliate the opponent rather than win his understanding; it seeks to annihilate rather than to convert. Violence is immoral because it thrives on hatred rather than love. It destroys community and makes brotherhood impossible. It leaves society in monologue rather than dialogue. Violence ends by defeating itself. It creates bitterness in the survivors and brutality in the destroyers. A voice echoes through time saying to every potential Peter, "Put up your sword." History is cluttered with the wreckage of nations that failed to follow this command.

If the American Negro and other victims of oppression succumb to the temptation of using violence in the struggle for freedom, future generations will be the recipients of a desolate night of bitterness, and our chief legacy to them will be an endless reign of meaningless chaos. Violence is not the way.

The third way open to oppressed people in their quest for freedom is the way of nonviolent resistance. Like the synthesis in Hegelian philosophy, the principle of nonviolent resistance seeks to reconcile the truths of two opposites—acquiescence and violence—while avoiding the extremes and immoralities of both. The nonviolent resister agrees with the person who acquiesces that one should not be physically aggressive toward his opponent; but he balances the equation by agreeing with the person of violence that evil must be resisted. He avoids the nonresistance of the former and the violent resistance of the latter. With nonviolent resistance, no individual or group need submit to any wrong, nor need anyone resort to violence in order to right a wrong.

It seems to me that this is the method that must guide the actions of the Negro in the present crisis in race relations. Through nonviolent resistance the Negro will be able to rise to the noble height of opposing the unjust system while loving the perpetrators of the system. The Negro must work passionately and unrelentingly for full stature as a citizen, but he must not use inferior methods to gain it. He must never come to terms with falsehood, malice, hate, or destruction.

Nonviolent resistance makes it possible for the Negro to remain in the South and struggle for his rights. The Negro's problem will not be solved by running away. He cannot listen to the glib suggestion of those who would urge him to migrate en masse to other sections of the country. By grasping his great opportunity in the South he can make a lasting contribution to the moral strength of the nation and set a sublime example of courage for generations yet unborn.

By nonviolent resistance, the Negro can also enlist all men of good will in his struggle for equality. The problem is not a purely racial one, with Negroes set against whites. In the end, it is not a struggle between people at all, but a tension between justice and injustice. Nonviolent resistance is not aimed against oppressors but against oppression. Under its banner consciences, not racial groups, are enlisted.

If the Negro is to achieve the goal of integration, he must organize himself into a militant and nonviolent mass movement. All three elements are indispensable. The movement for equality and justice can only be a success if it has both a mass and militant character; the barriers to be overcome require both. Nonviolence is an imperative in order to bring about ultimate community.

A mass movement of militant quality that is not at the same time committed to nonviolence tends to generate conflict, which in turn breeds anarchy. The support of the participants and the sympathy of the uncommitted are both inhibited by the threat that bloodshed will engulf the community. This reaction in turn encourages the opposition to threaten and resort to force. When, however, the mass movement repudiates violence while moving resolutely toward its goal, its opponents are revealed as the instigators and practitioners of violence if it occurs. Then public support is magnetically attracted to the advocates of nonviolence, while those who employ violence are literally disarmed by overwhelming sentiment against their stand.

COMPLETENESS OF CLASSIFICATION

In the following paragraph, Joseph Addison divides physical labor into two kinds; he makes a dichotomous (two-part) classification. All labor is either of one kind or the other.

> Bodily labor is of two kinds, either that which a man submits to for his livelihood, or that which he undergoes for his pleasure. The latter of them generally changes the name of labor for that of exercise, but differs only from ordinary labor as it rises from another motive.
>
> A country life abounds in both these kinds of labor, and for that reason gives a man a greater stock of health, and consequently a more perfect enjoyment of himself, than any other way of life. ("Recreation")

A dichotomous classification is necessarily complete because it divides everything into either A or B (X or not X). However, completeness is more difficult to achieve in a complex classification such as a scientific classification or the Dewey decimal system for classifying books in a library.

A scientific classification—like a simple analysis—must be complete, that is, each separate item must fall into its designated group with no loose ends. Thus a zoologist finds a place in his classification for *all* forms of animal life; a botanist does the same for plant life. Similarly, under the Dewey decimal system a library assigns every one of its holdings a general "number" heading: 900 if it is a history book, 700 if it deals with the arts, and so on. These numbers are then broken down further: 930 for ancient history; 940 for medieval and modern European history; and so on. A good classification embodies the dictum "a place for everything and everything in its place." Thus in the Dewey system, small items that are too specialized to have individual headings are grouped into categories such as General Works, Miscellaneous, and Literature of Other Languages. (The "other" includes all languages that have not been specifically named, so that no language spoken or written anywhere is overlooked; each has a theoretical "place" into which it "fits" within the library's classification system.)

In using classification for rhetorical purposes—as the formal basis of an essay—writers have more latitude than the scientists permit. Even so, note that in the following nonscientific classification of "Three Kinds of Discipline," the author covers the subject without any cross-ranking. A whole paragraph is devoted to "places where all three disciplines overlap."

THREE KINDS OF DISCIPLINE

John Holt

A child, in growing up, may meet and learn from three different kinds of disciplines. The first and most important is what we might call the Discipline of Nature or of Reality. When he is trying to do something real, if he does the wrong thing or doesn't do the right one, he doesn't get the result he wants. If he doesn't pile one block right on top of another, or tries to build on a slanting surface, his tower falls down. If he hits the wrong key, he hears the wrong note. If he doesn't hit the nail squarely on the head, it bends, and he has to pull it out and start with another. If he doesn't measure properly what he is trying to build, it won't open, close, fit, stand up, fly, float, whistle, or do whatever he wants it to do. If he closes his eyes when he swings, he doesn't hit the ball. A child meets this kind of discipline every time he tries to *do* something, which is why it is so important in school to give children more chances to do things, instead of just reading or listening to someone talk (or pretending to). This discipline is a great teacher. The learner never has to wait long for his answer; it usually comes quickly, often instantly. Also it is clear, and very often points toward the needed correction; from what happened he can not only see that what he did was wrong, but also why, and what he needs to do instead. Finally, and most important, the giver of the answer, call it Nature, is impersonal, impartial, and indifferent. She does not give opinions, or make judgments; she cannot be wheedled, bullied, or fooled; she does not get angry or disappointed; she does not praise or blame; she does not remember past failures or hold grudges; with her one always gets a fresh start, this time is the one that counts.

The next discipline we might call the Discipline of Culture, of Society, of What People Really Do. Man is a social, a cultural animal. Children sense around them this culture, this network of agreements, customs, habits, and rules binding the adults together. They want to understand it and be a part of it. They watch very carefully what people around them are doing and want to do the same. They want to do right, unless they become convinced they can't do right. Thus children rarely misbehave seriously in church, but sit as quietly as they can. The example of all those grownups is contagious. Some mysterious ritual is going on, and children, who like rituals, want to be part of it. In the same way, the little children that I see at concerts or operas, though they may fidget a little, or perhaps take a nap now and then, rarely make any disturbance. With all those grownups sitting there, neither moving nor talking, it is the most natural thing in the world to imitate them. Children who live among adults who are habitually courteous to each other, and to them, will soon learn to be courteous. Children who live surrounded by people who speak a certain way will speak that way, however much we may try to tell them that speaking that way is bad or wrong.

The third discipline is the one most people mean when they speak of discipline—the Discipline of Superior Force, of sergeant to private, of "you do what I tell you or I'll make you wish you had." There is bound to be some of this in a child's life. Living as we do surrounded by things that can hurt children, or that children can hurt, we cannot avoid it. We can't afford to let a small child find out from experience the danger of playing in a busy street, or of fooling with the pots on the top of a stove, or of eating up the pills in the medicine cabinet. So, along with other precautions, we say to him, "Don't play in the street, or touch things on the stove, or go into the medicine cabinet, or I'll punish you." Between him and the danger too great for him to imagine we put a lesser danger, but one he can imagine and maybe therefore want to avoid. He can have no idea of what it would be like to be hit by a car, but he can imagine being shouted at, or spanked, or sent to his room. He avoids these substitutes for the greater danger until he can understand it and avoid it for its own sake. But we ought to use this discipline only when it is necessary to protect the life, health, safety, or well-being of people or other living creatures, or to prevent destruction of things that people care about. We ought not to assume too long, as we usually do, that a child cannot understand the real nature of the danger from which we want to protect him. The sooner he avoids the danger, not to escape our punishment, but as a matter of good sense, the better. He can learn that faster than we think. In Mexico, for example, where people drive their cars with a good deal of spirit, I saw many children no older than five or four walking unattended on the streets. They understood about cars, they knew what to do. A child whose life is full of the threat and fear of punishment is locked into babyhood. There is no way for him to grow up, to learn to take responsibility for his life and acts. Most important of all, we should not assume that having to yield to the threat of our superior force is good for the child's character. It is never good for *anyone's* character. To bow to superior force makes us feel impotent and cowardly for not having had the strength or courage to resist. Worse, it makes us resentful and vengeful. We can hardly wait to make someone pay for our humiliation, yield to us as we were once made to yield. No, if we cannot always avoid using the Discipline of Superior Force, we should at least use it as seldom as we can.

There are places where all three disciplines overlap. Any very demanding human activity combines in it the disciplines of Superior Force, of Culture, and of Nature. The novice will be told, "Do it this way, never mind asking why, just do it that way, that is the way we always do it." But it probably *is* just the way they always do it, and usually for the very good reason that it is a way that has been found to work. Think, for example, of ballet training. The student in a class is told to do this exercise, or that; to stand so; to do this or that with his head, arms, shoulders, abdomen, hips, legs, feet. He is constantly corrected. There is no argument. But behind these seemingly autocratic demands by the teacher lie many decades of custom and tradition, and behind that, the necessities of dancing itself. You cannot make the moves of classical ballet unless over many years you have acquired, and renewed every day, the needed strength and suppleness in scores of muscles and joints. Nor can you do the difficult motions, making them look easy, unless you have learned hundreds of easier ones first. Dance teachers may not always agree on all the details of teaching these strengths and skills. But no novice could learn them all by himself. You could not go for a night or two to watch the ballet and then, without any other knowledge at all, teach yourself how to do it. In the same way, you would be unlikely to learn any complicated and difficult human activity without drawing heavily on the experience of those who know it better. But the point is that the authority of these experts or teachers stems from, grows out of their greater competence and experience, the fact that what they do *works,* not the fact that they happen to be the teacher and as such have the power to kick a student out of the class. And the further point is that children are always and everywhere attracted to that competence, and ready and eager to submit themselves to a discipline that grows out of it. We hear constantly that children will never do anything unless compelled to by bribes or threats. But in their private lives, or in extracurricular activities in school, in sports, music, drama, art, running a newspaper, and so on, they often submit themselves willingly and wholeheartedly to very intense disciplines, simply because they want to learn to do a given thing well. Our Little-Napoleon football coaches, of whom we have too many and hear far too much, blind us to the fact that millions of children work hard every year getting better at sports and games without coaches barking and yelling at them.

DISCUSSION AND EXERCISES

1. Evaluate King's classification of the types of resistance to oppression: Is it logically sound? Is the argument in favor of the third kind of resistance convincing? Use prewriting techniques to prepare to write a paragraph of your own in which you agree or disagree with King's position.

2. Write a paragraph (150-250 words), opening with the topic sentence "I can see three different types of students in this room." Instead of devoting a paragraph to each type (as in the full-length Holt essay), devote only two sentences—the first naming the type, the second adding specific details or examples of the type. In Francis Christensen's terms, this will be a three-level, coordinate sequence paragraph—one that moves from general to specific:

   > 1 Topic Sentence (general)
   >> 2 First type (specific)
   >>> 3 Details or examples (more specific)
   >> 2 Second type (specific)
   >>> 3 Details or examples (more specific)
   >> 2 Third type (specific)
   >>> 3 Details or examples (more specific)

3. Consider Holt's classification of discipline into three kinds.
   a. What is the purpose of this classification?
   b. Is it complete? Explain.
   c. Is there any cross-ranking? Any overlapping? Discuss the writer's explanation of overlapping: Is it vital?
   d. Examine paragraph divisions. Locate topic sentences. Describe paragraph sequences by numbering them according to Christensen's levels of generality.
   e. Consider the restored definition of discipline (pages 324–325). How does that definition fit into Holt's classification?
   f. Write a paragraph in which you classify discipline into two kinds, using as the basis for your classification that kind of discipline which you think is good and that which you consider bad.

ESSAY SUGGESTIONS

1. In an essay (500-750 words) classify people you know or know of into Jung's extravert and introvert types. You may wish to add a third category, the ambivert (one who balances or oscillates between extraversion and introversion). Use the prewriting techniques you have learned.

2. Write an essay (500-750 words) in which you warn against oversimplification by describing the many types of one of the following (as you have observed or experienced it):

intelligence	love	loyalty
freedom	beauty	charity
truth	goodness	courage
happiness		

3. In an essay (750-1,000 words) indicate the "common types" of any one of the following:
   a. Psychology/Sociology

dreams	class conflict	fads
memories	talent or aptitude	pressure groups
mental disturbances	ambition	communities
propaganda	success	status seekers
conformity	prejudice	

   b. Anthropology (customs in a given group)

marriage	courtship	hospitality
mourning	suicide	taboos
burials	drinking	

   c. Travel

   airplane
   road
   motor vehicle

   d. Law

law courts	prisons	evidence
law specialities	crime prevention	misdemeanors
crimes	assaults	

   e. Zoology

whales	reptiles
goats	monkeys
elephants	snakes

f. Botany

> plants   trees
> vegetables   shrubs

4. An Aaron Copland essay opens with the following sentence: "I can see three different types of composers in musical history, each of whom conceives music in a somewhat different fashion." Substitute for "composers in musical history" one of the following and write an essay (750-1,000 words). You may have to vary the number of types. Use the prewriting techniques you have learned before you begin to write.

> painters   novelists   students
> dancers   architects   teachers
> poets   photographers   doctors
> playwrights   artists   engineers

DISCUSSION AND EXERCISES

1. Read the following poem, which explores the consequences of postponing the fulfillment of a dream.

Dream Deferred

Langston Hughes

> What happens to a dream deferred?
>
> > Does it dry up
> > like a raisin in the sun?
> >
> > Or fester like a sore—
> > And then run?
> >
> > Does it stink like rotten meat?
> > Or crust and sugar over—
> > like a syrupy sweet?
> >
> > Maybe it just sags
> > like a heavy load.
> >
> > *Or does it explode?*

a. List the various similes used by Hughes and indicate in what ways they are effective.
b. Why, do you suppose, are all but one of the possible consequences framed as questions?
c. What is gained by italicizing the last line?
d. Does the poet provide an answer to his original question?

Continued

2. Write a paragraph (150-250 words) in which you contemplate the possible consequences of repressing any strong feeling or desire; base your speculations on your own experience or that of someone you know; shape your topic sentence in the form of a question, use the prewriting techniques you have learned, and develop the paragraph in terms of specific possibilities.

3. The young woman in the photograph below has just been crowned a beauty queen. Where does she go from here? Write a paragraph (150-200 words) in which you describe the consequences of winning the contest.

4. Consider Benjamin Compaine's "Computers and the New Literacy."
   a. To whom will the Computer Age belong? Why?
   b. Some people consider the computer a possible corrupting influence for school children. What presently respectable practices were considered similarly "corrupting" in the past? Do you feel that computers can corrupt? Why or why not?
   c. How has computer use grown over the past ten years?

d. What part do computers play in your life, if any?

e. Do you foresee that the computer will replace present literary skills such as reading and writing, or will it improve them? Explain.

5. Answer the following questions based on the essay "My Wood."

a. What is the purpose of this essay?

b. To whom is it addressed?

c. What is the tone?

d. What is the writer's relationship to the subject matter?

e. How does he want his reader to relate to the subject matter? Is he successful?

f. Comment on the following quotations. In what ways do they develop and illuminate the central meaning and purpose of the essay?

1. "It is not a large wood . . . and it is intersected, blast it, by a public footpath."

2. "It was a man of weight who failed to get into the Kingdom of Heaven."

3. "I could not afford to buy Mrs. Henessy out."

4. "Sometimes I think I will cut down such trees as remain in the wood, at other times I want to fill up the gaps between them with new trees."

5. "Possession is one with loss."

6. "I shall wall in and fence out until I really taste the sweets of property."

6. Answer the following questions about Mike Davis's "A Generation under Curfew."

a. What details does Davis select to support his view of the situation in Los Angeles? Which details are most memorable?

b. What, in Davis's opinion, are the most dramatic consequences of the last few years?

c. Find the place in the essay where Davis shifts his attention to the future. What transitional devices does he use to signal this shift?

d. What do the final two quotations add to the essay? Why do you think Davis chose to end this section of the book in this way?

ESSAY SUGGESTIONS

1. Write an essay (750-1,000 words) indicating what you think were, are, or will be the major effects or consequences of any one of the following (on the individual, the family, or society at large). (Be sure to use prewriting techniques before you actually begin to write.)

a. Inventions

the automobile	the airplane
the telephone	the electric light
the television	the microchip

Continued

b. Social changes

space travel	increased mixed marriages
human organ transplants	increased urbanization
fight against pollution	increased automation
increased drug usage	increased income tax
increased divorce rate	increased leisure
homelessness	the new morality
unemployment	

2. In an essay (750-1,000 words) describe the effect on your mind or sensibilities of one of the following:

the moon	current fashions
the sun	nightmares
hot weather	fatigue
cold weather	religion
noise	advertising
silence	exercise
prejudice	

3. Considering Compaine's article on "Computers and the New Literacy," write an essay (500-750 words) predicting how a college student's education will have changed in five or ten years as a consequence of the Computer Age.

4. Write an essay (500-750 words) describing the effect on you of some possession you have acquired (such as a word processor) or the consequences of some action ("breaking up"). Like Forster, you might try to suggest not only the personal but wider social consequences as well. You might also try to adopt Forster's organization.

5. Over 200,000 listened as Dr. Martin Luther King, Jr., spoke passionately and eloquently in the shadow of the Lincoln Memorial. The event was the March on Washington for Jobs and Freedom on August 28, 1963. He spoke of a dream that he had—one that would bring the nation's people together. "I have a dream that one day this nation will rise up and live out the true meaning of its creed: 'We hold these truths to be self-evident, that all men are created equal.' " Write an essay (750-1000 words) discussing the consequences of this memorable event, depicted on page 332.

6. Consider the photograph accompanying "A Generation under Curfew." Speculate on the future of the arrested persons. Write a short narrative (500 words) explaining the probable consequences of this arrest.

Question

15

HOW DOES X COMPARE TO Y?

PRINCIPLES OF COMPARISON

ORGANIZING A COMPARISON
    GRANT AND LEE: A STUDY IN CONTRASTS,
        BRUCE CATTON
    THEIR AMAZING GRACE, JERRY ADLER
    COMPARISON OF PARTS
        THAT LEAN AND HUNGRY
          LOOK, SUZANNE JORDAN
    SIMILARITIES AND DIFFERENCES
        THE GUMBO BATTLE, PETER FEIBLEMAN
    COMPARING POEMS
        DEATH BE NOT PROUD, JOHN DONNE
        DO NOT GO GENTLE INTO THAT
          GOOD NIGHT, DYLAN THOMAS
        TIMOR MORTIS CONTURBAT ME,
          R. L. CHAPMAN
        HERE, PAUL MONETTE

PRINCIPLES OF COMPARISON

Take any two people, objects, events, ideas, books, disciplines, countries, continents, planets; take any two periods of time, works of art, artists; take two of *anything* (provided there is a logical basis of comparison), and ask these questions: How does one compare with the other? How are they similar? How are they different? With these questions you "invent" a study in comparative analysis.

Before making a comparison, you should be aware of the way this word is often used. Strictly speaking, the word "comparison" refers to the act or process of examining *similarities,* while the word "contrast" refers to the examination of *dissimilarities* or differences. Traditional rhetoricians usually call the study you are about to undertake "comparison and contrast," but in popular usage the term *comparison* generally covers both activities and means "setting things side by side to show how they are alike or different," while the word *contrast* retains its sense of emphasizing differences. Also strictly speaking, a comparison may involve more than two subjects: you could theoretically set X alongside not only Y but also S, T, U, and V; or you could compare X with Y in the light of Z, and so on. We will concentrate on popular usage, since most of what should be said about comparison and contrast fits under this heading.

Read the following example, a short comparison of two presidents that shows how they were alike:

> Kennedy has been compared to Franklin Delano Roosevelt and he liked to pose in front of an F.D.R. portrait. In fact, some of his qualities more nearly recall Theodore Roosevelt, the apostle of the big stick, the strenuous life and the bully pulpit. Like T.R., for instance, Kennedy had a perhaps undue regard for Harvard and a craving for its approval. The only election he ever lost was one of the ones he wanted most to win—his first try for a seat on the Harvard Board of Overseers. He grimly ran again and his election to the Board was a cherished triumph. Like T.R., too, Kennedy fancied himself in the role of national taste maker—Roosevelt picked up Edwin Arlington Robinson and Kennedy adopted Robert Frost. Roosevelt let his rather rigid literary ideas get about and the Kennedys thought they ought to provide White House examples— Casals, Shakespeare and opera in the East Room—for the cultural uplift of the nation. . . .
>
> —Tom Wicker, *Kennedy*

Note that in this paragraph the two men are compared not merely *in general* but on the basis of *two specific qualities.* This is the basis of all good comparison. You should not simply say X is like Y; instead you should say X is like Y on the basis of the following specific points: 1, 2, 3, and so on—which is to say, in this case:

Kennedy was like Theodore Roosevelt in that both

1. regarded Harvard highly.
2. regarded themselves as taste makers.

Now note another comparison, this one showing—through an analogy—how two presidents were *different:*

> Lyndon Johnson's father once told him that he did not belong in politics unless he could walk into a roomful of men and tell immediately who was for him and who was against him. In fact, even the shrewd LBJ has not quite such occult power, but his liking for the story tells us something useful about him: he sets much store by instinct. No wonder, then, that it would be to his instincts—honed in the Texas hill country, sharpened in a life of politics, confirmed in his successful Congressional career—that he would often turn in the White House.
>
> This reliance on instinct enabled Johnson to put on the Presidency like a suit of comfortable old clothes. John Kennedy, on the other hand, came to it with a historical, nearly theoretical view of what was required of a strong President; he knew exactly what Woodrow Wilson had said about the office and he had read Corwin and Neustadt and he was unabashedly willing to quote Lincoln: "I see the storm coming and I know His hand is in it. If He has a place and work for me, I believe that I am ready."
>
> And Kennedy would add: "Today I say to you that if the people of this nation select me to be their President, I believe that I am ready." With eager confidence, Kennedy acquired a Presidential suit off the rack and put on a little weight to make himself fit it.
>
> —Wicker, *JFK and LBJ*

As a form of analysis, comparison is not merely a rhetorical technique; it is a natural, instinctive process that goes on constantly in everyone's mind. We think and learn by comparing the unfamiliar with the familiar; we come to terms with a new situation by comparing it with an old one; we get our bearings by comparing the past with the present. Whether we are more impressed by the similarities between two situations or the differences depends of course on the situations themselves. The ability to see through the differences to the underlying similarities—or through the similarities to underlying differences—is the mark not only of critical intelligence but of the creative mind at work. Psychologist William James wrote, "Some people are far more sensitive to resemblances and far more ready to point out wherein they consist, than others are. They are the wits, the poets, the inventors, the scientific men, the practical geniuses." Speaking specifically of Newton and Darwin, James said, "The flash of similarity between an apple and the moon, between the rivalry for food in nature and the rivalry for man's selection, was too recondite to have occurred to any but exceptional minds."

But even the unexceptional mind naturally makes comparisons: Comparative situations are common in everyday life (before and after, then and now, loss and gain, here and there, promise and fulfillment). Because nothing indicates more clearly how well a person has grasped a subject than the ability to detect similarities and differences among its parts (hence the popularity of How does X compare to Y? as an essay-type examination question), you should make an extra effort to master this form of discourse. It is not a difficult form if you approach it systematically; more than that, you can rely on it to produce interesting and engaging essays.

ORGANIZING A COMPARISON

There are several forms into which comparative analyses may conveniently be organized. There are also many variations within each form, for the forms are flexible, giving you ample freedom to shape your essay as you wish. What is important is that the essay always have a shape—a definite plan or pattern of development—so that it does not shift haphazardly back and forth: from X to Y; back to part of X; then more about Y; back to another part of X; and so on. Whatever shifting takes place must follow an orderly procedure.

Historian Bruce Catton below compares the Civil War's two military leaders, Ulysses S. Grant and Robert E. Lee. These two men, Catton tells us, represented "two conflicting currents" in the nation, currents that came together ultimately in a "final collision." Catton characterizes first Lee, then Grant, setting the two men side by side, so that the reader may judge them as though they were portraits hanging next to one another on the wall. The "wholes" can be outlined as follows:

   I. Robert E. Lee
     A. Background
     B. Personality
     C. Underlying aspiration
  II. Ulysses S. Grant
     A. Background
     B. Personality
     C. Underlying aspiration

In the final section of the essay, Catton shifts both his thesis and his principle of organization to show that underneath their striking differences, the two soldiers had "much in common." The author links this final section so well to the rest of the essay ("Yet it was not all contrast, after all") that the shift to likenesses, to reconciliation of apparent opposites, serves to deepen rather than dilute the study in contrast. We recognize that life is like that: Under two "conflicting currents" may run a common current.

GRANT AND LEE: A STUDY IN CONTRASTS

Bruce Catton

Introduction   When Ulysses S. Grant and Robert E. Lee met in the parlor of a modest house at Appomattox Court House, Virginia, on April 9, 1865, to work out the terms for the surrender of Lee's Army of Northern Virginia, a great chapter in American life came to a close, and a great new chapter began.

          These men were bringing the Civil War to its virtual finish. To be sure, other armies had yet to surrender, and for a few days the fugitive Confederate government would struggle desperately and vainly, trying to find some way to go on living now that its chief support was gone. But in effect it was all over when Grant and Lee signed the papers. And the little room where they wrote out the terms was the scene of one of the poignant, dramatic contrasts in American history.

Thesis: The two men were "oddly different."

They were two strong men, these oddly different generals, and they represented the strengths of two conflicting currents that, through them, had come into final collision.

Back of Robert E. Lee was the notion that the old aristocratic concept might somehow survive and be dominant in American life.

Lee

Lee was tidewater Virginia, and in his background were family, culture, and tradition . . . the age of chivalry transplanted to a New World which was making its own legends and its own myths. He embodied a way of life that had come down through the age of knighthood and the English country squire. America was a land that was beginning all over again, dedicated to nothing much more complicated than the rather hazy belief that all men had equal rights and should have an equal chance in the world. In such a land Lee stood for the feeling that it was somehow of advantage to human society to have a pronounced inequality in the social structure. There should be a leisure class, backed by ownership of land; in turn, society itself should be keyed to the land as the chief source of wealth and influence. It would bring forth (according to this ideal) a class of men with a strong sense of obligation to the community; men who lived not to gain advantage for themselves, but to meet the solemn obligations which had been laid on them by the very fact that they were privileged. From them the country would get its leadership; to them it could look for the higher values—of thought, of conduct, of personal deportment—to give it strength and virtue.

Lee embodied the noblest elements of this aristocratic ideal. Through him, the landed nobility justified itself. For four years, the Southern states had fought a desperate war to uphold the ideals for which Lee stood. In the end, it almost seemed as if the Confederacy fought for Lee; as if he himself was the Confederacy . . . the best thing that the way of life for which the Confederacy stood could ever have to offer. He had passed into legend before Appomattox. Thousands of tired, underfed, poorly clothed Confederate soldiers, long past the simple enthusiasm of the early days of the struggle, somehow considered Lee the symbol of everything for which they had been willing to die. But they could not quite put this feeling into words. If the Lost Cause, sanctified by so much heroism and so many deaths, had a living justification, its justification was General Lee.

Grant

Grant, the son of a tanner on the Western frontier, was everything Lee was not. He had come up the hard way and embodied nothing in particular except the eternal toughness and sinewy fiber of the men who grew up beyond the mountains. He was one of a body of men who owed reverence and obeisance to no one, who were self-reliant to a fault, who cared hardly anything for the past but who had a sharp eye for the future.

These frontier men were the precise opposites of the tidewater aristocrats. Back of them, in the great surge that had taken people over the Alleghenies and into the opening Western country, there was a deep, implicit dissatisfaction with a past that had settled into grooves. They stood for democracy, not from any reasoned conclusion about the proper ordering of human society, but simply because they had grown up in the middle of democracy and knew how it worked. Their society might have privileges, but they would be privileges each man had won for himself. Forms and patterns mean nothing. No man was born to anything, except perhaps to a chance to show how far he could rise. Life was competition.

Yet along with this feeling had come a deep sense of belonging to a national community. The Westerner who developed a farm, opened a shop, or set up in business as a trader, could hope to prosper only as his own community prospered—and his community ran from the Atlantic to the Pacific and from Canada down to Mexico. If the land was settled, with towns and highways and accessible markets, he could better himself. He saw his fate in terms of the nation's own destiny. As its horizons expanded, so did his. He had, in other words, an acute dollars-and-cents stake in the continued growth and development of his country.

Comment on the "most striking" contrast

And that, perhaps, is where the contrast between Grant and Lee becomes most striking. The Virginia aristocrat, inevitably, saw himself in relation to his own region. He lived in a static society which could endure almost anything except change. Instinctively, his first loyalty would go to the locality in which that society existed. He would fight to the limit of endurance to defend it, because in defending it he was defending everything that gave his own life its deepest meaning.

The Westerner, on the other hand, would fight with an equal tenacity for the broader concept of society. He fought so because everything he lived by was tied to growth, expansion, and a constantly widening horizon. What he lived by would survive or fall with the nation itself. He could not possibly stand by unmoved in the face of an attempt to destroy the Union. He would combat it with everything he had, because he could only see it as an effort to cut the ground out from under his feet.

So Grant and Lee were in complete contrast, representing two diametrically opposed elements in American life. Grant was the modern man emerging; beyond him, ready to come on the stage, was the great age of steel and machinery, of crowded cities and a restless, burgeoning vitality. Lee might have ridden down from the old age of chivalry, lance in hand, silken banner fluttering over his head. Each man was the perfect champion of his cause, drawing both his strengths and his weaknesses from the people he led.

Underlying similarities

Yet it was not all contrast, after all. Different as they were—in background, in personality, in underlying aspiration—these two great soldiers had much in common. Under everything else, they were marvelous fighters. Furthermore, their fighting qualities were really very much alike.

Each man had, to begin with, the great virtue of utter tenacity and fidelity. Grant fought his way down the Mississippi Valley in spite of acute personal discouragement and profound military handicaps. Lee hung on in the trenches at Petersburg after hope itself had died. In each man there was an indomitable quality . . . the born fighter's refusal to give up as long as he can still remain on his feet and lift his two fists.

Daring and resourcefulness they had, too; the ability to think faster and move faster than the enemy. These were the qualities which gave Lee the dazzling campaigns of Second Manassas and Chancellorsville and won Vicksburg for Grant.

Lastly, and perhaps greatest of all, there was the ability, at the end, to turn quickly from war to peace once the fighting was over. Out of the way these two men behaved at Appomattox came the possibility of a peace of reconciliation. It was a possibility not wholly realized, in the years to come, but which did, in the end, help the two sections to become one nation again . . . after a war whose bitterness might have seemed to make such a reunion wholly impossible. No part of either man's life became him more than the part he played in their brief meeting in the McLean house at Appomattox. Their behavior there put all succeeding generations of Americans in their debt. Two great Americans, Grant and Lee—very different, yet under everything very much alike. Their encounter at Appomattox was one of the great moments of American history.

Reporter Jerry Adler uses a similar approach in discussing the lives of Justice Thurgood Marshall and gospel musician Thomas Dorsey, two men who died in the same week. They lived very different lives, as Adler points out; he quite rightly uses contrast as the major method of development. Yet his larger point is the similarities they shared as black men born in the early twentieth century.

Adler's approach suggests a truth about comparing and contrasting as cognitive skills and expository modes. Each makes the most sense when there is an element of the other present. The differences between Grant and Lee are remarkable because they were both leading Civil War generals. An essay pointing out the differences between Robert E. Lee and Angela Lansbury, for example, would probably be an exercise in futility for both writer and reader; so would a paper that demonstrated the similarities between two Ford Mustangs or two bowls of homemade chicken soup. The task of the writer who seeks to compare two people, two objects, or two ideas is to discover unexpected similarities and surprising differences. Notice how Adler moves through the contrasting circumstances in the lives of Marshall and Dorsey to identify the common experiences that transcend their careers in law and music.

THEIR AMAZING GRACE

Jerry Adler

It is vouchsafed to each of us, the gift of transcendence, if we but know how to use it. Justice Thurgood Marshall, who died last week at 84, surely did; seldom has the language been put to higher use than when Marshall appeared before the Supreme Court and by force of argument overcame the legal subjugation of 16 million of his—our!—fellow Americans. And Thomas Dorsey, born nine years earlier and buried on the same day . . . well, he was a transcendent figure, too. From 30,000 churches across the land every Sunday, voices are raised in the music he put there, the words of salvation improbably joined to the rhythms of blues and stride piano to create the sound he called gospel. When Marshall opened the door to the promised land to his brothers and sisters, they were ready for it; they'd been singing about it in church for a generation already.

Their funerals were separated by the distance between Washington National Cathedral, in whose hushed vastness the very president must sit in silent contemplation of a power greater than his own, and Pilgrim Baptist Church in Chicago, where the humblest cabdriver may make the earth tremble with the volume of his faith. Marshall marched into history under the banner of Amos 5:24—"Let judgment run down like waters . . ."—which his eulogists almost unanimously selected as the appropriate verse to commemorate his time on earth; 10 hours later Dorsey was blasted heavenward by the T. A. Dorsey Gospel Chorus belting out "I'll Tell It Wherever I Go." History does not record whether the two men ever met, although it's certainly possible; Dorsey actively supported the

NAACP during the years Marshall was counsel to the organization's Legal Defense Fund. But as they made their separate ways through this world of pain, their lives surely touched one another's many times—at the funeral of Martin Luther King Jr., for one, where Marshall would have heard King's favorite hymn, "Precious Lord, Take My Hand," written by Dorsey 36 years earlier out of grief for the death in childbirth of his young wife.

What they shared, mostly, was membership in that extraordinary generation born around the turn of the century, a dismal time when Jim Crow laws, abetted by a singularly obtuse Supreme Court, were spreading across a third of the nation. They could look back, in other words, to their parents' generation, when the brief hope of Reconstruction glimmered, and ahead to a century whose burgeoning promise meant for them only more places (buses, movie houses . . .) to sit in the back. It was a fantastic leap of imagination in those years to envision a better life for the people politely called Negroes, and an act of cold courage to take concrete steps to bring it about. Yet from this generation came Kenneth Clark (born in 1914), the brilliant psychologist whose research helped Marshall prove his case against segregated schools; the novelists Zora Neal Hurston (1903) and Richard Wright (1908); Louis Armstrong (1900), Count Basie (1904) and Duke Ellington (1899). "They knew who they were," says John Hope Franklin, the black historian who was born in 1915, of Marshall and his contemporaries. "They had no insecurity, which made it possible to look beyond America's sick society."

Marshall was born in Baltimore in 1908. His family was, for that time and place, on the verge of aristocracy; his mother was a schoolteacher and his father a Pullman porter and later head steward at a wealthy country club on the shores of Chesapeake Bay. He attended Lincoln University, a small all-black school in

Pennsylvania, and graduated first in his class from the law school at Howard University in 1933. But in the eyes of the law, from Maryland south, that made him exactly equal to a black sharecropper, which is to say, nothing compared with a white who hadn't finished grade school. *Plessy v. Ferguson,* the seminal case authorizing separate-but-equal public accommodations for blacks and whites, had been decided in 1896; in the year of Marshall's birth the Supreme Court ruled in *Berea v. Kentucky* that a state could outlaw even voluntary integration at a private college. Decades later, that was one of the precedents Marshall fought as he constructed the chain of cases leading to the monumental triumph of *Brown v. Board of Education* in 1954.

It was on those cases—32 appearances before the Supreme Court, of which he won 29—that history judges Marshall as one of the greatest Americans of this century. He went on to other achievements, as federal judge, U.S. solicitor general, and in 1967 the first African-American to sit on the Supreme Court, where he was a leading spokesman for civil liberties (including the right to abortion) and against the death penalty. And the civil-rights movement went on to other battles, with other tactics. But as Eleanor Holmes Norton, the congressional delegate for the District of Columbia, says, "A lot of folks don't appreciate that Thurgood Marshall and his band of lawyers were the only civil-rights movement there was until the late 1950s."

It was vital to overturn segregation, but almost as significant that the victory go to a black man, so that no one could ever assert that equality was a gift extended to blacks by whites. And Marshall used the forms and institutions that were the traditional tools of his oppressors; his triumphs were of cold legal logic, which is why they have stood up so well. To establish the absurdity of separate-but-equal

education, he began with the seemingly minor question of law schools. A judge, he once explained, might believe that a segregated elementary school could be as good as an integrated one, but he would undoubtedly esteem legal education too highly to accept any such nonsense about law school. And his arguments were flawlessly understated (although he was a witty, sometimes ribald, storyteller in private); no one could ever suggest that Marshall had swayed the court by playing on its sympathies. He coined no great legal phrases, except one that is distinguished only for its utter simplicity: asked by Justice Felix Frankfurter to define "equal," Marshall replied: "Equal means getting the same thing, at the same time, and in the same place"—and when he put it that way, who could any longer deny it?

On the surface, Dorsey, the son of a Georgia preacher, lived a very different sort of life. Unlike Marshall, he rarely had much contact with white society, and devoted himself to a different and incomparably harder fight, the struggle for his own soul. By his own account it might have gone either way. In his youth Dorsey was "Georgia Tom," a well-known blues musician who played piano for Ma Rainey, and a composer of "hokum," blues numbers filled with ribald double-entendre. Around 1926, moved by the death of a friend, he essentially invented gospel with the song "If You See My Savior, Tell Him That You Saw Me." "I was doing all right for myself," he once recalled, "but the voice of God whispered and said you need to change." Evidently God didn't express a preference for any particular kind of music. "His promise to God was, 'I'll change the words'," says Michael W. Harris, Dorsey's biographer. "Blues was the only music he knew."

But if God didn't mind praise that happened to come in a 16-bar blues, Dorsey's fellow parishioners in Chicago, where he came to live in 1916, were less tolerant. Blacks who had escaped the rural South had no desire to be reminded of their roots. By the time of World War I most big-city black churches, says Harris, "were basically white churches with black members," complete with a classical orchestra devoted to playing the most somnolently decorous hymns in the canon. When Dorsey appeared, "people would say, 'You can't bring that music in here. That's what we danced to last night.' And he would turn around and say, 'It's *our* music'." In effect, Dorsey helped preserve a vital part of African-American culture that might otherwise have succumbed to assimilation; among his inheritors were a generation of soul singers from Aretha Franklin to Stevie Wonder and Ray Charles.

Out of deepest despair, comes transcendence: that was the message of Dorsey's life, as also, mutatis mutandis, of Marshall's. In 1932, a telegram about his wife's death summoned Dorsey home; by the time he arrived, his newborn son had died also. "Now, what should I do then and there?" he recalled decades later for the documentary film "Say Amen, Somebody." "People tried to tell me things that were soothing to me . . . but none of which have ever been soothing to me from that day to this." Yet of that experience came the transforming hymn "Precious Lord, Take My Hand":

> . . . *Lead me on, let me stand.*
> *I am tired. I am weak.*
> *I am worn. Through the storm,*
> *through the night, lead me*
> *on to the light.*

In a sense, time passed both men by eventually, as it must for anyone who lives into his ninth decade. Gospel music is no longer as central to African-American culture as it was in the early 1940s, when Mahalia Jackson and Dorsey toured together. Marshall ended his career as a lonely and sometimes bitter dissenter. And of course it was only a few years after *Brown* that the civil-rights movement moved from the courts to the legislatures and the streets, where other leaders came to prominence. Cultural fashions of recent years left him unmoved. "Marshall wasn't interested in collard greens and African history, he was interested in the rights of Americans," says essayist Albert Murray, 76. Sylvia Drew Ivie, who attended Howard's law school in the late 1960s, recalls Marshall coming to accept an award and being bearded by a militant student who called him an Uncle Tom. "It was one of the most humiliating moments I can remember," she says. "He was silent for a moment and then said, '*Boy,* I was litigating civil-rights lawsuits before you were born. Don't you ever use that name with me'."

Marshall, says his law-school classmate Oliver Hill, "never lost hope that things would get better." And he never lost sight of how much room there was for improvement. When asked in 1991 whether he felt "free at last," his response was tart: "Well I'm not free. All I know is that years ago . . . a Pullman porter told me that he had been in every city in this country . . . and he had never had to put his hand up in front of his face to find out he was a Negro. I agree with him." He is free at last now, even as Dorsey has gone on to be with his Lord; but we are still only half free, still struggling to be saved. From their lives let us take courage, as we reach . . . for transcendence.

Comparison of Parts

If your purpose is to show how parts of one subject "play off" against parts of the other, then you will structure your piece according to those specific parts, or points of interest. Had Catton wanted to organize his essay in terms of parts, he would have done so as follows:

    I. Background
       A. Lee
       B. Grant
    II. Personality
       A. Lee
       B. Grant
   III. Underlying aspiration
       A. Lee
       B. Grant

A comparison may involve many parts, one following another in rapid succession with intricate (though always orderly) weaving back and forth between X and Y, sometimes within a single sentence. We see this process at work in the following essay, which examines the comparative virtues of "fat" and "thin." Fat people are better, the author concludes, taking a highly provocative position by maintaining that "they're a hell of a lot *nicer* than the wizened and shriveled." Note how paragraphs alternate between how fat people and thin people relate to various *parts* of the total topic: "Thin people believe in logic," is the topic sentence of one paragraph, followed in the next paragraph with the topic sentence, "Fat people realize that life is illogical and unfair."

THAT LEAN AND HUNGRY LOOK

Suzanne Jordan

Caesar was right. Thin people need watching. I've been watching them for most of my adult life, and I don't like what I see. When these narrow fellows spring at me, I quiver to my toes. Thin people come in all personalities, most of them menacing. You've got your "together" thin person, your mechanical thin person, your condescending thin person, your tsk-tsk thin person, your efficiency-expert thin person. All of them are dangerous.

In the first place, thin people aren't fun. They don't know how to goof off, at least in the best, fat sense of the word. They've always got to be adoing. Give them a coffee break, and they'll jog around the block. Supply them with a quiet evening at home, and they'll fix the screen door and lick S&H green stamps. They say things like "there aren't enough hours in the day." Fat people never say that. Fat people think the day is too damn long already.

Thin people make me tired. They've got speedy little metabolisms that cause them to bustle briskly. They're forever rubbing their bony hands together and eying new problems to "tackle." I like to surround myself with sluggish, inert, easygoing fat people, the kind who believe that if you clean it up today, it'll just get dirty again tomorrow.

Some people say the business about the jolly fat person is a myth, that all of us chubbies are neurotic, sick, sad people. I disagree. Fat people may not be chortling all day long, but they're a hell of a lot *nicer* than the wizened and shriveled. Thin people turn surly, mean and hard at a young age because they never learn the value of a hot-fudge sundae for easing tension. Thin people don't like gooey soft things because they themselves are neither gooey nor soft. They are crunchy and dull, like carrots. They go straight to the heart of the matter while fat people let things stay all blurry and hazy and vague, the way things actually are. Thin people want to face the truth. Fat people know there is no truth. One of my thin friends is always staring at complex, unsolvable problems and saying, "The key thing is . . ." Fat people never say that. They know there isn't any such thing as the key thing about anything.

Thin people believe in logic. Fat people see all sides. The sides fat people see are rounded blobs, usually gray, always nebulous and truly not worth worrying about. But the thin person persists. "If you consume more calories than you burn," says one of my thin friends, "you will gain weight. It's that simple." Fat people always grin when they hear statements like that. They know better.

Fat people realize that life is illogical and unfair. They know very well that God is not in his heaven and all is not right with the world. If God was up there, fat people could have two doughnuts and a big orange drink anytime they wanted it.

Thin people have a long list of logical things they are always spouting off to me. They hold up one finger at a time as they reel off these things, so I won't lose track. They speak slowly as if to a young child. The list is long and full of holes. It contains tidbits like "get a grip on yourself," "cigarettes kill," "cholesterol clogs," "fit as a fiddle," "ducks in a row," "organize" and "sound fiscal management." Phrases like that.

They think these 2,000-point plans lead to happiness. Fat people know happiness is elusive at best and even if they could get the kind thin people talk about, they wouldn't want it. Wisely, fat people see that such programs are too dull, too hard, too off the mark. They are never better than a whole cheesecake.

Fat people know all about the mystery of life. They are the ones acquainted with the night, with luck, with fate, with playing it by ear. One thin person I know once suggested that we arrange all the parts of a jigsaw puzzle into groups according to size, shape and color. He figured this would cut the time needed to complete the puzzle by at least 50 per cent. I said I wouldn't do it. One, I like to muddle through. Two, what good would it do to finish early? Three, the jigsaw puzzle isn't the important thing. The important thing is the fun of four people (one thin person included) sitting around a card table, working a jigsaw puzzle. My thin friend had no use for my list. Instead of joining us, he went outside and mulched the boxwoods. The three remaining fat people finished the puzzle and made chocolate, double-fudged brownies to celebrate.

The main problem with thin people is they oppress. Their good intentions, bony torsos, tight ships, neat corners, cerebral machinations and pat solutions loom like dark clouds over the loose, comfortable, spread-out, soft world of the fat. Long after fat people have removed their coats and shoes and put their feet up on the coffee table, thin people are still sitting on the edge of the sofa, looking neat as a pin, discussing rutabagas. Fat people are heavily into fits of laughter, slapping their thighs and whooping it up, while thin people are still politely waiting for the punch line.

Thin people are downers. They like math and morality and reasoned evaluation of the limitations of human beings. They have their skinny little acts together. They expound, prognose, probe and prick.

Fat people are convivial. They will like you even if you're irregular and have acne. They will come up with a good reason why you never wrote the great American novel. They will cry in your beer with you. They will put your name in the pot. They will let you off the hook. Fat people will gab, giggle, guffaw, gallumph, gyrate and gossip. They are generous, giving and gallant. They are gluttonous and goodly and great. What you want when you're down is soft and jiggly, not muscled and stable. Fat people know this. Fat people have plenty of room. Fat people will take you in.

Similarities and Differences

Still a third organizational pattern, in some ways the most straightforward, involves a simple grouping of similarities and differences. Had Catton chosen this pattern, he would have followed the procedure outlined as follows:

    I. Differences between Lee and Grant
       A. Background

      1. Lee: tidewater Virginia
      2. Grant: Western frontier
   B. Personality
      1. Lee: an "English country squire" type
      2. Grant: a rugged individualist of the New World
   C. Underlying aspiration
      1. Lee: aristocratic
      2. Grant: democratic
II. Similarities between Lee and Grant
   A. Tenacity and fidelity to cause
      1. Lee
      2. Grant
   B. Daring and resourcefulness
      1. Lee
      2. Grant
   C. Ability to turn from war to peace
      1. Lee
      2. Grant

In most cases writers will present the position they want to stress in the later, more emphatic part of the essay. In the Catton piece, of course, contrast was the basic theme of the essay; similarities underlying the contrast provide a still deeper dimension of analysis and interpretation.

In the following reading, novelist Peter Feibleman incorporates his answers to the question *How does X compare to Y?* within a narrative that answers the question, *How did X happen?* He recalls a Sunday afternoon when he was a child in New Orleans and his friend Richard came over to share a bowl of gumbo. What is gumbo?, you may wonder. As Feibleman explains, there are different answers to that simple question.

THE GUMBO BATTLE

Peter Feibleman

The next day, Sunday, Richard returned to collect his portion of Saturday's loot—a bowl of gumbo. Good food is taken seriously even by children in New Orleans, and though fine dishes may be found at the nearest street corner, a good gumbo is still worth a trip from one end of town to the other, for gumbo is the classic Creole and Acadian dish—perhaps the greatest achievement of all South Louisiana kitchens. While the *roux* for the gumbo was being prepared, Richard and I played ball in the back yard. Suddenly from the kitchen the sound of an impending disaster brought us running in to witness a battle I still vividly remember.

It was a battle that grew out of an important, though often forgotten, rule of New Orleans cooking. The rule is simply this: there is no one way to do anything—or, to put it differently, there are at least 200 ways to do everything. A gumbo is a gumbo in much the way that a snowflake is a snowflake or a fingerprint a fingerprint. All gumbos look alike until you get close to them; then you find that no two are the same. South Louisiana cooking is inventive—it had to be, or it wouldn't have invented itself. New combinations of ingredients are always being tried by good Creole and Acadian cooks, and made to come out right by a sprig of this or a spoonful of that. Louisiana recipes, in fact, are only as good as the cooks who use them—and few Louisiana cooks ever consult anything in writing. They believe that you either know how to make a dish or you don't—and if you do, your neighbors won't agree with you anyway; so why write it down? Be polite about the cooking next door and they will be polite about yours. Be rude about it, and you invite open warfare.

What Richard and I had heard from the back yard was the first volley. Our cook, Thelma, had been chatting in the kitchen with her sister-in-law Ruby. Now Ruby was also a fine cook. This did not distinguish her; most New Orleans women are fine cooks, whether they happen to make their living at it or not. What did distinguish Ruby was that she had a preference for okra gumbo—and Thelma had just gone on record as believing that okra gumbo was made only by fools and other idiot types who have never learned that filé gumbo is far superior. Ruby, who had stopped by on her way home to make lunch for Thelma's brother, took her hat off, put her purse on the kitchen counter, smiled patronizingly and settled down for a battle royal.

To understand the clash between those women, you must know that there are two distinct categories of gumbo worshipers: those who believe that a gumbo should be thickened with fresh okra, and those who prefer it thickened with a substance called filé powder—a product originally made by the Choctaw Indians of Louisiana from the young leaves of the sassafras tree. The leaves were dried, pounded to a powder and pressed through a sieve; the result was then brought to New Orleans to be sold at the French Market. Early on, Creole cooks found that filé powder made an excellent thickener that gave their gumbos a new taste. But the filé can only be used at the last minute, just before the dish is served—otherwise the gumbo becomes stringy. Okra, on the other hand, can be put in at the beginning; simmered right along with the gumbo, it subtly alters the flavor. But—and this is the catch—you can't use both of them together: in combination, filé and okra overthicken the dish and lose their own flavors. So you must choose, and the choice on this Sunday was stark. Thelma slammed a black iron pot down on the left side of the stove; Ruby got another out of the cabinet and set it on the right burner. Both a filé gumbo *and* an okra gumbo were to be made, and Richard and I were to decide which was better. It was all very simple.

That is, it was simple until Ruby saw that Thelma was going to put chicken and ham into her gumbo along with the crabs. That procedure, according to Ruby, could only be followed by a woman ignorant enough not to know that a Creole crab gumbo was originally a "maigre" dish—a dish for a fast day—and should never contain meat. This information greatly amused Thelma. Between belly laughs, she explained to all and sundry (Richard and me) that she had never before met anyone so misguided as to confuse crab gumbo with an oyster or shrimp gumbo, which are true Lenten foods. She saw clearly that her brother must have married Ruby for some reason other than Ruby's abilities in the kitchen.

Now in other cultures and in other lands it may not be insulting for one woman to suggest that another woman's greatest talent lies outside the domain of the kitchen. In New Orleans it is about the worst thing you can say. Even women of ill fame are supposed to know how to cook. All great ladies know how to cook, though they usually have someone to cook for them. In fact, to *be* a woman in South Louisiana is to know how to cook, and you are a lot safer in casting aspersions on a woman's intelligence or even her appearance than you are in questioning her right to stand at a stove. I don't recall what words passed between Ruby and Thelma after that, but it didn't really matter—they were shouting too loud to hear each other anyway. I do recall that each stood facing the other, that neither of them seemed to look at the stove for the next hour—and that neither stopped cooking for an instant. By the end of the hour I had learned a great many new and gorgeously unrespectable words, and was ready to enjoy two totally different kinds of gumbo.

While Ruby and Thelma cried and made up, Richard and I enjoyed the spoils of war. Ruby's gumbo was composed of crabs, shrimp, onions, okra, chilies, bay leaf, thyme, Tabasco, water, salt and a touch of cayenne. It was a gumbo of the lake and the earth: rich and dark, yet smelling somehow of the purity of wind-blown water. When you put your face over it—as you should with all gumbos—and let the steam cloud hold you for a moment before you tasted it, you knew what the essence of shellfish smelled like. Then, when you put a spoonful in your mouth, the word pungent could never again hold the same meaning for you. You could not have imagined a pungency combined with sweetness and the taste of herbs, not to mention the sting of red pepper on the tongue, and the deep taste of crab. In its simplicity the dish was a marvel.

By contrast, Thelma's gumbo was less simple and pure, but fuller and rounder. In her anger at Ruby she had dismissed the crabs entirely and produced instead a gumbo based on chicken, ham and two dozen oysters that she had been saving to fry for dinner. The dish was prepared in about the same way as Ruby's, but without okra, with oyster liquor instead of water, and with a generous measure of filé powder spread over the top just before the gumbo was served. Richard and I happily ate bowlfuls of both gumbos, each with two spoonfuls of white rice at the center of the dark liquid to add substance and softness to the spicy meal. Gumbo is exactly that—a meal; it isn't really a soup and it isn't a solid. As we drank the liquid off, we ate the chicken and ham and the pieces of crab and the shrunken oysters and shrimp that lay at the bottoms of the bowls.

There are other good gumbos, made from turkey or rabbit or even squirrel. There is a pure shrimp gumbo (best with filé), a pure chicken gumbo and a pure oyster one. There is cabbage gumbo, and even a gumbo made with herbs and greens alone, called *gumbo aux herbes* or *gumbo z'herbes* . . . it is said to have been originated by the superstitious Creoles especially for Good Friday when, it was believed, you would have good luck for the coming year if you ate seven greens and met seven people during the day. In the bayous there are muskrat gumbos, and if you were to transplant an Acadian family to Maine there would doubtless be a lobster gumbo. In short, a gumbo can contain whatever you get your hands on—if your hands can cook. It is indeed the all-containing dish; as the Creoles put it, "Gumbo, c'est bon—c'est tout"—or, in English, "It's plain good, it's everything."

Comparing Poems

The following poems deal with the same theme—death. Beyond this basic similarity, there are many differences. Read the poems carefully and see how many points of likeness and difference you can detect.

DEATH BE NOT PROUD

John Donne

Death, be not proud, though some have called thee
Mighty and dreadful, for thou art not so;
For those whom thou think'st thou dost overthrow
Die not, poor Death, nor yet canst thou kill me.
From rest and sleep, which but thy pictures be,
Much pleasure; then from thee much more must flow,
And soonest our best men with thee do go,
Rest of their bones, and soul's delivery.
Thou art slave to fate, chance, kings, and desperate men,
And dost with poison, war, and sickness dwell,
And poppy or charms can make us sleep as well
And better than thy stroke; why swell'st thou then?
One short sleep past, we wake eternally
And death shall be no more; Death, thou shalt die.

DO NOT GO GENTLE INTO THAT GOOD NIGHT

Dylan Thomas

Do not go gentle into that good night,
Old age should burn and rave at close of day;
Rage, rage against the dying of the light.

Though wise men at their end know dark is right,
Because their words had forked no lightning they
Do not go gentle into that good night.

Good men, the last wave by, crying how bright
Their frail deeds might have danced in a green bay,
Rage, rage against the dying of the light.

Wild men who caught and sang the sun in flight,
And learn, too late, they grieved it on its way,
Do not go gentle into that good night.

Grave men, near death, who see with blinding sight
Blind eyes could blaze like meteors and be gay,
Rage, rage against the dying of the light.

And you, my father, there on the sad height,
Curse, bless, me now with your fierce tears, I pray.
Do not go gentle into that good night.
Rage, rage against the dying of the light.

Timor Mortis Conturbat Me
(The Fear of Death Disturbs Me)

R. L. Chapman

My Lord Death, hear this petition:
You are (Thou art?) a goodly lord,
I know cerebrally;
Handsomer than that grinning clanky clown
We show you as;
Goodly, opulently velvety dark
And somberly lovely.

Pray, Lord, when you extinguish me,
Do it micro-fast and from behind,
So he did not know what hit him.
And wait, if you can manage
In your cleansing economy,
Until I am old enough to be the elegant
Rarefied abstraction of a man,
A paper person so fined by abrasive years
As to be more symbolic than real.

Then strike, and hear him rustle as he falls.

Here

Paul Monette

everything extraneous has burned away
this is how burning feels in the fall
of the final year not like leaves in a blue
October but as if the skin were a paper lantern
full of trapped moths beating their fired wings
and yet I can lie on this hill just above you
a foot beside where I will lie myself
soon soon and for all the wrack and blubber
feel still how we were warriors when the
merest morning sun in the garden was a
kingdom after Room 1010 war is not all
death it turns out war is what little
thing you hold on to refugeed and far from home
oh sweetie will you please forgive me this
that every time I opened a box of anything
Glad Bags One-A-Days KINGSIZE was
the worst I'd think will you still be here
when the box is empty Rog Rog who will
play boy with me now that I bucket with tears
through it all when I'd cling beside you sobbing
you'd shrug it off with the quietest *I'm still
here* I have your watch in the top drawer

which I don't dare wear yet help me please
the boxes grocery home day after day
the junk that keeps men spotless but it doesn't
matter now how long they last or I
the day has taken you with it and all
there is now is burning dark the only green
is up by the grave and this little thing
of telling the hill I'm here oh I'm here

DISCUSSION AND EXERCISES

1. After noting specific points of similarity and difference in the preceding poems, write a one- or two-paragraph report of your findings. Be prepared to explain your choice of organizational pattern—for example, comparison of parts or of wholes.

2. Read the following meticulously organized paragraph on the two protagonists in Willa Cather's novel *Death Comes for the Archbishop.*

> Cather's two equally admirable priests, Latour and Vaillant, are opposites in almost countless ways. Latour is a man of reflection, for example, while Vaillant is a man of action. Latour is careful and thoughtful while Vaillant is impulsive. Latour loves a few very well while Vaillant is sympathetic with many people. Latour is an organizer while Vaillant is a builder and proselytizer. Latour is an aristocrat while Vaillant is a baker's son. Latour is a scholar and Vaillant is a preacher. Latour gardens while Vaillant cooks. Latour identifies with the Indians while Vaillant identifies with the Mexicans. Latour finds building a cathedral work for the head while Vaillant seeks lost souls "without pride and without shame[.]" Latour dies once of having lived and dies quietly as Indians squat silently in the nearby courtyard, while Joseph [Vaillant] cheats death repeatedly and then attracts thousands to the funeral which is not unlike a circus. Such a list of differences, though already long, could be extended further. But what is important is that Cather, like Pascal, accords her opposites equal respect; she concedes that neither is perfect and that each needs the other to function effectively.
>
> —Merrill M. Skaggs, "*Death Comes to the Archbishop:* Cather's Mystery and Manners," *American Literature,* October 1985

   a. Indicate in which ways the listing of differences is cast in parallel construction.
   b. Does the writer vary the parallelism at any point?
   c. Comment on the effectiveness of the last sentence of this passage.

3. Using a comparison of parts, write a paragraph or two comparing and contrasting a set of people you know well and respect but who have very different personalities: your parents, two siblings, two friends, two relatives, two teachers, two neighbors—or whoever.

4. In "Grant and Lee: A Study in Contrasts" the two generals are shown to be different and alike. Cite the specific points of difference and likeness, indicating whether they are organized methodically and logically.

5. Write a one-paragraph essay (150-250 words) showing that X is not like Y, on the basis of specific points. Choose one pair of topics from one of the following categories. (Note: The specific points of difference need not be factual details in every case; a "point" may be an example, an analogy, an attitude, as in the comparison of Kennedy and Johnson. The "points" may also be the ramifications of one main point.) Use the prewriting techniques you have learned.
   a. Warfare

   > conventional/guerrilla
   > Korea/Vietnam
   > atomic weapons/conventional weapons
   > atomic warfare/germ warfare
   > offensive/defensive

   b. Astronomy

   > astronomy/astrology
   > dawn/dusk
   > sun/moon
   > planet/star
   > Earth/Mars

   c. Eating

   > appetite/hunger
   > home cooking/college cafeteria
   > eating to live/living to eat
   > eating in the tropics/eating in the Arctic
   > eating/dining

   d. Fact and Fiction

   > detectives/detectives in movies and television
   > American Indians/Indians in movies and television
   > family life/family life on a television series
   > Marine Corps/movie marines
   > courtroom/courtroom on television

6. Analyze the organization of parts in "That Lean and Hungry Look." Do you think the alternation of paragraphs addressed to "fat" and "thin" is the most effective mode of presentation? Explain. Would "comparison of wholes" or "similarities and differences" have worked as well? Explain. Comment on the tone of the piece.

7. Write a one- or two-paragraph comparison of the adjacent pair of photographs of cyclists.

8. The following paired terms are close in meaning and therefore have to be distinguished from each other (either denotatively or connotatively). Write one or two paragraphs in which you cite the essential difference or differences between the terms in one of the following pairs:

talent/genius	induction/deduction
aptitude/talent	libel/slander
conscience/guilt	liberty/license
knowledge/wisdom	class/caste
intelligence/knowledge	dissent/rebellion
cooperate/collaborate	wit/humor

ESSAY SUGGESTIONS

1. Using the paragraphs you developed above, compose an essay (750-1,000 words) contrasting two people you know and respect but who have very different personalities. Be certain to organize your essay around a thesis, perhaps one that illuminates the parts of your own make-up that these two people affect.

2. Write an essay (500-1,000 words) in which you compare two men or two women, using as your organizational plan either comparison of wholes or comparison of parts. Use the prewriting techniques you have learned.

3. Drawing on your own experience, write an essay (500-1,000 words) on one of the following topics:
   a. Two things mistakenly believed to be alike
   b. A similarity (or difference) between two authors or two literary works (or two of anything) that no one, to your knowledge, has observed before.

4. Expand one of the paragraph exercises above into an essay of 500-750 words.

5. Write a defense (500-1,000 words) of "that lean and hungry look" in which you proclaim the superiority of thin people over fat people. Try to reply to points raised in Jordan's essay. Use the organization that best suits your purpose (comparison of wholes, comparison of parts, or similarities and differences).

Question

16

WHAT IS THE PRESENT STATUS OF X?

CONCERNING AN HISTORIC MONUMENT
NO NEWS FROM AUSCHWITZ,
A. M. ROSENTHAL

CONCERNING SPORTS—AND WOMEN
THE FIRST GIRL AT SECOND BASE,
SUSAN JACOBY

CONCERNING TRAVEL
THE LATEST FASHION IN TRAVEL,
JAN MORRIS

CONCERNING A RECENT EVENT
GIVING VOICE TO HURT AND BETRAYAL,
SETH MYDANS

Although it is an aspect of comparison, the question of *present status* is important enough to merit a chapter of its own. You have only to consider the variety of timely, thought-provoking "then and now" essays to know why writers use present status so often. Indeed, in every professional field or discipline, as well as in every area of ordinary life, we must periodically bring things up to date by asking *What is the present status of X?* or, in words we are more likely to use, *What is new about X?* or *What is happening with X?* or *How do people feel about X at the present moment?* or *How do I feel at the present time?* Whatever form it takes, the question leads to a special kind of comparison in which "now" is compared to "then."

We may properly ask the question, *What is its present status?* of almost any idea, habit, custom, condition, or belief. Is it "in" or "out"? Timely or obsolete? How is it different from or similar to what it was—and why? As Heraclitus pointed out more than two thousand years ago, the world is in a constant state of flux; nothing stands still; one never steps into the same stream twice. Thus there is always a story in an assessment of the present status of something.

CONCERNING AN HISTORIC MONUMENT

In the summer of 1958—thirteen years after the defeat of Nazi Germany—an American correspondent went to Auschwitz, the most hideous of the Nazi concentration camps (where four million prisoners, mostly Jews, were murdered during the Second World War), to describe its present status. What is it like *now*? This was the question that he answered in the following feature story, whose impact rests on the contrast between the ghastly activity of the past and the peaceful stillness of the present.

No News from Auschwitz

A. M. Rosenthal

The most terrible thing of all, somehow, was that at Brzezinka the sun was bright and warm, the rows of graceful poplars were lovely to look upon and on the grass near the gates children played.

It all seemed frighteningly wrong, as in a nightmare, that at Brzezinka the sun should ever shine or that there should be light and greenness and the sound of young laughter. It would be fitting if at Brzezinka the sun never shone and the grass withered because this is a place of unutterable terror.

And yet, every day, from all over the world, people come to Brzezinka, quite possibly the most grisly tourist center on earth. They come for a variety of reasons—to see if it could really have been true, to remind themselves not to forget, to pay homage to the dead by the simple act of looking upon their place of suffering.

Brzezinka is a couple of miles from the better-known southern Polish town of Oswiecim. Oswiecim has about 12,000 inhabitants, is situated about 171 miles from Warsaw and lies in a damp, marshy area at the eastern end of the pass called the Moravian Gate. Brzezinka and Oswiecim together formed part of that minutely organized factory of torture and death that the Nazis called Konzentrationslager Auschwitz.

By now, fourteen years after the last batch of prisoners was herded naked into the gas chambers by dogs and guards, the story of Auschwitz has been told a great many times. Some of the inmates have written of those events of which sane men cannot conceive. Rudolf Franz Ferdinand Hoess, the superintendent of the camp, before he was executed, wrote his detailed memoirs of mass exterminations and the experiments on living bodies. Four million people died here, the Poles say.

And so there is no news to report about Auschwitz. There is merely the compulsion to write something about it, a compulsion that grows out of a restless feeling that to have visited Auschwitz and then turned away without having said or written anything would be a most grievous act of discourtesy to those who died here.

Brzezinka and Oswiecim are very quiet places now; the screams can no longer be heard. The tourist walks silently, quickly at first to get it over with and then, as his mind peoples the barracks and the chambers and the dungeons and flogging posts, he walks draggingly. The guide does not say much either, because there is nothing much for him to say after he has pointed.

For every visitor, there is one particular bit of horror that he knows he will never forget. For some it is seeing the rebuilt gas chamber at Oswiecim and being told that this is the "small one." For others it is the fact that at Brzezinka, in the ruins of the gas chambers and the crematoria the Germans blew up when they retreated, there are daisies growing. There are visitors who gaze blankly at the gas chambers and the furnaces because their minds simply cannot encompass them, but stand shivering before the great mounds of human hair behind the plate glass window or the piles of babies' shoes or the brick cells where men sentenced to death by suffocation were walled up.

One visitor opened his mouth in a silent scream simply at the sight of boxes—great stretches of three-tiered boxes in the women's barracks. They were about six feet wide, about three feet high, and into them from five to ten prisoners were shoved for the night. The guide walks quickly through the barracks. Nothing more to see here.

A brick building where sterilization experiments were carried out on women prisoners. The guide tries the door—it's locked. The visitor is grateful that he does not have to go in, and then flushes with shame.

A long corridor where rows of faces stare from the walls. Thousands of pictures, the photographs of prisoners. They are all dead now, the men and women who stood before the cameras, and they all knew they were to die.

They all stare blank-faced, but one picture, in the middle of a row, seizes the eye and wrenches the mind. A girl, 22 years old, plumply pretty, blonde. She is smiling gently, as at a sweet, treasured thought. What was the thought that passed through her young mind and is now her memorial on the wall of the dead at Auschwitz?

Into the suffocation dungeons the visitor is taken for a moment and feels himself strangling. Another visitor goes in, stumbles out and crosses herself. There is no place to pray at Auschwitz.

The visitors look pleadingly at each other and say to the guide. "Enough."

There is nothing new to report about Auschwitz. It was a sunny day and the trees were green and at the gates the children played.

CONCERNING SPORTS—AND WOMEN

Things *ought* to have changed by now—but they haven't, according to feminist writer Susan Jacoby in the essay below. She is talking about the sports world and the dearth of women heroes with whom an athletically inclined young girl might identify. Note that this piece revolves around a contrast between early expectations ("the grand as if") as set against the ongoing present reality.

The First Girl at Second Base

Susan Jacoby

Between the ages of seven and ten, I spent a good deal of time dreaming of the day I would follow in the footsteps of my hero, Jacob Nelson (Nellie) Fox, and play second base for the Chicago White Sox. The crowd would roar as I stepped up to the plate in the bottom of the ninth with two out, runners on second and third, and the Sox trailing by one run. The roar would turn to whoops of joy as I, like the ever-reliable Nellie, punched a game-winning hit through the infield.

In endless conversations between innings at Comiskey Park, I badgered my grandfather about my desire to break the sex barrier in major league baseball. Nellie was small for a ballplayer—the sportscasters called him. "Little Nell"—and it was quite possible that I might grow up to be as tall as he was. If Jackie Robinson (another of my heroes) could become the first Negro in the big leagues, there was no reason why Susan Jacoby could not become the first girl on the diamond. No reason at all, my grandfather agreed. He was too softhearted to point out the facts of life to a granddaughter he had helped turn into a baseball nut.

Not all of my childhood heroes were sports figures, but they all had one thing in common: They were men. The most important nonsportsman in my pantheon was Franklin D. Roosevelt, who captured my imagination not because of anything he had done as President but because he had overcome polio. I associated heroism not only with courage but with the sort of courage that is expressed in a visible, physical way. I had never heard of any woman who embodied my notions of what a hero did and was.

When I questioned my women friends about their childhood heroes, an extraordinary number insisted they never had any. Of those who did remember, all but one acknowledged that their heroes had been men. It turned out that the exception—a woman who said Margaret Sanger had been her hero—was speaking from a newly acquired feminist consciousness rather than from any true memory of childhood.

When I asked men the same question, nearly all of them immediately produced long lists of heroes. All-male lists. Not a single man grew up with a woman for a hero. In fact, it seems that Eleanor Roosevelt was the only public woman (apart from movie stars) whose achievements impinged upon the consciousness of boys who were growing up in the 1930s, '40s, and '50s.

Growing up in a culture with male criteria for heroism undoubtedly exerts its influence on a boy's image of women. For a girl, though, the matter is more personal and more crucial: Her image of herself is at stake. Hero worship confined to the opposite sex—a phenomenon that seems to have been almost universal among women of my generation and almost nonexistent among men—poses a psychological problem on at least two levels.

On the surface level—the rational one—the problem is obvious and solvable. Reggie Jackson, who brought on a bad relapse of my baseball hero worship by hitting three home runs in the final game of this year's World Series, is just my age. I was not at all surprised to read in the sports pages that Jackie Robinson had been Reggie's hero as well as mine. The difference between us, of course, is that Reggie Jackson could grow up to play his hero's game.

The feminist movement has a sensible answer to the predicament of a girl who, having been born the wrong sex, can never grow up to be like her hero. Feminists say: "Give us our rightful place in the history books, establish equal opportunity for women now, and soon we'll have our share of heroes." Fair enough. A girl who dreams of achievement in sports or politics or law or medicine certainly has more women to emulate today than girls did when I was growing up.

The sensible feminist solution would be enough if a hero were only an object of emulation. The true function of the hero, however, lies in the realm of imagination. Most boys, after all, are no more likely to grow up to be Jackie Robinson than I was. Heroes give a child access to what the novelist Cynthia Ozick calls "the grand as if." When a young girl dreams of heroes, she dreams as if she were free: Limitations of height or weight or sex or race become irrelevant. A hero represents not so much a specific achievement as a whole range of human possibilities, an awe-inspiring glimpse of perfection.

On this level of awe and myth, it is difficult to develop a feminist alternative to the cultural values that have made both men and women regard heroism as a male characteristic. Heroism has almost always been linked with physical prowess and strength: Moral and physical courage are inseparable in most heroic sagas. This ideal of the hero places women at a disadvantage, because most societies have imposed severe restraints on public displays of female strength. Even today, when many of those restraints have crumbled, women are still at a disadvantage if the traditional concept of the hero is upheld. There is no getting around the fact that most men are stronger than most women.

Many adults talk about the need to smash traditional notions of heroism by stressing the moral rather than the physical aspects of courage. It sounds like a good idea, but I suspect these adults haven't been talking to many kids. In a sampling of my favorite ten-to-twelve-year-old girls, I elicited the name of just one woman hero: Billie Jean King. One of the girls expressed regret that her hero had trounced the aging Bobby Riggs rather than a man her own age. Two girls said their hero was the great Brazilian soccer player Pele, and two others, to my delight, mentioned Reggie Jackson. (I admit I spoke to the girls just a few days after the dramatic ending of the World Series.) One eleven-year-old said her ambition was to become a pilot and she was sorry America had never sent up a woman astronaut. So much for adult notions of dispensing with physical daring and achievement as standards of heroism.

There are people who think the end of the traditional hero would produce more realistic men and women. I doubt it. I still remember the pure joy I took in my baseball-playing fantasies. Doing well under extreme pressure was an important element in my fantasies, and that ideal is certainly suitable for any "realistic" adult. To dream as if you were free is a moving and beautiful experience—so beautiful that many adults feel obliged to forget it. I wish some of those dreams had come to me in the form of my own as well as of the opposite sex. Things ought to have changed by now, but it seems that barriers to women are more formidable in the world of heroes than in union hiring halls or executive suites.

CONCERNING TRAVEL

The following essay provides a witty description of the changing fashion in travel. While our grandparents may have taken a well-publicized Grand Tour or a pampering ocean cruise on a luxury liner, today's dedicated traveler heads for the remote Galápagos Islands and booby birds ("a place that almost nobody has been to, and a bird that practically no one has ever heard of"). Explaining that "class in holiday travel comes in cycles," Jan Morris points out with wry humor that the popular vacation place today is grubby, not glamorous. If you want to be a trendy traveler, she advises that you simply tell your travel agent "whether you prefer to freeze at the poles or boil in Equatoria, wade through swamps in search of amphibious reptiles or crouch in treetop blinds waiting for fruit bats." That's the "in" thing in travel today.

THE LATEST FASHION IN TRAVEL

Jan Morris

Not long ago a dear friend of mine who owns a travel agency invited me to join, as his guest, a group tour which was proving particularly popular, he said, among his more sophisticated clients. What could be more enjoyable? I asked myself. A week in Florence perhaps? A long meander through Japan? Wine tasting on the Côte d'Or? Unfortunately not. A short sharp trip to the Galápagos Islands was what he was offering, providing unrivaled opportunities, he assured me, for observation of the booby birds.

The *booby birds!* A world of great art, noble architecture, magnificent food, and lovely lazy beaches awaits the traveler out there, but what my friend's more urbane clients especially liked was ten days among the boobies of the Galápagos! "There's a nice little local boat," he said, "out of Guayaquil—not one of your luxury ships, of course, but with any luck you'll get a cabin to yourself."

It was a generous gift that he was offering me, for not only was the excursion extremely expensive, but it really was immensely popular. It exactly suited, it seems, the ethos of contemporary travel. It combined in just the right proportions a moderate degree of discomfort, at least the suggestion of adventure, a place that almost nobody has ever been to, and a bird that practically nobody has ever heard of. It was the very epitome of a classy traveling vacation, 1980s style.

For class in holiday travel comes in cycles. In our great-grandfathers' day the Grand Tour was the thing, and the vacationist boarded some grandiosely titled liner, *Leviathan* or *Majestic,* loaded with traveling trunks, patent medicines, and sketching materials, to potter amply around the trade routes in the process anomalously known as globetrotting. Our grandparents, on the other hand, much preferred the frivolity of the Ocean Cruise—cocktails in Naples Bay, badinage at the captain's table, fox-trot rendezvous beneath the starboard lifeboats, and all that Noël Coward stuff.

After World War II, individual travel was the only socially acceptable kind (picking up a rented Mercedes at Frankfurt, revisiting the old squadron airfield at Chipping-in-the-Marsh) until the pauper-plutocrats of the hippie generation made the communal journey to Katmandu an absolute *sine qua non* of chic fulfillment. Today it is perfectly O.K. to go somewhere by train, preferably the Orient Express to Venice, or take a gastronomic barge tour through the French canals, but unquestionably the *really* smooth thing to do is to go and watch the booby birds.

They need not actually be boobies, of course, or even for that matter birds, and the Galápagos Islands are not a compulsory venue. Anywhere sufficiently remote, uncomfortable, and unfamiliar will do, and today there is almost no journey to be made on earth, almost no adventure to be undertaken, that cannot be arranged for you by a competent professional travel agent. Confide in him. Tell him whether you prefer to freeze at the poles or boil in Equatoria, wade through swamps in search of amphibious reptiles or crouch in treetop blinds waiting for fruit bats.

He will soon find the tour to suit you, for at any moment of the year these days there are ships full of tourists plowing through ice floes, planes full of tourists landing on jungle airstrips, jeeps full of tourists pursuing the yak tents of Mongolian nomads, pony caravans of tourists slogging through the Andes, trucks full of tourists being pushed out of flooded Bhutanese rivers.

The fashionable cycle has come full circle. The Grand Tourists, setting out so pompously to the blast of the farewell siren, were traveling partly for pleasure, of course, and partly for show, but partly for self-improvement. They wanted to see for themselves the marvels of art and architecture they had only read about, to learn more about the less fortunate peoples of the world, and to come home culturally and mentally richer for the trip. Travel in those days was, as they used to say in the brochures, a Truly Educational Experience. It Broadened the Mind.

Today rather the same emotions govern our generation of sophisticated travelers, for in many ways ours is an earnest age too. Even the hippies claimed to be traveling for enlightenment, and today your truly worldly pleasure traveler would not dream of traveling just for pleasure's sake. Holidaying is no longer just getting away from it all; it is more like jogging, and if you are into marathons, you are almost certainly into booby birds.

Of course there is a degree of exhibitionism still. Few of us are altogether immune to the temptations of self-display, and it really must be rather gratifying to be able to say that at this time last week you were in the Antarctic, or sharing a camel chop with an Uzbek chieftain. (Twenty years ago I used to like to claim that I was the thirtieth European ever to set foot in Namche Bazar, in the Sherpa country; now that there is an excellent small Japanese tourist hotel a little way up to Khumbu Valley, on the glacial track to Everest, I talk about the experience rather less often.) But there is also, I think, something a little wistful to the trend. It is as though history has gone rather too far for purely frivolous travel, time is shorter than we used to think, and we should treat the world in a spirit of adventurous but respectful inquiry, while we still have it. They may seem a little comical, those stalwarts of the PTA gnawing at their stew in the outback, those associate professors buckling on their Lapland snowshoes, those company presidents bumping sandgrimed across the Kalahari, but there is a certain grandeur to their folly, all the same.

Doubtless the fashion will shift again anyway, one of these days, and we shall enter another phase of holiday travel. What will it be next? I wonder. Shall we sophisticates of the group tour all be looking at disused coal mines or superannuated steam pumps on Industrial Archaeology Projects? Shall we all be going to Bath or Baden-Baden, taking the waters once again? Shall we be cycling through the Low Countries, or mucking out the shearing sheds on Farm Participation Holidays?

Anything is possible, in the ceaseless rotation of traveling fashion, but in the meantime there are always the boobies.

"Right, then," my friend said. "See you at Guayaquil, Tuesday week. Mind you bring strong shoes."

But no, I was nowhere near Guayaquil Tuesday week. Grateful though I was for the invitation, I had boobied out.

CONCERNING A RECENT EVENT

Another way to approach this question is to ask it of a more recent event. Some changes become apparent over a long stretch of time, as Rosenthal demonstrates in the first essay in this chapter. With other events, the perspective of even a year can bring changes that are worth observing. Such is the approach taken by *New York Times* reporter Seth Mydans one year after the riots in Los Angeles that followed the verdicts in the Rodney King trial. Mydans focuses on the Korean-American neighborhoods of Los Angeles, which experienced a great deal of looting, vandalism, and destruction during the riots. Through interviews and a profile of a prominent lawyer, Angela Oh, Mydans gives a sense of the experiences of the entire community in the year following April 29, 1992.

GIVING VOICE TO HURT AND BETRAYAL

Seth Mydans

One year after the rioting that devastated the Korean community here in Los Angeles, Angela Oh, a prominent Korean American lawyer, has decided to learn to read and write the language of her parents.

She can speak Korean, said Miss Oh, a busy, no-nonsense professional who, as president of the Korean American Bar Association of Southern California, has emerged as a spokesman for her community. Learning to read it would also allow her to read the documents of her clients. It took her a while to confess: "Really, it's on a personal level. I want to read novels. You know that? That's my goal. Yes, I want to read novels and I want to read the poetry of the people."

The riots that erupted on April 29, 1992, were a watershed for Korean-Americans, bringing them up short in their headlong pursuit of economic success and forcing many of them, including Miss Oh, to rethink their place astride two cultures.

More than 2,000 Korean businesses were damaged or destroyed, totaling more than $350 million in damage, and only one in four have reopened a year later. The failure of the police to protect them and of the government to help them rebuild has bred deep resentment as well as a realization that Korean-Americans must work harder to be included in the political and social process of the country.

"Already in the first days after the riots last April, many of us were saying: This is our rite of passage into American society. This is our people's tragedy," said Miss Oh, 37, in an interview in her downtown law office. "It is what internment was to the Japanese.

"It's a little scary because I don't see where this one is going to end," she added. "There is a lot of animosity toward Koreans out there right now," from the public and even from some government agencies.

The place of Koreans in American society is lonely and precarious, she said, and has served as a convenient buffer between the racism of the white majority and the anger of the black minority. Just as Korean-owned businesses, which suffered nearly half the looting and vandalism in last year's violence, became an outlet for the rage of many rioters, Korean-Americans here now view themselves as "human shields" in a complicated racial hierarchy, she said.

"We stand between the African-Americans, who are really at the bottom rung, and the white community, which is at the top rung because they are at the top of the power structure," Miss Oh said. "That's why I hate the term 'model minority.' It really makes me blanch. It translates into being a human shield."

Instead of confronting the profound socio-economic problems blacks face, Miss Oh said, whites merely point to the industrious Koreans and say, "How come blacks aren't more like you guys? Why don't they help each other more? Why don't they work as hard as you do?"

In the midst of the city's ethnic and racial frictions, Korean-Americans are also glibly caricatured, and dismissed, as hard-working drones by those in power and resented by poor blacks. "We are perceived as being, as a people, greedy, selfish, insulated and unwilling to become a part of America," Miss Oh said. "That is how we are seen. It is very untrue in terms of the heart of the people."

A low point came this week in a two-hour televised town meeting that brought together representatives of many racial and ethnic groups. A Korean spokesman challenged Labor Secretary Ron Brown to find $20 million to help reopen hundreds of burned-out Korean-owned liquor stores.

The questioner drew derisive laughter when Mr. Brown responded that if the Federal Government had $20 million to spare, it certainly would not spend it to open liquor stores.

"That was a horrible moment," Miss Oh recalled. "But the problem is that there is a moral obligation that Los Angeles needs to make to the Koreans. These people lost everything. They had investments ranging from $180,000 to half a million dollars. Those losses for the most part could not be insured because they couldn't find carriers, or the carriers were bogus. How do you tell these people that lost half a million dollars that there is nothing you can do about it?"

One widely accepted lesson of the riot and its aftermath is that Korean-Americans must become more involved in politics and American society. "They need to begin to participate in other aspects of American life, other than the material," Miss Oh said. "Materialism was a very, very prominent characteristic in our community. People understand now that those things they have gathered can be taken away so easily."

Most political participation had been confined to making campaign contributions, she said. "That's not political power, as we saw," she said. "They learned that very painfully." When the crisis came, they lacked the clout to win a fair share in recovery efforts. While Koreatown has mostly rebuilt, most of the businesses located in the South Central neighborhood have not.

When Miss Oh's parents immigrated to Los Angeles as college students in the 1950's, there were only a few Koreans in this country. As her mother, a schoolteacher, and father, a laboratory technician, raised their five children— a lawyer, a doctor, a pharmacist, a dentist and an architect—the Korean population of the country swelled to nearly 700,000. The huge increase, particularly over the past decade, included mostly the small merchants whose influx to Los Angeles has created the largest Korean enclave outside Korea.

After receiving her law degree from the University of California at Davis in 1986, Miss Oh became active in civil rights and human rights causes. Since the riots, her criminal defense practice has included a larger number of Korean-Americans, and her awareness of their special needs has grown acute.

She is now defending a married couple charged with arson in the fire that burned their store a year ago. Unable to speak English or comprehend the American legal system, Miss Oh said, they are at the mercy of forces they do not understand.

Over the past year, she has increasingly taken it upon herself to give voice to the needs of her community. Influenced by the feminist movement, she says, she has broken with a cultural tradition of meek and dutiful womanhood to become an advocate, active in political campaigns, government commissions and women's rights groups.

Along with its needs, the potential cultural contributions of the Korean-American community have been overlooked, Miss Oh said, including areas such as literature and the arts. "Along with the politics and the economics and all that," she said, "I really think that the creativity that is needed at this point in the history of this country is going to come from other sources, from the guts of the people."

Like many in her community, Miss Oh says she remains suspended between the two cultures, unsure of her identity or her role. "I see myself as a Korean-American—not Korean, not American, but something quite different and undefined," she said. "But definitely I have in my gut a sense that I am valuable to this country."

DISCUSSION AND EXERCISES

1. Answer the following questions about "No News from Auschwitz."
   a. In A. M. Rosenthal's grimly moving essay, what is the basic and ironic contrast that makes everything seem "frighteningly wrong"?
   b. Point to other contrasting elements in this piece and show how they function as an organizing principle.
   c. Evaluate the function and effectiveness of the opening and closing paragraphs.
   d. In what way is the tone of this essay subdued?
   e. Discuss "restraint" as the fundamental rhetorical device of this essay. Cite specific examples of understatement, and speculate on what the piece might be like if the writer had not exercised restraint. Explain why the story would have been more or less effective.
   f. Discuss the simplicity of diction and the structure of the following sentences. Explain why you do or do not find them powerful.
      1. "And so there is no news to report about Auschwitz."
      2. "The guide does not say much either, because there is nothing much for him to say after he has pointed."
      3. "Nothing more to see here."
   g. Explain the grammatical structure of the following phrases and indicate what rhetorical function they serve.
      1. "A brick building where sterilization experiments were carried out on women prisoners."
      2. "A long corridor where rows of faces stare from the walls."
      3. "Thousands of pictures, the photographs of prisoners."
   h. Why does the writer single out and ponder the photograph of one prisoner—the "plumply pretty" blonde?
   i. What is the significance of the visitor who "crosses herself"? What extra dimension of meaning is introduced by this detail?
2. Write a one-paragraph (150-250 words) response to Rosenthal's essay. Consider the advantages and disadvantages of using a topic sentence at either the beginning (movement from general to specific) or the end of the paragraph (movement from specific to general). Be prepared to explain your decision.

3. Rhetorical Stance: Jan Morris, "The Latest Fashion in Travel"
   a. *Purpose:* What do you think to be the writer's purpose in this piece? What do you think she hopes to accomplish or communicate about "the ethos of contemporary travel"?
   b. *Occasion:* Appearing in the "Going to Extremes" travel department of *Vanity Fair* magazine, this column is one of a monthly series. Does the April issue sound appropriate for a piece of this kind? Characterize Morris's tone and point of view. Cite specific passages to support your answers.
   c. *Audience:* What sort of audience do you think Morris is addressing? How do you envision the readers of *Vanity Fair?*
   d. *Reader-Writer Relationship:* How does Morris see herself in relation to her audience? Is she "at a distance" or "one of them"? Is she critical? Approving?

4. In 1951, Ruth Orkin's photograph "American Girl in Florence, Italy, 1951" was a popular postcard. Write a two-paragraph "response" indicating how such a card was probably viewed then, followed by speculation as to its "present status."

American Girl in Florence, Italy, 1951
Ruth Orkin, International Center of Photography,
New York

ESSAY SUGGESTIONS

1. In an essay (500-1,000 words) describe the present status of a place that has changed drastically—for better or worse—since you first knew or heard about it. Use the prewriting techniques you have learned before you begin to write.

2. Contemplate Susan Jacoby's lament. Write an essay (500-1,000 words) in which you support or challenge her observation that "barriers to women . . . in the world of heroes" are still as formidable as ever

OR

Write an essay (500-1,000 words) in which you cite another area in which "Things ought to have changed . . ." but have not.

3. In an essay (500-1,000 words) compare travelers of the past (THEN) with travelers of today (NOW) as you view them. Assume whatever rhetorical stance you feel is appropriate.

4. In an essay entitled "On the Status of the Soul," Bertrand Russell once pointed out that we are losing such "fine old simplicities" as the belief in an immortal soul. In an essay (500-1,000 words) describe the present status, as you view it, of one of the following established "simplicities":

Be it ever so humble, there's no place like home.
Honor thy father and thy mother.
Love conquers all.
You can't keep a good man down.
There's always room at the top.
Cleanliness is next to godliness.
You can't teach an old dog new tricks.

5. Begin an essay (750-1,000 words) with the words, "What once was _____ is now _____ " and continue to describe the present status of some institution, belief, tradition, or unexamined attitude among any group which you are familiar with.

Question

17

HOW CAN X
BE SUMMARIZED?

SUMMARIZING IDEAS
  RACE MATTERS, CORNEL WEST

SUMMARIZING PLOT (SYNOPSIS)

SUMMARIZING EVENTS
  THE PARADOX OF THE SIXTIES,
    JAMES RESTON

SUMMARIZING IDEAS

How can I briefly and accurately restate the main points in a body of information? How can I see through to its essence? How can I strip it bare of details and implications? How can I condense and communicate its core meaning? These are the questions you ask about summarizing, an intellectual challenge and a skill that some people regard as mechanical and routine, not at all creative. Actually, no greater challenge to the intellect and no more accurate test of understanding exist than the ability to contemplate an idea and then restate it briefly in your own words. Indeed, to read and study efficiently, to do research, to take satisfactory notes, to write papers, critiques, and examinations, to grasp an idea and hold it in the mind—all require the ability to "boil down" materials and see their basic intentions, their main points, and the relation of these points to one another. Writing a summary is a demanding exercise in analysis and interpretation.

A significant and recurrent question is, then: *How can X be summarized?* Most often you will need an answer to complete a summary for a *section* of an essay you are working on rather than a whole essay, although there are occasions when summary is the main or total purpose of a piece of writing: in the "Week in Review" section of the Sunday *New York Times,* for example, and in *Time* and *Newsweek* magazines.

Reviewing the different situations and types of material that call for summary is useful. Observe at the outset that the basis of all summary is careful and repeated reading of the text you want to summarize and sustained critical thinking about what you have read. This process of probing to "the heart of the matter" will enable you to render the essence in a clear, concise, accurate restatement.

In trying to summarize more complex ideas—for example, a proposal that contains several parts plus a rationale—you must again commit yourself to several readings. You must again search carefully for the main points and the key terms that embody them, noting also recurrent words and phrases and summing-up sentences that might profitably be quoted.

In the following excerpt, which introduces a collection of his essays on race in America, Cornel West gives his overview of attitudes toward race. This essay represents, in one sense, a summary of views that will be developed further in the rest of West's book. As you read, identify the main ideas you would want to include in a summary.

RACE MATTERS

Cornel West

What happened in Los Angeles in April of 1992 was neither a race riot nor a class rebellion. Rather, this monumental upheaval was a multiracial, trans-class, and largely male display of justified social rage. For all its ugly, xenophobic resentment, its air of adolescent carnival, and its downright barbaric behavior, it signified the sense of powerlessness in American society. Glib attempts to reduce its meaning to the pathologies of the black underclass, the criminal actions of hoodlums, or the political revolt of the oppressed urban masses miss the mark. Of those arrested, only 36 percent were black, more than a third had full-time jobs, and most claimed to shun political affiliation. What we witnessed in Los Angeles was the consequence of a lethal linkage of economic decline, cultural decay, and political lethargy in American life. Race was the visible catalyst, not the underlying cause.

The meaning of the earthshaking events in Los Angeles is difficult to grasp because most of us remain trapped in the narrow framework of the dominant liberal and conservative views of race in America, which with its worn-out vocabulary leaves us intellectually debilitated, morally disempowered, and personally depressed. The astonishing disappearance of the event from public dialogue is testimony to just how painful and distressing a serious engagement with race is. Our truncated public discussions of race suppress the best of who and what we are as a people because they fail to confront the complexity of the issue in a candid and critical manner. The predictable pitting of liberals against conservatives, Great Society Democrats against self-help Republicans, reinforces intellectual parochialism and political paralysis.

The liberal notion that more government programs can solve racial problems is simplistic—precisely because it focuses *solely* on the economic dimension. And the conservative idea that what is needed is a change in the moral behavior of poor black urban dwellers (especially poor black men, who, they say, should stay married, support their children, and stop committing so much crime) highlights immoral actions while ignoring public responsibility for the immoral circumstances that haunt our fellow citizens.

The common denominator of these views of race is that each still sees black people as a "problem people," in the words of Dorothy I. Height, president of the National Council of Negro Women, rather than as fellow American citizens with problems. Her words echo the poignant "unasked question" of W. E. B. Du Bois, who, in *The Souls of Black Folk* (1903), wrote:

> They approach me in a half-hesitant sort of way, eye me curiously or compassionately, and then instead of saying directly, How does it feel to be a problem? they say, I know an excellent colored man in my town. . . . Do not these Southern outrages make your blood boil? At these I smile, or am interested, or reduce the boiling to a simmer, as the occasion may require. To the real question, How does it feel to be a problem? I answer seldom a word.

Nearly a century later, we confine discussions about race in America to the "problems" black people pose for whites rather than consider what this way of viewing black people reveals about us as a nation.

This paralyzing framework encourages liberals to relieve their guilty consciences by supporting public funds directed at "the problems"; but at the same time, reluctant to exercise principled criticism of black people, liberals deny them the freedom to err. Similarly, conservatives blame the "problems" on black people themselves—and thereby render black social misery invisible or unworthy of public attention.

Hence, for liberals, black people are to be "included" and "integrated" into "our" society and culture, while for conservatives they are to be "well behaved" and "worthy of acceptance" by "our" way of life. Both fail to see that the presence and predicaments of black people are neither additions to nor defections from American life, but rather *constitutive elements of that life.*

To engage in a serious discussion of race in America, we must begin not with the problems of black people but with the flaws of American society—flaws rooted in historic inequalities and longstanding cultural stereotypes. How we set up the terms for discussing racial issues shapes our perception and response to these issues. As long as black people are viewed as a "them," the burden falls on blacks to do all the "cultural" and "moral" work necessary for healthy race relations. The implication is that only certain Americans can define what it means to be American—and the rest must simply "fit in."

The emergence of strong black-nationalist sentiments among blacks, especially among young people, is a revolt against this sense of having to "fit in." The variety of black-nationalist ideologies, from the moderate views of Supreme Court Justice Clarence Thomas in his youth to those of Louis Farrakhan today, rest upon a fundamental truth: white America has been historically weak-willed in ensuring racial justice and has continued to resist fully accepting the humanity of blacks. As long as double standards and differential treatment abound—as long as the rap performer Ice-T is harshly condemned while former Los Angeles Police Chief Daryl F. Gates's antiblack comments are received in polite silence, as long as Dr. Leonard Jeffries's anti-Semitic statements are met with vitriolic outrage while presidential candidate Patrick J. Buchanan's anti-Semitism receives a genteel response—black nationalisms will thrive.

Afrocentrism, a contemporary species of black nationalism, is a gallant yet misguided attempt to define an African identity in a white society perceived to be hostile. It is gallant because it puts black doings and sufferings, not white anxieties and fears, at the center of discussion. It is misguided because—out of fear of cultural hybridization and through silence on the issue of class, retrograde views on black women, gay men, and lesbians, and a reluctance to link race to the common good—it reinforces the narrow discussions about race.

To establish a new framework, we need to begin with a frank acknowledgment of the basic humanness and Americanness of each of us. And we must acknowledge that as a people—*E Pluribus Unum*—we are on a slippery slope toward economic strife, social turmoil, and cultural chaos. If we go down, we go down together. The Los Angeles upheaval forced us to see not only that we are not connected in ways we would like to be but also, in a more profound sense, that this failure to connect binds us even more tightly together. The paradox of race in America is that our common destiny is more pronounced and imperiled precisely when our divisions are deeper. The Civil War and its legacy speak loudly here. And our divisions are growing deeper. Today, eighty-six percent of white suburban Americans live in neighborhoods that are less than 1 percent black, meaning that the prospects for the country depend largely on how its cities fare in the hands of a suburban electorate. There is no escape from our interracial interdependence, yet enforced racial hierarchy dooms us as a nation to collective paranoia and hysteria—the unmaking of any democratic order.

The verdict in the Rodney King case, which sparked the incidents in Los Angeles, was perceived to be wrong by the vast majority of Americans. But whites have often failed to acknowledge the widespread mistreatment of black people, especially black men, by law enforcement agencies, which helped ignite the spark. The verdict was merely the occasion for deep-seated rage to come to the surface.

This rage is fed by the "silent" depression ravaging the country—in which real weekly wages of all American workers since 1973 have declined nearly 20 percent, while at the same time wealth has been upwardly distributed.

The exodus of stable industrial jobs from urban centers to cheaper labor markets here and abroad, housing policies that have created "chocolate cities and vanilla suburbs" (to use the popular musical artist George Clinton's memorable phrase), white fear of black crime, and the urban influx of poor Spanish-speaking and Asian immigrants—all have helped erode the tax base of American cities just as the federal government has cut its supports and programs. The result is unemployment, hunger, homelessness, and sickness for millions.

And a pervasive spiritual impoverishment grows. The collapse of meaning in life—the eclipse of hope and absence of love of self and others, the breakdown of family and neighborhood bonds—leads to the social deracination and cultural denudement of urban dwellers, especially children. We have created rootless, dangling people with little link to the supportive networks—family, friends, school—that sustain some sense of purpose in life. We have witnessed the collapse of the spiritual communities that in the past helped Americans face despair, disease, and death and that transmit through the generations dignity and decency, excellence and elegance.

The result is lives of what we might call "random nows," of fortuitous and fleeting moments preoccupied with "getting over"—with acquiring pleasure, property, and power by any means necessary. (This is not what Malcolm X meant by this famous phrase.) Post-modern culture is more and more a market culture dominated by gangster mentalities and self-destructive wantonness. This culture engulfs all of us—yet its impact on the disadvantaged is devastating, resulting in extreme violence in everyday life. Sexual violence against women and homicidal assaults by young black men on one another are only the most obvious signs of this empty quest for pleasure, property, and power.

Last, this rage is fueled by a political atmosphere in which images, not ideas, dominate, where politicians spend more time raising money than debating issues. The functions of parties have been displaced by public polls, and politicians behave less as thermostats that determine the climate of opinion than as thermometers registering the public mood. American politics has been rocked by an unleashing of greed among opportunistic public officials—who have followed the lead of their counterparts in the private sphere, where, as of 1989, 1 percent of the population owned 37 percent of the wealth and 10 percent of the population owned 86 percent of the wealth—leading to a profound cynicism and pessimism among the citizenry.

And given the way in which the Republican Party since 1968 has appealed to popular xenophobic images—playing the black, female, and homophobic cards to realign the electorate along race, sex, and sexual-orientation lines—it is no surprise that the notion that we are all part of one garment of destiny is discredited. Appeals to special interests rather than to public interests reinforce this polarization. The Los Angeles upheaval was an expression of utter fragmentation by a powerless citizenry that includes not just the poor but all of us.

What is to be done? How do we capture a new spirit and vision to meet the challenges of the post-industrial city, post-modern culture, and post-party politics?

First, we must admit that the most valuable sources for help, hope, and power consist of ourselves and our common history. As in the ages of Lincoln, Roosevelt, and King, we must look to new frameworks and languages to understand our multilayered crisis and overcome our deep malaise.

Second, we must focus our attention on the public square—the common good that undergirds our national and global destinies. The vitality of any public square ultimately depends on how much we *care* about the quality of our lives together. The neglect of our public infrastructure, for example—our water and sewage systems, bridges, tunnels, highways, subways, and streets—reflects not only our myopic economic policies, which impede productivity, but also the low priority we place on our common life.

The tragic plight of our children clearly reveals our deep disregard for public well-being. About one out of every five children in this country lives in poverty, including one out of every two black children and two out of every five Hispanic children. Most of our children—neglected by overburdened parents and bombarded by the market values of profit-hungry corporations—are ill-equipped to live lives of spiritual and cultural quality. Faced with these facts, how do we expect ever to constitute a vibrant society?

One essential step is some form of large-scale public intervention to ensure access to basic social goods—housing, food, health care, education, child care, and jobs. We must invigorate the common good with a mixture of government, business, and labor that does not follow any existing blueprint. After a period in which the private sphere has been sacralized and the public square gutted, the temptation is to make a fetish of the public square. We need to resist such dogmatic swings.

Last, the major challenge is to meet the need to generate new leadership. The paucity of courageous leaders—so apparent in the response to the events in Los Angeles—requires that we look beyond the same elites and voices that recycle the older frameworks. We need leaders—neither saints nor sparkling television personalities—who can situate themselves within a larger historical narrative of this country and our world, who can grasp the complex dynamics of our peoplehood and imagine a future grounded in the best of our past, yet who are attuned to the frightening obstacles that now perplex us. Our ideals of freedom, democracy, and equality must be invoked to invigorate all of us, especially the landless, propertyless, and luckless. Only a visionary leadership that can motivate "the better angels of our nature," as Lincoln said, and activate possibilities for a freer, more efficient, and stable America—only that leadership deserves cultivation and support.

Before beginning to summarize this essay, we should imagine a hypothetical situation in which such a summary might be necessary. A summary, like any other piece of writing, gains its shape and purpose from a rhetorical situation—an audience and an occasion. Assume, then, that you are writing an essay that compares different contemporary analyses of race in the United States (perhaps for a political science or sociology course). You plan to use West's essay as one of several perspectives on race and racism in contemporary America. Because you need to write a compact and concise essay, you need to boil down West's complex ideas into a short paragraph. How can you do this without distorting its essential features?

One way to begin is by isolating key terms and concepts. The title is one place to begin, though since "Race Matters" is the title of both this essay and the book-length collection of essays which it introduces, it may not be as specifically useful as titles of other essays can be. Let's reflect on the title for a moment; it seems to have two meanings, doesn't it? Can you see how it can be read as both a noun phrase and a complete sentence? Why do you suppose West chose this double meaning? If West is arguing that race *does* matter in the United States, how might he try to develop his point? (Asking speculative questions such as these as you begin reading serves as what we might term *pre-reading,* a strategy that helps us read actively and effectively.) As we read through the essay, we can make a list of several recurring ideas: the pervasiveness of race in America, the problems in the ways American discuss race, the need to discuss race in connection with a range of social issues and problems.

If we examine the structure of the essay, we will recognize that it falls into several distinct parts. The first six paragraphs point out what West sees as failures in the ways race is discussed. As we look over those paragraphs, we see certain ideas that are repeated: criticism of both liberals and conservatives for their racial attitudes, objections to viewing black people as somehow separate from the rest of the country, a failure to face the issue of race openly. These conjectures about the unifying idea of the first section are proven accurate by the statement with which West closes this section, part of which he italicizes for greater emphasis: "Both [liberals and conservatives] fail to see that the presence and predicaments of black people are neither additions to nor defections from American life, but rather *constitutive elements of that life.*" Authors who signal so clearly their main ideas show by such sentences their honest concern that readers understand accurately their ideas.

Looking over the second part of West's essay, we can see another pattern of repeated main ideas, a pattern that contrasts with and therefore complements the first half. This pattern can be seen in such phrases as the following:

> a frank acknowledgment of the basic humanness and Americanness of each of us
> our interracial interdependence
> rootless, dangling people with little link to the supportive networks
> collapse of spiritual communities
> the notion that we are all part of one garment of destiny

Again and again, West returns to the idea of our connectedness as a positive good and a failure to acknowledge that connectedness as a root of our problems. As he describes economic problems, spiritual impoverishment, the random search for pleasure, and political opportunism, he returns to this sense of the common good. We seem to have identified a central pattern in West's thought: the juxtaposition of these contrasting ideas. In the last sentence of this excerpt, West returns to the situation with which he began and provides a summary statement of his main idea, explaining the way in which race matters in America: "The Los Angeles upheaval was an expression of utter fragmentation by a powerless citizenry that includes not just the poor but all of us."

Having identified the central point of West's essay, we organize our summary around it, adding additional information as needed. For our paper on contemporary analyses of race in United States, we might write a summary paragraph such as this:

Cornel West suggests that our analysis of racial issues in the United States too often polarizes blacks and whites and isolates black people from the common national experience. Both liberals and conservatives, in his view, make this mistake: liberals by thinking that money will solve black "problems," conservatives by dismissing these problems as moral issues unique to the black community. West urges us to develop a true community spirit that views the problems faced by black people as part of larger national problems: economic problems, spiritual impoverishment, the random search for pleasure, and political opportunism. The absence of a sense that we are part of "one garment of destiny" lies behind these problems and must be addressed so that we can reverse the social fragmentation that led to the Los Angeles unrest.

SUMMARIZING PLOT (SYNOPSIS)

The ability to write a plot summary, or synopsis, underlies much writing about literature, for we cannot discuss a literary work such as a novel or play unless we are sure that the reader knows its story line—the sequence of events that constitutes its action. We may relate the events in chronological order, adding neither interpretive asides nor explanations of the work's structure or underlying logic. Thus, in "outline" versions of major works of literature, the summary is a bare recital of unfolding events, as in the following one-paragraph summary of Chapter XXII in Book I of *Don Quixote* (Bass):

Don Quixote saw trudging towards him in the road twelve convicts linked together by a chain, manacled, and accompanied by four armed guards. Because these men were obviously not going to their destination of their own free will, the Don believed that this was a situation which called for the services of a knight-errant. He rode up and asked each convict what crime he had committed, receiving honest answers in return. Despite these accounts of roguery, the Don, according to his duty as a knight-errant, requested the guards to free the men. When they refused, he attacked them. The convicts, seizing this opportune moment, broke their chain and proceeded to stone the guards who finally took to their heels. Sancho, fearing that a posse of the Holy Brotherhood would set upon himself and his master, advised the Don to get away as fast as possible. But Don Quixote gathered the criminals around him and commanded them to present themselves to his lady Dulcinea del Toboso. However, unwilling to risk apprehension and already suspicious of the sanity of a man who would free convicts, they began to pelt the Don with stones. When they had felled him, they stripped him and Sancho of a goodly portion of their clothing, then departed leaving the Don in a sullen mood and Sancho trembling for fear of the Holy Brotherhood.

Naturally, the author omits all narrative details such as dialogue, description, and reflection from this one-paragraph summary. What is left is a bare-bones account of the action—a helpful tool for charting one's way through a long and involved novel such as *Don Quixote,* which contains many more details and episodes than one could possibly keep track of without a chapter-by-chapter outline.

Such outlines are available in various series, such as the one cited above. Some of these publications are accurate and reliable; others are filled with errors and distortions of the original text.

In any case, it is far better to make your own outlines, for in outlining a work, as mentioned earlier, you come to see its shape and the progressive unfolding of its purpose on a far deeper and more intimate level than a simple "reading through" would yield. Approached in this way, as an analytical "break-down" of what happened in a novel, the section-by-section plot summary is a helpful study aid.

Also useful is the overall plot summary, which sweeps across the terrain of an entire novel, reducing it to two pages, or even a single paragraph, as in the following:

> Don Quixote de la Mancha, the history of, a satirical romance by Miguel Cervantes, the first part of which appeared in 1605 and the second in 1615. A kindly and simple-minded country gentleman has read the romances of chivalry until they have turned his brain. Clad in a suit of old armor and mounted on a broken-down hack which he christens Rozinante, he sets out on a career of knight-errantry, assuming the name of Don Quixote de la Mancha. For the object of his devotion he chooses a village girl, whom he names Dulcinea del Toboso and as squire he takes an ignorant but faithful peasant, Sancho Panza. The ordinary wayfarers of the Spanish roads of the seventeenth century are transformed by the knight's disordered imagination into warriors, distressed damsels, giants, and monsters. For instance, he tilts on one occasion, at the sails of a group of wind-mills, thinking them living creatures, and his attempts to right fictitious wrongs and win chivalric honor among them lead him and his squire into ludicrous and painful situations. Yet amidst their discomfitures Don Quixote retains a dignity, a certain nobility, and a pathetic idealism, and Sancho a natural shrewdness and popular humor which endear them to the reader. In the second part the interest is fully sustained, and variety is introduced by the sojourn of the pair with a duke and duchess and Sancho's appointment as governor of the imaginary island of Baratoria. At the end, Don Quixote, as the result of a dangerous illness, recovers his senses, renounces all books of chivalry, and dies penitent. The book was begun as an attack on the absurdities of the late chivalric romances, not on the essential chivalric ideals. As the work progresses it becomes a picture of human nature, its absurdities and its aspirations, its coarse materialism and lofty enthusiasm.

The length of a summary does not determine its excellence. A good summary is as long as it *needs* to be in order to fulfill a given purpose. It may be objective and analytic or subjective and interpretive, again depending on the purpose. You may not want to intrude any judgments or comments on the work, but simply to tell it as it is—in brief space.

Generally, it is preferable to weave into the recital of bare facts an interpretive description of the work's underlying logic and theme. You will not usually summarize just to summarize but rather to provide plot background for a literary review or literary analysis.

In such cases the length of the plot summary will vary according to how important plot is in the development of your main theme, how much space you have available, and how much plot you are working with. Some stories have weak, virtually nonexistent plots, as the writer of the following summary notes:

> *Adolphe,* a romance by Benjamin Constant. The story has very little incident or action. The whole plot may be summed up in a few words: Adolphe loves Eleonore, and can be happy neither with her nor without her. The beauty of the author's style and the keenness and delicacy with which he analyzes certain morbid moods of the soul have placed this work among the masterpieces of French literature. The romance is almost universally believed to be an autobiography, in which Constant narrates a portion of the adventures of his own youth.

A summary that provides a background for a literary paper should not merely recite happenings ("first this happened, then this, then this"). Rather, it should explain *why* things happen as they do, how events are significant, and how they contribute to the pattern of the total work. The literary plot summary, in other words, should go beyond the superficial story line to analysis and interpretation. In such a summary you weave in your own view of the plot even as you recount the bare facts.

SUMMARIZING EVENTS

As mentioned earlier, the weekly news magazines and the "Week in Review" section of the Sunday *New York Times* are devoted specifically to summarizing events in time—a week, a month, or more. A presentation of highlights in relation to the broad sweep of events is fundamental to a good "capsule" summary of the news, a form that helps busy readers find out quickly what is happening or what has happened in the world.

The following ambitious summary, for example, attempts to touch upon major historic events, "surprises," and trends during the first sixty years of this century. Note that the writer sums up the past decade in a single term: "paradox."

THE PARADOX OF THE SIXTIES

James Reston

> This has been a century of stunning surprises, yet the resident seers and magicians here seem to think the seventies will be menacing but manageable. It is a puzzler. The mood of the capital about present problems is pessimistic, but the forecasts for the coming decade are fairly optimistic.
>
> No major war, retreat from Vietnam, probably a controlled war in the Middle East with the big powers on the sidelines, endless local and tribal conflict in Africa and maybe even in Latin America, more spheres of influence or Monroe Doctrines for the Soviet Union in Eastern Europe and for China in Southeast Asia; more people, more inflation, more trouble—in short, more of the same—but nothing apocalyptic. This seems to be the forecast of many thoughtful people in the capital.
>
> **The Historical Record**
>
> There is very little in the history of these last sixty years to justify this assumption that the human race has run out of spectacular stupidities. These sixty

years started with the decline of the British and French and ended with the triumph of the Mets—with two tragic wars and endless barbarities and futilities in between.

Herman Kahn and Anthony J. Wiener have kept the boxscore on the astounding surprises that took place in the first and second thirds of the century. It started, they note, with parliamentary democracy in pretty good shape, and Christianity on the rise. The Western world felt fairly optimistic and secure. Then in the first third of the century, the following:

The Russo-Japanese War; the First World War, which devastated Europe; the collapse of the five major dynasties (Hohenzollern, Habsburg, Manchu, Romanov and Ottoman); the rise of Communism and the Soviet Union and Fascism; the Great Depression; and the intellectual influence of Bohr, de Broglie, Einstein and Freud.

The Big Surprises

The second third of the century produced even more surprises: The Second World War; mass murders and evacuations beyond all previous dreams of human depravity; the collapse of the old empires; the reunification and centralization of China and its development of nuclear weapons; the emergence of two superpowers (the U.S. and the U.S.S.R), five large powers (Japan, West Germany, France, China and Britain); the new confrontation of Washington and Moscow in the cold war; and the emergence of new techniques, new post-Keynesian and post-Marxian economic theories.

Why, then, after all these apocalyptic events—why now when Washington is depressed about its frustrations over Vietnam, inflation, the blacks, the rebellious university whites—should thoughtful men and women here be taking a comparatively calm and even optimistic view of the seventies?

The Major Trends

Maybe it is merely wishful thinking or lack of imagination, and maybe the optimists are wrong, for there are many others who think the country and the world are hopelessly lost and divided and headed for chaos. But this does not seem to be the view of most reflective and experienced minds in the capital.

In fact, the majority seems to be suggesting that the sixties, for all the violence, defiance and confusion, were just violent and defiant and confused enough to force a reappraisal of past assumptions, and make the major powers think about adopting new attitudes and policies in defense of their vital interests.

Within their own geographical spheres of influence, the great powers are still demanding control, and in contested areas like the Middle East, they are still competing for influence in the most dangerous way, but on the big questions, which could produce a world and nuclear war, they are finally talking with a little more common sense.

The major trends elsewhere are also a little more rational. Europe is talking seriously again about cooperation and even economic integration; the war in Vietnam is not escalating but de-escalating; the Soviet Union is just worried enough about China's belligerent tone to reduce tensions in the West and avoid trouble on both fronts at the same time.

Accordingly, at least some observers think they see a new balance of power developing at the turn of the decade. The Congress is challenging the President's right to make war as he chooses; the Communist parties of the world are challenging Moscow's use of power against Czechoslovakia; the militant blacks and militant students in the United States are finding that violence by the minority produced counterviolence by the white majority.

So while all these struggles still go on, there is a feeling here that maybe they can be contained in the seventies, mainly because we learned in the sixties that violence doesn't always pay off, either at home or abroad.

DISCUSSION AND EXERCISES

1. *Summarizing Ideas.* In a paragraph of no more than 200 words sum up each of the following:
   a. Allen Gilbert's argument for abolishing college lectures (see "College Lectures Are Obsolete").
   b. "Sweet Truths About Sugar".
   c. One of the reviews in Question 19.
   d. One of the "functions" in Question 8.

2. *Summarizing Plot.* In a paragraph of 100-150 words summarize James Joyce's short story "Clay."

ESSAY SUGGESTIONS

1. Write an essay (750-1,000 words) in which you summarize the ideas presented in one of the essays in this book and comment on them (let half the essay be summary, the other half comment).

2. Write an essay (750-1,000 words) in which you summarize the plot of a short story, novel, play, film, or television drama; follow your summary with a two-paragraph evaluation (see Question 19, What is the value of X?).

3. Write an essay (750-1,000 words) summarizing events of the 1970s or the 1980s. As Reston characterizes the sixties (the decade is summed up in the term "paradox") try to find a word or phrase that will characterize each decade. You may want to attempt a comparison of the two decades. (See Question 15, How Does X Compare to Y?)

Question

18

HOW SHOULD X
BE INTERPRETED?

INTERPRETING AN ACTIVITY
  FOOTBALL—THE GAME OF AGGRESSION,
    GEORGE STADE

INTERPRETING BEHAVIOR
  HALLOWED BE THE MALL, KENNETH COLE

INTERPRETING A STORY
  CLAY, JAMES JOYCE
  INTERPRETATION OF JOYCE'S "CLAY,"
    FLORENCE L. WALZL

INTERPRETING A POEM
  ANYONE LIVED IN A PRETTY HOW TOWN,
    E. E. CUMMINGS
  *AN INTERPRETATION OF CUMMINGS' "ANYONE
  LIVED IN A PRETTY HOW TOWN,"*
    R. W. STALLMAN
  ADDITIONAL POEMS
    WINTER TREES, SYLVIA PLATH
    YOUR DEPARTURE VERSUS THE HINDENBURG,
      RICHARD BRAUTIGAN

INTERPRETING POPULAR CULTURE
  HONKY TONKING, MOLLY IVINS

Beyond definition, description, and analysis—and to a large extent dependent on these basic processes—is the more subtle business of interpretation, of explaining what is not immediately apparent; of taking facts and going beyond them to discover the deeper meaning or significance of a subject, the relationship of particulars to a general principle, the truth that lies beneath the surface.

INTERPRETING AN ACTIVITY

Take the subject of football, for example. On the face of it, football is simply a popular spectator sport, a national pastime, a "he-man" game filled with action and excitement. On a deeper level, however—as the writer of the following essay points out—football is more than a game. It is an acting-out of a basic and primitive human compulsion to gain and hold on to property. Note how the writer supports his interpretation by providing explicit facts about the game on the basis of an implicit general principle.

FOOTBALL—THE GAME OF AGGRESSION

George Stade

There are many ways in which professional football is unique among sports, and as many others in which it is the fullest expression of what is at the heart of all sports. There is no other major sport so dependent upon raw force, nor any so dependent on a complex and delicate strategy; none so wide in the range of specialized functions demanded from its players; none so dependent upon the undifferentiated athletic *sine qua non,* a quickwitted body; none so primitive; none so futuristic; none so American.

Football is first of all a form of play, something one engages in instinctively and only for the sake of performing the activity in question. Among forms of play, football is a game, which means that it is built on communal needs, rather than on private evasions, like mountain climbing. Among games it is a sport; it requires athletic ability, unlike croquet. And among sports, it is one whose mode is violence and whose violence is its special glory.

In some sports—basketball, baseball, soccer—violence is occasional (and usually illegal); in others, like hockey, it is incidental; in others still, car racing, for example, it is accidental. Definitive violence football shares alone with boxing and bullfighting, among major sports. But in bullfighting a man is pitted not against another man, but against an animal, and boxing is a competition between individuals, not teams, and that makes a great difference. If shame is the proper and usual penalty for failures in sporting competitions between individuals, guilt is the consequence of failing not only oneself and one's fans, but also one's teammates. Failure in football, moreover, seems more related to a failure of courage, seems more unmanning than in any other sport outside of bullfighting. In other sports one loses a knack, is outsmarted, or is merely inferior in ability, but in football, on top of these, a player fails because he "lacks desire," or "can't take it anymore," or "hears footsteps," as his teammates will put it.

Many sports, especially those in which there is a goal to be defended, seem enactments of the games animals play under the stimulus of what ethologists, students of animal behavior, call *territory* "the drive to gain, maintain, and defend the exclusive right to a piece of property," as Robert Ardrey puts it. The most striking symptom of this drive is aggressiveness, but among social animals, such as primates, it leads to "amity for the social partner, hostility for the territorial neighbor." The territorial instinct is closely related to whatever makes animals establish pecking orders: the tangible sign of one's status within the orders is the size and value of the territory one is able to command. Individuals fight over status, groups over *lebensraum* and a bit more. These instincts, some ethologists have claimed, are behind patriotism and private property, and also, I would add, codes of honor, as among ancient Greeks, modern Sicilians, primitive hunters, teen-age gangs, soldiers, aristocrats, and athletes, especially football players.

The territorial basis of certain kinds of sports is closest to the surface in football, whose plays are all attempts to gain and defend property through aggression. Does this not make football *par excellence* the game of instinctual satisfactions, especially among Americans, who are notorious as violent patriots and instinctive defenders of private property? (At the same time, in football this drive is more elaborated than in other sports by whatever turns instinct into art; football is more richly patterned, more formal, more complex in the functions of its parts, which makes football *par excellence* the game of esthetic satisfactions.) Even the unusual amity, if that is the word, that exists among football players has been remarked upon, notably by Norman Mailer. And what is it that corresponds in football to the various feathers, furs, fins, gorgeous colors by means of which animals puff themselves into exaggerated gestures of masculine potency? The football player's equipment, of course. His cleats raise him an inch off the ground. Knee and thigh pads thrust the force lines of his legs forward. His pants are tight against his rump and the back of his thighs, portions of his body which the requirements of the game stuff with muscle. Even the tubby guard looks slim of waist by comparison with his shoulders, extended half a foot on each side by padding. Finally the helmet, which from the esthetic point of view most clearly expresses the genius of the sport. Not only does the helmet make the player inches taller and give his head a size proportionate to the rest of him; it makes him anonymous, inscrutable, more serviceable as a symbol. The football player in uniform strikes the eye in a succession of gestalt shifts: first a hooded phantom out of the paleolithic past of the species; then a premonition of a future of spacemen.

In sum, and I am almost serious about this, football players are to America what tragic actors were to ancient Athens and gladiators to Rome: models of perennially heroic, aggressive, violent humanity, but adapted to the social realities of the times and places that formed them.

INTERPRETING BEHAVIOR

Probe beneath the surface of most human activities and you often uncover a wonderland worthy of Alice's journey behind the looking-glass. Our next writer, for instance, cites a college professor whose studies in religion and American culture led him to suggest that the modern shopping mall is the new religious and ceremonial center of urban America. Professor Ira Zepp calls the mall a "camouflage for the sacred" in modern life and substantiates his case by tracing the similarities between a typical mall and a Gothic cathedral.

Both, he tells us, have a common architectural layout, a common sense of sacred time and place, and a common function within the surrounding community. While not concealing the mall's shortcomings, Zepp offers an interpretation that may explain why all of us—young and old, rich and poor, student and teacher—"go there in droves."

Based on an interview, this essay maintains the reader's attention while probing deeper levels of meaning, for Kenneth Cole practices what one editor referred to as the writer's third law: "always tell a story." (The first law is "be concrete and precise," and the second is "pay attention to the sound of language.") Although the essay concerns ideas, it tracks, in narrative fashion, the evolution of Zepp's thinking: his early observations of malls, why he studied them, what his research revealed, how one insight generated others. Cole's questioning tone and insistent repetition of the phrase "a religious space" reflect a natural and ongoing incredulity that a shopping center might be fulfilling a spiritual function. We read on in some suspense. Will the thesis hold? The journey of the mind to understanding human behavior is no less an adventure for being internal, inward.

Hallowed Be the Mall

Kenneth Cole

Not long ago Ira G. Zepp Jr., a cheery-faced, bearded professor of religious studies at Western Maryland College, observed that the shopping mall—that most popular and familiar of modern marketplaces—was more than a mere commercial center. Detecting a similarity between "going uptown" on a Saturday night years ago in his hometown of Bel Air, Md., and "hanging out at the mall," he came to believe that malls are essentially small-town America gussied up—roofed over, air-conditioned, planted with trees and shrubs, hung with paintings, graced with sculptures, and protected by guards.

That observation led to still another. Intrigued that some 3,000 malls have sprung up since the 1956 opening of Northfield Mall in suburban Minneapolis, and that in 1985 shoppers purchased over $600 billion of goods in malls and shopping centers (over 50 percent of retail sales), and still further that Americans spend more time in malls than anywhere else except the home, workplace, and school, Zepp toured the country visiting and studying malls, some forty in all. For all their brassy materialism, he concluded after his travels, malls are more than shopping complexes: in essence, they satisfy a religious dimension of human experience and serve as a "camouflage of the sacred" in modern life. A mall is, in short, a religious space.

Zepp qualifies somewhat his use of the word *religious*. A Methodist minister trained at the Drew Theological School who did his Ph.D. study in the history of religion, Zepp doesn't use *religious* to refer to piety, faith in a supreme being, or adherence to a particular dogma, church, or denomination. Rather, he concerns himself with *homo-religiosus*, that is, the religious person in us, our tendency to embody the "religious impulse to center and order life, to invoke community and otherness by way of crosses and squares and circles, to create festivity and to play, to ritualize and symbolize life."

Since Zepp sees precisely that religious dimension in malls, he underscores their role as that "camouflage of the sacred." As he relates in his book, *The New*

Religious Image of Urban America: The Shopping Mall as Ceremonial Center, malls and outdoor festival marketplaces are an updated incarnation of the Gothic market-town cathedral, a place that is "interchangeably and simultaneously a ceremonial center, an alternative community, a carnival, and a secular cathedral."

A religious space.

Zepp's discovery of that parallel to Gothic cathedrals provided the first clue to the mall's religious dimension. A student of the work of Mircea Eliade, a world-renowned historian of religions, Zepp followed Eliade's contention that manifestations of the sacred occur everywhere and can involve any human activity. For instance, the ceremonial laying of a cornerstone replicates ancient rites in which priests dedicated a city square or temple as the *omphalos,* or world navel. Power from the sacred realm entered the profane world of everyday life through the *omphalos.*

"As I was looking at malls and visiting them," Zepp explains, "I happened to see there certain patterns and images that reflected some of Eliade's grand models. I had some students work with me, studying the malls and interviewing people." He tested his thesis first in his column for the local newspaper and then with a monograph on the *Sacred Places of Westminster,* about the natural and secular symbols and areas in and around the town where Western Maryland is located.

His study is the first to examine malls from the perspective of the phenomenology of religion, and he launched into it by "suspending judgment and values and trying to find the human intention." He looked at the shape and structure of malls, at their planned activities, their art and decoration, their use of time and space, and their social structure and implications.

"It's a human impulse to symbolize life, and to recognize in those symbols a sense of who we are," says Zepp. "Whenever this happens, it's a religious activity. I believe one of the reasons malls have grown rapidly and their popularity [has] increased is that they fulfill our need for order and orientation. Malls mean centering," particularly in those commuter developments and suburbs that often have no natural center or square.

Malls perform that centering duty in their circular or centering architecture that serves as a small-scale capitol or temple to collect power from the four compass points, the zenith, and the nadir, contends Zepp. This "architectural rhetoric" duplicates that of the medieval cathedrals, down to the use of cardinal axiology. As with the cathedrals, such architectural rhetoric is a sign of cosmological ordering.

"The design and layout of most modern shopping malls is a 'secular' version of the ancient prototype," says Zepp. "The quadrilateral design establishes the mall as a sacred space and assimilates and brings together all the surrounding territory."

And as with other sacred spaces, important symbols enhance the center: fountains (water of life); trees, shrubs, flowers, and plants (the cosmic tree); skylights and lamps (the lighted center of a monastery or stained glass illuminating the altar); and food courts (the bread of life).

"I'm not certain whether the developer or architect or customer or clerk is altogether conscious of it," he says, "but the centeredness of the mall is a way most of us find a certain microcosmic reflection of the world. The theory is that a square or circle or cross is a way of saying life is fundamentally safe. It's a miniaturization of the universe."

And with festivals and special events, malls also provide a sense of sacred time to correspond to the sacred space. In doing so, they promote a sense of community.

"Most malls are very sensitive to the community in which they reside, finally for profit, of course," Zepp says. "But there is a sensitivity to provide festive occasions for the community. They usually follow the religious seasons as well as the national seasons." For example, the huge Columbia (Md.) Mall each winter allows the local girl scouts in for a sleep-over; or there's the "Eggs-hibition" at Dallas's Galleria, a decorating contest and show of ostrich eggs each Easter and of course the usual Christmas promotions. Activities range from fund-raising events to concerts and programs highlighting service clubs to performances by local youth groups.

Thus malls reflect another characteristic of medieval cathedrals, that of a festival center. Zepp notes this tendency to festivity in the developers' move from constructing huge buildings to the creation of festival marketplaces, such as Baltimore's Harborplace, New York City's South Street Seaport, Norfolk's Waterside, and Boston's Faneuil Hall, all projects by James Rouse.

Art is another part of the mall's culture package. As Zepp points out, most malls have a major artwork as their centerpiece, whether it's Alexander Calder's mobile in Long Island's Smith Haven Mall, the big clock in Dallas's Prestonwood, the Japanese gardens in Los Angeles' Fox Hills Mall, the massive eagle of the CrossRoads Mall in Boulder, Colo., and even the abstract work reminiscent of whales' tails in the Livingston Mall.

"Every mall tends to have its own unique piece," Zepp says, "It's very interesting that the malls have attracted and commissioned this kind of work. People who would not go to a museum to see abstract art are compelled to look at it in malls, and the malls can get away with it. Of course, malls usually have more traditional art or crafts exhibitions about twice a year."

All these factors plus the sensuous display of merchandise have made malls a preferred gathering place. Studies by mall developers show that 40 percent of the people who go to malls never intend to purchase anything. And although merchandising is aimed at customers 25-50 years of age, the mall has become a favorite sanctuary for teenagers and old people. According to Zepp's interviews, teenagers visit in the evenings, and the elderly in the morning.

For the old, safety is a major attraction. Very little violent crime occurs in malls, and, as Zepp learned from a man in St. Petersburg, Fla., the mall is a place for older men to meet other men, to stroll measured miles or play checkers, and to reminisce while their wives shop—an updated version of the pot-bellied stove and cracker barrel in the local general store.

For teenagers, malls become a haven to enact the rituals of courtship, test independence, and sample the forbidden—all out of sight of parents but within a safe arena. "Meetcha at the mall," a phrase born at the youth-oriented Cherry Hill (N.J.) Mall, has become code for youthful mobility and initiation.

A Religious Space?

Zepp traces some of the mall's religious meaning to James Rouse, the most innovative and influential developer of malls and festival marketplaces. A highly successful planner, Rouse is what Zeppe terms the "mahatma of malls," and Rouse's philosophy of development, it happens, has an overtly religious impulse.

"Rouse belongs to the Church of the Savior in Washington, D.C." Zepp explains. "It's one of those small, committed Christian communities who mean business. You have to take two years of study, at least tithe, and give so many hours a week in community service. You have to be involved.

"Part of Rouse's acceptance as a member involved study of a book by Paul Jones, and what turned him on was Jones' phrase, 'co-creativity with God.' There was this whole liberal impulse coming out of his study that sent Rouse into trying to create 'people places.' Rouse has a real religious tone in what he says and writes about his work. It's not sectarian, but he clearly intended to build places where people feel at home and safe and welcome—places where people come first and not profits."

Zepp is quick to point out that Rouse, now retired and constructing festival areas whose profits go to low-income housing, intended to make a profit but created commercial complexes that became community centers.

Malls are not perfect, Zepp concedes. They don't overcome racial housing patterns and are generally a middle- and upper-class institution.

"There is a problem with racial discrimination based on economic discrimination," he says. "The mall is a mostly white institution. You do find some exceptions, such as the Mondawmin Mall in Baltimore, which is located in the black community and oriented toward it. But it's safe to say that poor people wouldn't feel at home in a mall." Zepp contends that tendency stems from the country's pattern of racism. During his hometown's Saturday nights years ago, blacks were not visible either, despite a small black community only two or three blocks from the center of Bel Air.

Then, too, while malls provide community focus, they don't naturally establish it. Their atmosphere is often too antiseptic, and, to an extent, the community created is not very social or organic. Furthermore, as Zepp puts it, "The malling of America becomes the mauling of communities." The cost of recreating small, plant-dominated environments inside a mall comes at the cost of destroying huge tracts of land for the building and its parking lot.

Even so, Zepp believes malls are generally inclusive. A few malls are designed for an elite clientele and carry expensive goods—among them the Mall at Short Hills, N.J., or Phipps Plaza in Atlanta—but the "vast majority of malls are middle-class, egalitarian, and democratic. Shopping is a democratic activity."

Yet malls are not a church, and the religious meanings of a mall's structure and organization are a far cry from those of the liturgy and sacraments. What does the rise of the mall as America's new religious image say about the church?

"Churches and religions reflect this same impulse, but perhaps our people have lost the inner meaning of some of those symbols and narrowed them and maybe even trivialized them. Malls highlight the loss of more traditional symbols and paradigms. In my own life, Eliade opened up some of the meanings of the more sectarian symbols in ways I'd never understood before."

Even religion can become idolatrous, says Zepp, by which he means that religion and its symbols come to reflect more the desire to rigidify meaning and narrow the gospel's role in the world than they do the desire to welcome interpretation and foster engagement in the world.

Now at work on a book about Martin Luther King, Jr., the subject of his Ph.D. dissertation and a previously published book, Zepp remains intrigued with malls as an institution of enduring power.

"One of the things that attracted me to this study was the sense of human community there. It certainly isn't an organic, dynamic community coming out of residence—like the Bel Air, Md., of my youth—but it may be the only alternative that suburban and urban people have today. And we go there in droves."

INTERPRETING A STORY

If analysis breaks down a subject, interpretation puts it together. To formulate a convincing interpretation, the writer must see the scattered parts of a subject as contributing on a deeper level to a unified whole. Seen in this light, all of literary criticism involves interpretation, a probing into the individual elements of a poem or story to see how they are related to one another and to the whole. What is the writer trying to tell us beyond the surface details? What larger statement is he or she making? How do the single details contribute to the statement? All of literature, like most other human activities, lends itself to interpretation. Take a relatively simple, seemingly pointless short story such as the following, and then judge one critic's interpretation of what the surface details add up to.

Clay

James Joyce

The matron had given her leave to go out as soon as the women's tea was over and Maria looked forward to her evening out. The kitchen was spick and span: the cook said you could see yourself in the big copper boilers. The fire was nice and bright and on one of the side-tables were four very big barmbracks. These barmbracks seemed uncut; but if you went closer you would see that they had been cut into long thick even slices and were ready to be handed round at tea. Maria had cut them herself.

Maria was a very, very small person indeed but she had a very long nose and a very long chin. She talked a little through her nose, always soothingly: *"Yes, my dear,"* and *"No, my dear."* She was always sent for when the women quarrelled over their tubs and always succeeded in making peace. One day the matron had said to her:

"Maria, you are a veritable peace-maker!"

And the sub-matron and two of the Board ladies had heard the compliment. And Ginger Mooney was always saying what she wouldn't do to the dummy who had charge of the irons if it wasn't for Maria. Everyone was so fond of Maria.

The women would have their tea at six o'clock and she would be able to get away before seven. From Ballsbridge to the Pillar, twenty minutes; from the Pillar to Drumcondra, twenty minutes; and twenty minutes to buy the things. She would be there before eight. She took out her purse with the silver clasps and read again the words *A Present from Belfast*. She was very fond of the purse because Joe had brought it to her five years before when he and Alphy had gone to Belfast on a Whit-Monday trip. In the purse were two half-crowns and some coppers. She would have five shillings clear after paying tram fare. What a nice evening they would have, all the children singing! Only she hoped that Joe wouldn't come in drunk. He was so different when he took any drink.

Often he had wanted her to go and live with them; but she would have felt herself in the way (though Joe's wife was ever so nice with her), and she had become accustomed to the life of the laundry. Joe was a good fellow. She had nursed him and Alphy too; and Joe used often say:

"Mamma is mamma but Maria is my proper mother."

After the break-up at home the boys had got her that position in the *Dublin by Lamplight* laundry, and she liked it. She used to have such a bad opinion of Protestants but now she thought they were very nice people, a little quiet and serious, but still very nice people to live with. Then she had her plants in the conservatory and she liked looking after them. She had lovely ferns and wax-plants and, whenever anyone came to visit her, she always gave the visitor one or two slips from her conservatory. There was one thing she didn't like and that was the tracts on the walks; but the matron was such a nice person to deal with, so genteel.

When the cook told her everything was ready she went into the women's room and began to pull the big bell. In a few minutes the women began to come in by twos and threes, wiping their steaming hands in their petticoats and pulling down the sleeves of their blouses over their red steaming arms. They settled down before their huge mugs which the cook and the dummy filled up with hot tea, already mixed with milk and sugar in huge tin cans. Maria superintended the distribution of the barmbrack and saw that every woman got her four slices. There was a great deal of laughing and joking during the meal. Lizzie Fleming said Maria was sure to get the ring and, though Fleming had said that for so many Hallow Eves, Maria had to laugh and say she didn't want any ring or man either; and when she laughed her grey-green eyes sparkled with disappointed shyness and the tip of her nose nearly met the tip of her chin. Then Ginger Mooney lifted up her mug of tea and proposed Maria's health while all the other women clattered with their mugs on the table, and said she was sorry she hadn't a sup of porter to drink it in. And Maria laughed again till the tip of her nose nearly met the tip of her chin and till her minute body nearly shook itself asunder because she knew that Mooney meant well though, of course, she had the notions of a common woman.

But wasn't Maria glad when the women had finished their tea and the cook and the dummy had begun to clear away the tea-things! She went into her little bedroom and, remembering that the next morning was a mass morning, changed the hand of the alarm from seven to six. Then she took off her working skirt and her house-boots and laid her best skirt out on the bed and her tiny dress-boots beside the foot of the bed. She changed her blouse too and, as she stood before the mirror, she thought of how she used to dress for mass on Sunday morning when she was a young girl; and she looked with quaint affection at the diminutive body which she had so often adorned. In spite of its years she found it a nice tidy little body.

When she got outside the streets were shining with rain and she was glad of her old brown waterproof. The tram was full and she had to sit on the little stool at the end of the car, facing all the people, with her toes barely touching the floor.

She arranged in her mind all she was going to do and thought how much better it was to be independent and to have your own money in your pocket. She hoped they would have a nice evening. She was sure they would but she could not help thinking what a pity it was Alphy and Joe were not speaking. They were always falling out now but when they were boys together they used to be the best of friends: but such was life.

She got out of her tram at the Pillar and ferreted her way quickly among the crowds. She went into Downes's cake-shop but the shop was so full of people that it was a long time before she could get herself attended to. She bought a dozen of mixed penny cakes, and at last came out of the shop laden with a big bag. Then she thought what else would she buy: she wanted to buy something really nice. They would be sure to have plenty of apples and nuts. It was hard to know what to buy and all she could think of was cake. She decided to buy some plumcake but Downes's plumcake had not enough almond icing on top of it so she went over to a shop in Henry Street. Here she was a long time in suiting herself and the stylish young lady behind the counter, who was evidently a little annoyed by her, asked her was it wedding-cake she wanted to buy. That made Maria blush and smile at the young lady; but the young lady took it all very seriously and finally cut a thick slice of plumcake, parcelled it up and said:

"Two-and-four, please."

She thought she would have to stand in the Drumcondra tram because none of the young men seemed to notice her but an elderly gentleman made room for her. He was a stout gentleman and he wore a brown hard hat; he had a square red face and a greyish moustache. Maria thought he was a colonel-looking gentleman and she reflected how much more polite he was than the young men who simply stared straight before them. The gentleman began to chat with her about Hallow Eve and the rainy weather. He supposed the bag was full of good things for the little ones and said it was only right that the youngsters should enjoy themselves while they were young. Maria agreed with him and favoured him with demure nods and hems. He was very nice with her, and when she was getting out at the Canal Bridge she thanked him and bowed, and he bowed to her and raised his hat and smiled agreeably; and while she was going up along the terrace, bending her tiny head under the rain, she thought how easy it was to know a gentleman even when he has a drop taken.

Everybody said: *"O, here's Maria!"* when she came to Joe's house. Joe was there, having come home from business, and all the children had their Sunday dresses on. There were two big girls in from next door and games were going on. Maria gave the bag of cakes to the eldest boy, Alphy, to divide and Mrs. Donnelly said it was too good of her to bring such a big bag of cakes and made all the children say:

"Thanks, Maria."

But Maria said she had brought something special for papa and mamma, something they would be sure to like, and she began to look for her plumcake. She tried in Downes's bag and then in the pockets of her waterproof and then on the hallstand but nowhere could she find it. Then she asked all the children had any of them eaten it—by mistake, of course—but the children all said no and looked as if they did not like to eat cakes if they were to be accused of stealing. Everybody had a solution for the mystery and Mrs. Donnelly said it was plain that Maria had left it behind her in the tram. Maria, remembering how confused the gentleman with the greyish moustache had made her, coloured with shame and vexation and disappointment. At the thought of the failure of her little surprise and of the two and fourpence she had thrown away for nothing she nearly cried outright.

But Joe said it didn't matter and made her sit down by the fire. He was very nice with her. He told her all that went on in his office, repeating for her a smart answer which he had made to the manager. Maria did not understand why Joe laughed so much over the answer he had made but she said that the manager must have been a very overbearing person to deal with. Joe said he wasn't so bad when you knew how to take him, that he was a decent sort so long as you didn't rub him the wrong way. Mrs. Donnelly played the piano for the children and they danced and sang. Then the two next-door girls handed round the nuts. Nobody could find the nutcrackers and Joe was nearly getting cross over it and asked how did they expect Maria to crack nuts without a nutcracker. But Maria said she didn't like nuts and that they weren't to bother about her. Then Joe asked would she take a bottle of stout and Mrs. Donnelly said there was port wine too in the house if she would prefer that. Maria said she would rather they didn't ask her to take anything: but Joe insisted.

So Maria let him have his way and they sat by the fire talking over old times and Maria thought she would put in a good word for Alphy. But Joe cried that God might strike him stone dead if ever he spoke a word to his brother again and Maria said she was sorry she had mentioned the matter. Mrs. Donnelly told her husband it was a great shame for him to speak that way of his own flesh and blood but Joe said that Alphy was no brother of his and there was nearly being a row on the head of it. But Joe said he would not lose his temper on account of the night it was and asked his wife to open some more stout. The two next-door girls had arranged some Hallow Eve games and soon everything was merry again. Maria was delighted to see the children so merry and Joe and his wife in such good spirits. The next-door girls put some saucers on the table and then led the children up to the table, blindfold. One got the prayer-book and the other three got the water; and when one of the next-door girls got the ring Mrs. Donnelly shook her finger at the blushing girl as much as to say: *O, I know all about it!* They insisted then on blindfolding Maria and leading her up to the table to see what she would get; and, while they were putting on the bandage, Maria laughed and laughed again till the tip of her nose nearly met the tip of her chin.

They led her up to the table amid laughing and joking and she put her hand out in the air as she was told to do. She moved her hand about here and there in the air and descended on one of the saucers. She felt a soft wet substance with her fingers and was surprised that nobody spoke or took off her bandage. There was a pause for a few seconds; and then a great deal of scuffling and whispering. Somebody said something about the garden, and at last Mrs. Donnelly said something very cross to one of the next-door girls and told her to throw it out at once: that was no play. Maria understood that it was wrong that time and so she had to do it over again: and this time she got the prayer-book.

After that Mrs. Donnelly played Miss McCloud's Reel for the children and Joe made Maria take a glass of wine. Soon they were all quite merry again and Mrs. Donnelly said Maria would enter a convent before the year was out because she had got the prayer-book. Maria had never seen Joe so nice to her as he was that night, so full of pleasant talk and reminiscences. She said they were all very good to her.

At last the children grew tired and sleepy and Joe asked Maria would she not sing some little song before she went, one of the old songs. Mrs. Donnelly said *"Do, please, Maria!"* and so Maria had to get up and stand beside the piano. Mrs. Donnelly bade the children be quiet and listen to Maria's song. Then she played the prelude and said *"Now, Maria!"* and Maria, blushing very much, began to sing in a tiny quavering voice. She sang *I Dreamt that I Dwelt,* and when she came to the second verse she sang again:

> *I dreamt that I dwelt in marble halls*
> *With vassals and serfs at my side,*
> *And of all who assembled within those walls*
> *That I was the hope and the pride.*
> *I had riches too great to count; could boast*
> *Of a high ancestral name,*
> *But I also dreamt, which pleased me most,*
> *That you loved me still the same.*

But no one tried to show her her mistake; and when she had ended her song Joe was very much moved. He said that there was no time like the long ago and no music for him like poor old Balfe, whatever other people might say; and his eyes filled up so much with tears that he could not find what he was looking for and in the end he had to ask his wife to tell him where the corkscrew was.

Interpretation of Joyce's "Clay"

Florence L. Walzl

Conflicting elements in Maria, the heroine of James Joyce's "Clay" in *Dubliners,* have led to contradictory interpretations of the character: as saint (William T. Noon, "Joyce's 'Clay': An Interpretation," *College English,* xvii, 1955, 93-95); as thematically disunified combination of laundress, witch, and Virgin Mary figure (Marvin Magalaner and Richard M. Kain, *Joyce: The Man, The Work, The Reputation,* New York, 1956, 84-91); and as unconsciously selfish troublemaker (Richard Carpenter and Daniel Leary, "The Witch Maria," *James Joyce Review,* iii, 1959, 3-7). I believe "Clay" is a thematic whole based on a set of contrasts relating to the two church holidays which provide the setting and to the two fortunes the heroine receives in a fortune-telling game.

The setting is Halloween, the night in folk tradition when the dead walk, and (by the anticipation of the heroine) All Saints' Day, a feast honoring all the blessed, both those proclaimed publicly in canonization and those completely unknown to the world. The fact that it celebrates, especially, the unheralded saints of ordinary life has a thematic relationship to the story, as does the walking abroad of spirits on All Hallows' Eve.

The plot of "Clay" is simple. A middle-aged spinster named Maria, a humble kitchen worker in a laundry, spends Halloween with a family, perhaps relatives, for whom she has been nursemaid. While blindfolded in a game of fortunes, she chooses the clay portending death. Her friends quickly hide this choice from her and substitute a prayer-book prophetic of a future convent life. The pathos is deepened by the contrast between the emptiness and futility of her life as it is and as it might have been. For this little laundress has the potential qualities of ideal woman and mother but their development has been stunted by the circumstances of her life.

In a sense, there are two Marias in this story: the Maria of the laundry and the Maria of the Halloween excursion. Within the confines of the laundry, several of Maria's qualities, her goodness, peaceableness, and loving motherliness, are greatly stressed. Both as a worker and a person her goodness is evident. She labors to make the scullery of the laundry a pleasant happy place: the kitchen is "spick and span," the fire "nice and bright," the barmbracks perfectly cut, the plants well-kept. She sees that each laundress is well served at teatime. She spends her hard-earned money buying cakes for the children of the family and plumcake for their elders. Much also is made of her peaceableness. "She was always sent for when the women quarrelled over their tubs and always succeeded in making peace." She always thinks the best of people. The matron of the laundry calls her a veritable peace-maker." Finally, she is loving and motherly. She evokes the affection of the rough washerwomen who all are "so fond of Maria." She likes to recall the children she formerly nursed who called her their "proper mother." She looks forward happily to the family evening with "all the children singing." Even her name suggests the Church's prototype of the ideal maid and mother in the Virgin Mary. This Maria with her alarm clock set for the early morning mass of All Saints' Day suggests the very kind of saint this feast was inaugurated to honor.

But Maria on her Halloween visitation seems quite different. Though her goodness and generosity within the rounds of the laundry are effective, outside it they are not. In her timidity and lack of experience she loses the plumcake that was to have been her gift to the family and irritates the children over its loss. Moreover, her very presence upsets the adults because they feel the pathos of her life. At one point, Joe's eyes so fill with tears that he cannot find the corkscrew for the family toast. Her peaceableness, which is so marked within the laundry, is also ineffective without. She annoys the salesgirl in the bakeshop, is unable to heal the breach between the two brothers, and unwittingly provokes three near-quarrels: over Alphy, over some nuts, and over her choice of the clay. Also the emotional frustration of her life and its lack of human love are emphasized. Through a series of incidents suggesting romance, Joyce indicates that romantic and maternal love remain undeveloped in Maria. The laundresses' teasing about the ring, the shop girls suggestion that the plumcake is for a wedding, the gallantry of the gentleman in the tram, and, above all, the verse from "I Dreamt That I Dwelt in Marble Halls" Maria forgets, a verse dealing with marriage proposals—all remind us of the sterility of her life. Finally, her appearance is that of "a very, very small person" with a "very long nose and a very long chin" which nearly meet. This Maria, ineffectual and trouble-making, suggests a Halloween witch.

What is Joyce's intent in this contrast which suggests saint and witch, life and death? I believe the answer is suggested in part by the two fortunes Maria receives at the party, the prayerbook and the clay—the first thematically associated with the saints' day, the second with the Halloween spirits. Both represent her future; both are death symbols.

The prayerbook, the fortune contrived by the family and forced upon her, is her immediate future, the life Irish society has molded for Maria. (In fact, her laundry job had been arranged for her by the family.) Her life in the laundry is a convent-like existence of narrow piety and goodness but without spiritual elevation, a life of small endeavors spent among women of a low class. Yet Maria had the potentialities for being the kind of heroic woman of full experience sainthood implies. . . .

Her hidden fortune, the clay, prophetic of death, suggests all that the ultimate future holds for her. In combination with Joyce's description of her as a Halloween wraith, it probably suggests also that she is not fully alive. Prevented by circumstances from full development of self, she represents virtue in an arrested state. Maria is one of the living dead of *Dubliners* who like Eliot's Hollow Men are "Shape without form, shade without colour,/Paralyzed force, gesture without motion."

INTERPRETING A POEM

Since poetry is the most compressed of all literary forms, it requires careful interpretation in order to be experienced in its deepest and fullest sense. The e. e. cummings poem reprinted below, for example, may appear on the surface to be mere nonsense, yet as critic R. W. Stallman points out, it is actually "rich in meanings." At the literal level it is a miniature short story: at the thematic level it makes a profound observation about how we live and how we love.

anyone lived in a pretty how town

e. e. cummings

anyone lived in a pretty how town
(with up so floating many bells down)
spring summer autumn winter
he sang his didn't he danced his did.   4

Women and men(both little and small)
cared for anyone not at all
they sowed their isn't they reaped their same
sun moon stars rain   8

children guessed(but only a few
and down they forgot as up they grew
autumn winter spring summer)
that noone loved him more by more   12

when by now and tree by leaf
she laughed his joy she cried his grief
bird by snow and stir by still
anyone's any was all to her   16

someones married their everyones
laughed their cryings and did their dance
(sleep wake hope and then)they
said their nevers they slept their dream   20

stars rain sun moon
(and only the snow can begin to explain
how children are apt to forget to remember
with up so floating many bells down)   24

one day anyone died i guess
(and noone stooped to kiss his face)
busy folk buried them side by side
little by little and was by was   28

all by all and deep by deep
and more by more they dream their sleep
noone and anyone earth by april
wish by spirit and if by yes.   32

Women and men(both dong and ding)
summer autumn winter spring
reaped their sowing and went their came
sun moon stars rain   36

An Interpretation of E. E. Cummings's
"anyone lived in a pretty how town"

R. W. Stallman

This poem, apparently obscure nonsense, is rich in meanings; and though it may appear difficult at first glance, it is actually very simple to understand. Cummings uses language "reflexively," every word being counterpointed against another. At the literal level of the language there is a narrative plot, a miniature short story. What makes the poem seem so strange or seemingly incomprehensible is its uncommon arrangement of common words, its wrenched syntax, and its coining of new words from old ones by reconverting their dictionary meaning and usage.

Cummings's case study is a certain anonymous fellow, a citizen of How* Town. The town disowns him. Why? Well, for one thing their conventions are shocked by his unconventional way of life. He simply does not conform. Of course they don't care for Mr. Anyone because they "cared for anyone not at all" (line 6); they care only selfishly for themselves alone. These people "both little [*i.e.*,

---

* The dictionary lists eight variant meanings for the word *how,* and all eight reverberate throughout the poem. Cummings uses the word as a noun. In the noun-sense the word means manner or method. But the meanings of *how* as adverb equally apply: 1. In what manner or way; 2. to what number or degree; 3. in what state or condition; 4. for what reason; 5. with what meaning, to what effect; 6. at what price, how dear; and 7. *how* meaning "what," as how about it? How Town is the conventional town of conformity to convention, where what counts is social manner or method, social degree, state or condition. In How Town what counts is how you do it, and the price is dear. In the sense of *how* as "why," the question asked by the person is what meaning has this way of life?

children] and small" (5) are small spiritually; which is why "*noone* loved him more by more" (12). And socially he didn't count because "anyone" married "noone." As for Miss "noone," she "loved him more by more." The non-lovers are the Someones who "married their everyones" (17). They play the social game, which is why they are Someones, but in conforming like "everyones" they have lost out in living, in loving life for its own sake. These Someones and Everyones do the conventional things in the conventional ways, and their life is a deadness and a monotony—"sleep wake hope and then"—because they live not at all spontaneously. And that is what sets them apart from Mr. Anyone. They "did their dance" (18), whereas he "*danced* his did" (4). they "*said* their nevers" (20), said their nevertheless, talked about what they didn't do and made excuses; whereas he "*sang* his didn't" (4). In short, "anyone *lived.*" For him How Town was "pretty how town," beautiful, beautiful "with up so floating many bells down"—life in both its ups and downs, it was all singsong to him. Anyone and Noone lived happily forever in the point-present now—not in How Town so much as in Now Town. She loved him "by now and tree by leaf" (13), all of him by every part of him; "anyone's any [thing] was all to her" (16). She "laughed his joy she cried his grief" (14); whereas the Someones married to their Everyones "laughed [at] their cryings" (18); their marriage is no marriage, merely an empty form. Even in death the lovers "dream their sleep" (30), belong to eternity and are reborn ("earth by april"); whereas the non-lovers even while living seem dead—"they slept their dream" (20). Caring "for anyone not at all/they sowed their isn't they reaped their same" (6-7). Their routine, clocked existence repeats itself through the cycles of time—"autumn winter spring summer"—with one season the same as another and later generations repeating the same old stenciled way of life (stanza 9). Time passes, mechanical time clocked by "sun moon stars rain" (lines 8 and 36), with the variant—stars rain sun moon (21)—to indicate the passing of time. The life of Someones and Everyones is never punctuated by memorable moments. No comma halts these "busy folk." And their children repeat the same blurred, indiscriminate, humdrum existence, they too "went their came" (35), wasting their coming by their busy going. Thus the bells, symbolizing Time, sound to them only as "dong and ding" (33), which is as dead men hear it, hollow, whereas to Mr. Anyone the bells sang, and he danced his life in lilt with them. Himself childlike in spontaneity, "children guessed" *how to live,* by his example—"but only a few/and down they forgot as up they grew" (9-10). Living is by loving, and loving is by losing oneself in another:

> little by little and was by was
> all by all and deep by deep
> and more by more they dream their sleep
> noone and anyone

But like Someones and Everyones, children become time-busy and "forget to remember" how to live, how to love. And that is how it goes in How to Live Town. The day Anyone died (stanza 7) "noone stooped to kiss his face."

Additional Poems

WINTER TREES

Sylvia Plath

The wet dawn inks are doing their blue dissolve.
On their blotter of fog the trees
Seem a botanical drawing—
Memories growing, ring on ring,
A series of weddings.

Knowing neither abortions nor bitchery,
Truer than women,
They seed so effortlessly!
Tasting the winds, that are footless,
Waist-deep in history—

Full of wings, otherworldliness.
In this, they are Ledas.
O mother of leaves and sweetness
Who are these pietas?
The shadows of ringdoves chanting, but easing nothing.

YOUR DEPARTURE VERSUS THE HINDENBURG

Richard Brautigan

Everytime we say good-bye
I see it as an extension of
       the Hindenburg
that great 1937 airship exploding
in medieval flames like a burning castle
       above New Jersey.
When you leave the house, the
shadow of the Hindenburg enters
to take your place.

INTERPRETING POPULAR CULTURE

It's easy to understand why an author would feel the need to interpret a short story by Joyce or a poem by e. e. cummings; it may be more difficult to see what there is to interpret in something as apparently simple as a country music song. Molly Ivins, however, finds there is more to "honky-tonk" music than meets the eye (or the ear). Ivins writes a syndicated newspaper column and often appears on public television or radio to "interpret" the events in Texas to the rest of the country. Caustic and liberal in her political outlook, Ivins seeks to stir controversy wherever she goes. What is an avowed feminist to do with what she sees as the deeply rooted sexism of so many country songs? After admitting her initial embarrassment at liking country music, Ivins offers her personal interpretation of the redeeming social value that she finds in these songs, and concludes that we may be spending too much time worrying about other people's taste in music.

HONKY TONKING

Molly Ivins

I can remember being embarrassed about liking country-western music, but I can't remember when I quit. It was a long time before they put Willie Nelson on the cover of *Newsweek*. Since there's a country song about everything important in life, there's one about this too—"I Was Country When Country Wasn't Cool."

Being hopelessly uncool is the least of the sins of country music. Back when I went to college, listening to Dave Brubeck and Edith Piaf was a fundamental prerequisite for sophistication, on a par with losing your virginity. Knowing a lot of Ernest Tubb songs didn't do squat for the reputation of the aspiring cosmopolite.

Country music was also politically incorrect. The folkies were on the right side of issues: Bob Dylan and Joan Baez sang at civil rights rallies; it seemed more than likely that Bull Connor listened to country.

The Beatles, Janis Joplin, the Jefferson Airplane, the Doors—everybody anybody listened to in the 1960s was against the Vietnam War. From the country side, Merle Haggard contributed "I'm Proud to Be an Okie from Muskogee." (Hippies quickly turned "Okie" into a longhair anthem and Kinky Friedman contributed a version entitled "I Am Just an Asshole from El Paso.")

And to be a feminist country music fan is an exercise in cultural masochism. There you are trying to uphold the personhood of the female sex, while listening to "She Got the Gold Mine, I Got the Shaft" or "Don't the Girls All Get Prettier at Closing Time." Women in country music are either saints or sluts, but they're mostly sluts. She's either a "good-hearted woman" or a "honky-tonk angel." There are more hard-hearted women in country music ("I Gave Her a Ring, She Gave Me the Finger"), despicable bimbos ("Ruuuby, Don't Take Your Love to Town"), and heartless gold diggers ("Satin Sheets to Lie On, Satin Pillow to Cry On") than the scholars can count. Even the great women country singers aren't much help. The immortal Patsy Cline was mostly lovesick for some worthless heel ("I Fall to Pieces") and Tammy Wynette's greatest contribution was to advise us "Stand by Your Man." (Tammy has stood by several of them.)

Not until the great Loretta Lynn, who is also musically lovelorn with great frequency but shows more spunk about it, did we hear some country songs that can be considered feminist. "Don't Come Home A-Drinkin' with Lovin' on Your Mind" is one of Loretta's better ass-kickin' anthems. The high-spirited spoof "Put Another Log on the Fire" is a classic parody of sexism: "Now, don't I let you wash the car on Sunday?/Don't I warn you when you're gettin' fat?/Ain't I gonna take you fishin' with me someday?/Well, a man can't love a woman more than that." Evidence of the impact of the Women's Movement on country music can be found in the hit song "If I Said You Had a Beautiful Body, Would You Hold It Against Me?"

But this is fairly limited evidence of redeeming social value in the genre. So what do we see in it? For one thing, how can you not love a tradition that produces such songs as "You Done Stompt on my Heart, an' Squished That Sucker Flat"?

(Featuring the refrain "Sweetheart, you just sorta/stompt on my aorta.") Or "Everything You Touch Turns to Dirt." Many cultures have popular song forms that reflect the people's concerns. In Latin cultures the *corridos,* written by immortal poets such as Garcia Lorca, give voice to the yearnings of the voiceless. In our culture, "Take This Job and Shove It" serves much the same function.

If you want to take the pulse of the people in this country, listen to country-western music. I first knew a mighty religious wave was gathering when I heard ditties like "Drop-kick Me, Jesus, Through the Goalposts of Life." I also knew the Moral Majority was past its prime and Pat Robertson would go nowhere when I heard "I Wrote a Hot Check to Jesus" on country radio, followed by "Would Jesus Wear a Rolex on His Television Show?"

Contrary to popular opinion, it is not easy to write country songs: many try and fail. One guy who never made it is Robin Dorsey from Matador, Texas. He went to Tech and had a girlfriend from Muleshoe about whom he wrote the love song "Her Teeth Was Stained but Her Heart Was Pure." She took offense and quit him over it, which caused him to write the tragedy-love song "I Don't Know Whether to Commit Suicide Tonight or Go Bowlin'."

Country music is easily parodied and much despised by intellectuals, but like soap operas, it is much more like real life than your elitists will admit. What do most people truly care about? International arms control? Monetary policy? Deconstructive criticism? Hell, no. What they care about most is love ("We Used to Kiss Each Other on the Lips, but Now It's All Over"). Betrayal ("Your Cheatin' Heart"). Revenge ("I'm Gonna Hire a Wino to Decorate Our Home"; "Who's Sorry Now?"). Death ("Wreck on the Highway"). Booze ("Four on the Floor and a Fifth under the Seat"; "She's Actin' Single, I'm Drinkin' Doubles"). Money ("If You've Got the Money, Honey, I've Got the Time"). Loneliness ("Hello, Walls"). Tragedy–love songs ("She Used My Tears to Wash Her Socks"; "My Bride's Wedding Dress Was Wash-and-Wear").

Now here we're talking major themes. In a song called "You Never Even Called Me by My Name," which author Steve Goodman labeled "the perfect country-western song," momma, trucks, trains, and prison are also suggested as mandatory country-western themes.

In this country we waste an enormous amount of time and energy disapproving of one another in three categories where only personal taste matters: hair, sports, and music. We need not review the family trauma, high dudgeon, tsk-tsking, and lawsuits caused over the years by hair and how people wear it. Consider the equally futile expenditure of energy in condemning other people's sports. And in music, good Lord, the zeal put into denouncing rock, sneering at opera, finding classical a bore, jazz passé, bluegrass fit only for snuff-dippers— why, it's stupefying. It's incomprehensible.

I am open to the argument that Ludwig van Beethoven has contributed more great music to the world than has Earl Scruggs. But there is a tiresome neoconservative argument these days that holds relativism responsible for all the evil in the modern world. These folks denounce the abandonment of absolute standards in everything—morality, taste, the postal service. As though the fact that people enjoy reading *The Three Musketeers* were a menace to Dante. I have felt the sting of their snotty scorn, the lash of their haughty sneers, and what I have to say is "You Are Just Another Sticky Wheel on the Grocery Cart of Life."

DISCUSSION AND EXERICISES

1. Sigmund Freud said that all behavior is a gesture—an "acting out" of deep-seated feelings and needs. Thus what we see on the surface is often (if not always) an expression of underlying "deeper meaning"; for example, football may be an expression of aggression. Speculate on what larger human purposes are being "acted out"—and satisfied—in five of the following activities:

stealing	playing a musical instrument	hiking
alcoholism	baseball	kite flying
stuttering	knitting	wrestling
lying	dancing	bullfighting
swearing	sailing	fishing
dreaming	skiing	playing pool
smoking	gambling	mountain climbing
promiscuity	hunting	singing
ice skating	boxing	doing a crossword puzzle

2. Write a paragraph (150-250 words) in which you interpret one of the above activities. Open with a general topic sentence; develop it into a coordinate sequence paragraph, a subordinate sequence, or a mixed construction. Be prepared to explain your choice.

3. Look again at Kenneth Cole's "Hallowed Be the Mall" and answer the questions below.
   a. How does Ira Zepp's definition of *religious* contribute to our understanding of malls as religious centers?
   b. What is the *omphalos* and why is its place in Mircea Eliade's theory important for accepting malls as religious spaces?
   c. How does the "architectural rhetoric" of malls "speak" to human beings?
   d. Why do malls attract people of all ages?
   e. Why is Zepp's term for James Rouse, "the mahatma of malls," fitting for Rouse's role in mall development and for the mall's religious significance?
   f. What are the shortcomings of malls?
   g. Study the opening paragraph. How does it "set up" the remainder of the essay?
   h. Why is *gussied* a particularly appropriate word choice in the final sentence of paragraph one?

4. Answer the following questions based on Joyce's "Clay."
   a. How did her fellow workers in the laundry regard Maria?
   b. What sort of things disturbed Maria?
   c. What sort of things gave her joy?
   d. Did Maria's responses to situations seem sincere or hypocritical? Explain.
   e. How did Maria feel about herself?
   f. How did strangers treat her?

g. Why did Joe and his family include Maria in the Hallow Eve festivities?

h. Did she enhance or detract from the party?

i. What was the significance of the clay in the dish?

j. What is the significance of Hallow Eve in the story?

k. Is Maria "a veritible peacemaker"? Why or why not?

l. Are things as they seem to be in this story? Explain.

5. Write a paragraph (200-250 words) in coordinate sequence using one of your answers to the above questions as your topic sentence. Write another paragraph in subordinate sequence.

6. Read "Winter Trees" and "Your Departure versus the Hindenburg" at least three times; read them aloud; note their images line by line.

7. Write a two-paragraph interpretation (300-500 words) of one of the above poems, citing words, images, and lines to support your view (as Stallman does in his interpretation of the Cummings poem).

8. Examine the photograph by Walker Evans on page 402. What are its most notable details and surface features? What do you think the photographer had in mind in creating this photograph? How can you interpret the details. Using specific details from the photograph, write a brief interpretation (300–500 words) of the photograph's meaning.

Question

19

WHAT IS THE
VALUE OF X?

EVALUATING A BOOK
 REVIEW OF A WEAVE OF WOMEN,
  BY E. M. BRONER, JOHN LEONARD
 SHAKESPEARE'S MOST RIDDLING CREATION
  (REVIEW OF *SHYLOCK: A LEGEND*
  AND ITS LEGACY, BY JOHN GROSS),
  JOHN SIMON

EVALUATING A FILM
 PREDATORS (REVIEW OF STEVEN SPIELBERG'S
  JURASSIC PARK), TERRENCE RAFFERTY
 SHAKESPEARE IN THE SUN (REVIEW OF KENNETH
  BRANAGH'S *MUCH ADO ABOUT NOTHING*),
  ANNE BARTON

EVALUATING A TELEVISION SHOW
 REVIEW OF DISCOVER: THE WORLD OF
  SCIENCE, MERRILL PANITT

When we ask about the value of something, we are moving still further beyond basic explanation into the greater complexities of judgment. Here we ask not simply, *What does X do?* but *What does X do that is worth doing?* and *How well does X do it?* The purpose is to appraise the worth, excellence, truth, beauty, or goodness of something. To what extent does X meet or fail to meet specific standards? In an evaluative essay you, the writer, always set the standards. Even if they are standards you have adopted from someone else, you have made them your own. Thus, the moment you address yourself to the question *What is the value of X?* you become a critic. Whether the subject is books, movies, art, or society at large, you evaluate it in the light of your own notion of what it is and *should* be. As you can see, then, writing a critique is a special challenge, for your evaluation will have significance only if you are open-minded, well informed, and fair—ready to back up your opinions, but not be opinionated.

Obviously, *What is the value of X?* is the guiding question behind most examples of critical writing and review. Whether you are concerned with books, movies, theater, music, or dance, you are expected to tell the readers of your review whether the offering in question is any good. Naturally, your opinion is, for the most part, exactly that—your *opinion*. This does not mean, however, that a good review cannot be objective. "I personally do not like courtroom drama," you might state, adding—if you want to be fair and to inform your audience of a truth larger and more important than your own likes and dislikes—that the courtroom scenes in one particular play are extraordinarily well done. To be a good reviewer, you must get outside yourself so that you see not only through your own eyes but also through the eyes of others. (See W. H. Auden on the function of a critic, Question 8.)

EVALUATING A BOOK

A good book review is informative, interpretive, and evaluative.

1. *It indicates the content and presumed purpose of the book.* The ability to write a good summary is important. More than that, if your review is to be fair, you must infer from the *fact* of the book what the author's intentions were—that is, *what* the author wanted to say and *how* he or she wanted it to be received. If, for example, a book is about poverty in Appalachia, you should not fault the author for lack of humor: clearly the book is not supposed to be funny. (One is reminded here of Mark Twain's spoofing criticism of the dictionary for its weak plot.)

2. *It assesses how successfully the author has achieved his or her purpose.* By examining rhetorical techniques, you can determine how well or how poorly the author has handled the material and how fully his or her purpose has been achieved.

3. *It judges the value of the book.* Is it any good? Do we have reason to be glad that it was written? Was its purpose worth achieving? What contribution, if any, does it make to our store of knowledge or aesthetic pleasure?

Only the first two considerations require a measure of objectivity, while the third depends on your own judgment, on your opinion of what is valuable and worthy. However you deal with these necessarily subjective aspects of reviewing, one thing is certain: you should not use the review as a showcase for your personal tastes and preferences, featuring these at the expense of the book itself. Your main function is to describe the book in such a way that your readers, who presumably have not read the book, can decide whether or not they want to read it. In addition, you can help to illumine the work so that readers can understand and appreciate it more deeply.

Most reviews follow a basic but flexible pattern:

Introduction
I. Description of the work
   A. what it is formally (novel, biography)
   B. what it is about (plot, character, theme)
II. Evaluation: to what extent it fulfills or fails to fulfill its purpose
   A. strengths   (this order may
   B. weaknesses   be reversed)
Conclusion

In the review cited below, for example, John Leonard of the *New York Times* adapts this organization to reflect his unqualified approval of E. M. Broner's novel *A Weave of Women*. Enthusiasm and description blend in his opening wrap-up evaluation of the novel as "an astonishment." Leonard then characterizes the novel—provocatively—as "a kind of epic poem, a recapitulation of the rhythms of female consciousness." Those not interested in epic poems or female consciousness need read no further; the reviewer's function is to inform, not force: Leonard has so far done his duty.

In succeeding paragraphs he supports his favorable judgment by interpreting the novel in terms of selected details. Note that he does not give the kind of point-by-point plot summary which is not only dull but also damaging to the book: It destroys all suspense for the prospective reader. Note also that throughout the review Leonard compares the novel under consideration to other novels, thereby placing it within a familiar framework while at the same time indicating how it is different, indeed unique.

Review of *A Weave of Women*, by E. M. Broner

John Leonard

Even from the author of such a fine first novel as *Her Mothers*, *A Weave of Women* is an astonishment. E. M. Broner seeks nothing less than to achieve, in a kind of epic poem, a recapitulation of the rhythms of female consciousness. It is circular and sinuous and ceremonial. I know of nothing else quite like it, although certain other recent examples of what might be called "apocalyptic communalism" come occasionally to mind—such books as Marge Piercy's *Dance the Eagle to Sleep*, Monique Wittig's *Les Guerilleres* and Doris Lessing's *The Four-Gated City*. Miss Broner, however, is interested in health; she proposes a myth of nurture.

Her 15 women do their weaving in a stone house in the Old City in Jerusalem in 1972. Simha, the only mother among them, is more or less the spiritual leader of the commune, but we are told that "each of the 15 women is saddled to a different horse, reined to another life: Terry to action; Gerda to molecules and numbers, exactness and abstraction; Gloria to self-glorification; Deedee to deaths and resurrections; Antoinette and Joan to the word; Dahlia to the note; Mickey to passion and regret; Hepzibah to the soul; Vered to responsibility; Tova to performance; among the wayward girls, Rina and Shula to respectability and Robin to confusion." They are "Temple Priestesses, renewing themselves and saving lives."

From England, Ireland and the United States, from Poland and Germany, and, of course, from Israel, variously wounded and searching, they have come or been brought to the stone house, where they make ceremonies. They dream up new ways of ridding their house of demons, of marrying their men and burying their dead. They invent "counterholidays" and the "hymenotomy," an equivalent of circumcision. They march and agitate and exact revenge. They are enemies of the state and the rabbinate, for what official politics and what official religion have done to women. They are creating new songs, a new therapy, a new religion, a healing cycle, out of scraps of Shakespeare and the Psalms. One betrays the circle and is excommunicated. One is murdered and mourned. One crosses the desert to the sea with a one-legged stork, and gives herself to a Bedouin prince. One, at the Wailing Wall, in a passage that seems to combine Isaac Bashevis Singer with Marc Chagall, turns into a pigeon.

We meet the women as a group before we are introduced to them as individuals, with their private stories. But even at the beginning, each voice is distinct, so that when it is finally matched with its story the effect is of intensification, proof, exegesis, a circle within the circle, almost a series of jazz riffs. The men, necessarily, are less distinct; they are peripheral to the circle, and often storyless. But they are particularized; the Arab student, the kibbutznik, the silk salesman, the despairing brother and the orthodox fanatic. They belong to the geography of the novel, not to its ideology.

And what a geography it is. One thinks: Of course, everything would have to start all over again in Jerusalem, with ideas of God and Africa and pure light. "Something about The Land," Miss Broner says, "makes this possible. In the Judean Hills one walks on stilts. Prophets come to the city to preach or people, after a sojourn in the city, decide they are prophets." Not the least of the many accomplishments is this sense of place, of fact and grit, on which her mysticism drapes itself. There is the shadow, the curse, of the mountain, but there is also the mountain. There are demons in the house, but there is also the house. There are Psalms, but also the law. When such a sense of place, a way with detail, joins with a sneaky sense of humor, we are no longer in the countries of Marge Piercy, Monique Wittig and Doris Lessing. War and madness yield to healing and music. Humor is subversive, just as beauty is beyond discussion. This circle is very large indeed, and all-encompassing. Its rhythm, its heartbeat, is renewal.

Any novel as ambitious as *A Weave of Women* is equally vulnerable. As the women sit around inventing their ceremonies, it is possible for the reader to nod off or to scoff, to resent the programmatic ringing of the thematic bells, to demand progression and to miss the point. Miss Broner, I think, insists on being watched and listened to, like the seasons and Bach. Repetition is indispensable to weaving; we are not involved in a narrative sprint and a gold medal. These women, we are told "intend a large deed." That deed will prove to be another exodus, a crossing of borders. The borders this time are of consciousness.

I hope there are many readers with the requisite patience, to hear *A Weave of Women* through to its affirmations. What seems new and distressing—the communal fiction, the abolition of the individual artist, the rejection of the authority of a point of view is actually at least as old as *The Canterbury Tales,* and probably much older, before we invented Canterbury, going all the way back to the caves where the shadows were explained and, perhaps, we bought the explanations of storytellers of the wrong sex.

In reviewing a nonfiction book, you must answer the same three questions: What is the content and purpose of the book? How skillfully does the author execute his or her purpose? Was the purpose worth achieving? To answer these, the reviewer must often answer the questions *How can X be summarized?* and *How should X be interpreted?* An effective evaluation is based on information and ideas generated from an effective summary and an effective interpretive analysis. It goes beyond mere summary, however, to communicate the reviewer's opinion of the book, supported by detailed references to the book itself.

The order in which you answer these questions is not important so long as they are all covered in a systematic fashion. You'll note that in John Simon's review of a book on the Shakespearean character Shylock, his basic evaluation comes fairly early, at the start of the fifth paragraph: "What makes Gross's book so valuable is that it is a true work of popularization." He proceeds through his review by taking each section of the book in turn, offering his summary and analysis of each new section. A book reviewer can organize his or her review in a number of ways. To be effective, the organization should be clear and easily followed by the reader.

SHAKESPEARE'S MOST RIDDLING CREATION
(REVIEW OF *SHYLOCK: A LEGEND AND ITS LEGACY*)

John Simon

Villains, on the whole, do not have critical books devoted to them. Not even villains created by Shakespeare. Richard III, royal scoundrel that he is, is still written about mostly by wrangling historians, debating whether or not he did in the little princes in the Tower. For a mere literary villain—and one who, unlike Lucifer or Mephistopheles, is not supernatural—to earn book-length appraisal is a remarkable feat; in the whole Shakespearean canon it has happened only to Iago and Shylock. Both of them continue to fascinate the learned and the layman alike: practicing critics and academic theoreticians, novelists, playwrights, poets, and journalists of every stripe.

Yet Iago and Shylock are very different characters. Iago preoccupies our minds because his malignity seems to be, if not exactly motiveless, vastly disproportionate to any offense incurred. Shylock, on the other hand, is now thought to have many plausible reasons for acting as he does, some of them cogent enough to make him hardly a heavy at all. With Iago, the problem is to find the motivation; with Shylock, to disentangle the true cause from an embarrassment of riches.

Interestingly, both these cynosures of exegetic enthusiasm are embroiled in matters of race or religion. Iago is obliged to serve a black superior; Shylock is a Jew forced to endure Christian contumely. It may be that this added spice helps keep them at the forefront of popularity. But not that alone: Marlowe's Barabas, in *The Jew of Malta,* and Shakespeare's own Aaron the Moor hold, and have held, only modest interest. And because Iago's evil is beyond dispute, whereas Shylock is often counted on the side of the angels (if that isn't too Christian a way of putting it), the Jew emerges as more interesting than the ensign.

Shylock and the play that houses him continue to exercise their spell as the ambiguity of his status, like that of his real-life coreligionists, refuses to be resolved. It is now nigh on two millennia that anti-Semitism, which is perfectly reflected in anti-Shylockism, has continued to thrive, if not on the scale of pogroms, diasporas, and holocausts, then in various more subtle yet sinister ways that show no sign of abatement. And *The Merchant of Venice,* and the Jew at its center, are its literary fulcrum. By a teasing coincidence, the American publisher of John Gross's absorbing *Shylock: A Legend and Its Legacy* has recently also brought out Philip Roth's latest, *Operation Shylock.* And Wendy Wasserstein's new Broadway hit, *The Sisters Rosensweig,* contains a saucy allusion to Shylock. Meanwhile, attempts to ban Shakespeare's play from production, high-school curricula, and even public-library shelves never cease. Shylock is as honored in the breach as in the observance.

What makes Gross's book so valuable is that it is a true work of popularization. Deluded souls often equate popularization with vulgarization, although the difference is enormous. Vulgarization oversimplifies and indulges in grandstanding; popularization does not pretend to solve the insoluble but merely lays out the difficulties clearly, makes the complexities accessible. It also transcends specialization, the chief obstacle to popular interest. The joy of this *Shylock* is that it is several books in one: despite its relative brevity, it covers the ground of several types of study.

Part One is a survey of what Shakespeare actually wrote in *The Merchant of Venice,* what his sources were, how he altered them, and what his own very particular contribution was. The play is analyzed and explicated not only from Gross's point of view but also from that of Shakespeare's contemporaries, and we get persuasive accounts both of how the various plots and sub-plots interact and reinforce one another and of how they struck the Elizabethan audience.

In Part Two, Gross sketches in, with broad but not slapdash strokes, the stage history and critical-scholarly annals of the play and its most problematic character: Shylock, the Jewish moneylender. We get brief but evocative accounts of how the play was mounted in Britain, the United States, and several other countries over the next two or three centuries; who the main interpreters of Shylock were and how they portrayed him; and what were the scholarly underpinnings and critical and popular reception of these conflicting—often even self-contradictory—interpretations, given that actors often created widely varying Shylocks in the course of their careers.

Clearly, what is at stake here is whether Shylock is a total dyed-in-the-gaberdine villain, a villain with qualifications, a heroic personage with more or less serious flaws, or an almost faultless figure whose only blemishes are his hatred of Christians and inordinate love of money, to both of which excesses a Christian society has driven him. Shylock and his fellow Venetians are caught in a timeless seesaw: as the esteem for Shylock goes up, that for the Christians goes down, and vice versa. And the interpretations on the stage and in the study are, of course, interpenetrative.

Part Three brings us to modern times, when the rise of communism, fascism, and Nazism, and, eventually, genocide change the backdrop against which the play and its Jew are enacted and evaluated. Here the book takes on a hallucinatory relevance. But Gross, an exemplarily circumspect assessor—as just as Portia, as Jewish as Shylock, and abler to see both sides of the question than anyone in the play and most outside it—never overdramatizes. Although he brings in his own views when appropriate, he never becomes self-important; better yet, he never becomes boring. The study ends with a summary of his opinions and conclusions: modest, intelligent, and tactful. He resolves what can decently be resolved, and leaves the rest up to the reader—who is now, thanks to Gross, immensely more qualified to make up his own mind.

Before I go into specifics, I must stress one more virtue of this monograph: its courage to digress, to become a multigraph. If there was something especially interesting about an actor or a writer involved with the topic at hand—something, however, not having direct bearing on the play or on Shylock—Gross does not shy away from relating it, concisely and racily, as the whole book is written. Surely a study of the history and art of Pompeii by the same token gains from a description of the wildflowers sprouting among the ruins. Thus, while talking about, say, the novelist Israel Zangwill's involvement with one actor's portrayal of Shylock, Gross cannot resist quoting the actor Herbert Beerbohm Tree's description of Zangwill: "his face shining like Moses, his teeth like the Ten Commandments, all broken."

The main motifs of *The Merchant of Venice* are old, if not ancient. Though a couple of them go back only as far as the fourteenth-century Italian collection *Il Pecorone,* the pound-of-flesh story harks back to ancient India or Persia. By Shakespeare's time Jews had for centuries been banned from England and, with the added fear of the unknown, were hated all the more. Further, the terms "Jew" and "usurer" were virtually synonymous to Elizabethan ears. Considering all this, Shakespeare did fairly well by Shylock: he did not make him repulsive physically or even horrible psychically. Had he been a mere stereotype, like Marlowe's Barabas, Shylock would not have held the stage for 400 years.

Though Gross gives us plausible derivations for Shylock's unusual name, he admits that none of them is wholly compelling. But what sets Shylock off even more than his name is a style much plainer than that of the other characters: he is, in fact, the first Shakespearean figure to speak prose for noncomic purposes. Although Gross admires the "Hath not a Jew" speech, and appreciates its humanizing value, he shrewdly observes that it is not a justification for everything its utterer does. And though Shakespeare's notion of legal procedure in the trial scene is totally bizarre, there is no dearth of legal experts huffing and puffing this way and that to defend contradictory aspects of the juridical confusion. And Gross reminds us that the conclusion of the play is not only as near to music as words can get (which is why Berlioz and Vaughan Williams, among others, set it) but also, in Lorenzo's famous speech, pure religious sentiment, the only instance of it in the text.

Part Two of the book is the most rollicking, as Gross adduces and assesses the conflicting literary interpretations that the play and its chief antagonist (Shylock is hardly the protagonist) gave rise to, and the amusingly diverse impersonations that Shylock underwent in the theater. In the study and on the stage his fortunes fluctuated as feverishly as the stock exchange in parlous times. On the boards the first great reversal occurred when Charles Macklin, in 1741, wrested Shylock away from the comedians, who had turned him into a mere sinister buffoon, and made him into a creature of fulgurating ferocity—eliciting from George II, who wished to scare the House of Commons into submission, the query to Walpole, "Vat you tink of sending dem to see dat Irishman play Shylock?" But no sooner had the public enjoyed this frisson than along came the coldly dignified, though still dangerous, Shylock of John Philip Kemble, of whom William Hazlitt remarked that he was "an icicle on the bust of tragedy."

Next came the rascally Shylock of G. F. Cooke, the actor who inspired Edmund Kean not only to emulate him but also to rescue his coffin from an unadorned grave in New York and "during the reburial . . . to abstract one of his toe bones," later to compel "other actors at Drury Lane to kneel down and pay homage to it," Gross writes. "After that he kept it permanently displayed on his mantelpiece, as a kind of sacred relic, until Mrs. Kean threw it away in disgust." Crazy people, these thespians—another of the entertaining subtexts of the book. Kean was to be the great Romantic Shylock, horrifying but magnificent; Samuel Taylor Coleridge remarked that watching him was "like reading Shakespeare by flashes of lightning." Kean's complex interpretation was the impetus for new scholarly perceptions of the good sides of Shylock, and Gross cites evidence that by the middle of the nineteenth century the idea of an impressive, half-sympathetic Shylock had taken hold at least of the intelligentsia.

The first genuinely philo-Semitic Shylock was that of the English actor Junius Brutus Booth, who performed him all over America, though he reverted in later years to a vicious Shylock, such as the less murderous but more talented of his famous sons, Edwin, was to embody all along. It was left to Henry Irving, however, to start out with a demonic Shylock and then over the years humanize him, until, in 1884, he perceived and interpreted him as, he declared, "the type of a persecuted race; almost the only gentleman in the play, and the most ill-used." For a moment he even snatched from Antonio the privilege of becoming the play's Christ figure. The reaction had to set in, and soon James Spedding and other scholars, and Henry James and other critics, upbraided Irving for this denaturing of Shakespeare's intent. In the end Irving, too, seems to have reverted to a harder, harsher Shylock.

Whereupon the academics picked up the gauntlet; it devolved upon George Sampson, the author of *The Concise Cambridge History of English Literature,* to affirm that "Irving's Shylock is implicit in the play." The idea developed among scholars that Shakespeare "builded better than he knew," as Brander Matthews, of Columbia University, argued, and in the theater Richard Mansfield was said by William Winter to be playing Shylock with one eye on the "Hebrew" section of the audience. In the 1930s J. Dover Wilson and H. B. Charlton evolved the prevalent modern view: that the play and Shylock were marked by a continual clash, as Charlton put it, between "the proposals of Shakespeare's deliberate will and the disposals of his creative imagination." In other words, Shakespeare's genius instinctively did something better than merely catering to the audience's notions, although that was its starting point.

I cannot here pursue in detail Gross's animated travelogue on the opinions and performances of a passing parade of writers and performers, fascinating reading though it makes. In Part Three of the book we enter modern times, and here the story and Gross's telling of it rise to such heights that one reads *Shylock* as if it were the biography of some major Jewish historical figure whose experiences encompassed everything from Freud's couch to Marx's political laboratory, from the Rothschildian world of high finance to the Nazis' death camps. Gross accompanies Shylock even beyond the Western world, to Africa and Asia. Most telling, perhaps, is the account of Karen Blixen (Isak Dinesen), in *Out of Africa,* of her conversation with Farah, her beloved Somalian retainer. Farah, though it is unusual for a Somali to take sides with fictional characters, sympathized with Shylock until the end, when he felt that the man let himself be cheated of that little bit of flesh for all that money. When Baroness Blixen remonstrated, Farah explained, "Memsahib, he could have used a red-hot knife. That brings out no blood."

Gross lustily catalogues the absurdities with which Marxists and Freudians saddled Shylock and the play. Though Marx himself made plenty of foolish remarks, Freud was—prudently or pusillanimously—silent about Shylock. Other Freudians, however, lost no time in reinterpreting—coming up with, among other things, a homosexual Antonio in love with Bassanio. But the most interesting pages, inevitably, concern the rise of deadly modern anti-Semitism, as reflected in attitudes toward Shylock. Whereas Israel Zangwill could still quote a Victorian gentlewoman's relatively benign remark that "of course Shylock is the only Jew most of us know personally," by 1920 an Englishman named E. S. Spencer had published a book titled *Democracy or Shylocracy?* which he called "a graphic exposure of Jewish corruption in Finance, Politics and Society." As Gross writes, "Shylock the usurer became Shylock the banker; Shylock the avenger was transformed into Shylock the conspirator. . . . After 1917, the Jewish devil became a Bolshevik and a plutocrat in equal measure." In due time Louis–Ferdinand Céline, in his horrible tract *L'Ecole des Cadavres,* described New York as "the most clamorous Shylockery in the world."

It may be surprising that Shakespeare was the only enemy author not banned by the Nazis in 1939; but, then, they subscribed to the notion that he was a crypto-German. What is not surprising is that *The Merchant of Venice* was one of the most performed plays in the Third Reich. Yet the Nazis did not do the kind of violence to the play that various modern mountings by such new-style directors as Jonathan Miller, Bill Alexander, and (in Germany) Peter Zadek have wreaked. Then, too, there are the revisionist authors and poets. Gross is at his most diverting describing a poem by a British poetess in which Shylock ends up "as a vehicle for the *chagrin d'amour* of Fiona Pitt–Kethley." As for modern scholarship, this is a time when "qualified and multifaceted views seem more rewarding." Thus, "where the key words were once 'justice' and 'mercy,' 'gold' and 'love,' they are now (among others) 'skeptical,' 'tension,' 'discrepancy,' 'distancing' and 'demystify.'" There are even reputable scholars who would abandon the play altogether.

In summarizing his own views, as derived from his study of so many others', Gross concludes that Shakespeare, "a shrewd and successful businessman," may have "had a lurking sympathy with Shylock's economic realism." And Shakespeare,

> though he may often have started from stereotypes, seldom ended up with them. . . . Shylock might easily have been a small character— someone, say, like the villainous Don John in *Much Ado About Nothing.*

But he is a big character, like Falstaff—someone who bursts the bounds of the play in which he appears.

You might say that bounds, like bonds, can be broken when an advocate as skilled as Portia or John Gross argues the case.

Although there are tiny slip-ups here and there (Hofmannsthal did not emphasize "atmosphere" by capitalizing it—*all* German nouns are capitalized; one doesn't "ogle at" a lead casket, one simply ogles it; Dr. Lopez was hanged, not "hung"; in 1550 there were fewer, not "less," than a thousand Jews in the ghetto), *Shylock* is about as lucid, elegant, witty, judicious, and informative an inquiry as ever was packed into roughly 350 pages of generously large print. But easy to read above all, because of John Gross's unostentatiously flowing style.

EVALUATING A FILM

Like a book reviewer, a film reviewer serves as intermediary between the film and the prospective viewer. This is what the film is about, you tell your readers, indicating not only basic plot line, character, and action but also what you take to be the intention of the director. You should also discuss technique (camera work, lighting, and so on) and quality of the performances (who plays what major roles and how well or how poorly they are performed). Finally, you should tell readers whether or not you think the film is worth seeing.

We offer here two film reviews, one of the popular blockbuster *Jurassic Park,* the other of a film with a more limited audience: an adaptation of Shakespeare's *Much Ado about Nothing.* What these two reviews have in common is that they delve beneath the surface of the films they discuss, weighing each element carefully. Film reviews on television or in popular magazines are often no more than brief plot summaries, but a good film review can do much more than tell us whether we will like a certain movie or not; it can help us understand the film and our reaction to it in a more substantive way.

PREDATORS

(REVIEW OF STEVEN SPIELBERG'S *JURASSIC PARK*)

Terrence Rafferty

The dinosaurs in Steven Spielberg's *Jurassic Park* are the handiwork of a small army of special-effects technicians, and the beasts look pretty good, at least in comparison to their nearest movie kin, the galumphing atomic-mutant monsters that crunched Japanese cities under their feet in the cheap horror-matinée pictures of the fifties and early sixties. Spielberg's state-of-the-art dinos (whose characteristics are based on the current theory that the animals were warmblooded, and therefore much more active and more versatile than had previously been believed) are a lot speedier than Godzilla and his hyperthyroid-reptile colleagues, and that enables the filmmaker to create dynamic stalk-and-chase sequences. The carnivorous animals in *Jurassic Park*—which include a massive, toothy Tyrannosaurus rex, a venom-spitting dilophosaur, and a pack of tenacious velociraptors—are efficient, resourceful predators: good scream-generators, in movie terms, because they're both intelligent and relentless, like the best serial killers. The placid herbivores don't figure in the plot at all; their appearances are confined to a handful of mawkish sense-of-wonder shots in the intervals between bouts of terror. But in *Jurassic Park* neither the benign beasts nor the scary monsters inspire anything close to awe, even with the aid of audience stimulants like surging symphonic music (by the shameless John Williams) and repeated closeups of wide-eyed, openmouthed actors. Spielberg's monsters have a showroom shine, and they're zippier than the old models, but the novelty wears off fast; for all the ingenuity of the movie's engineering, *Jurassic Park* doesn't have the imagination—or the courage—to take us any place we haven't been a thousand times before.

It's just a creature feature on amphetamines, and its natural audience—as usual for Hollywood blockbusters—is people who have never seen a movie or who want only to see the same story again and again: kids, that is, and grownups who yearn to relive the dumb thrills of their first moviegoing experiences. We're all capable of reverting to childish responses from time to time, but most of us like to feel that we can't be had too easily—that the filmmakers should have to *work* a little if they want us to suspend our adult disbelief and start squealing and cheering and stamping our feet like twelve-year-olds. *Jurassic Park* assumes that we're going to react exactly as we're intended to: everything feels programmed, as if by computer whizzes who think that a piece of software this simple can't go wrong. (It doesn't seem to have occurred to anyone involved in this picture that human beings are more readily bored by predictability than machines are.) Michael Crichton's novel, on which the movie is based, is a rather elegantly designed diversion: science-fiction-thriller junk, but with a narrative so intricately constructed that we don't mind being taken for a ride. But the screenplay, which is credited to Crichton and David Koepp, reduces the story to its bare bones—people running away from hungry animals. The movie *Jurassic Park* turns back the clock on its own source: it's interested in only the most primitive horror-movie effects, and the storytelling is so basic that it's virtually prehistoric.

The action takes place on an island off the coast of Central America, where a wealthy entrepreneur, John Hammond (Richard Attenborough), has set up an amusement park that features live dinosaurs. The animals have been cloned from DNA recovered from fossilized mosquitoes that once sucked dino blood. When he has a few full-grown animals (of six species) roaming the island, behind electrified fences that are controlled by a sophisticated computer system, Hammond invites a few people down for an inspection tour: a couple of paleontologists (Sam Neill and Laura Dern); a chaos-theory mathematician (Jeff Goldblum); a lawyer (Martin Ferrero), who represents some large investors in the park; and his own grandchildren, Tim (Joseph Mazzello) and Lex (Ariana Richards). In the middle of the tour, the island's power goes out—an act of sabotage by Jurassic Park's loathsome computer expert (Wayne Knight)—and no one can figure out how to turn it back on. Pretty soon, the T. rex is crashing through the now unelectrified barriers and picking up people in its giant jaws, the dilophosaur is spewing its inky poison, and the six-foot-tall velociraptors are scurrying around everywhere, converging on their victims with frightening speed. (The raptors work together like a basketball team with a murderous full-court press.) Some people die; others don't. The moral is: You shouldn't mess with nature, even for a noble purpose like creating large-scale, lucrative entertainment for children.

This message is not fresh, despite being dressed up in gaudy chaos-theory jargon about the inherent instability of complex systems. And the conceit of a theme park gone haywire is one that Crichton tried out on a smaller scale in the 1973 movie *Westworld,* which he wrote and directed. For Spielberg fans, *Jurassic Park* is like an album full of new, slickly rearranged versions of the director's greatest hits. Most obviously, the movie recalls *Jaws,* but several of the action set pieces—one involving a truck teetering in the branches of a tree, and one having to do with a suddenly reëlectrified fence—are in the style of the cliffhanger-serial thrills in the Indiana Jones pictures, and the scenes in which the children gape at gentle dinos like the long-necked brachiosaurs cover the *Close Encounters* and *E.T.* bases. Crichton and Spielberg haven't come up with anything fundamentally new in *Jurassic Park;* they've just cloned themselves (with a few strands of conventional monster-movie DNA thrown into the genetic cocktail), and they clearly believe that the audience can no longer tell the difference between the real thing and a lab-hatched replica. But conviction can't be faked, even in popular art. When the spark of enthusiasm—of wit, or obsession, or simple joy in invention—isn't there, a movie takes on a dead, glassy look, like the insomniac stare of the killer robot that Yul Brynner played in *Westworld. Jurassic Park* has a couple of effectively frenetic suspense sequences and one terrific visual joke (involving a charging T. rex and a rearview mirror), but over all the picture feels lifeless. The cinematography, by Dean Cundey, is drab; the exposition is perfunctory (most of the scientific information we need to know is conveyed in an insultingly jokey animated segment featuring Mr. DNA); the characters are endowed with a maximum of two traits apiece, and the actors are hung out to dry on those tiresomely reiterated idiosyncrasies; the dialogue consists largely of strained, witless wisecracks (often delivered by characters who should be speechless with fear or pain); and the plotting is so rushed and porous that it undermines the picture's momentum.

Jurassic Park isn't as sorry a mess as Spielberg's last movie, the unspeakable *Hook.* It's the same kind of mess, though: an immensely gifted filmmaker's strenuous, confused attempt to recapture past glory. There are only so many ways for a movie to get a big rise out of a big audience, and Spielberg had most of them down cold by the time he made his sixth feature, *E.T.,* in 1982. Since completing that perfect piece of Hollywood entertainment, he's been treading water. Hit-makers of Spielberg's magnitude (in music as well as in movies) often suffer puzzling creative slumps, because the relationship between a commercial enter-tainer and his audience is a tricky one: you might even say that it's inherently unstable. When an artist is aiming for universal acceptance, he's constantly gauging the desires of an unknown, generalized audience, and that's dangerous territory: if his calculations are off, and the audience doesn't want what he thinks it wants, he's stuck with a flop, and, worse yet, a trivial flop—a mousetrap that didn't spring. At a certain point, the technical challenges that face pure pop craftsmen like Spielberg become enervating: it's difficult to do the same tricks over and over—especially if you've already performed them so beautifully that there's no real room for improvement. The movie-magic program that Spielberg has devised in *Jurassic Park* may work for him this time, but he's playing a loser's game.

One of the wittiest things about Crichton's book is its portrayal of Jurassic Park's prime mover, Hammond. In the novel, he's a greedy, arrogant entrepreneur: he's in the live-dinosaur business for profit and for the godlike sense of power that this expensively engineered world can give him. He's a predator himself, and it's deeply satisfying to read, at the end of the book, of the grisly death inflicted on him by the stronger animals that he has brought into being. The movie's Hammond, however, is a cuddly, kindhearted old dreamer, whose primary motive in constructing Jurassic Park is to provide joy and education for all the world's children. He's meant to be a poignant figure, and in this version he's not gnawed to a bloody pulp by maddened beasts; he leaves the island by helicopter, taking one last, forlorn look back at the ruins of his grand, benign, misguided vision. This complete reversal in the portrayal of Jurassic Park's creator is perhaps the clearest indication of the moviemakers' capacity for self-delusion. We're supposed to be moved by this billionaire's disappointment at the failure of a gigantic and criminally stupid entertainment project: he's a decent man who just wanted to put a smile on our faces and make a nice buck. He reflects, that is to say, the American movie industry's sentimental sense of itself. And he *survives,* along with the other good people who deserve happy endings. Survival—with self-esteem—is what big-budget studio filmmaking is all about, and the movie community's ability to congratulate itself on mediocre, cold-blooded creations like *Jurassic Park* is perhaps its most essential adaptive mechanism. Hollywood's scaly denizens don't believe in the possibility of extinction; they think they're actually living in a land that time forgot.

SHAKESPEARE IN THE SUN
(REVIEW OF KENNETH BRANAGH'S *MUCH ADO ABOUT NOTHING*)

Anne Barton

Much Ado About Nothing (1598) is one of the most resolutely urban of Shakespeare's comedies. The house of Leonato, Governor of Messina, stands in a Sicilian city of churches, law courts, and jails, where crowded streets as well as private dwellings need to be patrolled and kept quiet at night—however inefficiently—by Constable Dogberry and his shambling subordinates. Although Leonato's town house, like that of his brother Antonio, is grand enough to boast a spacious garden, in which some of the action takes place, no one in this play ever escapes to the equivalent of *As You Like It*'s Forest of Arden, the wood near Athens of *A Midsummer Night's Dream,* or even Petruchio's country estate in *The Taming of the Shrew.* Outside the tightly knit family world of Leonato's Messina, but never visited in the play, there seem to be only that unidentified battlefield on which Don Pedro, Prince of Arragon, has just defeated his bastard brother, the vicious and disaffected Don John, and those Italian cities in which Leonato's other aristocratic guests were born: Florence in the case of Count Claudio, Don Pedro's youthful favorite, Padua in that of Benedick, the prince's older and comically misogynistic companion.

In the film version of *Much Ado About Nothing,* adapted as well as directed by Kenneth Branagh (who also plays Benedick), Messina has disappeared. Shakespeare's main plot, about Leonato's daughter, Hero, the young girl falsely accused of unchastity and cast off by her fiancé, Claudio, on their wedding day, and the subsidiary action involving Benedick and Leonato's niece, Beatrice, arch-enemies maneuvered by their friends into love, both unfold at or near a ravishing rose-red villa in Italy's Chianti country: "Vignamaggio," once the home of Leonardo da Vinci's Mona Lisa Gherardini.

From the very beginning—a picnic in an olive grove—Branagh's version of *Much Ado* is boldly rural and open-air. "Church" weddings happen out of doors, and even the few scenes set "inside" tend to place characters in interior courtyards open to the sky, or on balconies and upper loggias framing a panorama of the Tuscan hills. There are losses involved in Branagh's decision here—not least a virtual obliteration, beneath the generalized bucolic bonhomie, of Shakespeare's carefully structured social hierarchy—but there are gains as well.

The movie is visually stunning. The other advantages are largely those stressed by Branagh himself in his *Much Ado About Nothing: Screenplay, Introduction, and Notes on the Making of the Movie,* the book released simultaneously with the film. Branagh reports that in 1988, when he toured the United Kingdom as Benedick in a stage version directed by Judi Dench for his own Renaissance Theatre Company, he was struck during one performance by how much "the play seemed to beg to live outside, in a vivid, lush countryside." In publicity for the film, he has elaborated on this feeling:

> I wanted to come to Italy for its sensual quality. To feature wine, grapes, bread, cheese and the simple way of life. Reduce it to a primitive passion where people live in the sun, eat, drink, and have sex. The sun changes the rhythm of the way you act and think about the characters.

The movie produced five years after Branagh's stage production has, indeed, an arresting sensuousness and vitality. This *Much Ado* is flooded not just with sun, food, and physical desire, but with music of various kinds, including choric ensembles. "Sigh no more, ladies," the bittersweet lyric sung just once in Act II of Shakespeare's play, becomes something like a leitmotif as it returns yet again in Patrick Doyle's catchy setting, while even the tonsured Friar Francis (sympathetically played by Jimmy Yuill) turns out, as he assists in the rites of atonement around the "dead" Hero's tomb, to be a deft hand at the guitar. There is also a great deal of communal, and spiritedly informal, dance. It is all very fresh and beguiling, and one must have a heart of stone to object that Leonato's house and garden sometimes seem to be accommodating an improbable number of jolly locals unaccounted for in Shakespeare's play, busily folding up laundry, or whirling hand in hand through cypress alleys and among the fountains, topiary, and statues.

The exigencies of Shakespeare's plot make it necessary for a cloud momentarily to darken all this *al fresco* joyousness (literalized in the film by a colossal electric storm the night before Hero's wedding) as Keanu Reeves's silkily sinister Don John moves into action. A proto-Iago figure who would really like to poison everyone at Leonato's overflowing banquet table, he has to be content with breaking off the wedding by slandering the bride, to the dismay of all concerned, including his brother, Don Pedro, who arranged the match. Branagh, who states in his book about the movie that he wanted "a certain fairy tale quality to emerge," finds it easy to accept Don John's essentially unreal evil—not, after all, unlike that of the cold Duke in Thurber's *The Thirteen Clocks,* who announces that "We all have flaws, and mine is being wicked." What he seems anxious to expunge are those far more troublesome doubts raised by the character and behavior of Shakespeare's

Claudio: doubts that would complicate and qualify the sunny ending of Branagh's film.

Like Proteus in *The Two Gentlemen of Verona*, Angelo in *Measure for Measure*, and Bertram in *All's Well That Ends Well*, Claudio is one of Shakespeare's cads: a young man who behaves abominably to a loving and generous woman, causes her great suffering, and then, after a perfunctory repentance, is dismissed with her into a happiness he scarcely seems to deserve. Long before the appearance of feminism, the outrage of Shakespeare's Beatrice over the way Claudio waits to expose her cousin Hero until the church ceremony itself—"What? bear her in hand until they come to take hands, and then with public accusation, uncovered slander, unmitigated rancor—O God, that I were a man! I would eat his heart in the market-place"—was something audiences and readers, male and female alike, needed no prompting to endorse.

There are other deficiencies visible in "the most exquisite Claudio": his mercenary concern, before he embarks on his love suit, about whether Hero is

Leonato's sole heir; the ease with which, instead of wooing Hero himself, he allows Don Pedro to do so in his name during the masked ball; his inclination to believe Don John's accusation immediately, even before he overhears his henchman Borachio's midnight courtship of Margaret (Hero's waiting gentlewoman) disguised as Hero, at her mistress's bedroom window; the callousness of his attempts to jest with Benedick after Hero's supposed death, and the alacrity with which he agrees, after Don John's plot has been uncovered, to marry another daughter of Leonato's house. Although a variety of separate excuses can be offered for Claudio's actions—not least the fact that Don Pedro also credits his brother's lie—he still does not add up to anything like Romeo. Indeed, it takes an extensive and strategic cutting of Shakespeare's text, together with surging violins in Doyle's musical score, to bring Hero's lover even within hailing distance of Juliet's.

—

In drastically shortening *Much Ado* for the screen, Branagh has stripped out not only most of the verse Shakespeare positioned so carefully in this predominantly prose comedy, but also the play's intricate double-entendres. For the fast-moving verbal bawdy of the original, he substitutes an equally fast-moving but far simpler visual sexuality. The result, more accessible to modern audiences, is arguably better suited to cinema as a form. It also serves, crucially, to render Robert Sean Leonard's Claudio much less sophisticated and knowing than Shakespeare's character. Leonard's performance, it has to be said, is distinctly wooden. Behind it, however, Branagh's own reading of the part shines clear, raising—not for the only time in the film—the question of how attentive he has been to character clues in Shakespeare's text. Leonard's Claudio is meant to be a very young man, barely past adolescence, who remains (despite his precocious feats as a soldier in Don Pedro's wars) emotionally vulnerable and unsure. His romantic idealism springs from an innocence that vies with that of Kate Beckinsale's Hero, a young woman who comes across (for all Branagh's insistence in an interview that he was "keen not to produce a Hero who was wimpish, not just a victim") as equally featureless, and certainly very immature.

It is one of the virtues of Branagh's *Much Ado* that, unlike some Shakespeare films—Peter Greenaway's *Prospero's Books* comes immediately to mind—in which it is hard to see how anyone not already familiar with the plot could possibly piece it together from the movie—it tells the story of the play very clearly. In achieving this clarity, Branagh has not only added and transposed scenes, but smoothed out many of the twists and turns in the comedy, including the initial misapprehension, encouraged by Don John, that Don Pedro intends to marry Hero himself. In the screen version, no one but Claudio ever entertains this idea, so that Benedick's "But did you think the Prince would have served you thus?" becomes an exasperated inquiry, instead of being, as it is in Shakespeare, an attempt to commiserate. The effect is to increase the sense of Claudio's naive gullibility, an overreadiness to jump to conclusions that helps to explain the speed with which, later, he will credit the allegation that Hero is false.

A movie audience, too, that has been allowed to join Claudio, Don John, and the Prince as they watch a particularly lusty Borachio (Gerard Horan) making vigorous love to Imelda Staunton's Margaret on Hero's balcony (a scene Shakespeare calculatedly did not stage) is far more likely to forgive the violence of

Claudio's response. As for Claudio's heartless witticisms in the first scene of Act V, they have been tactfully omitted.

Paradoxically, Branagh displaces what is genuinely disturbing in Shakespeare's comedy onto Dogberry, a clown part written originally for the great Elizabethan comic actor Will Kemp. His conception of this character looks remarkably like desperation. Branagh himself has confessed to being scarred by his earlier stage failure to make *As You Like It*'s Touchstone funny. The indications are that he also worried, in this respect, about Dogberry, and so decided not to try. In the movie, moreover, he had the further problem, given a setting confined to Leonato's rural estate, of deciding what to do with a constable, his sidekick Verges, and an entire crew of night watchmen explicable only in an urban setting. Cutting (particularly drastic in these scenes), although it removes some of the specific embarrassments, could never be more than a partial solution. Hence, as it seems, the necessity to transform Michael Keaton, as Dogberry, into a menacing, sadistic, and profoundly unamusing thug.

—

In his youthful autobiography, *Beginning,* published in 1989, and in subsequent statements, including some connected with the film of *Much Ado,* Branagh has consistently emphasized not only the importance of *being* as opposed to *demonstrating* a character, that favorite maxim of twentieth-century drama schools and rehearsal rooms, but what he calls the "utter reality of characterization." Film cameras, he has asserted, are particularly ruthless in the way they expose "artificial 'witty' acting—flutey voiced young gallants with false laughs and thighs made for slapping." The present movie, "based on character," was not to be like that, both because Branagh deplores such performances in general, and because "it is the detail of humanity amongst the participants that helps make *Much Ado* one of Shakespeare's most accessible works."

Shakespeare invested Dogberry with quite a lot of humanity. Benedick complains of Beatrice at one moment in Act V, "Thou hast frighted the word out of his right sense, so forcible is thy wit." Dogberry is continually terrorizing the English language, but out of incompetence, not wit. A man engaged in a non-stop struggle with those polysyllabic words he loves but can never get right, he uses them to bolster up an authority of which he is inordinately proud, but in which he feels anything but secure. If he patronizes the elderly Verges, his second in command and most appreciative audience, it is always with affection. The nature and strength of the bond between the two men is never in doubt. In one of those lightning glimpses of a character's past typical of Shakespeare (but cut in the film) Dogberry provides a clue to his pomposity. He is, he explains, not only an officer, but

> . . . which is more, a householder; and, which is more, as pretty a piece
> of flesh as any in Messina, and one that knows the law, go to! and a rich
> fellow enough, go to! and a fellow that hath had losses; and one that hath
> two gowns and everything handsome about him.

There is a tiny life history here, providing a vivid and clear basis on which to build the character. Dogberry has, at some time, experienced financial disaster, then an uphill battle to regain social standing, self-esteem, and the modest prosperity of which he is now so proud. It is both comic and, for Dogberry, a terrible thing when one of Don John's henchmen, his villainy unexpectedly brought to light by a police force that normally sleeps on the beat, tells the constable in public, "You are an ass"—not just an insult, but a monosyllabic one at that.

Keaton's interpretation of Dogberry would appear to take off from the constable's observation in Act III that "an two men ride of a horse, one must ride behind." He and Ben Elton's badly acted Verges customarily arrive and depart, linked together, to the accompaniment of a clatter of hoofs—or, as Branagh puts it in the screenplay,

> From out of a mad dark night come galloping on imaginary horses two
> comic psychopaths: the physical malaprops, taking with utter serious-
> ness their role as Cassidy and Sundance of the local constabulary.

It is not entirely clear how law enforcers can believe themselves to be outlaws, but more worrying is the way Branagh (who also invokes Patton talking to the troops, Perry Mason, and John Wayne to characterize Dogberry) has with these two parts reduced the "humanity" on which he places so much stress to a matter of "comic" malaprops. Not so comic either. Borachio and his partner, Conrade (Richard Clifford), are not a pretty sight after their interrogation by the law. When the demented Dogberry begins to operate on Verges's eyes with his thumbs (because Verges has threatened to upstage him), it seems for a moment that some of the Cornwall and Gloucester footage has strayed in from a film Branagh has yet to make—of *King Lear.*

———

The audiences, however, who will surely pack the theaters over the next few months to see *Much Ado* will be there not for Dogberry and Verges, but for Branagh's Benedick, and Emma Thompson's Beatrice. The Hero and Claudio plot may be at the center of Shakespeare's play; but at least since the reign of Charles I, when Leonard Digges was referring to Beatrice and Benedick as well-known theatrical crowd-pullers, and the king himself carefully crossed out the title *Much Ado About Nothing* in his personal copy of the First Folio, replacing it with *Beatrice and Benedick,* the older pair of lovers have claimed the lion's share of attention—and also the star performers.

In the present movie, Beatrice and Benedick become even more fascinating by virtue of the off-screen facts. Branagh, whose talent and hard work have conducted him, while still in his early thirties, from working-class poverty in Protestant Belfast to control of an impressive mini-empire in theater and film (while inviting comparison as an actor with Olivier) and Emma Thompson, the former Cambridge undergraduate fresh from an Oscar for her performance as Margaret Schlegel in *Howards End,* are, we know, in real life husband and wife. Phyllida Law, as it happens, who plays Hero's attendant Ursula, is also Emma Thompson's mother, but the real focus of attraction—as in the Richard Burton/Liz Taylor *Taming of the Shrew,* or Olivier's stage production of *Antony and Cleopatra* with Vivien Leigh—is bound to be that perennially engaging spectacle of a couple becoming husband

and wife in fiction who already are so in fact. A situation exploited on the English stage ever since the Restoration, when the appearance of actresses (including such married theater couples as Susanna and William Mountfort) first made the phenomenon possible, it places Branagh and Thompson firmly in a line that also includes Humphrey Bogart and Lauren Bacall, the Lunts, and more recently, in what has become a far less attractive example of the imaginary spilling over into the real, Woody Allen and Mia Farrow.

Emma Thompson's burgeoning reputation can only be enhanced by this film. She is an enchanting Beatrice: vibrant, spirited, and quick, but manifestly with hidden depths. Branagh, so ready to deprive Dogberry of his past, has wisely given full measure to those hints in the text which suggest that Beatrice has previously given her heart to Benedick ("Marry, once before he won it of me with false dice") and come away badly hurt. Her aggressive behavior toward him now, that "merry war" of words between the two, in which she usually comes off best, conceals both a determination not to be wounded in that way again, and a smoldering love that Hero and her attendant Ursula can easily fan into fire simply by making her believe that Benedick feels the same for her.

As Don Pedro, Claudio, and Leonato, by means of a similar trick, have already brought Benedick to realize his true feelings for Beatrice, by whom he remains obviously obsessed, their happiness waits only upon a mutual and open declaration of love. That, ironically, the public shaming of Hero by Claudio provokes. Benedick not only believes in Hero's innocence (which even her own father did not) because Beatrice does; he consents at her request to challenge Claudio to a duel, thus dividing himself at a stroke from his old, accustomed world of cynical, barracks room humor and male camaraderie.

Thompson's beautifully nuanced performance projects in abundance that quality essential to so many of Shakespeare's comedy heroines: a transparent goodness that never becomes sentimental or smug. A mistress of many moods, she manages to be both comic and touching in the big "overhearing" scene in the orchard, then deadly serious—and a little frightening—in her distress and anger on Hero's behalf. Actresses often have trouble avoiding titters from the audience when Beatrice so abruptly asks Benedick, after their first kiss, to "Kill Claudio," but Thompson's emotional intelligence, and a sudden deepening of vocal register on the line, adroitly fend off the danger. Admirable too is her handling of that tense moment in Act II when she jests her way into a marriage proposal from Denzel Washington's Don Pedro, suddenly realizes that he means it, and needs with grace and sensitivity to extricate them both.

The film contains a number of outstanding performances: Richard Brier's Leonato, Yuill's Friar, Clifford's Conrade, Law's Ursula, Reeves's Don John. It also suffers from some bad ones, for which miscasting occasionally seems to blame. Hero's uncle Antonio, for instance, is a frail and elderly man, who gamely if a little comically challenges Claudio to what must be a most unequal fight. But the hulking Brian Blessed, none the worse for his recent ascent of Everest (much publicized in England), looks in the part as though his sneeze would be enough to knock Leonard's Claudio down for the count. The best acting, however, comes from Washington as Don Pedro and Thompson, as much in small details as in their overall handling of their parts. His face, in every scene in which he appears, speaks volumes. Her probing and wise reading of the two stanzas of "Sigh no more, ladies," at the very beginning of the movie, is worth considerably more than its elaborate reappearances as a song.

To single out Thompson and Washington in this way is not to slight Branagh as Benedick. His is a creditable, interesting performance which, in the chapel scene, becomes genuinely moving. It is hard not to feel, however, that despite having played the part before, and the precautionary measure of asking his former instructor Hugh Cruttwell to monitor his acting in rehearsals, Branagh this time, trying to play Benedick while also directing the film, has bitten off more than he can chew. With so much on his hands, he ends up making basic performance mistakes of just the kind he inveighs against in his introduction to the screenplay, and in the early pages of *Beginning* has mocked himself for committing as a novice: generalizing mood, demonstrating Benedick's character, as opposed to living it through. The problem focuses itself in his prose soliloquies. Branagh, so good at communicating the plot of the play generally, seems as an actor oddly unresponsive to the story line of the character in these speeches, as it changes and unfolds before our eyes in a small space.

Part of the problem here would seem to be his insistence upon looking everywhere except into the camera. This refusal to address soliloquy to an audience in the way Shakespeare intended, although it is even easier to do so in film than on the stage, is in line with the naturalism of Branagh's entire approach. But it cuts him off from us, making Benedick seem like a man suddenly talking to himself because he is in a generalized "state." Branagh has some fine moments—the highly charged simplicity of his "I do love nothing in the world so well as you," in the chapel scene with Beatrice, or his comic squawk of outrage from the cypress alley in which he is concealed, rapidly transformed into an unconvincing bird imitation, as he overhears Don Pedro accuse him of having "a contemptible spirit." (The word means nothing worse than "contemptuous" in Shakespeare, but the modern sense produces a nice bit of business, and only a pedant would object.) But overall, this is a disappointingly exterior Benedick.

Here it contrasts markedly, not only with Emma Thompson's Beatrice, but with Washington's haunting, wonderfully inward Don Pedro: a performance of great dignity and depth. Washington's dialogue with Beatrice in Act II provides one of the few moments of real intimacy in a film which in general prefers the communal to the private. (Branagh has even, in the interests of pace, cut the lovely, domestic scene between the three women in Hero's apartment on her wedding morning.) Contained and humorous in the early part of the play, Washington later makes Don Pedro's affronted Spanish honor very real. Unforgettable too is the silent eloquence of his pain in the monument scene, and his guilt at the end when, like Prospero with Caliban, he must confront the fettered Don John: a thing of irredeemable darkness, that he must "acknowledge mine." Although directorially underplayed (the camera rests for only a split second on Washington, standing alone by the chapel as the revels begin), his absence from the final dance seems both very Shakespearean and right.

—

Imaginative, intelligent, and brilliantly filmed, Branagh's *Much Ado* deserves a big success, not only for those reasons, but because it is likely to make many people—especially the young—understand that Shakespeare can be vital, interesting, moving, and fun. In *Beginning*, Branagh says of his Renaissance Theatre Company that "the appeal was intended to be very broad. We wanted to present popular art. Not poor art or thin art or even 'arty' art, but popular art that would expand the mind and the senses and really entertain." That manifesto might have been written for this film, and it is not an easy brief. Certainly it is possible to complain that although *Much Ado* is one of Shakespeare's shorter plays, Branagh has "thinned" his original more than was needed: that by abbreviating the dance sequences (especially the interminable one at the end) he might have found room for more of Shakespeare's text.

There is something wrong when tangos and an extended ring around the maypole mean sacrificing lines like Leonato's agonized

> *mine, and mine I loved, and*
> *mine I praised,*
> *And mine that I was proud on—*

or the great heralding of dawn as the comedy lifts toward resolution at the end of the monument scene:

> *Good morrow, masters, Put your*
>   *torches out.*
> *The wolves have preyed, and look,*
>   *the gentle day,*
> *Before the wheels of Phoebus,*
>   *round about*
> *Dapples the drowsy east with*
>   *spots of grey.*

We are talking here about only a few minutes of playing time, but they are a crucial few. A different kind of "thinning" oversimplifies or sentimentalizes character, and bans other kinds of Shakespearean complexity from Branagh's resolutely "fairytale" world.

Olivier's classic, and visually even more astonishing, film of *Henry V,* although it too cut a considerably longer play to make it simpler and more positive, nevertheless retained a much greater proportion of text—and ambiguity—than Branagh has. Branagh is not yet Olivier, either as a director or actor. His own film of *Henry V,* although highly praised, is most unlikely to look as good after almost half a century as its great predecessor. Branagh's *Much Ado* is significantly better than his *Henry V.* But he will need to take on and master a good deal more of what is challenging and difficult in Shakespeare, while retaining popular appeal, before that frequently made comparison with Olivier rings true. But it says a great deal for him—and for the future of the plays both on stage and screen—that he should already be coming so close.

EVALUATING A TELEVISION SHOW

Like a book or film review, a good television review will be informative, interpretive, and evaluative, as the following review of the documentary, *Discover: The World of Science,* demonstrates. Bright, lively, and impeccably organized, it starts out by indicating the presumed purpose of the show: to explain—in clear, nontechnical language that the lay person can understand—the latest discoveries and developments in science.

It then assesses how successfully the show achieves its purpose: "It's a fascinating show," the reviewer tells us, with "a flexible format" and a "deftly written script" that carries out its "near-impossible mission of explaining complex subject matter brightly and smoothly by talking *to,* rather than *down* to, the audience." Is such a purpose *worth* achieving (the third and final basis of judgment)? Most assuredly, says the reviewer, summing up the value of such a show in an amusingly direct comment on the sponsor's investment: "Money well spent."

Note how distinctively the reviewer's voice dominates the review, especially in paragraph three where he scolds "wise guys" and "scoffers" who "ridicule the idea of spoon-fed science." A whole series of provocative questions—a science quiz of sorts— challenges such viewers to *just watch this show and see how wrong you are!* Could any of us resist tuning in?

REVIEW OF *DISCOVER: THE WORLD OF SCIENCE*

Merrill Panitt

Scientists have their own language. They communicate effectively with one another, but when it comes to explaining their work to laymen, it's as if they're speaking in a strange tongue. They must go back to basics and lead us from there if we're to have any idea of what they're talking about. And usually there isn't enough time—or enough interest on our part—to warrant the effort.

As the sciences advance and their impact on our society increases, we find ourselves living in a world we barely understand. Which is why *Discover: The World of Science,* the PBS series that deals with discoveries and developments in science and nature in an intelligible manner, is so timely. This year's second of five hour-long episodes is scheduled for Monday, Nov. 14, on most PBS stations. The rest will be seen once a month through February at the convenience of your local PBS station manager.

There are undoubtedly those who ridicule the idea of spoon-fed science as further evidence of the television audience's inability to grasp anything deeper than a sitcom or a cop show. To those scoffers we say, "OK, wise guys, how does a solar-powered vehicle work? What makes lightning? What's the advantage of an insulin pump? How come there are so many different species of honey creepers on Hawaii, which started as molten lava? What's a black hole and how do astronomers go about finding one? What's relaxation response and how can it help athletes? How are we talking to dolphins and how are they answering? *Do you know?* Huh?"

Viewers who watched some of last season's *Discover* episodes have the answers or, in some cases, at least know how scientists are trying to find the answers. And while they may not be able to lecture on positive and negative charges in clouds and how they react to form lightning, they do understand the experiments being conducted to solve the mystery of lightning.

It's a fascinating show, largely because the producers, Graham Chedd and John Angier, have adopted a flexible magazine format that permits them to spend only as much time as is necessary on each segment. The host and narrator is Peter Graves, who, with a deftly written script, carries out his near-impossible mission of explaining complex subjects brightly and smoothly by talking *to,* rather than *down* to, the audience.

Among this season's segments: students at California Polytech building and operating a human-powered helicopter with a 140-foot blade; how—and why— red wolves are being reintroduced into a North Carolina forest preserve; a demonstration of new scientific methods of identifying criminals; the bizarre creatures (including giant clams and 3-foot worms) that exist in areas permeated by volcanic hydrogen sulfide a mile and a half beneath the surface of the ocean; and what makes a boomerang come back.

Discover is for people of all ages who enjoy learning about our world and what scientists are doing to further our understanding of it. The show is "made possible" by GTE, the utilities conglomerate. Money well spent.

DISCUSSION AND EXERCISES

Analyze and evaluate the reviews in this chapter by answering the following questions:

1. Do they provide readers with sufficient information to make a sound judgment of their own?

2. In what ways do the reviewers support their own evaluations (evidence, logical reasoning)?

3. Describe the tone of each review and indicate whether it is appropriate. Does it win readers' "good will"?

4. Comment on each reviewer's style and the overall readability of each review.

5. How effective are the opening and closing sentences of each review?

6. Comment on rhetorical stance.

ESSAY SUGGESTIONS

1. Write a review (500-1,000 words) of a book, a film, or a television show that interests you. Remember that writing a review requires not only the ability to evaluate but also many other composite skills. Be prepared, then, to draw on both the models cited above and the following as well:

   a. *your ability to describe* and to assemble details (see question 1, *How can X be described?*)

   b. *your ability to assemble facts* (see question 6, *What are the facts about X?*)

   Continued

c. *your ability to summarize* (see question 17, *How can X be summarized?*)

d. *your ability to interpret* (see question 18, *How should X be interpreted?*)

2. Write a review (500-1,000 words) of a new television show, following the tone and organization of Merrill Panitt's review of *Discover: The World of Science.*

3. Watch your favorite television show, taking notes for a review. Watch another show that you have heard is not good and again take notes. Employing prewriting techniques to assemble your thoughts, write a comparison-and-contrast essay of 750-1,000 words that reviews (see Question 15: *How Does X Compare to Y?*) the two programs with respect to one another.

Question

20

WHAT CASE CAN BE MADE FOR OR AGAINST X?

THE NATURE OF ARGUMENT
> *COLLEGE LECTURES ARE OBSOLETE,*
> ALLAN H. GILBERT

THE STRUCTURE OF ARGUMENT
> *SHAME ON ADS THAT USE CULTURE TO*
> *SELL LIQUOR,* NICOLE HARRIS

FUNDAMENTALS OF LOGIC
> DEDUCTION AND INDUCTION

ARGUMENT BY ANALOGY
> *THE GREAT WHITE MYTH,* ANNA
> QUINDLEN
> COMMON LOGICAL FALLACIES

ARGUING FOR AND AGAINST
> *ANIMAL RESEARCH: AN UNNECESSARY*
> *EVIL?* ANN SQUIRE
> *ON EXPERIMENTING WITH ANIMALS,*
> GEORGE BERNARD SHAW
> *A HUMANE AND SCIENTIFIC NECESSITY,*
> ROBERT J. WHITE

MODERN ARGUMENT: THE EDITORIAL
A WORD FOR THE NEW YORK ACCENT,
RICHARD SHEPARD

HUMANIZING ARGUMENT: ROGERIAN STRATEGY
INAUGURAL ADDRESS, BILL CLINTON

TESTING YOUR ARGUMENT: A CHECKLIST
IN DEFENSE OF VOLUNTARY
EUTHANASIA, SIDNEY HOOK
COMMUNICATION: ITS BLOCKING AND
ITS FACILITATION, CARL R. ROGERS

THE NATURE OF ARGUMENT

Aristotle said, "If it is a disgrace to a man when he cannot defend himself in a bodily way, it would be odd not to think him disgraced when he cannot defend himself with reason." It is reason—and mainly reason—that you must marshal when you answer the question, What case can I make for or against X? In trying to build a case, you move beyond plain exposition into the more active and agressive realm of argumentation, an ancient and honored form of discourse: You try not merely to explain but also to defend or refute what logicians call a "proposition," statement that usually includes conflict and controversy. Unlike a plain statement of fact ("John Smith is the mayor of Squedunk"), readers cannot look up, verify, and establish a proposition once and for all. Instead, a proposition is debatable: It may or may not be true ("The mayor of Squedunk is corrupt and should be thrown out of office"). In making such a judgment about what *ought* to be done, you assume the burden of proof. You must therefore marshal evidence and exert rigorous reasoning in support of your proposed course of action; you must persuade your readers or listeners that the proposition is necessary and just; and you must win them over to your side by making them see that your side is their side—that you have common cause with them. You must recognize that all reform requires collective action, that you alone, for example, cannot sweep the corrupt mayor of Squedunk out of office: you will need help.

Obviously, of all forms of discourse, argumentation is the most morally compelling and significant. In addition, it is far more demanding and comprehensive than the other forms not only because it requires rigorous reasoning and persuasive tactics, but also because it frequently embraces other forms: definition, description, comparison, analysis, narration, characterization, interpretation, and evaluation. All these forms may enter into argumentation. Indeed, in answering What case can I make for or against X? you may include all these forms—plus some others not mentioned.

In making a case, then, you should try to raise as many pertinent points as possible, for the content of the argument—the evidence that substantiates your position—as well as the rigor of your reasoning—will establish and prove your case.

Also remember that in no form of writing is it more important to use the strengths of language to the best possible effect. Stylistic failings such as undefined terms that create ambiguity, confusing grammatical constructions, vague allusions, and pompous, overlong sentences will alienate those you might otherwise convince. Bad writing, in other words, can kill a case as surely as lack of evidence or fallacious reasoning.

Is and *Ought* Propositions

Basically, you use two different kinds of propositions in argument: the *is* proposition (as assertion of opinion or value) and the *ought* proposition (a proposal for action). Most of the illustrative essays in this chapter combine the two types of arguments, establishing the fundamental causal relationship that underlies most argumentation:

Because A *is* the case, B *ought* to be done.

Woodrow Wilson's historic address to Congress in 1917 asking for a declaration of war against Germany uses this logical formulation, which may be summarized this way:

> Because Germany's aggressive submarine action against American commerce is an act of warfare against both the United States and mankind [an assertion of opinion or value], America *ought* to enter World War I [a proposal for action], which action would make the world "safe for democracy" [the projected conclusion].

President Wilson's aim in this classic example of making a case for a specific action was to win the assent of members of Congress, to convince them that what he asserted was true and just, worthy of wholehearted and unconditional support.

Similarly in the following essay Allan H. Gilbert combines *is* and *ought* propositions to make a spirited case against a hallowed academic tradition, the college lecture.

COLLEGE LECTURES ARE OBSOLETE

Allan H. Gilbert

The advertising pamphlet of a well-known American university recently showed a picture of a professor presenting chemistry to some hundreds of students. Except for the costumes and the ugly angularity of the room, it might have been an academic scene in 1450, before the invention of printing. In 1766 Dr. Johnson remarked:

> I cannot see that lectures can do as much good as reading the books from which the lectures are taken.

And in 1781 he still thought:

> Lectures were once useful, but now, when all can read, and books are so numerous, lectures are unnecessary.

Yet after two hundred years, the modern professor has not overtaken Dr. Johnson. He has not discovered that printing has been invented—not to mention Xerox®, etc. The old-time methods are good enough for him. Academic photographers are especially amusing in that they delight in showing the most blatantly up-to-date subjects, such as physics, presented as in Abelard's Paris. Obviously this applies not to the occasional public lecture, but to the twice-a-week throughout the term.

What Is Wrong About Lectures?

1. Even a good speaker will not always be correctly heard by his audience. Horns toot, students cough. And sometimes professors mumble. Even in the notes of graduate students the well-known Professor Fredson Bowers has appeared as Fritz and Brower, and Nike of Samothrace as the Decay of Sammy's Face.

2. What is written on a blackboard—often in professorial scribble—cannot be perfectly copied. Time presses; even modern lighting is not all-revealing; perfect vision is not universal.

3. A student trying to take excellent notes cannot think about their content; he must not lag. He is like the telegrapher of whom Edison tells. The man received, in dots and dashes, the news of Lincoln's assassination; when he went out on the street, he learned that such news had been reported. In the days of monotype composition for newspapers, I knew the man who set the gossip column for the local paper. When the paper appeared, he read it as something new to him. Such must be the mind of the student who takes notes so good that he can attain the ideal of giving back in his blue book what the lecturer has said. The Welsh professor of mediaeval literature, Dr. Ker, is said to have remarked: "How can I give less than 90 for my own words?"

4. Lectures prepared long since and read from yellowed paper cease to call on the professor's brain. His class in the morning need not call him from the idiot box in the evening. The chairman of a department in which I served once read the same lecture to a class for the third successive time. . . . It is reported of a Harvard professor that he moved to the door and put his hand on the knob for his last sentence. No student could catch him. Revision would disarrange the schedule and desecrate the sentences which, through many repetitions, the professor has come to regard as truth. He is a human tape recorder. The students are tape-receivers. . . .

5. The college lecturer seldom has a prepared audience. How often can a lecturer on Shakespeare, for example, be sure that his hearers have read the play on which he speaks? If he can read aloud, he may read to his class with profit, but then he ceases to be a lecturer. The unprepared audience (or the audience not eager to learn the subject, and not impatient of failure to help them do so) affects the lecturer. He wishes to break through their boredom. So he tends to become an entertainer, giving a show. There is much in the story that the faculty of a well-known college for men opposes the admission of women because—evidently being old fogies—they imagine they would be deprived of the bawdy jokes supposed to amuse their captive audiences. But how often do professorial jokes illustrate the subject in hand? Or the popular lecturer turns to oratory. Newspaper pictures of some popular teachers who recently have gathered publicity by dismissal, show them making gestures suited to the soap box or the pulpit. An academic Savonarola or Billy Sunday or Graham may rouse in a few hearers an emotional desire to learn. Such a desire, when it lasts, prepares a youth to study and to seek aid from a teacher, but it is not teaching. Colleges, like the rest of life, need their share of emotion, but their primary business is intellectual. A man given over to his own convictions and beliefs is not a teacher because he cannot see both sides of a subject.

6. Especially for commuting students, attendance at lectures is a serious burden. If the teacher has lectures prepared, let them be mimeographed. Then the student can study them at home. Or let the professor require the student to read the books from which the lectures are drawn. They can be bought for less money than commuting requires; and the student is not wasting his time in a bus or automobile.

7. In the lecturer's audience, the student tends to become a mere numbered unit, deprived of power to question, much less to object. He is trained to accept the dicta of the professor—a habit worse than that of going to the library to find "a book"—author unobserved—from which to copy. At least the library offers more

than one book, and even the most facile pedagogue is likely to take more pains with dicta to be printed than with those merely to be pronounced in the uncritical isolation of the lecture hall, before students who—if they wish good marks—will not murmur publicly against what they are told. The lecture inculcates passivity of mind. The student is a spectator, with no part in the game, except that he selects the lecture course because it is called a crib.

8. The book, even when mimeographed, is better than any student's notes. There are no hiatuses for sickness, empty pens, noise. As Dr. Johnson said: "If your attention fails and you miss part of a lecture, you are lost; you cannot go back as you can upon a book."

Furthermore, the best lectures are most likely to attain printing. If a professor has lectures better than any printed book or even group of printed books, can he be defended for restricting them to his own university, instead of giving them to mankind? Are we to suppose that there are in America a hundred sets of lecture notes superior to anything in print? Is not the student better off with A. C. Bradley's own vindication of Falstaff—however absurd it is—than with the Shakespeare professor's diluted version of it? If the professor cannot do better than the authors on his reading list, why not omit the lectures and attend to the reading list?

9. Something can be said for the living presence of the lecturer. But this is again revivalistic; the college lecturer is supposed to be teaching a subject. There is, too, a presence behind the written word, usually stronger, though less immediate than that on the platform. Does the student come to college for the personality of Professor X, or to learn? Indeed the professor who gives a course in himself is handicapped by the insignificance of his subject. "A good book is the precious life blood of a master spirit." How often are lecture-writers such spirits?

10. The important poets have been so richly annotated that even the most expert scholars can now add little detailed comment. Fortunate is the lecturer on Milton who can improve on Professor Hughes' notes. The lesser authors have been carefully worked. How many teachers of Herrick can correct any of Professor Patrick's notes, or explain difficulties he has not elucidated? As to more general comment, a lecturer may indeed warn his pupils against much that has been written on great authors, but how many lecturers are capable of anything else than riding with the tide? Poetry exists to be read; the lecture pushes it into the class of something to be talked about rather than experienced. (Non-lecture teaching is somewhat less subject to this danger.)

The Remedy

Perfect teaching will appear when we have teachers who have entered into their subjects and students eager to learn. With these, we would not need to bother about systems. Without them, not much can be done. We have always had, and always shall have, lawyers not aware of the nature of law, generals unaware of the nature of war, professors of physics who have not found out what their subject is, teachers of Chaucer and Dante who do not, as Benedetto Croce has said, sympathize with their authors. Yet something external can be done against lecturitis.

Let a teacher who sufficiently believes in his own greatness put his lectures in print to be revised frequently as he grows wiser. Then he can abandon his robes of glory, and the student will have more accurate statements and clearer diagrams, which he can copy at his leisure, if that will implant them in his memory.

In a normal lecture course, let us suppose thirty lectures per term, and 150 students. At that rate, each student gets of the professor's public time 1/150 of thirty hours, or 1/5 of an hour. If the professor abandons his rostrum, he has time to meet each student individually for ten minutes a term. The student is warned to prepare. The assistants who gather about such courses are consulted on what the student may profitably ask. Some students would treasure throughout life the memory of ten minutes' serious talk with an eminent professor.

I know students at some of our large places who have gone through their four years without ever speaking on their studies with a man of professorial rank. Such undergraduates deal with junior teachers, graduate students, some of them brilliant, but many of them destined to be mediocrities or failures. Yet from the class of a thousand, the hundred and fifty with the best records can still meet the eminent professor. Such a teacher, relieved from the strain of the large lecture—not entirely removed by the loud speaker—would usually be willing to go beyond the hundred and fifty. If freed from the ceremonial lecture, the pupil has two hours a week free for studying books, mimeographed or printed, and scientific specimens. He does not—in the computer age—spend thirty hours a term writing by hand. Nothing good in the present system need be abolished. The students in the big class can still be divided into small sections, presided over by the best junior teachers the college will pay for.

The survival of the lecture, for nearly five hundred years after the invention of printing, exhibits the unimaginative, unobserving professorial mind. Hidebound professors still read lectures to three or four students, even to one. This seems more ludicrous in nuclear physics than in the humanities, but does not reveal a more imperceptive mind. John Philip Holland, the father of the submarine, said that naval officers (who yield little to professors in holding to what has been) disliked the submarine because it provided no quarter deck to strut on. Do professors cling to lectures because they offer a rostrum to strut on and a lectern to sprawl over?

Lively and provocative as this argument is, are there not logical grounds on which readers could challenge its indictment of the lecture system? Are all lectures *necessarily* read "from yellowed paper"? Are all lecturers *necessarily* "human tape recorders"? Are all students *necessarily* "human tape-receivers"? Are mimeographed copies of a lecture read by students privately in the library *necessarily* more profitable than personal delivery in a lecture? (May not students fall asleep in the library as well as the lecture hall?) What about the creative lecturer who communicates fresh insights so compellingly that students "catch fire"—as they could not from the printed page? Cannot more be said about the possibilities and value of person-to-person classroom encounter? Must the lecture be an extended monologue? Is Gilbert talking about *some* kinds of lectures and lecturers of *all* kinds?

THE STRUCTURE OF ARGUMENT

We should note that although Gilbert wrote his essay in the twentieth century, its organization follows the classic three-part structure that provided the ground plan for Greek and Roman orators—and which is still useful today.

I. Introduction

The introduction, consisting of single sentence or of several paragraphs, includes one or more of the following:

A. *Exordium:* The beginning or opening words, designed to win attention and good will by introducing the case in an interesting and favorable light (a quotation, personal reference, story)

B. *Exposition or narration:* An account of the history of the case (what gave rise to the present problem; how the issues developed)

C. *Direct statement of the case* (the *proposition* to be proved or defended)

D. *Division of proofs:* An *outline* of how the writer will present the evidence ("first I will explain . . . and then I will demonstrate . . .")

II. Body

A. *Confirmation* of one's case by presenting evidence in its favor

1. facts
2. reasons
3. statistics
4. testimony of experts
5. opinions
6. reports
7. examples
8. logical reasoning (deductive and inductive)
9. analogy

B. *Refutation* of opposing views by demonstrating that they are:

1. untrue
2. illogical
3. self-contradictory
4. ambiguous (terms are not clearly defined)
5. dishonest (a deliberate attempt to deceive)
6. absurd

III. Conclusion

A. *Recapitulation* and *summary* of argument: To repeat is to reinforce points, and to make certain readers have not misunderstood them

B. *Peroration:* A final, heightened appeal for support

This classical structure has proven so effective that authors have adapted it for a variety of uses. In the shorter piece below, written as a column in the *Detroit Free Press,* we can identify many of the features of classical argument. Nicole Harris catches our attention with the reference to Janet Jackson, then introduces her main point— that advertisers should not use "culturally significant artifacts" to reach and exploit the African-American audience. She interweaves the elements of confirmation and refutation, then, in her peroration, urges more positive views of African-American life.

SHAME ON ADS THAT USE CULTURE TO SELL LIQUOR

Nicole Harris

When I turned to the Black Entertainment Television channel recently, Janet Jackson's funky dance steps were not yet on the screen. Instead, the latest commercial spot for Schlitz malt liquor was trying to coax me into picking up a bottle or a six-pack.

I have a serious problem with any ads for malt liquor. For one thing, they seemed to be exclusively targeted at African-Americans. Walk down the streets of any predominantly African-American neighborhood and try to count the number of billboards or posters advertising malt liquor. You may run out of fingers and toes.

But there was something different about this commercial that grabbed my attention and provoked my anger. African kente cloth was being used to market Schlitz malt liquor. The actors were in kente cloth hats and vests. The male actor placed a kente cloth sash around the neck of an admiring female, while there were background shots of an African drum. All to the rhythm of a contemporary rap tune and appearances of the raging Schlitz malt liquor bull symbol.

Advertisers are using culturally significant artifacts to reach their target audience, having evolved from creating the stereotypical images of basketball-playing, boom box–toting, singing and dancing black kids.

And it's catching on quickly. Coca-Cola's "Always" campaign includes a spot in which a group of young men are singing a hip, a cappella tune and holding bottles of Coke. The first shot, however, is a kitchen scene with an African Ashanti fertility doll in the background. Now Ashanti dolls are being used to sell more Coke.

Even print ads are jumping on the bandwagon. One of Polaroid's latest ads includes a man dressed in African-print garb looking at pictures in an album.

Advertisers and their clients argue that it's just a matter of using customary strategies to attract a particular consumer.

"The notion of Afrocentrism is very high in the target audience" for malt liquor, said Rob Jackson of Burrell Advertising Agency, the largest African-American ad agency and the creators of the Schlitz ad.

"Kente cloth was just one of the things that we identified that tells the black consumer that we are speaking to them."

Ed Boyd, spokesman for Stroh, maker of Schlitz, said: "I don't see any difference between using kente cloth in the '90s and using an Afro in an ad during the '70s."

The Afro was one of many symbols of an antiestablishment attitude in the '70s. But kente cloth means more—and should be accorded more respect than it's getting in these ads. The wearing of kente cloth symbolizes a connection to cultural heritage, a chance to commemorate traditions.

The term kente means woven. Different countries in Africa have their own patterns and colors. African families would wear a particular cloth so they could be easily identified. The gold, red and green pattern that is popular in the United States today was the cloth worn by the Ashanti royalty in Ghana.

It is highly inappropriate to link the rich history of kente cloth with the selling of malt liquor. One celebrates a culture of a people while the other leads to destruction.

A report, Marketing Booze to Blacks, published in 1987 by the nonprofit Center for Science in the Public Interest—showed that while African Americans consume less alcohol than whites, drinking among blacks results in higher rates of certain alcohol-related problems.

For instance, the U.S. surgeon general reports the death rate for African Americans from cirrhosis of the liver is twice the rate for whites. And there is an alcohol connection to many other devastating problems in the community, from spousal and child abuse to high crime rates.

Jackson argues that since the art of brewing originated in Africa, the relationship portrayed in the ad is accurate.

But I don't want to see kente cloth reduced to a commercial symbol for African Americans, like the raging bull is an icon for Schlitz malt liquor.

"It's a legitimate concern," said Don Coleman of Don Coleman and Associates, an African-American advertising agency in Southfield.

"We have been given a steady diet of singing, dancing, and drinking so that instead of using good marketing experience and judgment—some advertisers use symbols and sometimes they're not the right ones."

And since most large corporations are relying on African-American agencies to create these commercials, these agencies ought to be more cautious about the messages they're sending. They ought to know it is good business to use their cultural heritage to develop a message that will hit home more successfully. Not every African American wears kente cloth, and I don't know anyone who has an Ashanti fertility doll in the kitchen.

So many aspects of African-American life have not been portrayed in advertisements.

"There's an extended family scene, positive experiences of a single family household," Coleman said. "Let's portray these positively."

If advertisers concentrated on those everyday images and left the cultural artifacts out of the marketing mix, they would be hitting the target.

FUNDAMENTALS OF LOGIC

Deduction and Induction

Making a case for or against something always entails choices. The most appropriate way depends on the particular subject and situation, the particular readers, and the particular purpose in the writer's mind. These factors are relative. What remains constant and predictable are the two basic lines of reasoning along which argument inevitably proceeds. They are *deduction*—inferring a particular fact from a general truth (for example, since deciduous plants are known to shed their leaves in winter, you can expect the deciduous dogwood that you planted in the yard last spring to shed its leaves this winter) and *induction*—moving from particular facts to generalizations (for example, since I have tasted thirty green apples and each one was sour, I conclude that all green apples are sour). In actual experience the two modes run into one another, as Thomas Huxley demonstrated in his essay "Thinking Scientifically." Thus:

1. You examine thirty green apples.
2. Each one is sour.

(induction)   3. You generalize: green apples are sour.
                4. You pick up apple thirty-one, which is also green.
(deduction)   5. You infer that this apple—which you have not yet tasted—will also
                   be sour.

Interdependent as they are, each mode of reasoning has distinctive features, and therefore should be examined individually.

Deduction In deductive reasoning we lay down *premises,* certain statements we know or strongly believe are true; from these premises we then derive a *conclusion.* Deduction, then, involves a closely linked *chain of reasoning:*

	A B
Major Premise:	All human beings are mortal.
	C A
Minor Premise:	Socrates is a human being.
	C B
Conclusion:	Socrates is mortal.

The line of reasoning in this *syllogism* (as we call a three-part statement of this kind) is logically valid because, given the two premises, the conclusion necessarily follows. In fact, the conclusion merely states *explicitly* what is already stated *implicitly* in the premises. The conclusion then derives logically and formally from the premises; in this case it points to the axiomatic truth that "things equal to the same things are equal to each other." Thus in the example above, A equals B; C equals A; therefore ($\therefore$) C equals B.

Although formal rules for syllogisms exist, we need not go into them. Our interest is in compositional logic, not in logic per se. Furthermore, common sense—that inborn quality of mind that enables us to follow a logical line of reasoning even if we have never heard the word "logic" before—often alerts us to logical errors. We can tell, for example, that thinking is askew when the premises state that *some* of X is undesirable, and the inference drawn is that *all* of X is undesirable:

> Some people are cruel.
> John is a person.
> $\therefore$ John is cruel.

Obviously, John might not belong in the group of "cruel people." The conclusion changes "some" to "all."

This leap from "some" to "all" is an especially common logical error, or *fallacy;* most people will not specify "some" even when they mean it. Instead they will say, "People are cruel." Such a statement is patently unfair. It can create ill feeling toward whole groups, when in truth only some members are blameworthy: because some students cheat on examinations, we should not conclude—as a sensational magazine story might maintain—that "college kids are dishonest."

Similarly, common sense tells us that another gross error has been committed in the following statement:

All human beings are mammals.
All monkeys are mammals.
All monkeys are human beings.

Logicians call this "the fallacy of the undistributed middle"*; but here again we need not name the logical flaw to see that it has been committed: we know that things belonging to the same general class are not necessarily identical. In this case, the fact that humans are mammals and monkeys are also mammals simply means that they, along with many other animals, share a larger biological category, as the logician's circular diagram shows:

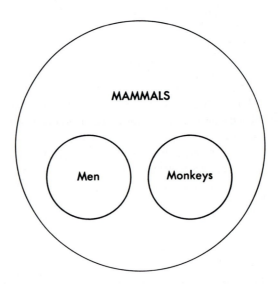

No one would fail to spot the fallacy of the undistributed middle in this example (we *know* monkeys are not people!), but the fallacy is not usually so easy to detect. Indeed it may be (and frequently is) used in a subtle and insidious way to create spurious arguments, such as that of guilt by association:

All communists support the ABC Plan.
Jack Smith supports the ABC Plan
∴ Jack Smith is a communist.

---

*In logic "distributed" means that a term refers to *all* members of the designated class. Thus, in the fallacy of the undistributed middle, the middle term of our syllogism ("human beings") does not refer to *all* members of the class. A syllogism consists of three terms: the predicate, subject, and middle term. The predicate appears in the major premise and conclusion, the subject in the minor premise and conclusion, and the middle term, which links the subject and predicate, appears *only* in the two premises.

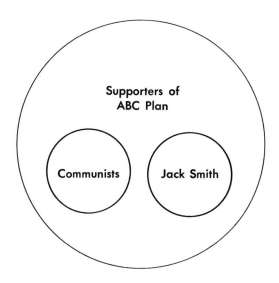

Syllogism is a logician's term, but the process of thought that it describes is hardly specialized; whenever you infer one idea from another, you are using a syllogism. If the reasoning is correct, the syllogism is valid—that is, the conclusion follows logically from the premises. But is it true? That is quite another question, since it is possible for a syllogism to be *valid* (correct in its formal reasoning) but factually *false*.

Thus the following two syllogisms are valid (given the premises, the conclusions may logically be inferred); yet the first one is nonsense and the second is patently false because the premises are false:

>   All unicorns are girls.
>   All boys are unicorns.
> ∴ All boys are girls.

>   All weaklings are fools.
>   All people are weaklings.
> ∴ All people are fools.

Clearly, it is important to examine the premises of an argument before making a judgment. For example, someone accuses a member of Congress of accepting graft by arguing that "it is a widely known fact that members of Congress take graft, so why should this member of Congress be any different? It should be obvious immediately that the basic premise is open to question. *Is* it widely known and is it a *fact* that all members of Congress accept graft? The attack conceals a faulty syllogism:

>   All members of Congress take graft.
>   Mr. X is a member of Congress.
> ∴ Mr. X takes graft.

Yes, the reasoning is valid; but the major premise is questionable, thereby dictating that the conclusion will be false.

Induction As noted above, when we reason inductively we follow the method of moving from particular facts that are objectively verifiable (what we can test, observe, or experience) to a broad generalization. We see the sun rise in the east and set in the west . . . once . . . twice . . . three times . . . four . . . five . . . six . . . seven. Finally we take the "inductive leap," the assertion of the general truth that the sun rises in the east and sets in the west and in all likelihood can be counted on to do so tomorrow, the next day, the day after that.

You can make a good inductive leap only when you have observed a sufficient number of particular instances. This number varies from situation to situation. The perfect induction is one in which the observer has taken into consideration every member of the class of things to which the proposition refers. This is clearly impossible in many cases and unnecessary in most cases; a fair sampling of typical instances chosen at random usually leads to a reliable enough generalization. For example, fifteen sour green apples certainly provide a reasonable basis for the generalization "green apples are sour." Yet if all the apples tasted came out of one orchard, or even one group of orchards located in one section of the country, we must wonder, Is it just *these* green apples that are sour? Perhaps green apples in other sections of the country are as sweet as red ones. A fair sampling of apples should include apples from different parts of the country, thereby eliminating the possibility that special geographical or climatic conditions produce sour green apples.

Scientific investigators require a relatively large sampling—perhaps hundreds, thousands, or in some cases tens of thousands of subjects (especially in medical research)—before they can safely draw any generalizations.

In any induction, observers must guard against hasty generalizations made without a sufficient number of examples. This is perhaps the most widespread fallacy in popular thinking. Like the error in deductive reasoning that takes us from "some" to "all," this error in inductive reasoning can produce or reinforce prejudice. A person who is already prejudiced against a minority group (blacks, Jews, Chicanos) is predisposed to conclude after noting even a few "offenses" in the group that "that's the way they *all* are."

ARGUMENT BY ANALOGY

In argument by analogy, often regarded as a form of induction, you can draw a crucial comparison in one inductive leap. Urging the United States to join the Allied cause in the First World War, Woodrow Wilson pointed to the fact that Russia had done so. In comparing his proposed action for the United States with Russia's earlier action, Wilson was making an analogy, telling Congress that just as Russia wisely joined the Allied cause, so should we. The reasoning here proceeds from one specific instance to a similar specific instance.

There is no doubt that analogical reasoning serves an important function in argumentation. It makes a point simply and economically (if Russia found it impossible to deal with Germany, why should the United States find it any easier?). Analogy is also vivid and may strike a strongly persuasive note when all direct reasoning fails. The story is told, for example, of the union organizer in the early days of the labor movement who, after reciting all rational reasons for joining the movement, finally won a prospective member by drawing a vivid and amusing analogy: "The top crowd's pressin' down! The bottom crowd's pressin' up. Whaddayou wanna be, a hamburger?"

Aside from its dramatic impact, you can determine the value of inductive analogy only by closely examining the two things being compared. Are they in fact similar in the essential characteristics relating to the conclusion? Does the generalization underlying the analogy stand up to logical analysis? In his book *Thinking Straight,* Monroe Beardsley points to what he calls a "simple and crude example" of how analogy may mislead.

> One old gambit of the temperature orator was to say: "The delicate membranes of the stomach are like the delicate membranes of the eye; if you want to see what alcohol does to your stomach, just pour some gin in your eye." Now we may grant that there are *some* resemblances between eye tissue and stomach tissue: the question is whether these are *relevant* resemblances. In other words, the question is whether there is some true generalization like "Everything that hurts the eye will hurt the stomach" that will allow us to infer that if gin hurts the eye it will also hurt the stomach.
>
> So we might reply to him, "So you mean that *everything* that hurts the eye will also hurt the stomach?" He may wish to narrow the suggested generalization from "everything" to "every liquid," or in some other way. But unless he is willing to subscribe to *some* relevant generalization, he simply hasn't got what it takes to draw the conclusion he wants. We are therefore justified in saying to him, "If your argument proved anything, it would prove just as well that lemonade, vinegar, and hot coffee are bad for the stomach because they will hurt the eye. Doesn't that show that there must be important *differences* between the eye and stomach, so that what is true of one is not necessarily true of the other?"
>
> —Monroe Beardsley, *Thinking Straight*

The important thing to remember about analogy is this: the fact that two things are alike in some respect does not necessarily mean they are alike in others. Mental processes and bodily processes, for example, are comparable but not identical; therefore the following analogy represents a deceptive argument in favor of censorship: "We don't allow poisonous substances to be put into our foods, so why should we permit books to be published that will poison the minds of our citizens?" Do you see the dangerously authoritarian generalization that underlies this argument? It is just as unsound as the old defense of monarchy which maintained that since the earth revolved around the sun, circular motion was "natural"; consequently, by analogy, monarchy was a "natural" form of government because the subjects revolved around their monarch (Huppé and Kiminsky, *Logic,* 204).

In the essay below, *New York Times* columnist Anna Quindlen examines some of the ways people in the United States view affirmative action. Often, argues Quindlen, people generalize from a few successful black Americans and assume that the board rooms and professional schools of America are filled with black men and women who have been "given" those positions. Quindlen matches such anecdotal evidence with facts and figures.

The Great White Myth

Anna Quindlen

In a college classroom a young white man rises and asks about the future. What, he wants to know, can it possibly hold for him when most of the jobs, most of the good positions, most of the spots in professional schools are being given to women and, most especially, to blacks?

The temptation to be short, sarcastic, incredulous in reply is powerful. But you have to remember that kids learn their lessons from adults. That's what the mother of two black children who were sprayed with white paint in the Bronx said last week about the assailants, teenagers who called her son and daughter "nigger" and vowed they would turn them white. "Can you imagine what they are being taught at home?" she asked.

A nation based on laws, we like to believe that when they are changed, attitudes will change along with them. This is naive. America continues to be a country whose people are obsessed with maintaining some spurious pecking order. At the bottom are African-Americans, taught at age twelve and fourteen through the utter humiliation of having their faces cleaned with paint thinner that there are those who think that even becoming white from a bottle is better than not being white at all.

Each generation finds its own reasons to hate. The worried young white men I've met on college campuses in the last year have internalized the newest myth of American race relations, and it has made them bitter. It is called affirmative action, a.k.a. the systematic oppression of white men. All good things in life, they've learned, from college admission to executive position, are being given to black citizens. The verb is ubiquitous: given.

Never mind that you can walk through the offices of almost any big company and see a sea of white faces. Never mind that with all that has been written about preferential treatment for minority law students, only about 7,500 of the 127,000 students enrolled in law school last year were African-American. Never mind that only 3 percent of the doctors in this country are black.

Never mind that in the good old days preferential treatment was routinely given to brothers and sons of workers in certain lines of work. Perceptions of programs to educate and hire more black citizens as, in part, an antidote to decades of systematic exclusion have been inflated to enormous proportions in the public mind. Like hot-air balloons, they fill up the blue sky of the American landscape with the gaudy stripes of hyperbole. Listen and you will believe that the construction sites, the precinct houses, the investment banks are filled with African-Americans.

Unless you actually visit them.

The opponents of affirmative action programs say they are opposing the rank unfairness of preferential treatment. But there was no great hue and cry when colleges were candid about wanting to have geographic diversity, perhaps giving the kid from Montana an edge. There has been no national outcry when legacy applicants whose transcripts were supplemented by Dad's alumnus status—and cash contributions to the college—were admitted over more qualified comers. We somehow discovered that life was not fair only when the beneficiaries happened to be black.

And so the chasm widens. The old myth was the black American incapable of prosperity. It was common knowledge that welfare was purely a benefits program for blacks; it was common knowledge although it was false. The percentage of whites on public assistance is almost identical with the percentage of blacks.

The new myth is that the world is full of black Americans prospering unfairly at white expense, and anecdotal evidence abounds. The stories about the incompetent black co-worker always leave out two things: the incompetent white co-workers and the talented black ones. They also leave out the tendency of so many managers to hire those who seem most like themselves when young.

"It seems like if you're a white male you don't have a chance," said another young man on a campus where a scant 5 percent of his classmates were black. What the kid really means is that he no longer has the edge, that the rules of a system that may have served his father well have changed. It is one of those good-old-days constructs to believe it was a system based purely on merit, but we know that's not true. It is a system that once favored him, and others like him. Now sometimes—just sometimes—it favors someone different.

Common Logical Fallacies

Before looking at further examples of argumentation, we should consider some common logical fallacies. You should recognize that logical flaws are not necessarily *rhetorical* flaws. In fact, logical flaws may be extremely effective in their impact on readers. Lies, if they are bold enough, generate drama and excitement; emotional appeals often touch readers' hearts so deeply that they don't even try to understand.

But these, of course, are tricks designed to fool and blind readers. The good argument is based on reason and uses emotion only to reinforce reason; the good argument not only makes a case for or against its subject, it also illuminates it so that readers—whether they agree or disagree with the argument—will at least learn more about the issues.

Circular Reasoning To assume in the premise what you are supposedly trying to *prove* in the course of your argument is to argue in a circle—or beg the question. It has been observed that "the function of logic is to demonstrate that because one thing or group of things is true, another must be true as consequence." (See Davis, "Logic.") But in a circular argument there is no progression; the same thing is said in different words: "We shall always be ruled by the will of the people because we have a democratic form of government." This statement establishes nothing because the people's will is already assumed in the word "democratic."

Equivocation To equivocate is to change the meaning of a word in the course of an argument or to use an ambiguous word in two different senses (whether deliberately or unintentionally) as in the following:

> Science has discovered many laws of nature. This is proof that there is a God, for a law implies the existence of a lawgiver, and God is the great Lawgiver of the universe.

Observe the confused and careless use of the word "law": first it is used with the scientific meaning of uniform behavior in nature; then it is used prescriptively to refer to regulations enforcible by a higher authority (Ruby, *Making Sense* 32-33).

Evading the Issue   This fallacy takes several forms:

Distraction

Raising extraneous considerations, such as emotions or sentiments can turn the course of an argument away from the main issues. Thus in making a case for the democratic form of government, the arguer may eulogize George Washington and the other founding fathers, extolling their personal courage and foresight. Such distractions may divert readers' attention and make them forget the real issues.

Ad hominem

Another way to evade the issue is to direct the argument against the character of the person making the case rather than the case itself. This fallacy is common and sinister ("You cannot trust Smith's reform bill because he has had questionable rightist leanings . . . and there is his divorce . . . and that suspicious suicide attempt . . .").

Name-Calling

Still another evasive smear tactic (and verbal trick) is calling an opposing view by a "bad name," thereby suggesting that it is in reality bad. Thus an attempt to improve welfare legislation may be labeled "starry-eyed idealism" or "sheer romanticism," that will turn our government into a "welfare state."

Appeal to Pity

When General Douglas MacArthur, pleading his case before the American people, cited the old refrain "Old soldiers never die, they just fade away," he was resorting to the popular and often successful ruse of making himself pitiful in order to win sympathy. Obviously, this focusing on "poor old me" is another way of evading substantive issues.

Fallacious Appeal to Authority   To cite a Nobel Prize-winning chemist as an authority on civil rights legislation is to misunderstand the meaning of the word "authority." An authority's opinion is meaningful only when it concerns his or her special field of competence; otherwise the so-called authority is simply an ordinary citizen like the rest of us—neither wiser nor more foolish.

Fallacy of the Undistributed Middle   (See Deduction.)

False Analogy   (See Argument by Analogy.)

Hasty Generalization   (See Induction.)

Non Sequitur   When a conclusion does not follow from its premises, there has obviously been a serious slip in the deductive reasoning process.

> All artists are creative.
> Jackson is an artist.
> ∴ Jackson should be subsidized.

We can make this broken line of reasoning conform to a logical pattern by thinking it through carefully. We should say, if the conclusion we want to render valid is as follows, this:

> All creative artists deserve to be subsidized.
> Jackson is a creative artist.
> ∴ Jackson should be subsidized.

Both syllogisms contain the same conclusion; but in one case it does not follow from the premises, and in the other it does. To correct a non sequitur, we must remember that a conclusion is valid not in and of itself but within the context of its own terms—i.e., within the body of the syllogism.

Oversimplification This is a root fallacy in which the arguer ignores the complexities of a problem so that he or she may solve it more easily.

Either . . . Or
This is a device in which the arguer states that there are two and only two alternatives in a given situation: *Either* you vote for the mayor's tax reform bill *or* you permit the city to become bankrupt. This allows for no intermediate choices although in fact there may be other possibilities.

Post Hoc, Ergo Propter Hoc ("After this, therefore because of this")
This error in cause-and-effect analysis was described earlier.

Personifying Abstractions This fallacy involves both oversimplification and verbal distortion. It suggests that "Science tell us . . ." or "History teaches . . ." or "Poets believe . . ." as if each of these were a single person speaking with one voice instead of a complex abstraction representing many different points of view.

ARGUING FOR AND AGAINST

In the service of a cause, writers typically muster all their powers of reason and persuasion to make their case. In defending their positions they concede as little as possible, and what concessions they do allow they try to turn to their advantage. In attacking their opposition, they challenge the very premises of the other side, question their opponents' motives, and occasionally resort to invective or ridicule. In the three essays below on the ethics of animal research, the writers go "all out." By turns deductive and inductive, alternately calm and reasonable, then passionately indifferent to reason, they attempt to inspire assent—i.e., to *move* readers into their camp.

Dr. Ann Squire, vice president for education at the American Society for the Prevention of Cruelty to Animals, argues against vivisection—the use of animals in experiments— claiming that the findings of animal research can be misleading and that alternatives exist that provide better results for less cost. She characterizes the scientific community's insistence on animal subjects as merely a cruel habit, objectionable principally on the grounds that animals are "sentient beings with the capacity for suffering." Even though some animal experiments yield useful information, it is not "ethically acceptable," in her view, "to subject animals to the cruelty involved in much medical research."

ANIMAL RESEARCH: AN UNNECESSARY EVIL?

Ann Squire

Should we eliminate the use of animals in biomedical research? It seems that any reasonable person would respond, "Of course we should, provided we can answer our questions in another way." The purpose of biomedical research is to gather facts that will help scientists unlock the mysteries of disease. Research on animals is simply a means to that end, not an end in itself. Where biomedical researchers and animal advocates differ is in how appropriate, necessary and ethically acceptable they consider animal experimentation to be.

While the ASPCA's long term goal is the elimination of all animals from invasive biomedical research, our immediate goals are to improve conditions for animals currently in labs, reduce the number of animals used and encourage the development of nonanimal alternatives.

Undependable Subjects

Any discussion of this subject raises several questions, the most pragmatic being: Are animal studies useful? That is, are animals really good models for human diseases?

In certain cases, the answer may be yes. Sometimes, however, using animals as predictors of human responses can have misleading—and potentially tragic—consequences.

For example, thalidomide, a tranquilizer introduced in the 1950s and quickly taken off the market, causes birth defects in humans but not in rats. Because people differ from animals in often unpredictable ways, results of animal tests can be irrelevant when applied to humans.

And although researchers proclaim the importance of animal studies in cancer, Alzheimer's disease and heart disease, much of what we know about these afflictions has come from human population studies, postmortems and clinical testing on people. In fact, one of the researchers involved in the first human implant of the Jarvik-7 artificial heart remarked that more was learned from this operation than from all the preceding research on the device (which included dozens of implants in animals).

Sentient Creatures

A more fundamental question is: Even if certain animal models do provide scientists with useful information, is it ethically acceptable to subject animals to the cruelty involved in much medical research? We think not.

Animals are used in research because of their similarity to humans, but this very similarity should make us hesitant to force animals to endure experiments that would be morally objectionable if performed on people.

While researchers praise animal models for their scientific value, they tend to forget that animals, like humans, are sentient beings with the capacity to suffer. That some animal experiments may provide useful medical information does not change the fact of that suffering, and does not automatically justify it.

Before undertaking an animal experiment, each researcher should ask himself whether the cost in animal suffering is likely to be outweighed by a direct health benefit. If the answer is no, the experiments should not be done, or should be redesigned so as to eliminate the use of animals.

Better Alternatives

Are there ways of doing biomedical research that do not require the use of animals? We have already seen that population studies and human clinical testing can provide better information than that available from animal tests. Sophisticated new techniques such as CAT (computerized axial tomography) and PET (positron emission tomography) have increased our ability to study humans directly, without resorting to potentially misleading animal models. *In vitro* techniques, mathematical and computer modeling and use of single-celled organisms are some of the other alternatives that hold great promise for reducing the number of animals used in biomedical research.

Not only are these alternative methods often more accurate and always more humane than animal tests, they are much less expensive. Simply maintaining a colony of chimpanzees for use in research can cost hundreds of thousands of dollars each year. Since most biomedical research is ultimately funded by the taxpayer, each of us has a financial (if not an ethical) interest in pressing for development of cheaper, nonanimal alternatives.

Breaking the Habit

If many nonanimal alternatives are more accurate, more humane and less expensive, why do biomedical researchers continue to cling to animal models, especially in the face of rising public sentiment against animal research?

It is largely a matter of habit and training. Most animal researchers have learned through years of schooling to view animals as part of an arsenal of laboratory equipment. Given this background, it is hardly surprising that many researchers rely on animal models and treat their subjects as pieces of equipment rather than as living, feeling beings.

Unfortunately, this makes it unlikely that needed changes will come solely from within the scientific community. It is, therefore, up to a less desensitized public to demand a reduction in the number of animals used in research, as well as more humane treatment of those animals still in laboratories.

An increased reliance on alternatives will have many benefits: better science, less cost to the taxpayer and, perhaps most important, a better life for millions of animals.

Playwright George Bernard Shaw (1856-1950) employs another strategy on behalf of the antivivisectionist movement. He first assaults the "unimpeachable" logic of animal experimenters by extending the implications of their "right to knowledge" argument to its limits, finding that the "right" conflicts with social law and practice. He then argues by analogy: is it justifiable for a man to experiment on an adult woman in order to learn how long she would survive at 500° Fahrenheit? The obvious answer is intended to discredit the premise that the right to knowledge is not only fundamental but *crucial*.

ON EXPERIMENTING WITH ANIMALS

George Bernard Shaw

The right to know is like the right to live. It is fundamental and unconditional in its assumption that knowledge, like life, is a desirable thing, though any fool can prove that ignorance is bliss, and that "a little knowledge is a dangerous thing" (a little being the most that any of us can attain), as easily as that the pains of life are more numerous and constant than its pleasures, and that therefore we should all be better dead. The logic is unimpeachable; but its only effect is to make us say that if these are the conclusions logic leads to, so much the worse for logic, after which curt dismissal of Folly, we continue living and learning by instinct: that is, as of right. We legislate on the assumption that no man may be killed on the strength of a demonstration that he would be happier in his grave, not even if he is dying slowly of cancer and begs the doctor to despatch him quickly and mercifully. To get killed lawfully he must violate somebody else's right to live by committing murder. But he is by no means free to live unconditionally. In society he can exercise his right to live only under very stiff conditions. In countries where there is compulsory military service he may even have to throw away his individual life to save the life of the community.

It is just so in the case of the right to knowledge. It is a right that is as yet very imperfectly recognized in practice. But in theory it is admitted that an adult person in pursuit of knowledge must not be refused it on the ground that he would be better or happier without it. Parents and priests may forbid knowledge to those who accept their authority; and social taboo may be made effective by acts of legal persecution under cover of repressing blasphemy, obscenity, and sedition; but no government now openly forbids its subjects to pursue knowledge on the ground that knowledge is in itself a bad thing, or that it is possible for any of us to have too much of it.

But neither does any government exempt the pursuit of knowledge, any more than the pursuit of life, liberty, and happiness (as the American Constitution puts it), from all social conditions. No man is allowed to put his mother into the stove because he desires to know how long an adult woman will survive at a temperature of 500° Fahrenheit, no matter how important or interesting that particular addition to the store of human knowledge may be. A man who did so would have short work made not only of his right to knowledge, but of his right to live and all his other rights at the same time. The right to knowledge is not the only right; and its exercise must be limited by respect for other rights, and for its own exercise by others. When a man says to Society, "May I torture my mother in pursuit of knowledge?" Society replies "No." If he pleads, "What! Not even if I have a chance of finding out how to cure cancer by doing it?" Society still says, "Not even then." If the scientist, making the best of his disappointment, goes on to ask may he torture a dog, the stupid and callous people who do not realize that a dog is a fellow-creature, and sometimes a good friend, may say Yes, though Shakespeare, Dr. Johnson and their like may say No. But even those who say "You may torture *a* dog" never say "You may torture *my* dog." And nobody says, "Yes, because in the pursuit of knowledge you may do as you please." Just as even the stupidest people say, in effect, "If you cannot attain to knowledge without burning your mother you must do without knowledge," so the wisest people say, "If you cannot attain to knowledge without torturing a dog, you must do without knowledge."

Answering both Squire and Shaw is neurophysiologist Dr. Robert J. White, who has used animal experimentation to develop techniques for brain surgery. Under personal attack personally for the purported excesses of his experiments, White responds with a variety of tactics. He argues that animal experiments are necessary for the survival of the human race and even applauds his opposition for raising ecological issues. He helps his case by narrowing his defense of animal experimentation to neurological science. He also rejects the very premises of the antivivisectionists, opening with a stirring quotation from Charles Norton Eliot to define his own position. Later he dismisses the logic of "a philosophy that places such a premium on animal life even at the expense of human existence and improvement." Scolding his critics for their "vituperative treatment" of him, White charges them with "prejudice against medicine" and possibly "psychiatric aberrations."

Hoping to defuse the charges made against animal experiments, White describes the actual procedures involved. Although his response does not defend experiments for consumer and beauty products, White's detailed presentation of vivisection aims at measure and fairness. He even marshals evidence against those supposedly better alternatives to vivisection mentioned by Squire.

Finally, in citing Albert Schweitzer, the ideal humanitarian of his generation, White charts the connection between law, government funding, and research, admitting that his greatest fear is that the antivivisectionists could—if they "win assent"—seriously jeopardize further progress in medical science.

A Humane and Scientific Necessity

Robert J. White

The humanity which would prevent human suffering is a deeper and truer humanity than the humanity which would save pain or death in the animal.

—Charles W. Eliot

The quotation above from that distinguished intellectual and former Harvard University president, written decades ago, continues to crystallize clearly the basic position of medical science toward the employment of animals in research and teaching. I would state it more simply: the alleviation of human suffering justifies the sacrifice of lower animals. Because this statement is as valid today as it was then, and yet has so little impact on the public conscience, I am almost reluctant to shed the mantle of clinical and professional detachment and take up the cudgels against that ill-defined, elusive Hydra—the antivivisection movement. To a degree, my inertia is also derived from my conviction that medical science has always seemed to assume a low-profile posture in justifying the utilization of lower animals for research and education (as it has so often done with other public health issues); it has invariably waited until one of those vigorous cyclic antivivisection campaigns, using the most advanced techniques in news management, has reached its apogee before attempting to combat the pernicious effects on public and congressional opinion. And then, unfortunately, it has employed almost exclusively its own scientific journals as the instruments for presenting its position to an already prejudiced audience. While the scientific community has lobbied successfully in congressional committees against restrictive legislation directed at medical research, it has neglected to present to the American public its case for the continuation of animal experimentation with sufficient force and clarity to eliminate the ever-present danger of government control of biological research through the limitation of animal availability and experimental design. The intelligent citizenry of this country must be educated not only regarding the already multiple advantages of medical research but, what is more important, the absolute necessity of continued proliferation of biological research.

Man, in a sense, has unwittingly painted himself into an ecological corner, and without the opportunity of biological testing in lower animals he may be unable to extract himself from his polluted environment. Acknowledging man's equally wanton disregard of animal life, as he has slowly but inevitably poisoned this planet (to say nothing of our careless attrition of individual species to the point of extinction), I do not intend that this essay should be, by any stretch of the imagination, construed as an indictment of the broad humanitarian movement; quite the contrary, for many of its objectives, particularly in the ecological field, are not only most laudable but fully subscribed to by many within the scientific community. Rather, my proprietary interest here is to emphasize need for animal experimentation in neurological research. As a consequence, my confrontation is exclusively with those societies, collectively known as the antivivisection movement, whose single unifying principle is the almost religiously held tenet that it is morally wrong to use lower animals in medical research and teaching. Professor Saul Bevolson, in tracing the historical development of the antivivisection movement in this country, demonstrates that the movement, while spawned and nurtured by the humanitarian establishment, is, in reality, separate in organizational structure. Dr. Maurice Visscher has felt the necessity of characterizing the antivivisection movement as a spectrum with certain gradations of moral and ethical absoluteness with regard to man's right to sacrifice lower animal life for scientific knowledge and medical advancement. Thus, this philosophical spectrum is anchored at one end by the abolitionists who see no justification under any circumstances for the employment of the nonhuman animal for scientific study, and at the other extreme by the regulatory antivivisectionists who would place external controls (obviously governmental) on medical research by limiting the type and number of animals utilized, and demanding review of the experimental methods with particular reference to purpose and duplication. Make no mistake, in spite of their highly publicized concern for the housing and veterinary care of research animals, the true thrust of these organizations is directed toward the eventual elimination from medical investigation and research of all nonhuman subjects.

As a concerned scientist and as a practicing neurosurgeon, I am simply unable to plumb the depths of a philosophy that places such a premium on animal life even at the expense of human existence and improvement. It would appear that this preoccupation with the alleged pain and suffering of the animals used in medical research may well represent, at the very least, social prejudice against medicine or, more seriously, true psychiatric aberrations. Regardless of the social or psychiatric shortcomings of the antivivisectionists, it has always amazed me that the biological profession is forced into a position of periodically preparing defense briefs on animal experimentation (unfortunately appearing only in scientific journals) as a result of the Herculean efforts of these societies, while the meat-packing industry, which slaughters millions of animals annually, seldom if ever finds it necessary to defend its activities.

As I write this article, I relive my vivid experiences of yesterday when I removed at operation a large tumor from the cerebellum and brain stem of a small child. This was a surgical undertaking that would have been impossible a few decades ago, highly dangerous a few years ago, but is today, thanks to extensive experimentation on the brains of lower animals, routinely accomplished with a high degree of safety.

The human brain is the most complex, the most superbly designed structure known. Before it, all human scientific and engineering accomplishment pales. Our understanding of its intimate functions, such as intelligence and memory, is extremely limited. Even the more easily characterized capabilities of sensory reception and motor activity are only now being elucidated. Without the use of the experimental animal, particularly a species whose central nervous system is similar to that of man, we simply cannot decipher the mysteries of cerebral performance. Without this knowledge of brain function, we will never be able to develop new and improved methods for the treatment of neurological diseases, so many of which now must be placed in an incurable category. Even today the surgery of the brain is in its infancy, and on many occasions the critical tolerance between success and failure in human cerebral operations is narrow. Yet this gap can be significantly increased through properly oriented research. These serious considerations moved Dr. Harvey Cushing, the eminent brain surgeon, to remark, "Those who oppose the employment of animals for such purposes . . . leave us the only alternative of subjecting our fellow man, as a lesser creature, to our first crude manipulations."

In a more personal sense, I have a score of my own to settle with these misguided societies that for decades have been attempting to confuse the public about the true purpose of animal experimentation by depicting the medical and veterinary scientist as the most cruel of men, seeking every opportunity to visit pain and suffering on defenseless laboratory creatures. The more aggressive of the organizations, which are committed to the total abolition of animal research, have recently installed me as their *célèbre terrible,* monster-scientist, perpetrator of abominable crimes. And thus I join the distinguished company of such legendary scientists as Claude Bernard, Louis Pasteur, Lord Lister, Victor Horsley and Alfred Blalock! Dr. Catherine Roberts herself has already prejudged my work and me by earnestly stating, "The details of his experiments are so horrifying that they seem to reach the limits of scientific depravity." Fortunately, my researches do not stand alone in her sweeping condemnation of medical science, for in the same article she described organ transplantation and profound hypothermia[1] as "life degrading scientific achievements." I am sure that she, as well as other staunch antivivisectionists, would be willing to include in this list: open-heart surgery, control of infection, surgical metabolism[2] and shock studies since literally thousands of animals were sacrificed in the development of these lifesaving techniques. In a sense, condemnation of these achievements amounts to condemnation of the most meaningful advances in medicine and surgery in the last thirty years.

What of our own experiments, which have evoked such vituperative treatment at the hands of the antivivisection press? Here are the "shocking" details.

In 1964, we were successful for the first time in medical history in totally isolating the subhuman primate brain outside of its body and sustaining it in a viable state by connecting it with the vascular system of another monkey or with a mechanical perfusion circuit that incorporated engineering units designed to perform the functions of the heart, lungs and kidneys while simultaneously circulating blood to and from the brain. We were overjoyed since scientists had attempted to construct such a model surgically for the last one hundred years without success. As late as the 1930s Dr. Alexis Carrel, the Nobel laureate, with the collaboration of Colonel Charles Lindberg, had been able to support the viability of almost all body organs in an isolated state with simple perfusion equipment that forcefully propelled nonsanguineous nutrient fluid through the blood vesels of the separated issue. Only the nervous system, because of its complexity and delicacy, escaped their magnificent scientific capabilities. Parenthetically, it should be mentioned that Dr. Carrel had his problems with the antivivisectionists of his time.

With further refinements in operative technique, perfusion/structural design and blood processing, we were able to demonstrate normalization of intrinsic electrical activity and metabolic performance of the isolated monkey brain for extended periods of time. We now had the methodology to unlock many of the subtle mysteries surrounding cerebral function that heretofore had resisted all attempts at solution because of the difficulties of neurogenically and vascularly isolating the entire brain *in situ.* What is perhaps of greater importance in terms of understanding and treating neurological disease, we could now easily impose on our brain models abnormal clinical states such as infarction, circulatory arrest, infection and malignancy with absolute control of environmental circumstances and with a real hope of elucidating their effects on brain tissue alone. Once the characteristics of these states were defined, these same models would be of inestimable value in developing new and meaningful therapeutic regimens aimed at eliminating these clinical disease states.

As we set about exploring and documenting the capabilities of the isolated brain in an atmosphere not unlike the conditions described for the fifth level in Michael Crichton's book *The Andromeda Strain,* we gradually became aware of a growing public interest in the preparation, an interest that intensified after our success in transplanting the brain in the experimental animal in 1966. A succession of competent medical journalists visited our laboratories and subsequently prepared a number of highly informative and reasoned articles dealing with our investigative efforts. I personally have always approved of this kind of

---

[1]*profound hypothermia:* very low body temperature, induced in a part of the body to aid surgery
[2]*surgical metabolism:* problems of a surgical patient that are related to nutrition and physical and chemical processes

interchange. In spite of our best efforts to assist in the preparation of the textual material, however, an unreviewed and unauthorized article written by Orianna Fallaci appeared in *Look* (November 28, 1967), in which this well-known interviewer attempted to humanize the monkey by depicting it as a small child. This single article (or lengthy excerpts from it) has now enjoyed world-wide publication and translation. Besides her treatment of the monkey as a small patient, Miss Fallaci's detailed description of the preoperative preparation (including the induction of anesthesia) and her vivid portrayal of the isolated brain model apparently struck a sympathetic and responsive chord among the membership of the antivivisection societies in this country as well as throughout the world. Like Mary Shelley, Miss Fallaci had created a Doctor Frankenstein and an up-to-date monster, at least as far as the antivivisectionists are concerned. True, this tale has its amusing—if not outlandish—elements, but its overall effect is tragic, since Miss Fallaci's creations are not only as facititous as Mary Shelley's, but in reality the direct antithesis of the Frankenstein legend.

Admittedly, the nervous system is the most difficult body organ system to investigate, not only because of its intrinsic complexity but also because, somewhere within its billions of cells and fibers, pain and suffering are represented. For this reason, the neurophysiologist is, on occasion, unable to avoid producing some discomfort in his animal when he is specifically studying pain in any or all of its complicated ramifications within the neural system. Actually, the isolated brain model is completely denervated by virtue of the fact that all pain pathways have been surgically severed; consequently, this brain model enjoys a completely painless existence by all known physiological criteria.

Since the isolated brain is incapable of perceiving these modalities, one can only wonder at the creditability and objectivity of the antivivisection prose, which has been so uncomplimentary in its descriptions of this subhuman research model.

The nervous system—the repository, so to speak, of pain and suffering, but, more important, of the qualities and capabilities that uniquely distinguish an organism—is most critical to this discussion since direct surgical or electronic manipulation or chemical modification of this system in the experimental animal offers to the antivivisectionist the most logical area for condemnation of biological research. At issue here would not be the indiscriminate infliction of pain and suffering (these experiments are basically free of pain), but rather purposeful alteration of the innate behavior of the organism in order to advance our knowledge of emotion, memory and intelligence, with the final phase again being the interpretive extrapolation of this information to the human and to human mental functioning. As yet we have heard little from the antivivisectionists regarding the inappropriateness of these experiments with reference to animal welfare. It may be however, that their historical fixation on the "twin sins" of pain and suffering in neurological investigation has blinded them to the realities of modern experimental research. Just as I must vigorously dissent from the antivivisection philosophy (and the belief of certain physiologists) that the production of some pain, no matter how minimal, is never justified, so too I cannot conceive of the development of a valid argument opposing behavioral research, if only for the simple reason that mental illness cannot successfully be treated until mental performance is understood.

To circumvent the employment of nonhuman animals in medical research, the antivivisection movement has recently turned for assistance to science itself. It has been suggested that many of the physiological and biochemical studies conducted on animals could be programmed for computer analysis and thereby reduce and eventually eliminate the need for the living experimental preparations. Actually, computers, since their inception, have been used in biological research and, with their growing complexity, have markedly extended the frontiers of investigation. If anything, computer availability has contributed to the increasing demand for animals for research.

An equally unrealistic approach to the elimination of animal experimentation has been based on the cell culture work of Professor Sureyat Aygun, Director of the Bacteriological Institute of the University of Ankara, and a leading antivivisection proponent. The theory here is that, with proper culture techniques, cells or embryos could eventually be developed into entire organ systems. The technological advances and expense necessary to accomplish such a program to replace present-day animal research facilities are unachievable. There is no more need to seek alternatives to the use of lower animals for medical research than to search for nonflesh substitutions for meat in our diets. While it may well be true that ecological "facts of life" could eventually require the elimination of certain endangered species from both the laboratory and commercial market, there is nothing to suggest that some suitable species cannot be substituted. Even Dr. Albert Schweitzer recognized in his own unique philosophical scheme of things that scientific experiments with animals were necessary for the alleviation of human ills.

The American public demonstrates its overwhelming support of medical research by annually contributing millions of dollars through direct federal financing and private subscription; yet this same public is tragically unaware that progress in medical science is continually threatened by the antivivisection movement. At the urging of a small but determined group of antivivisectionists, the United States Congress is constantly considering legislation that, if enacted into law, will seriously restrict the freedom of individual scientists participating in medical research, in the same way that laws have so seriously hampered similar research in Britain. Since, through research grants to qualified individuals and institutions, the federal government provides the major financial support for medical investigation in this country, all laws affecting the conduct of such research are of paramount importance to the health of the entire citizenry. Unless American medicine and its allied biological professions cast off their mantles of detachment and undertake the responsibility of educating through established lines of communication our citizens to the necessities of medical research, the antivivisection movement may eventually win the day.

In the final analysis, there is no way that I can personally resolve or even arbitrate the impasse that exists between the theology of the antivivisection movement and the immutable stance of practicality maintained by biological research, since like R. D. Guthrie, I believe that the inclusion of lower animals in our ethical system is philosophically meaningless and operationally impossible and that, consequently, antivivisection theory and practice have no moral or ethical basis.

MODERN ARGUMENT: THE EDITORIAL

One may think of the newspaper or magazine editorial as the modern counterpart of the classical oration in that it is basically an argument presented by the editors of a publication, a case drawn for or against an issue of timely, often pressing significance. Both *is* and *ought* propositions lie at the heart of the editorial, a clear, cogent, and systematic review of the controversial issues involved.

Ultimately, the editorial writer asks the reader to think or act in a given way, as in the following 1966 *New York Times* editorial, a witty defense of that maligned mark of identity, the New York accent. By examining why people seem to so dislike this way of speaking, Richard Shepard links the accent to the rhythms and character of the city itself. Suggesting that this accent is as worthy of preservation as an old building, Shepard connects this habit of language with a sense of history and identity.

A WORD FOR THE NEW YORK ACCENT

Richard Shepard

They've been trying to abolish it for years. Teachers attack it. Students resist it. Users regret it, but it's harder to give up than smoking. It and obscenity may often keep you off the air. It's altogether unforgivable.

"It," of course, is the New York accent. It's probably the city's longest-lived landmark and it is the one that everyone is trying to stamp out.

A fine German accent may bolster a psychiatrist's fee. A crisp British accent simply cries for a lecture tour. Regional variations across the city line command affectionate toleration. To speak as they do in Dixie—as long as it's intelligible—is a sentimental plus. The New England twang conjures up visions of democracy in the raw, small townsmen going to meetings and debating about raising money by lottery. The pioneer spirit infests the Western drawl, even when it emanates from a mouth that never shouted at a cow. Modified Midwestern is to us what Florentine is to Italian, the standard, the stated norm that few from elsewhere can more than approximate.

But they abominate the New York accent. New Yorkers abominate it, too. In school, patient teachers, with frustrating results, try to extirpate local aberrations, such as *oi* for *er, er* for *oi,* the *dese, dems* and *doses,* the *whatcha* for *what are you* and the lamentable, mystifying disappearance of the *r* that makes *Noo Yawkers* rush to *fi-uhs* when the *alahm* bell rings.

Add to this, ethnic variants with rising intonations and brutally mis-emphasized consonants and the city emerges as a linguistic disaster area, a desperate zone of pear-shaped poverty, in which even sizable federal aid will show no pronounced results. There are many degrees of disability; many New Yorkers have contrived to color their diction with accepted resonances and inflections, along with such critical minima as clear expression of *th's* and careful avoidance of caricature-like vocal extremes.

Now, is the New York accent really all that bad? The answer, doubtless, is a resounding yeah. But it need not be so; that is a culturally bred reaction and nothing that a little positive thinking can't cure.

Happily, we have become a great nation and our immigrants have turned into true-blue Yankees, looking for roots. There is a passion for antiques dating back to colonial days and homes with Ol' Virginny columns. We are in a preservation mood. We want to preserve old buildings. Why not old accents?

It is not as if the New York accent doesn't suit the environment. It is a rough-cut affair, matching the jagged skyline. It is as noisily slurred as a subway rush. It is as guttural as a traffic jam.

It is the dialect that unifies the fastest town in the world. It wastes no time on colorful metaphors and drawled verities. It runs toward a deed, a deal or a dollar, anything that has a goal from the most concrete transaction to the most abstruse research. It is not a time-waster. It is the hurry-up, short-order accent of America.

This doesn't make it the best. But it doesn't make it the worst, either. Granted, New Yorkers should vocalize so that they may be understood by other English-speaking peoples (who have their problems, too, as anyone who has looked in on the Midlands can attest).

But must our accent be rooted out? Under New York's landmark laws, certain ancient buildings may be built anew inside but not a brick on the outside may be touched. Is there no way to harness the accent and its vigor to reach a happy medium that will allow for some internal refurbishing while preserving the rugged exterior? (Something between Mayor Lindsay and Zero Mostel?)

It's one of the few things left to us that is untaxed and that we may call our own.

—*The New York Times,* November 5, 1966

HUMANIZING ARGUMENT: ROGERIAN STRATEGY

Even Aristotle, who defined man as a rational animal, recognized that man is not *always* rational. Sometimes—indeed frequently—he is exactly the opposite: he is emotional, irrational, existentially adrift; he feels lonely, frustrated, helpless, isolated, threatened on all sides. Recognizing this deeper and darker dimension of human nature—that it is pervasive in all people however mighty their accomplishments and lofty their positions—psychotherapist Carl R. Rogers has proposed that we incorporate the recognition into our rhetoric. He asks that we modify our traditionally aggressive and intellectually derived principles of persuasion to accommodate newer and more profound psychological insights into the way people really feel and think.

One set of rhetoricians (See Young, Becker, and Pike, *Rhetoric*), acting on Rogers's advice, describes "Rogerian strategy" as an approach to argument which reduces threat and subsequent defensiveness, thereby encouraging both parties in an argument to try to "encounter" one another, to enter "reciprocally and empathetically" into the other's position. Compared to the strictly "win" tactics of traditional argumentation, Rogerian strategy

> ...is based on quite different assumptions about men and...has quite different goals. It rests on the assumption that a man holds to his beliefs about who he is and what the world is like because other beliefs threaten his identity and integrity. Hence, the first requirement for changing beliefs is the elimination of this sense of threat. If this assumption is true, then the weaknesses of the other strategies are apparent. A

strong sense of threat may render a person immune to even the most carefully reasoned and well developed argument. Likewise, attempts to condition him or to explain away his beliefs become very threatening once he discovers what is happening to him. From the Rogerian point of view, man has free will, but his ability to consider alternative positions is limited if he feels threatened. The primary goal of this rhetorical strategy is to reduce the reader's sense of threat so that he is *able* to consider alternatives to his own beliefs. The goal is thus not to work one's will on others but to establish and maintain communication *as an end in itself* (*Rhetoric*).

By shifting the primary emphasis of argument from working one's will on others to establishing and maintaining lines of communication, Rogerian rhetoricians make possible new goals, particularly the goal of working toward consensus rather than a one-sided win. The significance of this strategy is obvious to anyone surveying the national and international scene.

Profound changes are taking place in the system of Western values that has for centuries guided conduct and provided social stability and continuity between generations. Thus it becomes more and more difficult to reason from ethical assumptions that are generally accepted. Truth has become increasingly elusive and men are driven to embrace conflicting ideologies. Ours is an age of isms. As a result of rapid and mass means of communication and transportation, our world is becoming smaller, and all of us are learning to become citizens of the world, confronting people whose beliefs are radically different from our own and with whom we must learn to live (*Rhetoric*).

No wonder, then, that Rogerian rhetoricians remind us that "it has become imperative to develop a rhetoric that has as its goal not skillful verbal coercion but discussion and exchange of ideas" (*Rhetoric*).

Perhaps no rhetorical occasion calls for a more skillful attempt to establish a consensus around common goals than does the inauguration of a President of the United States. We have already seen, in Chapter 4, the process by which President John F. Kennedy crafted an inaugural address that would appeal to all Americans. Following an often contentious campaign that may have gone on a year or more, the victorious candidate must help to establish a sense of unity among disparate parties so that the work of governing the nation may proceed. The skillful use of the strategies of Rogerian rhetoric were perhaps never more evident than in Abraham Lincoln's Second Inaugural Address, given in January 1865, three months before his death, when the Civil War was moving toward its close. Anticipating the need to reunite the fractured nation, Lincoln looked toward a common future of reconciliation, in words that have become immortal:

With malice toward none; with charity for all; with firmness in the right as God give us to see the right, let us strive on to finish the work we are in; to bind up the nation's wounds; to care for him who shall have borne the battle and for his widow, and his orphans—to do all which may achieve and cherish a just and lasting peace among ourselves, and with all nations.

The nation was at peace on January 20, 1993 when Bill Clinton took the presidential oath of office. Like those of his predecessors, Clinton's inaugural address attempted to transcend partisan differences by articulating common goals. See which Rogerian strategies you can identify at work in this speech.

INAUGURAL ADDRESS

Bill Clinton

My Fellow Citizens: Today, we celebrate the mystery of American renewal. This ceremony is held in the depth of winter. But, by the words we speak and the faces we show the world, we force the spring. A spring reborn in the world's oldest democracy that brings forth the vision and courage to reinvent America.

When our founders boldly declared America's independence to the world and our purposes to the Almighty, they knew that America, to endure, would have to change.

Not change for change's sake, but change to preserve America's ideals—life, liberty, the pursuit of happiness. Though we march to the music of our time, our mission is timeless.

Each generation of Americans must define what it means to be an American.

On behalf of our nation, I salute my predecessor President Bush for his half-century of service to America, and I thank the millions of men and women whose steadfastness and sacrifice triumphed over depression, fascism and communism.

Today, a generation raised in the shadows of the Cold War assumes new responsibilities in a world warmed by the sunshine of freedom but threatened still by ancient hatreds and new plagues.

Raised in unrivaled prosperity, we inherit an economy that is still the world's strongest, but is weakened by business failures, stagnant wages, increasing inequality and deep divisions among our own people.

When George Washington first took the oath I have just sworn to uphold, news traveled slowly across the land by horseback and across the ocean by boat. Now, the sights and sounds of this ceremony are broadcast instantaneously to billions around the world.

Communications and commerce are global; investment is mobile; technology is almost magical, and ambition for a better life is now universal. We earn our livelihood in America today in peaceful competition with people all across the Earth.

Profound and powerful forces are shaking and remaking our world, and the urgent question of our time is whether we can make change our friend and not our enemy.

This new world has already enriched the lives of millions of Americans who are able to compete and win in it. But when most people are working harder for less, when others cannot work at all, when the cost of health care devastates families and threatens to bankrupt our enterprises, great and small, when fear of crime robs law-abiding citizens of their freedom and when millions of poor children cannot even imagine the lives we are calling them to lead—we have not made change our friend.

We know we have to face hard truths and take strong steps. But we have not done so. Instead, we have drifted, and that drifting has eroded our resources, fractured our economy and shaken our confidence.

Though our challenges are fearsome, so are our strengths. Americans have ever been a restless, questing, hopeful people. And we must bring to our task today the vision and will of those who came before us.

From our revolution to the Civil War, to the Great Depression to the civil rights movement, our people have always mustered the determination to construct from these crises the pillars of our history.

Thomas Jefferson believed that to preserve the very foundations of our nation, we would need dramatic change from time to time. Well, my fellow Americans, this is our time. Let us embrace it.

Our democracy must be not only the envy of the world but the engine of our own renewal. There is nothing wrong with America that cannot be cured by what is right with America.

So today, we pledge an end to the era of deadlock and drift—and a new season of American renewal has begun.

To renew America, we must be bold.

We must do what no generation has had to do before. We must invest more in our own people, in their jobs and in their future, and at the same time cut our massive debt. And we must do so in a world in which we must compete for every opportunity.

It will not be easy; it will require sacrifice. But it can be done, and done fairly, not choosing sacrifice for its own sake, but for our own sake. We must provide for our nation the way a family provides for its children.

Our founders saw themselves in the light of posterity. We can do no less. Anyone who has ever watched a child's eyes wander into sleep knows what posterity is. Posterity is the world to come—the world for whom we hold our ideals, from whom we have borrowed our planet, and to whom we bear sacred responsibility.

We must do what America does best: offer more opportunity to all and demand more responsibility from all.

It is time to break the bad habit of expecting something for nothing, from our government or from each other. Let us all take more responsibility, not only for ourselves and our families but for our communities and our country.

To renew America, we must revitalize our democracy.

This beautiful capital, like every capital since the dawn of civilization, is often a place of intrigue and calculation. Powerful people maneuver for position and worry endlessly about who is in and who is out, who is up and who is down, forgetting those people whose toil and sweat sends us here and pays our way.

Americans deserve better. And in this city today, there are people who want to do better. So I say to all of you here, let us resolve to reform our politics, so that power and privilege no longer shout down the voice of the people. Let us put aside personal advantage so that we can feel the pain and see the promise of America.

Let us resolve to make our government a place for what Franklin Roosevelt called "bold, persistent experimentation," a government for our tomorrows, not our yesterdays.

Let us give this capital back to the people to whom it belongs.

To renew America, we must meet challenges abroad as well as at home. There is no longer clear division between what is foreign and what is domestic—the world economy, the world environment, the world AIDS crisis, the world arms race—they affect us all.

Today, as an old order passes, the new world is more free but less stable. Communism's collapse has called forth old animosities and new dangers. Clearly, America must continue to lead the world we did so much to make.

While America rebuilds at home, we will not shrink from the challenges, nor fail to seize the opportunities, of this new world. Together with our friends and allies, we will work to shape change, lest it engulf us.

When our vital interests are challenged, or the will and conscience of the international community is defied, we will act—with peaceful diplomacy whenever possible, with force when necessary. The brave Americans serving our nation today in the Persian Gulf, in Somalia, and wherever else they stand are testament to our resolve.

But our greatest strength is the power of our ideas, which are still new in many lands. Across the world, we see them embraced—and we rejoice. Our hopes, our hearts, our hands are with those on every continent who are building democracy and freedom. Their cause is America's cause.

The American people have summoned the change we celebrate today. You have raised your voices in an unmistakable chorus. You have cast your votes in historic numbers. And you have changed the face of the Congress, the presidency and the political process itself.

Yes, you, my fellow Americans, have forced the spring.

Now, we must do the work the season demands.

To that work I now turn, with all the authority of my office. I ask the Congress to join with me. But no president, no Congress, no government can undertake this mission alone.

My fellow Americans, you, too, must play your part in our renewal.

I challenge a new generation of young Americans to a season of service—to act on your idealism by helping troubled children, keeping company with those in need, reconnecting our torn communities. There is so much to be done—enough, indeed, for millions of others who are still young in spirit to give of themselves in service, too.

In serving, we recognize a simple but powerful truth: We need each other. And we must care for one another.

Today, we do more than celebrate America; we rededicate ourselves to the very idea of America:

An idea born in revolution and renewed through two centuries of challenge;

An idea tempered by the knowledge that, but for fate, we—the fortunate and the unfortunate—might have been each other;

An idea ennobled by the faith that our nation can summon from its myriad diversities the deepest measure of unity;

An idea infused with the conviction that America's long, heroic journey must go forever upward.

And so my fellow Americans, as we stand at the edge of the 21st Century, let us begin with energy and hope, with faith and discipline, and let us work until our work is done. The scripture says, "And let us not be weary in well-doing, for in due season, we shall reap, if we faint not."

> From this joyful mountaintop of celebration, we hear a call to service in the valley.
>
> We have heard the trumpets. We have changed the guard. And now—each in our own way, and with God's help—we must answer the call.

TESTING YOUR ARGUMENT: A CHECKLIST

Whatever case you may make for or against any subject, you should test your argument against the following questions:

1. Have you defined the terms? (See *What Does X Mean?*)
2. Have you established exactly what the argument is about? That is, have you stated the proposition clearly and indicated precisely what issues are to be defended and refuted?
3. Are you certain that the facts and assumptions are correct?
4. Have you offered sufficient evidence—facts, statistics, illustrations, testimony—that will further illuminate and substantiate each point as well as the overall position? (See *Gathering Information.*)
5. Are generalizations fair and reliable?
6. Do conclusions follow logically from the premises?
7. Have you cited reliable authorities?
8. Is the presentation rhetorically effective, that is, clear, cogent, well organized?
9. Have you examined *every* important aspect of the case? Aristotle maintained that we should be able to argue on either side of a question—not because we are without personal conviction or commitment but because only then can we feel certain that no aspect of the case has escaped us.
10. Is the tone appropriate to the subject, the occasion, and the purpose you are trying to achieve? Have you taken Rogerian strategy into consideration; in other words, have you tried to reduce threat and defensiveness by entering empathetically into your opponent's position? Is your overall approach flexible, reasonable, and sympathetic, rather than rigid, dogmatic, unnecessarily and irritatingly disputatious?

Note how successfully the following essay meets the criteria of sound—indeed *powerful*—argument. Whether or not you agree with the writer's position in favor of euthanasia, you cannot help but be moved by his relentless logic and genuine fervor.

In Defense of Voluntary Euthanasia

Sidney Hook

A few short years ago, I lay at the point of death. A congestive heart failure was treated for diagnostic purposes by an angiogram that triggered a stroke. Violent and painful hiccups, uninterrupted for several days and nights, prevented the ingestion of food. My left side and one of my vocal cords became paralyzed. Some form of pleurisy set in, and I felt I was drowning in a sea of slime. At one point, my heart stopped beating; just as I lost consciousness, it was thumped back into action again. In one of my lucid intervals during those days of agony, I asked my physician to discontinue all life-supporting services or show me how to do it. He refused and predicted that someday I would appreciate the unwisdom of my request.

A month later, I was discharged from the hospital. In six months, I regained the use of my limbs, and although my voice still lacks its old resonance and carrying power I no longer croak like a frog. There remain some minor disabilities and I am restricted to a rigorous, low-sodium diet. I have resumed my writing and research.

My experience can be and has been cited as an argument against honoring requests of stricken patients to be gently eased out of their pain and life. I cannot agree. There are two main reasons. As an octogenarian, there is a reasonable likelihood that I may suffer another "cardiovascular accident" or worse. I may not even be in a position to ask for the surcease of pain. It seems to me that I have already paid my dues to death—indeed, although time has softened my memories they are vivid enough to justify my saying that I suffered enough to warrant dying several times over. Why run the risk of more?

Secondly, I dread imposing on my family and friends another grim round of misery similar to the one my first attack occasioned.

My wife and children endured enough for one lifetime. I know that for them the long days and nights of waiting, the disruption of their professional duties and their own familial responsibilities counted for nothing in their anxiety for me. In their joy at my recovery they have been forgotten. Nonetheless, to visit another prolonged spell of helpless suffering on them as my life ebbs away, or even worse, if I linger on into a comatose senility, seems altogether gratuitous.

But what, it may be asked, of the joy and satisfaction of living, of basking in the sunshine, listening to music, watching one's grandchildren growing into adolescence, following the news about the fate of freedom in a troubled world, playing with ideas, writing one's testament of wisdom and folly for posterity? Is not all that one endured, together with the risk of its recurrence, an acceptable price for the multiple satisfactions that are still open even to a person of advanced years?

Apparently those who cling to life no matter what, think so, I do not.

The zest and intensity of these experiences are no longer what they used to be. I am not vain enough to delude myself that I can in the few remaining years make an important discovery useful for mankind or can lead a social movement or do anything that will be historically eventful, no less event-making. My autobiography, which describes a record of intellectual and political experiences of some historical value, already much too long, could be posthumously published. I have had my fill of joys and sorrows and am not greedy for more life. I have always thought that a test of whether one had found happiness in one's life is whether one would be willing to relive it—whether, if it were possible, one would accept the opportunity to be born again.

Having lived a full and relatively happy life, I would cheerfully accept the chance to be reborn, but certainly not to be reborn again as an infirm octogenarian. To some extent, my views reflect what I have seen happen to the aged and stricken who have been so unfortunate as to survive crippling paralysis. They suffer, and impose suffering on others, unable even to make a request that their torment be ended.

I am mindful too of the burdens placed upon the community, with its rapidly diminishing resources, to provide the adequate and costly services necessary to sustain the lives of those whose days and nights are spent on mattress graves of pain. A better use increases the opportunities and qualities of life for the young. I am not denying the moral obligation the community has to look after its disabled and aged. There are times, however, when an individual may find it pointless to insist on the fulfillment of a legal and moral right.

What is required is no great revolution in morals but an enlargement of imagination and an intelligent evaluation of alternative uses of community resources.

Long ago, Seneca observed that "the wise man will live as long as he ought, not as long as he can." One can envisage hypothetical circumstances in which one has a duty to prolong one's life despite its costs for the sake of others, but such circumstances are far removed from the ordinary prospects we are considering. If wisdom is rooted in knowledge of the alternatives of choice, it must be reliably informed of the state one is in and its likely outcome. Scientific medicine is not infallible, but it is the best we have. Should a rational person be willing to endure acute suffering merely on the chance that a miraculous cure might presently be at hand? Each one should be permitted to make his own choice—especially when no one else is harmed by it.

The responsibility for the decision, whether deemed wise or foolish, must be with the chooser.

DISCUSSION

1. Discuss Allan H. Gilbert's essay "College Lectures Are Obsolete." Consider arguments in favor of the lecture system.
2. Read the letter below and answer the questions that follow.

A LETTER TO THE EDITOR

(1) With a great show of moral indignation, it was recently revealed that 47 percent of Monroe College students "cheated" on quizzes, prelims, and examinations. Since then, readers of *The Bulletin* have been deluged with pious commentaries. Isn't it about time someone asked whether our modern Puritans aren't being overly righteous in this matter? A little giving or taking of information on an examination, or the use of a few crib notes, is not such a bad thing as some prudish minds would have us think. The very fact that so many loyal Monroe students indulge in this is evidence that it can't be very wrong.

(2) On the contrary, copying or the use of crib notes seems quite pardonable in many courses. In a course which requires remembering a lot of facts, why not use crib notes? It's only a difference of degree between using them and using some elaborate system for memorizing facts. Both are artificial means to help you remember.

Continued

(3) If we view the problem from another angle, we can see that what is so smugly denounced as "dishonesty" may actually reveal foresight—which is certainly a praise-worthy trait. If you were going into an unknown wilderness, you would take along the things you knew were needed for survival, wouldn't you? Taking crib notes into the unknown territory of an examination shows the same foresight. Now suppose also that one of your companions on this expedition desperately needed water or food or help of some sort. You'd do what you could for him, wouldn't you? Helping someone on an examination isn't any different.

(4) To put the question another way, suppose we define charity as "giving to a person in need." Isn't one, therefore, performing an act of charity during an examination when one gives some "needy" person the desired information? The fact that one isn't giving money or food doesn't make the act any less charitable.

(5) If we inquire *who* is stirring up this fuss over alleged "cheating," we find it's the faculty—in other words, the persons who have selfish interests to protect. Obviously, they flunk students to make them repeat the course and thus to keep it filled.

(6) Finally, to take a long-range view, why should colleges get all excited over what they choose to call "cheating" when there are much more urgent things for them to worry about? When the very existence of our democracy is being threatened by Communism, why fret about the source of Johnny X's information on an exam in ancient history?

—Name Withheld

a. What is the writer's main point? State the reasons given in support of it.
b. What is the writer's implied definition of cheating? Comment on its adequacy as a definition?
c. What is the writer's view of people who denounce cheating? What purpose does this view serve in the argument?
d. What is the implied premise or underlying assumption of: "The very fact that so many loyal Monroe students indulge in this is evidence that it can't be very wrong"?
e. Identify and briefly describe the fallacy in paragraph 2.
f. What kind of argument does the writer use in paragraph 3? Appraise its soundness.
g. Comment on the argument used in paragraph 4 and again in paragraph 6.

3. Discuss the advantages and possible disadvantages of Benjamin Franklin's advice. Do his rules preclude the kind of confident assertion necessary to win the reader's agreement and assent? Explain the psychological value of Franklin's approach.

4. Analyze and evaluate the editorial below in terms of the following:

Title
Opening sentence/closing sentence
Organization
Soundness of argument
Use of Rogerian strategy

TIME TO START SAVING THE SOIL

We are accustomed to think of soil destruction as a problem confronting other lands and other times: the inexorable spread of the Sahara Desert, the parching of lands in India, the American Dust Bowl of the 1930s. But as a United Nations conference in Nairobi, Kenya, begins to assess the global problem of the loss of arable lands, it is sobering to note that even in this country, the reputed world leader in modern agricultural practices, the land is eroding away.

Over the past two centuries, erosion has ruined some 200 million arable acres, more than half as much land as we currently have under cultivation. Today an estimated one-third of our croplands are losing topsoil at a rate too great to be sustained without eventually reducing productivity. Crop yields continue high only because of the use of fertilizers and modern technology and management methods. Water alone carried off nine tons of soil per average acre of American cropland in 1975; five tons are generally considered the upper limit tolerable over a sustained period in even deep soils. Wind has added to the destruction, and some observers fear conditions are ripe for another dust bowl.

How can this be—some four decades after Franklin D. Roosevelt launched the nation on the path toward soil conservation? The answers lie in economics. Farmers seek to maximize their immediate crop yields by planting continuous single crops and eliminating protective cover crops. They are often reluctant to adopt costly conservation practices.

The Agriculture Department and key congressional committees have begun a major reassessment of the nation's soil conservation programs. The House and Senate have already approved bills designed to help stem the loss of land. The approaches so far have been essentially voluntary; they seek to persuade the farmer to adopt conservation practices through education, technical assistance and cost-sharing incentives.

That may not be enough. Compulsion may be needed. The farm bloc would of course oppose mandatory regulations, but the time has probably come to insist that farmers follow good soil conservation practices as a condition of receiving farm loans, crop insurance, price supports and other federal aid. Conserving the nation's land is too important to be left to the individual farmer.

5. Select an editorial from your local or college newspaper and analyze as in question 4 above.

6. Analyze Ann Squire's "Animal Research: An Unnecessary Evil?" by answering the following questions:
   a. What does Squire accomplish in her first two sentences, particularly in the phrase, "any reasonable person would respond"?
   b. How does Squire make her point about the dependability of animals as predictors for human responses?
   c. Look at Squire's citation concerning the Jarvik-7 heart and examine the logic of its point. Is the argument sound?

Continued

    d. Examine the last paragraph of Squire's section "Sentient Creatures." What is the implied response if scientists ask themselves the question she suggests and they answer yes instead of the no she provides? What are the implications of that unanswered alternative for Squire's argument about the intrinsic value of animals?

    e. Do you accept Squire's reasoning that scientists "view animals as a part of an arsenal of laboratory equipment"? If so, why? If not, why not? What experiences do you bring to the issue that influence your response? Is Squire manipulating your response? If so, in what ways?

    f. Speculate as to why Squire orders her four points—undependable subjects, sentient creatures, better alternatives, breaking the habit—as she does? Is it the most effective sequence she could have chosen?

    g. Note that Squire opens her argument with a question and starts each section of it with a question. Why does she do this? Is it an effective strategy? How so?

7. Analyze George Bernard Shaw's "On Experimenting with Animals," using the questions below as a guide:

    a. What expectations does Shaw establish with his first sentence and use of the cliché "ignorance is bliss"? Does he fulfill expectations, frustrate them, or play on them?

    b. Which of the persuasive techniques does Shaw employ in the argument developed in paragraph three?

    c. What is the essential argument embedded in Shaw's statement that even those who permit animal experimentation "never say, 'You may torture *my* dog?'"?

    d. Shaw frequently wrote in a mocking, ironic tone. Cite evidence of this in this essay, indicating specific word choices and phrases that help create such a tone.

8. Analyze Robert White's "A Humane and Scientific Necessity."

    a. What does White gain for his position by spending much of his first paragraph explaining science's inertia in the face of attacks from antivivisectionists?

    b. Whether or not the human race is "painted . . . into an ecological corner," speculate about why White makes necessity a cornerstone of his argument. What does he add by praising the "humanitarian movement" in general for its call for ecological sanity? Is White in sympathy with that movement? Explain.

    c. Does White see any differences within the antivivisectionist camp? Do differences matter to him? Explain.

    d. In raising the issue of meat-packing plants, what is White's actual point?

    e. Quoting Dr. Harvey Cushing on the need for animal experiments in neurophysiology, White establishes an either-or situation: either we are allowed to experiment on animals or we must inflict "our first crude manipulations" on humans. Decide whether or not this either-or situation is an instance of the logical fallacy known as the excluded middle. Discuss.

    f. Why do you think White introduces his defense of his own experiments by listing the names of eminent scientists?

    g. Which, if any, of White's "shocking details" do you find actually shocking? How do they support or undermine his argument?

    h. What does White gain for his position by turning from the issue of vivisection itself to a concern for federal funding and the reference to animal-based research in Great Britain? What do you think he is appealing to—perhaps unconsciously?

9. What—in your opinion—are the main strengths of Sidney Hook's "...Defense of Voluntary Euthanasia"? What points can be made in rebuttal? Organize a case *against* voluntary euthanasia.

10. Read the following news item carefully, noting the many complications in the situation. Indicate how a Rogerian rhetorician might analyze the explosive problems described—and how they might have been avoided.

> Having written about his lacerating experience in a forthcoming Anchor/Doubleday book, *Academic Turmoil,* due next month, Theodore L. Gross, former dean of humanities at City College and now provost at the Capitol Campus of Penn State outside of Harrisburg, can be a little more objective about it all, though both his voice and manner suggest that it has been rough going for the last two years.
>
> It all started with an article that appeared in the Feb. 4, 1978, issue of the *Saturday Review* with the startling headline, "How to Kill a College" and an illustration of a bloody dagger plunged into the heart of academe. The article was a sober assessment of the open admissions program at City College, which the then-dean had advocated but which he felt had been less than successful. But the trappings of the piece, the headline and illustration, neither of which he was responsible for, evidently sensationalized the entire issue. The result, among other things, brought confrontations with organized student groups on campus and severe criticism from the president of the college, Robert E. Marshak, with whom Dean Gross had had cordial relations.
>
> Mr. Gross was removed as dean and though he could have returned to an earlier position of professor of English, he accepted the offer made to him by Penn State to take the Capitol Campus post.
>
> "I did not realize that the president would take the piece so personally," Mr. Gross said. "It was a piece about open admissions. It was not a personal matter. Had I known what would develop, I would have written the essay but held off from publishing it until it was a book."
>
> The book is now in, and it tells not only what Mr. Gross wanted to say about open admissions and higher education and its relation to pre-college schooling, but it includes also a blow-by-blow account of the events that followed publication of the article.
>
> He is still for open admissions. "We don't have any choice in regard to the program," the educator said. "It is pragmatic and it is education as practiced in America. It can be sloppy, it can be messy, but there is about it a sense of promise, of openness that is marvelous and tremendously exciting." He sees his book as a 1970s case history and hopes it will offer guidance to inner-city educators.
>
> Taking a long look back now, would he say that these recent events constitute a triumph or failure?
>
> "Neither," said the former dean, "A circumstance of life."
>
> —Lask, "Publishing"

ESSAY SUGGESTIONS

1. In an essay (750-1,000 words) reply to Allan H. Gilbert's essay "College Lectures Are Obsolete." Support the position or assert a contrary position in favor of the lecture system. Prepare to write this essay by using the prewriting techniques you have learned.

2. Write an essay (750-1,000 words) arguing against another aspect or procedure of our educational system that might be considered obsolete or otherwise inadequate (the grading system, required courses, awarding of degrees, formal class meetings). Be sure to locate specific issues and to include in the body of your argument not only evidence in behalf of your case, but evidence refuting points of opposition. Attempt to weave in a Rogerian strategy, if possible.

3. In an essay (500-750 words) make a case against any -ism of your choice (atheism, romanticism, racism) by showing that it is either self-contradictory (a logical flaw) or self-defeating (a moral flaw). Use analogies to develop your argument.

4. Fill in the space(s) of one of the headlines below and write an editorial for your college or local newspaper (500-750 words).

Give the _____ a Chance

Time to Start _____

Hold That _____ at _____

5. Write an editorial (500-750 words) on any subject of timely or urgent concern.

6. Choose one of the controversial topics listed below and write an essay (750-1,000 words) in which you take a definitive position and argue your case as persuasively as possible.

capital punishment
nuclear energy plants
trade with communist countries
family choice about comatose relatives
confidentiality for AIDS patients
English as the official American language
abortion upon demand
prayer in the schools
defendants' rights
tobacco-crop subsidies
legalization of drugs

Be certain to do appropriate research before beginning your essay so that you understand the issues involved and the major arguments for both sides.

7. Once you have chosen a side to take in any of the above debates, write an argumentative essay (750-1,000 words) from the viewpoint of the opposition, trying to be as forceful and as powerful as anyone arguing that stance with real conviction.

8. Write a reply (500-1,000 words) to Sidney Hook's "In Defense of Voluntary Euthanasia" in which you take either an opposing or a re-affirming position.

9. Write a Letter to Editor (300-500 words) or an essay (750-1,000 words) entitled "A Case for _____" or "In Defense of _____."

10. Read the essay below, originally a paper presented by Carl Rogers at Northwestern University's Conference on Communications (October 11, 1951). Evaluate the arguments in behalf of the main thesis that "the major barrier to mutual interpersonal communication is our very natural tendency to judge, to evaluate, to approve or disapprove, the statement of the other person, or the other group." Test out Rogerian strategy by setting up with a classmate an experimental argument in which you try, as Rogers suggests, "creating a situation in which each of the different parties come to understand the other from the *other's* point of view."

Using the results of your experiment, plus Rogers's argument in support of his thesis, write an argument of your own (750-1,000 words) entitled "The Case For Rogerian Strategy," or "The Case Against Rogerian Strategy."

COMMUNICATION: ITS BLOCKING AND ITS FACILITATION

Carl R. Rogers

It may seem curious that a person whose whole professional effort is devoted to psychotherapy should be interested in problems of communication. What relationship is there between providing therapeutic help to individuals with emotional maladjustments and the concern of this conference with obstacles to communication? Actually the relationship is very close indeed. The whole task of psychotherapy is the task of dealing with a failure in communication. The emotionally maladjusted person, the "neurotic," is in difficulty first because communication within himself has broken down, and second because as a result of this his communication with others has been damaged. If this sounds somewhat strange, then let me put it in other terms. In the "neurotic" individual, parts of himself which have been termed unconscious, or repressed, or denied to awareness, become blocked off so that they no longer communicate themselves to the conscious or managing part of himself. As long as this is true, there are distortions in the way he communicates himself to others, and so he suffers both within himself, and in his interpersonal relations. The task of psychotherapy is to help the person achieve, through a special relationship with a therapist, good communication within himself. Once this is achieved he can communicate more freely and more effectively with others. We may say then that psychotherapy is good communication, within and between men. We may also turn that statement around and it will still be true. Good communication, free communication, within or between men, is always therapeutic.

It is, then, from a background of experience with communication in counseling and psychotherapy that I want to present here two ideas. I wish to state what I believe is one of the major factors in blocking or impeding communication, and then I wish to present what in our experience has proven to be a very important way of improving or facilitating communication.

I would like to propose, as an hypothesis for consideration, that the major barrier to mutual interpersonal communication is our very natural tendency to judge, to evaluate, to approve or disapprove, the statement of the other person, or the other group. Let me illustrate my meaning with some very simple examples. As you leave the meeting tonight, one of the statements you are likely to hear is, "I didn't like that man's talk." Now what do you respond? Almost invariably your reply will be either approval or disapproval of the attitude expressed. Either you respond. "I didn't either. I thought it was terrible," or else you tend to reply, "Oh, I thought it was really good." In other words, your primary reaction is to evaluate what has just been said to you, to evaluate it from *your* point of view, your own frame of reference.

Or take another example. Suppose I say with some feeling, "I think the Republicans are behaving in ways that show a lot of good sound sense these days," what is the response that arises in your mind as you listen? The overwhelming likelihood is that it will be evaluative. You will find yourself agreeing, or disagreeing, or making some judgment about me such as "He must be a conservative," or "He seems solid in his thinking." Or let us take an illustration from the international scene. Russia says vehemently, "The treaty with Japan is a war plot on the part of the United States." We rise as one person to say "That's a lie!"

This last illustration brings in another element connected with hypothesis. Although the tendency to make evaluations is common in almost all interchange of language, it is very much heightened in those situations where feelings and emotions are deeply involved. So the stronger our feelings, the more likely it is that there will be no mutual element in the communication. There will be just two ideas, two feelings, two judgements, missing each other in psychological space. I'm sure you recognize this from your own experience. When you have not been emotionally involved yourself, and have listened to a heated discussion, you often go away thinking, "Well, they actually weren't talking about the same thing." And they were not. Each was making a judgement, an evaluation, from his own frame of reference. There was really nothing which could be called communication in any genuine sense. This tendency to react to any emotionally meaningful statement by forming an evaluation of it from our own point of view is, I repeat, the major barrier to interpersonal communication.

But is there any way of solving this problem, of avoiding this barrier? I feel that we are making exciting progress toward this goal and I would like to present it as simply as I can. Real communication occurs, and this evaluative tendency is avoided, when we listen with understanding. What does that mean? It means to *see the expressed idea and attitude from the other person's point of view, to sense how it feels to him, to achieve his frame of reference in regard to the thing he is talking about.*

Stated so briefly, this may sound absurdly simple, but it is not. It is an approach which we have found extremely potent in the field of psychotherapy. It is the most effective agent we know for altering the basic personality structure of an individual, and improving his relationships and his communications with others. If I can listen to what he can tell me, if I can understand how it seems to him, if I can see its personal meaning for him, if I can sense the emotional flavor which it has for him, then I will be releasing potent forces of change in him. If I can really understand how he hates his father, or hates the university, or hates communists—if I can catch the flavor of his fear of insanity, or his fear of atom bombs, or of Russia—it will be of the greatest help to him in altering those very hatreds and fears, and in establishing realistic and harmonious relationships with the very people and situations toward which he has felt hatred and fear. We know from our research that such empathic understanding—understanding *with* a person, not *about* him—is such an effective approach that it can bring about major changes in personality.

Some of you may be feeling that you listen well to people, and that you have never seen such results. The chances are very great indeed that your listening has not been of the type I have described. Fortunately I can suggest a little laboratory experiment which you can try to test the quality of your understanding. The next time you get into an argument with your wife, or your friend, or with a small group of friends, just stop the discussion for a moment and for an experiment, institute this rule: "Each person can speak up for himself only *after* he has first restated the ideas and feelings of the previous speaker accurately, and to the speaker's satisfaction." You see what this would mean. It would simply mean that before presenting your own point of view, it would be necessary for you to really achieve the other speaker's frame of reference—to understand his thoughts and feelings so well that you could summarize them for him. Sounds simple doesn't it? But if you try it you will discover it is one of the most difficult things you have ever tried to do. However, once you have been able to see the other's point of view, your own comments will have to be drastically revised. You will also find the emotion going out of the discussion, the differences being reduced, and those differences which remain being of a rational and understandable sort.

Can you imagine what this kind of an approach would mean if it were projected into larger areas? What would happen to a labor-management dispute if it was conducted in such a way that labor, without necessarily agreeing, could accurately state management's point of view in a way that management could accept; and management, without approving labor's stand, could state labor's case in a way that labor agreed was accurate? It would mean that real communication was established, and one could practically guarantee that some reasonable solution would be reached.

If then this way of approach is an effective avenue to good communication and good relationships, as I am quite sure you will agree if you try the experiment I have mentioned, why is it not more widely tried and used? I will try to list the difficulties which keep it from being widely utilized.

In the first place it takes courage, a quality which is not too widespread. I am indebted to Dr. S. I. Hayakawa, the semanticist, for pointing out that to carry on psychotherapy in this fashion is to take a very real risk, and that courage is required. If you really understand another person in this way, if you are willing to enter his private world and see the way life appears to him, without any attempt to make evaluative judgments, you run the risk of being changed yourself. You might see it his way, you might find yourself influenced in your attitudes or your personality. This risk of being changed is one of the most frightening prospects most of us can face. If I enter, as fully as I am able, into the private world of a neurotic or psychotic individual, isn't there a risk that I might become lost in that world? Most of us are afraid to take that risk. Or if we had a Russian communist speaker here tonight, or Senator Joe McCarthy, how many of us would dare to try to see the world from each of these points of view? The great majority of us could not *listen;* we would find ourselves compelled to *evaluate,* because listening would seem too dangerous. So the first requirement is courage, and we do not always have it.

But there is a second obstacle. It is just when emotions are strongest that it is most difficult to achieve the frame of reference of the other person or group. Yet it is the time the attitude is most needed, if communication is to be established. We have not found this to be an insuperable obstacle in our experience in psychotherapy. A third party, who is able to lay aside his own feelings and evaluations, can assist greatly by listening with understanding to each person or group and clarifying the views and attitudes each holds. We have found this very effective in small groups in which contradictory or antagonistic attitudes exist. When the parties to a dispute realize that they are being understood, that someone sees how the situation seems to them, the statements grow less exaggerated and less defensive, and it is no longer necessary to maintain the attitude, "I am 100% right and you are 100% wrong." The influence of such an understanding catalyst in the group permits the members to come closer and closer to the objective truth involved in the relationship. In this way mutual communication is established and some type of agreement becomes much more possible. So we may say that though heightened emotions make it much more difficult to understand *with* an opponent, our experience makes it clear that a neutral, understanding, catalyst type of leader or therapist can overcome this obstacle in a small group.

This last phrase, however, suggests another obstacle to utilizing the approach I have described. Thus far all our experience has been with small face-to-face groups—groups exhibiting industrial tensions, religious tensions, racial tensions, and therapy groups in which many personal tensions are present. In these small groups our experience, confirmed by a limited amount of research, shows that this basic approach leads to improved communication, to greater acceptance of others and by others, and to attitudes which are more positive and more problem-solving in nature. There is a decrease in defensiveness, in exaggerated statements, in evaluative and critical behavior. But these findings are from small groups. What about trying to achieve understanding between larger groups that are geographically remote? Or between face-to-face groups who are not speaking for themselves, but simply as representatives of others, like the delegates at Kaesong? Frankly we do not know the answers to these questions. I believe the situation might be put this way: As social scientists we have a tentative test-tube solution of the problem of breakdown in communication. But to confirm the validity of this test-tube solution, and to adapt it to the enormous problems of communication-breakdown between classes, groups, and nations, would involve additional funds, much more research, and creative thinking of a high order.

Even with our present limited knowledge we can see some steps which might be taken, even in large groups, to increase the amount of listening *with,* and to decrease the amount of evaluation *about.* To be imaginative for a moment, let us suppose that a therapeutically oriented international group went to the Russian leaders and said, "We want to achieve a genuine understanding of your views and even more important, of your attitudes and feelings, toward the United States. We will summarize and resummarize these views and feelings if necessary, until you agree that our description represents the situation as it seems to you." Then suppose they did the same thing with the leaders in our own country. If they then gave the widest possible distribution to these two views, with the feelings clearly described but not expressed in name-calling, might not the effect be very great? It would not guarantee the type of understanding I have been describing, but it would make it much more possible. We can understand the feelings of a person who hates us much more readily when his attitudes are accurately described to us by a neutral third party, than we can when he is shaking his fist at us.

But even to describe such a first step is to suggest another obstacle to this approach of understanding. Our civilization does not yet have enough faith in the social sciences to utilize their findings. The opposite is true of the physical sciences. During the war when a test-tube solution was found to the problem of synthetic rubber, millions of dollars and an army of talent was turned loose on the problem of using that finding. If synthetic rubber could be made in milligrams, it could and would be made in the thousands of tons. And it was. But in the social science realm, if a way is found of facilitating communication and mutual understanding in small groups, there is no guarantee that the finding will be utilized. It may be a generation or more before the money and the brains will be turned lose to exploit that finding.

In closing, I would like to summarize this small-scale solution to the problem of barriers in communication, and to point out certain of its characteristics.

I have said that our research and experience to date would make it appear that breakdowns in communication, and the evaluative tendency which is the major barrier to communication, can be avoided. The solution is provided by creating a situation in which each of the different parties come to understand the other from the *other's* point of view. This has been achieved, in practice, even when feelings run high, by the influence of a person who is willing to understand each point of view emphatically, and who thus acts as a catalyst to precipitate further understanding.

This procedure has important characteristics. It can be initiated by one party, without waiting for the other to be ready. It can even be initiated by a neutral third person, providing he can gain a minimum of cooperation from one of the parties.

This procedure can deal with the insincerities, the defensive exaggerations, the lies, the "false fronts" which characterize almost every failure in communication. These defensive distortions drop away with astonishing speed as people find that the only intent is to understand, not judge.

This approach leads steadily and rapidly toward the discovery of the truth, toward a realistic appraisal of the objective barriers to communication. The dropping of some defensiveness by one party leads to further dropping of defensiveness by the other party, and truth is thus approached.

This procedure gradually achieves mutual communication. Mutual communication tends to be pointed toward solving a problem rather than toward attacking a person or group. It leads to a situation in which I see how the problem appears to you, as well as to me, and you see how it appears to me, as well as to you. Thus accurately and realistically defined, the problem is almost certain to yield to intelligent attack, or if it is in part insoluble, it will be comfortably accepted as such.

This then appears to be a test-tube solution to the breakdown of communication as it occurs in small groups. Can we take this small-scale answer, investigate it further, refine it, develop it and apply it to the tragic and well-nigh fatal failures of communication which threaten the very existence of our modern world? It seems to me that this is a possibility and a challenge which we should explore.

PART III

Beyond the Short Paper

Chapter 5   Generating a Longer Paper

Chapter 6   Researching a Longer Paper

Chapter 7   Writing a Longer Paper

Chapter 5

GENERATING
A LONGER PAPER

ANSWERING MANY QUESTIONS

TO INFORM
   SPEAKING WITH A SINGLE TONGUE
      JARED DIAMOND

TO INTERPRET
   ISAAC NEWTON, I. BERNARD COHEN

TO PERSUADE
   LETTER FROM BIRMINGHAM JAIL
      THE REV. MARTIN LUTHER KING, JR.

ANSWERING MANY QUESTIONS

To focus our attention, we have treated papers of 500–1000 words as though they took their impulse from the need to answer a single one of the twenty questions. Subquestions may be very useful to writers in exploring and expanding their topics, but a paper of only a few pages generally needs the unity of purpose and clear organization that comes from providing a clear answer to a single topic.

We have also seen, however, that one question often leads naturally to another and another; writers who are in touch with their subjects will learn to listen for the questioning voice that encourages future exploration. When attempting to sustain a paper for more than a few pages, you'll find that linking questions together enables you to give a fuller and more compelling account of your subject than if you had limited yourself to a single question. Combining several of the twenty questions can be useful in a variety of writing assignments:

- to not only describe the basic steps of a process but also explain the deeper meanings of a process and its ultimate result and value
- to describe a character, not only in broad brush strokes as in a sketch, but also with the nuances of detail that fill out the portrait
- to explore an issue beyond its most obvious features—presenting both the facts and *how* they got to be facts, *why* and *with what consequences*
- to examine systematically the many facets of an explanation, an interpretation, or an argument

When the questions are used in such a way, they serve as strategies to meet a larger rhetorical purpose—to inform, to interpret, or to persuade, for example. In this chapter, we present three examples of extended essays that exhibit this combination of responses.

TO INFORM

This article, which originally appeared in *Discover* magazine, examines thousands of languages in danger of extinction because the last speakers of those languages are dying off. As you read it, note that it begins as an answer to the question, What is the present status of X? What other questions did the author, Jared Diamond, ask and answer in the process of developing his answer to this primary question? Look for the points in the article where he moves from one question to another. How does he signal these shifts in direction to his readers?

SPEAKING WITH A SINGLE TONGUE

Jared Diamond

"Kópipi! Kópipi!" In jungle on the Pacific island of Bougainville, a man from the village of Rotokas was excitedly pointing out the most beautiful birdsong I had ever heard. It consisted of silver-clear whistled tones and trills, grouped in slowly rising phrases of two or three notes, each phrase different from the next. The effect was like one of Schubert's deceptively simple songs. I never succeeded in glimpsing the

singer, nor have any of the other ornithologists who have subsequently visited Bougainville and listened spellbound to its song. All we know of the kópipi bird is that name for it in the Rotokas language and descriptions of it by Rotokas villagers.

As I talked with my guide, I gradually realized that the extraordinary music of Bougainville's mountains included not only the kópipi's song but also the sounds of the Rotokas language. My guide named one bird after another: *kópipi, kurupi, vokupi, kopikau, kororo, keravo, kurue, vikuroi.* . . . The only consonant sounds in those names are *k, p, r,* and *v.* Later I learned that the Rotokas language has only six consonant sounds, the fewest of any known language in the world. English, by comparison, has 24, while other languages have 80 or more. Somehow the people of Rotokas, living in a tropical rain forest on one of the highest mountains of the southwest Pacific, have managed to build a rich vocabulary and communicate clearly while relying on fewer basic sounds than any other people.

But the music of their language is now disappearing from Bougainville's mountains, and from the world. The Rotokas language is just one of 18 languages spoken on an island roughly three-quarters the size of Connecticut. At last count it was spoken by only 4,320 people, and the number is declining. With its vanishing, a 30,000-year history of human communication and cultural development is coming to an end.

That vanishing exemplifies a little-noticed tragedy looming over us: the possible loss of 90 percent of our creative heritage, linked with the loss of 90 percent of our languages. We hear much anguished discussion about the accelerating disappearance of indigenous cultures as our Coca-Cola civilization spreads over the world. Much less attention has been paid to the disappearance of languages themselves and to their essential role in the survival of those indigenous cultures. Each language is the vehicle for a unique way of thinking, a unique literature, and a unique view of the world. Only now are linguists starting seriously to estimate the world's rate of language loss and to debate what to do about it.

If the present rate of disappearance continues, our 6,000 modern languages could be reduced within a century or two to just a few hundred. Time is running out even to study the others. Hence linguists face a race against time similar to that faced by biologists, now aware that many of the world's plant and animal species are in danger of extinction.

To begin to understand the problem, we should take a look at how the world's languages are divided up. If the global population of about 5.5 billion humans were equally distributed among its 6,000 tongues, then each language would have roughly 900,000 speakers—enough to give each language a fair chance of survival. Of course, the vast majority of people use only one of a few "big" languages, such as Mandarin Chinese, English, or Spanish, each with hundreds of millions of native speakers. The vast majority of languages are "little" ones, with a median number of perhaps only 5,000 speakers.

Our 6,000 languages are also unevenly distributed over the globe. Western Europe is especially poorly endowed, with about 45 native languages. In 1788, when European settlement of Australia began, aboriginal Australia was considerably richer: it had 250 languages, despite having far fewer people than Western Europe. The Americas at the time of Columbus's arrival were richer yet: more than 1,000 languages. But the richest region of the globe, then and now, is New Guinea and other Pacific islands, with only 8 million people, or less than .2 percent of the world's population, but about 1,400 languages, or almost 25 percent of the world's total! While New Guinea itself stands out with about 1,000 of those languages, other neighboring archipelagoes are also well endowed—Vanuatu, for example, with about 105, and the Philippines with 160.

Many New Guinea languages are so distinctive that they have no proven relationship with any other language in the world, not even with any other New Guinea language. As I travel across New Guinea, every 10 or 20 miles I pass between tribes with languages as different as English is from Chinese. And most of those languages are "tiny" ones, with fewer than 1,000 speakers.

How did these enormous geographic differences in linguistic diversity arise? Partly, of course, from differences in topography and human population density. But there's another reason as well: the original linguistic diversity of many areas has been homogenized by expansions of political states in the last several thousand years, and by expansions of farmers in the last 10,000 years. New Guinea, Vanuatu, the Philippines, and aboriginal Australia were exceptional in never having been unified by a native empire. To us, the British and Spanish empires may be the most familiar examples of centralized states that imposed their state language on conquered peoples. However, the Inca and Aztec empires similarly imposed Quechua and Nahuatl on their Indian subjects before A.D. 1500. Long before the rise of political states, expansions of farmers must have wiped out thousands of hunter-gatherer languages. For instance, the expansion of Indo-European farmers and herders that began around 4000 B.C. eradicated all preexisting Western European languages except Basque.

I'd guess that before expansions of farmers began in earnest around 6000 B.C. the world harbored tens of thousands of languages. If so, then we may *already* have lost much of the world's linguistic diversity. Of those vanished languages, a few—such as Etruscan, Hittite, and Sumerian—lingered long enough to be written down and preserved for us. Far more languages, though, have vanished without a trace. Who knows what the speech of the Huns and the Picts, and of uncounted nameless peoples, sounded like?

As linguists have begun surveying the status of our surviving languages, it has become clear that prognoses for future survival vary enormously. Here are some calculations made by linguist Michael Krauss of the University of Alaska at Fairbanks. Presumably among the languages with the most secure futures are the official national languages of the world's sovereign states, which now number 170 or so. However, most states have officially adopted English, French, Spanish, Arabic, or Portuguese, leaving only about 70 states to opt for other languages. Even if one counts regional languages, such as the 15 specified in India's constitution, that yields at best a few hundred languages officially protected anywhere in the world. Alternatively, one might consider languages with over a million speakers as secure, regardless of their official status, but that definition also yields only 200 or so secure languages, many of which duplicate the list of official languages. What's happening to the other 5,800 of the world's 6,000?

As an illustration of their fates, consider Alaska's 20 native Eskimo and Indian languages. The Eyak language, formerly spoken by a few hundred Indians on Alaska's south coast, had declined by 1982 to two native speakers, Marie Smith (age 72) and her sister Sophie Borodkin. Their children speak only English. With

Sophie Borodkin's death last year at the age of 80, the language world of the Eyak people reached its final silence—except when Marie Smith speaks Eyak with Michael Krauss. Seventeen other native Alaskan languages are moribund, in that not a single child is learning them. Although they are still being spoken by older people, they too will meet the fate of Eyak when the last of those speakers dies; in addition, almost all of them have fewer than 1,000 speakers each. That leaves only two native Alaskan languages still being learned by children and thus not yet doomed: Siberian Yupik, with 1,000 speakers, and Central Yupik, with a grand total of 10,000 speakers.

The situation is similar for the 187 Indian languages surviving in North America outside Alaska, such as Chickasaw, Navajo, and Nootka. Krauss estimates that 149 of these are already moribund. Even Navajo, the language with by far the largest number of speakers (around 100,000), has a doubtful future, as many or most Navajo children now speak only English. Language extinction is even further advanced in aboriginal Australia, where only 100 of the original 250 languages are still spoken or even remembered, and only 7 have more than 1,000 speakers. At best, only 2 or 3 of those aboriginal languages will retain their vitality throughout our lifetime.

In monographs summarizing the current status of languages, one encounters the same types of phrase monotonously repeated. "Ubykh [a language of the northwest Caucasus] . . . one speaker definitely still alive, perhaps two or three more." "Vilela [sole surviving language of a group of Indian languages in Argentina] . . . spoken by only two individuals." "The last speaker of Cupeño [an Indian language of southern California], Roscinda Nolasquez of Pala, California, died in 1987 at the age of 94." Putting these status reports together, it appears that up to half of the world's surviving languages are no longer being learned by children. By some time in the coming century, Krauss estimates, all but perhaps a few hundred languages could be dead or moribund.

Why is the rate of language disappearance accelerating so steeply now, when so many languages used to be able to persist with only a few hundred speakers in places like traditional New Guinea? Why do declining languages include not only small ones but also ones with many speakers, including Breton (around 100,000) and even Quechua (8.5 million)? Just as there are different ways of killing people—by a quick blow to the head, slow strangulation, or prolonged neglect—so too are there different ways of eradicating a language.

The most direct way, of course, is to kill almost all its speakers. This was how white Californians eliminated the Yahi Indian language between 1853 and 1870, and how British colonists eliminated all the native languages of Tasmania between 1803 and 1835. Another direct way is for governments to forbid and punish use of minority languages. If you wondered why 149 out of 187 North American Indian languages are now moribund, just consider the policy practiced until recently by the U.S. government regarding those languages. For several centuries we insisted that Indians could be "civilized" and taught English only by removing children from the "barbarous" atmosphere of their parents' homes to English-language-only boarding schools, where use of Indian languages was absolutely forbidden and punished with physical abuse and humiliation.

But in most cases language loss proceeds by the more insidious process now underway at Rotokas. With political unification of an area formerly occupied by sedentary warring tribes comes peace, mobility, intermarriage, and schools. Mixed couples may have no common language except the majority language (for example, English or Pidgin English in Papua New Guinea, the nation to which Bougainville belongs). Young people in search of economic opportunity abandon their native-speaking villages and move to mixed urban centers, where again they have no option except to speak the majority language. Their children's schools speak the majority language. Even their parents remaining in the village learn the majority language for its access to prestige, trade, and power. Newspapers, radio, and TV overwhelmingly use majority languages understood by most consumers, advertisers, and subscribers. (In the United States, the only native languages regularly broadcast are Navajo and Yupik.)

The usual result is that minority young adults tend to become bilingual, then their children become monolingual in the majority language. Eventually the minority language is spoken only by older people, until the last of them dies. Long before that end is reached, the minority language has degenerated through loss of its grammatical complexities, loss of forgotten native words, and incorporation of foreign vocabulary and grammatical features.

Those are the overwhelming facts of worldwide language extinction. But now let's play devil's advocate and ask, So what? Are we really so sure this loss is a terrible thing? Isn't the existence of thousands of languages positively harmful, first because they impede communication, and second because they promote strife? Perhaps we should actually *encourage* language loss.

The devil's first objection is that we need a common language to understand each other, to conduct commerce, and to get along in peace. Perhaps it's no accident that the countries most advanced technologically are ones with few languages. Multiple languages are just an impediment to communication and progress—at least that's how the devil would argue.

To which I answer: Of course different people need some common language to understand each other! But that doesn't require eliminating minority languages; it only requires bilingualism. We Americans forget how exceptional our monolingualism is by world standards. People elsewhere routinely learn two or more languages as children, with little effort. For example, Denmark is one of the wealthiest and most contented nations in the world. Danes have no problem doing business profitably with other countries, even though practically no one except the 5 million Danes speaks Danish. That's because almost all Danes also speak English, and many speak other foreign languages as well. Still, Danes have no thought of abandoning their tongue. The Danish language, combined with polylingualism, remains indispensable to Danes being happily Danish.

Perhaps you're thinking now, All right, so communication doesn't absolutely require us all to have a single language. Still, though, bilingualism is a pain in the neck that you yourself would rather be spared.

But remember that bilingualism is practiced especially by minority language speakers, who learn majority languages. If they choose to do that extra work, that's their business; monolingual speakers of majority languages have no right or need to prevent them. Minorities struggling to preserve their language ask only for the freedom to decide for themselves—without being excluded, humiliated, punished, or killed for exercising that freedom. Inuits (Eskimos) aren't asking U.S.

whites to learn Inuit; they're just asking that Inuit schoolchildren be permitted to learn Inuit along with English.

The devil's second objection is that multiple languages promote strife by encouraging people to view other peoples as different. The civil wars tearing apart so many countries today are determined by linguistic lines. Whatever the value of multiple languages, getting rid of them may be the price we have to pay if we're to halt the killing around the globe. Wouldn't the world be a much more peaceful place if the Kurds would just agree to speak Arabic or Turkish, if Sri Lanka's Tamils would consent to speak Sinhalese, and if the Armenians would switch to Azerbaijani (or vice versa)?

That seems like a very strong argument. But pause and consider: language differences aren't the sole cause, or even the most important cause, of strife. Prejudiced people will seize on any difference to dislike others, including differences of religion, politics, ethnicity, and dress. One of the world's most vicious civil wars today, that in the land that once was Yugoslavia, pits peoples unified by language but divided by religion and ethnicity: Orthodox Serbs against Catholic Croats and Muslim Bosnians, all speaking Serbo-Croatian. The bloodiest genocide of history was that carried out under Stalin, when Russians killed mostly other Russians over supposed political differences. In the world's bloodiest genocide since World War II, Khmer-speaking Cambodians under Pol Pot killed millions of other Khmer-speaking Cambodians.

If you believe that minorities should give up their languages in order to promote peace, ask yourself whether you believe that minorities should also promote peace by giving up their religions, their ethnicities, their political views. If you believe that freedom of religion but not of language is an inalienable human right, how would you explain your inconsistency to a Kurd or an Inuit? Innumerable examples besides those of Stalin and Pol Pot warn us that monolingualism is no safeguard of peace. Even if the suppression of differences of language, religion, and ethnicity did promote peace (which I doubt), it would exact a huge price in human suffering.

Given that people do differ in language, religion, and ethnicity, the only alternative to tyranny or genocide is for people to learn to live together in mutual respect and tolerance. That's not at all an idle hope. Despite all the past wars over religion, people of different religions do coexist peacefully in the United States, Indonesia, and many other countries. Similarly, many countries that practice linguistic tolerance find that they can accommodate people of different languages in harmony: for example, three languages in Finland (Finnish, Swedish, and Lapp), four in Switzerland (German, French, Italian, and Romansh), and nearly a thousand in Papua New Guinea.

All right, so there's nothing inevitably harmful about minority languages, except the nuisance of bilingualism for the minority speakers. What are the positive advantages of linguistic diversity, to justify that minor nuisance?

One answer is that languages are the most complex products of the human mind, each differing enormously in its sounds, structure, and pattern of thought. But a language itself isn't the only thing lost when a language goes extinct. Each language is indissolubly tied up with a unique culture, literature (whether written or not), and worldview, all of which also represent the end point of thousands of years of human inventiveness. Lose the language and you lose much of that as well.

Thus the eradication of most of the world's accumulation of languages would be an overwhelming tragedy, just as would be the destruction of most of the world's accumulated art or literature. We English-speakers would regard the loss of Shakespeare's language and culture as a loss to humanity; Rotokas villagers feel a similar bond to their own language and culture. We are putting millions of dollars into the effort to save one of the world's 8,600 bird species, the California condor. Why do we care so little about most of the world's 6,000 languages, or even desire their disappearance? What makes condors more wonderful than the Eyak language?

A second answer addresses two often-expressed attitudes: "One language is really as good as another," or conversely, "English is much better than any of those fiendishly complicated Indian languages." In reality, languages aren't equivalent or interchangeable, and there's no all-purpose "best language." Instead, as everyone fluent in more than one language knows, different languages have different advantages, such that it's easier to discuss or think about certain things, or to think and feel in certain ways, in one language than another. Language loss doesn't only curtail the freedom of minorities, it also curtails the options of majorities.

Now perhaps you're thinking, Enough of all this vague talk about linguistic freedom, unique cultural inheritance, and different options for thinking and expressing. Those are luxuries that rate low priority amid the crises of the modern world. Until we solve the world's desperate socioeconomic problems, we can't waste our time on bagatelles like obscure Indian languages.

But think again about the socioeconomic problems of the people speaking all those obscure Indian languages (and thousands of other obscure languages around the world). Their problems aren't just narrow ones of jobs and job skills, but broad ones of cultural disintegration. They've been told for so long that their language and everything else about their culture are worthless that they believe it. The costs to our government, in the form of welfare benefits and health care, are enormous. At the same time, other impoverished groups with strong intact cultures—like some recent groups of immigrants—are already managing to contribute to society rather than take from it.

Programs to reverse Indian cultural disintegration would be far better than welfare programs, for Indian minorities and for majority taxpayers alike. Similarly, those foreign countries now wracked by civil wars along linguistic lines would have found it cheaper to emulate countries based on partnerships between proud intact groups than to seek to crush minority languages and cultures.

Those seem to me compelling cultural and practical benefits of sustaining our inherited linguistic diversity. But if you're still unconvinced, let me instead try to persuade you of another proposition: that we should at least record as much information as possible about each endangered language, lest all knowledge of it be lost. For hundreds, perhaps thousands, of the world's 6,000 languages, we have either no written information at all, or just brief word lists. If many of those languages do indeed vanish, at least we'd have preserved as much knowledge as possible from irreversible loss.

What is the value of such knowledge? As one example, consider that relationships of the languages that survive today serve to trace the history of human development and migrations, just as relationships of existing animal and plant species trace the history of biological evolution. All linguists agree, for instance, that we can trace existing Indo-European languages back to an ancestral Proto-Indo-European language spoken somewhere in Europe or western Asia around 6,000 years ago. Now some linguists are trying to trace languages and peoples back much further in time, possibly even back to the origin of all human language. Many tiny modern languages, the ones now most at risk of vanishing unrecorded, have proved disproportionately important in answering that question that never fails to interest each of us: Where did I come from?

Lithuanian, for example, is an Indo-European language with only 3 million speakers, and until recently it struggled against Russian for survival. It's dwarfed by the combined total of 2 billion speakers of the approximately 140 other Indo-European languages. Yet Lithuanian has proved especially important in understanding Indo-European language origins because in some respects it has changed the least and preserved many archaic features over the past several thousand years.

Of course, dictionaries and grammars of Lithuanian are readily available. If the Lithuanian language were to go extinct, at least we'd already know enough about it to use it in reconstructing Indo-European language origins. But other equally important languages are at risk of vanishing with much less information about them recorded. Why should anyone care whether four tiny languages, Kanakanabu, Saaroa, Rukai, and Tsou, spoken by 11,000 aborigines in the mountains of Taiwan, survive? Other Asians may eventually come to care a lot, because these languages may constitute one of the four main branches of the giant Austronesian language family. That family, consisting of some 1,000 languages with a total of 200 million speakers, includes Indonesian and Tagalog, two of Asia's most important languages today. Lose those four tiny aboriginal languages and these numerous Asian peoples may lose one-quarter of the linguistic data base for reconstructing their own history.

If you now at last agree that linguistic diversity isn't evil, and might even be interesting and good, what can you do about the present situation? Are we helpless in the face of the seemingly overwhelming forces tending to eradicate all but a few big languages from the modern world?

No, we're not helpless. First, professional linguists themselves could do a lot more than most of them are now doing. Most place little value on the study of vanishing languages. Only recently have a few linguists, such as Michael Krauss, called our attention to our impending loss. At minimum, society needs to train more linguists and offer incentives to those studying the languages most at risk of disappearing.

As for the rest of us, we can do something individually, by fostering sympathetic awareness of the problem and by helping our children become bilingual in any second language that we choose. Through government, we can also support the use of native languages. The 1990 Native American Languages Act actually *encourages* the use of those languages. And at least as a start, Senate Bill 2044, signed by former President Bush last October, allocates a small amount of money—$2 million a year—for Native American language studies. There's also a lot that minority speakers themselves can do to promote their languages, as the Welsh, New Zealand Maori, and other groups have been doing with some success.

But these minority efforts will be in vain if strongly opposed by the majority, as has happened all too often. Should some of us English-speakers not choose actively to promote Native American languages, we can at least remain neutral and avoid crushing them. Our grounds for doing so are ultimately selfish: to pass on a rich, rather than a drastically impoverished, world to our children.

DISCUSSION AND EXERCISES

1. Identify the paragraphs in the article that answer the following questions.
   a. How can X be described?
   b. How did X happen?
   c. What are the facts about X?
   d. How is X made or done?
   e. What are the causes of X?
   f. What are the consequences of X?
   g. How does X compare to Y?
   h. What is the present status of X?
   i. What is the value of X?
   j. What case can be made for or against X?

2. Explain what each of the following sentences means and how it helps to develop Diamond's ideas.
   a. Who knows what the speech of the Huns and the Picts, and of uncounted nameless peoples, sounded like?
   b. Just as there are different ways of killing people—by a quick blow to the head, slow strangulation, or prolonged neglect—so too are there different ways of eradicating a language.
   c. Perhaps we should actually *encourage* language loss.
   d. If you believe that minorities should give up their languages in order to promote peace, ask yourself whether you believe that minorities should also promote peace by giving up their religions, their ethnicities, their political views.
   e. Each language is indissolubly tied up with a unique culture, literature (whether written or not), and worldview, all of which also represent the end point of thousands of years of human inventiveness.
   f. What makes condors more wonderful than the Eyak language?

3. How does Diamond compare languages becoming extinct and species becoming extinct? In what ways are cultural and biological extinction similar? In what ways are cultural and biological extinction different?

4. Note the places where Diamond uses questions in his article. Do they make the article more interesting or easier to read? Why or why not?

TO INTERPRET

Like the short character sketch, the extended characterization focuses on a single individual, posing the questions, What kind of person is this? What makes him or her tick? The extra length of the extended study enables you to probe more deeply into the complexities of your subject and to compose a fuller portrait, richer in descriptive detail, illustrative episode, and possible interpretations. Even so, like the 500-word sketch, the 2,500-word character study should have a unifying thread; it should point to the quality or qualities that define the person and provide a key to his or her character (Question 3, What kind of person is X?).

This article on the great seventeenth-century scientist Isaac Newton, provides a straightforward, chronologically organized account of this "strange solitary figure" whose inner life and motivations were "hidden even from his contemporaries." In this article, as in the two other papers, you will observe that the writer has drawn upon a variety of questions to round out his subject—a character analysis and interpretation of a mysterious loner whose "voyagings through strange seas of thought" changed the face of science and our vision of the universe.

Isaac Newton

I. Bernard Cohen

The mind and personality of Issac Newton challenge any historian. Newton was a strange, solitary figure, and the wellsprings of his behavior were hidden even from his contemporaries. A biographer of his time compared Newton to the River Nile, whose great powers were known but whose source had not been discovered. Nevertheless, the few facts we have about his early life do allow some speculation about Newton's character and development.

He was born prematurely, a physical weakling. It is said that he had to wear a "bolster" to support his neck during his first few months, that no one expected him to live. Newton later was fond of saying that his mother had said he was so tiny at birth that he could have been put into a quart mug.

Newton's father died three months before he was born. When the boy was less than two years old, his mother remarried, and he was turned over to his aged grandmother. He lived on an isolated farm, deprived of parental care and love, without the friendly companionship and rivalry of brothers and sisters. The late Louis T. More, author of the best-known modern biography of the man, held that much of Newton's "inwardness" could be attributed to his lonely and unhappy childhood.

Born in 1642, Newton grew up in an era when England was still tasting the "terrors of a protracted and bitter civil war." Raiding and plundering parties were common. His grandmother was "suspected of sympathy to the royal forces." In the face of these real terrors and "the frights of his imagination," he could not have received much comfort from his grandmother or the hired laborers on the farm. Naturally enough, as More observed, the boy turned to "the solace of lonely meditation" and developed a strong habit of self-absorption. A girl who knew him in his youth described him as a "sober, silent, thinking lad" who "was never known scarce to play with the boys abroad, at their silly amusements."

He evidently overcame his physical weakness by the time he reached school age, for a schoolmate reported that Newton challenged a bully who had kicked him in the belly to a fight and "beat him till he would fight no more"—winning out because he had "more spirit and resolution." The bully stood high in the class, and

Newton was so determined "to beat him also at his books" that "by hard work he finally succeeded, and then gradually rose to be the first in the school."

When Newton was 14, his mother took the boy back into her home, her second husband having died. She conceived the idea of making him a farmer, but the experiment proved an unqualified failure. Newton found farming totally distasteful. Instead of attending properly to his chores, he would read, make wooden models with his knife, or dream. Fortunately for science, his mother gave up the attempt and allowed him to prepare for Cambridge University.

At the age of 18, Newton entered Trinity College. In his early years at the University he was not outstanding in any way. Then he came under the influence of Isaac Barrow, a professor of mathematics and an extraordinary man. He was an able mathematician, a classicist, an astronomer and an authority in the field of optics. Barrow was one of the first to recognize Newton's genius. Soon after his student had taken a degree, Barrow resigned his professorship so that Newton might have it. Thus at 26 Newton was established in an academic post of distinction and was free to pursue his epoch-making studies.

He had already sown the seeds of his revolutionary contributions to three distinct fields of scientific inquiry: mathematics, celestial mechanics and physical optics. After his graduation from the University he had returned to his home at Woolsthorpe for 18 months of work which can fairly be described as the most fruitful 18 months in all the history of the creative imagination. Newton's subsequent life in science consisted to a large degree in the elaboration of the great discoveries made during those "golden" months. What Newton did at Woolsthorpe is best stated in his words:

"In the beginning of the year 1665 I found the method for approximating series and the rule for reducing any dignity [power] of any binomial to such a series [i.e., the Binomial theorem]. The same year in May I found the method of tangents of Gregory and Slusius, and in November [discovered] the direct method of Fluxions [i.e., the elements of the differential calculus], and the next year in January had the Theory of Colours, and in May following I had entrance into the inverse method of Fluxions [i.e., integral calculus], and in the same year I began to think of gravity extending to the orb of the Moon...and having thereby compared the force requisite to keep the Moon in her orb with the force of gravity at the surface of the earth, and found them to answer pretty nearly...."

As a by-product of his analysis of light and colors, which he had shyly kept to himself, Newton invented a reflecting telescope, to free telescopes from the chromatic aberration of the refracting lens. He made a small version of his new telescope for the Royal Society of London, and was shortly elected, at the age of 30, as a Fellow of the Royal Society, the highest scientific honor in England.

Newton was understandably overwhelmed by his sudden public recognition. He had been loath to announce his discoveries, but within a week after his election to the Society he asked permission to communicate an account of the "philosophical discovery" which had induced him "to the making of the said telescope." With a disarming lack of false modesty, he said that in his judgment he had made "the oddest, if not the most considerable detection, which hath hitherto been made in the operations of nature."

Newton's letter to the Royal Society, "containing his new theory of light and colours," was sent to London on February 6, 1672. This paper can claim a number of "firsts." It was Newton's initial publication; it founded the science of spectroscopy, and it marked the beginning of a sound analysis of color phenomena. Briefly, what Newton showed is that a prism separates white light into its component colors, associated with specific indices of refraction, and that a second prism can recombine the dispersed light and render it white again. These magnificent experiments provided a new departure for the formulation of theories about the nature of color. Yet the paper did not win for Newton the universal applause that he had sought. The Royal Society was bombarded with letters disputing Newton's conclusions. Some of the objectors were unimportant, but others were men of stature: Christian Huygens, Robert Hooke. With astonishing patience. Newton wrote careful letters answering each objection. But he won over only one of his opponents—the French Jesuit Father Pardies.

The controversy had an acid effect on Newton's personality. He vowed that he would publish no further discoveries. As he wrote later to Leibnitz: "I was so persecuted with discussions arising from the publication of my theory of light, that I blamed my own imprudence for parting with so substantial a blessing as my quiet to run after a shadow." And yet he did later continue to publish; he wanted the applause of the scientific world. This ambivalence was not overlooked by Newton's enemies. The astronomer John Flamsteed, who broke with Newton, described him as "insidious, ambitious, and excessively covetous of praise, and impatient of contradiction....I believe him to be a good man at the bottom; but, through his nature, suspicious."

At Cambridge Newton was the very model of an absent-minded professor. His amanuensis, Humphrey Newton (no relative), wrote that he never knew Newton "to take any recreation or pastime either in riding out to take the air, walking, bowling, or any other exercise whatever, thinking all hours lost that were not spent in his studies." He often worked until two or three o'clock in the morning, ate sparingly and sometimes forgot to eat altogether. When reminded that he had not eaten, he would go to the table and "eat a bite or two standing." Newton rarely dined in the college hall; when he did, he was apt to appear "with shoes down at heels, stockings untied, surplice on, and his head scarcely combed." It was said that he often delivered his lectures to an empty hall, apparently with as much satisfaction as if the room had been full of students.

After the controversy, Newton withdrew from the public eye as a scientist. He served the University as its representative in Parliament and worked away in private at chemistry and alchemy, theology, physics and mathematics. He became acquainted with Leibnitz, but refused to give his great contemporary any exact information about his discoveries in mathematics. Today it is generally agreed that the calculus was discovered more or less independently by both Newton and Leibnitz, but the two men and their partisans quarreled acrimoniously over priority, and Newton accused Leibnitz of plagiarism. Newton conceived a jealous proprietary interest in every subject he studied, and almost every achievement of his creative life was accompanied by some quarrel.

In 1684 came the famous visit to Newton by the astronomer Edmund Halley. He had a problem concerning the gravitational attraction between the sun and the planets. Halley and Hooke had concluded from Johannes Kepler's accounting of planetary motions that the force of attraction must vary inversely with the square of distance between a planet and the sun. But they had been unable to prove their idea. "What," Halley asked Newton, "would be the curve described by the planets on the supposition that gravity diminished as the square of the distance?" Newton answered without hesitation: "An ellipse." How did he know that? "Why," replied Newton, "I have calculated it." These four words informed Halley that Newton had worked out one of the most fundamental laws of the universe—the law of gravity. Halley wanted to see the calculations at once, but Newton could not find his notes. He promised to write out the theorems and proofs. Under Halley's insistent urging he completed a manuscript for the Royal Society. Thus was born the *Philosophiae Naturalis Principia Mathematica,* known ever since simply as the *Principia.*

Just before its publication a crisis arose when Hooke laid claim to the inverse-square law. Newton threatened to withdraw the climactic chapters of work, but Halley mollified him and the great classic went to press intact. Halley's credit in this enterprise is enormous. He not only got Newton to write the work but also saw it through the press and paid the cost of publication, although he was not a wealthy man.

The *Principia* is divided into three "books." In the first Newton laid down his three laws of motion and explored the consequences of various laws of force. In the second he explored motion in various types of fluids; here he was somewhat less successful, and much of his work had to be revised in the succeeding decades. In the third he discussed universal gravitation and showed how a single law of force explains at once the falling of bodies on the earth, the motion of our moon or of Jupiter's satellites, the motions of planets and the phenomenon of tides.

One of the most vexing problems for Newton was to find a rigorous proof that a sphere acts gravitationally as if all its mass were concentrated at its center. Without this theorem, the whole theory of gravitation would rest on intuition rather than precise calculation. For instance, in the simple case of an apple falling to the ground—the occasion of the central idea of gravitation according to Newton's own account—what is the "distance between" the earth and the apple? Here the calculus came into play. Newton considered the earth as a collection of tiny volumes of matter, each attracting the apple according to the inverse-square law of gravitation. Then he summed up the individual forces and showed that the result was the same as if the earth were a point mass, as if all the matter of the earth were shrunk into a tiny region at its center.

Newton suffered some kind of "nervous breakdown" after the completion of the *Principia.* He complained that he could not sleep, and said that he lacked the "former consistency of his mind." He wrote angry letters to friends and then apologized; he protested bitterly to John Locke, for example, that the philosopher had attempted to "embroil him with women."

In 1696 Newton abandoned the academic life for the position of Warden, later Master, of the Mint. Honors for his scientific achievements continued to come to him: he was knighted in 1705 and served many years as president of the Royal Society. But the last quarter century of his life produced no major contributions to science. Some say that his creative genius had simply burned out. Others argue that after having founded the science of physical optics, invented the calculus and shown the mechanism of the universe, there just wasn't anything left for him to do in the realm of science.

Although he made no important discoveries, Newton's last years were not barren of ideas. Now famous and honoured, he felt secure enough to offer many public speculations on scientific problems. He suggested various possible hypotheses as to the "cause" of gravitation and speculated on the nature of the "ether," the size of the constituent units of matter, the forces of electricity and magnetism, the cause of muscular response to the "commands of the will," the origins of sensation, the creation of the world, the ultimate destiny of man. In the century after Newton, physical experimenters followed up many of his bold speculations.

Newton is often described as the inaugurator of the "Age of Reason." Alexander Pope expressed the sentiment of his time in the famous lines:

> Nature and Nature's laws lay hid in the night:
> God said, Let Newton be! and all was light.

DISCUSSION AND EXERCISES

1. What picture does the reader get of the seventeenth century? What was the political situation, and how did it affect Newton's life?

2. If he were born today, how different would Newton's life and work be? What advantages and disadvantages would he encounter? Might he achieve more or less than he did in the seventeenth century? Explain.

3. Some have said that in the last quarter of his life, Newton's creative genius burned out. Others have said that there "just wasn't anything left for him to do in the realm of science." Which statement do you find the most credible? Discuss.

4. List some of the general sources from which Cohen drew his facts about Newton. What effect does the reference to such sources have on the piece? Speculate on the effect of formal footnotes: Would they enhance or detract from overall readability and credibility?

5. How do the small details about Newton enhance the portrait (for example, "He was so tiny he could have been put into a quart mug"; "He would go to the table and eat a bite or two standing")?

6. What adjectives reveal Cohen's attitude toward Newton? How would you describe that attitude? What is your attitude toward Newton?

7. How effective are the lines by Pope at the end of the article? Do they serve as appropriate summary and conclusion? Explain.

8. Analyze the paragraph sequences in the essay, noting the patterns of the paragraphs and their movement from beginning to end.

TO PERSUADE

One of the rhetorical treasures of this century is the Reverend Martin Luther King, Jr.'s "Letter from Birmingham Jail." A brilliant argument supporting the nonviolent struggle for freedom, King's essay repays careful study. Calmly convincing in tone, patiently reasoned throughout, the "Letter" is King's reply to eight prominent clergymen who had jointly published a statement denouncing his nonviolent protest marches, demonstrations, voter registrations, and sit-ins as "unwise and untimely."

An ordained Baptist minister with a doctorate in theology, King was addressing an audience of his peers, appealing to them as spiritual colleagues and developing his ideas with a wealth of Biblical allusions. No wonder, then, that some likened his letters to those of St. Paul. That King, like Paul, was writing from prison heightens this plea for racial equality, a cause to which King dedicated his life and for which he ultimately lost it.

King set down the first draft of this letter—in his own understated description—"under somewhat constricting circumstances." Specifically, he began it, as he would later report, ". . . on the margins of the newspaper in which the [clergymen's] statement appeared while I was in jail, . . . continued on scraps of writing paper supplied by a friendly Negro trustee, and concluded on a pad my attorneys were eventually permitted to leave me." Before presenting it to a wider audience, King "indulged in the author's prerogative of polishing it for publication."

The final version, as one commentator has aptly observed, "is a model of careful and reasonable analysis of a very complex situation. It succeeds largely because it remains concrete." King also systematically treats one issue after another, "refusing to be caught up in passion or posturing. King remains grounded in logic. He is convinced that his statement of his view will convince his audience" (Jacobus, *Ideas*).

As you read "Letter from Birmingham Jail," note the succession of questions that King addresses to his subject, returning to them time and time again as new occasions and contexts arise. For example, he asks What are the causes of X? at five separate points. In repeatedly providing reasons for his position and (it would seem) in intuitively following Rogerian strategy, Dr. King humanizes his argument by recognizing that his readers are apt to feel threatened and defensive. By reaching out to them in the patiently reasoning tone that characterizes the entire letter, he deflects any defensiveness by anticipating it, transcending the need for defense. "I will tell you," King says, "how these grievances came into being (How is X made or done?); and I will further show you their consequences." King calls upon one dimension of explanation after another: these are the facts and these are the types; this is the purpose and here is my summary. This long, richly textured position on civil rights obviously grew out of a creative combination of pointed questions addressed to the subject at hand plus a steady forward progression toward a moving and climactic conclusion.

Letter from Birmingham Jail

The Rev. Martin Luther King, Jr.

April 16, 1963

My Dear Fellow Clergymen:

While confined here in the Birmingham city jail, I came across your recent statement calling my present activities "unwise and untimely." Seldom do I pause to answer criticism of my work and ideas. If I sought to answer all the criticisms that cross my desk, my secretaries would have little time for anything other than such correspondence in the course of the day, and I would have no time for constructive work. But since I feel that you are men of genuine good will and that your criticisms are sincerely set forth, I want to try to answer your statement in what I hope will be patient and reasonable terms. [1]

Question 12:
What are the causes
of X?

I think I should indicate why I am here in Birmingham, since you have been 2
influenced by the view which argues against "outsiders coming in." I have the
honor of serving as president of the Southern Christian Leadership Conference, an
organization operating in every southern state, with headquarters in Atlanta,
Georgia. We have some eighty-five affiliated organizations across the South, and
one of them is the Alabama Christian Movement for Human Rights. Frequently we
share staff, educational and financial resources with our affiliates. Several months
ago the affiliate here in Birmingham asked us to be on call to engage in a nonviolent
direct-action program if such were deemed necessary. We readily consented, and
when the hour came we lived up to our promise. So I, along with several members
of my staff, am here because I was invited here. I am here because I have
organizational ties here.

But more basically, I am in Birmingham because injustice is here. Just as the 3
prophets of the eighth century B.C. left their villages and carried their "thus saith the
Lord" far beyond the boundaries of their home towns, and just as the Apostle Paul
left his village of Tarsus and carried the gospel of Jesus Christ to the far corners of
the Greco-Roman world, so am I compelled to carry the gospel of freedom beyond
my own home town. Like Paul, I must constantly respond to the Macedonian call
for aid.

Question 16:
What is the present
status of X?

Moreover, I am cognizant of the interrelatedness of all communities and 4
states. I cannot sit idly by in Atlanta and not be concerned about what happens in
Birmingham. Injustice anywhere is a threat to justice everywhere. We are caught
in an inescapable network of mutuality, tied in a single garment of destiny.
Whatever affects one directly, affects all indirectly. Never again can we afford to live
with the narrow, provincial "outside agitator" idea. Anyone who lives inside the
United States can never be considered an outsider anywhere within its bounds.

You deplore the demonstrations taking place in Birmingham. But your 5
statement, I am sorry to say, fails to express a similar concern for the conditions that
brought about the demonstrations. I am sure that none of you would want to rest
content with the superficial kind of social analysis that deals merely with effects
and does not grapple with underlying causes. It is unfortunate that demonstrations
are taking place in Birmingham, but it is even more unfortunate that the city's white
power structure left the Negro community with no alternative.

Question 9:
What are the
component parts
of X?

In any nonviolent campaign there are four basic steps: collection of the facts 6
to determine whether injustices exist: negotiation; self-purification; and direct
action. We have gone through all these steps in Birmingham. There can be no
gainsaying the fact that racial injustice engulfs this community. Birmingham is
probably the most thoroughly segregated city in the United States. Its ugly record
of brutality is widely known. Negroes have experienced grossly unjust treatment
in the courts. There have been more unsolved bombings of Negro homes and
churches in Birmingham than in any other city in the nation. These are the hard
brutal facts of the case. On the basis of these conditions, Negro leaders sought to
negotiate with the city fathers. But the latter consistently refused to engage in
good-faith negotiation.

Question 6:
What are the facts
about X?

Then, last September, came the opportunity to talk with leaders of Birming- 7
ham's economic community. In the course of the negotiations, certain promises
were made by the merchants—for example, to remove the stores' humiliating
racial signs. On the basis of these promises, the Reverend Fred Shuttlesworth and

the leaders of the Alabama Christian Movement for Human Rights agreed to a moratorium on all demonstrations. As the weeks and months went by, we realized that we were the victims of a broken promise. A few signs, briefly removed, returned; the others remained.

Question 10:
How is X made or done?

As in so many past experiences, our hopes had been blasted, and the shadow of deep disappointment settled upon us. We had no alternative except to prepare for direct action, whereby we would present our very bodies as a means of laying our case before the conscience of the local and the national community. Mindful of the difficulties involved, we decided to undertake a process of self-purification. We began a series of workshops on nonviolence, and we repeatedly asked ourselves: "Are you able to accept blows without retaliating?" "Are you able to endure the ordeal of jail?" We decided to schedule our direct-action program for the Easter season, realizing that except for Christmas, this is the main shopping period of the year. Knowing that a strong economic-withdrawal program would be the by-product of direct action, we felt that this would be the best time to bring pressure to bear on the merchants for the needed change.

Then it occurred to us that Birmingham's mayoralty election was coming up in March, and we speedily decided to postpone action until after election day. When we discovered that the Commissioner of Public Safety, Eugene "Bull" Connor, had piled up enough votes to be in the run-off, we decided again to postpone action until the day after the run-off so that the demonstrations could not be used to cloud the issues. Like many others, we waited to see Mr. Connor defeated, and to this end we endured postponement after postponement. Having aided in this community need, we felt that our direct-action program could be delayed no longer.

Question 12:
What are the causes of X?

You may well ask: "Why direct action? Why sit-ins, marches and so forth? Isn't negotiation a better path?" You are quite right in calling for negotiation. Indeed, this is the very purpose of direct action. Nonviolent direct action seeks to create such a crisis and foster such a tension that a community which has constantly refused to negotiate is forced to confront the issue. It seeks so to dramatize the issue that it can no longer be ignored. My citing the creation of tension as part of the work of the nonviolent-resister may sound rather shocking. But I must confess that I am not afraid of the word "tension." I have earnestly opposed violent tension, but there is a type of constructive nonviolent tension which is necessary for growth. Just as Socrates felt that it was necessary to create a tension in the mind so that individuals could rise from the bondage of myths and half-truths to the unfettered realm of creative analysis and objective appraisal, so must we see the need for nonviolent gadflies to create the kind of tension in society that will help men rise from the dark depths of prejudice and racism to the majestic heights of understanding and brotherhood.

Question 8:
What is the essential function of X?

The purposes of our direct-action program is to create a situation so crisis-packed that it will inevitably open the door to negotiation. I therefore concur with you in your call for negotiation. Too long has our beloved Southland been bogged down in a tragic effort to live in monologue rather than dialogue.

Question 3:
What kind of person is X?

One of the basic points in your statement is that the action that I and my associates have taken in Birmingham is untimely. Some have asked: "Why didn't you give the new city administration time to act?" The only answer that I can give to this query is that the new Birmingham administration must be prodded about

8

9

10

11

12

as much as the outgoing one, before it will act. We are sadly mistaken if we feel that the election of Albert Boutwell as mayor will bring the millennium to Birmingham. While Mr. Boutwell is a much more gentle person than Mr. Connor, they are both segregationists, dedicated to maintenance of the status quo. I have hope that Mr. Boutwell will be reasonable enough to see the futility of massive resistance to desegregation. But he will not see this without pressure from devotees of civil rights. My friends, I must say to you that we have not made a single gain in civil rights without determined legal and nonviolent pressure. Lamentably, it is an historical fact that privileged groups seldom give up their privileges voluntarily. Individuals may see the moral light and voluntarily give up their unjust posture; but, as Reinhold Niebuhr has reminded us, groups tend to be more immoral than individuals.

Question 16:
What is the present
status of X?

We know through painful experience that freedom is never voluntarily given by the oppressor; it must be demanded by the oppressed. Frankly, I have yet to engage in a direct-action campaign that was "well timed" in the view of those who have not suffered unduly from the disease of segregation. For years now I have heard the word "Wait!" It rings in the ear of every Negro with piercing familiarity. This "Wait" has almost always meant "Never." We must come to see, with one of our distinguished jurists, that "justice too long delayed is justice denied."[1]

13

We have waited for more than 340 years for our constitutional and Godgiven rights. The nations of Asia and Africa are moving with jetlike speed toward gaining political independence, but we still creep at horse-and-buggy pace toward gaining a cup of coffee at a lunch counter. Perhaps it is easy for those who have never felt the stinging darts of segregation to say, "Wait." But when you have seen vicious mobs lynch your mothers and fathers at will and drown your sisters and brothers at whim; when you have seen hate-filled policemen curse, kick and even kill your black brothers and sisters; when you see the vast majority of your twenty million Negro brothers smothering in an airtight cage of poverty in the midst of an affluent society; when you suddenly find your tongue twisted and your speech stammering as you seek to explain to your six-year-old daughter why she can't go to the public amusement park that has just been advertised on television, and see tears welling up in her eyes when she is told that Funtown is closed to colored children, and see ominous clouds of inferiority beginning to form in her little mental sky, and see her beginning to distort her personality by developing an unconscious bitterness toward white people; when you have to concoct an answer for a five-year-old son who is asking: "Daddy, why do white people treat colored people so mean?"; when you take a cross-country drive and find it necessary to sleep night after night in the uncomfortable corners of your automobile because no motel will accept you; when you are humiliated day in and day out by nagging signs reading "white" and "colored"; when your first name becomes "nigger," your middle name becomes "boy" (however old you are) and your last name becomes "John," and your wife and mother are never given the respected title "Mrs."; when you are harried by day and haunted by night by the fact that you are a Negro, living constantly at tiptoe stance, never quite knowing what to expect next, and are plagued with inner fears and outer resentments; when you are forever fighting a degenerating sense of

14

[1] The jurist referred to here is Earl Warren, who adapted the line from the English writer Walter Savage Landor: "Justice delayed is justice denied."

"nobodiness"—then you will understand why we find it difficult to wait. There comes a time when the cup of endurance runs over, and men are no longer willing to be plunged into the abyss of despair. I hope, sirs, you can understand our legitimate and unavoidable impatience.

Question 14:
What are the types of X?

You express a great deal of anxiety over our willingness to break laws. This is [15] certainly a legitimate concern. Since we so diligently urge people to obey the Supreme Court's decision of 1954 outlawing segregation in the public schools, at first glance it may seem rather paradoxical for us consciously to break laws. One may well ask: "How can you advocate breaking some laws and obeying others?" The answer lies in the fact that there are two types of laws: just and unjust. I would be the first to advocate obeying just laws. One has not only a legal but a moral responsibility to disobey unjust laws. I would agree with St. Augstine that "an unjust law is no law at all."

Question 15:
How does X compare to Y?

Now, what is the difference between the two? How does one determine [16] whether a law is just or unjust? A just law is a man-made code that squares with the moral law or the law of God. An unjust law is a code that is out of harmony with the moral law. To put it in the terms of St. Thomas Aquinas: An unjust law is a human law that is not rooted in eternal law and natural law. Any law that uplifts human personality is just. Any law that degrades human personality is unjust. All segregation statutes are unjust because segregation distorts the soul and damages the personality. It gives the segregator a false sense of superiority and the segregated a false sense of inferiority. Segregation, to use the terminology of the Jewish philosopher Martin Buber, substitutes an "I-it" relationship for an "I-thou" relationship and ends up relegating persons to the status of things. Hence segregation is not only politically, economically and sociologically unsound, it is morally wrong and sinful. Paul Tillich has said that sin is separation. Is not segregation an existential expression of man's tragic separation, his awful estrangement, his terrible sinfulness. Thus it is that I can urge men to obey the 1954 decision of the Supreme Court, for it is morally right; and I can urge them to disobey segregation ordinances, for they are morally wrong.

Let us consider a more concrete example of just and unjust laws. An unjust [17] law is a code that a numerical or power majority group compels a minority group to obey but does not make binding on itself. This is *difference* made legal. By the same token, a just law is a code that a majority compels a minority to follow and that it is willing to follow itself. This is *sameness* made legal.

Let me give another explanation. A law is unjust if it is inflicted on a minority [18] that, as a result of being denied the right to vote, had no part in enacting or devising the law. Who can say that the legislature of Alabama which set up that state's segregation laws was democratically elected? Throughout Alabama all sorts of devious methods are used to prevent Negroes from becoming registered voters, and there are some counties in which even though Negroes constitute a majority of the population, not a single Negro is registered. Can any law enacted under such circumstances be considered democratically structured?

Sometimes a law is just on its face and unjust in its application. For instance, [19] I have been arrested on a charge of parading without a permit. Now, there is nothing wrong in having an ordinance which requires a permit for a parade. But such an ordinance becomes unjust when it is used to maintain segregation and to deny citizens the First-Amendment privilege of peaceful assembly and protest.

I hope you are able to see the distinction I am trying to point out. In no sense do I advocate evading or defying the law, as would the rabid segregationist. That would lead to anarchy. One who breaks an unjust law must do so openly, lovingly, and with a willingness to accept the penalty. I submit that an individual who breaks a law that conscience tells him is unjust, and who willingly accepts the penalty of imprisonment in order to arouse the conscience of the community over its injustice, is in reality expressing the highest respect for law. [20]

Of course, there is nothing new about this kind of civil disobedience. It was evidenced sublimely in the refusal of Shadrach, Meshach and Abednego to obey the laws of Nebuchadnezzar, on the ground that a higher moral law was at stake. It was practiced superbly by the early Christians, who were willing to face hungry lions and the excruciating pain of chopping blocks rather than submit to certain unjust laws of the Roman Empire. To a degree, academic freedom is a reality today because Socrates practiced civil disobedience. In our own nation, the Boston Tea Party represented a massive act of civil disobedience. [21]

Question 7: What does X mean?

We should never forget that everything Adolf Hitler did in Germany was "legal" and everything the Hungarian freedom fighters did in Hungary was "illegal." It was "illegal" to aid and comfort a Jew in Hitler's Germany. Even so, I am sure that, had I lived in Germany at the time, I would have aided and comforted my Jewish brothers. If today I lived in a Communist country where certain principles dear to the Christian faith are suppressed, I would openly advocate disobeying that country's anti-religious laws. [22]

Question 5: What is my personal response to X?

I must make two honest confessions to you, my Christian and Jewish brothers. First, I must confess that over the past few years I have been gravely disappointed with the white moderate. I have almost reached the regrettable conclusion that the Negro's great stumbling block in his stride toward freedom is not the White Citizen's Counciler or the Ku Klux Klanner, but the white moderate, who is more devoted to "order" than to justice; who prefers a negative peace which is the absence of tension to a positive peace which is the presence of justice; who constantly says: "I agree with you in the goal you seek, but I cannot agree with your methods of direct action"; who paternalistically believes he can set the timetable for another man's freedom; who lives by a mythical concept of time and who constantly advises the Negro to wait for a "more convenient season." Shallow understanding from people of good will is more frustrating than absolute misunderstanding from people of ill will. Lukewarm acceptance is much more bewildering than outright rejection. [23]

I had hoped that the white moderate would understand that law and order exist for the purpose of establishing justice and that when they fail in this purpose they become the dangerously structured dams that block the flow of social progress. I had hoped that the white moderate would understand that the present tension in the South is a necessary phase of the transition from an obnoxious negative peace, in which the Negro passively accepted his unjust plight, to a substantive and positive peace, in which all men will respect the dignity and worth of human personality. Actually, we who engage in nonviolent direct action are not the creators of tension. We merely bring to the surface the hidden tension that is already alive. We bring it out in the open, where it can be seen and dealt with. Like a boil that can never be cured so long as it is covered up but must be opened with all its ugliness to the natural medicines of air and light, injustice must be exposed, [24] with all the tension its exposure creates, to the light of human conscience and the air of national opinion before it can be cured.

Question 20:
What case can be made for or against X?

In your statement you assert that our actions, even though peaceful, must be condemned because they precipitate violence. But is this a logical assertion? Isn't this like condemning a robbed man because his possession of money precipitated the evil act of robbery? Isn't this like condemning Socrates because his unswerving commitment to truth and his philosophical inquiries precipitated the act by the misguided populace in which they made him drink hemlock? Isn't this like condemning Jesus because his unique God-consciousness and never-ceasing devotion to God's will precipitated the evil act of crucifixion? We must come to see that, as the federal courts have consistently affirmed, it is wrong to urge an individual to cease his efforts to gain his basic constitutional rights because the quest may precipitate violence. Society must protect the robbed and punish the robber.

25

Question 18:
How should X be interpreted?

I had also hoped that the white moderate would reject the myth concerning time in relation to the struggle for freedom. I have just received a letter from a white brother in Texas. He writes: "All Christians know that the colored people will receive equal rights eventually, but it is possible that you are in too great a religious hurry. It has taken Christianity almost two thousand years to accomplish what it has. The teachings of Christ take time to come to earth." Such an attitude stems from a tragic misconception of time, from the strangely irrational notion that there is something in the very flow of time that will inevitably cure all ills. Actually, time itself is neutral; it can be used either destructively or constructively. More and more I feel that the people of ill will have used time much more effectively than have the people of good will. We will have to repent in this generation not merely for the hateful words and actions of the bad people but for the appalling silence of the good people. Human progress never rolls in on wheels of inevitability; it comes through the tireless efforts of men willing to be co-workers with God, and without this hard work, time itself becomes an ally of the forces of social stagnation. We must use time creatively, in the knowledge that the time is always ripe to do right. Now is the time to make real the promise of democracy and transform our pending national elegy into a creative psalm of brotherhood. Now is the time to lift our national policy from the quicksand of racial injustice to the solid rock of human dignity.

26

Question 9:
What are the component parts of X?

Question 15:
How does X compare to Y?

You speak of our activity in Birmingham as extreme. At first I was rather disappointed that fellow clergymen would see my nonviolent efforts as those of an extremist. I began thinking about the fact that I stand in the middle of two opposing forces in the Negro community. One is a force of complacency, made up in part of Negroes who, as a result of long years of oppression, are so drained of self-respect and a sense of "somebodiness" that they have adjusted to segregation; and in part of a few middle-class Negroes who, because of a degree of academic and economic security and because in some ways they profit by segregation, have become insensitive to the problems of the masses. The other force is one of bitterness and hatred, and it comes perilously close to advocating violence. It is expressed in the various black nationalist groups that are springing up across the nation, the largest and best-known being Elijah Muhammad's Muslim movement. Nourished by the Negro's frustration over the continued existence of racial discrimination, this movement is made up of people who have lost faith in

27

America, who have absolutely repudiated Christianity, and who have concluded that the white man is an incorrigible "devil."

I have tried to stand between these two forces, saying that we need emulate neither the "do-nothingism" of the complacent nor the hatred and despair of the black nationalist. For there is the more excellent way of love and nonviolent protest. I am grateful to God that, through the influence of the Negro church, the way of nonviolence became an integral part of our struggle. [28]

If this philosophy had not emerged, by now many streets of the South would, I am convinced, be flowing with blood. And I am further convinced that if our white brothers dismiss as "rabble-rousers" and "outside agitators" those of us who employ nonviolent direct action, and if they refuse to support our nonviolent efforts, millions of Negroes will, out of frustration and despair, seek solace and security in black-nationalist ideologies—a development that would inevitably lead to a frightening racial nightmare. [29]

Question 12:
What are the causes of X?

Oppressed people cannot remain oppressed forever. The yearning for freedom eventually manifests itself, and that is what has happened to the American Negro. Something within has reminded him of his birthright of freedom, and something without has reminded him that it can be gained. Consciously or unconsciously, he has been caught up by the *Zeitgeist,* and with his black brothers of Africa and his brown and yellow brothers of Asia, South America and the Caribbean, the United States Negro is moving with a sense of great urgency toward the promised land of racial justice. If one recognizes this vital urge that has engulfed the Negro community, one should readily understand why public demonstrations are taking place. The Negro has many pent-up resentments and latent frustrations, and he must release them. So let him march; let him make prayer pilgrimages to the city hall; let him go on freedom rides—and try to understand why he must do so. If his repressed emotions are not released in nonviolent ways, they will seek expression through violence; this is not a threat but a fact of history. So I have not said to my people: "Get rid of your discontent." Rather, I have tried to say that this normal and healthy discontent can be channeled into the creative outlet of nonviolent direct action. And now this approach is being termed extremist. [30]

Question 7:
What does X mean?

But though I was initially disappointed at being categorized as an extremist, as I continued to think about the matter I gradually gained a measure of satisfaction from the label. Was not Jesus an extremist for love: "Love your enemies, bless them that curse you, do good to them that hate you, and pray for them which despitefully use you, and persecute you." Was not Amos an extremist for justice: "Let justice roll down like waters and righteousness like an ever-flowing stream." Was not Paul an extremist for the Christian gospel: "I bear in my body the marks of the Lord Jesus." Was not Martin Luther an extremist: "Here I stand; I cannot do otherwise, so help me God." And John Bunyan: "I will stay in jail to the end of my days before I make a butchery of my conscience." And Abraham Lincoln: "This nation cannot survive half slave and half free." And Thomas Jefferson: "We hold these truths to be self-evident, that all men are created equal . . . ." So the question is not whether we will be extremists, but what kind of extremists we will be. Will we be extremists for hate or for love? Will we be extremists for the preservation of injustice or for the extension of justice? In that dramatic scene on Calvary's hill three men were crucified. We must never forget that all three were crucified for the [31] same crime—the crime of extremism. Two were extremists for immorality, and thus fell below their environment. The other, Jesus Christ, was an extremist for love, truth and goodness, and thereby rose above his environment. Perhaps the South, the nation and the world are in dire need of creative extremists.

[32] I had hoped that the white moderate would see this need. Perhaps I was too optimistic; perhaps I expected too much. I suppose I should have realized that few members of the oppressor race can understand the deep groans and passionate yearnings of the oppressed race, and still fewer have the vision to see that injustice must be rooted out by strong, persistent and determined action. I am thankful, however, that some of our white brothers in the South have grasped the meaning of this social revolution and committed themselves to it. They are still all too few in quantity, but they are big in quality. Some—such as Ralph, McGill, Lillian Smith, Harry Golden, James McBride Dabbs, Ann Braden and Sarah Patton Boyle—have written about our struggle in eloquent and prophetic terms. Others have marched with us down nameless streets of the South. They have languished in filthy, roach-infested jails, suffering the abuse and brutality of policemen who view them as "dirty nigger-lovers." Unlike so many of their moderate brothers and sisters, they have recognized the urgency of the moment and sensed the need for powerful "action" antidotes to combat the disease of segregation.

[33] Let me take note of my other major disappointment. I have been greatly disappointed with the white church and its leadership. Of course, there are some notable exceptions. I am not unmindful of the fact that each of you has taken some significant stands on this issue. I commend you, Reverend Stallings, for your Christian stand on this past Sunday, in welcoming Negroes to your worship service on a nonsegregated basis. I commend the Catholic leaders of this state for integrating Spring Hill College several years ago.

Question 5:
What is my
personal response
to X?

[34] But despite these notable exceptions, I must honestly reiterate that I have been disappointed with the church. I do not say this as one of those negative critics who can always find something wrong with the church. I say this as a minister of the gospel, who loves the church; who was nurtured in its bosom; who has been sustained by its spiritual blessings and who will remain true to it as long as the cord of life shall lengthen.

[35] When I was suddenly catapulted into the leadership of the bus protest in Montgomery, Alabama, a few years ago, I felt we would be supported by the white church. I felt that the white ministers, priests and rabbis of the South would be among our strongest allies. Instead, some have been outright opponents, refusing to understand the freedom movement and misrepresenting its leaders; all too many others have been more cautious than courageous and have remained silent behind the anesthetizing security of stained-glass windows.

[36] In spite of my shattered dreams, I came to Birmingham with the hope that the white religious leadership of this community would see the justice of our cause and, with deep moral concern, would serve as the channel through which our just grievances could reach the power structure. I had hoped that each of you would understand. But again I have been disappointed.

Question 4:
What is my memory
of X?

[37] I have heard numerous southern religious leaders admonish their worshipers to comply with a desegregation decision because it is the law, but I have longed to hear white ministers declare: "Follow this decree because integration is morally right and because the Negro is your brother." In the midst of blatant injustices

inflicted upon the Negro, I have watched white churchmen stand on the sideline and mouth pious irrelevancies and sanctimonious trivialities. In the midst of a mighty struggle to rid our nation of racial and economic injustice, I have heard many ministers say: "Those are social issues, with which the gospel has no real concern." And I have watched many churches commit themselves to a completely other-worldly religion which makes a strange, un-biblical distinction between body and soul, between the sacred and the secular.

Question 1:
How can X be
described?

I have traveled the length and breadth of Alabama, Mississippi and all the other southern states. On sweltering summer days and crisp autumn mornings I have looked at the South's beautiful churches with their lofty spires pointing heavenward. I have beheld the impressive outlines of her massive religious-education buildings. Over and over I have found myself asking: "What kind of people worship here? Who is their God? Where were their voices when the lips of Governor Barnett dripped with words of interposition and nullification? Where were they when Governor Wallace gave a clarion call for defiance and hatred? Where were their voices of support when bruised and weary Negro men and women decided to rise from the dark dungeons of complacency to the bright hills of creative protest?" [38]

Question 5:
What is my
personal response
to X?

Yes, these questions are still in my mind. In deep disappointment I have wept over the laxity of the church. But be assured that my tears have been tears of love. There can be no deep disappointment where there is not deep love. Yes, I love the church. How could I do otherwise? I am in the rather unique position of being the son, the grandson and the great-grandson of preachers. Yes, I see the church as the body of Christ. But, oh! How we have blemished and scarred that body through social neglect and through fear of being nonconformists. [39]

There was a time when the church was very powerful—in the time when the early Christians rejoiced at being deemed worthy to suffer for what they believed. In those days the church was not merely a thermometer that recorded the ideas and principles of popular opinion; it was a thermostat that transformed the mores of society. Whenever the early Christians entered a town, the people in power became disturbed and immediately sought to convict the Christians for being "disturbers of the peace" and "outside agitators." But the Christians pressed on, in the conviction that they were "a colony of heaven," called to obey God rather than man. Small in number, they were big in commitment. They were too God-intoxicated to be "astronomically intimidated." By their effort and example they brought an end to such ancient evils as infanticide and gladiatorial contests. [40]

Question 16:
What is the present
status of X?

Things are different now. So often the contemporary church is a weak, ineffectual voice with an uncertain sound. So often it is an archdefender of the status quo. Far from being disturbed by the presence of the church, the power structure of the average community is consoled by the church's silent—and often even vocal—sanction of things as they are. [41]

Question 13:
What are the
consequences of X?

But the judgment of God is upon the church as never before. If today's church does not recapture the sacrificial spirit of the early church, it will lose its authenticity, forfeit the loyalty of millions, and be dismissed as an irrelevant social club with no meaning for the twentieth century. Every day I meet young people whose disappointment with the church has turned into outright disgust. [42]

Perhaps I have once again been too optimistic. Is organized religion too inextricably bound to the status quo to save our nation and the world? Perhaps I [43] must turn my faith to the inner spiritual church, the church within the church, as the true *ekklesia* and the hope of the world. But again I am thankful to God that some noble souls from the ranks of organized religion have broken loose from the paralyzing chains of conformity and joined us as active partners in the struggle for freedom. They have left their secure congregations and walked the streets of Albany, Georgia, with us. They have gone down the highways of the South on tortuous rides for freedom. Yes, they have gone to jail with us. Some have been dismissed from their churches, have lost the support of their bishops and fellow ministers. But they have acted in the faith that right defeated is stronger that evil triumphant. Their witness has been the spiritual salt that has preserved the true meaning of the gospel in these troubled times. They have carved a tunnel of hope through the dark mountain of disappointment.

Question 5:
What is my
personal response
to X?

Question 12:
What are the causes
of X?

Question 10:
How is X made or
done?

Question 17:
How can X be
summarized?

I hope the church as a whole will meet the challenge of this decisive hour. But [44] even if the church does not come to the aid of justice, I have no despair about the future. I have no fear about the outcome of our struggle in Birmingham, even if our motives are at present misunderstood. We will reach the goal of freedom in Birmingham and all over the nation, because the goal of America is freedom. Abused and scorned though we may be, our destiny is tied up with America's destiny. Before the pilgrims landed at Plymouth, we were here. Before the pen of Jefferson etched the majestic words of the Declaration of Independence across the pages of history, we were here. For more than two centuries our forebears labored in this country without wages; they made cotton king; they built the homes of their masters while suffering gross injustice and shameful humiliation—and yet out of a bottomless vitality they continued to thrive and develop. If the inexpressible cruelties of slavery could not stop us, the opposition we now face will surely fail. We will win our freedom because the sacred heritage of our nation and the eternal will of God are embodied in our echoing demands.

Question 12:
What are the causes
of X?

Before closing I feel impelled to mention one other point in your statement [45] that has troubled me profoundly. You warmly commended the Birmingham police force for keeping "order" and "preventing violence." I doubt that you would have so warmly commended the police force if you had seen its dogs sinking their teeth into unarmed, nonviolent Negroes. I doubt that you would so quickly commend the policemen if you were to observe their ugly and inhumane treatment of Negroes here in the city jail; if you were to watch them push and curse old Negro women and young Negro girls; if you were to see them slap and kick old Negro men and young boys; if you were to observe them as they did on two occasions, refuse to give us food because we wanted to sing our grace together. I cannot join you in your praise of the Birmingham police department.

Question 19:
What is the value
of X?

It is true that the police have exercised a degree of discipline in handling the [46] demonstrators. In this sense they have conducted themselves rather "nonviolently" in public. But for what purpose? To preserve the evil system of segregation. Over the past few years I have consistently preached that nonviolence demands that the means we use must be as pure as the ends we seek. I have tried to make clear that it is wrong to use immoral means to attain moral ends. But now I must affirm that it is just as wrong, or perhaps even more so, to use moral means to preserve immoral ends. Perhaps Mr. Connor and his policemen have been rather nonviolent in public, as was Chief Pritchett in Albany, Georgia, but they have used the moral means of nonviolence to maintain the immoral end of racial injustice. As T.S. Eliot has said: "The last temptation is the greatest treason: To do the right deed for the wrong reason."

I wish you had commended the Negro sit-inners and demonstrators of Birmingham for their sublime courage, their willingness to suffer and their amazing discipline in the midst of great provocation. One day the South will recognize its real heroes. They will be the James Merediths, with the noble sense of purpose that enables them to face jeering and hostile mobs, and with the agonizing loneliness that characterizes the life of the pioneer. They will be old, oppressed, battered Negro women, symbolized in a seventy-two-year-old woman in Montgomery, Alabama, who rose up with a sense of dignity and with her people decided not to ride segregated buses, and who responded with ungrammatical profundity to one who inquired about her weariness: "My feet is tired, but my soul is at rest." They will be the young high school and college students, the young ministers of the gospel and a host of their elders, courageously and nonviolently sitting in at lunch counters and willingly going to jail for conscience' sake. One day the South will know that when these disinherited children of God sat down at lunch counters, they were in reality standing up for what is best in the American dream and for the most sacred values in our Judaeo-Christian heritage, thereby bringing our nation back to those great wells of democracy which were dug deep by the founding fathers in their formulation of the Constitution and the Declaration of Independence.

Never before have I written so long a letter. I'm afraid it is much too long to take your precious time. I can assure you that it would have been much shorter if I had been writing from a comfortable desk, but what else can one do when he is alone in a narrow jail cell, other than write long letters, think long thoughts and pray long prayers?

If I have said anything in this letter that overstates the truth and indicates an unreasonable impatience, I beg you to forgive me. If I have said anything that understates the truth and indicates my having a patience that allows me to settle for anything less than brotherhood, I beg God to forgive me.

I hope this letter finds you strong in the faith. I also hope that circumstances will soon make it possible for me to meet each of you, not as an integrationist or a civil-rights leader but as a fellow clergyman and a Christian brother. Let us all hope that the dark clouds of racial prejudice will soon pass away and the deep fog of misunderstanding will be lifted from our fear-drenched communities, and in some not too distant tomorrow the radiant stars of love and brotherhood will shine over our great nation with all their scintillating beauty.

Yours for the cause of Peace and Brotherhood,
Martin Luther King, Jr.

DISCUSSION AND EXERCISES

1. Notice that King answers all but one of the twenty questions. Which one is that? Has King implied this question anywhere? Had King written a longer letter might he have

woven in this question and answer? Discuss the places where two questions work together. Can you find additional instances where a pair of questions might have worked together? Cite other questions King asks. In paragraph 21, for example, he is clearly asking, What other examples can you cite of civil disobedience?

2. What is King's purpose in writing this letter? Why is he so careful to begin by defining his audience? In the beginning he refers to his audience as "men of good will." What does he say later that indicates to the reader that King does not really trust their "good will"? What indicates that King may actually have intended this letter for a larger audience?

3. Show how King's letter follows the three-part structure used by Greek and Roman orators (as described in What case can be made for or against X?). Note the equivalents of exordium, exposition; direct statement of case, and division of proofs; locate confirmation (facts, reasons, statistics, logical reasoning, analogy), refutation, concession, recapitulation and peroration. Discuss.

4. What evidence of deductive and inductive reasoning do you find? Discuss.

5. In many places King uses the device of analogy: "the drawing, in one inductive leap, of a crucial comparison." Locate these places and indicate whether he uses analogy in place of direct reasoning or as a supplement. Do you find any examples of false analogy? Explain.

6. According to Rogerian strategy, you can understand another position only if you see it from "the other's point of view." Describe King's point of view and indicate in what ways he tries to see the situation from "the other's point of view" (the eight clergymen, the Birmingham police, the townspeople). Apply Rogerian strategy by putting yourself in the place of King, the demonstrators, the police, Southerners in general, and the clergy.

7. Comment upon the straightforwardness and simplicity of the introduction. How does this first paragraph set the tone for the rest of the letter?

8. Evaluate the virtuoso "suspended sentence" in paragraph 14. (It begins on page 493 with the words "But when you have seen vicious mobs . . . " and concludes on page 494 with "—then you will understand why we find it difficult to wait.")What binds this sentence into a unified whole? In what sense does this compare to Christensen's description of sentences in coordinate sequence ("like things in like ways")?

9. Evaluate the effectiveness of the image that closes paragraph 43: "They have carved a tunnel of hope through the dark mountain of disappointment."

10. Indicate how King achieves strong emphasis in the following sentence from paragraph 44: "Abused and scorned though we may be, our destiny is tied up with America's destiny."

11. How does King use word repetitions to unify paragraph 45?

Continued

13. Discuss the effectiveness of King's "conclusion," viewing paragraphs 45 through 48 as a first concluding block, and paragraphs 48 through 50 as the final block. This letter, addressed originally to eight clergymen, has since become one of the most widely anthologized works of our time. Why do you think this letter has such an appreciative audience? What special audience would be particularly responsive?

14. Identify the following terms and explain why King obviously felt no need to provide footnotes for his original letter. Why is it necessary to make adjustments for different audiences?

Tarsus	The Millenium
Hungarian Freedom Fighters	The Muslim Movement
Elijah Muhammad	Nebuchadnezzar

Also identify the following people:

Socrates	Reinhold Niebuhr	St. Augustine
St. Thomas Aquinas	Martin Buber	Paul Tillich
Amos	Martin Luther	John Bunyan
Abraham Lincoln	Thomas Jefferson	Paul
T. S. Eliot	James Meredith	

ESSAY SUGGESTIONS

1. Write a letter—an extended argument (2,500-3,500 words)—in which you protest an injustice—a deeply held belief of your own. Develop your argument in terms of what "ought" to be done. Let King's argument serve as your model for organization, tone, logical development, and rhetorical effectiveness. Assume that your audience, like King's, is not openly hostile to your position.

2. Write an extended argument on what you support or take issue with King's position on civil disobedience. Pay close attention to King's distinction between laws that are morally right and those that are morally wrong (do you agree with this distinction?). Would you be moved to defend or protest any laws now in effect or proposed? Build your argument carefully and logically: provide as much supporting material (such as facts and statistics) as possible.

Chapter

6

RESEARCHING
A LONGER PAPER

DETERMINING SUBJECT AND PURPOSE

USING THE LIBRARY
      CATALOGS
      GENERAL REFERENCE BOOKS
      SUBJECT-SPECIFIC REFERENCE BOOKS
      PERIODICAL INDEXES AND ABSTRACTS
      GOVERNMENT PUBLICATIONS

DEVELOPING A RESEARCH STRATEGY

PLANNING YOUR TIME

GATHERING INFORMATION
      FOR A SHORT PAPER
      FOR A LONGER PAPER

IDENTIFYING AND EVALUATING SOURCES

TAKING NOTES
      DIRECT QUOTATION
      PARAPHRASE
      SUMMARY
      PHOTOCOPYING

AVOIDING PLAGIARISM

Frequently in your college career, and even afterward, you will need to do research on a subject. Sometimes your research will lead you to prepare a formal paper or report, sometimes not. But in either case, the process is essentially the same. To do effective and efficient research you must have an inquiring mind and must understand libraries and reference sources.

To be a good researcher you must be part scholar, part reporter: you must be able to locate electronic, printed and manuscript sources that contain the facts you need within the libraries accessible to you. You must have a kind of nose for news. You should develop the ability to see which you must discard because they do not contribute to the special thesis of your piece. This screening process is evidence that invention does not end when research begins. Even as you are gathering the special information that will constitute the substance of your paper, you are rounding it out and reshaping it. You may even revise your original thesis somewhat in the light of the materials you collect during this active research period.

Most often you will gather more information for a research paper than you use. This may seem wasteful, but it is really a necessary part of the research procedure because you are learning about your subject, developing a perspective on your materials and an awareness of the context from which they are drawn. Without this broader view, you may not be able to distinguish what is relevant from what is not. Furthermore, all the facts that you know about your subject, even those that do not appear in the finished piece, contribute to its total impact, for they give you confidence in your knowledge of your subject and authority in your writing.

At the same time, you must not allow yourself to get bogged down in research. There is a point at which you must decide "this is enough"—even if it does not seem *quite* enough. In most cases, no matter how conscientiously you have explored your subject, there will be some aspect of it you would like to pursue further, something else you would like to know. Arbitrarily but firmly you must call an end to research and move on to put your research to use—perhaps by writing about the subject for a college class or an employer, reporting on it orally, or simply integrating it into your own personal body of knowledge. In most cases, when your goal is to write a paper on your subject (and often when your goal is to make an oral report), you will begin writing, however tentatively, while you are still doing research—setting up a way to begin or to conclude or even shaping some self-contained middle section.

Charles Schulz, creator of the "Peanuts" comic strip, has commented aptly on the necessity of limiting research to what is feasible within the allotted time. Because Schulz believes that a comic strip should constantly introduce the reader to "new areas of thought and endeavor," which "should be treated in an authentic manner," he is constantly engaged in research:

> I never draw about anything unless I feel I have a better than average knowledge of my subject. This does not mean that I am an expert on Beethoven, kite-flying, or psychiatry, but it means that as a creative person, I have the ability to skim the surface of such subjects and use just what I need (73-74).

To skim the surface of a subject and dip down only where and when there is usable information pertinent to your purpose is a skill you should learn so that you can cope with the thousands of pages you will consult during your college years alone.

DETERMINING SUBJECT AND PURPOSE

At the outset, before you ever go to the library, you should have a clear idea of what kind of research project you will do. That involves deciding (or being told) whether your purpose is to survey and report on what others have said, or to take a stand, make a recommendation, or otherwise influence your reader in some way. Both are acceptable approaches to research projects.

The survey paper requires that you investigate as completely as possible the various aspects of a topic and then report the facts of what others have said as objectively as possible. You do not advance a view of your own but rather interpret and present the views of others—although you do need a central focus.

The persuasive research paper, like other kinds of persuasive writing, argues for a particular view or moves toward a consensus. In such a paper you do more than accumulate and present factual information: you offer an opinion that you support by means of your library research.

When you have decided about the purpose of your research, consider your topic. Some topics lend themselves to research better than others. Avoid topics that are too personal: you cannot very well do research on a topic that focuses on your own experience or on your own preferences. For instance, you will probably not be able to research effectively a topic such as Why Southern California is the best location for a family vacation. Unless your instructor tells you otherwise, beware of topics that are so current that there is likely to be little information available except that in newspapers and current weekly magazine sources. Such topics almost always lack the benefit of the perspective many commentators can give them and you will find your own paper rests largely on your own opinion. A paper on the Whitewater scandal written while testimony was still being given before Congressional committees would not have had the benefit of the reports of those committees, the commentary on those reports, and so on. Avoid "one-source" papers as well: any topic that relies on a single source is too narrow, or else your library does not have sufficient material to support research on that topic.

A further word of advice: be kind to yourself and to your reader. Select a subject you are really interested in; you are going to be working on it for a long time. It should be substantial enough and imaginative enough to appeal to a group of intelligent, mentally active adults, if that is your audience. Abortion, censorship, and other time-tested controversies will probably interest such readers *only* if you can offer a fresh approach.

USING THE LIBRARY

Knowing your way around a library and understanding its various reference sources are indispensable to you as you begin to research your selected topic. An important aspect of research technique is being able to find what you want as quickly as possible without wasting time looking up unusable information. Library materials are roughly of two kinds: primary and secondary. "Primary" refers to firsthand sources: original manuscripts, letters, diaries, journals, notebooks, research reports written by researchers themselves, statistics issued by the people who compiled them, reports of interviews, and so on. Articles and books are considered primary if the content is essentially original with the authors. Secondary materials are largely derivative. They are assembled from a variety of outside sources. Thus all major reference works such as encyclopedias and almanacs are secondary; so are essays, articles, and books whose major purpose is to report on, analyze, or interpret the findings of original researchers.

A reference book differs from an ordinary book in that you do not read it sequentially but rather turn to it with a special purpose in mind, thumbing as quickly as possible to the place that will provide the information you need.

In the sections that follow, reference materials are grouped under seven main headings:

1. Catalogs
2. General Reference Books
    A. Encyclopedias
    B. Biographical Works
    C. Dictionaries
    D. Yearbooks and Almanacs
    E. Atlases and Gazetteers
3. Subject-Specific Reference Books
4. Periodical Indexes and Abstracts
    A. General Indexes
    B. Special Subject Indexes
    C. Abstracts
5. Government Publications

There are two broad types of reference works: those that give information about a subject and those that tell you where to find information.

Catalogs

All libraries list the items they possess in some form of catalog. Most college and university libraries now offer their catalogs in an on-line form, accessible through computer terminals in the library. In many cases, you can also reach this information by dialing up the library's catalog from your home computer using a modem. Some libraries offer all or part of their catalog on microfilm or microfiche, or even in a card catalog. Because on-line catalog systems vary widely, we can only give you a general sense of the ways you can retrieve information from a particular system. You'll need to make an appointment with a librarian or attend a training session to learn the most efficient ways of using your particular system. Even if the basic operation of your on-line system is fairly easy to grasp, you'll find that a librarian can help you learn more complex searches that will make your research even easier.

The catalog is the index to the library. Each entry, whether on an actual card or in a computer database, represents a particular library holding—a book, periodical, or other reference source—and contains such vital information as author, title, subject, publisher, place and date of publication, and number of pages. Card catalogs generally have at least three cards for each holding—one each for author, title, and subject. Depending on the design of your online system, you will be able to search for holdings under these three headings and more. We offer two typical catalog entries: one from a card catalog (Figure 6–1), one from an

The Dewey Decimal System

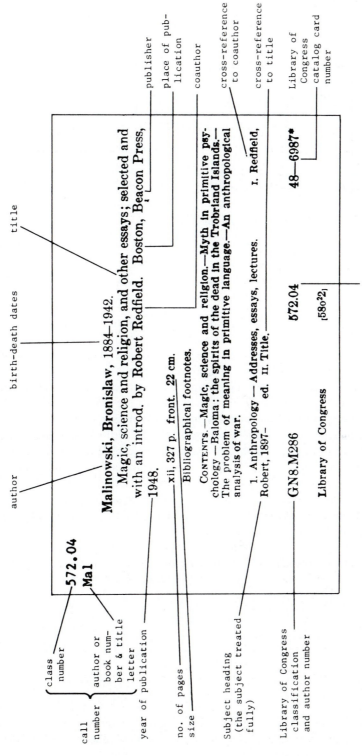

author   birth-death dates   title   publisher   place of publication   coauthor   cross-reference to coauthor   cross-reference to title   Library of Congress catalog card number

572.04
Mal

Malinowski, Bronislaw, 1884–1942.
   Magic, science and religion, and other essays; selected and with an introd. by Robert Redfield. Boston, Beacon Press, 1948.
   xii, 327 p. front. 22 cm.
   Bibliographical footnotes.
   CONTENTS.—Magic, science and religion.—Myth in primitive psychology.—Baloma: the spirits of the dead in the Trobriand Islands.—The problem of meaning in primitive language.—An anthropological analysis of war.

   1. Anthropology — Addresses, essays, lectures.   I. Redfield, Robert, 1897–   ed. II. Title.

GN8.M286   572.04

Library of Congress   [580²]   48—6987*

class number
author or book number & title letter
call number
year of publication
no. of pages
size
Subject heading (the subject treated fully)
Library of Congress classification and author number
Dewey classification

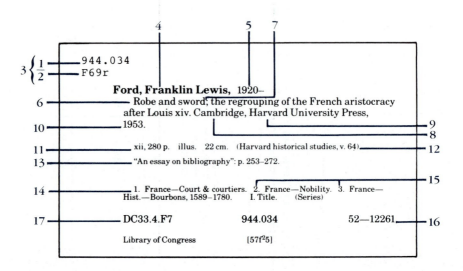

online catalog (Figure 6–2). Whether you're using an on-line catalog or a card catalog, it's a fairly easy process to find out where a specific book or other item is located.

What does take some thought, however, is tracking down *all* the material in the library that pertains to your subject, for this is not always evident from a first quick look under the obvious main headings. Here again you must be aware of various subheadings under which the catalog may list relevant works. Some subheadings are indicated on the main entry card itself as illustrated in Figure 6–1 ("Anthropology—Addresses, essays, lectures"). For further information you can refer to these subject cards. In addition to being ingenious about subheadings, you must be imaginative and knowledgeable enough about your subject to figure out alternate designations. If it is "cinema techniques" you want to know about, for example, then you should surely think of turning to "Motion Pictures," "Film," or perhaps "Movies." By referring to *Subject Headings . . . of the Library of Congress,* a large volume owned by most libraries and installed near the card catalog, you will get an idea of the variety of cross-references possible for most subjects.

Once you've found the main entry for a source you're interested in, you should take some time to evaluate the information there to determine how useful that book or other item will be in your particular research project. Carefully examine the following:

Date of publication: Is the work too old to be useful?
Author: Is he or she known to you? Does he or she have a reputation in this field? Is the book likely to be a trustworthy treatment of the topic?
Publisher: Is it a reputable press or a fly-by-night vanity press, which will publish almost anything as long as the author will pay for it?
Number of pages: Is the book too long or too short for your purposes?
Title and subtitle: Does the wording suggest a tone or approach that would be particularly appropriate or inappropriate for your purpose?

Another important step in beginning your research is to have a consultation with a research librarian, who will help you evaluate the information you're discovering and suggest

sources you may have overlooked. No matter how accessible and user-friendly your library is, the librarian will probably be able to suggest additional resources both in your library and the larger community.

General Reference Books

When you have finally found your topic and are ready to gather information, you would be wise to turn at the outset to a general encyclopedia, for it will provide a helpful overview of the subject, a description of its essential nature and its scope. More than that, it will verify whatever facts you have on hand and fill in some of the details, thereby bringing you up to date on your subject and either reinforcing your interest in it or actually discouraging you from pursuing the topic further. If the encyclopedia confirms that your subject is promising, copy the bibliography, for it will give you a good start as you search the catalog of the library's holdings, and then its general and special reference books.

A. Encyclopedias The best—and best-known—all-around reference work is the encyclopedia, which provides background materials for almost any field of knowledge. Do you want to know about white supremacy in Africa? the fiscal crisis of Catholic parochial education? the world's consumption of raw materials? All these questions call for initial consultation with a broad treatment of the subject. This is exactly what the encyclopedia offers in the form of a relatively short, condensed article, in many cases written by a specialist and signed.

The best general encyclopedias include the following:

The New Encyclopaedia Britannica: A Survey of Universal Knowledge. 30 vols. Chicago: Encyclopaedia Britannica, Inc., 1992.
  Supplemented annually by the *Britannica Book of the Year.*
Encyclopedia Americana (International Edition). 30 vols. Danbury, Conn.: Grolier, 1989. Supplemented annually by the *Americana Annual.*
Chambers's Encyclopaedia. New rev. ed. Oxford and New York: International Learning Systems, 1973.
  Supplemented annually by Chambers's *Encyclopaedia World Survey.*
Collier's Encyclopedia. 24 vols. New York: Crowell-Collier, 1986.
  Supplemented by *Collier's Year Book.*

Whatever encyclopedia you use, several facts are worth remembering:

1. Although the major encyclopedias are not thoroughly revised each year, most of them undergo a process of continuous revision whereby each printing embodies some changes. In most cases, therefore, the information gathered from a reputable encyclopedia is relatively up-to-date. For up-to-the minute information, however, you must consult a periodical—an abstract, article, or news report. (See Periodical Indexes and Abstracts, pages 516–517).

2. Every encyclopedia contains an explanation of its own code: its abbreviations, a key to the initials on the signed articles, index conventions, and so on. You should consult this code at the outset of research so that you can understand the information you gather.

3. The major encyclopedias contain bibliographies (lists of other works on a given subject or other places where you may find information), plus a detailed index, usually

located in the last volume. Researchers are not always aware of these supplementary aids; students often ignore the main index, in particular, because they hurriedly turn to the main entry where they can usually—but not always—find most of the needed information. Proper use of the encyclopedia also involves cross-referencing. If your topic is the chateau country of France, for example, you should follow each of the suggested cross-references to individual chateaux as they are mentioned in the main entry (Amboise, Chenonceaux). Then you should proceed—on your own—to look up other entries that *might* provide more information: you might investigate individual kings, for example, who built or restored chateaux (Charles VIII, Louis XII, Francis I), or you might turn to the individual towns in which chateaux are located. Your ingenuity at cross-referencing may determine whether your paper contains simply the usual and expected information or that extra dimension that raises it above the ordinary.

B. Biographical Works If your topic involves a prominent person or persons (an historical character, an inventor, a literary figure), you should begin your research by compiling biographical data. General biographical works may be universal in scope (like the first two in the following list) or they may be limited to individuals of a particular nationality, geographical location, or professional position. For our purposes—in fact for most purposes—the main distinction is whether the person in question is living or dead.

Persons Living

> *Current Biography,* 1940-date. New York: Wilson, 1940-date.
>> Published monthly and gathered into annual volumes, each of which contains lively profiles of about 400 new personalities.
> *Who's Who,* 1849-date. London: Black, 1849-date.
>> Published annually, this famous dictionary of notable living Englishmen and a few distinguished persons of other countries gives brief facts and addresses.
> *Who's Who in America,* 1899/1900-date. Chicago: Marquis, 1899-date.
>> This American counterpart of the British *Who's Who* is published every other year, along with a supplementary *Who's Who of American Women,* 1958-date. (See also separate volumes of *Who's Who* that cover different regions of the United States: *Who's Who in the East, Who's Who in the South and Southwest, Who's Who in the Midwest,* and so on. See also volumes covering various other nations such as *Who's Who in Australia, Who's Who in Modern China, Who's Who in Latin America.*)

Other contemporary biographical sources are organized according to profession and include such volumes as the following:

> *American Men and Women of Science*
> *The Directory of American Scholars*
> *Twentieth Century Authors*
> *Contemporary Authors*
> *Who's Who in American Politics*
> *Dictionary of Scientific Biography*

Persons No Longer Living

Dictionary of American Biography. 20 vols. New York: Scribner, 1927-1980. 8
Supplements to 1990.

Long, detailed articles, written by prominent scholars and accompanied by
a bibliography of sources (most of them primary), chronicle the lives and
accomplishments of distinguished Americans. See also *Facts About the Presidents, American Authors (1600-1900),* and *Notable American Women, 1607-1950.*

Dictionary of National Biography. Ed. Sir Leslie Stephen and Sir Sidney Lee. London:
Smith, Elder and Co., and Oxford University Press, 1885-date.

The British counterpart of (and model for) the *Dictionary of American
Biography* (D.A.B.), the D.N.B. is the most complete and accurate guide to the
lives of important Britons of the past.

(See also such helpful sources as *Who Was Who, British Authors of the
Nineteenth Century, British Authors Before 1800, European Authors, 1000-1900,*
and *World Authors.*)

Persons living and Dead

Webster's Biographical Dictionary. Springfield, Mass.: Merriam, 1980.

Chambers's Biographical Dictionary. Rev. ed. New York: St. Martins, 1974. (See also
entries under individual names in the general encyclopedias.)

C. Dictionaries At the outset of research, look up key terms to find out their conventional
boundaries of meaning. Will you want to stay within these boundaries or will you want to
use certain terms in an unorthodox sense, either more or less restricted than usual? As we see
in Question 1, What does X mean? you can vary word usage provided you indicate at the
outset that you are using the term in a special sense, one that meets the particular needs of
the paper.

Before you can make any such statement, however, you must see what the dictionary—
preferably an unabridged dictionary—has to say. You may even find it necessary to discover
how the meaning of a particular word has changed over the years: maybe a past meaning will
be specially relevant to your purpose; maybe it will be worth adopting or adapting. Four good
standard dictionaries provide information of this kind: three are general, one historical.

Webster's Third New International Dictionary of the English Language. 3d ed. unabridged. Ed. Philip Gove. Springfield, Mass.: Merriam, 1993.

One of the great English dictionaries—the first to be published under the
direct and commanding influence of modern linguistic science—*Webster's Third*
contains almost half a million words, 100,000 of which are new entries or new
meanings for older entries. Some early critics maintained that this dictionary
would never replace Webster's more traditional Second Edition (1934), but it
has.

The Random House Dictionary of the English Language. Unabridged 2d ed. Ed. Stuart
Berg Flexner. New York: Random House, 1987.

A computer-produced, highly legible dictionary containing 260,000 words.

The American Heritage Dictionary of the English Language. Ed. William Morris. New York: American Heritage Publishing Co., Inc., and Boston: Houghton Mifflin Co., 1992.

An entirely new and highly readable dictionary, copiously illustrated.

New English Dictionary on Historical Principles. Ed. Sir James A. H. Murray. 10 vols. and supplement. Oxford: Clarendon Press, 1888-1933. Reissued, 1933, in 13 vols. under the title *Oxford English Dictionary* (OED), 2d ed. 1989.

(See also the one-volume *Oxford University Dictionary,* 3d ed., revised with addenda and corrections. Oxford: Clarendon Press, 1959.)

This great dictionary, the most scholarly lexicographical achievement in the English language, which took years of cooperative scholarship to complete, was compiled on a different plan and serves a different purpose from that of the ordinary dictionary. It traces the history of every word in the language (its meaning, spelling, pronunciation) from the time it first appeared as an English word (perhaps 800 years ago) to the present, giving illustrations of its usage at the various stages of its career.

D. Yearbooks and Almanacs Yearbooks and almanacs, published each year, contain a wealth of general information and statistics, much of it based on primary materials from government bulletins and abstracts.

Facts on File, A Weekly Digest of World Events with Cumulative Index. New York: Facts on File, Inc., 1930-date.

An extremely helpful, time-saving weekly digest of the news, arranged under such headings as world affairs, arts, economy, science, education, religion. It has been said that *Facts on File* is a *current* encyclopedia, keeping the reader abreast of the latest developments in all fields, particularly in the United States.

(See also *Keesing's Contemporary Archives,* a weekly diary of world events, published in London but worldwide in scope.)

The New York Times Encyclopedic Almanac. New York: The New York Times, 1970–date.

Comprehensive and reliable, this recently introduced encyclopedic almanac offers all the useful features of an almanac (statistics on every phase of American life, from the Supreme Court to sports) based on the research and educational resources of the *New York Times.* Issued annually.

The World Almanac and Book of Facts. New York: Newspaper Enterprise Association, 1868-1876, 1886–date.

Statesman's Year-Book: Statistical and Historical Annual of the States of the World. London: Macmillan, 1864–date.

An exceptionally useful manual containing information and statistics on the governments of the world—their rulers, constitutions, forms of government, population, commerce, state finance, defense, production, industry.

(See also the *Worldmark Encyclopedia of the Nations* (1988), which provides supplementary materials to the *Statesman's Year-Book* and presents helpful information on the newer countries and on famous persons in each country's history. See also yearbooks for individual countries and continents, such as *Europa Year Book: A World Survey, Canadian Almanac and Directory, South American Handbook.*)

E. Atlases and Gazetteers There are general and special atlases, some of which are listed below:

General

> *Hammond Medallion World Atlas*
> *Rand McNally Commercial Atlas*
> *Rand McNally Cosmopolitan World Atlas*
> *McGraw-Hill International Atlas*
> *The Times Atlas of the World*

Special

> *Atlas of American History*
> *Atlas of World History*
> *Atlas of the Historical Geography of the United States*
> *Atlas of the Sky*

A gazetteer is a dictionary of places that provides information about history, population, trade, industry, cultural institutions, natural resources. See, for example:

> *Columbia-Lippincott Gazetteer of the World*
> *Webster's New Geographical Dictionary*
> *The Times Index-Gazetteer of the World*

Subject-specific Reference Books

In addition to general references, many special reference works are devoted to individual fields such as history, political science, and literature. Each of these fields has its own body of materials—encyclopedias, handbooks, indexes, abstracts, almanacs, yearbooks, dictionaries, and so on—that you can locate through a general reference guide like Constance Winchell's standard *Guide to Reference Books* or one of the smaller "pocket guides." These overall subject guides are your single most helpful research aids, for they acquaint you with the major writings in your chosen field and list not only encyclopedias and handbooks but also bibliographies, abstracts, and periodical indexes that tell you where you can find further information (discussed below under Periodical Indexes and Abstracts).

How many subject areas have their own reference shelf of special materials? It would be impossible to list them all here, for there are separate reference works devoted to almost every discipline, activity, profession, occupation, and recreation; handbooks and encyclopedias are available for you in every field and every field-within-a-field you can imagine. However, you might note some of the more common subject headings under which special reference works are likely to be listed:

Subject Heading	*Representative Reference Works*
Philosophy	*Encyclopedia of Philosophy*
Psychology	*Annual Review of Psychology*
Religion	*Encyclopedia of Religion and Ethics*
	(See separate encyclopedias for Catholic, Jewish, etc.)
Social Sciences	*Sources of Information in the Social Sciences*
	International Encyclopedia of the Social Sciences
	Dictionary of Sociology
	Biennial Review of Anthropology
	(See separate reference works in political science, economics, law, education, etc.)
Physical Sciences	*The Harper Encyclopedia of Science*
	McGraw-Hill Encyclopedia of Science and Technology
	A Guide to the Literature of Chemistry
	The International Dictionary of Applied Mathematics
	Encyclopaedic Dictionary of Physics
	Glossary of Geology and Related Sciences
Natural Sciences	*The Encyclopedia of Biological Sciences*
	Gray's Manual of Botany
	Mammals of the World
	Glossary of Genetics and Other Biological Terms
Technology	*McGraw-Hill Encyclopedia of Science and Technology*
	A Guide to Information Sources in Space Science and Technology
	(See separate reference works under medical science, engineering, agriculture, business, etc.)
Fine Arts	*Encyclopedia of World Art*
	A Guide to Art Reference Books
	Grove's Dictionary of Music and Musicians
	Encyclopedia of Jazz
Literature	*The Reader's Adviser: A Guide to the Best in Literature*
	(See also bibliographies, dictionaries, directories, handbooks, biographies, criticism, history, drama, poetry, fiction, etc.; see also national literatures: English, American, French, etc.)
Language and Linguistics	*The World's Chief Languages*
	Language in Cultures and Society
	A History of the English Language
	Dictionary of Linguistics
History	*An Encyclopedia of World History*
	Oxford Classical Dictionary
	(See under historical periods: ancient, medieval, etc.; see also national histories: English, American, etc.)

Periodical Indexes and Abstracts

When you want to find out the latest information on a given subject (the influence of drugs on mental alertness, critical opinion of a current production of *King Lear,* or new facts about the moon), you must turn to periodical indexes that list articles, reports, reviews, essays, news stories, speeches, bulletins, and editorials that have appeared in periodicals—journals, magazines, and newspapers. In some cases, you may want to turn to this resource immediately, for what is new about your subject may be the most important thing you need to learn—the very core of your paper as well as your reason for writing it.

You can expect the periodical indexes to put you in touch with the most recent and up-to-date information. In that special type of index known as an "abstract," you will also find a brief summary of what the articles and essays contain.

Major periodical indexes can be divided into general and specialized (according to subject areas).

A. General Indexes

Readers' Guide to Periodical Literature New York: Wilson, 1905–date.

Social Science Index and Humanities Index. New York: Wilson, 1975–date. Formerly known as *Social Sciences and Humanities Index,* 1965–1974.

New York Times Index. New York: New York Times Corp., 1851–date.

Essay and General Literature Index. New York: Wilson, 1900–date.

Book Review Digest. New York: Wilson, 1905–date.

Book Review Index. Detroit: Gale Research, 1965–date.

B. Special Subject Indexes Here again, it is impossible to list all the separate indexes devoted to particular subjects. To locate the one most useful to your purpose, consult one of the general guides to the literature such as Winchell's *Guide to Reference Books* (mentioned earlier), or the less formal but eminently readable *How and Where to Look It Up.*

A few representative subject indexes are:

Applied Science and Technology Index. New York: Wilson, 1958–date. Formerly *Industrial Arts Index,* 1913–1958.

Art Index. New York: Wilson, 1929–date.

Business Periodicals Index. New York: Wilson, 1958–date.

Education Index. New York: Wilson, 1929–date.

Film Literature Index, 1973–date.

Index of Religious Periodical Literature. Ed. American Theological Library Assn. Princeton, N.J.: Princeton Theological Seminary, 1953–date.

The Music Index. Detroit: Information Service, Inc., 1949–date.

Public Affairs Information Service Bulletin. New York: Public Affairs Information Service, 1915–date.

Psychological Index, 1894–1935. 42 vols. Princeton, N.J.: Psychological Review Co., 1895–1936. (Continued by *Psychological Abstracts*)

C. Abstracts

Abstract of English Studies
America: History and Life: A Guide to Periodical Literature (with abstracts)
Biological Abstracts
Chemical Abstracts
Historical Abstracts
   Now being published in two parts: *Modern Abstracts,* 1775–1914; and *Twentieth Century Abstracts,* 1914–date.
Mathematical Reviews
Mineralogical Abstracts
Psychological Abstracts
Religious and Theological Abstracts
Science Abstracts (physics and electrical engineering)
Sociological Abstracts

Government Publications

The United States government is probably the largest and most versatile publisher in the world, printing and processing in a single year more books, booklets, periodicals, newsletters, leaflets, films, and filmstrips; more annual reports, research documents, transcripts (of congressional hearings, for example), manuals, handbooks, bibliographies, indexes, dictionaries, catalogs, checklists, and statistical compilations than any single commercial publisher or any foreign government.

Few people are aware of the enormous amount of information available through the Government Printing Office, either free or at very low cost. A brief listing of recent titles suggests how far-ranging this information is: *Science and the City, Mini-gardens for Vegetables, Family Budgeting, The Nature of Ocean Beds, Raising Raccoons, Home Construction, Space, National Parks, Living Death: The Truth About Drug Addiction, FDA* (Food and Drug Administration) *on Oral Contraceptives, Story of the Mississippi Choctaws, Pocket Guide to Japan, Fables from Incunabula to the Present.* In truth, government publications touch on nearly every field, especially in the areas of history, travel, and the social, physical, and biological sciences.

To tap this rich source of authoritative and up-to-date primary source material, you should be familiar with the main bibliographies and indexes issued by the government and some of the more recent and important guides.

> U.S. Superintendent of Documents. *Monthly Catalog of United States Government Publications.* Washington, D.C.: Government Printing Office, 1895–date.
> *Price Lists of Government Publications.* Washington, D.C.: Government Printing Office, 1895–date.
> U.S. Bureau of the Census. *Statistical Abstract of the United States.* Washington, D.C.: Government Printing Office, 1878–date.
>   This matchless compendium of statistics covers the political, social, economic, and industrial organization of the country, including vital statistics, and figures on population, immigration, finance, employment, etc. It is the basic source of

statistical information of all kinds from which most other sources (yearbooks, almanacs) get their information.

Subject Guide to Major United States Government Publications. Chicago: American Library Association, 1987.

Covers important government publications from the earliest period to the publication date, arranged by subject.

Leidy, W. Philip. *A Popular Guide to Governmental Publications.* 4th ed. New York: Columbia University Press, 1976.

Covers the most popular government publications issued 1961–66, arranged by subject.

Palic, Vladimir M. *Government Publications and Their Use.* New York: Oxford University Press, 1977.

Contains descriptions of catalogs and indexes, bibliographies, congressional publications, constitutions (federal and state), court decisions, presidential papers, etc.

Libraries organize their government materials differently: some catalog them in the regular card catalog, as they would any other library material; others keep them in a separate file, or official United States government depository, classifying them as Government Documents or Government Publications. The reference librarian can explain the system used in the individual library.

DEVELOPING A RESEARCH STRATEGY

Once you have found a subject and done some preliminary checking in general reference sources, you are in a better position to determine how much research you need to do. Obviously, the amount and depth of your research will depend upon the purpose to which you intend to put that research.

It is at this point that you should take some time to limit your subject. Consider the projected length of your paper and the time you have available; then adjust your scope so that you can treat your subject with some depth. Aim for a focused statement you can use to guide your continued research. Although you will probably find that you have to limit your subject further as you find out more about it, making some early decisions will save you unnecessary work. For example, if you were initially interested in writing about the negative effects of smoking, you might now be ready to limit your subject to, say, the ways smoking damages one's body. And as you investigate that topic, you may decide to limit it to an area as narrow as how an expectant mother's smoking affects her unborn child. A review of the discussion earlier in this book on *limiting the subject and focusing it* will help you shape your research paper and formulate your thesis statement.

PLANNING YOUR TIME

This is also the time to make a schedule. Even if your assignment is to produce a short paper of 500-750 words, you can hardly do this overnight. And if you are to produce a fully developed term paper, you will certainly need several weeks to complete all the work involved. After establishing a schedule, you still have to find and evaluate sources, take notes, organize your materials, make a working plan, draft your paper, revise it, and prepare the final manuscript.

If you are writing your paper for a composition class, your instructor may set up a schedule for you, stating dates by which you will need to submit your working bibliography, note cards, and a working plan and/or first draft, as well as the date the final draft is due. For other classes, and for research projects after college graduation, you will usually be told only the completion date (and will submit only the final version of your work). A sensible schedule would provide approximately twenty percent of your scheduled time to each stage of the research process. Therefore, if your American History instructor assigns a term paper at the beginning of the term and names a due date ten weeks in the future, you can feel comfortable about your progress if you know what you should accomplish at the end of each two-week period. Plan to prepare your working bibliography by the end of the fourth week and to have completed taking notes by the end of the sixth. Draft your paper by the end of the eighth week. You then have two weeks to revise the paper and type or word-process it in its final form. Too often students realize only at the end of the seventh or eighth week that their papers are due in two or three weeks and rush about trying to accomplish in that brief span what they could have done easily in ten weeks. Furthermore, term papers will often be due in other classes at nearly the same time, and few students can write three or four good papers in three weeks. Following a carefully planned schedule may not assure you of a superbly written paper, but it will allow you the time to prepare one that represents your best effort.

GATHERING INFORMATION

For a Short Paper

The weekly, biweekly, or semiweekly writing assignment that usually runs from 500 to 1,000 words often requires library research. Let us take an average 500-750-word paper (two to three pages) and call it a "short" paper. You can gather information for this writing assignment in approximately three to four hours of library research. You should allow—*at least*—an equal amount of time for writing the paper and revising. Thus, the average writing assignment requires from six to eight hours of total effort. Since virtually all writing assignments have a deadline, they are self-limiting: what you need to do, in other words, becomes a function of what you *can* do within the prescribed time. Recognizing this fact will put the paper in perspective and helps you make a realistic assessment of how much you can hope to cover and what you can conceivably accomplish.

Let us consider how you might go about gathering information for four possible topics, each an answer to a specific question.*

1. How does X compare to Y?
   Title: The Peace Corps—Then and Now

---

*You do not need to consult all references listed in each instance; sometimes one or two provide sufficient information. Should you want to extend the piece to a long paper, however, these bibliographies would represent the bare essentials. Although it is obvious, in most cases you should also look into the card catalog under appropriate headings. Even if you do not have time to read a whole book on a subject, you may find separate chapters directly pertinent to your purpose.

List of Possible Sources:

Encyclopedia Americana
Government publications (See "Federal Depository" in college library, which contains recent government reports, pamphlets, bulletins, programs, etc.)
Public Affairs Information Service Bulletin (PAIS)
New York Times Index
Readers' Guide to Periodical Literature

2. What is the present status of X?
   Title: A New View of the Soul*

List of Possible Sources:

Encyclopedia of Philosophy
The Dictionary of Religious Terms
Encyclopedia of Religion and Ethics
The New Schaff-Herzog Encyclopedia of Religious Knowledge
Handbook of Denominations in the United States
Religious and Theological Abstracts

3. How is X made or done?
   Title: How Artificial Snow Is Made

List of Possible Sources:

Science News Yearbook (annual)
Encyclopaedia Britannica
McGraw-Hill Encyclopedia of Science and Technology
   (see supplementary yearbooks)
      or
Van Nostrand's Scientific Encyclopedia
Weather and Climate
Applied Science and Technology Index
Readers' Guide to Periodical Literature

4. What case can be made for or against X?
   Title: The Case Against Multiple-Choice Tests

List of Possible Sources:

Encyclopedia of Educational Research
Mental Measurements Yearbook
Psychological Abstracts
Education Index
Readers' Guide to Periodical Literature
Catalog (under "Educational Tests," "Testing," etc.)

---

*You could easily extend this topic, in particular, into a long piece dealing with different concepts of the soul at different periods in history or among different religions. See *Handbook of Denominations in the United States* and encyclopedias and dictionaries of the various religions.

For a Long Paper

Doing researching for a long paper may require as much as thirty or forty hours in the library. Even if you simply cannot devote that much time to a term paper assignment, you should plan on at least fifteen to twenty hours of research for a paper that will run between 3,000 and 5,000 words. It is impossible, of course, to set exact specifications; the demands of the subject vary, along with the background knowledge of the writer.

The following list of possible sources for projected term paper topics gives an indication of the extent of research necessary for a typical term paper.

Term Paper 1: Description-Narration Title: The Assassination of Malcolm X

1. Biographical sources

   Current Biography
   Who Was Who in America
   Biography Index

2. Newspaper and magazine accounts

   New York Times Index
   Readers' Guide to Periodical Literature

3. Essays and commentaries in journals, anthologies, etc.

   Essay and General Literature Index
   Social Science and Humanities Index
   America: History and Life: A Guide to Periodical Literature

4. Catalog

   See under "Malcolm X: Biography; Bibliography."

5. Reference books

   Black American Reference Book
   Encyclopedia of Islam

Term Paper 2: Extended Characterization-Interpretation Title: The World of Pablo Picasso

1. Biographical sources

   Chambers's Biographical Dictionary, rev. ed.
   Webster's Biographical Dictionary

2. Encyclopedias and dictionaries

   Encyclopedia of World Art
   Encyclopedia of Modern Art
   Dictionary of Art and Artists
   Dictionary of Art
   Dictionary of Modern Painting

3. Bibliographies and indexes

Readers' Guide to Periodical Literature (for articles in national magazines)
New York Times Index
The Art Index
A Guide to Art Reference Books

4. Picasso's artistic development—some specific works

Ashton, Dore. *Picasso on Art.* New York: Viking Press, 1972.
Barr, Alfred H., Jr. *Picasso: Fifty Years of His Art.* Rev. and enl. ed. New York: Museum of Modern Art, 1974.
Chevalier, Denis. *Picasso: Blue and Rose Periods.* New York: Crown, 1969.
Gallwitz, Klaus. *Picasso at 90: The Late Work.* New York: Putnam, 1971.
Gedo, Mary W. *Picasso: Art as Biography.* Chicago: 1980.
——————— *The Success and Failure of Picasso.*
Schiff, G., ed. *Picasso in Perspective.* Englewood Cliffs, N.J.: Prentice-Hall, 1974.

5. Catalog

For individual biographies, check under "Picasso, Pablo." For background information, check under "Art History," "Modern Art," "Twentieth-Century Art."

Term Paper 3: Extended "Facts About . . ." Title: The Latest Facts About Twins

1. Basic background reference

Encyclopaedia Britannica (See under "Genetics, Human")
McGraw-Hill Encyclopedia of Science and Technology
International Encyclopedia of Psychiatry, Psychology, Analysis, and Neurology

2. Bibliographies and indexes

Index Medicus
Social Sciences Index
Sociological Abstracts
Psychological Abstracts
Readers' Guide to Periodical Literature
New York Times Index

3. Catalog

See under "Twins"; also "Birth (Multiple)," "Brothers & Sisters," "Diseases in Twins," "Human Genetics," "Heredity"

Term Paper 4: Extended Argument Title: The Case Against Capital Punishment

1. Basic reference

International Encyclopedia of the Social Sciences

2. Bibliographies and indexes

   Readers' Guide to Periodical Literature
   New York Times Index
   Public Affairs Information Service Bulletin (PAIS)
   Social Sciences Index
   Sociological Abstracts
   CIS/INDEX: Index to Congressional Publications and Public Laws

3. Government document

   Monthly Catalog

4. Catalog

IDENTIFYING AND EVALUATING SOURCES

The next step in the research process is to prepare a working bibliography—a list of all the sources you can find in your library (and perhaps in nearby libraries) that are pertinent to your topic. You will probably not need all of them, but compiling a list of everything available is useful, particularly if you discover you must modify your topic.

Before you begin, you may wish to provide yourself with 3 × 5 inch cards on which to list the sources you find. Cards are more flexible than lists on notebook paper since you can easily group them according to books and periodicals, alphabetize them, discard them, and so on. Some researchers prefer cards of two different sizes, one size for sources and another for notes; other researchers simply use different colors of the same size card.

If you have looked up your subject in an encyclopedia, you probably copied down the bibliography you found there. Transfer those entries to a bibliography card using whatever system of documentation your instructor requires. Consistently writing entries in the prescribed style expedites the preparation of your final bibliography. The examples below follow the style established by the Modern Language Association, or MLA.

```
Quinn, Arthur Hobson.   Edgar Allen Poe, A Critical
Biography.   New York:   Appleton-Century-Crofts,
1941.
```

```
Chivers' Life of Poe.  Ed. Richard Beale Davis.
 New York: E. P. Dutton & Co., 1952.
```

```
Poe, Edgar Allen.  "The Philosophy of Composition,"
Graham's Magazine (Apr. 1846), rpt. in James A.
Harrison, ed., The Complete Works of Edgar Allen
Poe. Vol. XIV.   New York: AMS Press, Inc., 1965,
pp. 193-208.
```

Next, check the Library of Congress Subject Headings (LCSH). This index lists the headings the library uses to catalog its books by subject. If you need help, ask a reference librarian.

When you have found the subject headings related to your topic, go to the catalog and look for holdings by subject. Carefully note the call number of any pertinent book on your bibliography card and, if you will be using more than one library, a code to show in which library you found it. If your library has any subject bibliographies on your topic, be sure not to overlook them.

When you have exhausted the subject headings, go to the stacks to find the subject bibliographies. These specialized bibliographies often list hard-to-find sources that are unlikely to be catalogued under the subject headings you have been searching. Sit down with the most recent and comprehensive bibliography and list on your cards the sources they provide on your subject, from both books and periodicals.

Now you are ready to check the catalog to see which of these sources and of those in the encyclopedia's bibliography are available in your library. Note the call number for each. If you have time, and if being very thorough is important for your research, you should check whether any nearby libraries have the sources your library does not. Many libraries subscribe to a computer database system that lists nationwide where a particular book can be found and most college and university libraries make that system available to students. If no library in your area has the book, and if you really need it, you can request it by Interlibrary Loan; remember, however, that you may have to wait two to three weeks for the book to arrive and also pay a modest postage fee.

Of course, books alone are not sufficient sources for good research. You should also use periodical literature since the latest information is there. Most students are familiar with the *Readers' Guide to Periodical Literature,* which lists articles in popular and general-interest publications. But for more advanced research, you should consult one of the specialized indexes of publications in a particular discipline. Begin with the most recent volumes of these indexes and work backward. Depending on how thorough you must be, you might work back only as far as the last year covered by the most recent subject bibliography available to you. When you have finished using the periodical indexes, you should check which journals and magazines your library subscribes to and which you will have to consult in another library. If no library in your area has a particular periodical volume you need, and if you are willing to pay the photocopying charge, you can request a copy of the article you want through the Interlibrary Loan Service.

In most cases, when you have located all the books and articles you can find, you have finished your research and can begin to take notes. Occasionally, however, you must first consult other kinds of sources: newspapers, databases, computer programs, recordings, maps, and so on. *Newsbank* indexes weekly on microfiche current topics from a variety of daily newspapers and provides a copy of the articles indexed. As most college libraries also subscribe to the *New York Times* on microfilm, if you need up-to-the minute material you can also consult the *New York Times Index.* In addition, most college and university libraries now have the capability of searching commercial databases for citations to relevant material. Although these searches are fast and, if properly designed, very efficient, they can be expensive. If you are considering a database search, make your first step a conference with a librarian experienced in designing such searches to keep your cost at a minimum and to garner as much appropriate data as possible for your investment.

Your working bibliography now contains numerous items, some of which you will use, many of which you will not. To decide which items will help you most, always keep in mind the focus you have chosen for your paper. Sift through your cards noticing the date of publication of each source. For topics that are current scientific or technical, the most recent information is usually most important. For other topics, the dates of your sources may be irrelevant.

Have you heard of the author? Are there multiple entries in your working bibliography for that author? Check quickly in a recent edition of *Who's Who* to see if he or she is listed. Is the author a regular contributor to the journal in question? Read the preface of the book as well as the introduction to determine the author's stance. If it seems one-sided or biased, you may have to check additional materials that are not.

As you take notes on the sources you have chosen, look carefully at the final paragraphs of articles, where the writers have generally summed up their conclusions. Note what one writer says about another. You will find one author's criticism or praise of another's work useful in evaluating sources. Again, be alert to any biases each may display. You should also scan the index of your sources. Not only do indexes list the major points covered in a book but they also contain references to what other authors have said on the subject. Look at the table of contents to assess how the author has analyzed the subject. Skim through bibliographies and footnotes to see if the author has consulted a balanced set of references. Try to ensure that your own set of sources include balanced views as well. If the bibliography is annotated, read the annotations of any sources you will consult.

Who is the publisher of the material? If the source is a book, note who published it. Is it a reputable press? Some books published at the author's expense are not reliable, nor are those that are published by presses advocating specific philosophies. For example, publications of fringe groups tend to ignore evidence that disproves their stance. If the source is an article, in what periodical did it appear? You might expect an article appearing in *Mother Jones* to take an entirely different approach—and a much more irreverent tone—than one appearing in *The National Review*. Make note of different points of view and judge your materials accordingly.

TAKING NOTES

The importance of familiarizing yourself with the library's major reference tools is obvious. At the same time, however, you should recognize that the vast resources of the Library of Congress itself are of little use if you do not know how to extract from them the information you need. Your goal should be to compile as much information on your topic as you need, and to do so in such a way that you will not have to return to the library once you have taken notes on all your sources. In order to develop your particular topic into a sound and informative paper, you must know how to take good notes, for they are obviously the foundation on which you will construct the paper itself. When the time comes to sit down and write the paper—when you must make certain points or provide certain data—good notes will enable you to thumb through them quickly and locate the information you need.

The writing process is a lot easier when you have taken accurate, ample, and well-organized notes. If you have not, you are in serious trouble, for without good notes you will not be able to write a good research paper, just as a bricklayer cannot build a strong and attractive building if the individual bricks are not themselves strong and attractive.

When do you begin? Avoid taking notes too soon—during the preliminary background-reading period in encyclopedias, for example. You may want to write down certain basic facts, figures, and dates about your subject, but beyond this you should generally hold your pencil until you have an overall feeling for your subject. Only after you have consulted more specialized references, which will probably provide more timely and useful information, should you *begin* note-taking in earnest.

Where do you begin? It is usually a good idea first to take notes from your most promising sources, but you should expect that not all of those will prove useful. Many a researcher has been surprised by a bibliographic reference that seems to address precisely the topic he or she has chosen only to find that the actual book or article refers to an entirely different branch of the topic: an article titled "Costuming in Early Drama" may refer to Greek drama rather than to early English drama, the researcher's concern. You can skim promising articles and scan the table of contents of books to decide whether they are worth reading carefully. In fact, it is a good idea to read reference materials at different rates and levels of intensity, depending on how promising they seem. You may have to skim page after page of a book without taking a single note, and then come upon a section or a separate article so relevant and reliable that you must pause two or three times per page to take notes.

Good note-taking is a skill closely related to writing. As a good note-taker, therefore, you should not mindlessly copy a paragraph of text, word for word. On the contrary, you should actively *think* about what you are reading and try to figure out exactly what it means and how it may contribute to your topic. Only after you have identified its possible use are you ready to put pencil to pad—or perhaps a small stack of 3×5 or 4×6 cards. And your first notation on each card should be the name of the author or an abbreviated title of the work you are using so that you can readily identify the source of your notes.

Once you have identified a specific source and how it can contribute to your topic, you must decide whether to quote the information directly, paraphrase it, or summarize it.

Direct Quotation

You should usually use direct quotation sparingly, for it introduces into the fabric of your prose an alien style that will be immediately noticeable to the reader, like a thread of a different color or size. Reserve direct quotation, then, for material that is controversial, elegantly stated, or unusually important. If you decide that a particular piece of information is worth quoting directly, be sure to copy it carefully, word for word, comma for comma, onto your note card. Then enclose what you have copied in quotation marks so that there will be no mistake later about whether the words are yours or another's. Finally, note the exact page numbers from which the quotation is taken. (See Sample Card 1, opposite page.)

Paraphrase

An alternative to the direct quotation is the paraphrase, a valuable means of simplifying complex material, clarifying technical language, or interpreting and evaluating ideas.

```
                         Poe / Theory of Poetry

Poe saw "Beauty" as the proper province of the poem and
"Sadness" as the proper tone:
                    Beauty of whatever kind, in its supreme
                    development, invariably excites the
                    sensitive soul to tears.  Melancholy
                    is thus the most legitimate of all the
                    poetical tones.

                              Philos. of Comp., p. 198
```

Sample Card 1

Paraphrasing requires not only that you read the source carefully but also that you understand it well enough to re-state its central idea in your own words, acknowledging—at the same time in a citation—that the idea is not your own. Consider the following statement about Edgar Allan Poe from Chivers' *Life of Poe:*

> His hair was as dark as a raven's wing. So was his beard—which he always kept shaved.

Those sentences might be paraphrased as follows:

> Poe was dark-haired and fastidious about his appearance.

Because you must acknowledge the source of this idea if you use it, note the exact page number on which it appears. Occasionally in paraphrasing an idea you can incorporate particularly memorable words or phrases from the original provided they are enclosed in quotation marks. Thus a note card paraphrasing a source might read like Sample Card 2.

```
                              Poe / Early Years

The only major American writer of his time to spend part of
childhood at school in England.  Apparently healthy:  a good
athlete; boxer; represented his school at racing competition;
story often told of how he could swim up to six miles, against
the tide and under a hot June sun.  Also a top student with
a "keen disciplined mind."  Yet as reminiscences from school-
mates indicate, he was "not popular in the usual sense of the
word."  (p. 84)

                              Quinn's EAP, pp. 65-85
```

Sample Card 2

Summary

In general, try to compress the information you take down from a reference source into a summary, so that when you are ready to use it you will be able to express the idea in your own words, maintaining, at the same time, the author's intention. This practice will reduce the possibility of distortion or inadvertent plagiarism (see Avoiding Plagiarism). Summarizing shortens or condenses a large body of information or notes the gist of what has been said. When you summarize, you may take down large chunks of information by employing a few well-chosen words or a single phrase. The phrase on sample note card 3, "slender and dark" summarizes a much longer description of Poe's physical appearance. Summary does not require complete sentences, nor even complete words. Feel free, then, to use whatever abbreviations you find helpful but be sure to avoid abbreviations that are so exotic or extreme that you later forget what they stand for! Again, carefully note the number(s) of the page or pages you have summarized from the source. (See Sample Card 3.)

Of course, you can also combine these techniques on a single note card, though doing so may make the note fairly long. Sample Cards 4 and 5 combine summary, paraphase, and direct quotation in a single note.

Another kind of note may include not only the data you have gleaned from reading, but your own observations and responses on it as you read. You should set off your own remarks in brackets on the source card so that you can distinguish later between what the authority said and what you said—or you might prefer jotting down your own ideas on an appropriately headed separate card.

```
Chivers' Life                                    Poe/Appearance

Neat and tidy, nervous in manner. Slender and dark--long
slender neck, slender arms and graceful hands. Broad forehead,
oval face, violet eyes with long lashes, strong chin, even
white teeth. Very good looking.
                                                      (53-58)
```

Sample Card 3

```
                               Poe / Personal Appearance

Neat and tidy, nervous in manner.  Slender and dark:  "His hair
was dark as a raven's wing.  So was his beard--which he always
kept shaved." (p. 53)  Broad forehead; long slender neck which
"made him appear, when sitting, rather taller than he really
was." (p. 54)  Slender arms and hands, gracefully tapered:  "In
fact, his hands were truly remarkable for their roseate softness
and lily-like, feminine delicacy." (p. 56)  Oval face, violet
```

Sample Card 4

```
                        Poe / Personal Appearance

eyes with long lashes, strong chin, even white teeth:  "really
handsome...especially when he smiled." (p. 57)  Strange smile:
"...there was this peculiarity about his smile...it did not
appear to be the result of gladness of heart altogether...but
...of that apollonian disdain which seemed to say, what you
'see through a glass darkly, I behold through the couched eyes
of an illuminated Seer.'"

                        - Chivers' Life of Poe, pp. 53-58
```

Sample Card 5

Although using a separate card for every note increases the flexibility of your notes, occasionally one idea may occupy more than one card or may need a combination of note-taking methods. When a note does occupy more than the front of a single card, continue it on a second card headed like the first and indicate that it is the second. (See Sample Cards 4 and 5.) Do not write on the back. Unfailingly, when you are at the writing stage, seeking a specific point of information, it will be on the *other* side of the card you are looking at—and you will not find it.

Not only should you write each note in your own words (unless a passage deserves to be quoted exactly), you should carefully label it according to the special category of information it deals with. By classifying your notes as you go along, you create order out of the mass of materials that confronts you. You cannot take it *all* down. You need only what relates to your topic. Once you have made at least a tentative decision about your topic and its main headings, your notes pick up these headings and perhaps even break them down into smaller subheadings (for example, Poe/Early years/Relationship with mother). Later on you can sort related page headings into separate groups (an "early years" group subdivided into "relationship with parents," "school," "early influences"; a "theory of poetry" group; a "marriage" group; a "drinking problem" group; a "financial reverses" group). When you organize notes this way, you can see your paper taking shape, even before you have begun writing. You can also judge your materials more easily. You are able to assess where you have enough information (on Poe's theory of poetry, let us say) and where you may want to do further research to avoid confusing "gaps" (Was Poe a dipsomaniac or a drunkard? Is there a difference between the two?). If you take notes conscientiously you may end up with more notes than you will actually use, but if you are reasonably selective along the way, you will not pile up an unsurmountable mountain of extraneous information.

Finally, as you read, summarize, paraphrase, and quote, try to maintain an attitude of healthy skepticism. You can perform a valuable service—both for yourself and for your readers—by remaining critical of your sources, probing them to discover what has *not* been covered. Does the author ignore important points? What are they? Why might they have been left out? What other point of view can one take? Does this source agree or disagree with other sources and why or why not? Questions like these can help you focus your own paper more critically and creatively, opening the possibility of making a real contribution to your subject.

Photocopying

Why, you may ask, is it still necessary to take notes in the library when you can photocopy relevant parts of sources—or even entire articles—and take them home to work on at leisure? The answer is simple: Photocopying can be costly; beyond that, it is a mindless effort which simply delays your real confrontation with a source. For even after it has been copied, you still have to read your source, take notes, interpret your notes, etc. For a few long, direct quotations you might cut up the photocopy and paste the exact quotation on a card, but generally speaking photocopying will offer you only a short-term convenience: Use it selectively.

AVOIDING PLAGIARISM

Plagiarism is an ugly practice, which most students try to avoid but may inadvertently commit if they are not aware of what plagiarism *is*. You should have no uncertainties on this score, however, for the offense is serious. Plagiarism is literally a crime, a form of theft in which one person steals the words of another—in ignorance, perhaps, of the fact that "phraseology, like land and money, can be individual personal property, protected by law" (Williams and Stevenson, *Research* 126). Plagiarism can also involve ideas: you might take someone else's ideas, put them into your own words, and say they are yours. But they are *not* yours, and courtesy as well as honesty requires that you acknowledge this fact with a simple phrase, such as "according to":

> *According to Northrop Frye,* the writer's ability to shape life into a literary form comes not from life but from previous contact with literature. Frye makes this point in his essay "Nature and Homer."

Even if it seems to you, after having read it, that you could have thought of that idea yourself, remember that *you did not* and that you therefore owe a credit line to Mr. Frye, whether you have used his exact words or not. You have borrowed his idea. As a conscientious writer, you must always be on guard against violations of this kind. You should be aware, for instance, that it was not anybody-at-all or nobody-in-particular, but *specifically* H. L. Mencken who maintained that "No quackery has ever been given up by the American people until they have had a worse quackery to take its place." This observation, with its fine cynical edge, was passed along by Gilbert Seldes in *The Stammering Century,* a history of quacks and cultists in nineteenth-century America. Seldes credited Mencken with the statement even though it is not a direct quotation and Seldes was not even certain whether Mencken made the remark in print or in private conversation.

Another subtle and often unwitting form of plagiarism involves *slightly changing* someone else's statement (substituting a different word here and there, shifting phrases, inverting clauses) and then presenting the passage as one's own. Here again it is important to recognize that this is not permissible. A paraphrase in your own language and style still deserves your credit.

Most students realize they must use quotation marks when they pick up an exact sentence or two, but they may not realize that this practice holds true even for a simple phrase or even for a single word: if that word is significant, you should place it in quotes. It was the critic Gilbert Murray, for example, who wrote an essay called "Literature and Revelation." If you were to follow Murray in this—that is, to treat literature as "revelation" and introduce the term as such into your writing, with all the richness of meaning that accompanies it, you should credit Murray: "Another way to view literature, as Gilbert Murray has pointed out, is as 'revelation'." (A citation should indicate precisely in what article Murray said this.)

Of course, you can arrive independently at an idea such as Murray's. "I just thought up that idea myself," you might say. "I wrote about literature as revelation because that's the way I saw it. I don't even know who Gilbert Murray is." The point is that you *should* know; you should know who has written on your chosen subject before you did; you should have read Murray's essay as part of a routine check of the literature in the *Essay and General Literature Index* or one of the literary bibliographies listed according to topic. Indeed, very few ideas are totally original. The honest and conscientious writer, student and professional alike, realizes this and always begins a piece of writing by searching the literature to see what has already been said on his or her projected subject. By conducting this preliminary search of the literature, you gain two advantages: you stimulate your own thinking and possibly learn something new; you also find out what has already been written. Knowing this, you will not naively present as new and original an idea that is, in fact, old and familiar. This does not mean that no one can write about literature as revelation because Murray has already done so. It *does* mean that anyone writing on the subject should know what Murray said at an earlier date, and go on from there.

To summarize: credit should be given in the following instances—either in an endnote or in the body of text:

1. When you directly quote someone else.
2. When you use someone else's ideas or opinions (unless they are common knowledge).
3. When you use someone else's examples.
4. When you cite statistics or other facts someone else has gathered.
5. When you present evidence or testimony taken from someone else's argument.

Chapter

7

WRITING A
LONGER PAPER

DRAFTING YOUR PAPER

CITING SOURCES
 SUMMARY AND PARAPHRASE
 DIRECT QUOTATION

DOCUMENTATION
 IN-TEXT NOTES
 FOOTNOTES AND ENDNOTES
 FINAL BIBLIOGRAPHY

EXTENDED HISTORICAL PROCESS ANALYSIS
 THE MOLLY MAGUIRE MOVEMENT,
 MELODY RAMMEL

EXTENDED CAUSAL EXPLANATION
 IRELAND: WHEN ECONOMIC AND
 CULTURAL AGENDAS CLASH,
 MATTHEW RINDFLEISCH

By the time you have finished taking notes, you should have ample information to write your paper. In fact, you may also have pieces of the paper already drafted; perhaps you drafted solutions for particularly thorny explanations while you were taking notes or jotted down a promising introduction or conclusion when it occurred to you. Set those aside for now, and assemble your note cards. Sort them according to the headings you recorded at the top. You may wind up with a dozen or more piles of cards. Review each stack of cards and read through the notes you have taken. Set aside any that do not seem pertinent—but do not discard them; you may need them. If you have done a good job of creating headings for your cards, you should be able to create a rudimentary working outline simply by placing them in a workable order. (Review the section titled Organizing a Subject.)

One advantage to handling your outline this way is that you can try out several different organizational patterns to see which is the most satisfactory. At this point it is also a good idea to determine which headings emerge as most important, most numerous or most significant. If those headings fall into a logical pattern, you should normally make those the main headings of your outline. If they do not, choose other, more coherent categories for which you have sufficient data.

Obviously, the paper you write will be shaped to a considerable certain extent by the information you have collected. For instance, you will undoubtedly find that some of your piles contain too few cards to be useful as headings. If the information on these cards is valuable, take some time to determine what a heading might be and relabel the cards. Other piles will be larger than you anticipated and will require that you formulate subheadings. Some cards, no longer pertinent to the thrust of your paper, should be discarded.

DRAFTING YOUR PAPER

In the section titled Beyond Twenty Questions, we saw that the writer profits from pressing a topic still further to wring from it an answer to the question, What is the main point I want to make? This answer, when formulated as a statement, will focus the reader's attention—and the writer's concern—on one single point that governs all else in the paper. Formulating a thesis is perhaps the single most important—and most difficult—task in writing a research paper.

Here again, your note cards should give you some help, particularly if they contain your own comments and reactions. First, and most important, your comments indicate how you were thinking about your subject as you took your notes. With what did you agree? disagree? What ideas of your own did a writer's comment prompt? What did you find most interesting? Second, the notes you took reflect how authorities on your subject view the main issues. What do these writers consider most important? Are there relationships among these sources that can prove fruitful for you? Are there gaps that they have not addressed? Don't let the views of authorities override your own; instead explore them for clues suggesting which aspects of your subject you want to emphasize.

As you *gather* ideas about what your main point is and how you want to support it, formulate that thesis into a one-sentence statement that you can test against your rough outline. When that statement fits your vision of your subject and takes into account most of your important points, you have not merely found but *actively formulated* your thesis. You may need to refine it, and adjust the outline accordingly, but you are ready to begin a first draft.

Drafting a research paper is much like drafting any other paper. You write as rapidly and as fluently as you can, making your statements as succinctly as possible without sacrificing the flow of your prose to search for a precise word or a more felicitous structure. (That can be done in revising.) Just get your ideas down on paper quickly in an order that approximates as nearly as possible the working outline you prepared. If you find yourself getting bogged down in a particularly difficult section, just go on to the next one that you feel comfortable with. You don't have to write all the sections of your paper in sequence. Although many writers find that a sound introduction helps to keep them on track, some write the introduction last, when they know exactly what they are going to say. Other writers draft the end of the paper first to establish the direction of the entire paper.

CITING SOURCES

The main difference between drafting a research paper and any other kind of paper is that in a research paper you must give credit for any statements you draw from the sources you consulted, statements you have taken care to work into your own prose as seamlessly as possible. Material you have summarized lends itself easily to citation.

Summary and Paraphrase

When you use information you have summarized from a source, simply cite each source you use each time you use it. For example, in her paper "The Mollie Maguire Movement," Melody Rammel summarizes background material from three sources. Notice how she makes the summary a part of her own prose and how she gives credit at the end of the summary.

> By the middle 1800s the farmer's animosity toward the landlords and agents reached the boiling point. The most popular explanation of the movement's origin is that Molly Maguire, a widowed tenant farmer, organized a movement to resist the rent system and to run the English ruling party out of Ireland. Her followers, adopting the name "Mollie Maguires," formed a secret society. Dressing up as women, they would launch surprise attacks on land agents which often escalated into violent beatings and even murders (Adamic, 12; Roy, 93; "Molly Maguires," 678).

You can work paraphrase into a paper in much the same way, either by naming the source in the text of the essay or by citing it at the close of the paraphrase:

> Thomas Brooks, a labor historian, thinks the terrorist faction formed when attempts to unionize the Irish miners failed (48).

> According to the newspapers, the victims of these crimes were usually foremen and officials, and only mine owners' property was destroyed (Rayback, 132).

Direct Quotation

Direct quotation is more difficult to manage: you must set each quote in a context that makes clear your reason for using it, and weave each smoothly into your own writing style in order to maintain a smooth flow. The most common—although often least effective—way to do this is to introduce a quotation by naming the person quoted:

> Labor historian Sidney Lens wrote of the faction, "Without a union to absorb their pain and relieve their fury, a few zealots took to terror" (17).

When you quote a second time from a source, you need not repeat the full name or the credentials:

> With the defeat of unionism, Brooks writes, "the young Irish hotheads in the Mollies turned to derailing mine cars and burning breakers. Then they took to the hills to snipe at mine supers and unpopular foremen" (48).

Notice how Melody Rammel provides a context for the above quotation. Whenever you can, you should try to work the sentence you quote into the syntax of your own sentence:

> According to his reasoning, he had to keep the railroad "from the arbitary control of an irresponsible trades union" (Lens, 25).

Although you must include within quotation marks the author's words exactly as they appear in the source, you can modify a quotation if you meticulously indicate with ellipses where you have left words out and with brackets ([]) where you have interpolated words or punctuation. Ellipses indicate omissions by the use of spaced dots, three for internal omissions, four for omission at the end of a sentence. For example, you might want to smooth the inclusion of a quotation in your paper by changing the syntax slightly. In the example below, a verb becomes a verbal to avoid a comma splice, and the quotation is shortened to include only the points most important for the writer's purpose:

> Life went on much as it had for centuries, "Hundreds of families [rising] in the morning to breakfast on a crust of bread and a glass of water....Day after day, men, women, and children went to adjoining woods to dig roots...to keep body and soul together...." (Roy 93)

The author's original intent must never be changed by any addition or deletion. For instance, it would be intellectually dishonest to change Rayback's original intent by converting *either* and *or* to *neither* and *nor*, even if the change were scrupulously acknowledged:

Intellectually dishonest

> "The 'members' who testified as to the purposes of the order were [n]either Pinkerton detectives [n]or criminals who had joined the order after 1875."

You should keep direct quotations to a minimum, both in number and extent. Generally, you should not use more than a couple of long, inset quotations, even in a 3,000 word paper. When you do use long quotations (more than four lines), indent the quotation ten spaces from the left margin (MLA style) and double-space it. You ordinarily introduce such quotations with a colon or a comma.

DOCUMENTATION

In-text citations and bibliographies provide a set procedure for crediting your sources, telling readers exactly where you obtained information on your subject. In order to simplify and standardize the process of documentation, most writers use one of two established forms, either the form in the newest *MLA* (Modern Language Association) *Handbook* or that in the *Publication Manual of the American Psychological Association,* Third Edition (1983). The writer chooses the one that better serves his or her purpose—or that the instructor assigns. Writers in the humanities generally follow MLA style, whereas those in the sciences use a variety of discipline-specific styles. In the social sciences, psychologists, of course, follow APA style and writers in education, sociology, political science, home economics, linguistics, and physical education use the variations of APA style corresponding to the practices of the leading journals in those fields. Writers in the fine arts, history, and philosophy use a footnote or endnote system which follows the recommendations found in the *Chicago Manual of Style,* 14th ed., 1994.[1] After determining which one you are using (or are required to use) you should use it consistently throughout. This book uses the latest MLA in-text style. As pointed out in the section on plagiarism (pages 532–533), you should document all information you have taken from sources, whether summarized, paraphrased, or quoted.

In-Text Notes

The MLA in-text system is very simple. You give the reference within parentheses immediately following the material you are quoting or referring to. You include only the author's last name and the appropriate page number, without the indication p., pp., or pg. If you mention the author's name in the text, you leave it out of the reference. If you are using more than one work by an author, you also include an abbreviated title of the work you are documenting. You will find plentiful examples of these parenthetical references in this book.

> Thomas Brooks (1964), a labor historian, thinks the terrorist faction formed when attempts to unionize the Irish miners failed. (48)

APA style, also a version of in-text citation, differs only slightly from MLA style. Instead of simply using the author's name and the page number, you cite the author's name, the date of the publication, and the page number preceded by p. or pp. The three items are separated by commas and enclosed in parentheses. An APA citation never uses the title. Like the MLA style, APA style omits the author's name if it is mentioned in the text of the paper, retaining only the date and the page number.

> According to the newspapers, the victims of these crimes were usually foremen and officials, and only mine owners' property was destroyed. (Rayback, 1959, p. 132)

> According to his reasoning, he had to keep the railroad "from the arbitrary control of an irresponsible trades union." (Lens, 1973, p. 25)

---

[1] The *Chicago Manual* acknowledges the difficulties footnotes present and recommends them with reservation: "When the publisher and the author, aware of the costs and the technical hazards, have agreed on the use of footnotes, the author can minimize the problems that will arise in page makeup by limiting both the number of footnotes per page and the length of individual notes" (410).

Labor historian Sidney Lens (1973) wrote of the faction, "Without a union to absorb their pain and relieve their fury, a few zealots took to terror." (p. 17)

Roy (1907) has noted the following:

Hundreds of families rose in the morning to breakfast on a crust of bread and a glass of water. . . . Day after day, men, women, and children went to adjoining woods to dig roots . . . to keep body and soul together. (p. 93)

Footnotes and Endnotes

You may use notes for explanations and additional comments you wish to include, but that would interrupt the continuity of thought in the text. Indicate these notes with consecutive superscript numbers in the text. Place the notes themselves, also indicated by superscript numbers, either at the bottom of the pages on which they are mentioned or all together at the end of the chapter or paper.

Final Bibliography

Both the MLA and the APA systems require that you list all of the works you have cited in the text in a cumulative bibliography at the end of the paper. They differ slightly as to the title of the list and the form of the listings. MLA calls this list "Works Cited," whereas APA calls it "References."

In MLA style, Works Cited lists all references alphabetically by author's last name. Alphabetize a work with more than one author according to the first author's surname. If you list more than one work by a single author, order these alphabetically *according to the title of the work* and replace the author's name with three hyphens followed by a period (---.). Alphabetize anonymous works according to the title. Indent the second and subsequent lines of all references and double-space throughout.

In APA style, References also lists all works alphabetically by author's last name. Again if a work has more than one author, alphabetize by the first author's surname. However, if the first author has participated in several works with different co-authors, alphabetize the work *first by the first author's surname and then by the second author's surname.* If you list more than one work by a single author or group of authors, arrange them according to *date of publication,* oldest first. Alphabetize anonymous publications by title unless the work identifies the author as anonymous. If it does, *and only if,* use "Anonymous" in place of the author's name. APA style also requires that the volume number of a journal be italicized.

Examples of listings for both MLA and APA style follow.

MLA Style
Book—single author
Moi, Toril. *Sexual/Textual Politics: Feminist Literary Theory.* London: Methuen, 1985.
Book with two authors
Wellek, Rene, and Austin Warren. *Theory of Literature.* New York: Harcourt, 1949.
Book with three authors
Samuel, Raphael, Ewan MacColl, and Stuart Cosgrove. *Theatres of the Left 1880-1935: Worker's Theatre Movements in Britain and America.* London: Routledge, 1985.

Book with more than three authors
Britton, James, et al. *The Development of Writing Abilities (11–18)*. Schools Council Research Studies. London: Macmillan, 1975.

Work of more than one volume
Poe, Edgar Allan. *Collected Works of Edgar Allan Poe*. Ed. Thomas Ollive Mabbott. 3 vols. Cambridge, MA: Belknap-Harvard UP, 1969–1978.

Edition of another author's work
Blake, William. *Selected Poetry and Prose of William Blake*. Ed. Northrop Frye. New York: Modern Library-Random, 1953.

Edited collection or anthology
Redmond, James, ed. *Drama, Sex, and Politics*. Cambridge: Cambridge UP, 1985.

Translation
Schopenhauer, Arthur. *The Wisdom of Life and Other Essays*. Trans. Bailey Saunders and Ernest Belfort Box. New York: Dunne, 1901.

Reprint
Anderson, Ruth Leila. *Elizabethan Psychology and Shakespeare's Plays*. 1927. New York: Russell, 1966.

Geffen, Arthur. "Profane Time, Sacred Time, and Confederate Time in *The Sound and the Fury*." *Studies in American Fiction 2* (1974). Rpt. in Arthur F. Kinney, ed. *Critical Essays on William Faulkner: The Compson Family*. Boston: Hall, 1982. 249–257.

Pamphlet
United States. National Endowment for the Humanities. *Science, Technology & Human Values*. Washington: GPO, [1979].

Essay in an edited collection
Kahrl, Stanley. "Secular Life and Popular Piety in Medieval English Drama." In Thomas J. Heffernan, ed. *The Popular Literature of Medieval England*. Knoxville: U of Tennessee P, 1985. 85–107.

Article in encyclopedia
R[oberts], S[idney (Castle)], [Sir], and J[ames] L[owrey] Cl[ifford]. "Samuel Johnson." *Encyclopaedia Britannica: Macropaedia*. 1974 ed.

Article in journal with continuous pagination
Briscoe, Marianne G. "Some Clerical Notions of Dramatic Decorum in Late Medieval England." *Comparative Drama* 19 (1985): 1–13.

Article in journal with separate pagination
Flores, Lauro. "Narrative Strategies in Rolando Hinojosa's *Rites and Witnesses*." *Revista Chicano-Riquena* 12. 3–4 (1984): 170, 179.

Magazine article—weekly
Henry, William A., III. "Reliving a Poignant Past: Neil Simon's Best Comedy Looks Homeward." *Time* 15 Dec. 1986: 72–78.

Magazine article—monthly
Percy, Walker. "The Diagnostic Novel: On the Uses of Modern Fiction." *Harper's* June 1986: 39–45.

Unsigned magazine article
"Faculty Leaders: A Salute." *Change* July/Aug. 1986: 33–36.

Newspaper article
Harmetz, Aljean. "How Some Films Combine Bad Reviews and Good Money." *New York Times* 27 June 1987, sec A:9.

APA Style
Book—single author
Aronson, E. (1972). *The social animal.* San Francisco: Freeman.
Book with two authors
Woods, M.L. & Moe, A.J. (1981). *Analytical reading inventory* (2d ed.). Columbus: Merrill.
Book with three authors
Beck, F., Moffat, D. B., & Lloyd, J. B. (1973). *Human embryology and genetics.* Oxford: Blackwell Scientific.
Book with more than three authors
Blake, R. R., Mouton, J. S., Tomaino, L., & Gutierrez, S. (1979). *The social worker grid.* Springfield, IL: Charles C. Thomas.
Work of more than 1 volume
Modgil, C. & Modgil, S. (Eds.). (1976–1983). *Piagetan research: Compilation and commentary* (Vols. 1-8). Windsor, Ont.: NFER.
Edited collection or anthology
Germain, C. (1970). Casework and science: A historical encounter. In R. Roberts & R. Nee (Eds.), *Theories of social casework* (pp. 3–32). Chicago: University of Chicago Press.
Translation
Piaget, J. (1980). *Adaptation and intelligence* (S. Eames, Trans.). Chicago: University of Chicago Press.
Reprint
Jung, C. G. (1984). *Dream analysis: Notes of the seminar given in 1928–1930.* Ed. William McGuire. Princeton: Princeton University Press. (Original work published 1938.)
Pamphlet
American Public Welfare Assn., Dept. Health, Education, & Welfare. (1979). *Standards for foster family services systems for public agencies.* Washington, DC: U.S. Government Printing Office.
Essay in edited collection
Germain, C. (1970). Casework and science: A historical encounter. In R. Roberts & R. Nee (Eds.), *Theories of social casework.* Chicago: University of Chicago Press.
Article in journal with continuous pagination
Secord, P. & Beckman, C. (1964). "Interpersonal congruency, perceived similarity, and friendship." *Sociometry, 27,* 111–127.
Article in journal with separate pagination
Kassam, Yusuf. (1986). Adult education, development and international aid: Some issues and trends. *Convergence, 19*(3), 1–11.
Magazine article—weekly
Wolff, A. (1986, Nov. 19). The recruiting file. *Sports Illustrated,* pp. 32–41.

Magazine article—monthly
Neugarten, B. & Neugarten, D. A. (1987, May) The changing meaning of age. *Psychology Today,* pp. 29–33.
Unsigned magazine article
CD-ROM starter kit geared to libraries. (1986, September). *T.H.E. Journal,* p. 109.
Newspaper article
McGinley, L. (1987, July 3) Flash point: Airline officials clash with FAA on fire-safety proposal. *The Wall Street Journal,* p. 11.

EXERCISES

1. Prepare a bibliography of general references you would consult in order to write a short essay (500–750 words) on one of the following topics:

   Why the Taj Mahal Was Built
   A Brief of the Alligator
   Four Types of American Prisons
   Carrie Nation: A Character Study
   The Facts About Smoking
   The Function of the Pituitary Gland
   The Present Status of Pop Art
   What Is Propaganda?
   The Poverty Program: Then and Now
   A Critical Estimate of Edward Albee

2. Compile a bibliography of eight to twelve reference works you would consult in preparation for writing a term paper on one of the following:
   a. The Case Against (or for) Capital Punishment
   b. A Critical Estimate of Tennessee Williams
   c. Hiroshima in Retrospect (an analysis and evaluation of causes and consequences)
   d. The Lincoln and Kennedy Assassinations: A Comparative Study

3. Take notes on the following essays (see the Contents in this text), treating them as if they were source materials for a paper you are writing on a related subject:

   Jonathan Spence, "The Earthquake"
   David Randolph, "Five Basic Elements of Music"
   George Stade, "Football—The Game of Aggression"
   I. Bernard Cohen, "Isaac Newton"

EXTENDED HISTORICAL PROCESS ANALYSIS

In tracing the development of the nineteenth-century labor movement, named for a widowed Irish tenant farmer, Molly Maguire, the student who wrote the term paper below followed the lines of process analysis—an orderly, chronologically organized account of an historical event. Note how judiciously the writer separates fact from speculation, document-ing her materials by citing authorities, historians, and published reports to support opposing views. Consider how she maintains distance and objectivity throughout. The subject remains controversial, she concludes, indicating that even today we cannot be certain "whether the Mollies were actually a terrorist group" or simply a secret society. What is incontrovertible is that the Mollie Maguires exerted a powerful and memorable influence on the labor movement in the United States. (Note the use of the new Modern Language Association documentation style.)

THE MOLLIE MAGUIRE MOVEMENT

Melody Rammel

In nineteenth-century Ireland, tenant farmers worked on estates owned by absentee landlords living in England and managed by on-site agents. Tenant farmers, kept at a level of near-poverty, were regarded by the agents as the dregs of society and treated as such. These farmers were so impoverished that they were frequently evicted for nonpayment of rent. [1]

By the middle 1800s, the farmers' animosity toward the landlords and agents reached the boiling point. The most popular explanation of the movement's origin is that Molly Maguire, a widowed tenant farmer, organized a movement to resist the rent system and to run the English ruling party out of Ireland. Her followers, adopting the name "Mollie Maguires," formed a secret society. Dressing up as women, they would launch surprise attacks on land agents which often escalated into violent beatings and even murders (Adamic 12; Roy 93; "Molly Maguires" 678). [2]

Eventually, the Mollie Maguires had control of entire counties. The landlords used their political connections to force the authorities into action. Alleged Mollie Maguire members were rounded up, tried, convicted and sentenced to harsh punishment. Suffering under these pressures and hoping to escape their poverty, many Irish farmers emigrated to America in the middle and late 1800s. [3]

The new settlers concentrated in the mining areas of Pennsylvania where work was plentiful and there were enough of their countrymen to carry on Irish traditions. Here they established a benevolent secret society, the Ancient Order of Hibernians, which was officially chartered in Pennsylvania in 1871 as a group to promote friendship, unity and Christian charity among members (Rayback 132). The primary focus of the organization was to maintain a charity fund to support the aged, sick, and infirm. In order to become a member, a person had to be Irish or of Irish descent, a good Roman Catholic, and of good moral character. The Hibernians' constitution read in part, "The Supreme Being has implanted in our natures tender sympathies and most humane feelings toward our fellow-creatures in distress; and all the happiness that human nature is capable of enjoying must flow from and terminate in the love of God and our fellows" (Adamic 13). [4]

The miners, most of whom were Irish, soon found that their economic and societal status was not changed by their migration. For the most part, they were Roman Catholic, while the mine bosses were almost all English or Welsh Protestants. In America, as in their homeland, they were considered the lowest of social classes. [5]

As the miners' disillusionment increased, a small terrorist faction broke off from the Hibernians. Adopting the violent methods and the name of the Mollie [6]

Maguires, its intent was to run the Welsh and English miners, mine bosses, and police out of the district ("Molly Maguires" 678). Thomas Brooks, a labor historian, thinks the terrorist faction formed when attempts to unionize the Irish miners failed. With the defeat of unionism, Brooks writes, "the young Irish hotheads in the Mollies turned to derailing mine cars and burning breakers. Then they took to the hills to snipe at mine supers and unpopular foremen" (48). Years after the Mollie movement ended, on the eve of a trial of I.W.W. members, President Theodore Roosevelt said, "I think that the Western Federation of Miners is a body just like the Molly Maguires of Pennsylvania. That there are a number of good, honest and stupid men in the ranks I have no doubt, just as I have no doubt that this was true of the Molly Maguires; but the moving spirit is to be described as representing 'a revolt against economic and social injustice' only in the sense that we thus describe a band of road agents who rob a coach" (qtd. in Foner 11). Labor historian Sidney Lens wrote to the faction, "Without a union to absorb their pain and relieve their fury, a few zealots took to terror" (Lens 17).

The Mollies numbered about 450 at the height of their power in the 1870s. They regarded themselves as superior to other foreigners in the district and demanded the easiest jobs in the mines. According to Louis Adamic's account of class violence in America, if a foreman refused their demands, he would probably die a violent death. Mine bosses who would not hire Irishmen were also murdered (14). [7]

Adamic also reports that a Mollie member could order death for a mine boss by filing a complaint with the proper committee, which would then vote on the proposed assassination. Once approved, the committee would assign two or more Mollie members from another area to carry it out. If a member refused to carry out a death order, he himself would be killed by fellow members (16). [8]

Thus the name "Mollie Maguires" became a synonym for terror. People in the mining districts would not leave their homes after dark, and they would go forth during the daylight hours only if armed. In January 1877, the American Law Review observed in an article about the coal regions of Pennsylvania: "From their dark and mysterious regions there came forth to the outside world an appalling series of tales of murder, arson, and violent crime of every description" (qtd. in Adamic 14). The Miners' Journal reported 63 unsolved murders in the Eastern Pennsylvania coal region between January 1860 and April 1867 (qtd. in Lens 16). [9]

Several Mollie leaders also headed the Miners' and Laborers' Benevolent Association, a group which organized the Long Strike of 1875. Pent-up bitter feelings turned the strike into a bloody labor war with the Mollie members and strikebreakers hired by the railroad and mine owners on the front lines. Miners who tried to return to work were threatened with murder by Mollie members. Such threats were not new to strikers. A laborer in 1853 had written in the London Times about his fear of being a "marked man" if he crossed the picket line (Ford 283). Strikebreakers who dared to cross the Mollie picket lines were beaten to death (Adamic 13; Lens 24). [10]

Franklin Benjamin Gowen, an ambitious young Irish attorney, was the head of the Legal Department of the Reading Railroad, the largest transporter of coal in the area, and therefore the main target of the Mollies' vandalism. Gowen, an antiunion ex-district attorney, became president of the railroad just before the start of the Long Strike. Gowen later admitted to spending four million dollars of the railroad's money to break the Long Strike. According to his reasoning, he had to keep the railroad "from the arbitrary control of an irresponsible trades union" (qtd. in Lens 23). Even so, [11] during one seven-month period, Gowen recorded 92 incidents of arson, derailed trains, assaults, threats, and murders (qtd. in Lens 25).

Some observers, like Sidney Lens, believe that "many if not most of these illegal acts were instigated by the operators and perpetrated by their agents" (25). During the Long Strike, Edward Coyle, a union head and Hibernian leader, was found murdered on Reading Railroad property. A mine boss killed another Hibernian member. A mine foreman shot at random into a crowd of strikers. None of these people were ever convicted (24). Lens is not the only historian who feels that Gowen himself had much to do with the violence during the Long Strike. "Gowen appeared to realize that violence connected with the strike could be meshed with the violence long attributed to the Molly Maguires," Wayne G. Broehl, Jr., writes, "and the two tied up into a neat package for clubbing all union activities under the guise of preserving law and order" (qtd. in Lens 24). [12]

The Long Strike actually lasted only five to seven months, after which the miners were forced to give in because their families were dying (Lens 24). Former miner Andrew Roy described the Mollie families: [13]

> Hundreds of families rose in the morning to breakfast on a crust of bread and a glass of water, who did not know where a bite of dinner was to come from. Day after day, men, women and children went to adjoining woods to dig roots and pick up herbs to keep body and soul together, and still the strike went on. The end came in the unconditional surrender of the miners. The force of nature could no further go (93).

Even after the strike ended the violence went on. Riots broke out and the murders, assaults, robberies and arson continued. According to the newspapers, the victims of these crimes were usually foremen and officials, and only mine owners' property was destroyed (Rayback 132). [14]

During the strike, Frank Gowen had contacted the Pinkerton Detective Agency for help in destroying the Mollie organization. Allan Pinkerton sent a young detective named James McParlan to do the job. McParlan, a young Irish-Catholic immigrant, was a gregarious, red-headed tenor who could dance a jig and hold his own in a drinking contest or barroom brawl. His work-background included stints as a factory laborer, teamster, wood-chopper, coachman and policeman. McParlan was probably America's first labor spy (Brooks 48-49). Using the alias "James McKenna" he went into the mine district disguised as a tramp, a recent immigrant from Ireland, and a member of the Irish Mollies. Establishing his new identity in a hotel in Pottsville that was owned by a reputed Mollie member, "McKenna" made his appearance memorable by hard drinking, dancing and singing a Mollie ballad well-known in the homeland. The Mollies accepted him as one of their own group and he distinguished himself as a leader in many of their violent acts. In fact "McKenna" was soon elected secretary of his district, primarily on his reputation as a proponent of violence and terrorism. After three years of Mollie membership, McParlan's true identity was discovered and he had to leave the coal fields on the run. His almost daily letter reports to the Pinkerton headquarters proved to be enough to undermine the entire Mollie organization (Roy 94; Lens 11). [15]

In late 1875 and early 1876 the Mollie members arrested during the Long Strike were brought to trial. McParlan and other Pinkerton operatives gave most of the [16] testimony leading to conviction. It was corroborated by Mollie Maguire members (also on the Pinkerton/Gowen payroll) who turned state's evidence in exchange for immunity from prosecution (Adamic 19). McParlan's "evidence" led to the arrest of 70 Mollie members, 12 convictions of first degree murder, four of second degree murder, four of accessory murder and six of perjury (Roy 94). Gowen, a former district attorney, took an active role in the trials as a prosecutor.

The Mollie members who had received immunity testified that the purpose [17] of the group was to get members elected to public offices that handled money. They also said that there were 6,000 Mollie lodges in the United States and that the organization was "criminal in character." Historian Joseph Rayback commented, "The 'members' who testified as to the purposes of the order were either Pinkerton detectives or criminals who had joined the order after 1875" (132). The rest of the testimony was also faulty and contradictory. At one point, a witness testified that he saw a union head (and Mollie member) kill a mine boss. When the accused man stood up, however, the witness testified that it was not the person he saw commit the murder. Incredibly, the falsely accused man was convicted and executed (Lens 28).

Some historians have characterized the Mollie Maguire trials as witch hunts [18] which served the purpose of the mine owners. On June 21, 1877, Pennsylvania had a "Day With a Rope." Two thousand people watched the hanging of six men on a double gallows near Pottsville. All of the men were members of the Ancient Order of Hibernians. Four other Hibernian members were hanged at Mauch Chunk on the same date. During the rest of the year, seven more Mollies were executed at scattered sites in the state. Even as late as January 1879, two men were hanged for their alleged roles as Mollies during the Long Strike (Lens 9-10).

The Mollie trials and executions changed the nation's image of the labor union [19] movement. As the organization came to an end, the country had a picture of miners as murderers, arsonists, and rioters (Rayback 37; Foner 41). The nation's newspapers celebrated the end of the movement. On May 9, 1876, the Pittsburgh Gazette wrote, "The Mollie Maguires represented the spirit of French Communism and enforced their views by secret murders. The principle involved was simply that of permitting them to dictate the operations of labor. Their men were to be employed, their prices admitted and their directions obeyed. . . ." Lens comments, "Plainly and simply, the miners were guilty of wanting a union" (25).

The day following the "Day With a Rope," news media applauded the executions: [20]

The Chicago Tribune: "A Triumph of Law and Justice"
The Philadelphia Times: "Justice at Last"
The Miners' Journal (published by mine owners): "What did they do? Whenever prices of labor did not suit them they organized and proclaimed a strike" (qtd. in Lens 10).
The New York Commercial and Financial Chronicle: "Labor is under control for the first time since the war." (The war referred to was the Long Strike.) (qtd. in Rayback 133)

Labor authorities and historians have never agreed on whether the Mollies were [21] actually a terrorist group. Andrew Roy, mining geologist and ex-chief mine inspector in Ohio, wrote of the Mollies in 1907, "The anthracite region had been infested for several years by a desperate class of men, banded together in secret, oath-bound association, known as the Mollie Maguires. Murder inspired these wicked men. They met in secret places and, under the influence of intoxicating liquor, planned incendiarism and murder" (12). Many others hold the opposing view. On June 30, 1877, the Irish World, a nationalist paper, claimed that the trials and executions were a set-up. The paper said the coal mine owners had invented and popularized the myth of the Mollies because they "found it necessary to frighten the country with a bugbear" (qtd. in Lens 11). Labor historian Joseph Rayback agrees with this opinion and writes that, except for the trial testimony, there was no evidence of a large, widespread number of Mollie lodges or of Mollie political involvement. He also writes that the violence in the mine fields did not begin until after the railroad brought the Pinkerton detectives into the fields. According to Rayback, many of the victims were union leaders and ordinary miners. Rayback concludes that "the Mollies were a figment of Pinkerton's and coal operators' imagination": they were invented to destroy unionism (132-133). Another historian, Herbert Harris, believes that the Mollies and Hibernians were a harmless secret fraternal order (Lens 12).

Sidney Lens thinks the Mollies were set up by the coal mine owners. "All that is certain," he maintains, "is that the men referred to as Molly Maguires were Irish, were members of the Ancient Order of Hibernians, were miners or sympathizers, and were participants in the strikes. Doubtless they engaged in violence, but they were as frequently the victims as the victimizers" (12). Philip Foner, author of a multivolume history of the American labor movement, writes that the Pennsylvania miners were "railroaded to the gallows, trade unionism in the anthracite regions [was] set back for many years, and the cause of organized labor throughout the country injured" (41). [22]

The passage of time has not settled the argument or lessened the Mollies' fame in labor circles. Whether they were terrorists or family men desperately trying to secure a decent wage and better working conditions, the Mollies changed the course of labor history by their very existence. Years after the movement, Eugene V. Debs, the radical labor leader, wrote of the Mollies, ". . . they were the neglected children of poverty, the product of a wretched environment. The men who perished upon the scaffold as felons were labor leaders, the first martyrs to the class struggle in the United States" (qtd. in Adamic 20). [23]

Works Cited

Adamic, Louis. Dynamite: The Story of Class Violence in America. Gloucester: Peter Smith, 1963.

Brooks, Thomas R. Toil and Trouble: A History of American Labor. New York: Delacorte, 1964.

Foner, Philip S. History of the Labor Movement in the United States. 4 vols. Vol. 4. New York: International Publishers, 1965.

Lens, Sidney. The Labor Wars. New York: Doubleday, 1973.

"Molly Maguires." Encyclopaedia Britannica, 1976.

Rayback, Joseph G. A History of American Labor. New York: Macmillan, 1959.

Roy, Andrew. A History of the Coal Miners of the United States. Columbus: J. L. Trauger Printing Co., 1907.

DISCUSSION AND EXERCISES

1. Indicate how many of the twenty questions the writer has called upon to develop her "process analysis."

2. How did the Mollie Maguire movement originate? When were the insurgents at the height of their power? Characterize the movement at that point.

3. Describe The Long Strike. How does the writer depict its impact on the miners and their families in day-to-day living? What was the outcome of the strike?

4. How do historians characterize the Mollie Maguire trials? What was the impact on the Labor Movement? What was the attitude of the nation's newspapers?

5. Characterize tone and point of view. Does the writer take sides? Do you get the impression that she is for or against the Mollie Maguire Movement?

6. The writer of this term paper draws heavily on factual data such as statistics and dates. How does she keep the piece from being dry or dull and lifeless?

7. How do the first and final paragraphs work together? Characterize the concluding quotation in terms of its tone, meaning, and effectiveness as a final statement and unifying device.

ESSAY SUGGESTIONS

1. Suggested writing topic: The Women's Suffrage Movement in the United States (1848–1920) (2,500–3,500 words).

   Trace the development of this early wave of the contemporary women's liberation movement. Begin with the first women's suffrage convention held in Seneca Falls, New York, in 1848, citing proponents and opponents of the movement, prominent crusaders, and early successes (in 1869 the territory of Wyoming was the first in the nation's history to grant women the right to vote). Develop your historical analysis further by showing how other states followed suit and how World War I contributed to the ultimate passage in 1920 of the Nineteenth Amendment to the Constitution. Bring the analysis up to date by assessing the impact of this movement on our own time.

   For a discussion of research procedures and library resources, read the section titled Gathering Information.

2. Additional topics for an extended historical analysis (2,500–3,500 words) include the following:
   a. The Women's Liberation Movement of our time (1960s to the present)
   b. The Abolitionist Movement of the 1800s (to abolish slavery)
   c. Prohibition (from the organization of the Prohibition Party in 1869 to the repeal of the Eighteenth Amendment in 1932)
   d. The Civil Rights Movement of the 1960s

> e. Any other self-contained educational, social, or political movement in American history or in the history of a foreign nation with which you are familiar (for example, the rise of the Nazi party in Germany in the 1930s)

EXTENDED CAUSAL EXPLANATION

In explaining the effects of economic conditions on Ireland's cultural identity, Matthew Rindfleisch, the author of the research paper below, followed the lines of causal explanation—an informal but not exhaustive approach to causal analysis. Notice how he brings together information from a variety of sources (including his own personal experiences in Ireland) to support his explanation of economic forces that shape the debate over Ireland's past, present, and future. (Note also the use of American Psychological Association documentation style, a form of citation common in the social sciences.)

IRELAND: WHEN ECONOMIC AND CULTURAL AGENDAS CLASH

Matthew Rindfleisch

Within the Irish community, there has currently been a great deal of debate over the classical cultural lines that have dominated the community's thinking for decades, indeed centuries. It has come to light that John Majors, the present prime minister of the United Kingdom, has been privately negotiating with the Irish Republican Army (I.R.A.) and Northern Ireland. It has also been revealed that the European Community (E.C.) has tried to build financial packages that treat Northern and Southern Ireland as a single region for aid rather than as separate ones. And, Southern Ireland continues to consider removing the legal precedence that the Catholic Church holds in its constitution.

Perhaps, what is most remarkable about the situation of the "Irish Question" is the economic impetus for "resolution" to it. One would think that the culturally reinforced models of Ireland vs. Great Britain, Southern Ireland vs. Northern Ireland, and Ireland vs. Europe would have been bigger obstacles on the political scene than they have been. But, it really comes as no surprise when considering the whole of Irish economic history. Time and time again, these cultural lines have been reamalgamated in the global economic furnace. And, in turn, Ireland's identity has been trimmed by outside economic influences and grafted with outside cultural influences.

The question arises, then, whether on the dawn of this—to continue the metaphor—new pruning of and grafting to the Irish nation can be tolerated without killing it. Can Ireland survive as an economic means and cultural means unto itself? It is not being asked if Ireland can survive as an isolated social entity; it is being asked if Ireland can maintain enough of its identity to preserve a sense of Irishness. As will be revealed in the analysis, Ireland has the potential of becoming a sort of economic crossroads for the E.C. and the U.S. but at the same time risks being overrun culturally by them; what remains of Irish culture gets trod underfoot.

It is good then to enquire into the path of Ireland's cultural lines from an economic standpoint. It is also good to question the influence of these lines on the sense of Irishness that remains. From these questions, it is hoped to obtain a clear sketch of the economic drives in Ireland's past that resulted in cultural fallouts, such as the "Irish Question," from perspectives both within the Irish community (Northern and Southern Ireland) and from outside of the Irish Community (Europe, America, and, more specifically, Great Britain).

Let us begin at the time when one of the first lines was made: that between the North and the South. Its roots can be traced all the way back to 1699 when the export of woolen goods from Ireland was prohibited from entering the English market. Munck (1993) summarizes the reason for the prohibition:

> England was now entering a period of mercantilism which preceded capitalism and was based on the country's strong navy and the exploitation through trade of other economies, such as the Irish one. For mercantilism to be effective as a replacement for direct plunder, it was necessary to restrict production in the periphery, for example, Ireland. (p. 6)

This restriction led necessarily to England generating its own wool supply. Sheep farming became a federally aided market. And when sheep farmers began to invade the lands of the Scottish and English farmers, these same Scottish and English farmers, who happened to be Protestant, began to emigrate to the prosperous county of Ulster. Thus, the seeds of religious partition in Ireland were sown.

Wool was not the only commodity restricted; cattle (in 1663), glass manufacturing (1670), and brewing (1670) were also hampered with prohibitive duties. This might lead one to think of Ireland's economic development as nefariously stunted by English intervention. But, at the same time, linen exports were hitting all time highs (23,000 yards in 1683 and 520,000 yards in 1705). Ireland's population was booming at two and a half million. The problem, as will be discussed more fully later in a modern context, was that the only development that was encouraged in Ireland was dependent development, i.e. development in business firms that essentially catered to foreign interests. This form of development would continue to thrive and plague Ireland's economic status up to and including the modern era.

What cemented this dependency was the Act of Union of Britain and Ireland (1800) in which British economic and legal regulation of Ireland became formalized. Until this time, during the 1700s, Ireland was reciprocating the Industrial Revolution in England and enjoying one of its more expansive centuries. Its linen and spinning industries were becoming mechanized, making Belfast the flagship of the Irish economy. Potatoes had arrived onto the Irish farm market and Irish nationalism was at a high. Ireland was achieving status as an export power. However, Ireland's economic dependency on England was also at a high. Eighty five percent of Irish exports headed for England in 1800.

Why the Act of Union was significant to dependent development can be seen through its indoctrination of Irish and British economic unification. At this time, England was the most advanced industrial economy in the world. The act of economic unification retarded the industrial movement in Ireland, as O'Malley (1989) explains:

> Unprotected industries generally could not develop smoothly from relatively small beginnings on the eve of, or after, the start of mechanisation

elsewhere, into successful large scale producers. Rather, only the few largest, most favoured regional centres of an industry at the time when mechanisation got under way were able to develop successfully, disposing of lesser competitors as they did so. (p. 40)

In other words, the overwhelming scale of England's industry wiped out Irish firms that were not big enough. Munck goes further: "The free operation of market forces meant death or emigration for a whole layer of the population and effectively blocked the development of a balanced, integrated and dynamic national economy" (p. 18). Thus, the few remaining industrial firms in Ireland were linen and shipbuilding (and, amusingly, tea-drying equipment by Davidson and Co), firms that were large enough and unique enough to survive in free market conditions. It was not until Irish independence—and thereby another cultural line—that Irish industrial development for the sake of its own economy would be renewed. As Marx (1971) observed, "Every time Ireland was about to develop industrially, she was crushed and reconverted into a purely agricultural land" (p. 132).

An important aside for Ireland's culture that became more apparent and crystallized during the time of Irish independence was that of religion. While during this period it bore no economical onus, religion is now, if anything, the key cultural factor in the Irish identity consequently influencing modern economic policy, and thereby merits analysis in its formation as such.

Ireland grew up nationally in many ways with Catholicism both as its ally and mentor. Ireland came to be allies with Catholicism through the Penal Laws of the late seventeenth century. These laws, essentially, set out to eliminate the Catholic Church and impart authority to the established church of Anglicanism. Instead, they made Catholicism into an underdog and a hero. In fact, one of the bans instituted by the Penal Codes was specifically economic in scope. Irish Catholics were disallowed from inheriting a farm intact: it had to be divided between all the male children. Thus, Catholic land ownership fell from 90 percent in 1600 to 14 percent in 1703 to 5 percent in 1770 (Rossiter, 1992 p. 80).

The Church went on to support the Irish political movement through such groups as David O'Connell's Catholic Association (1823). These groups concentrated on the repeal of the Act of Union, and, in turn, painted the Church in the role of political advocate. This sculpted a relatively different mold for the Catholic Church of Ireland from that of its European counterparts who had been politically linked with a feudalistic and aristocratic frame of mind.

The Catholic Church strengthened its hold over the Irish mind during the Great Famine during 1845-49. While the English mismanaged the ample food supplies of the country, the Church created an avenue of devotional relief for the poor by offering vocations, i.e. a way out of starvation for the overly numerous families. The Catholic Church continued to dampen population booms, as Rossiter points out:

The Church came to play a major socioeconomic role in the Irish peasantry's drive to reduce population growth. The custom of subdivision of land in pre-famine years was ended, and single inheritance became the norm. Late marriage for those lucky enough to inherit or receive a dowry was universal, and the remaining siblings either remained celibate or emigrated. The Church's role in the policing of sexuality and the creation of a strict puritanical climate was essential in this enterprise. (p. 81)

Thus, the Church's holy men and women more than tripled in number during this time and established a regime that was large and thriving during 1921.

What happened during the partition of Ireland was the solidification of a cultural line that had already been traced in the religious landscape. Indeed, it could be said that the political and religious sentiments fed each other in their respective development. Southern Ireland was largely concentrated with Catholic small-scale farming, and the manufacturing places of Ulster and the other five counties remained Protestant—quite economically considering their dependence on Britain's investment and market.

The political arena reciprocated this division with leaders and policies that matched the religions of the regions they represented. James Craig, the first Prime Minister of the Northern State, set to create "a Protestant state for a Protestant people" (Rossiter, p. 81). Southern Ireland legislated a large number of moral codes that ranged from literature and film to contraception and divorce (Censorship of Films Act, 1923; Censorship of Publications Act, 1935; and Criminal Law Act (contraception), 1935).

This partition or "independence" of 1922 was obviously significant for the cultural aspects of religion and politics and, of course, had economic precedents and created future economic ramifications. Henceforward, the economic analysis of Ireland would be split in two: one devoted to the South and another to the North. This transformation should be noted as radically jarring, for dependent development had grown deeply and, if not extricated, at least needed to be contained.

The fundamental change from a region in the U.K. to an independent state had a debilitating economic effect on Southern Ireland that is clearly seen from an industrial perspective. Kennedy, Giblin, and McHugh (1988) state:

> Despite the great rural exodus, however, the population of Ireland in the early 1920s remained largely a rural one with only one-third of people living in towns. Why did Ireland not succeed in developing a larger industrial base? It may be pointed out, of course, that if Ireland is viewed not as a separate country, but merely as a region within the United Kingdom—as it was in fact up to 1921—then the failure to develop a stronger industrial base appears less unusual. Among the larger European countries, regions as big as Ireland remained industrially underdeveloped. (p. 8)

The problem here is that Ireland was becoming a separate country. Otherwise, this would be perfectly adequate if not for the Irish nationalism in the South and the British unionism in the North. Kennedy, Giblin, and McHugh go on to say:

> In the six counties that became Northern Ireland, the share of the labour force in industry, at about 35 per cent, approached the British level, and even within Northern Ireland, industrial activity centered largely in and around Belfast. In the remainder of the country, which was to become the Irish Free State, the industrial labour force was only 13 per cent of the total, a low figure in comparison with any other Western European nation. (p. 8)

It was also extremely poor footing to begin a nation on in the Industrial Era. While this might seem to draw Ireland even deeper into dependent development, Irish nationalism, a cultural force, would steer Ireland's first bouts with economic policy toward protectionism.

Ireland's protectionism began with the election of the Fianna Fail party to office in 1932. This party was devoted to Ireland's self-sufficiency to the point of sacrifice. As Fianna Fail's leader, de Valera (1928), stated, "If the servant was displeased with the kicks of the master and wanted to have his freedom, he had to make up his mind whether or not he was going to have that freedom, and give up the luxuries of a certain kind which are available to him by being in that mansion" (p. 3).

And so, it implemented a policy to provide employment and reduce emigration, but it did not create this protectionist plan for infant industries, which would ultimately be expected to be competitive internationally to garner Ireland's industrial image. Instead, Fianna Fail's policies favored food as Ireland's main export and not industrial goods. The enforcement of these policies was basically accomplished through heavy tariffs on imports, many ranging from 50 to 75 percent, but import licences and quotas (which did help industry too) were deployed as well.

This government then took on the greater task of trying to separate itself economically from Britain in what later became called the Economic War. In 1932, de Valera, in line with his nationalistic philosophies, decided that the land annuities that were still being paid to the British due to the various, still existing Land Acts should remain with the Irish Exchequer. Granted, previously in 1926 Mr. Blythe, the Irish Minister for Finance, and Mr. Churchill, the British Chancellor of the Exchequer, had already explicitly recognized the Irish government's continued obligation to hand over these land annuities in an agreement.

So, riding upon the popularity of its stance on land annuities and the advice of Keynes who said, "Let goods be homespun wherever it is reasonably and conveniently possible, and above all, let finance be primarily national" [Munck, p. 28], the Irish government withheld its first installment of about 2.5 million pounds on July 1, 1932. While this sum was of no great concern, the Great Depression was affecting everyone and the British responded quickly and harshly with a 20—eventually 30—percent duty on the South's agricultural goods being imported to Britain. The Irish government responded in 'self-defense' by imposing duties on British coal, cement, iron goods, and steel goods among others to what wound up covering one-third of the import trade from Britain—a relatively modest reply.

The Economic War would last until 1938 and during this time Fianna Fail took steps that eventually covered industrial goods under the umbrella of self-sufficiency. The Control of Manufactures Act of 1932 ensured that in all new manufacturing companies 51 percent of shares should be in local hands. There was also a considerable extension of state-sponsored bodies in industry with the Industrial Credit Company in 1933; Ceimici Teoranta, a chemical manufacturer, in 1934; Aer Lingus, the Irish airline, in 1936; and the Irish Life Assurance Company and the Irish Tourist Board in 1939.

But Ireland, whose economy essentially was made or broken by the export-import business, surely suffered during this battle. Irish exports suffered a steady loss from 1931 until 1935 with a trade of 36.3 million pounds down to 19.9 million. While import prices also declined, they fell much less after 1931 than export prices, so that the terms of trade deteriorated by more than a quarter between 1931 and 1934, and even by 1938 had recovered only 20 percent of the 1931 level. The volume of imports did not decline nearly as much as the exports, due to the need to purchase machinery to support the new self-sufficient industries.

What ended the Economic War were the 1938 Defence, Financial, and Trade Agreements in which a great deal was done to turn things back to business-as-usual, and yet which was also a profitable venture for the Irish. On the annuities question, the Irish government agreed to pay 10 million pounds in final settlement of all British claims, the estimated value being somewhere between 80 and 100 million pounds. The U.K. agreed to abolish the penal duties imposed during the Economic War. It also re-established commonwealth preferential duties for Ireland. In turn, the Irish agreed to remove the counter-duties also established during the Economic War. So, on the whole, Ireland came out relatively ahead with its primary export purchaser returned and its protective, as opposed to penal, duties on imports intact.

It may seem questionable that Britain was so giving to Ireland in the Agreements, but as Kennedy says:

> Form the British viewpoint, there had been economic losses in the reduction in Irish imports of coal and machinery, but political considerations—in particular its desire to retain Ireland within its sphere of influence—were probably of even greater consequence to Britain. It seemed foolish to Chamberlain, the British Prime Minister, to persist in an economic dispute with its nearest neighbour at a time of crisis in Europe which was likely to culminate in war. (p. 49)

The sentiment was appreciated and it softened the edge upon the cultural line that had hardened during the Thirties. Irish nationalism had proven itself as far as it would go and had essentially failed to redirect trade to another market. If anything, Ireland had validated its dependence, which deepened during the Second World War, and, as Kennedy smartly quips, "had succeeded in changing only the nature but not the fact, of Ireland's dependence on the outside world" (p. 52). Britain, then, provided a bunker of trade during World War II, a time—due to Ireland's chosen neutrality—when isolation and self-sufficiency were enforced.

This view, however, was inverted during the late 1950s with a focus on outward re-orientation. What is meant by outward-looking or outward re-orientation is a stress upon free trade, exports, and foreign goods (O'Malley, 1989, p. 72). It is this view that has set the scale of Ireland's economic view up to the present time.

It most decisively began in 1958 with the election of the Fianna Fail party to leadership. Take note that this was not the party of the 1930s separatists; its party composition had changed to those with the old British-linked commercial interest and those with the new capitalist interest tied to American investment. This was primarily due to the fact that, for the first time, agriculture had lost its role as the main employer of labor in Ireland. This would warp not only political policy but economic and cultural policy as well. The question that would come out of shift in employment is: after centuries of type-cast in the role of the farmer, how well would Ireland do in the role of the industrialist? Indeed, could Ireland even survive in such a role? The Irish responded by looking to the outside for ideas and money to support this role.

From 1958 to 1973 (when Ireland was admitted into the E.C.), Ireland experienced a vast increment of successful trade. The agricultural output increased by 50 percent. Foreign capital was incurred and resulted in an average 23 percent per annum increase in manufactured goods (Munck, p. 32). Industrial output doubled and for once emigration had trickled and, in fact, by 1973 had reversed to a small immigration. Ireland appeared ready to be a full partner in the E.C.

There were costs incurred during this boom that would be accentuated during the recessions of the 1970s and 1980s. One of the largest costs came with the large amount of borrowing that the Irish government did in order to finance large-scale industrial development and to attract foreign firms' interest with tax breaks and incentives. The state became the chief sponsor of investment—nearly 50 percent—for development. When the recessions hit, government spending withdrew and what profit the government drew from development went to its increasing debt in foreign energy. Industrial development was forced to look elsewhere for funding.

By drawing foreign investment, it seemed that many of Ireland's problems were solved, but Ireland's financial dependence only deepened. The problem was that while foreign firms provided tools and jobs, they did not provide profit. Profits were patently invested not in the country where the company's plants stood but back in the company's originating country. It was this system that brought American investment to fifty percent of all foreign investment, but it was a system that was like a form of clear-cutting the forest, and Ireland could not rejuvenate.

What seems as a result of this dependence is that Ireland's culture is necessarily to follow. With U.S. dollars fuelling a great deal of Ireland's industry, one has to wonder what culture this currency brings with itself. As Mary Robinson stated in her address to the Cultures of Ireland Group:

> One notices throughout Ireland a keen preoccupation with the Irish identity, with what it means to be Irish. This has roots in our turbulent past and in the continuing division of the present day. It also stems, however, from the rapid social and economic changes experienced by most Western countries in recent times and from the readjustments dictated by our deepening involvement with our European neighbours. There is a growing recognition that we are living in a world whose contours are changing with breath-taking speed and in which the safe certainties of the past are constantly being challenged. (Longley, 1991, p. 5)

But more importantly, can an economic crossroads, i.e. between the U.S. and Britain, maintain itself?

Recently, in American music and film (Enya and Sinead O'Connor; Far and Away and The Commitments), there has been an increased fascination with the Irish identity. One might consider it a backlash of our increased financial interest. One might even also consider this an outpouring of Irishness in definition of itself. But, is it really? Remembering that the plot for The Commitments centers on the foibles of an Irish band trying to get its American Motown musical act together and that Far and Away focuses on an Irishman trying to reach America for the Great Land Rush in Oklahoma; and remembering, too, that a few years ago Sinead O'Connor moved from Dublin to Los Angeles, and that Enya's American film repertoire ranges from Far and Away to My Life, I am more tempted to label it more appropriately as America's fascination with itself in relation to the other's perspective, as opposed to America's fascination with the other, or even the other's fascination with itself.

But yet I'm tempted to say I have hope for Irish culture in hearing and seeing such films as The Crying Game and In the Name of the Father, films that have nothing to do with America. However, I notice that both of these films center on the conflict between Britain and Ireland. Once again, Ireland is not working in definition in and of itself. It is working in terms of itself with the other named Britain. This is reflective of Ireland's more immediate concern in dealing with its problems with the E.C.

This constantly focuses my attention on the fact that, with the gales of economic "progress" forcing the doors of Ireland open to many other cultural influences, will Ireland's cultural base crumble or become dependent as has its economic base throughout its history? To analogize, if America and Britain have fairly large scales of cultures and Ireland's scale of culture is not so large, will it be overwhelmed by the American and British scales? The sheer bounty of American and British culture leaves little international media space for Ireland to talk about itself for itself. This is important, for if a culture does not take the time to define itself within its own terms, that culture and others will be unable to understand it or accept it. How is the culture even sure it is, in fact, a culture?

I am constantly reminded throughout this analysis of a woman I met in Ireland during the fall. I was in one of the federally-sponsored gift shops in Kilkenny and I was teasing the cashier about her wearing the price tags on her wrist after sale. She laughed at herself and when I asked her about what she would do after this, she replied, "I'll move on, I guess. I don't really care where it is, but I know it won't be here." It shocked me and made me wonder about the youth of Ireland (under age 27) who make up more than 50 percent of the population. Considering the steady trickle of emigration that has always plagued Ireland and the Irish youth's patriotic malaise, it makes me think despairingly. Ireland's culture could be left as a ghost town that is carefully preserved, not developed, by the aged who wish to remain.

REFERENCES

de Valera, E. (1928) Fianna Fail and its economic policy. Dublin: National Executive of Fianna Fail.

Kennedy, K. A., Giblin, T. & McHugh, D. (Ed.). (1988) The economic development of Ireland in the twentieth century. New York: Routledge.

Longley, E. (Ed.). (1991) Culture in Ireland: Division or diversity? Belfast: Institute of Irish Studies.

Marx, K. & Engels, F. (1971) Ireland and the Irish question. (R. Dixon, Trans.) Moscow: Progress.

Munck, R. (1993) The Irish economy: Results and prospects. Boulder: Pluto Press.

O'Malley, E. (1989) Industry and economic development: The challenge for the latecomer. Dublin: Gill and Macmillan.

Rossiter, A. (1992) "'Between the devil and the deep blue sea': Irish women, Catholicism, and colonialism." In Sahgal, G. & Davis, Y. (Eds.), Refusing holy orders: Women and fundamentalism in Britain. London: Virago.

DISCUSSION AND EXERCISES

1. What economic factors lay behind the division of Ireland into North and South? What are the different causes that contributed to the separation?

2. In what ways has Ireland's economic development been based on dependence? What have the effects of that dependence been?

3. In what ways has religion impacted economic development? Have other cultural factors had a similar impact?

4. Evaluate the use of outside sources. Why did the writer choose to paraphrase some sources and quote others?

5. Explain the effectiveness of the closing personal example. When is such a personal perspective appropriate in academic writing?

ESSAY SUGGESTIONS

1. Suggested writing topic: The Influence of the Sixties on American Cultural Values (1500–2000 words.)

   Explore the influence of this important decade on current social values focusing on social programs, family structures, minority issues, or educational values. Develop your causal explanation by providing a summary of social values in the area you choose to focus on as they existed at the beginning of the Sixties and as they exist now. Find evidence of the influence of the Sixties to account for the differences observable in the Eighties.

   For a discussion of research procedures and library resources, read Chapter 6, Researching a Longer Paper.

2. Additional topics for an extended causal explanation (1,500–2,000 words) include the following:

   a. Yuppies: Who are they? Where did they come from?
   b. The resurgence of political conservatism, 1975–1985
   c. The national deficit
   d. Any other self-contained educational, social, or political movement in American history or in the history of a foreign nation with which you are familiar (for example, the rise of apartheid in South Africa).
   e. See also suggested topics following Question 12, What are the causes of X?

PART
IV

A GUIDE TO EFFECTIVE LANGUAGE

Chapter 8   Using Paragraphs Effectively

Chapter 9   Using Sentences Effectively

Chapter 10   Using Words Effectively

Chapter 11   Writing Correct Sentences

Chapter 12   Editing and Proofreading

Chapter

8

USING PARAGRAPHS EFFECTIVELY

PARAGRAPH COHERENCE
TRANSITIONAL DEVICES

PARAGRAPH PATTERNS
COORDINATE SEQUENCE
SUBORDINATE SEQUENCE
MIXED SEQUENCE
PLACEMENT OF TOPIC SENTENCE

As any experienced writer knows, asking the right questions and finding interesting answers is only part of producing an effective piece of writing. Through the nuts and bolts of writing paragraphs, sentences, and words we give our ideas the concrete form that allows us to communicate them to our readers. In the next five chapters, we will examine the many resources writers have at their disposal to communicate their ideas clearly, vigorously and memorably to their readers. As we proceed, we'll draw on the insights of Hugh Blair, an eighteenth-century rhetoric teacher from Scotland, whose observations on writing and style remain useful to writers seeking to improve their work.

PARAGRAPH COHERENCE

Coherence literally means "sticking together." Thus a piece of writing is coherent when all its parts stick together, when the writer arranges and connects the individual words, phrases, and sentences so that a clear pattern of thought emerges.

Readers, who are "always in trouble," as E. B. White once noted, have no time or inclination to play games, to reassemble the parts of a complete thought; they must accept the writer's composition as they read it. If important pieces are missing so that the elements do not interlock (such as gaps in thought or puzzling jumps from one idea to another), readers cannot see the shape of the writer's thought.

As a conscientious writer, then, you must try to communicate more than the basic raw material of your ideas. You must try to communicate relationships: Why does point three follow point two and not vice versa? Does the example cited at the end of the paragraph illustrate the whole paragraph or only the last point? Is the second point the cause or the effect of the first? And what does reason three have to do with reason two? Are they of equal importance, or is one subordinate to the other?

Don't make your reader guess what these connections could be. Make certain not only that your readers can share the main idea of your paragraph (unity) but also that they can follow your particular train of thought from beginning to end (coherence).

You can achieve coherence in your writing in three basic ways:

1. By arranging materials according to an appropriate ordering principle.
2. By maintaining a consistent tone and point of view.
3. By providing transitions from one idea to another.

We have discussed ordering principles and consistent tone in Chapter 3. Let us here examine the use of transitions more closely.

Transitional Devices

These and other common transitional devices appear here in categories that to some extent necessarily overlap.

Referring back: as we have seen, on the whole, as mentioned above, as stated previously, as I have said, it seems then

Looking ahead: then, later, next, after, afterward, thereafter, finally, now, consequently, to sum up

Establishing causal connections: the result, in conclusion, to conclude, because, for, since, consequently, accordingly, hence, thus, therefore

Time markers: now, then, later, soon, before, next, afterward, finally, meanwhile, thereafter, at the same time

Place markers: here, there, at this point, below, beside, next to, behind, in front, outside, inside

Comparing and establishing degree: and, similarly, in like manner, in the same way, just as, so . . . that, also, more than, less than, beyond this

Qualifying, conceding, or contrasting: but, nevertheless, on the other hand, however, despite this, still, on the contrary, conversely, if, as if, granted that, unless, whether, anyhow, although, even though, yet

Adding and intensifying: first, second, third; a, b, c,; 1, 2, 3; to repeat, in addition, moreover, and, also, still, again, similarly, furthermore, finally, really, indeed

Introducing an illustration: thus, to illustrate, for example, for instance

Repeating a key word: This device keeps the main idea before the reader and carries the thread of meaning throughout a passage.

Using synonyms: Instead of repeating a key word so that it becomes monotonous, you may use suitable synonyms that continue the same thought.

Using proper pronoun reference: Another substitute for the repetition of key nouns and another way of connecting ideas is to use pronouns in place of nouns.

Maintaining same subject throughout paragraph: You can often continue the same subject from sentence to sentence, thereby maintaining a steady focus throughout the paragraph.

Establishing repetitive or parallel sentence patterns: In addition to repeating key words and ideas, you may repeat the grammatical structure of your sentences to reinforce the unity of your thoughts and promote their flow.

Linking last sentence of one paragraph with first sentence of next: This natural, frequently intuitive method maintains coherence between paragraphs. Sometimes you may need connecting words (such as "then again" or "on another occasion"), but often the direction of the thought provides its own continuity.

PARAGRAPH PATTERNS

The following procedure will help you apply the principles of good paragraphing. Follow these three steps:

First: Observe the workings of some recurrent paragraph patterns drawn from the work of established writers.

Second: Practice these patterns until you have mastered them.

Third: Go on to more complex and innovative forms as skill and inclination dictate, and as your instructor suggests.

You should recognize a truth at the outset—a truth every writer becomes aware of—that paragraph patterns are infinitely various. Writers are entitled to create any pattern they are capable of creating, provided it works, fulfills the purpose for which it was designed, and does what the writer wants it to do. This is the ultimate practical test of all writing.

Beginning writers, however, start with what they know will work—what has worked in the past and what is still working for contemporary prose writers. After mastering these fundamental forms, the beginner, of course, is no longer a beginner. The forging of an individual, personal, perhaps powerful style lies ahead for those who continue to polish their prose. Expanding their knowledge of the infinite resources of language, they will see options open at every level: word, sentence, paragraph.

This presentation is modeled on the generative approach of Francis Christensen whose study of the paragraphs of established writers is especially valuable because it is *inductive*. That is, it is based on what writers actually do to make their writing effective, rather than on what prescriptive "experts" *think* they do or think they *should* do. Furthermore, Christensen shows us realistically and specifically how writers achieve their purposes.

Christensen's method of diagramming paragraphs is the one we shall follow here. He positions the sentences of the paragraph one under the other (like the lines of a poem), numbering them to indicate their level of generalization. Number one is the "top" (or topic) sentence, the sentence ". . . on which the others depend, the sentence whose assertion is supported or whose meaning is explicated or whose parts are detailed by the sentences added to it" (*A New Rhetoric*).

First, let us look at a basic type of paragraph, familiar to us all. It moves in a straight line from the general to a series of specifics.

1 Many of the Founding Fathers were passionate lovers or practitioners of music.
   2 Jefferson used to rise at five in the morning to practice the violin; his expense books record many a purchase of "the latest minuets" and of fiddle strings for string quartet sessions, and he was well acquainted with the technique and construction of various instruments.
   2 Samuel Adams organized the people of Boston into secret singing clubs to stir up enthusiasm for independence.
   2 And Thomas Paine wrote at least two fine songs, "The Liberty Tree" and "Bunker Hill."
   2 In addition to having made a famous ride, Paul Revere might go down in history as having been the engraver of the first volume of original hymns and anthems ever published in this country.
   2 And Benjamin Franklin—most versatile of all—not only was a writer of ballad verses and a music publisher, but even invented a new musical instrument—the glass Armonica, for which Gluck, Mozart, and Beethoven composed a number of pieces.

—Elie Siegmeister, "Music in Early America"

Coordinate Sequence

Christensen calls patterns of this type a *coordinate sequence* because all sentences following the topic sentence are coordinate; that is, they are equal in rank to one another, all serving the same function. In this case each of the Founding Fathers (Jefferson, Adams, Paine, Revere, and Franklin) provides an example of the same general category: They are all "lovers or practitioners of music."

At the same time, as you may have already figured out yourself, the coordinate sentences in this paragraph are all *subordinate* to the topic sentence; that is, they are all at lower levels of generality.

Thus within the boundaries of each separate sentence, the writer presents each Founding Father as grammatical subject followed by an appropriately active verb:

> Jefferson used to rise . . .
> Samuel Adams organized . . .
> . . . Thomas Paine wrote . . .
> . . . Paul Revere might go down in history . . .
> . . . Benjamin Franklin . . . not only was writer . . . but invented . . .

It is not difficult to perceive the advantages of casting all subordinate sentences in a coordinate sequence in parallel construction: like things should be said in like ways. The very structure of the sentences reinforces the likeness of their meaning and function and indicates at each step that the author is about to present another item in the series. In the paragraph above, for example, the parallel construction announces at the start of each sentence that the writer is about to present another Founding Father (note the traditional "and's" used in the third and fourth sentences). Of course some variation is necessary to prevent monotony; thus we see the writer shifting in sentence five to a modifying prepositional phrase as sentence opener ("In addition to making a famous ride, Paul Revere . . ."). Writers must use common sense and instinct here: the best of devices used too frequently or mechanically becomes obtrusive and irritating.

Note, finally, that the writer signals us at the end of the paragraph to let us know that we are coming to the last entry. Obviously he assigns Benjamin Franklin to this most emphatic final position because Franklin was—of all Founding Fathers—the "most versatile." The writer clearly has organized his paragraph according to order of climax.

The simple structure of the coordinate sequence makes a significant point about the nature of orderly writing and the ordered mind behind such writing. In the following paragraph, for example, the writer tells us in the topic sentence that "There are three kinds of analytic group therapy." Only a very careless writer, insensitive to the expectations created in a reader, would not then proceed to list the kinds. Note that here again the writer lists like things in like ways, using parallel construction to introduce each item in the coordinate series. Note also that the last sentence is subordinate to the next-to-the-last sentence in this otherwise coordinate series.

> 1 There are three different kinds of analytic group therapy.
>   2 One concerns itself with the psychoanalysis of the individual in groups, as represented by Alexander Wolf.
>   2 The second variety of analytic group therapy is psychoanalysis of the entire group as a whole, as represented by the technique of Jacob Moreno.
>   2 The third variation of analytic group therapy is analysis by the group as developed by Michael Foulkes, DeMare, James Anthony and others.
>   3 It is this type of analytic group therapy with which I identify.
> —Martin Grotjahn, *The Art and Technique of Analytic Group Therapy*

The paragraph below provides another example of the coordinate sequence in which like things are said in like ways.

1 This is the essence of the religious spirit—the sense of power, beauty, greatness, truth infinitely beyond one's own reach, but infinitely to be aspired to.
  2 It invests men with pride in a purpose and with humility in accomplishment.
  2 It is the source of all true tolerance, for in its light all men see other men as they see themselves, as being capable of being more than they are, and yet falling short, inevitably, of what they can imagine human opportunities to be.
  2 It is the supporter of human dignity and pride and the dissolver of vanity.
  2 And it is the very creator of the scientific spirit; for without the aspiration to understand and control the miracle of life, no man would have sweated in a laboratory or tortured his brain in the exquisite search after truth.

—Dorothy Thompson (cited in Christensen, *Notes* 59)

The simple coordinate sequence—a topic sentence followed by a series of coordinate sentences with like things put in like ways—"is a natural point for starting to master paragraph structure," says Christensen. "It is a simple kind of structure, but you may have to fight an ingrained habit of putting down what comes naturally" (*A New Rhetoric,* 164).

You will find, if you give it a fair try, that the form itself provides discipline and direction, helping you guard against digressions or gaps in thought. The form also helps to sort and order your ideas both in the prewriting stage and while you are writing. Indeed, once you have assimilated the form, your memory and imagination will more easily dredge up old ideas and dream up new ones. The approach is appropriately described as *generative:* one idea generates another in an ongoing sequence.

Subordinate Sequence

In a subordinate sequence the added sentences have different structural relationships to the topic sentence: they do not comment directly on the topic sentence. Instead, each succeeding sentence is a direct comment on its immediate predecessor. In such a paragraph—as you will see in the example below—the topic sentence serves essentially as a point of departure from which every succeeding sentence moves further and further away. Each sentence is then seen to be *subordinate* to its predecessor and is numbered accordingly:

1 The process of learning is essential to our lives.
  2 All higher animals seek it deliberately.
    3 They are inquisitive and [they] experiment.
      4 An experiment is a sort of harmless trial run of some action which we shall have to make in the real world . . . whether it is made in the laboratory by scientists or by fox cubs outside their [den].
        5 The scientist experiments and the cub plays; both are learning to correct their errors of judgment in a setting in which errors are not fatal.
          6 Perhaps this is what gives them both their air of happiness and freedom in these activities.

—J. Bronowski (cited in Christensen, *Notes* 60)

To draw an analogy, we might say that sentences in a coordinate sequence—all relating back in the same way to the topic sentence—are children of the same parent; whereas sentences in a subordinate sequence—each relating back to its immediate predecessor—represent succeeding generations of the same parent. They are descendants, as it were; or, in rhetorical terms, they *descend* progressively to lower and lower levels of generalization, each providing a still more specific comment on the generalization contained in the original "top" or topic sentence.

You must be careful in a subordinate sequence to establish connecting links among the descendants. Indeed you must guard against digression at each and every point. In the subordinate sequence the question of coherence—the sticking together of parts—may become a problem.

Let us look at the Bronowski paragraph cited above to see how he avoided this problem, how he provided the links that keep his main thought moving in a straight and steady line of development, moving toward the progressively more specific. His topic sentence provides a general base on which a block of thought takes shape:

Level 1: The process of learning is essential to our lives.

He announces the subject simply and directly. Even though the succeeding sentences of the paragraph will move away from this general statement, he scrupulously maintains a connecting thread throughout.

Level 2: All higher animals seek it deliberately.

This sentence is a comment on the first, an amplification or development of it at a more specific level since it specifies who seeks the process: "all higher animals" (a detail) and *how* they seek it: "deliberately" (another detail). The writer has provided two added specifics within the frame of a sentence connected to the preceding sentence by the pronoun "it," which clearly refers back to "the process of learning."

Level 3: They are inquisitive and [they] experiment.

Although this sentence moves the reader still further from the topic sentence, it is not confusing. The pronoun "they" clearly refers back to "higher animals," explaining *why* they seek to learn: "They are inquisitive" (a specific reason); and *how* they seek to learn: "they experiment" (a specific detail). Note how skillfully Bronowski weaves in the basic materials of paragraph development.

Level 4: An experiment is a sort of harmless trial run of some action which we shall have to make in the real world . . . whether it is made in the laboratory by scientists or by fox cubs outside their [den].

He joins this sentence to its predecessor by repetition of the key word "experiment." As the last word of sentence three and the first word of sentence four, "experiment" provides an unmistakable link in the ongoing progression. True, this sentence departs further and further from the topic sentence, but note how closely connected the departing steps are to one another. Specifically, the level four sentence *defines* a key word in level three. Level four also tells *who* experiments: "scientists" and "fox cubs" (specific examples); and *where* each experiments: "in the laboratory" or "outside their [den]" (specific details).

> *Level 5:* The scientist experiments and the cub plays; both are learning to correct their errors of judgment in a setting in which errors are not fatal.

Here again repetition of key words serves as a connecting link. The writer now describes the actions of the previously mentioned "scientist" and "fox cub" more specifically in terms of *what* they do: "the scientist experiments and the fox cub plays" (specific examples); *what* they are learning: to "correct their errors" (additional detail); and *where* they are learning: in a nonfatal setting (final detail).

> *Level 6:* Perhaps this is what gives them both their air of happiness and freedom in these activities.

With the opening word "perhaps" the writer clearly speculates on what he has just said. Three pronoun references ("this," "them," and "their") plus one demonstrative adjective ("these") bind this last sentence in the paragraph to its predecessor. The earlier description of the setting as one in which errors are not fatal implies the new detail that both scientist and fox cub enjoy an "air of happiness and freedom." This same detail might well serve as transition to a new paragraph dealing with the pleasures of learning under controlled conditions.

As you can see, a subordinate sequence achieves unity and coherence when the writer makes judicious use of transitions: repetition of key words, pronoun references, and so on. Even in a simple narrative—and narrative paragraphs are often subordinate—transitions are what keep the story *moving*. Note how the pattern works in the following paragraph.

Repetition of key word	1 *Starlings* are notoriously difficult to "control."
Pronoun references	2 The story is told of a man who was bothered by *starlings* roosting in a large sycamore near his house.
Pronoun references, synonym	3 *He* said he tried everything to get rid of *them* and finally took a shotgun to three of *them* and killed them.
Demonstrative adjective, repetition of key word	4 When asked if *that* discouraged the *birds,* he reflected a minute, leaned forward, and said confidentially, "*Those three* it did." (Dillard, *Pilgrim*).

By viewing the paragraph as a linked sequence of sentences—as in the above examples—Christensen provides a quick and useful test of paragraph unity, one that we can easily apply to our own writing. As we reread the first draft of a paragraph we have written, we can ask, Does every sentence (that is, every link in the sequence) connect with the sentence that precedes it and the sentence that follows? If not, if a sentence is neither coordinate with any sentence before it nor subordinate to the sentence immediately preceding it, then it does not belong in the paragraph (it breaks the sequence) and we should either move it elsewhere or set it off in parentheses. In these cases, as Christensen puts it, "the paragraph has begun to drift from its moorings, or the writer has unwittingly begun a new paragraph."

In the properly unified paragraph, then, all the sentences deal with the same subject but at various levels of generality. A comment, for example, will be subordinate to the sentence on which it is commenting; an explanation or example of the comment will be subordinate to the comment, and so on. The paragraph moves and takes shape in terms of how each added sentence relates—either coordinately or subordinately—to the sentence that precedes it.

Mixed Sequence

Purely coordinate or subordinate sequences are not, as we might expect, as common as those in which the sequence is mixed, although one form or the other usually dominates.

Note, for example, that in the paragraph (page 564) dealing with different types of analytic group therapy, the topic sentence ("There are three different kinds of analytic group therapy") suggests that the paragraph will provide a series of three coordinate sentences. Having provided these, the writer wants the reader to know that he will discuss only the last item in the coordinate series further. To tell us this, he shifts downward from a level-two sentence to a final level-three.

Similarly, in the paragraph below, the writer—having committed himself at the outset to a coordinate sequence—shifts regularly within that sequence of level-two sentences to level-threes, which provide specific examples of the points made at level two. The paragraph provides a perfect example of that subtler movement—that ebb and flow between the general and specific—which characterizes the more complex paragraphs of our best writers.

Mixed sequence, based on coordination

1 The atmosphere that stirs expectation, that tantalizes the secret hunches that all theater-goers have, is composed of many things, some tangible and some not so very.
  2 Titles count.
    3 ("Sixth Finger in a Five Finger Glove" is not a good title; "The Strong Are Lonely" is not a good title; "Bells Are Ringing" is a good title.)
  2 Personalities count.
    3 (I've always liked that nice Walter Pidgeon.)
  2 Subject matter counts.
    3 (Do I want to see a play tonight about treachery in a prison camp?)
  2 Timing counts.
    3 (I may want to see a play about treachery in a prison camp next year, or I may have wanted to see one last year, but—tonight?)
  2 Circumstances count.
    3 (Is it Eugene O'Neill's last play, and what did he say about his family?)
  2 Curiosity counts.
    3 (What in heaven's name can "The Waltz of the Toreadors" be like?)
The curve of the moon counts.

—Walter Kerr, "How to Beat the Critics"

You can see how the alternating of level-two and level-three examples in the above paragraph rounds it out so that it offers more than a laundry-list itemization. Similarly in the next paragraph the writer pauses at one point—and only at one point—to develop his level-two item with a specific example and further details.

Mixed sequence, based on coordination

1 It is commonplace that most artists of outstanding originality and creative power have met lack of appreciation or abuse in their lifetimes.

2 We know that Beethoven's latest and finest works seemed to his comtemporaries to be meaningless meanderings of senility aligned with deafness, that Rembrandt's paintings were judged to be "Gothic and crude" by the autocrats of good taste in France.

2 We know the obloquy which the Post-Impressionist painters were required to face.

3 Even in 1925 Cézanne was described by one American critic as "commonplace, mediocre, and a third-rate painter," and in 1934 his work was characterized by another as "meager and unfulfilled art," while an English critic of some prominence has published his judgement that when you have seen one you have seen them all.

2 We know the indignation which was aroused at the beginning of the century by the new enthusiasm for African sculpture.

2 We remember the bewildered ridicule of "modern" music—Stravinsky and Bartók, even of Scriabin and Sibelius—which is now accepted and "placed."

2 We remember the controversies aroused by D. H. Lawrence and James Joyce, the repudiation of Eliot, Pound, Auden.

[Summing-up] This is not a new thing in critics who have led the vociferous opposition to the new.

—Harold Osborne, *Aesthetics and Criticism*

Now note in the following paragraph how a writer introduces a coordinate series into a subordinate sequence; in this case the coordinate elements come at the end of the paragraph.

Mixed sequence, based on subordination

1 The timing of New York's entry into casino gambling raises another, basic question: Can it really provide significant economic stimulus to decaying localities?

2 Officials assume favorable answers, but with little evidence.

3 Unless casinos bring a flood of visitors to the state, they will simply reshuffle local assets.

4 Does Mayor Koch believe that Manhattan casinos will increase tourism?

4 Will new hotels rise here for gamblers when Atlantic City and Las Vegas are already in the business and further competition impends?

4 Would such gambling drain other city entertainments, such as theaters and restaurants?

—*New York Times* Editorial, "Gambling on the Facts in New York"

Mixed paragraphs such as these are especially interesting and worthy of close study, for as Christensen says, they suggest "careful calculation of what could be left to the reader and what must be made more explicit." Obviously the writer treats those points that contain several subordinate sentences at greater length because he or she feels that they need clarification or emphasis. The inclusion of further information (details, examples, illustrations, and so on) provides the additional mass that tells the reader "take note: this is difficult; it needs further explaining" or "this is important, and therefore I want to linger over it."

Thus in the mixed sequence below, the writer stops the subordinate thrust of the sequence at two points, moving on to complete the sequence only after the pauses have achieved their purpose.

Mixed sequence, based on subordination

1 Whether we like it or not, ours is an Age of Science.
2 It is also like every other epoch of history, an Age of Private Experience.
3 In this second half of the twentieth century what can a writer do about these inescapable historical facts?
3 And what, as a conscientious literary artist and a responsible citizen, ought he to do about them?
4 His first duty, of course is to write as well as he can.
5 Much of our experience comes to us, so to say, through the refracting medium of art.
6 If that art is inept, our experience will be vulgarized and corrupted.
6 Along with unrealistic philosophy and religious superstition, bad art is a crime against society.
4 The writer's next duty is to learn something, if only superficially and in patches, about the methods and results of advancing science.
5 This knowledge should then be correlated with private experience and the shared traditions of culture, and the amalgam should be treated as a new kind of raw material for the creation of new varieties of the familiar literary forms.

—Harper's

Strictly speaking, the well-constructed, well-developed paragraph may assume an indefinite number of forms: it is impossible to encompass all possible paragraphs in a single description. But basically, as Christensen (*Notes,* 57) has written, the paragraph is "a sequence of structurally related sentences"—that is,

. . .sentences related to one another by coordination and subordination. If a first sentence of a paragraph is the topic sentence, the second is quite likely to be a comment on it, a development of it, and therefore subordinate to it. The third sentence may be coordinate with the second sentence . . . or subordinate to it. The fourth sentence may be coordinate with either the second or third (or with both if they themselves are coordinate. . .) or subordinate to the third. And so on.

Deciding how much to tell the reader at any point—where an added subordinate sentence is necessary or where another coordinate statement might clarify or emphasize an important idea—is up to the judgment of the individual writer. There is no formula that spells out the proper proportions of a paragraph. Even so, the writer can benefit enormously by familiarity with the "additive approach," for very often all that is necessary to improve a passage of prose is further development or amplification at a given level. Thus, says Christensen, addressing this remark to the teacher of writing, "there is nothing arbitrary or unnatural about urging the student to add levels, usually of a lower order of generality, in order to produce a texture rich enough to contain and display his subject" (*Symposium*, 60-88). John Lord reinforces this idea when he tells us in his study of the paragraph that "all good writing is a constant weaving up and down between the concrete and the abstract, as well as a constant forward movement from a beginning through a middle to an end" (*Paragraph*, 73).

Placement of Topic Sentence

Note that a paragraph may have no introductory topic sentence, that is, no announced statement of its theme, as in the following paragraph. Note also, however, that a topic sentence does indeed lurk in the second level-two sentence, beginning with "In Italy. . . ."

2 In Spain, where I saw him last, he looked profoundly Spanish.
  3 He might have passed for one of those confidential street dealers who earn their living selling spurious Parker pens in the cafés of Málaga or Valencia.
    4 Like them, he wore a faded chalk-striped shirt, a coat slung over his shoulders, a trim, dark moustache, and a sleazy, fat-cat smile.
    4 His walk, like theirs, was a raffish saunter, and everything about him seemed slept in, especially his hair, a nest of small wet serpents.
  3 Had he been in Seville and his clothes been more formal, he could have been mistaken for a pampered elder son idling away a legacy in dribs and on drabs, the sort you see in windows along the Sierpes, apparently stuffed.
2 In Italy he looks Italian; in Greece, Greek: wherever he travels on the Mediterranean coast, Tennessee Williams takes on a protective colouring which melts him into his background, like a lizard on a rock.
2 In New York or London he seems out of place, and is best explained away as a retired bandit.
  3 Or a beach comber: shave the beard off any of the self-portraits Gauguin painted in Tahiti, soften the features a little, and you have a sleepy outcast face that might well be Tennessee's.

—Kenneth Tynan (cited in Christensen, *Notes*, 71-72)

Very often the structure and impetus of an idea may carry over from paragraph to paragraph so that the paragraph needs no formal transition or topic sentence. In fact, a writer may promote readability by distributing a single idea over several paragraphs. In the following selection, for example, the topic sentence—"Sebastiana was devoted to Tanguy, in a silent, inarticulate way"—controls four relatively short paragraphs, each bringing out a different aspect of her devotion, and each serving as a kind of level-two sentence. The final three sentences serve as a concluding commentary or "terminator."

Sebastiana was devoted to Tanguy, in a silent, inarticulate way. She watched over him and took care of him. Every day, during the midday break, everyone saw her arrive with "the kid's" dinner. She had a half-hour's walk each way to bring him his food, but she was determined he must get something hot inside him. She always managed to get something which she considered a "luxury"—a slice of ham, perhaps, or a little cheese. She arrived proudly carrying her bundle and sat on a big stone, in the shade, beside Tanguy. Other workers used to have jokes at her expense, and tell her she was "past the age for that kind of thing." She let them talk, and did not even take the trouble to reply. She was desolate at seeing Tanguy so ill and dejected, and she continued to look after him with extraordinary tenderness.

She spent a great deal of time finding classical music for him in the radio programs, pretending to adore Bach and Beethoven. In the evening, after Tanguy had come home, they would sit before dinner in the little courtyard and chat. When he was reading the paper or listening to music, she sat quietly, without moving or speaking.

They never expressed their affection openly. Sebastiana's love remained dumb; like Gunther, she never gave external reality to her tender feelings except through the unimpeachable eloquence of her actual behavior. She lived for Tanguy as she would have lived for her own son, watched over him while he slept, took care of his clothes, gave him the kind of food he liked best (as far as she could), and tried to find amusements for him. On Sundays they sometimes picnicked on the beach, well away from the crowd.

He told her about everything. She listened in silence and smiled at him tenderly. All her understanding came from her heart, for she was the maternal instinct personified. Tanguy, on his part, loved and admired her because she was fair and honest. He loved her uncalculating generosity and her tranquil expression. She was sensible rather than clever, but she almost always knew what was right.

—Michel del Castillo, *Child of Our Time*

Although the topic or "top" sentence does generally lead off the paragraph, it may also conclude it. In the following paragraph, Willa Cather deliberately saves her topic sentence for the end of the paragraph so that the reader—having been offered a series of vivid images—can arrive with the writer at a summing-up generalization.

2 Ivy's red skin was flecked with tiny freckles, like rust spots, and in each of his hard cheeks there was a curly indentation, like a knot in a treehole—two permanent dimples which did anything but soften his countenance.

2 His eyes were small, and an absence of eyelashes gave his pupils the fixed, unblinking hardness of a snail's or a lizard's.

2 His hands had the same swollen look as his face, were deeply creased across the back and knuckles, as if the skin were stretched too tight.

1 He was an ugly fellow, Ivy Peters, and he liked being ugly.

—Willa Cather, *The Lost Lady*

To summarize, each paragraph should have its appropriate pattern and sufficient duration to do full justice to its subject; it should also develop its thought (answer its question) systematically, with a variety of materials that give the paragraph substance and texture (levels of generalization); and it should not drop the thought until, as Herbert Read wrote, it has been "seen in all profitable lights." Furthermore, the writer should develop these thoughts at a steady, reasonably accelerated pace so that the writing *flows*. To quote Read (61) again:

> There is about good writing a visual actuality. It exactly reproduces what we should metaphorically call the contour of our thought. The metaphor is for once exact: thought has a contour or a shape. The paragraph is the perception of this contour or shape.
>
> The writer has toward his materials, words, the same relation that an artist, say a modeller, has toward his material, clay. The paragraph is a plastic mass, and it takes its shape from the thought it has to express: its shape *is* the thought.

DISCUSSION AND EXERCISES

1. Coordinate Sequence

1. Students wrote both paragraphs below using the same topic sentence, "Sweet are the uses of adversity." Christensen commended one paragraph, and critized the other. Analyse the paragraphs and distinguish between the two, explaining your choice. Note that even in the commendable paragraph Christensen observes that "the shape is faulty at . . . one point" (*New Rhetoric,* 164–65). See if you can locate that point and comment.

   a. "Sweet are the uses of adversity," for it is in misfortune that a man is truly revealed. Adversity gives rise to dreams and hopes which prosperity might never incite. Adversity educates and strengthens the mind, eliciting talents which under more fortunate circumstances might have lain dormant. Adversity following prosperity challenges a comeback, giving the future a purpose and placing a new value on the lost success. Without experiencing adversity it is difficult to appreciate prosperity. Finally, it is in adversity that the truly noble spirit shines brightest—both that of the afflicted and that of his loyal friend who stands by in spite of everything.

   b. "Sweet are the uses of adversity." The poet John Keats struggled with sorrow and adversity experienced in the finite world. Keats searched for the ideal, but came to the conclusion sorrow and suffering must be accepted as part of the human experience. Beauty must die in order to have existence, for beauty fixed would be cold and inhuman. Alluding to his two poems, "To Autumn" and "Ode to a Nightingale," Keats resolved that autumn, too, has its song. Adversity is a part of living that makes one's human experiences more complete.

2. Use each of the following topic sentences as the basis for a coordinate sequence paragraph (add three or four sentences to each topic sentence). Try to order your

Continued

materials appropriately, say, "like things in like ways," use transitions where needed, and employ slight variations in structure where they will improve the flow and avoid monotony.

a. Sweet are the uses of adversity.

b. There are many things I like about my generation.

c. There are at least three different types of love.

d. There are countless ways to improve the quality of life on this campus.

e. I have several favorite books.

3. Write ten more coordinate sequences using the following quotations as topic sentences and adding as many sentences as you need to develop the idea.

a. It never rains but it pours.

b. Politics does indeed make strange bedfellows.

c. What's in a name?

d. There is no place more delightful than home.

e. The pen is mightier than the Saturday Night Special.

f. Knowledge is power.

g. Nothing is so much to be feared as fear itself.

h. Foresake not an old friend, for the new is not comparable to him.

i. Second thoughts are best.

j. The heroes, the saints, and the sages—they are those who face the world alone.

2. Subordinate Sequence

1. Write subordinate sequences using the following quotations as "points of departure": add as many levels as you need to complete your idea. Remember that in developing a subordinate sequence you do not refer back directly to the topic sentence, but only to the preceding one. Your idea should move forward steadily.

a. A man's reach should exceed his grasp.

b. It is better to have loved and lost than never to have loved at all.

c. Variety is not always the spice of life.

d. A classic is something that everybody wants to have read and nobody wants to read.

e. I laughed till I cried.

f. False words are not only evil in themselves, but they infect the soul with evil.

g. Nothing great was ever achieved without enthusiasm.

h. The reward of a thing well done is to have done it.

i. He . . . thought the moon was made of green cheese.

j. The mass of men lead lives of quiet desperation.

2. Even topic sentences that might initially suggest a coordinate series may generate a subordinate series. If the writer wishes to, he or she may use a second sentence to focus on only one aspect of the topic. Let us begin this assignment with one such example.

    1 Sweet are the uses of adversity.

      2 *I remember the day I discovered the truth of this famous line from Shakespeare.*

Note that the second sentence now enables you to narrate the events of that particular day. Add a comparably limiting second sentence to each of the following.

a. There is one book I'll never forget.

b. The sense of greatness keeps a nation great.

c. According to an old song title, "Saturday Night Is the Loneliest Night of the Week."

3. Mixed Sequence

1. Use the topic sentences below to write mixed sequences, following the pattern indicated for each paragraph.

a. The atmosphere that stirs expectation, that tantalizes the secret hunches that all movie-goers have, is composed of many things, some tangible and some not so very. (1,2,3,2,3,2,3,2,3,2,: See paragraph "How to Beat the Critics," page 568).

b. There are many things I like about my generation. (1,2,2,2,3,4,5)

c. Whether we like it or not, ours is an Age of Anxiety. (1,2,3,3,4,5,6,6,4,5: See paragraph on "Age of Science," page 570).

d. He had changed. (1,2,2,3,3,4,5) or (1,2,3,4,4,4,4)

e. Some people simply don't learn from experience. (1,2,3,3,2,3,2,3,4,5)

2. Number the following paragraphs to determine their pattern (mixed sequences based on coordination or subordination); then write a paragraph following the same pattern, using a topic sentence of your own, or selecting one of the quotations provided in the exercises above.

a. Never in the history of English letters has there been a more dedicated participant in the literary feuds of his day than the great and cantankerous Dr. Samuel Johnson, who stomped noisily through eighteenth-century London, demolishing arguments and smashing reputations with enormous vigor and gusto. Usually his verbal abuse was enough to smite the unworthy, but sometimes the impatient Doctor resorted to physical violence. ("There is no arguing with Johnson," the novelist, Oliver Goldsmith, said, "for when his pistol misses fire he knocks you down with the butt end of it.") Once, when a waiter used his dirty fingers instead of the proper tongs to drop a lump of sugar into the Doctor's tea, Johnson tossed the glass through the window and was about to do the same with the waiter, when a friend appeared and calmed him. On another occasion, the manager had placed a chair on a side stage especially for Dr. Johnson's use. Another man, finding the seat empty, sat in it, and then made the unpardonable error of failing to relinquish it to its rightful holder. Faced with this effrontery, the powerful Dr. Johnson simply picked up the chair, with the man still in it, and threw both chair and occupant in the pit.
— Myrick Land, *The Fine Art of Literary Mayhem*

b. A surprising number of people of Hiroshima remained more or less indifferent about the ethics of using the bomb. Possibly they were too terrified by it to want to think about it at all. Not many of them even bothered to find out much about what it was like. Mrs. Nakamura's conception of it—and awe of it—was typical. "The

Continued

atom bomb," she would say when asked about it, "is the size of a matchbox. The heat of it is six thousand times that of the sun. It exploded in the air. There is some radium in it. I don't know just how it works, but when the radium is put together, it explodes." As for the use of the bomb, she would add, "Shikata ga nai," a Japanese expression as common as, and corresponding to, the Russian word "nicheve": "It can't be helped. Oh, well. Too bad." Dr Fujii said approximately the same thing about the use of the bomb to Father Kleinsorge one evening, in German: "Da ist Nichts zu machen. There's nothing to be done about it."

—John Hersey, *Hiroshima*

4. Identifying Paragraph Patterns

1. Characterize the following paragraphs as coordinate, subordinate, or mixed. Number the various "levels of generality."

a.   The English language has not begun its life entirely devoid of Greek and Roman influence. Far back in the Dark Ages it drew in Latin and Greek words to cover activities which were not native to its people—religious, social, political—and even the names of foreign foods and drinks. *Church* and *kirk* come from the Greek; so do *bishop, monk, priest,* and *wine.* Many Latin words entered indirectly at the Conquest, through Norman-French. Then, as the Middle Ages flowed towards the Renaissance, English began to grow in the same way, and for the same reasons, as French: very largely under the influence of French. Chaucer was the chief figure in this process.

—Gilbert Highet, *The Classical Tradition*

b.   What are qualities that make language live? *Feeling* is one. A writer's ability to feel life deeply, to be responsive to it. The *power over language,* the gift to use words significantly and to form them in ways to give them meaning and impact. Also the quality of *style,* a writer's personal way with words, as intimate a part of a good writer as the size and shape of his nose. *Knowledge* is another quality that elevates writing into literature, so that the reader is memorably informed and made aware of new worlds. *Insight* is still another quality—a writer's ability to illuminate experience, to light up the dark places so that the reader sees life more clearly. And lastly what Dobie calls *perspective,* so that in reading one is aware of relationships both in space and time.

—Lawrence Clark Powell, *The Little Package*

c.   "There is hardly any activity, any enterprise, which is started with such tremendous hopes and expectations, and yet which fails so regularly, as love," wrote Erich Fromm. I think that part of the reason for this failure rate is that too often people are speaking different languages when they speak of love. The problem is not how much love they feel, but which kind. The way to have a mutually satisfying love affair is not to find a partner who loves "in the right amount," but one who shares the same approach to loving, the same definition of love.

—John Alan Lee, "The Styles of Loving"

d.   As I said earlier, the average writer sets out to commit an act of literature. He thinks that his article must be of a certain length or it won't seem important. He thinks how it will look in print. He thinks of all the people who will read it. He thinks that its style must dazzle. No wonder he tightens: he is so busy thinking of his awesome responsibility to the finished article that he can't even start!

—William Zinsser, "On Writing Well"

e.   Her doctor had told Julian's mother that she must lose twenty pounds on account of her blood pressure, so on Wednesday nights Julian had to take her downtown on the bus for a reducing class at the Y. The reducing class was designed for working girls over fifty, who weighed from 165 to 200 pounds. His mother was one of the slimmer ones, but she said ladies did not tell their age or weight. She would not ride the buses by herself since they had been integrated, and because the reducing class was one of her few pleasures, necessary for her health and free, she said Julian could at least put himself out to take her, considering all she did for him. Julian did not like to consider all she did for him, but every Wednesday night he braced himself and took her.

—Flannery O'Conner, "Everything That Rises Must Converge"

f.   The chronicler of Petrarch's life must record high hopes coupled with bitter disappointments. The poet spent a lifetime lyricizing an idealized and unattainable love, finally concluding that "Commerce with women, without which I had sometimes thought I could not live, I now fear more than death. . . . When I reflect on what woman is, a temptation quickly vanishes." He worked for the restoration of an imperial Rome, only to decide that it was a city which sold for gold the blood of Christ. He wanted an ivory tower in which to write masterpieces, but wandered restlessly through a dozen towns on a lifetime odyssey, which Bishop retraced in preparing his book. (Mrs. Bishop's pen impressions of these towns illustrate and enhance the volume.) He sought to emulate Virgil by rallying Italy to greatness with an epic poem on Scipio Africanus, only to have contemporaries hoot at it and tempt him to burn it. He strove for immortality through erudite works in Latin, but he won it with Italian rimes to a woman he had never touched.

—Robert J. Clements, "Laurels in Lieu of the Lady"

g.   Out on Safaris, I had seen a herd of Buffalo, one hundred and twenty-nine of them, come out of the morning mist under a copper sky, one by one, as if the dark and massive, iron-like animals with the mighty horizontally swung horns were not approaching, but were being created before my eyes and sent out as they were finished. I had seen a herd of Elephant travelling through dense Native forest, where the sunlight is strewn down between the thick creepers in small spots and patches, pacing along as if they had an appointment at the end of the world. It was, in giant size, the border of a very old, infinitely precious Persian carpet, in the dyes of green, yellow, and black-brown. I had time after time watched the progression across the

Continued

plain of the Giraffe, in their queer, inimitable, vegetative gracefulness, as if it were not a herd of animals but a family of rare, long-stemmed, speckled gigantic flowers slowly advancing. I had followed two Rhino on their morning promenade, when they were sniffing and snorting in the air of the dawn—which is so cold that it hurts in the nose—and looked like two very big angular stones rollicking in the long valley and enjoying life together. I had seen the royal lion, before sunrise, below a waning moon, crossing the grey plain on his way home from the kill, drawing a dark wake in the silvery grass, his face still red up to the ears, or during a midday-siesta, when he reposed contentedly in the midst of his family on the short grass and in the delicate, spring-like shade of the broad Acacia trees of his part of Africa.

—Isak Dinesen, *Out of Africa*

h.   In its days of glory, Hollywood was much more than a symbol. It was a power, a velvet-gloved tyranny exerted over most of the globe. And it could show its despotism in whimsical ways. When, around 1910, the movies began their trek westward to California, actors found the celluloid collars that were conventional wear at the time too hot; so they affected soft-collared shirts. Men across the world aped the new screen style so obediently that within a year or two the celluloid-collar industry was finished forever. A quarter of a century later, the male-underwear business experienced a similar crisis when Clark Gable removed his shirt in *It Happened One Night* to reveal that he wore no undershirt. In women's style the tyranny was inevitably even more severe and continuous. Gloria Swanson's gown, the length of Mary Pickford's hair, Theda Bara's mascara or Clara Bow's rouge, Jean Harlow's peroxide, Joan Crawford's shoulders, Veronica Lake's peekaboo, Jane Russell's profile, Marilyn's wiggle. Taken together, these women affected the look of an entire generation.

—David Robinson, "The Movies"

Chapter

9

USING SENTENCES EFFECTIVELY

COMPOSING SENTENCES
  COMBINING SENTENCES
  EXPANDING SENTENCES

REVISING FOR AN EFFECTIVE STYLE
  REVISING FOR UNITY
  REVISING FOR ECONOMY
  REVISING FOR EMPHASIS
  REVISING FOR VIGOR
  REVISING FOR RHYTHM

FORGING A BETTER STYLE

Improving sentences is a formidable job, but you can do it if you take the trouble to contemplate them critically—that is, to see how they actually work on paper and what options you have for effective change and revision. Only in this way can you improve your writing style, for the rhetorical strengths that contribute to what we call "readability" operate principally on the level of the sentence. No matter how interesting a subject is, no matter how carefully you organize it, no matter how soundly you develop it, any subject cannot turn into a good essay unless you embody each element of thought in a smooth-flowing series of clear, forceful sentences.

Logically, writers may think in paragraphs or units of thought, but concretely they spin out their ideas sentence by sentence—subject/verb/object by subject/verb/object. This is the typical English prose sentence, which writers vary as they feel a need for a change in rhythm and pace. The writer provides the reader with ideas sentence by sentence, from subject to predicate, and adds various modifications and qualifications along the way. Every sentence advanced beyond the primer stage of "See Spot run!" contains more than a bald subject committed to a particular action. The writer always weaves conditions and descriptions into the assertion that deepen and enrich its core meaning.

Dr. Samuel Johnson said that "most men think indistinctly and therefore cannot speak with exactness." To some extent this is true, but it is also true that your special function as a writer is to overcome this human deficiency. Before setting down your thoughts on paper, you have a special obligation to probe your mind until you see your ideas clearly as a distinct and unified whole. Then your special obligation is to try out different forms for each sentence to see which one most exactly reproduces the idea as it exists in your mind. Only after you have made clear thinking *visible on paper* are you justified in claiming the time and attention of a reader.

COMPOSING SENTENCES

A sentence is a sequence of separate words and word clusters—that is, phrases and clauses. How these words are arranged on paper determines what they mean. A careful and skillful arrangement in which the separate parts fit together to form a cohesive structure is clear; an arrangement in which the parts are loosely and haphazardly thrown together is unclear, perhaps incomprehensible. Working toward clarity, then, means constructing sentences in which meaning flows logically and smoothly from one sentence element to the next, thereby enabling the reader to follow and grasp the exact contour of the writer's thought as well as its bare substance.

Combining Sentences

No single skill will promote good writing more than the ability to condense and consolidate sentences that do not carry sufficient meaning to be set apart as separate sentences. This section examines ways to combine sentences that are loosely written and needlessly repetitive. Only after you have mastered this skill can you produce tight, well-constructed sentences that you can then *creatively* expand; in other words, that you can expand not by mere words but by the artful weaving in of added meaning and modification.

Sentence combining involves the reduction of a full sentence to one of the following sentence elements:

1. Relative Clause

Example: The fighting fish is small and quarrelsome.
                    The fighting fish lives in the waters around the Malay Archipelago.
Improvement: The fighting fish, which is small and quarrelsome, lives in the waters around the Malay Archipelago.

2. Prepositional Phrase

Example: Benjamin Franklin was born in Boston, Massachusetts. His birthday was January 17, 1706.
Improvement: Benjamin Franklin was born in Boston, Massachusetts, on January 17, 1706.

3. Participial Phrase

Example: The blizzard paralyzed the city. It piled up drifts as tall as houses. It blocked roads and highways. It kept residents indoors where they were safe and warm.
Improvement: The blizzard paralyzed the city, piling up drifts as tall as houses, blocking roads and highways, and keeping residents indoors where they were safe and warm.

4. Absolute Phrase

Example: The dancer soared across the stage. Her head was held high. Her arms were raised. Her legs were extended like the wings of a bird.
Improvement: The dancer soared across the stage, her head held high, her arms raised, her legs extended like the wings of a bird.

Absolutes help us to weave narrative and descriptive details into a sentence, thereby providing a full rather than a fragmented image. Absolutes also help us to move from a general subject (a dancer) to specific aspects of the subject (her head, arms, legs).

5. Appositves

Example: My neighbor is Mrs. Jones. She is the oldest living resident of our town.
Improvement: My neighbor, Mrs. Jones, is the oldest living resident of our town.

6. Subordinate Clause

Example: Honor was important to both Stamm and Zodomirsky. As a result of it they were both hurt in a duel.

Improvement: Because honor was important to both Stamm and Zodomirsky, they were both hurt in a duel.

Expanding Sentences

Like the paragraph, writing the sentence is a generative or "additive" process; that is, a building or adding on to a basic unit. In the paragraph, as we have seen, the basic unit is a topic or lead sentence; in a sentence, the basic unit is a main clause. Like a topic sentence, a main clause is generally stated in general or abstract terms to which the writer adds specific modifiers (subordinate clauses, adjective clusters, verb clusters, prepositional phrases) that expand and enrich the meaning of the predication.

Expanding a Minimal Sentence   There are six basic ways in which we may add to or expand a minimal sentence.

1. Compounding what is called the "head" term in a subject/verb/complement pattern:

   Example: Fresh fruit is good.
   Head word: fruit
   Expansion: Fresh fruit and vegetables are good.

2. Juxtaposing appositive phrases to the head term:

   Expansion: Fresh fruit, a rare treat in any season, is good.

3. Using verbals or verbal phrases (participles, gerunds, infinitives) in the subject/verb/complement pattern:

   Expansion: Oozing with natural juices, fresh fruit is good.

4. Using noun clauses to serve as the subject or complement in the subject/verb/complement pattern:

   Expansion: Whoever eats fresh fruit says that it is good.

5. Using an adjective or adjective clause to modify the head term of the subject or complement in the subject/verb/complement pattern:

   Expansion: Wherever it comes from, fresh fruit is good.

6. Using an adverb or adverb clause to modify the verb in the subject/verb/complement pattern:

   Expansion: Fresh fruit is always good.

Levels of Generalization   Christensen points out that "What you wish to say is found not in the noun but in what you add to qualify the noun....The noun, the verb, and the main clause serve merely as a base from which the meaning will rise. The modifier is the essential part of any sentence"(4). The sentence, then, like the paragraph, frequently exhibits levels of generalization, as the following subordinate sequence illustrates:

1 He dipped his hands in the bichloride solution and shook them, (main clause)
  2 a quick shake, (noun cluster)
    3 fingers down (absolute)
      4 like the fingers of a pianist above the keys. (prepositional phrase)
                    —Sinclair Lewis (cited in Christensen, *Notes,* 9)

Coordinate and mixed sequences—such as the following—illustrate further the many shapes that sentences, like paragraphs, may assume:

1 He could sail for hours,
  2 searching the blanched grasses below him with his telescopic eyes, (verb cluster)
  2 gaining height against the wind, (verb cluster)
  2 descending in mile-long, gently declining swoops when he curved and rode back, (verb cluster)
  2 never beating a wing. (verb cluster)
                —Walter Van Tilberg Clark (cited in Christensen, *Notes,* 10)

1 Joad's lips stretched tight over his teeth for a moment, and
1 he licked his lips,
  2 like a dog, (prepositional phrase)
    3 two licks, (noun cluster)
      4 one in each direction from the middle. (noun cluster)
                    —John Steinbeck (cited in Christensen, *Notes,* 11)

1 It was as though someone, somewhere, had touched a lever and shifted gears, and
1 the hospital was set for night running,
  2 smooth and silent, (adjective and adjective)
  2 its normal clatter and hum muffled, (absolute)
  2 the only sounds heard in the whitewalled room distant and unreal: (absolute)
    3 a low hum of voices from the nurses' desk, (noun cluster)
      4 quickly stifled, (verb cluster)
    3 the soft squish of rubber-soled shoes on the tiled corridor, (noun cluster)
    3 starched white cloth rustling against itself, (noun cluster) and outside,
    3 the lonesome whine of wind in the country night (noun cluster) and
    3 the Kansas dust beating against the windows. (noun cluster)
                    —Student (cited in Christensen, *Notes,* 11-12)

Although it may seem strange to see sentences laid out in this almost mathematical manner, a well-constructed sentence lends itself to schematization, for any well-constructed sentence has a plan or design. The practiced writer frequently creates the design spontaneously as the product of a well-ordered and trained mind, accustomed to bending words to its will. Just as frequently, however, the design is a result of the careful reworking and polishing of a rough first draft.

In any case, we should keep Christensen's schema in mind, for it describes more accurately than the traditionally "diagrammed" sentence how we actually write: we accumulate information as we go along; word follows word on the page; these words unite into clusters, phrases, clauses; separate parts combine to form a total statement—a sentence.

EXERCISES

1. Combine the following groups of sentences by reducing some of them to relative clauses, subordinate clauses, prepositional or participial phrases, absolutes, or appositives.
   a. Ballet is one of the most beautiful and graceful of the arts. Ballet requires great athletic ability.
   b. John F. Kennedy was assassinated. Three other presidents have been assassinated. Kennedy was the last one.
   c. The speaker mesmerized the audience. He gazed at them with his electric-blue eyes. He spoke in a rhythmic chant. He raised his arms repeatedly. He looked as if he wanted to supplicate the heavens.
   d. The city was in shambles. Telephone lines were down everywhere. The streets were littered with debris. Some of the debris consisted of fallen branches, pieces of glass from shattered windows, and assorted objects. They had detached themselves from roofs of houses and parked cars.
   e. Minsk is a city of over one million inhabitants. It lies at the confluence of rivers no longer navigable. The rivers have silted up.
   f. I recently overheard someone use the term "prejudice." It was used in a manner that made me angry. I was angry at the narrowmindedness of the speaker.
   g. People are becoming indifferent to the penny. The penny is a medium of monetary exchange. People believe the penny no longer has any real value.
   h. William Faulkner was an American novelist. He has sometimes been called "the voice of the modern South."
   i. In the second section complications are introduced by Mariana. She begs Zodomirsky not to duel. This begging causes Zodomirsky to face a conflict between his honor as a man and his love for Mariana.

2. Expand the following sentences in the six basic ways a minimal sentence may be expanded. (See examples under the heading Expanding Sentences.)
   a. Sunny afternoons are pleasurable.
   b. Thoughtless friends are a problem.
   c. Dangerous sports are exciting.
   d. Clothes make the man.
   e. Women are asserting their rights.
   f. Computers are becoming indispensable.

3. Generate your own sentences according to the pattern illustrated on page 583, under the heading Levels of Generalization. Substitute the following main clauses:
   a. She raised the book above her head and brandished it . . . (follow a 1, 2, 3, 4 subordinate sequence)
   b. He could diet for months . . . (follow a 1, 2, 2, 2, 2 coordinate sequence)

c. His knuckles whitened as he gripped the arm of the seat . . . (follow a 1, 1, 2, 3, 4 sequence here)
d. It was as though someone had pulled a lever at mignight and suddenly the campus was awake and running . . . (follow a 1, 2, 2, 2, 3, 3, 3, 3, 3 mixed coordinate sequence)

REVISING FOR AN EFFECTIVE STYLE

Experienced writers go beyond making sure that their prose is error-free: they polish and hone each sentence and each paragraph to make sure that all sentences are unified and economical, clear and cogent and properly emphatic, vigorous and euphonious and rhythmically "right":

Revising for Unity

A sentence, however elaborated by modifications and qualifications, should be essentially about *one thing*.

> For the very nature of a Sentence implies one proposition to be expressed. It may consist of parts, indeed; but these parts must be so closely bound together as to make the impression upon the mind of one object, not of many.
>
> —Blair, Lecture XI

Thus the reader, who can take in only one idea at a time, can grasp the writer's one idea before moving on to the next. A sentence is unified, then, if it clearly conveys its one main idea; a sentence is not unified if it tries to crowd in so many details that no single idea emerges as *the* idea of the sentence. Similarly, a sentence is not unified if its parts are illogically arranged or if there is needless shifting within the sentence from one subject to another. Consider now each of these impediments to sentence unity.

Avoid Overcrowding When we talk about unity, we are actually concerned with something inside the writer: his or her idea as it forms in the mind and takes shape on paper. Is it one unified idea that takes a clearly defined shape? Or do many ideas—only vaguely related and vaguely expressed—crowd into one another to form an amorphous mass that buries rather than exhibits its meaning, as in the following sentence?

> We think that there is footloose in society, in the enthusiasms with which people become missionaries for the various things in which they take a deep personal interest, a great capacity for helping the other fellow along, and we believe that any leisure-time service should consider its function not alone to the promotion of specific activities, such as athletics, or the arts, but that we should consider as a leisure-time field, in which a great many will find happy outlets for their energies, the pursuit of information or of intellectual culture, not as a matter of schooling but as a matter of post-school avocational interest, and that others can only be served by affording organized outlets for their own leisure enjoyment, in being helpfully

identified with causes and movements which are appealing to them, in capacities of service to their group as individuals, or to society at large.

To convert this gibberish into well-formed phrases and clauses, we must first isolate the main point, focus it sharply, and state it clearly. Then we must organize the details so that they follow in an orderly sequence. At the same time, we must eliminate meaningless generalities ("post-school avocational interest"). Having done all this, we are ready to convert these "notes" into an intelligibly written statement. In this case we will need more than one sentence:

> *Improvement:*   Most people appear to enjoy helping other people: notice how enthusiasts (say, tennis players) try to convert others to their pastime. A leisure-time agency could easily utilize this natural missionary impulse by building a program of social service into its regular program of athletic and cultural activities. Such a program would provide an organized outlet for people who want to do good for individuals in their own communities or for society at large.

Avoid Piled-Up Phrases Like the overcrowded sentence (of which it is a variation), the sentence with too many prepositional phrases, one piled on top of the other, confuses the reader because no single coherent idea emerges. There is no rule concerning the number of prepositional phrases that can comfortably fit in a sentence, but a long string of phrases generally produces a rambling effect. In such cases the writer should eliminate some of the phrases and replace others with single adjectives or adverbs.

> *Example:*   Words are the efforts made by an individual to crystallize his or her ideas and thoughts in order to express them in manner suitable to the mind of a rational creature.
>
> *Improvement:*   Words represent an individual's effort to crystallize and express his or her ideas in a rational manner (or simply "rationally").

Avoid Illogical Arrangement Long, rambling sentences are not the only violators of unity. The following short sentence also fails to convey meaning because the hodgepodge arrangement of words on paper simply does not add up to one unified, well-thought-out idea. Indeed, it is impossible to infer from the following exactly what the writer *meant*—or was trying to say.

> If one moves into the sentient, aware sense of intellectual self-development, here too are found barriers to attainment.

Meaningless, confused, sentences generally issue from one of two problems: either your thoughts are tangled, or they are not coming out on paper as clearly as you envisioned them. In either case you must work with the sentence itself, examining it critically word by word and asking Does it make the clear, logical, unified statement that I have in mind? If not, how can I make it say what I want it to say and not something else? Only after you have answered these questions can you begin to revise your sentences so that they will convey meaning effectively, so that they will not fall apart in the reader's mind. The writer of the sentence cited above has to rethink the idea because the form it took on paper does not make a logical statement.

Another kind of illogical arrangement that may be classified as a violation of unity grows out of a careless, illogical combination of subject and predicate. Rhetoricians call this "faulty predication," a common problem illustrated by the following:

The first step in hiking is comfortable shoes and light clothing.

The writer of this sentence should have asked, as he or she critically reread the first draft, "Are shoes and clothing steps in hiking?" Of course not. The sentence should read:

The first step in preparing for a hike is to get comfortable shoes and light clothing.
> or
Before setting out on a hike, one should put on comfortable shoes and light clothing.

Neither of the improved versions is a model of rhetorical splendor, but at least each states a simple idea clearly and accurately, whereas in the original sentence the predicate does not sensibly complete the meaning initiated by the subject.

Revising for Economy

Loose writing is often said to be a reflection of loose thinking; if so, verbosity is a root flaw. Frequently, however, loose writing is a sign not so much of loose thinking as of not enough work, specifically not enough reworking and revising of the original sentence. That first spontaneous overflow simply cannot be trusted to convey meaning in a clear, concise, and effective manner. "With years of practice," as editor Norman Cousins has observed, "a man may be able to put down words swiftly and expertly. But it is the same kind of swiftness that enables a cellist, after having invested years of effort, to negotiate an intricate passage from Haydn" (479).

Those of us who are not experts will probably need more than one try at most sentences, for people are naturally wordy. Indeed, as George Orwell observed in "Politics and the English Language," "It is easier—even quicker once you have the habit—to say *In my opinion it is not an unjustifiable assumption that* than to say *I think.*"

We cannot very well trim our conversation as we go along, nor can we go back and edit it. When we write, however, we can and must do exactly that: we must return to the sentences we have written and rework, recast, rewrite them until they are lean, crisp, and concise, free of what Flaubert so justifiably deplored as fatty deposits. Such "tight" sentences have far more impact on the reader: "'Beware the anger of a quiet man' is superior to 'A quiet man's anger is especially to be feared,' for the same reasons and in the same way that a short, straight shaft is better than a long, crooked one in most machine operations" (Burgess).

Admittedly it is always harder to condense than to write; still there are concrete ways to go about the "boiling down" process. As we have seen, we can combine sentences and thereby eliminate unnecessary words as well as condense full sentences into sentence elements and long sentence elements into shorter ones. Let us consider each of these processes in some depth.

Eliminate Unnecessary Words

Avoid Indirect Expressions

Example:	Probably the *Encyclopaedia Britannica* would provide one with the choicest information since it spends almost five pages expounding upon Shelley. (20 words)
Improvement:	The *Encyclopaedia Britannica,* with five full pages on Shelley, is probably the best source. (14 words)
Example:	Without words and what they communicate both connotatively and denotatively, human beings would be reduced to the level of lower primates. (21 words)
Improvement:	Without language human beings would be reduced to the level of the lower primates. (14 words)
Example:	The agnostic is one who holds that he has no knowledge of God; indeed that the human mind is incapable of knowing whether there is or is not a God. (30 words)
Improvement:	An agnostic maintains that the human mind cannot know whether or not God exists. (14 words)

Avoid Useless Repetition

Example:	The believer sees not only the human world, but instead the believer also sees the divine world. (17 words)
Improvement:	The believer sees both the human world and the divine. (10 words)
Example:	The main portion of the story dealt with Robert Peel's political life, an aspect of his life that was very active. (21 words)
Improvement:	The main portion of the story dealt with Robert Peel's very active political life. (14 words)
Example:	The average person in high school is a combination of both of these types, having a balance of both of these types of characteristics. (24 words)
Improvement:	The average high school student combines the characteristics of both types. (11 words)

Avoid Negative Phrasing

Example:	I find myself not in agreement with you. (9 words)
Improvement:	I disagree with you. (4 words)
Example:	I do not have much faith in his honesty. (9 words)
Improvement:	I distrust him. (3 words)
Example:	She was not very often on time. (7 words)
Improvement:	She usually arrived late. (4 words)
	or
	She usually was late. (4 words)

Example:	I do not expect to be misunderstood. (7 words)
Improvement:	I expect to be understood. (5 words)

Avoid Ineffective Intensifiers ("Really") and Qualifiers ("Rather")

Example:	*A Farewell to Arms* was the novel that really first made Hemingway a commercial success. (15 words)
Improvement:	*A Farewell to Arms* was Hemingway's first commercially successful novel. (10 words)
Example:	The most powerful force in all the world is love. (10 words)
Improvement:	The most powerful force in the world is love. (9 words)
Example:	He was a somewhat quiet man. (6 words)
Improvement:	He was a quiet man. (5 words)

Avoid Anticipatory Phrases Such As "It is," "There Was"[1]

Example:	It is for the above-mentioned reasons that I abandoned the project. (11 words)
Improvement:	For the above-mentioned reasons I abandoned the project. (8 words)
Example:	There were crowds of people milling about. (7 words)
Improvement:	Crowds of people were milling about. (6 words)
Example:	The reason that he voted for the independent candidate was that she had an antiwar record. (16 words)
Improvement:	He voted for the independent candidate because she had an antiwar record. (12 words)

Avoid Redundance

Example:	His shirt was blue in color. (6 words)
Improvement:	His shirt was blue. (4 words)
Example:	The professor introduced a new innovation. (6 words)
Improvement:	The professor introduced an innovation. (5 words)

Avoid Deadwood (Words That Carry No Meaning)

Example:	In many cases students are now working along the lines of discussing controversial issues with the administration. (17 words)
Improvement:	Many students are now discussing controversial issues with the administration. (10 words)
Example:	She is working in the interest of political unity. (9 words)
Improvement:	She is working toward political unity. (6 words)
Example:	That society is an interesting one. (6 words)
Improvement:	That society is interesting. (4 words)

---

[1]This principle generally applies, although with notable exceptions: specifically when the extra words contribute to the rhythm of the sentence or when they help to build the sentence toward an appropriately emphatic climax.

Example: She was aware of the fact that he had not returned her paper. (13 words)

Improvement: She was aware that he had not returned her paper. (10 words)

Here is a list of common deadwood expressions that pad rather than add to the meaning of a sentence:

along the lines of	in the interest of
to the extent that	of the nature of
the fact that	owing to the fact that
seems to me to be	with reference to
of the character that	tends to be
on the level of	may be said to be

Note how easily many such useless and cumbersome expressions can be abbreviated.

at that time	then
at some future time	after
in the event that	if
is aware of	knows
by virtue of	through
owing to the fact that	because
in spite of the fact that	despite
he is a man who	he
is likely to	may
was of the opinion that	believed
the question as to whether	whether
to be desirous of	to want
the great percentage of	most
to be deficient in	to lack
in a slow manner	slowly
there is no doubt that	undoubtedly
it may be assumed that	supposedly
as an example or an example is	for example
to take into consideration	to consider

Condense Long Sentence Elements

Reduce Clause to Phrase

Example: If we follow such a policy it may have the desired effect of convincing our competitors that we mean business. (20 words)

Improvement: Following this policy may convince our competitors that we mean business. (11 words)

Reduce Clause to Appositive

Example: Einstein, who was one of the most brilliant men of all time, behaved in a manner that was warm and human. (21 words)

Improvement: Einstein, one of the most brilliant men of all time, was a warm human being. (15 words)

Reduce Clause to Adjective

Example: He was introducing considerations that had nothing to do with the case. (12 words)

Improvement: He was introducing extraneous considerations. (5 words)

In summary, we should aspire to spareness and leanness of style, taking care not to go to the other extreme of making our style so spare as to be telegraphic:

> We shall always find our Sentences acquire more vigour and energy when . . . retrenched: provided always that we run not into the extreme of pruning so very close, as to give a hardness and dryness to style. For here, as in all other things, there is a due medium. Some regard, though not the principal, must be had to fullness and swelling of sound. Some leaves must be left to surround and shelter the fruit.
>
> —Blair, Lecture XII

Revising for Emphasis

In a properly emphatic sentence every word and every group of words are given what Blair calls "due weight and force." To some extent you can build into the grammatical construction of the sentence the clues as to what is most important in the sentence and what is less important.

Put Main Idea in Main Clause It is an oversimplification to say that you should always place the main idea in the main clause, and subordinate points in the subordinate clause, but it represents a helpful technique. If, for example, you have two points of information to present in a sentence—(1) that you were walking in the park, and (2) that you saw a thief steal a woman's purse—you certainly would want to emphasize the second point for that is clearly the *news* of the sentence: that you were witness to a theft. Thus you would be wise to subordinate the background information by placing it in a subordinate rather than in a coordinate position:

Example: I was walking in the park and I saw a man snatch a woman's purse.

Problem: This coordinate construction distributes importance equally to both halves of the sentence. Actually, however, the two halves are not equal and should not be made to seem so. The first clause should be made subordinate.

Improvement: As I was walking in the park, I saw a man snatch a woman's purse.

Use Emphatic Positions You can also achieve proper emphasis in a sentence by positioning important elements. The beginning of the sentence and, especially, the end are the emphatic positions. In the unfolding of a sentence, as in the unfolding of an essay, the last words stand out and impress themselves most forcibly on the reader. To fail to take advantage of this, to allow a sentence to trail off with empty qualifying phrases, insignificant afterthoughts, or weak monosyllables such as "it," "was," "done," "is," "etc.," is not only to ignore an extremely important psychological resource but also to create a sense of anticlimax, of a sentence continuing past its natural and proper end.

Example:	The advances of the future must be made in the moral as well as the technological sphere, according to the commencement speaker.
Improvement:	According to the commencement speaker, the advances of the future must be made in the moral as well as the technological sphere.
Example:	Hawthorne was haunted throughout his life by the evil deeds his ancestors had done.
Improvement:	Hawthorne was haunted throughout his life by the evil deeds of his ancestors.
Example:	The word is the basic unit of language and what we communicate with.
Improvement:	The word is the basic unit of language with which we communicate.

Note that in the last example the final preposition has been moved to a less prominent middle position. This was done not because the final preposition is in itself bad, as the old rule proclaims ("Never end a sentence with a preposition"), but rather because it is an unemphatic word that ends the sentence weakly. Actually, where idiom demands it, a final preposition is acceptable:

I did not know what to put it in.

Where idiom does not demand a final preposition, however, it should be avoided, along with all small "inconsiderable words" as Blair terms them, referring to adverbs, participles, conjunctions.

> For besides the want of dignity which arises from those monosyllables at the end, the imagination cannot avoid resting for a little on the import of the word which closes the sentence; and as those prepositions [and other weak words] have no impact of their own but only serve to point out the relations of other words, it is disagreeable for the mind to be left pausing on a word which does not by itself produce any idea nor form any picture in the fancy.
>
> —Blair, Lecture XII

Vary Normal Word Order Because the normal and familiar pattern of the English sentence is subject/verb/object ("I don't like him"), any variation in this pattern calls attention to itself and emphasizes the point being expressed ("Him I don't like"). The second sentence wrenches subject and object out of their expected positions. The subject no longer opens the sentence; the object no longer follows the verb. Instead the word "him" opens the sentence—an unusual location for a pronoun in the objective case. Clearly, this sentence informs the reader that this is no ordinary dislike, just as this is no ordinary sentence. The inexperienced writer might try to get the point across by using weak intensifiers ("I really dislike him very much"); the simple transposition of pronouns is far more economical and successful.

Achieving emphasis through transposition is not necessarily a conscious process. The strength of our feelings often dictates a spontaneous switching of terms:

That I cannot believe!
Oh, the troubles I've had!
Never will I do that again!

We can also make conscious use of this device in such simple transpositions as the ones listed below, all of them effective as emphasizers of what might otherwise be mundane observations.

Cold was the night.
Come winter and we'll see the fall of snow.
Of this plan, he knew nothing.

First a warning, musical; then the hour, irrevocable. [referring to Big Ben striking]
—Virginia Woolf, *Mrs. Dalloway*

Revising for Vigor

Closely allied to economy and emphasis is vigor: a lean, tightly constructed sentence with movement and energy built into its structure. Such a sentence, as Bishop Whately wrote long ago, will "stimulate attention, excite the Imagination, and . . . arouse the feelings" (*Elements*). You will probably write a vigorous sentence in the active rather than in the passive voice and will choose a strong, substantial verb rather than a weak, colorless verb such as "is," "was," "does," or "has."

Use Active Voice "Voice" indicates whether the subject of a sentence acts or is acted upon, whether the subject is the doer of the action or the receiver.

I hit the ball.

This sentence is in the active voice because the subject, "I," is the actor or doer.

The ball was hit.

This one is in the passive voice because the subject, "ball," receives the action of being hit.

Once we are aware of the distinction between active and passive voice, we cannot fail to see that in general the active voice is more lively and assertive than the passive, which tends—as the term "passive" suggests—to lack immediacy.

Example:	The test was taken by the students.
Improvement:	The students took the test.
Example:	College students were recruited by the township and a new project was begun.
Improvement:	The township recruited college students and set up a new project.

Sentences in the active voice are stronger and more emphatic for two reasons. First, they are more economical: the active voice generally requires fewer words. Second, the active voice emphasizes the *real* subject because the *real* subject is also the *grammatical* subject: "students" in the first example above is the *real* subject of the sentence, not "test." But we should also recognize that in some cases the passive voice is preferable: when the doer of the action is unknown ("The house was robbed"); when the receiver of the action, rather than the doer, has to be emphasized ("Shoplifters will be prosecuted"); and in formal report writing, where it is conventional for a writer to be anonymous ("The test was run and the following results obtained").

Despite these important exceptions, you should try, whenever possible, to strengthen and enliven your sentences by converting unnecessary and awkward passives into the active voice.

Concentrate Activity in Verbs   Another way to invigorate and at the same time tighten a sentence is to concentrate its action in substantial, well-chosen verbs, avoiding wherever possible weak verbs, such as "is," "was," "has," and "does." Shakespeare habitually used strong verbs rather than the weak state-of-being forms ("is" and "was"). When he did use them, he exacted from them their deepest existential meaning: "To be or not to be, that is the question."

The careless writer often uses a weak, roundabout verb form or inadvertently wastes the action of the sentence on a noun.

Example:	He felt an obvious hatred for the new recruit.
Improvement:	He obviously hated the new recruit.
Example:	Thoreau became a complete recluse from society in his shack at Walden Pond.
Improvement:	Thoreau secluded himself in his shack at Walden Pond.
Example:	In this anthology are some of the best haiku and tanka verse ever written.
Improvement:	This anthology contains some of the best haiku and tanka verse ever written.
Example:	There were two contributing factors to this situation.
Improvement:	Two factors contributed to this situation.
Example:	There was a car moving in circles around the speedway.
Improvement:	A car circled the speedway.

Note that when we exploit the peculiar power of the verb to invigorate a sentence, we have at the same time tightened the sentence by reducing the number of words and phrases. We have also pinpointed the action of the sentence on one vivid verb, instead of wasting it on a noun ("Thoreau became a recluse") or a participle ("a car moving").

Choose Specific, Concrete Words   A third way to promote vigor in the sentence is to use words that are specific and concrete rather than general and abstract ("the tall, red-haired soldier at the end of the line" rather than "that man over there"). (See Choosing the Right Word in Chapter 10.)

Revising for Rhythm

Although rhythm is usually associated with poetry, it is a feature of prose writing as well. Indeed, anyone who has ever listened to a sentence read aloud knows that it is a unit not only of meaning but also of rhythm and sound. There is no better guide to good writing than the ear, because what sounds good usually reads well. Conversely, what is jarring, overly intricate, or unpronounceable is usually hard to read and just as hard to understand. Thus it is wise to test your sentences on your ear, to *listen* to the sound of the words—both individually and in combination—and to *feel* their rising and falling action. As one writer has noted,

> . . .an author who would please or move his readers will often wish to do so by sound as well as sense. Here rhythm becomes important. Feeling tends to produce rhythm; and rhythm, feeling. Further, a strong rhythm may have a hypnotic effect, which holds the reader, as the Ancient Mariner held the wedding guest; prevents his attention from wandering; and makes him more suggestible. (Lucas, 215)

Basically, prose rhythm defies strict analysis and is probably "dictated by some inner pressure, hardly felt at the time, just as the rhythms of poetry seem to come into the head almost unbidden" (Boulton, 68). We may speculate that rhythm is associated with physical sensations: the writer's rate of breathing, heartbeat, pulse, metabolism. Similarly for the reader, a good sentence meets what Flaubert called "the needs of respiration." The sentence must "breathe" correctly—provide pauses where needed, changing pace, slowing down, speeding up. "A good sentence," Flaubert concluded, "should be like a good line of poetry, *unchangeable,* just as rhythmic, just as resonant."

Certainly the musical quality of the sentence cannot be denied, but neither can it be described easily in a short space. It will suffice to quote Blair once again, for his observations on "harmony"—though brief—are quite appropriate.

> Let us consider agreeable sound, in general, as the property of a well-constructed Sentence. . . . This beauty of musical construction in prose, it is plain, will depend upon two things; the choice of words, and the arrangement of them.
>
> I begin with the choice of words; on which head, there is not much to be said, unless I were to descend into a tedious and frivolous detail concerning the powers of the several letters, or simple sounds, of which Speech is composed. It is evident, that words are most agreeable to the ear which are composed of smooth and liquid sounds, where there is a proper intermixture of vowels and consonants; without too many harsh consonants rubbing against each other; or too many open vowels in succession, to cause a hiatus, or disagreeable aperture of the mouth. It may always be assumed as a principle, that whatever sounds are difficult in pronunciation, are, in the same proportion, harsh and painful to the ear. Vowels give softness; consonants strengthen the sound of words. The music of Language requires a just proportion of both; and will be hurt, will be rendered either grating or effeminate by an excess of either. Long words are commonly more agreeable to the ear than monosyllables. They please it by composition, or succession of sounds which they present to it: and, accordingly,

the most musical languages abound most in them. Among words of any length, those are the most musical which do not run wholly either upon long or short syllables, but are composed of an intermixture of them; such as, *repeat, produce, velocity, celerity, independent, impetuosity.*

The next head, respecting the Harmony which results from a proper arrangement of the words and members of a period, is more complex, and of greater nicety. For, let the words themselves be ever so well chosen, and well sounding, yet, if they be ill disposed, the music of the Sentence is utterly lost. . . . In English, we may take, for an instance of a musical Sentence, the following from Milton, in his Treatise on Education:

> We shall conduct you to a hill-side, laborious indeed, at the first ascent; but else, so smooth, so green, so full of goodly prospects, and melodious sounds on every side, that the harp of Orpheus was not more charming.

> Every thing in this Sentence conspires to promote the Harmony. The words are happily chosen; full of liquid and soft sounds; *laborious, smooth, green, goodly, melodious, charming:* and these words so artfully arranged, that were we to alter the collocation of any one of them, we should, presently, be sensible of the melody suffering. For, let us observe, how finely the members of the period swell one above another. "So smooth, so green,"—"so full of goodly prospects, and melodious sounds on every side";—till the ear, prepared by this gradual rise, is conducted to that full close on which it rests with pleasure;—"that the harp of Orpheus was not more charming."
>
> —Blair, Lecture XIII

Rhythm and harmony are matters too complex to contemplate here with any thoroughness. We shall simply consider four basic rhetorical devices that contribute to the rhythmic and euphonious arrangement of sentence elements: (1) parallel construction: (2) balanced antithesis; (3) order of climax; (4) variation in sentence length, pattern, and type.

Parallel Construction More than any other single resource available to the writer, parallel construction—repetition of sentence elements ("I came, I saw, I conquered")—provides a basis for rhythm in prose. Listen to these familiar words from Lincoln's Gettysburg Address: "...we cannot dedicate, we cannot consecrate, we cannot hallow this ground." Rhythmically, this sentence approaches poetry, as we can hear by noting the measured beat in each clause:

we cannot dedicate,

we cannot consecrate,

we cannot hallow this ground.

Or, if you wish to stress different syllables:

we cannot dedicate,

we cannot consecrate,

we cannot hallow this ground.

Expressing like ideas in like grammatical form improves a sentence on almost every count. It tightens, enlivens, and unifies. It also makes the sentence more emphatic and coherent, because likeness of form enables the reader to recognize more readily likeness of content: each item in a parallel series announces itself as a companion to the others—a comparable action:

They were walking, running, leaping. (three participles)

Because the meaning of such a sentence is reinforced by its structure and rhythm, a direction issued in parallel form is easier to grasp:

Walk, do not run, to the nearest exit. (two imperative verbs)

Similarly, a longer sentence that contains a series of observations or many details and qualifications is held together by a framework of parallelism.

> The only advice...that one person can give another about reading is to take no advice, to follow your own instincts, to use your own reason, to come to your own conclusions.
>
> —Virginia Woolf, *The Second Common Reader*

(Note the series of four infinitives: "to take . . . to follow . . . to use . . . to come. . . .")

> Jealousy of Mr. Elliot had been the retarding weight, the doubt, the torment. That had begun to operate in the very hour of first meeting her in Bath; that had returned, after a short suspension, to ruin the concert; and that had influenced him in every thing he had said and done, or omitted to say and do, in the last four-and-twenty hours.
>
> —Jane Austen, *Persuasion*

(Note that in the first sentence above the three complements of "had been" are nouns presented in order of rising intensity: "weight," "doubt," "torment." In the second, longer sentence the parts are held in place by the three long "that" clauses, in the last of which there is parallelism within the parallel: "every thing he had said and done, or omitted to say and do. . . . ")

Parallelism combined with repetition of key words produces an especially tight and emphatic rhythmic unit.

> No fact, however interesting, no image, however vivid, no phrase, however striking, no combination of sounds, however resonant, is of any use to a poet unless it fits: unless it appears to spring inevitably out of its context.
>
> —Northrop Frye, "New Directions from Old"

It can be easy to overlook both the semantic and rhythmic significance of arranging like ideas in parallel form. When the items themselves correspond to one another, the reader expects to find the words in corresponding form and is disappointed if they are not.

Example:	They liked to go to the movies, hiking in the mountains, and on long rainy days they would sleep the whole afternoon.
Problem:	The writer has expressed three comparable activities in three different grammatical forms: an infinitive phrase, a participial phrase, and a clause.
Improvement:	They liked to go to the movies, to hike in the mountains, and on long rainy days to sleep the whole afternoon.
	or
	They liked going to the movies, hiking in the mountains, and—on long rainy days—sleeping the whole afternoon.
Example:	The course grade is based on three factors: what you do in the final examination, writing a term paper, and classwork.
Problem:	Here again, three ideas of equal importance are expressed in three different grammatical forms: a relative clause, a participial phrase, and a single noun.
Improvement:	The course grade is based on three factors: a final examination, a term paper, and classwork.

Balanced Antithesis   It has long been recognized that when two ideas stand in opposition to each other (the "either . . . or"), the contrast or tension between them can be emphasized by setting them forth in a form of parallelism called *balanced antithesis.*

> Either we live by accident and die by accident; or we live by plan and die by plan.
> —Thornton Wilder, *The Bridge of San Luis Rey*

> The tragedy of life is not that man loses but that he almost wins.
> —Heywood Broun

> Talent, Mr. Micawber has; money, Mr. Micawber has not.
> —Charles Dickens, *David Copperfield*

(Note that Dickens has achieved further emphasis by inverting normal word order.)

The force and binding power of balanced antithesis rest basically on parallel constructions in which the writer repeats key words in an opposite context. Note the impact, for example, of President John F. Kennedy's famous statement.

> Ask not what your country can do for you; ask what you can do for your country.

One way to emphasize a balanced antithesis is to pair words through alliteration:

> Both poems are didactic: one preaches, one praises.

> Yonder is one whose years have calmed his passions but not clouded his reason.
> —Samuel Johnson, *Rasselas*

Balanced antithesis should not, however, be overused. Herbert Read noted, "used with discretion [balanced antithesis] adds point and vivacity to expression; but when abused it becomes tedious and artificial." (40)

Order of Climax

> But in a larger sense we cannot dedicate, we cannot consecrate, we cannot hallow this ground.

Note that, in addition to casting this sentence in a parallel construction, Lincoln carefully organized its three verbs in climactic order, moving from the least commitment ("to dedicate" is to set aside ground); to a deeper commitment ("to consecrate" is to declare the ground sacred); to the very deepest commitment ("to hallow" is to perpetually honor the ground as holy). Thus, Lincoln fulfilled the requirements of a rhythmic as well as a properly emphatic statement; he did not allow his sentence to fall off at the end. Indeed, he arranged the verbs so that they would grow both in meaning and in rhythmic impact. The importance of rising action cannot be overstressed, for it rests on the natural human expectation that items in a series will intensify as they progress. Surely it was this recognition that led Jane Austen in the sentence cited earlier to describe jealousy in progressively more oppressive terms: first as a "retarding weight," then as a "doubt," and finally as a "torment." To reverse the order (a "torment," a "doubt," or "retarding weight") would create an anticlimax—a letdown instead of buildup. Thus, as Blair wrote, the writer should always make certain that the "members" of a sentence

> . . . go on rising and growing in their importance above one another. This sort of arrangement. . . . is always a beauty in composition. From what cause it pleases is abundantly evident. In all things we naturally love to ascend to what is more and more beautiful, rather than to follow the retrograde order. Having had once some considerable object set before us, it is with pain we are pulled back to attend to an inferior circumstance. . . . The same holds in melody . . . : that a falling off at the end always hurts greatly. For this reason particles, pronouns, and little words, are as ungracious to the ear, at the conclusion, as I formerly showed they were inconsistent with strength of expression. It is more than probable that the sense and sound here have a mutual influence on each. That which hurts the ear seems to mar the strength of meaning; and that which really degrades the sense, in consequence of this primary effect appears also to have a bad sound.
>
> —Blair, Lecture XIII

Variation in Sentence Length, Pattern, and Type A succession of declarative sentences written in the conventional subject/verb/object order, with an average length of fourteen to twenty words, or two lines apiece, would produce a droning monotone. After a while the sameness of rhythm and pattern, the lack of emphasis, would dull the reader's senses and send his or her attention elsewhere. Note the tiresome succession of short, choppy sentences in the following paragraph:

> Hemingway's works abound in war, violence, and death. Hemingway had first-hand experience with all three. He took in two world wars. He also participated in

smaller wars. They made him see death without disguise. He had no heroic illusions. [Note gap in thought here.] Life and death were intermingled in the minds of his characters.

Most writers intuitively vary sentence length because the mind in the process of composition tends to express itself in unequal "waves" of thought. Note in the following paragraph, for example, how John Steinbeck's sentences range in length from three words to forty-two:

Sentence Length

Average (27 words)	When I was very young and the urge to be someplace else was on me, I was assured by mature people that maturity would cure this itch.
Short (12 words)	When years described me as mature, the remedy prescribed was middle age.
Average (25 words)	In middle age I was assured that greater age would calm my fever and now that I am fifty-eight perhaps senility will do the job.
Short (3 words)	Nothing has worked.
Average (20 words)	Four hoarse blasts of a ship's whistle still raise the hair on my neck and set my feet to tapping.
Long (42 words)	The sound of a jet, an engine warming up, even the clopping of shod hooves on pavement brings on the ancient shudder, the dry mouth and vacant eye, the hot palms and the churn of stomach high up under the rib cage.
Average (15 words)	In other words, I don't improve; in further words, once a bum always a bum.
Short (6 words)	I fear the disease is incurable.

—John Steinbeck, *Travels with Charley*

Similarly, most writers tire of the typical declarative sentence and vary the pattern of their prose with the addition of a rhetorical question, an imperative, an exclamation.

I hate to hear people saying, "He is young, he must wait; he will get plenty of chances." How do they know? Could Keats have waited, or Shelley, or Byron, or Burns?

—J. A. Spender, *The Comments of Bagshot*

Writers also tire of the usual subject/verb/object pattern and automatically alter it so that sentences open differently—sometimes with the subject, other times with a prepositional phrase, an adverb, a subordinate clause.

Sometimes in history, a nation collapses not because of its own flaws but because of the attacking nation's tremendous strength. Was this but the latest example? For years, from Berlin, I had watched Nazi Germany's mercurial rise in military might, which the sleeping democracies in the West did little to match. I had followed, too, at firsthand, Hitler's cynical but amazingly successful diplomacy, which had so easily duped the West and paved the way for one quick military conquest after another. But still the French debacle was quite incomprehensible. Not even the German generals I had talked with in Berlin expected it.

—William Shirer, *The Collapse of the Third Republic*

The most dramatic wrenching of normal word order occurs in the periodic or suspended sentence, wherein the writer postpones the predication to the end of the sentence, thereby achieving a kind of "suspense."

The fighter who stays in the ring as long as he can stand on his feet, the man who keeps his business alive while his clothes are threadbare and his stomach empty, the captain who clings to his ship while there is a plank left afloat—that is Washington.

—W. E. Woodward, *George Washington, the Image and the Man*

Because the reader does not know what a suspended sentence is about until the end, he or she will surely get lost or simply give up along the way unless the writer establishes a rhythmic unity that holds the sentence together and moves it toward its climax. This can be achieved only by observing strict parallelism, as in the following example:

How is it that I, who had the biggest Big League Gum collection in the East, who can still recite the lineup of the 1931 World Series (though there isn't much demand for it), who missed supper rather than miss the ball scores on WOR at 7 P.M., who never read the great novels because of a boyhood spent reading baseball news and "The Baseball Magazine" instead—how is it that I, the despair of my parents for an addiction that shut out almost every other field of knowledge, the bane of my sisters for the simulated major league doubleheaders that I played against the side of the house every day with a rubber ball, can hardly bring myself to follow the game today?

—William Zinsser, *Pop Goes America*

Sentences like these gain enormously in emphasis and vigor by virtue of their suspension—the "long and steady climb upward over successive terraces of clauses" (Potter)—followed by the final swift descent to the point of the sentence. Certainly the cadence of such a sentence captures the reader, so that it elicits a whole new dimension of rhythmic as well as mental response.

Not all sentences are as dramatically suspended as the preceding examples. Frequently the writer introduces a short delay, using words that may seem unnecessary but that serve a rhythmic purpose.

It was not until the other day, when I returned on a visit to Coney Island, that I recalled an important episode of my youth which had been buried all these years.

—Isaac Rosenfeld, in "Coney Island Revisited"

At first we might question the seemingly useless "It was" opening of the preceding sentence. But if we study it more carefully, we will see that this normally poor construction works here; it enables the writer to build a short rhythmic suspense that has more impact than the direct and economical and flat alternative:

> I recalled an important, long-buried episode of my youth the other day when I returned on a visit to Coney Island.

To some extent it is true that a series of short, simple sentences conveys an impression of speed, whereas longer sentences, as Herbert Read noted, "give an air of solemnity and deliberation to writing" (35). Actually, long sentences may move swiftly, provided they are well constructed and flow smoothly and harmoniously from one word group to another. Take the two virtuoso examples that follow:

This sentence closes Lytton Strachey's biography of Queen Victoria:

> Perhaps her fading mind called up once more the shadows of the past to float before it, and retraced, for the last time, the vanished visions of that long history—passing back and back, through the cloud of years, to older and ever older memories—to the spring woods of Osborne, so full of primroses for Lord Beaconsfield—to Lord Palmerston's queer clothes and high demeanor; and Albert's face under the green lamp, and Albert's first stag at Balmoral, and Albert in his blue and silver uniform, and the Baron coming in through a doorway, and Lord M. dreaming at Windsor with the rooks cawing in the elmtrees, and the Archbishop of Canterbury on his knees in the dawn, and the old King's turkeycock ejaculations, and Uncle Leopold's soft voice at Claremont, and Lehzen with the globes, and her mother's feathers sweeping down towards her, and a great old repeater-watch of her father's in its tortoise-shell case, and a yellow rug, and some friendly flounces of sprigged muslin, and the trees and the grass at Kensington.
>
> —Lytton Strachey, *Queen Victoria*

This long sentence moves back steadily in time, as the writer imagines the queen's "fading mind" moving back through memory to retrace the "vanished visions" of her long life. As her memories pass "back and back, through the cloud of years," so this single sentence moves back and back in a continuous flow of images. One long life is thus encompassed in one long tightly organized sentence that captures in its unity the unity and rhythm of the life it describes.

Here is another seemingly endless descriptive sentence, this one suspended:

> If the eyes are too big, and they are twice too big, and if they surround a nose that cannot be subdivided, and if the body parts might have been assembled by a weary parent on Christmas Eve, and if the teeth are borrowed from a rabbit soliciting carrots, and if the voice could summon sentry dogs, and if she does not walk so much as lurch, glide and jerk in continuing peril of collapsing like a rag doll dismissed by a bored child, and if on top of that she is saddled with being Judy Garland's first of three children by her second of five marriages, then how can the bearer of these oddments, how can this girl put together in the Flea Market, how can

Liza Minnelli, at 23, threaten to become the major entertainment figure that she is becoming? (Thompson)

This sentence is clearly playful as well as descriptive. By piling *if*-clause upon *if*-clause, the writer has tried to intensify the mystery ("Who is this strange creature?" we wonder), and by building on a repetitive "and if . . . and if," he has established an almost breathless musical refrain, moving us, we are led to expect, to some sort of crescendo. Instead, the sentence falls off at the end, contrary to conventional principles of emphasis and harmony. Nonetheless, the sentence succeeds almost despite itself, for it brings us down to earth, again rhythmically. The subject, after all, is not of momentous import (note that most of the words are short and simple); the writer's weak ending seems to tell us that he knows he has been a bit overdramatic, but he has been writing in a spirit of fun. There is clearly a tongue-in-cheek element in this sentence. It is in itself a little essay, light and playful in tone.

FORGING A BETTER STYLE

As Blair points out in the following passage, the best way to forge a better style is to write slowly and carefully, never aiming directly for speed. At the same time, we must not be too plodding.

Many rules concerning style I have delivered, but no rules will answer the end, without exercise and habit. At the same time, it is not every sort of composing that will improve style. This is so far from being the case, that by frequent, careless, and hasty composition, we shall acquire certainly a very bad style; we shall have more trouble afterwards in unlearning faults, and correcting negligences, than if we had not been accustomed to composition at all. In the beginning, therefore, we ought to write slowly and with much care. Let the facility and speed of writing, be the fruit of longer practice. Says Quintilian, with the greatest reason, "I enjoin, that such as are beginning the practice of composition, write slowly and with anxious deliberation. Their great object at first should be, to write as well as possible; practice will enable them to write speedily. By degrees, matter will offer itself still more readily; words will be at hand; composition will flow; every thing as in the arrangement of a well-ordered family, will present itself in its proper place. The sum of the whole is this; by hasty composition, we shall never acquire the art of composing well; by writing well, we shall come to write speedily."

We must observe, however, that there may be an extreme, in too great and anxious care about words. We must not retard the course of thought, nor cool the heat of imagination, by pausing too long on every word we employ. There is, on certain occasions, a glow of composition which should be kept up, if we hope to express ourselves happily, though at the expense of allowing some inadvertencies to pass. A more severe examination of these must be left to be the work of correction. For, if the practice of composition be useful, the laborious work of correcting is no less so: it is indeed absolutely necessary to our reaping any benefit from the habit of composition. What we have written, should be laid by for some little time, till the ardour of composition be past, till the fondness for the expressions we have used be worn off, and the expressions themselves be forgotten; and then, reviewing our work with a cool and critical eye, as if it were the performance of another we shall discern many imperfections which at first escaped us. Then is the season for pruning redundances; for weighing the arrangement of sentences; for attending to the juncture and connecting particles; and bringing style into a regular, correcting and supported form. This *"Limoe Labor,"* must be submitted to by all who would communicate their thoughts with proper advantage to others; and some practice in it will soon sharpen their eye to the most necessary objects of attention, and render it a much more easy and practicable work than might at first be imagined.

—Blair, Lecture XIX

DISCUSSION AND EXERCISES

1. Locate the weaknesses in the following sentences, and rewrite each sentence to improve it.
   a. Just as scientific progress has dispelled the belief that an "evil spirit" causes the headache, so has it replaced the former cure of boring holes in the skull with aspirin.
   b. There are more single women than men in the United States, according to the Census Bureau.
   c. Most of the churches have large congregations that are rather wealthy.
   d. In 1870 Pavlov conducted an investigation of the pancreatic nerves and was awarded a gold medal for it.
   e. One old cottage in particular attracted my attention. It was a huge white structure with four gables, one at each corner.
   f. Milton, who was one of the most scholarly men of all time, devoted a good part of his life to activities in the sphere of politics.
   g. She began singing in a coffeehouse in Boston at the age of nineteen.
   h. The author's central purpose is a view of human behavior.
   i. It is important to keep in mind what sin and guilt meant in Hawthorne's use.
   j. He was a man of heroic soul, keen intellect, and quiet wit.
   k. There is a noticeable lack of friends in his life.
   l. On returning to the deck, the sea became dark and turbulent.
   m. The French engineers proposed an alternative plan. Their plan called for the construction of a semicircular dam two hundred fifty feet wide which cost eighty million dollars.
   n. There are two basic means of communication of which one is speaking and the other is the use of the written word.
   o. The English hate frogs, but the French love frogs and hate the English, and cut off their hind legs and consider them a great delicacy.
   p. The next morning he was found lying on the floor by a cleaning women.
2. Comment on the following passages and indicate what factors contribute to their rhetorical effectiveness.

a. When youth is gone, every man will look back upon that period of life with infinite sorrow and regret. It is the bitter sorrow and regret of a man who knows that once he had a great talent and wasted it, of a man who knows that once he had a great treasure and got nothing from it, of a man who knows that he had strength enough for everything and never used it.

—Thomas Wolfe

b. The world of Homer is unbearably sad because it never transcends the immediate moment; one is happy, one is unhappy, one wins, one loses, finally one dies. That is all. Joy and suffering are simply what one feels at the moment; they have no meaning beyond that; they pass away as they came; they point in no direction; they change nothing. It is a tragic world but a world without guilt for its tragic flaw is not a flaw in human nature, still less in an individual character, but a flaw in the nature of existence.

—W. H. Auden, Introduction to *The Portable Greek Reader*

c. I who am blind can give one hint to those who see -- one admonition to those who would make full use of the gift of sight: Use your eyes as if tomorrow you would be stricken blind. And the same method can be applied to the other senses. Hear the music of voices, the song of a bird, the mighty strains of an orchestra, as if you would be stricken deaf tomorrow. Touch each object you want to touch as if tomorrow your tactile sense would fail. Smell the perfume of flowers, taste with relish each morsel, as if tomorrow you could never smell and taste again. Make the most of every sense; glory in all the facets of pleasure and beauty which the world reveals to you through the several means of contact which Nature provides. But of all the senses, I am sure that sight must be the most delightful.

—Helen Keller, *Three Days to See*

d. They went down to the camp in black, but they came back to the town in white; they went down to the camp in ropes, they came back in chains of gold; they went down to the camp with their feet in fetters, but came back with their steps enlarged under them; they went also to the camp looking for death, but they came back from thence with assurance of life; they went down to the camp with heavy hearts, but came back with pipe and tabor playing before them.

—John Bunyan, *Life and Death of Mr. Badman*

e. We sailed early in January, and for nearly a year we wandered from country to country. I saw Egypt. I saw the Pyramids, at noon and at sunset, by moonlight, and at sunrise. I saw the Tombs of the Kings, and the great Temple a Karnak. I saw the lovely vanished Temple of Philae. I saw the coast of Asia Minor, and the harbor of Smyrna. I sailed on the Aegean Sea. I saw the Isles of Greece, and the Acropolis. I saw the Golden Horn in the sunrise, and the minarets and the cypresses of Constantinople. I saw Italy. I saw Switzerland. I saw Paris. I saw England in summer. I saw the frozen lakes of Norway, and the midnight sun over the ice fields.

—Ellen Glasgow, *The Woman Within*

Chapter

10

USING WORDS EFFECTIVELY

WORDS: THE WRITER'S TOOL

CHOOSING THE RIGHT WORD
    THE NATURAL WORD
    THE CONCRETE WORD
    THE ACCURATE WORD
    THE FRESH WORD
    THE FIGURATIVE WORD
    THE CONNOTATIVE WORD

WORDS: THE WRITER'S TOOL

Despite the limitations of language, words are the writer's only tool. It is not surprising then that words preoccupy and even obsess the writer: not simply their meaning but their sound, shape, texture, rhythm. Like strains of melody presenting themselves unbidden to the composer, words whirl about in the writer's mind, resound in the inner ear, impinge on the consciousness—as if they were real beings with lives of their own. Indeed, some writers even personify words, as the Mexican poet Octavio Paz has done in his observation that

> the easiest thing in the world is to break a word in two. At times the pieces continue to live with a frantic life, ferocious, monosyllabic. It's wonderful to throw that handful of newborns into the circus: they jump, they dance, they bound and rebound, they scream tirelessly, they raise their colored banners.

Ordinary people do not have this almost mystical affinity for words; they do not see them as "colored banners," but rather as conveyors of meaning, and properly so, for it is here that our concern should begin: with words that convey meaning most simply, clearly, and forcefully. Thus, as Lincoln said in his second Inaugural Address:

> With malice toward none, with charity for all, with firmness in the right as God gives us to see the right, let us strive on to finish the work we are in, to bind up the nation's wounds, to care for him who shall have borne the battle and for his widow and his orphan, to do all which may achieve and cherish a just and lasting peace among ourselves and with all nations.

Note the simplicity of the diction here; each word is *right* because it is appropriate not only to the speaker, but also to his subject and to the occasion for the address. There are no long, pretentious adjectives, no vague terms, no clichés, no fiery declamations. The inspired eloquence of the utterance can best be appreciated when we read George Orwell's parody of pretentious language:

> We want to terminate this conflict and have an equitable peace. We do not desire a vindictive peace but one that will restore the country to unity. We believe that we are right and are determined to gain the victory and have a fair peace. After the cessation of hostilities we must not forget to take care of the veterans and the dependents of those killed or wounded in the struggle.

CHOOSING THE RIGHT WORD

You cannot—on order or even on exhortation—increase your sensitivity to words or enlarge your word-stock. Only as you read and pay attention to words, as words assume a prominent place in your thinking, will the right word be available when you need it; only then will the struggle for that word seem worthwhile. In the meantime, however, you can improve your writing by committing yourself to certain broad categories of words: to the natural word as opposed to the pretentious or trite; to the concrete word as opposed to the vague; to the exact word as opposed to the approximate. We shall consider each of these in turn.

The Natural Word

George Orwell once advised the writer never to use a long word if a short one will do. This sweeping rule ignores those exceptions where a long word has a better sound or helps to establish a better rhythm in the sentence. Modern prose style is generally straightforward and relaxed, designed to capture the rhythms of everyday speech, to serve readers rather than to impress them, to talk to them rather than to pontificate. The modern prose stylist, as Bonomy Dobrée points out in *Modern Prose Style*, "is trying to be more honest with himself," is aiming at a style "that will faithfully reflect [the] mind as it utters itself naturally."

In this sense, the unknown author of Ecclesiastes was writing in a modern vein when composing the following verse:

> I returned, and saw under the sun, that the race is not to the swift, nor the battle to the strong, neither yet bread to the wise, nor yet riches to men of understanding, nor yet favour to men of skill; but time and chance happeneth to them all.

In his essay "Politics and the English Language" Orwell praises this passage as an example of "good English"—simple, direct, concrete, smoothly flowing, harmonious, *natural*. By way of contrast Orwell offers a stiff, jargon-ridden variation, written by an imaginary but "typical" bad writer, a stylist of "the worst sort":

> Objective considerations of contemporary phenomena compel the conclusion that success or failure in competitive activities exhibits no tendency to be commensurate with innate capacity, but that a considerable element of the unpredictable must invariably be taken into account.

"This is a parody," Orwell admits, "but not a very gross one." He goes on to explain why Ecclesiastes is preferable:

> It will be seen that I have not made a full translation. The beginning and ending of the sentence follow the original meaning fairly closely, but in the middle the concrete illustrations—race, battle, bread—dissolve into the vague phrase "success or failure in competitive activities." This had to be so, because no modern writer of the kind I am discussing—no one capable of using phrases like "objective consideration of contemporary phenomena"—would ever tabulate his thoughts in that precise and detailed way. . . . Now analyse these two sentences a little more closely. The first contains forty-nine words but only sixty syllables, and all its words are those of everyday life. The second contains thirty-eight words of ninety syllables: eighteen of its words are from Latin roots, and one from Greek. The first sentence contains six vivid images, and only one phrase ("time and chance") that could be called vague. The second contains not a single fresh, arresting phrase, and in spite of its ninety syllables it gives only a shortened version of the meaning contained in the first. (*Shooting,* 84-85)

In an attempt to be "formal" and to seem properly "authoritative," many students write stiff, dehumanized prose such as that which Orwell parodies. They must repress any impulse to use a word such as "transpire," for example, when they mean "take place." They must also repress the tendency to write phrases like "objective consideration of contemporary phenomena" or "commensurate with innate capacity" or "considerable element of the unpredictable." They only need to read these passages aloud and *listen* to them to know that they are hardly faithful reflections of "the mind as it utters itself naturally."

The Concrete Word

In addition to raising semantic problems, general and abstract terms cause rhetorical problems, for they create dense, lifeless prose lacking in precision and energy. We cannot avoid such prose altogether, for a certain amount of classifying of ideas and experiences is necessary to all discourse. Nonetheless, every time we choose a word we can make a determined effort to be as specific and concrete as the subject will allow. In his *Philosophy of Style,* Herbert Spencer suggested that we avoid sentences like: "In proportion as the manners, customs, and amusements of a nation are cruel and barbarous, the regulations of their penal code will be severe." Instead, said Spencer, we should write a sentence like: "In proportion as men delight in battles, bull-fights, and combats of gladiators, will they punish by hanging, burning, and the rack."

The point to keep in mind is that most people do not think in general or abstract terms but in concrete particulars. Thus when readers encounter generalizations or abstractions, they tend to translate them into specific images of their own choosing. Conscientious writers, who do not want readers filling in their prose for them, will therefore write in concrete images. It is no accident that in Antony's speech over Caesar's body, Shakespeare—who wanted to excite in his audience the utmost horror—has Antony talk in the most highly particularized language: "those honorable men [not who merely *killed* Caesar, but] whose *daggers* have *stabbed* Caesar" (Whately, 322).

The following examples illustrate another way in which the general may be rendered more specific, the abstract more concrete, by adding details:

Example: My father and I argue about everything.
Improvement: My father and I argue about everything from politics and civil rights to the relationship between parents and children.

Example: The meal was delicious.
Improvement: The shrimp gumbo was hot and spicy, the roasted chicken rich with fresh rosemary and thyme, the salad a cool medley of fresh greens kissed by a delicate vinaigrette, the triple chocolate mousse sweet and creamy; in short, the meal was delicious.

The Accurate Word

To use words with any exactness, you must be painstaking. The first word that comes to mind is not always the best one. To try to clarify your meaning by rephrasing what you have just written—prefacing it with "in other words" or "that is to say"—does not help much. The precisely right word used in precisely the right place will say once and for all what you need to say.

Discussing "right" words in the abstract is difficult, for they depend on specific writing situations. Some general principles, however, may be set down.

1. Make certain that the word you choose is literally correct and used in the customary way. In the following examples the writers have made nearly right but ultimately wrong choices:

Example:	Her selfishness is prevalent throughout the story.
Improvement:	Her selfishness is *evident.* . . .

Example:	There is a sadness that emits from the character's every action.
Improvement:	There is a sadness that *issues.* . . .

Example:	I banged my fist on the table, thereby instilling pain throughout my arm.
Improvement:	I banged my fist on the table, thereby *inflicting.* . . .

Example:	They are utterly ignorant to her fears.
Improvement:	They are utterly ignorant *of* her fears.

Example:	I found his poems unmeaningful.
Improvement:	I found his poems *meaningless.*

Example:	The fishing trip had a remedial effect on their spirits.
Improvement:	The fishing trip had a *restorative effect.* . . .

2. Choose a word that is appropriate in tone and level of usage (formal, informal, colloquial, slang). Although modern prose style tends to be informal and relaxed, you should not introduce words that are clearly out of place in the context of your piece. Certainly anyone with the slightest sensitivity to words will recognize that the verb in the following sentence is ill-chosen.

Plato's dialogues stuff the student's mind with new ideas.

The verb "stuff" in this sentence clearly has the wrong tone and the wrong connotation for any discourse that is not deliberately ironic. One may *stuff* one's mouth with food or *stuff* a bag with equipment, but readers of Plato do not have their minds *stuffed.*

Similarly, in the following sentence there is an awkward combination of three different levels of usage: formal, informal, and slangy:

Students remember that despite the multitudinous tasks that confront them, they must somehow get their work done; they cannot permit themselves to goof off, even for a day.

Today there are no fixed rules governing correctness; slang expressions and colloquialisms are often included in so-called formal writing. As the National Council of Teachers of English announced in 1952, "All usage is relative." The correct or best expression always depends on many factors: What the writer is saying (a description of a soccer scrimmage or stoic philosophy); how the writer says it (written or spoken); to whom and on what occasion the writer says it (a bull session with a roommate or a presentation of a paper before an honors committee). Ultimately, the writer must exercise his or her own taste and judgment and a sense of what is appropriate, acceptable, and comfortable in a given context.

3. Choose a word that has suitable connotations. Your own sensitivity to words must be your guide here.

Example:	In their simple-mindedness, children are free of racial and religious prejudice.
Problem:	"Simple-mindedness" suggests that children are foolish, that they simply do not understand the complexities of the situation—and that if they did, they too would be prejudiced.
Improvement:	In their *innocence,* children are free of racial and religious prejudice. ("Innocence" is preferable here because it suggests—as the writer wanted to suggest—purity rather than ignorance.)

Example:	In his novels Faulkner lashes out at racial prejudice.
Problem:	"Lashes out" implies violence and lack of control.
Improvement:	In his novels Faulkner *attacks* racial prejudice. ("Attack" does not carry the connotation of uncontrollable fury but rather of a more measured and thoughtful action against an opposing evil.)

4. In an official or formal context, choose the *single, exact* word in place of a series of words.

Example:	He was introducing considerations that had nothing to do with the case.
Improvement:	He was introducing *extraneous* considerations.

Example:	They cut themselves off from the main group.
Improvement:	They *detached* themselves from the main group.

Example:	There are many factors contributing to the deficiencies in my writing, the most outstanding one being my unwillingness to work.
Improvement:	Many factors contribute to my writing deficiencies, most notably my *laziness.*

5. Avoid ill-sounding combinations of words. Although good readers read silently, they "hear" the sounds of the words. You should avoid inadvertent rhymes and words that have the same sound but different meanings (homonyms) because they are distracting.

Example:	Another explanation of his motivation can be found in his observation that. . .
Problem:	Too many -*tion* endings.

Example:	Those who lean toward leniency. . .
Problem:	Awkward repetition of *lean* sound.

Example:	The sole purpose of his soul-searching address was. . .
Problem:	Homonyms.

Example:	It must be clear that the fear of the atmosphere. . .
Problem:	Inadvertent rhyme.

6. Avoid awkward variations. "Repetition is bad," said Mark Twain, "but inexactness is worse." Guard against using an inexact or awkward variation of a word simply to avoid repetition.

Example: Having considered Faulkner's vision, let us now go on to a consideration of the characters who exemplify the theory.

Improvement: (Repeat the word "vision" in place of "theory.")

7. Avoid quaint and archaic terms.

Example: We should treat the medium of writing with respect, nay with reverence.

Improvement: We should treat the medium of writing with respect, *even* (or "as well as" or "indeed") with reverence.

The Fresh Word

The right word is one that is fresh and new, one that has not been repeated so often that it becomes a cliché. Though most clichés have a kernel of truth to them (that's why they've become so popular, after all), they've become, as Walker Percy once wrote, like worn poker chips, their edges worn away from much use. The effective writer learns to find fresh ways to express fresh ideas and works to root out clichés when they sprout like dandelions on a well-tended lawn.

A cliché is an expression that was once original and apt, a new and vivid metaphor, perhaps, that later acquires "an unfortunate popularity." The *Oxford English Dictionary* calls the cliché "a stereotyped expression, a commonplace phrase." We can add to this definition the adjectives "trite," hackneyed," "overworked," "worn out"—"a coin so battered by use as to be defaced" (cited in Partridge, 2).

> Some are foreign phrases (*coup de grâce; et tu, Brute*). Some are homely sayings or are based on proverbs ("You can't make an omelet without breaking eggs," *blissful ignorance*). Some are quotations ("To be or not to be, etc.";	"Unwept, unhonored, and unsung"). Some are allusions to myth or history (*Gordian knot, Achilles' heel*). Some are alliterative or rhyming phrases (*first and foremost, high and dry*). Some are paradoxes (*in less than no time, conspicuous by its absence*). Some are legalisms (*null and void, each and every*). Some are playful euphemisms (*a fate worse than death, better half*). Some are figurative phrases (*leave no stone unturned, hit the nail on the head*). And some are almost meaningless small change (*in the last analysis, by the same token*). (Bernstein, 104)

You cannot banish clichés altogether from your speech and writing; but you should weed clichés out of your writing with patience and diligence before they destroy all possibility of meaningful discourse. Stock phrases are the enemy of thought: people will repeat them mechanically without thinking about what they are saying. Note the following conglomerate:

> It was a deep dark secret that I would not for the life of me have revealed to a soul; certainly not to any Tom, Dick, or Harry that happened by, like a ship passing in the night.

Because the reader of the cliché expects the language to proceed according to a set pattern, humorists twist or reverse the pattern and thwart the expectation. Thus wits have come up with: "She's as pure as the driven slush"; "It is better to have loved and lost then never to have lost at all"; "None but the brave desert the fair"; "Bachelors never make the same mistake once"; "Work is the curse of the drinking class." Bergen Evans has said that these anticlichés are "golden transmutations of some of the world's dullest lead."

The Figurative Word

No language has enough words to express the infinite variety of human ideas, feelings, and experiences. Because people instinctively recognize this, they try to expand and strengthen their power of expression by creating new ways of saying what they mean, specifically by using figures of speech—nonliteral expressions of meaning in which they say one thing in terms of something else.

> I think a poet is just a tree—
> it stands still and rustles its
> leaves; it doesn't expect to lead
> anyone anywhere.
> —Boris Pasternak

When I say, for instance, "That a good man enjoys comfort in the midst of adversity"; I just express my thought in the simplest manner possible. But when I say, "To the upright there ariseth light in darkness"; the same sentiment is expressed in a figurative style; a new circumstance is introduced; light is put in the place of comfort, and darkness is used to suggest the idea of adversity. In the same manner, to say, "It is impossible, by any search we can make, to explore the divine nature fully," is to make a simple proposition. But when we say, "Canst thou, by searching, find out God? Canst thou find out the Almighty to perfection? It is high as heaven, what canst thou do? deeper than hell, what canst thou know?" This introduces a figure into style; the proposition being not only expressed, but admiration and astonishment being expressed together with it.
> —Hugh Blair, *Lectures on Rhetoric and Belles Lettres*

Because figures of speech issue from the deepest recesses of the imagination, they cannot be learned. You can simply note the figures of other writers and hope that in sensitizing yourself and giving free play to your own imagination, you too will be inspired to create word-pictures. Let us examine some of the more common forms of figurative language.

Metaphor
(identification of
one thing with
another)

> To an imaginative person, what is a map? The silhouette of a chimera or a spot of colour? Trivial comparisons are futile, so be careful. What is South America? A pear upside down.
> —Adolfo Costa Du Rels, *Bewitched Lands*

> In his financial operations, Monsieur Grandet was part tiger and part boa constrictor. He would crouch in ambush watching his prey until it was time to spring with open jaws; then, having swallowed the

gold, he would slowly digest it, like a snake, impassive, methodical, cold to any human touch.

—Honoré de Balzac, *Eugénie Grandet*

(Note also the simile here: "*like* a snake"; see "simile," below.)

Living was a field of grain blowing in the wind on the side of a hill. Living was a hawk in the sky. Living was an earthen jar of water in the dust of the threshing with the grain flailed out and the chaff blowing. Living was a horse between your legs and a carbine under one leg and a hill and valley and a stream with trees along it and the far side of the valley and hills beyond.

—Ernest Hemingway, *For Whom the Bell Tolls*

No man is an island, entire of itself; every man is a piece of the continent, a part of the main.

—John Donne, *Meditation XVII*

Rhetorical question

Be not righteous over much, neither make thyself over wise:
Why shouldest thou destroy thyself?
Be not over much wicked, neither be thou foolish:
Why shouldest thou die before thy time?

—Ecclesiastes 7:16-17

Implicit or submerged metaphor

Youth is the time to go flashing from one end of the world to the other both in mind and body; to try the manners of different nations; to hear the chimes at midnight.

—Robert Louis Stevenson

Outside the weather was winter, the trees medieval presences arching gray through gray.

—John Updike, "Museums and Women"

About the middle of the nineteenth century, in the quiet sunshine of provincial prosperity, New England had an Indian summer of the mind; and an agreeable reflective literature showed how brilliant that russet and yellow season could be.

—George Santayana, *Character and Opinion in the United States*

A kind of splendid carelessness goes with surpassing power. The labor of the file was not for Aeschylus as it was not for Shakespeare.

—Edith Hamilton, *The Greek Way*

Simile (comparison of one thing with another joined by "like" or "as")

Their prose—Tolstoy's sentences, heavy as blocks of granite; Chekhov's rhythms, soft as autumn leaves; Dostoievsky's moaning and quivering like telegraph wires at night—revealed itself to me in all its beauty of language and depth and richness of meaning.

—Yevgeny Yevtushenko, *A Precocious Autobiography*

Human potentialities, so poignant and literally crucial in adolescence really are trapped and vitiated in a mass society. But American society, just because it is so very mass, is attached to mass institutions like a factory to its parking lot, or a church to its graveyard.

—Edgar Z. Friedenberg, *Coming of Age in America*

Personification (attribution of human characteristics to inanimate objects or ideas)

Wit is a lean creature with a sharp inquiring nose, whereas humor has a kindly eye and comfortable girth.

—Charles Brooks, "Wit and Humor"

Falseness withered in her presence, hypocrisy left the room.
—Adlai Stevenson, eulogizing Eleanor Roosevelt

Death came for her, ashamed of itself.
—Bertolt Brecht, *Brecht on Brecht*, arr. and tr. George Tabori

The Connotative Word

Language is rich in meanings, not only a word's formal dictionary definition, its *denotation*, but also in the associated overtones called *connotations*. All words, no matter how bloodless they seem on the surface—words such as "circular" or "flat"—are nonetheless capable of evoking emotional responses. Some words, of course, are richer in connotation than others. Take the word "house," for example, a relatively straightforward term referring to a dwelling place, a physical structure. Now take the word "home"; it too refers to a dwelling place, but the connotations of this word suggest the special place it is: the place where the family lives, where, as Robert Frost wrote, when you have to go there they have to take you in. On Christmas and Easter vacations, you do not go to a house; you go home.

Many words change in connotation over time. The word *propaganda* once suggested a reliable and trustworthy source of information; now it implies thought manipulation and deception. Semantic games result from juggling with the connotations of words, as in Bertrand Russell's famous "I am firm; you are stubborn; he is pig-headed." All three terms have more or less the same *core* meaning (denotation); by cleverly manipulating the *overtone* of meaning (connotation), users can shade their statements into a commendation or a criticism. Consider the following pairs of words, which have essentially the same denotation. Do they mean the same thing, though?

debate	dispute	antique	old-fashioned
relax	loaf	slender	skinny
reflect	daydream	voluptuous	fat
carefree	unconcerned	restrained	repressed
statesman	politician	chatting	yakking
sweet	saccharine	intellectual	egghead
childlike	childish		

In most contexts the connotations of the words in the left columns would be favorable, whereas those in the right would be less favorable. You can see how useful and dangerous a tool connotation can be in the hands of those who would like to misinform without really lying. For example, during the late 1940s a news magazine, openly Republican in policy, would refer repeatedly to Democratic President Truman's friends as "cronies" (suggesting backroom, poker-playing types). Later, when Republican President Eisenhower was in office, however, the magazine spoke solemnly and respectfully of the president's "long-time associates" (suggesting dignified colleagues in high political office).

One of the strangest, most tragic accounts of mistaken connotation comes out of World War II. It involves a reply reportedly received through the official news agency of Japan in response to the surrender ultimatum issued by the Allies at Potsdam. The reply contained the Japanese word *mokusatsu,* which the Domei agency translated into the English word "ignore," thereby implying that the Emperor's regime would not consider surrender under any circumstances. In truth, however, the word *mokusatsu* suggests that one is not flatly dismissing or *ignoring* but only "reserving an answer until a decision is reached." If this careless translation of *mokusatsu,* which failed to incorporate the special connotations of this word, did in fact "confirm America's resolve to drop the atomic bomb, the error may well have been the most costly linguistic blunder in human history" (Girsdansky, 88).

EXERCISES

1. Rewrite the following sentences, in concrete or specific terms, to create a more vivid impression in the reader's mind.
   a. He seemed happy.
   b. She seemed lovely.
   c. She seemed intelligent.
   d. He seemed rebellious.
   e. He seemed tired.
   f. She seemed angry.
   g. He seemed restless.
   h. They seemed frightened.
   i. They seemed nervous.
   j. The countryside was beautiful.
   k. The city was awful.
   l. The campus was in a turmoil.
   m. The dormitory was noisy.
   n. The room was crowded.
   o. He had the patience of Job.

2. Improve the following sentences by changing one or more words.
   a. The park is rather circular, with momentous oak trees.
   b. The reversal of Robert Jordan in *For Whom the Bell Tolls* is Frederic Henry in *A Farewell to Arms.*
   c. Thomas Wolfe was abhorred by what he saw in society.
   d. One notices the author's occupation with this theme.

    e. He carries out his life in accordance with Faulkner's vision of fate and moral responsibility.

    f. The memory of Ben's death was so vivid that Wolfe was able to duplicate it in his novel with all its poignancy.

    g. The most beneficial source was *The International Index*.

    h. The room seemed to him to have too much in it.

    i. Many writers are too flowery and superfluous, so that the point they are trying to convey is lost in the garbage of irrelevant material.

    j. For a complete terminology of a word, see an unabridged dictionary.

    k. Oftentimes I yearn for the good old days.

    l. The speaker of the poem relates how he felt the loss of the pleasures he had once enjoyed.

    m. Hemingway looked very deeply into the nature of courage.

    n. He was admired for his stubborn principles.

    o. Mrs. Compson's last speech in *The Sound and the Fury* reiterates our assumptions about her.

    p. Most high school students are all the same.

    q. Words are one of the most essential sophistications humanity has devised.

3. Try to revitalize the following clichés by creating a "play" or "twist" on the words.

    a. Home is where the heart is.

    b. It never rains but it pours.

    c. The more the merrier.

    d. As ye sow, so shall ye reap.

    e. Hell hath no fury like a woman scorned.

    f. All work and no play makes Jack a dull boy.

    g. A fool and his money are soon parted.

    h. Spare the rod and spoil the child.

    i. People who live in glass houses shouldn't throw stones.

    j. Beggars can't be choosers.

4. Connotations

    Consider the following words, all with good connotations. Cite for each a bad counterpart: a word that means approximately the same thing denotatively but *not* connotatively.

cautious	satisfied	leader
courageous	passion	cooperation
retaliation	discuss	independent
compromise	individualist	patriotism
liberty	clever	reformer
subtle	dissent	nonconformist

Chapter

11

WRITING CORRECT
SENTENCES

Learning Grammar

Reviewing the Grammar
    of the Sentence
        Subjects
        Predicates
        Relationships of Words
        Sentence Types

Revising for Correctness
        Grammatical Form
        Sentence Integrity
        Sentence Coherence

Writers seldom think consciously about the structure of a sentence as they are writing it. Instead words seem simply to accompany the ideas as they take shape in the mind. It is in revision that writers consciously manipulate language to make sure they have said exactly what they mean as precisely and clearly as possible, to make certain furthermore that they have not committed an error in basic grammar, sentence integrity, or coherence. Revision provides the opportunity not only to correct such errors but also to make sure that ideas appear in the best dress the writer can give them. In this chapter, we'll review some basic grammatical principles and examine how effective writers use them to constuct sentences that meet readers' expectations of correctness.

LEARNING GRAMMAR

We learn in school how to compose paragraphs and essays, but we master the grammar of the sentence in early childhood, long before we are even conscious of the learning process. Whether it issues from our tongue or pen, the sentence appears as a spontaneous creation of the individual consciousness, a result of a lifetime's experience with language, not just the needs of the moment. Indeed, although many people feel uneasy about grammar, the fact is that all native speakers have a deep awareness of the basic structure of English. If you doubt this, consider Lewis Carroll's famous "Jabberwocky" from *Through the Looking-Glass,* which begins:

> 'Twas brillig and the slithy toves
> Did gyre and gimble in the wabe:
> All mimsy were the borogoves,
> And the mome raths outgrabe.

When Alice hears these lines she says: "Somehow it seems to fill my head with ideas—only I don't know exactly what they are!" Actually, the ideas are *patterns*—the structural or grammatical meanings that stand out unmistakably because the lexical meanings have been obliterated. That is, the words themselves do not mean anything, but the *forms* of the words and their arrangement within the line stir the mind to vague recognition. Let us see how this works. First of all, there are certain real words that frame the nonsense words. The verse starts with "it was" ("'Twas"). Ask yourself, what kind of word could follow "'Twas" in this particular line? Certainly not a verb. "'Twas *walked*"? Nobody would ever combine such words in English. Our intuition leads us to such expressions as "the night before Christmas," or "it was an evening in May." Which is to say that "brillig" is probably a time expression and "slithy" is probably an adjective followed by the noun "toves."

> 'Twas an evening in May and the happy girls
> Did dance and frolic in the snow:

Some such statement is being made here. We know it; we feel it; it could not be otherwise. Whatever particular words you might choose to fill in here, they would all have the same *form:* they would be time expression, adjective, noun/verb, verb, noun. The same principles apply to the next two lines:

> All mimsy were the borogoves,
> And the mome raths outgrabe.
>
> All (adjective) were the (noun),
> And the (adjective) (noun) (verb).
>
> All happy were the carolers,
> And the young boys rejoiced.

How do we know and why do we feel that these kinds of words fit into these particular places? As modern linguists point out (see Francis), we are responding here to the structural or grammatical meanings that we learned as children, long before we could read or write. We heard words in certain positions within an utterance: the subject came first, followed by an action, then by an object or adjective. We learned to identify the territories where we could expect to encounter one or another form. In other words, we learned the basic grammatical process of the English language: word order.

We also learned that certain kinds of words changed in set ways; some might have an *s* sound attached to end, and, when they did, certain other words would change their form to be in *agreement* with them. Thus we feel that "borogoves" is plural; it has an *s* ending, and the verb that precedes it is a verb that goes with a plural noun. If "borogoves" were singular, the verb preceding it would be "was," not "were."

It does not matter what the individual word denotes here: "borogoves" could mean "cars" or "handkerchiefs." In either case—in *any case*—the structural or grammatical meaning (the terms are interchangeable) remains constant: an *s* ending signals plurality, and an alteration in verb form signals a particular relationship between the verb and the noun. Collectively these changes in form are known as *inflection.* Inflection is the second most important structural device in the English language.

There is a third formal device. Function words such as "the," "and," "by" have no concrete meaning when they stand alone but serve an important function within the context of a sentence. There they help to indicate how substantive words—that is, words with a full referential meaning, such as "water" and "sink"—are related: "The water is *in* the sink"; "The shoes are *under* the bed." Function words are *determiners,* or *formal markers,* that help us to identify other words in the sentence and indicate how other words are functioning: as verbs? nouns? adjectives? After all, what a word *is* depends on how it functions in the sentence: one may *jump* across a puddle (verb); one may take a big *jump* (noun); or one may watch a referee at a basketball game toss up a *jump* ball (adjective).

When we find a "the" or "a" preceding words such as "toves" or "wabe," we know that they are words to which an *s* can be added, words that we, using traditional terminology, call "nouns." Thus, when we substitute for "borogoves" we automatically do so with another noun. Similarly, by using the function word "and" at the beginning of the fourth line—"and the mome raths outgrabe"—the writer is telling us that the fourth line conveys a parallel assertion to the assertion in line three, "All mimsy were the borogoves." The past tense "were" (rather than "are") in line three is therefore carried over, by virtue of the connective "and" (a conjunction), to line four. The "borogoves *were,*" and the "mome raths" also appear to have completed some action in the past.

REVIEWING THE GRAMMAR OF THE SENTENCE

Grammar, very simply, is the structure of a language or the study of how a language works. This review of the basic grammar of the sentence moves from a consideration of the function of various parts of a sentence to a discussion of the way the parts are combined to form phrases, clauses, and sentences. The section concludes with a review of the principles of sentence correctness.

A sentence is composed of a subject and a predicate, alone or in combination with one or more of the following: a direct object, an indirect object, a subject complement, an object complement, modifiers (adjectival or adverbial), and connectives.

Subjects

According to the familiar schoolroom definition, the subject (S) of a sentence names the person, thing, or concept spoken about. It can be identified by asking Who or what is doing the action? But this definition ignores a fundamental problem: sentences are often constructed so that the grammatical subject is different from the actual topic of the sentence—the notional subject. (See Gregory Colomb and Joseph Williams, 95.)

The announcer reported that the hurricane would soon reach Miami.

A more reliable definition is that the grammatical subject of a sentence is the element that changes position (or immediately follows a form of *to be*) when the sentence is converted to a question.

Did the announcer report that the hurricane would soon reach Miami?

Subjects are generally nouns or noun substitutes—pronouns, gerunds, infinitives, or clauses.

Noun:	The *woman* is busy.
	Chicago is cold in winter.
	Is *Chicago* cold in winter?
Pronoun:	*She* is busy.
	It is cold in winter.
	Is *she* busy?
Gerund:	*Talking* with friends makes me happy.
	Does *talking* with friends make me happy?
Infinitive:	*To know* me is to love me.
	Is *to know* me to love me?
Clause:	*What I am doing* makes me happy.
	Does *what I am doing* make me happy?

Almost any word or group of words, however, can serve as a subject. For example, a word normally used as an adverb can be used as a noun:

Now is the time.

So too can a prepositional phrase (although awkward, it is correct):

> *After graduation* is too late to think about a career.

What is important is not a rigid classification of a word as, say, an adverb or of a phrase according to its form, but rather its use in the sentence. Whatever fits the subject slot is a subject.

Predicates

The predicate—a verb (V) plus its object (O) or complement (C), if any—makes an assertion about the subject and generally carries the greatest weight of meaning. A verb is a word that functions in the sentence as the predicate or as part of the predicate.

Verbs   Verbs are conventionally defined as words that assert action or state of being. A more precise definition would incorporate the fact that verbs *predicate* some action of the subject: that is, they make a statement ("She worked hard"), ask a question ("Are you coming?"), or issue a command or direction ("Fold the batter into a cakepan").

Auxiliaries

Though most people recognize auxiliaries as verbs, they are not precisely verbs but rather verb markers. They include the forms of *be, have, do, can, may, will, shall, must,* and *ought to.* Each of the first three can stand as the main verb in a sentence, but these auxiliaries, like the other six, also combine with regular or irregular verbs to form the various tenses and to indicate emphasis or continuation. The other auxiliaries cannot stand as the main verb in a sentence; they combine with *have* or *be* or with lexical verbs to show ability, obligation, intention, and so forth.

> We *do* that frequently.
> They *ought to* be here.

Regular and Irregular Verbs

English verbs have five main forms (often called principal parts): base (also called present or infinitive), -s form (third person singular, present tense), -ed form (past tense), -ing form (present participle), and -en form (past participle). The main difference between regular and irregular verbs is how each forms the past tense. Regular verbs simply add -ed to the base form to make the past tense (help, helped). Irregular (lexical) verbs form the past tense by changing the root vowel (give, gave).

Transitive and Intransitive Verbs

Verbs are transitive or intransitive. A *transitive* verb requires an *object* to complete its meaning.

> d.o.
> The professor *asked* a question.

An *intransitive* verb does not require an object to complete its meaning.

> They *moaned* and *cried.*

The same verb may sometimes be used transitively or intransitively.

> d.o.
> Mary *paints* pictures. (transitive)
> Mary *paints* beautifully. (intransitive)

Linking Verbs

Linking verbs (sometimes called "state of being" verbs)—for example, *feel, seem, be, appear, become, smell, taste*—are considered intransitive because they serve merely to connect or "link" a subject with its subject complement.

> She *felt* happier than ever.
> He *was becoming* anxious.
> It *smelled* terrible.

Tense

Verbs are inflected to indicate tense, or time. English basically has two simple tenses which are inflected. The other four "tenses" (compound tenses) are formed by combining a past participle with an auxiliary. Because the simple tenses with the compound tenses indicate six different time senses, we often say that English has six tenses.

> *Present:* She *asks* no questions.
> *Past:* She *asked* no questions.
> *Future:* She *will ask* no questions.
> *Present Perfect:* She *has asked* no questions.
> *Past Perfect:* She *had asked* no questions.
> *Future Perfect:* She *will have asked* no questions.

Present tense is often used to express universal truth ("All people are mortal"), habitual action ("He longs for final answers"), or an historical or literary present ("Shakespeare writes of universal human values.")

Voice

The transformation to passive voice can be performed only with transitive verbs; intransitive verbs are never passive. As we have seen, a transitive verb in the *active* voice has a direct object.

> d.o.
> The police officer *put* a parking ticket on the car.

We can transform a verb to the *passive* voice when we convert the object to the subject by casting the verb into a phrase consisting of a form of the verb *to be*, followed by a past participle.

> A parking ticket *was put* on the car by the police officer.

Note that the subject of a verb cast in the active voice performs an action, while the subject of a verb cast in the passive voice receives an action.

Mood

In English, verbs have three moods: indicative, subjunctive, and imperative. The mood indicates the writer's attitude about the action—whether it is to be understood as fact (indicative), as possible or desirable (subjunctive), or as a necessity (imperative).

Indicative: makes a statement or assertion (The car *needs* repair), asks a question (Does the car *need* repair?)

Subjunctive: suggests actions that are probable, possible, or contrary to fact or desire. Once used in many constructions, the subjunctive mood is now used in a limited number of forms: in the present and past tense of the verb *to be* (If I *were* you, I would repair the car.), in *that* clauses pertaining to parliamentary motions, or in recommendation or resolution statements:

I move that the car *be* repaired.
She recommended that he *repair* the car.
Resolved that this car *be* repaired.

Imperative: issues a command, request, or directive (*Repair* the car.)

Objects A sentence may contain a direct object, both a direct and an indirect object, or neither. Unless a sentence contains a transitive verb, it will not contain an object. We can identify a direct object by asking who or what receives the action. We can usually identify an indirect object by asking to whom or for whom the action is done.

Mark ordered a dozen *roses*. (direct object)
Mark ordered *her* a dozen roses. (indirect object)

Notice that indirect objects occur only in the presence of direct objects.

Complements Sentences may contain subject or object complements. *Subject complements* occur with linking verbs and are nouns (or noun substitutes) or adjectives that complete the meaning of the subject.

She seemed *haughty*. (adjective)
Einstein was a *genius*. (noun)

Object complements refer to the direct object and may also be either nouns (or noun substitutes) or adjectives.

George painted the fence *white*. (adjective)
The article called him a *patriot*. (noun)

Modifiers Variety and nuance in sentences are often achieved by adding modifying words, phrases, and clauses. Basically, there are two types of modifiers: adjectival and adverbial.

Adjectives
Adjectives are words that modify (qualify, quantify, describe, or limit) nouns and pronouns.

The *four* boys rode their *new* bikes.

Frequently, a word that ordinarily functions as another part of speech may be converted to adjectival use.

In order to lose weight, she went to a *milk* farm.

Here the word *milk,* normally a noun and sometimes a verb ("She *milked* the cow"), is being used as an adjective. Similarly, nouns in the possessive case ("*Gloria's* room," "the *boy's* trousers") and such pronouns as *this, that, her, our, your* may serve an adjectival function ("*Our* clothes are wet"); so may certain phrases and clauses, as we shall see.

Adverbs
Adverbs are words that modify (qualify, quantify, describe, or limit) verbs, adjectives, or other adverbs.

He drank his milk *slowly.*
The milk was *terribly* sour.
He drank his milk *very* slowly.

In addition, adverbs may modify gerunds, participles, and infinitives.

Adverbs generally indicate place (*nowhere, here*), definite time (*now, yesterday*), indefinite time (*often, always, seldom, never*), degree (*very, exactly, quite, almost*), and manner (*quietly, softly, stealthily*).

Sometimes an adverb may qualify an entire sentence.

Clearly, that man is incompetent.
Surely you don't mean that.
I *certainly* do mean it.

Many adverbs are formed simply by adding *-ly* to an adjective: *rapid* (adjective), *rapidly* (adverb). However, many adverbs do not have a final *-ly,* as you can see above in the list of adverbs signifying place, time, and manner. Still other adverbs have the same form as their corresponding adjectives. The word *slow,* for instance, may be used as either adjective or adverb. Contrary to what many people think, the road sign "Go Slow" is grammatically correct.

Connectives (Function Words) As the term suggests, connectives serve mainly to connect other words in the sentence and to show their relationship. Having no meaning of their own apart from their function in the sentence, the two major kinds of connectives, prepositions and conjunctions, are often called "function words."

Prepositions
Prepositions connect nouns or noun equivalents to show how they are related to some other part of the sentence or to the whole sentence.

She walked *into* the room two minutes *before* class ended.
Up the street a man was watering his lawn

The preposition and the noun (which may have its own modifiers) constitute a modifying unit, the noun serving as the so-called object of the preposition.

There are many prepositions in the English language (such as *out, in, to, toward, under, over, between, in front of, in back of*), and their use is generally established by idiom and usage. Sometimes usage is so lax and regionally determined that one may communicate the same idea by using different prepositions ("I got *up* from the bed," "I got *down* from the bed," "I got *out* of bed").

One rule, however, has no exceptions: a pronoun following a preposition must be in the objective case. Many people violate this rule by using the expression "between you and *I*" in the belief that *I* is somehow more elegant than plain *me*. To avoid such overcompensation, it may be helpful to think of the analogous expression "between *us*," for which "between *we*" would never be used.

There is an old prohibition against ending a sentence with a preposition, which grew out of a mistaken belief that English grammar must imitate Latin grammar. Winston Churchill is said to have dismissed this "rule" as "the sort of English up with which I will not put" (Gowers, 131). As a general guideline, use a final preposition if the sentence sounds more natural and idiomatic and retains proper emphasis.

Conjunctions
Acting as function words, conjunctions connect words, phrases, or clauses. There are two kinds of conjunctions: coordinating and subordinating.

Coordinating conjunctions (*and, but, or, nor, for, yet*) connect words or word groups of equal grammatical rank.

> The girl *and* the boy were skating.
> It is a warm *but* cloudy day.
> Did you open the front door *or* the living room window?

In using a coordinating conjunction, make certain that the elements on both sides of the conjunction are of equal rank: If the conjunction joins two single words they should be the same part of speech; if two word groups are joined, both should be either phrases or clauses (see the discussion of parallelism on pages 596–597).

Subordinating conjunctions (*if, since, because, when, although*, and so on) connect sentence elements that are of unequal rank—specifically, main and subordinate clauses—and show their relationship. The following list presents the most commonly used subordinating conjunctions, grouped according to the specific relationships they establish.

Comparison: *than, as . . . as*

> She has no more feeling than a stone.

Condition: *If, unless, whether, as long as, provided that*

> If the rain continues, the picnic will be postponed until Saturday.

Concession or contrast: *though, although, even though*

> Although the archeologists dug steadily for six months, they failed to find any artifacts.

Degree or comparison: *as, just as, as much as, as . . . as, than*

They carried as much food and water to the survivors as they could.
John ranked higher on the College Boards than Jim ranked last year.

Manner: *as, as if, as though*

She studied for the exam as she had been instructed.

Place: *where, wherever*

Wherever you go in California, you are certain to see spectacular scenery.
I found my gloves where I had left them.

Purpose: *so that, in order that*

I have written full instructions on the board so that the exam can begin on time.

Reason or cause: *because, since, as*

They laughed because they were enjoying themselves.

Time: *when, until, before, while, since, as*

While they were attending the lecture, fire broke out in the basement.

Conjunctive adverbs simultaneously connect main clauses and provide an adverbial modifier. The chief conjunctive adverbs include single words (*however, furthermore, thus, therefore, indeed, consequently, nonetheless, moreover*) and transitional phrases (*for example, in addition, in fact, on the other hand, on the contrary, at the same time, that is*). In contrast to subordinating conjunctions, conjunctive adverbs generally relate two main clauses and are preceded by a semicolon rather than a comma:

The weather bureau was issuing storm warnings hourly;
nevertheless, the crew decided to set sail and hope for the best.

Relationships of Words

Phrases   A phrase is a group of words that functions as a unit but does not contain a subject and predicate. A phrase may be classified according to its own construction and according to the part of speech for which it performs a function.

Prepositional Phrase
A preposition introduces a prepositional phrase; it functions as an adjective or adverb.
Adjectival: modifies a noun or pronoun

The girl *in the bright green dress* entered the room.
Her yellow hat, *with its purple feathers,* attracted our attention.

Adverbial: modifies a verb, adverb, or adjective

The man walked *through a long, dark tunnel.*
Drive carefully *on icy streets.*
The bread was still hot *from the oven.*

Verbal Phrase
A verbal phrase consists of a verb form plus other words; it functions as a noun, an adjective, or an adverb.
Gerund: often called a "verbal noun"; always ends in -*ing;* functions as a noun; takes objects, complements, and modifiers.

> *Stealing someone else's lines* is plagiarism.
> *Stealing with a grand flourish* is still stealing.
> My favorite exercise is *dancing the polka.*

Participle: often called a "verbal adjective"; modifies a noun or pronoun.

> The woman *banging on the door* was obviously terrified.
> *Having been rejected,* he plunged into a depression.

Infinitive: functions as a noun, an adjective, or an adverb.

> *To see* is *to believe.* (noun)
> Jan is an artist *to be admired.* (adjective)
> The meat was marinated *to make it tastier.* (adverb)

Absolutes A group of words containing a noun followed by a modifier, an absolute usually expresses a cause or a condition or else offers additional information about the main clause.

> We'll go on a picnic today, *weather permitting.*
> Lee flushed angrily, *his foot tapping.*

Because absolutes may modify whole clauses or entire sentences, they are also called "sentence modifiers" or "parenthetical phrases."

> *The sun having come out,* we prepared for our picnic.
> We were both concerned, *Joan about the food and I about the weather.*

Clauses A clause is a group of related words containing both a subject and a predicate and forming a sentence or part of a sentence.

Main Clauses
Main (or independent) clauses can stand alone as simple, separate sentences.

> The man called my name, and I called his name in return.
> They have made sensible plans; furthermore, they know how to implement them.
> No higher praise can be given than this: he was a man who lived by principle.

Subordinate Clauses
A subordinate (or dependent) clause is a clause that contains some word which keeps it from being able to stand alone as a sentence (and links it to some element of the sentence of which it is a part).

> . . . when a parent accompanies them.

The sense of this clause depends on the rest of the sentence; therefore, it is clearly a subordinate clause. However, when subordinate clauses are read in connected discourse, it is rarely so easy to see that they do not stand alone.

> Sixteen-year-olds can get a permit when a parent accompanies them.
> I thought when I got there she would already have arrived.

Unless you can recognize which clauses can stand alone and which cannot, there is no reliable way to identify a subordinate clause. However, a simple—though not always reliable—method is to look for a subordinating conjunction or relative pronoun and then check to see if what follows contains both a subject and a predicate. Most subordinate clauses begin this way although occasionally the *that* introducing a noun clause or the *who, whom, which,* or *that* introducing an adjective clause will be understood (see the examples above and below). In such a case, the appropriate conjunction can always be inserted before the clause in question without disturbing the sense of the sentence.

Subordinate clauses may be used as adjectives, adverbs, or nouns. An *adjective clause* modifies a noun or a pronoun and is generally introduced by a relative pronoun *(who, whom, which, that)* or by a relative adverb *(where, when, why):*

> This pen, *which I found in the library,* belongs to Lee.
> The store *where I bought the dress* is closed for the afternoon.
> She is a girl *I cannot understand.* (relative pronoun *whom* omitted)

An *adverbial clause* is introduced by a subordinating conjunction, which indicates the exact relationship between the subordinate idea and the main idea:

> His friends gave a party *when he returned.*
> She agreed to go *although she had grave reservations.*

A *noun clause* functions like a noun and—like an adjective clause—is generally introduced by *who, whom, which, that;* also by *whichever, whoever, whomever, where, when, why.*

> *Whoever telephoned for an appointment this morning* has just called back.
> He said *that he would arrive at noon.*
>   or
> He said *he would arrive at noon.* (conjunction *that* may sometimes be omitted)

Using subordinate clauses effectively will enhance your writing, enabling you to combine facts in varied sentence patterns which show more exact relationships than the mere stringing together, in a coordinate sequence, of one idea after another.

> Coordination: I went downtown and it rained.
> Subordination: When I went downtown, it rained.

Sentence Types

Sentences may also be classified in four categories on the basis of the clauses they contain: simple, compound, complex, compound-complex.

Simple A simple sentence contains only one subject and one predicate—that is, one main clause, with no subordinate clauses. Such a sentence may contain modifying phrases, however.

> I decided to go home.
> Tired and dejected, I decided to go home.

Compound A compound sentence contains at least two subjects and two predicates— that is, two or more main clauses, with no subordinate clauses. A compound sentence is actually two independent sentences linked by a semicolon and/or by a coordinating conjunction (*and, but, for, or, nor, yet*) or conjunctive adverb (*however, therefore,* and so on).

> She was a sophomore; he was a junior.
> She wanted to leave the stage, but the audience would not stop applauding.
> The reviews of the show were poor; however, the word-of-mouth reports were excellent.

The compound sentence is useful when you wish to express two thoughts that are of approximately equal value or that are contrasting or opposing aspects of a single idea. The pairing of independent clauses into a compound sentence provides a structure that clarifies the relationship between the clauses.

Complex A complex sentence contains one main clause and one or more subordinate clauses.

> Although the reviews of the show were poor, the word-of-mouth reports were excellent.

Use a complex sentence when you wish to show more precisely the relationship between ideas—specifically, when you wish to give greater stress or importance to one part of the sentence. In such cases it is advisable to subordinate grammatically that which is actually subordinate or less important. (See Revising for Emphasis.)

Compound-Complex A compound-complex sentence contains at least two main clauses and at least one subordinate clause.

When the flowers arrived, she placed them in a large vase; thus she enjoyed the rest of the afternoon, gazing at his fragrant gift.

REVISING FOR CORRECTNESS

Errors that occur in writing are generally of three kinds: errors in grammatical form, errors in sentence integrity, and errors in sentence coherence.

Grammatical Form

Most errors in grammatical form involve problems with agreement, pronoun case, verb tense, and use of the comparative and superlative degrees of adjectives and adverbs.

Agreement of Subject and Verb

1. A verb should agree with its subject in person and number.

Many zoo animals (third person plural subject) live (plural verb) in crowded cages.
She (third person singular subject) lives (third person singular verb) in the country.

2. Two or more subjects connected by *and* require a plural verb.

A noun and a verb are necessary in a sentence.

Exception: When two singular subjects connected by *and* present a single idea, the verb may be singular.

His pride and joy is his new car.
Ham and eggs is my favorite breakfast.

3. When two or more subjects are connected by *or*, *either . . . or*, or *neither . . . nor*, the verb agrees with the subject nearest to it.

Either the men or the woman is guilty.
Neither Jim nor his brothers are guilty.

4. A collective noun referring to a group as a unit requires a singular verb; a collective noun referring to individuals in a group acting separately requires a plural verb.

The class is attentive.
The class are going their separate ways.

The public is easy to reach.
The public are writing letters to the radio station.

5. Nouns plural in form but singular in meaning require a singular verb.

The news is bad.
Economics is a popular subject.
Politics is an art.
Ethics, like politics, is not a science.
The Magnificent Ambersons is a fine film.

6. Words stating time, money, fractions, weight, and amount are generally singular and require a singular verb.

Thirty days is a long time.
Five dollars is the price.
Two-thirds of nine is six.
Twenty pounds is not considered excessive.
Twelve miles is a long walk.

7. A prepositional phrase that follows a subject does not affect the number of the verb.

The size of the pictures in the album is small.
The cost of his pranks was paid by his parents.

8. A relative pronoun used as a subject may be either singular or plural, depending on the number of its antecedent.

John is one of those men who always complain. (antecedent of *who is men*)
John is the only one of those men who always complains. (antecedent of *who* is *one*)

9. Singular pronouns require singular verbs: *each, everyone, everybody, anyone, anybody, someone, somebody, no one, nobody, one, another, anything, either, neither.*

Each of the students is gifted.
Neither of the candidates shows any promise.

The pronoun *none* is singular or plural according to context.

None of the students was willing to reply.
None of the students were able to attend.

10. Since *every* **and** *many a* **before a word or series of words are viewed as modifiers, they should be followed by singular verbs.**

Every man, woman, and child in town is invited.
Many a person in this situation has given up.

11. A singular subject followed by *with, in addition to, as well as,* **and** *including* **requires a singular verb.**

The woman, as well as the three men in the car, was injured.
Maria, as well as Jim, is leaving for the weekend.

12. In *here is/here are* **and** *there is/there are* **constructions, the noun following the verb is considered the real subject and therefore determines the person and number of the verb. A singular subject obviously requires a singular verb:**

Here is your coat.

Similarly, a plural subject requires a plural verb:

There are thirty students in the class.

When the first element of a compound subject is singular, the choice between a singular or plural verb is a matter of taste:

There was (or *were*) joy and tears in her eyes.

Agreement of Pronoun and Antecedent A pronoun should agree with its antecedent in person, number, and gender. That is, a pronoun and the noun to which it refers should match.

The chairman (third person, singular, masculine) submitted his (third person, singular masculine) report.

The women (third person, plural, feminine) left their (third person, plural) books on the shelf.

Mary and Carlos (compound subject) handed in their (plural) papers.

The sales pitch for aspirin (third person, singular, neuter) emphasized its (third person, singular, neuter) pain-killing properties.

Like securing agreement of subject and verb, guaranteeing agreement of pronoun and antecedent is not always as easy as it sounds. Below are guides to follow for common agreement situations that may cause difficulty.

1. Collective nouns that refer to a group as a unit require singular pronouns; those that refer to individuals in a group acting separately require plural pronouns.

The jury announced its verdict.

The audience applauded their hero.

2. The indefinite pronouns *each, either, neither, somebody, anybody, nobody, someone, anyone,* and *no one* require a singular pronoun; *everyone* and *everybody* take a singular or plural pronoun depending on meaning.

No one knew where to find his or her coat.

Everyone reported his and her grades.

  or

Everyone reported their grades.

Linguist Martha Kolln ("Everyone's Right to Their Own Language," *College Composition and Communication,* Feb. 1986, 100-102) points out that certain indefinite pronouns—in particular *everyone* and *everybody*—act in sentences the same way that collective nouns act. That is, they may refer to persons who are members of a group but who act separately (as, for instance, members of an audience may). She suggests that when such is the case, the plural pronoun may be used and that in many instances the singular pronoun is inappropriate. She gives the example "At first *everyone* in the room was singing; then *they* began to laugh." The conservative usage is still to use the singular.

Another difficulty occurs with indefinite pronouns. Since English has no single pronoun to indicate both male and female, *he* has traditionally been used to refer to both genders. Such usage is essentially inaccurate, however, because the reference may be to a woman as well as to a man. There are several ways to avoid this problem. One is to pluralize.

As a finale, they all threw their hats in the air.

Another possibility is to use *his or her* as the example below does.

As a finale, everyone threw his or her hat in the air.

Yet another solution is to rephrase the sentence.

As a finale, hats of every sort were tossed into the air.

3. The impersonal *one* may be followed by *his or her,* but take care not to overuse this solution.

One should watch his or her manners.

An alternate and more conservative usage provides more consistency and accuracy.

One should watch one's manners.

4. Who refers to persons, *which* to things, and *that* to persons or things.

I voted for the candidate who (that) gave the most logical speeches.
I bought the car which (that) was most economical.
I prefer the cat that has orange stripes.

The importance of definite, unambiguous pronoun reference cannot be overemphasized. For further discussion and illustrations, see "Sentence Coherence."

Pronoun Case Forms Pronouns and—to a lesser extent—nouns undergo *inflection,* a change of form to indicate their specific meaning or grammatical function in the sentence. The inflectional form of a noun or pronoun is referred to as its *case;* a subject (except the subject of an infinitive or of a participle that is in the objective case) is required to be in the *subjective,* or nominative, case *(woman/she);* an object is required to be in the *objective* case *(woman/her).* The *possessive,* or genitive, case form is indicated in nouns by the use of an apostrophe and in pronouns by a change in form *(woman's/hers).*

Nouns and some indefinite pronouns vary their case form only to show possession:

The *girl's* book was lost on the train.
Anybody's mother would have felt the same way.

The following six pronouns require different and distinctive forms in all three cases:

Subjective	I	we	he, she	they	who
Possessive	my (mine)	our (ours)	his, her (hers)	their (theirs)	whose
Objective	me	us	him, her	them	whom

You should keep several other principles of case in mind:

1. The personal pronouns *it* and *you* are inflected only to show possession: *its, your, yours.*

2. A pronoun used in apposition should be in the same case as the noun or pronoun to which it is in apposition.

They put the blame on the two of us, John and *me.*

3. The case of a pronoun is determined by its function in its own clause.

She will invite *whoever* can come. (pronoun subject of clause)
She will invite *whomever* she wants. (pronoun object of clause)
I will talk to *whoever* is in the office. (pronoun subject of clause)

4. In standard written English the pronoun *whom* is consistently used when its position in the sentence requires the objective case.

The student *whom* he advised has finally registered. (*Whom* is direct object of *advised.*)
To *whom* are you addressing that question? (*Whom* is object of preposition *to.*)

Exceptions: In informal usage—in speech or when the pronoun opens the sentence (where the subjective case is normally the rule)—the use of *who* has become acceptable, indeed idiomatic.

> *Who* did I see you with last night?
> She is a student *who* I admire greatly.

In many instances it is possible to avoid the controversy and confusion that surround the use of *who/whom* by simply editing the pronoun out of the sentence.

> She is a student I admire greatly.
> Are you talking about any particular writer? (rather than the correct but awkward-sounding *Whom are you talking about?*)

On similar grounds, writers who object to the conventionally correct use of the subjective case of a pronoun used as subject complement of the linking verb *be* ("Can it be *they?*") can sidestep the issue by recasting the sentence ("Do you hear them coming?"). "It's me" (as opposed to the grammatically pure "It is I") has already been established as an idiom, but can be avoided by simply answering, "Speaking."

5. The case of a pronoun following *than, as,* or *but* is determined by whether the pronoun is the subject or object of the verb that follows, whether that verb is explicitly stated or only implied.

> She is older than *I* (am).
> They call her more often than (they call) *me*.

Verb Tense Probably the most serious mistakes writers make with verb tense involve choosing the correct form in setting up the logical sequence of tenses in a compound or complex sentence.

Illogical Sequence of Verbs

When sentences contain more than one verb—as in complex sentences—and when those verbs indicate actions taking place at different times, the sequence in which the tenses are presented reflects very precisely the time relationships between the verbs. But not every combination is logical; because the tense of the verb in the independent clause governs that, in the dependent clause, only certain combinations can logically occur:

1. If the verb in the independent clause is in the present tense, the verb in the dependent clause

a. indicates action occurring at the same time if it is also in the present tense:

> Elizabeth *knows* that she *wants* to take Latin.
> Elizabeth *knows* that she *does want* to take Latin.
> Elizabeth *knows* that she *is going* to take Latin.

b. indicates action occurring at an earlier time if it is in the past tense:

I *think* that she *asked* the same question earlier.
I *think* that she *did ask* the same question earlier.
I *think* that she *was asking* the same question earlier.

    c. indicates continuous action from the past to the present if it is in the present perfect tense:

He *says* that they *have lived* there for centuries.
He *says* that they *have been living* there for centuries.

    d. indicates action yet to happen if it is in the future tense:

My car *needs* a tune up because I *will drive* it across country.
My car *needs* a tune up because I *will be driving* it across country.

    2. If the verb in the independent clause is in the past tense, the verb in the dependent clause.

    a. indicates a general truth if it is in the present tense:

Jefferson *argued* that we *are* all created equal.

    b. indicates earlier action if it is in the past tense:

They *lived* in an apartment after they *moved* to Sandusky.

    c. indicates action begun and completed in an earlier past if it is in past perfect tense:

We *understood* that the supplies *had been exhausted* during the first hour.

    3. If the verb in the independent clause is in the present or past perfect tense, the verb in the dependent clause must be in the past tense:

My bank account *has shrunk* since I *started* paying my own tuition.
My bank account *had shrunk* before I *started* paying my own tuition.

    4. If the verb in the independent clause is in the future tense, the verb in the dependent clause

    a. indicates simultaneous action if it is in the present tense:

They *will leave* when they *are* ready.

Note that the future tense in the dependent clause is not only unnecessary, but can also be confusing:

They will leave when they will be ready.

    b. indicates earlier action if it is in the past tense:

They *will get* good grades if they *answered* the questions correctly.

    c. indicates future action earlier than the verb of the independent clause if it is in the present perfect tense:

Gas *will explode* again from Lake Nyos unless the government *has taken* the proper precautions.

5. If the verb in the independent clause is in the future perfect tense, the verb in the dependent clause indicates future time whether it is in present or present perfect tense:

The government *will have installed* a pipe to drain off unwanted carbon dioxide gas by the time this decade *ends*.
The government *will have installed* a pipe to drain off unwanted carbon dioxide gas by the time this decade *has ended*.

For a discussion of the importance of carefully controlling verb tense and of how confusing shifts in voice, tense, and mood of the verb can be, see the discussion of sentence coherence, pages 585–587.

Adjectives and Adverbs: Comparative and Superlative Degrees Adjectives and adverbs are capable of showing degree; that is, they can indicate the extent to which they modify a word. Adjectives and adverbs have three levels of degree: positive, comparative, and superlative. The positive degree shows no comparison, the comparative degree indicates differing levels between two things, and the superlative among three or more. The degrees are indicated by the use of *-er* or *more* (or *less*) for the comparative and *-est* or *most* (or *least*) for the superlative.

Positive: His stereo is *loud*.
                 Mark plays *beautifully*.
                 Those bookends are not *useful*.

Comparative: His stereo is *louder* than mine.
                 Mark plays *more beautifully* than Pete.
                 Those bookends are *less useful* than these.

Superlative: His stereo is the *loudest* in the whole apartment complex.
                 Mark plays the *most beautifully* of all the guitarists I know.
                 The ornamental bookends are the *least useful* of all of them.

No hard and fast rule can be stated for when to use the *-er* or *-est* ending and when to combine the adjective or adverb with *more* or *most*. In general, most one-syllable adjectives and a few one syllable adverbs form the comparative and superlative degree by the addition of -er and -est, whereas most other adverbs and the longer adjectives combine with *more* or *most*. There are exceptions to this rule of thumb, however, so if you are uncertain of how to form a particular comparative or superlative, consult your dictionary.

More crucial are the problems of the incomplete comparison and of the double comparison. When you use the comparative degree, state both elements of the comparison so that the sentence is clear. We have become used to incomplete comparisons in advertising, but they still have not gained acceptance in writing because they leave too much opportunity for confusion.

Incomplete:	I like her better.
Improved:	I like her better than I like Susan.
	I like her better than I used to.

Not only must your comparisons be complete, but you must avoid double comparisons. If an adjective or adverb has an *-er* or *-est* ending, it is already inflected for the comparative or superlative degree, and the addition of *more, less, most,* or *least* does not add intensity. If your intent is to intensify a comparative or superlative, do so with the addition of a different modifier.

Double:	That dog is the most meanest dog in the neighborhood.
Improved:	That dog is undoubtedly the meanest dog in the neighborhood.

Additional difficulties arise with irregular adjectives and adverbs. *Good* and *well* both have the comparative and superlative *better* and *best,* and *bad* and *badly* both have the comparative and superlative *worse* and *worst.* This duplication may have contributed to usage problems in both sets. *Good* and *bad* are used as adjectives with linking verbs and not as adverbs. *Well* and *badly* are used as adverbs.

Alex looks *good* in blue.
Alex does not look *bad* in green.
The lawnmower runs *well.*
The grass needs mowing *badly.*

In recent years, however, the distinction between *bad* and *badly* has begun to blur and many people accept "The lawnmower runs bad," at least in informal speech. The most conservative course, naturally, is to continue to observe the distinction. (For a discussion of adverbs that have the same form as their corresponding adjectives, see page 625.) Of the other irregular adjectives, *many, much,* and *some* also share forms (*more* and *most*) for the comparative and superlative degrees. *Little* (*less, least*) offers few problems except as *less* is confused with *fewer* (*less* means *how much* and accompanies a singular noun, whereas *fewer* means *how many* and accompanies a plural noun).

Sentence Integrity

A standard English sentence contains at least one complete subject and one complete predicate, properly punctuated. When a sentence contains more than one complete subject and predicate, it must also contain either a subordinating conjunction or relative pronoun to indicate dependent clauses or else it must contain the punctuation necessary to separate independent clauses. Deviations from the standard may confuse the reader and suggest that the writer has been careless and negligent.

The three most common problems in sentence integrity are fragments, comma splices, and fused sentences. Properly speaking, comma splices and fused sentences are punctuation errors, but because they often reflect a writer's unawareness of basic sentence structure, they are best dealt with as problems of sentence integrity.

1. Sentence Fragment

a. Treating a participial phrase or verbal as if it were a whole sentence

Fragment: Calling frantically to the men on the pier, and pointing to the injured swimmer.

In this case the participial phrases should be replaced by at least one verb:

Correct: He called frantically to the men on the pier, pointing to the injured swimmer.

> or

Calling frantically . . ., he pointed . . . .

Fragment: She wanted to get *A*'s in all her subjects. Being competitive and ambitious.

Being is a verbal; the participial phrase modifies *she.*

Correct: Being competitive and ambitious, she wanted to get *A*'s in all her subjects.

b. Treating a subordinate clause like a main clause

Fragment: They wanted to return home as quickly as possible. Where they knew they would be welcome.

The *where* clause is subordinate and should be joined to its main clause by a comma.

Correct: They wanted to return home as quickly as possible, where they knew they would be welcome.

Exceptions

Divergence from the standard complete sentence is acceptable when you are trying to achieve some special effect, as in the following instances.

1. In the case of the imperative, where the subject is "understood."

    Don't go. (subject "understood" to be *you*)

2. An answer to a question.

    Was she angry? Not at all.

3. An exclamation.

    Never!
    What a joy!

4. Part of running dialogue.

    "They looked the other way. Didn't want to know the truth."

5. A descriptive word or phrase, set off for emphasis.

    The mountains were lofty and ice-capped. An awesome sight.

6. Part of a stream of consciousness in which the thought processes naturally flow in fragments.

> This late age of the world's experience had bred in them all, all men and women, a well of tears. Tears and sorrows; a perfectly upright and stoical bearing.
>
> —Virginia Woolf, *Mrs. Dalloway*

2. Comma Splice

This violation of sentence integrity occurs when a comma (rather than a period, semicolon, or colon) is used between two main clauses, thereby "splicing" the sentence.

Comma Splice:	She simply could not answer the question, it confused her completely.
Correct:	She simply could not answer the question. It confused her completely.
	or
	She. . .question; it. . . completely.
	or
	She. . . question, for it. . . completely.

When a comma rather than a semicolon is used before a conjunctive adverb (*however, therefore, thus, nevertheless,* and so on), a comma splice results.

Comma Splice:	I wanted to go, however, I could not raise the fare.
Correct:	I wanted to go; however, I could not raise the fare.

Exceptions

1. When the clauses are very short and closely related, a comma may be used to separate them.

> That year my brother was eight, my sister was ten.

2. Comma splices are acceptable when you are trying to achieve some special effect as in stream of consciousness in which the thoughts naturally tumble over each other.

> He carried him into the hut and Major de Spain got light on a paper spill from the buried embers on the hearth and lit the lamp and Boon put Sam on his bunk and drew off his boots and Major de Spain covered him and the boy was not there, he was holding the mules, the sound one which was trying again to bolt since when the wagon stopped Old Ben's scent drifted forward again along the streaming blackness of air, but Sam's eyes were probably open again on that profound look which saw further than them or the hut, further than the death of a bear and the dying of a dog.
>
> —William Faulkner, "The Bear"

3. Fused Sentence

This violation of sentence integrity consists in writing two sentences with no punctuation between them (no period or semicolon) and no coordinating conjunction.

Fused:	She got to the game on time that kind of punctuality was unusual for her.
Correct:	She got to the game on time. That kind of punctuality was unusual for her.
	or
	She got to the game on time; that kind. . . .

Exception

Fused sentences, like fragments and comma splices, are acceptable in a stream of consciousness that attempts to recapitulate the somewhat disordered and associative processes of raw thought:

> . . . that big heathen I first noticed him at dessert when I was cracking the nuts with my teeth I wished I could have picked every morsel of that chicken out of my fingers it was so tasty and browned and as tender as anything. . .
>
> —James Joyce, *Ulysses*

Sentence Coherence

To begin working toward a coherent sentence in which the main clause and its added elements flow smoothly and logically into one another—you must avoid the pitfalls listed below, each of which involves carelessness or misplacement of an added element.

Misplaced Modifiers It was a misplaced modifier that created the amusing song title of some years ago, "Throw Mama from the Train a Kiss." Similarly, it was a misplaced modifier (plus a few missing words) that produced the inadvertently humorous letter written by a serviceman's wife to the welfare service at Lackland Air Force Base: "In accordance with your instructions, I have given birth to twins in the enclosed envelope."

Word order is the principal grammatical process of the English language (the difference in meaning between "Dog bites man" and "Man bites dog" is simply a matter of how identical words are positioned); therefore it is vital that the writer arrange words on paper so that they show accurate relationships. Modifiers should be near the terms they modify, and related ideas should be close together; otherwise they may latch on to some other sentence element where they will not make sense.

Notice how easily the following sentences—each containing a misplaced modifier—can be improved either by repositioning the modifier or by restructuring the sentence slightly so that the reader can readily see what words and word groups are intended to go together:

Example:	He saw an accident that he reported yesterday.
Problem:	What does "yesterday" modify—the accident or the time of the report?
Improvement:	Yesterday he saw an accident, which he immediately reported.
	or
	He immediately reported the accident (that) he saw yesterday.
Example:	She was the kind of girl who could accept the fact that she was pigeon-toed with a smile.
Improvement:	She was the kind of girl who could accept with a smile the fact that she was pigeon-toed.

Example:	He was born while the Korean War was in progress in the United States.
Improvement:	He was born in the United States while the Korean War was in progress.

In improving sentences with a dangling modifier, the writer must either change the placement of the modifier or revise the syntax of the main clause in the sentence.

Example:	Having just returned from a long cruise, the city seemed unbearably hot.
Problem:	In *A Dictionary of American–English Usage,* Margaret Nicholson cites this as an example of the often inadvertently funny dangling participle. "The city had not been on the cruise," Nicholson points out—thereby voicing the English teacher's classic protest. Participles must be attached to the noun responsible for the action or they will "dangle." On this ground she revises the sentence to read:
Improvement:	Having just returned from a long cruise, we found the city unbearably hot.

A prohibitive attitude toward the dangling participle will be familiar to almost all students, for the construction has long been universally condemned—unfairly so, according to many contemporary writers on usage and style who point out that in most instances the so-called dangling modifier (it may be a gerund or an infinitive as well as a participle) is often modifying the entire main clause, not just the single noun subject. Thus, according to Bergen and Cornelia Evans in *A Dictionary of Contemporary American Usage* (New York: Random House), it is not misleading or unclear to say, "Looking at the subject dispassionately, what evidence is there?" They claim that "this is the idiomatic way of making statements of this kind and any other construction would be unnatural and cumbersome."

The general principle to follow is simply this: if a dangling modifier makes the meaning obscure or absurd you should rewrite the sentence so that it makes immediate sense. The reader should never have to reread the sentence in order to get it right. Thus, in order to be absolutely free of ambiguity, a sentence such as "After finishing college, my family moved to New York" should be improved to read "After I finished college, my family moved to New York."

Mixed Constructions   Sometimes a writer begins a sentence with one construction in mind and then, somewhere along the way, carelessly shifts to another.

Example:	Students know that by getting together to discuss a problem how they can avoid violence.
Improvement:	Students know that by getting together to discuss a problem they can avoid violence.

The second version of this sentence is an improvement because the second half of the sentence fulfills the expectation raised in the first half—namely that the subordinating conjunction "that" will be followed by a new subject and predicate. These grammatical terms may mean little or nothing to the average reader who has either forgotten or never really understood grammatical terminology, but the reader nonetheless responds to structural signs.

I believe that someone is knocking at the door.
> or

I believe that Harry will call.
> *not*

I believe that how hard you try is good.

In this last sentence, as in the example cited above, the subordinating conjunction "that" is followed by a second subordinating conjunction, "how." The result is momentary confusion in the reader's mind, for halfway along in the sentence the signals shift abruptly. The implied promise of the sentence has not been fulfilled; the reader's expectations have been thwarted.

It is important to avoid this kind of awkwardness in sentence construction. Actually, carelessness rather than ignorance creates such problems, for, as Lewis Carroll has shown us, all native speakers are unconsciously familiar with the basic structure of English.

Avoid Other Unnecessary Shifts We have seen that any change in the pattern of a sentence that surprises and stops the reader—even for a fraction of a second—or that disappoints an expectation set up in the early part of the sentence is a violation of coherence, the "sticking together" of the parts that makes the sentence a sound, consistent, and easy-to-read unit. In addition to shifts in the basic pattern of the sentence that produce hybrid construction, there are other kinds of shifts. They are not as obviously bad as those described above, but equally unnecessary and undesirable because they break up the flow and therefore the coherence of the sentence. These are shifts in voice, tense, mood, and person; we shall consider each of them in turn.

Shift in Voice

Example:	When the townspeople heard that the mayor had resigned, a general meeting was called.
Problem:	In the above sentence the writer has needlessly shifted from active to passive voice—and this, in turn, has involved a shift in subject from "townspeople" to "meeting." Both of these shifts interfere with the smooth, natural flow of the sentence.
Improvement:	When the townspeople discovered that the mayor had resigned, they called a general meeting.

Shift in Tense

Example:	They come into the room and began opening up the books that are on the table.
Problem:	the writer shifts carelessly from present to past to present tense.
Improvement:	They come into the room and begin opening up the books that are on the table.
	> or
	They came into the room and began opening up the books that were on the table.

Shift in Mood

Example: First discuss the problem; then you should take action.

Problem: A needless shift in mode or mood—from imperative, which issues a command or request, to subjunctive, which expresses obligation.

Improvement: First discuss the problem; then take action.

Shift in Person

Example: A student should know the provisions of the Civil Rights Act, for one cannot be a good citizen unless you keep up with current legislation.

Problem: The writer shifts from "student" to "one" to "you."

Improvement: A student should know the provisions of the Civil Rights Act, for he or she cannot be a good citizen unless he or she keeps up with current legislation.

                     or

               You should know the provisions of the Civil Rights Act, for you cannot be a good citizen unless you keep up with current legislation.

Blair sums up the case against unnecessary shifts:

> During the course of the Sentence, the scene should be changed as little as possible. We should not be hurried by sudden transitions from person to person, nor from subject to subject. There is commonly, in every Sentence, some person or thing, which is the governing word. This should be continued so, if possible, from the beginning to the end. . . . Should I express myself thus:
>
> > After we came to anchor they put me on shore, where I was welcomed by all my friends who received me with the greatest kindness.
>
> In this Sentence, though the objects contained in it have a sufficient connexion with each other, yet by this manner of representing them, by shifting so often both the place and the person, *we* and *they* and *I* and *who,* they appear in such a disunited view that the sense of connexion is almost lost. The Sentence is restored to its proper unity . . . in . . . the following manner:
>
> > Having come to anchor, I was put on shore, where I was welcomed by all my friends and received with the greatest kindness.[1]

Avoid Unclear Reference Still another violation of sentence coherence grows out of unclear pronoun reference, a common flaw in student writing. "Reference" suggests that the meaning of a pronoun depends on its antecedent. Strictly speaking, a pronoun is a word used in place of a noun; therefore, unless the reader knows precisely what noun or noun clause, what overall idea the pronoun is replacing, the sentence will be neither clear nor coherent.

---

[1]Note the dangling modifier here. Do you find it offensive? Can a person ("I") "come to anchor"?

Example:	The women were stopped and questioned by company guards. They then went to the police who refused to protect them. This attitude has also been reported in other towns.
Problem:	The direct antecedent of "they" in the second sentence is "guards." Yet (as we realize on a second reading), the pronoun is supposed to refer to "women." Still another problem: "This attitude" is not clear. Does the writer mean "this *hostile* attitude"—or what? The pronoun references do not provide a clear and definite guide to meaning because the writer has been careless about antecedents of the personal pronoun and has not supplied enough information to indicate precisely what the demonstrative adjective "this" refers to. It is up to the writer to say *specifically* what he or she means here. The reader should not be asked to fill in a noun and adjectives.
Improvement:	After being stopped and questioned by company guards, the women went to the police, who refused to protect them. A similar indifference on the part of the police has been reported in other towns.

Another unclear, ambiguous reference:

Example:	Jim's father was president of the college, which gave him considerable prestige.
Problem:	Does "him" refer to Jim's father? Technically it does, but is that what the writer means? (The reference of "which" is also vague.)
Improvement:	Because his father was president of the college, Jim enjoyed considerable prestige.

Avoid Unnecessary Splits Sentence flow or coherence is impaired by the careless separation or splitting of words that belong together, as in the following examples:

Subject Split from Its Verb

Example:	Zodomirsky, shocked and grieved at the death of Mariana, becomes a monk.
Improvement:	Shocked and grieved at the death of Mariana, Zodomirsky becomes a monk.

Verb Split from Its Object

Example:	She sipped slowly and contentedly the warm cocoa.
Improvement:	Slowly and contentedly she sipped the warm cocoa.

Verb Split from Its Auxiliaries

Example:	He had long ago known the woman.
Improvement:	He had known the woman long ago.
	or
	Long ago he had known the woman.

We should note here that not all splits are bad. Sometimes, as in the following sentence, the writer deliberately suspends the predication—the signal of the sentence's direction—without losing the flow or continuity of thought.

"Alienation," a term once confined to philosophy, law, psychiatry, and advanced literary criticism, has entered the daily vocabulary.

Avoid Weak Connectives Avoid small, loose connectives that detract from the impact of a statement. As an example, we may look at Wilson Follett's observation in *Modern American Usage* on the use of "as."

The novice's resort to *as* with the meaning *since* or *because* is always feeble. It makes trivial what follows. Webster (1934 edition) remarks: "*As* assigns a reason even more casually than *since*." What is worse, the untrained or heedless writer turns to this weak subordinating link to introduce a co-ordinate clause or what should be his main clause. In either case he ruins emphasis. *It was a comparatively unproductive year, as he was dogged by ill health and domestic worries.*

As Wilson Follett concluded, in place of *as* we should substitute the word *for.*

Similarly, the word "so" is a loose connective, more suited to rambling conversation than to writing.

So I told him I was *so* angry I could barely contain myself. And *so* he finally admitted he was *so* sorry he could hardly stand it. And *so* I said "forget it." *So* we made up and *so* I'm seeing him again tonight.

Where "so" is used as an intensifier ("I was *so* happy") it can usually be eliminated without loss, for like most so-called intensifiers ("I really was happy," "I truly was so very happy") it does not work. In fact, it may produce a reverse effect by creating uneasiness and suspicion. "Exactly how happy is *so* happy?" the reader may wonder. "Why is the writer being vague and seemingly inarticulate and insistent?"

The use of "so" to introduce a clause of purpose or a clause of result is equally ineffective, although the usage is clearly established in informal conversation.

I wanted to see the town so I asked them to take me along.
The glass was broken so I had to get another.

Even here the link provided by "so" is weak and can be made more emphatic by using "so that."

The glass was broken so that I had to get another.

Better still, the first half of the sentence can be subordinated.

Because (or since) the glass was broken, I had to get another.

GRAMMAR QUIZ

Read the following sentences carefully and determine which ones are grammatically correct and what errors have been committed in the incorrect sentences. How *should* they read? (*No rephrasing is necessary.*)

1. She writes much better than me.
2. Each voter must make their own decision about who to vote for.
3. Stealing someone else's words are plagiarism.
4. If I were more confident of my stand on foreign trade, I would run for Senator.
5. Turkey and stuffing are a traditional Thanksgiving treat.
6. The mechanic said that neither the carburator nor the timing were properly adjusted.
7. They objected to me cooking cabbage every Thursday.
8. At the end of the road stands a large red maple and a gnarled oak.
9. They enrolled in college after they are serving in the military.
10. Margaret is the least reasonable of the two sisters.
11. Those coats are there for whoever needs them.
12. Each of his performances were electrifying.
13. I have as much of an interest in this subject as they.
14. Each of the students announces their own preferences.
15. The physics professor is one of those teachers whom is always prepared.
16. The zookeeper took the peanuts from Bill and I.
17. She dropped the glass she was always clumsy.
18. Being that he was the first one to think of the solution.
19. It is important that she be allowed to remain onstage with the orchestra.
20. I asked him nicely, he still wouldn't agree.
21. Just ahead of me are the rest of the class.
22. It is the responsibility of we students to make the class lively.
23. I am simply trying to make my point more clear.
24. Twelve months are a long time to wait.
25. My favorite pet is the dog who has floppy ears.

Chapter

12

EDITING AND PROOFREADING

PUNCTUATION
    LINKING PUNCTUATION
    SEPARATING PUNCTUATION
    ENCLOSING PUNCTUATION
    PUNCTUATION INDICATING OMISSIONS

MECHANICS
    CAPITALIZATION
    ITALICS
    ABBREVIATIONS AND CONTRACTIONS
    NUMBERS

SPELLING

PUNCTUATION

The following chart demonstrates at a glance the fundamental principles of sentence punctuation; it is followed by a brief summary of the main points of punctuation usage.

1. Sentence. Sentence.
2. Main clause; main clause.
3. Main clause: main clause.
4. Main clause, $\begin{Bmatrix} \text{and} \\ \text{or} \\ \text{but} \\ \text{for} \\ \text{nor} \end{Bmatrix}$ main clause.
5. Main clause; $\begin{Bmatrix} \text{so that} \\ \text{therefore} \\ \text{however} \\ \text{then} \end{Bmatrix}$ main clause.
6. Main clause subordinate clause.
7. Subordinate clause, main clause.
8. Introductory word or phrase, main clause.
9. Main clause subordinate clause; main clause.
10. Main clause; subordinate clause, main clause.

As you can see, the rules of punctuation are neither numerous nor complicated. They must be adhered to *with exactness,* however, for as linguist Harold Whitehall has pointed out, "The traditional purpose of punctuation is to symbolize by means of visual signs the patterns heard in speech" (119). In other words, punctuation marks do the work of vocal inflections in conveying critical distinctions in meaning, as between "He's a great guy!" and "He's a great guy?"

Punctuation marks serve readers in much the same way that road signs serve drivers: they let readers know where they are and keep them moving in the right direction. Whitehall has noted (119) that the most important function of punctuation is "to make grammar graphic" and that it fulfills this function in four ways:

1. by *linking* parts of sentences and words

   semicolon
   colon
   dash
   hyphen

2. by *separating* sentences and parts of sentences

   period
   question mark
   exclamation point
   comma

3. by *enclosing* parts of sentences

paired commas
paired dashes
paired parentheses
paired brackets
paired quotation marks

4. by *indicating* omissions

apostrophe
omission period or dot
triple periods or dots

Let us consider each of these marks in its turn.

Linking Punctuation

Use a Semicolon (;)

1. To link main clauses that could otherwise occur as separate sentences, especially if they are parallel in structure and emphasis:

I insisted on a camping trip; no other vacation interested me.

2. To link main clauses joined by a conjunctive adverb (for example, *moreover, therefore, indeed, also, instead, likewise, meanwhile, hence, nevertheless, consequently*):

I mailed in a deposit; however, I received no reply.

3. To link word groups when one or more contains heavy internal punctuation:

My department chairman, John Webster, plans to travel through most of southern Europe; through all of the Near East; and, if he has the time, along the northern, western, and southern coasts of Africa.

Caution: Do not use a semicolon to introduce a list or to set off a dependent clause from an independent clause.

According to Whitehall, the semicolon distributes emphasis more or less equally between the preceding and following statements; whereas the colon throws emphasis forward toward the following statement.

Use a Colon (:)

1. To introduce a summary or a list; generally the introductory clause should be a main clause:

He carried a suitcase filled with books: the plays of Shakespeare, the novels of George Eliot, the poems of Keats, the essays of Montaigne, and the collected cartoon strips of Charles Schulz.

2. To introduce an extended quotation (use a comma if the quotation is a single sentence or part of a sentence):

> He said: "I cannot begin to think about returning home. My work is barely under way; in fact, today I had my first chance to examine the data. The preliminary findings are certainly promising."

3. To introduce a formal statement or question:

> The committee met to consider a sobering question: What shall we do if the president resigns?

Caution: Do not use a colon to introduce a list that is a complement or an object of the verb of the sentence, or which is the object of a preposition.

NOT   The ingredients are: tomato paste, onions, garlic, and green pepper.

BUT   The ingredients are tomato paste, onions, garlic, and green pepper.

NOT   Many breeds of dogs were represented at the show such as: dachshunds, poodles, cocker spaniels, and dobermans.

BUT   Many breeds of dogs such as dachshunds, poodles, cocker spaniels, and dobermans were presented at the show.

Use a Dash (—)

1. To introduce a final clause that summarizes, explains, amplifies, or provides an unexpected addition to what has gone before.

> Freedom of speech, freedom of worship, freedom from want, freedom from fear—these form the foundation of a democratic state.
> He was modest, shy, simply dressed—and absolutely obsessed with the subject of sex.

2. To indicate a break in thought or in speech:

> Periodically—I'd say about every two months—he writes me to ask for a loan. I—I don't know what to say.

3. To stress or reinforce an idea:

> She was good—too good.

4. To indicate several referents of a pronoun if the pronoun is the subject of a summarizing clause.

> Wolfe, Faulkner, and Joyce—these were the writers he took as his models.

Whitehall explains that the dash, unlike the anticipatory colon, throws the reader's attention back to the original statement.

Word processing note: On a typewriter, it is customary to indicate a dash by typing two hyphens (--). Many computer programs and printers, however, are capable of printing a true dash. (On Macintosh computers, for example, holding down the option and shift keys while striking the hyphen key produces a true dash.) Consult your computer documentation to use this more professional-looking option.

Use a Hyphen (-)

1. To designate compound words or to separate certain prefixes and suffixes from their root words:

brother-in-law	self-government
six-year-old	ex-governor
five-story	governor-elect
soft-spoken	great-grandfather

Since usage varies and is often divided, consult a current dictionary of your choice.

2. To indicate continuation of a word divided at the end of a line. (Always check the dictionary to make certain you are dividing the word where the syllables break.)

3. To link the elements of compound numbers from twenty-one to ninety-nine and to link the elements of fractions:

sixty-eight dollars
two-thirds of a nation

4. To link nouns or modifiers which are being used in a compound sense:

It was a well-run school.
The year-end dinner-dance was a great success.
There were cradle-to-grave benefits.
Her reasons were all-too-human.

Many formerly hyphenated words have become fused into single units, such as *seaweed* and *bookkeeper.* Where there is no precedent, the best policy is to hyphenate when you feel that hyphenation will make your meaning clearer.

Separating Punctuation

Use a Period (.)

1. To separate declarative subject-predicate sentences (including mild commands) from sentences that follow. One can *hear* the end of a declarative sentence, for there is a distinct drop in the voice from high to low pitch:

The lake is light blue.
Do not be late.

2. To conclude a statement that may not be in conventional subject-predicate form but which clearly falls in pitch and thereby generates a pause:

The more, the merrier.

Use a Question Mark (?)

1. To separate questions and quoted questions from their following context. Because the grammatical meaning of the question mark is "answer needed," it should be used to indicate all forms of query:

> Did she say that?
> She said what?
> Can you pass the course? is the main question.
> He asked me, "Are you leaving tonight?"

2. To express more than one query in the same sentence:

> Did she say that? or you? or who?

Use an Exclamation Point (!)

1. To separate exclamatory sentences expressing surprise, incredulity, admiration, or other strong emotion from their following context:

> How lovely!
> What a surprise!
> I can't believe it!
> O Lord, save thy people!

Use a Comma (,)

1. To separate elements in a sentence that might cause confusion or fail to make sense if considered in combination:

> Instead of hundreds, thousands came.
> To Mary, Clark was very friendly.
> What the answer is, is hard to say.
> Out of every hundred, fifty were rejected.

2. To separate main clauses that are joined by a coordinating conjunction (*and, but, or, nor, for*);

> She attended all the lectures, but she could not get to the laboratory sessions.

3. To separate introductory words, phrases, or dependent clauses from the main clause and thereby to facilitate reading:

> Luckily, she arrived in time.
> Up to that time, she had never taken a math course.
> Before gathering shells, we went for a swim.
> Although he intended no harm, his behavior created chaos in the classroom.

4. To separate coordinate adjectives and words, phrases, and clauses in a series:

> The rich, bright, penetrating sound of the organ filled the cathedral with the complex harmonies of a Bach fugue.

They wanted bread, cheese, salami, and wine.
He looked after the baby, cleaned, and cooked.
After looking through my desk, after phoning the lost and found office, after questioning everyone in the building, I finally found my notebook.
I came, I saw, I conquered.[1]

5. To set off nonrestrictive[2] or parenthetical words, phrases, or clauses in a sentence:

The financial risk, he reported, was enormous.
Chapter One, which deals with definition, serves as an introduction to all forms of discourse.
But: The chapter that deals with definition serves as an introduction to all forms of discourse. (No comma is necessary here because the clause *that deals with definition* is restrictive—that is, essential to identify the chapter being referred to.)

6. To set off words or phrases in apposition:

That man, the owner of the bookstore, will never reduce his prices.

7. To set off works or phrases in contrast:

He needs sympathy, not anger.

8. To set off absolute expressions:

The course having ended, the students prepared to leave the campus. (nominative absolute)
Indoors or out, tennis is a healthful sport. (absolute phrase)
Well, let's get started. (mild interjection)
We don't have a chance, do we? (echo question)

9. To indicate the omission of an "understood" verb in a compound sentence:

Byron was a poet; Beethoven, a composer.
My brother lives in New Jersey; my sister, in New York.

10. To set off a noun or phrase in direct address:

Madame President, the vote has been counted.

11. To set off *yes* and *no* when used at the beginning of a sentence:

No, I cannot leave the building.

---

[1]When a complete predication is made in two or three words, or when the predications form a unit of expression (such as a proverb or familiar saying), commas may be used in place of periods or semicolons.
[2]Restrictive modifiers are essential to the meaning of a sentence: The professor who had taken off her glasses answered the question. (That is, among others this particular professor, the one who removed her glasses, answered the question.) Nonrestrictive modifiers are not essential but merely elaborate; they could be eliminated without altering the basic meaning of the sentence: The professor, who had taken off her glasses, answered the question. (That is, the professor who answered also—and incidentally—removed her glasses.)

12. To separate a direct quotation from its context:

    "I cannot go," she told him.

13. To separate elements in dates and place names:

    She was born December 15, 1954, in Sioux City, Iowa, and lived there for ten years.

14. To separate initials or the abbreviations of academic degrees from the rest of a sentence:

    Brown, J.S., and Jones, B.D., are listed in the student directory.
    Thomas Hale, M.D., and James Hale, D.D.S., will open their clinic next week.

Do *Not* Use a Comma

1. To separate compound predicates or pairs of words, phrases, or dependent clauses joined by a coordinating conjunction:

    She was born in Sioux City and lived there for ten years.
    Do you want cake or pie?
    I tried to call or to come as quickly as possible.
    Students who want to pass the course but who are unable to grasp basic concepts must attend review sessions.

2. To separate main clauses.

3. To separate two nouns, one of which identifies the other; in such cases the appositive is so closely related to the noun as to be considered a part of it:

    The booklet "Fixing Furniture" is on the coffee table.
    My sister Jane leaves for school on Monday.
    Carter's boat *The Nautilus* will be ready in June.

4. To separate an appositive that is part of a name:

    I remember reading about Richard the Lion-Hearted.

5. To separate an appositive that contains several words in a series, punctuated by commas; in such instances use dashes instead:

    We looked for them—John, Harry, Jim, and Kate—for almost four hours.

6. To separate the month and year in a date:

    The bridge was opened in June 1960.

Enclosing Punctuation

Enclosing punctuation consists of paired commas, dashes, parentheses, brackets, and quotation marks, all of which "are used to enclose elements outside the main structure of a sentence. They represent a triple scale of enclosure, in which paired commas enclose elements most closely related to the main thought of the sentence and parentheses those elements least closely related" (Whitehall, 128). Paired dashes enclose elements whose connection falls between the two extremes of closeness. Brackets are essentially a special kind of parentheses, and quotation marks are used mainly to enclose direct reports of spoken words.

Use Paired Commas (, . . . ,)

1. To enclose nonrestrictive sentence elements—that is, elements that are not essential because they do not identify the word they modify, but merely add information about it:

> The boat, which was red, sank under the first wave.
> *But:* The boat that we built ourselves sank under the first wave.

2. To enclose interpolated or transitional words or phrases:

> The truth, as a matter of fact, is none of your business.
> Your report, I conclude, is based on secondary sources.
> That notion, however, has no basis in fact.

Use Paired Dashes (—. . .—)

1. To enclose elements that are not as closely related to the main thought of the sentence as are those contained within paired commas, but not as incidental to the main thought as are those within parentheses:

> My subject—related to anthropology, yet not strictly anthropological—concerns a tribe of New Zealanders now almost extinct.

In general, dashes emphasize the parenthetical material more than commas do; parentheses, less.

2. To provide emphasis or suspense:

> She said—and she must have known it all along—that he had won first prize.

3. To mark a sudden break or abrupt change in thought:

> If I fail the boards—which heaven forbid!—I will have to take them again next year.
> He said—and no one could contradict him—that the dates had been miscalculated.

4. To replace paired commas when the enclosed word group contains heavy comma punctuation:

> A representative from each department—English, History, Zoology, Political Science, Anthropology, and Psychology—attended the meeting.

Use Parentheses (. . .)

1. To enclose material clearly not part of the main thought of the sentence, and not a grammatical element of the sentence, yet important enough to be included:

   > The standard Austen text (based on a collation of the early editions by R.W. Chapman) should be cited in the footnotes.

2. To enclose an explanatory word or phrase that is not part of the main statement:

   > The unconscious (not to be confused with the subconscious) was definitively explored by Sigmund Freud.

3. To enclose references and directions:

   > The data (see Chart 13) indicate that the incidence of polio is decreasing.

4. To enclose the numbering elements of a series:

   > The aims of the new party were (1) to gather together local dissidents; (2) to formulate common goals; and (3) to promote these goals through political activism.

5. To enclose figures repeated to ensure accuracy:

   > Enclosed is fifty dollars ($50.00) to cover the cost of our tickets.

Use Brackets [. . .]

1. To insert additions or comments in a quoted passage:

   > "She [Edith Wharton] addressed herself to the novel of manners."
   > She testified that she had, as she put it, "never seen the man in her life [I actually saw them together in the cafeteria last week] nor even heard his name spoken."

2. To enclose *sic,* indicating that an error in a quotation has been noted but not changed:

   > "Zelda Fitzgerald's *Save Me the Waltz* was published in 1934 [*sic*]."

3. To indicate parentheses within parentheses:

   > The general impression of the central Washington topography is that of a land scoured by a powerful geologic scrub-brush (hence the term "channelled scablands" [Bush, personal interview, 1970]).

Use Quotation Marks (". . .")

1. To enclose direct quotations (use paired single quotation marks to enclose a quotation within a quotation):

   > The reply was a firm "Yes."
   > Jim said, "I am leaving," but she refused to believe him.

"When I asked her to come home," he explained, "she told me, 'Never again'."

2. To enclose technical terms used in a nontechnical context:

His tendency to "disassociate" suggested a possible psychological disorder.

3. To enclose terms used in an idiomatic or deprecatory sense, such as hackneyed expressions, slang, sarcasm (such usage should be sparing):

The "reward" was a ten-dollar fine.
She appeared to think it was "the thing to do."

4. To enclose words used as words (an alternative is to italicize or underscore such words):

How hot is "hot"?

5. To enclose titles of essays, short stories, short poems, chapters of a book, newspaper and magazine articles:

I suggest that you read Milton's "Lycidas."
Is Dorothy Parker's "The Waltz" really about a waltz?

Remember the proper positioning of quotation marks:

1. Quotation marks are always used *in pairs;* for every opening quotation mark, there must be a closing one.

2. Quotation marks always go outside commas and periods:

She said, "Let's go now," and then I heard a crash.
She heard someone say, "The party is over."

3. Quotation marks always go inside semicolons and colons:

He told me plainly, "It was all your fault"; but I knew better.
She wanted to "pack them all up": the books, the furniture, the equipment.

4. Quotation marks may go inside or outside the question marks and exclamation points, depending on the intended meaning:

He asked me, "Where are my books?" (The question mark applies only to the quotation.)
Did he really say, "Those are my books"? (The question mark does not apply to the quotation, but rather to the whole sentence.)
But: Did he really ask you, "Where are my books?" (A second question mark is not used after the quotation mark.)
He said, "What a great book!" (The exclamation point applies only to the quotation.)
How wonderful it was to hear him say, "You have passed the course"! (The exclamation point does not apply to the quotation, but rather to the whole sentence.)

Punctuation Indicating Omissions

Use an Apostrophe (')

1. To indicate contractions or omitted letters:

   > you've (you have)
   > o'clock (of the clock)
   > it's (it is)

2. To form plurals of letters, figures, symbols, and words used as words:

   > She received three *A*'s.
   > Her *e*'s and *l*'s look alike.
   > The beginning writer has trouble making *8*'s.
   > His *and*'s are usually *&*'s.

3. To indicate the possessive case of nouns and pronouns:

   a. Add *'s* to form the possessive case of all singular nouns:

   > cat's, girl's, man's lady's, Jones's, Keats's, Dickens's

   When a noun ends in an *s* sound, the option exists of adding only an apostrophe, omitting the second *s*. In such instances be sure to place the apostrophe *after* the *s* that is part of the noun:

   > Keats' *or* Keats's (not *Keat's*)
   > Jones' *or* Jones's (not *Jone's*)
   > James' *or* James's (not *Jame's*)

   The choice of which form to use depends on how it sounds (does "Dickens's novels" *sound* better to your ear than "Dickens' novels"?) Whenever the addition of an *s* creates real difficulty in pronunciation, add only the apostrophe:

   > Aristophanes', Mars', mistress'

   b. Add an apostrophe alone to form the possessive of most plural nouns:

   > boys', hats', sailors', musicians'

   Nouns that end in *s* in the singular must add *es* for the plurals; to form the possessive, place the apostrophe after the final *s:*

   > The Joneses' books are for sale.
   > Ladies' hats are on the fourth floor.

   The relatively few plurals that do not end in *s* must add *s* to form the possessive:

   > people's, men's, women's, children's, oxen's, mice's

   c. Add *'s* to the final word of compound nouns:

   > secretary-treasurer's report

brother-in-law's room (singular possessive)
brothers-in-law's rooms (plural possessive)

d. Add *'s* only to the last noun to show joint possession in a series of nouns:

soldiers and sailor's home
Tom, Dick, and Harry's apartment

e. Add *'s* to each noun to show separate possession in a series of nouns:

Tom's, Dick's, and Harry's apartments

f. Add an apostrophe or *'s* to the last component of an indefinite pronoun:

somebody else's desk
others' classes

4. To indicate the omission of initial centuries in dates:

the class of '45

Do *Not* Use an Apostrophe

1. To form the possessive of personal pronouns:

his, hers, theirs, its, whose

Do not confuse the possessive pronoun *its* with the contraction *it's* ("it is"):

Its wing is broken.
It's a broken wing.

Similarly, do not confuse the possessive pronoun *whose* with the contraction *who's* ("who is"):

Who's on the telephone?
Whose telephone should I use?

2. To form plurals of spelled-out numbers and of words that already contain an apostrophe:

threes and fours
a list of don'ts

Do add *'s*, however, if it makes the plural easier to read:

which's and *that's*

3. After words ending in *s*, such as names of countries and other organized bodies that are more descriptive than possessive.

United Nations Assembly
United States policy
merchants market

4. To form the simple plural of a noun:

The Smiths and Joneses arrived late. (*Not* The Smith's and Jones's arrived late.)

Use an Omission Period or Dot (.)

1. To indicate abbreviation:

   Mr. L. B. Matthews
   B.A., M.S., M.D., Ph.D.
   R.F.D.
   U.S.

   When a sentence ends with an abbreviated word, use only one period to punctuate both the abbreviation and the sentence:

   Please send my packages C.O.D.

Do *Not* Use an Omission Period

1. After Roman numerals:

   III   IV   XXX

2. With abbreviated names of well-known government agencies, labor organizations, and the like:

   NIH (National Institute of Health)
   UMW (United Mine Workers)
   OPEC (Organization of Petroleum Exporting Countries)

Use Triple Periods or Dots, Called Ellipses (. . .)

1. To indicate omission of words or phrases from a quoted text:

   "On the other hand, when Marx the reformer spoke, . . . we get a wholly different conception of the function of the theory and of its claim to truth."
   "The ultimate aim is to bring about a more intelligent use of language. . . ."
   (The first period punctuates the sentence, and the last three periods indicate the omission of the words that followed in the original text.)

2. To indicate omission in content, in order to leave something to the reader's imagination or to create an atmosphere (use sparingly to avoid a mannered effect):

   They rowed on . . . past the meadow . . . past the old decaying castle . . . on and on they rowed.

MECHANICS

Capitalization

1. Capitalize the first word of every sentence of a direct quotation, and generally, of each line of a poem.

2. Capitalize all proper nouns—the names of persons, places, and official organizations:

> Dwight Eisenhower
> Beijing, China
> Union Station (but: *the railroad station in Washington*)
> British Commonwealth: the Commonwealth (but not when used in a general sense: *a commonwealth of nations*)
> Bureau of the Census; the Census Bureau (but not when used in a general sense: *the census bureau in Laurel*)

3. Capitalize the names of specific geographic locations and features:

> the North Atlantic states, the East, the South (but not when used merely to indicate direction or position: *north, south, east, west*)
> the Promised Land
> the Continent (but not when merely descriptive: *continental boundaries*)

4. Capitalize days, months, holidays, historic events (but not seasons):

> Monday, January, Fourth of July, War of 1812, spring, summer, fall, winter

5. Capitalize titles of all books—literary works, official publications, documents, formal acts and treaties:

> *The Oxford Companion to English Literature* (do not capitalize prepositions, conjunctions, or articles within a title)
> *American Journal of Science*
> Treaty of Ghent

6. Capitalize specific school courses and all language courses or references to languages (but not general subject areas: math, science, literature):

> Survey of English Literature

7. Capitalize titles preceding names and the names of offices when they are used as titles:

> Doctor Perez (but not an occupation itself: *doctor, engineer, chemist*)
> Ambassador George (but not when used in a general sense: *ambassador-at-large*)
> President Lincoln (*President* is always capitalized when it precedes the name of a president of the United States: President Kennedy; the term is *not* capitalized when used in a general sense: *the president of the United States; the president of a college*)

Italics Use Italics (Underline):

1. To indicate the titles of books, plays, newspapers, magazines, paintings, sculpture, the names of ships and aircraft:

> *Madame Bovary, Othello,* the *Boston Globe, The New Yorker,* the *Mona Lisa,* the *Queen Mary,* the *Spirit of St. Louis*

2. To indicate foreign words and phrases:

> *ad hoc*
> *ad infinitum*
> *madre*
> *bonjour*
> *savoir-faire*
> *Zeitgeist*

Many foreign words and phrases become completely assimilated into English and may be printed roman, rather than italic.

> papier-mâché
> en route
> ibid.

3. To indicate words or phrases used as words or phrases (quotation marks may be used instead of underlining, but whichever form you use, be consistent throughout):

> How hot is *hot*?
> He said *honey* so many times that it began to sound like a nonsense word.

Abbreviations and Contractions

Abbreviations should be avoided except where convention specifically dictates their usage. Contractions, a form of abbreviation whereby an apostrophe replaces an omitted letter (you're for you are), should also be avoided except in dialog or in informal essays, where contractions provide the more relaxed and natural tone suitable for such writing.

Abbreviations may be used to designate

1. Established titles and degrees:

> Mr., Mrs., Ms., B.A., Ph.D.

2. Time:

> It was 4:30 A.M.

3. Established organizations or agencies:

> UNESCO, CIA, CARE

4. Certain standard foreign phrases:

> i.e. (that is)
> e.g. (for example)
> etc. (and so on)

Numbers

Although usage varies somewhat, the following is a reasonably reliable guide to the use of numbers.

1. Use numbers for dates, street addresses, telephone and social security numbers and the like, chapters of a book, decimals, percentages, and fractions (in a mathematical context; see item 5, below):

> January 22, 1970, or 22 January, 1970 (not *January 22nd*);
> Chapter 14
> .12 or 0.12
> 12 percent
> ¼, ⅓ (not *¼th, ⅓rd*)

2. Use numbers to indicate measurement or weight:

> The room was 14×12 feet.
> She weighed 115 pounds.

3. Use numbers in a sentence containing a series of figures:

> He calculated the following totals: 18, 14, 12, 19, and 15.

4. Use numbers to indicate time, always adding A.M. or P.M.:

> The meeting adjourned at 4:15 P.M.

5. Use words when no more than two words are required to pronounce a figure:

> twelve, forty-two, nine thousand, one-half, ten million
> Jane is twenty years old.

6. Use numbers when more than two words are required to pronounce a figure:

> $10.86; 9,842; 354

7. Never begin a sentence with a number:

> Twelve students were reported missing. (not *12 students . . .*)
> In 1912 he had his first success. (not *1912 marked . . .*)

SPELLING

Because English spelling is not only not phonetic but also exasperatingly irregular, we must trust to memory and to the clear mental picture of words that most of us gain during our many years of schooling and independent reading. There are many intelligent people, however, who simply cannot retain the image of the correct spelling of a word. Whatever the reason for this inability, a simple prescription is in order: A dictionary or comparable word guide must always be kept within easy reach. There is no overemphasizing the importance of accurate spelling. So strong is the concern about spelling in American schools and in society at large that anything less than complete accuracy tends to brand the writer as careless and unreliable, if not subliterate.

In addition to consulting a dictionary regularly, you may find it helpful to study the following list of commonly misspelled words in order to check your memory and reinforce correct practice.

Commonly Misspelled Words

absence	exorbitant	parceled
accommodate	friend	peculiar
all right	fulfilled	persistent
already	governor	persuade
analogous	grammar	polluted
appalled	grievous	possession
apparatus	guarantee	preceding
argument	harass	preferable
ascendance	height	preferred
balance	independent	prejudice
believe	ingenious	principal (compare *principle*)
benefited	interpretation	privilege
breath (compare *breathe*)	interruption	questionnaire
capital (capitol)	irresistible	quite (compare *quiet*)
cemetery	its (compare *it's*)	receive
changeable	judgment	recommend
choose (compare *chose*)	likable	recurrence
committed	loneliness	referring
consensus	lose	relevant
correspondent	maintenance	repetition
defensible	mathematics	resemblance
definite	miscellaneous	reverence
dependent	mischievous	rhyme
desirable	misspell	seize (compare *siege*)
development	movable	separate
devise (compare *device*)	necessary	similar
disappearance	neighbor	stationary (compare *stationery*)
disastrous	ninety	succeed
dissension	noticeable	than (compare *then*)
effect (compare *affect*)	occasionally	their (compare *there*)
embarrass	occurrence	tyranny
environment	occurred	whose (compare *who's*)
exaggerate	offense	your (compare *you're*)
exhilarate	ommitted	
existence	parallel	

EXERCISES

1. Revise the following opening paragraphs taken from narrative essays. Tighten sentences by combining them and by getting rid of excess verbiage.

   a. It was cool, refreshing evening, and highly welcomed after a long, tedious day of sightseeing in the humid city of Budapest. The sky was cloudy and a sweet fragrance of rain was in the air. The city was calm and peaceful.

   b. It was a typical late August day, the sun was shining bright but the air was dry. You could almost sense Autumn was coming and with Autumn, another school year. For me, it was my first, as I was going into first grade. I was excited about starting school and I couldn't stop talking about it. I needed many things for school: pencils, paper and erasers. Since I was going to be a student, I needed a pair of nice shoes. My birthday was in a few days so my Grandmother bought me an early present. The shoes were Hushpuppy loafers, the kind that didn't have any laces. I was so proud of them that I wanted to show all my friends the shoes as soon as we got home from the store.

   c. It was a very dark and rainy night when we set out to a destination unknown. We had heard that there was to be a very big party near one of our neighboring schools. My two friends and myself got off to a late start from home. It was about 11:30 when we finally started out for the party. We only had a general idea of where the party was being held. One of my friends was driving, I was in the passenger seat, and my other friend was in the back seat. The car was a yellow Fiat.

2. Edit the following paper, written by a student at Drew University, focusing on such specific features as title, introduction and conclusion, overall organization, paragraph division and organization, paragraph development, sentence structure, and choice of words. Is the essay clear? Unified? Coherent? Does it flow smoothly and gracefully? What needs to be deleted, added, or repositioned? Try to assess the strengths of this paper; then note and diagnose weaknesses. Finally, revise and rewrite so as to produce a distinctly improved piece.

TEENAGE SUICIDE

The teenage years present considerable stress, due to the adolescent's search for psychological identity and independence. Preparation for a new social role as an adult also heightens his/her vulnerability to suicidal tendencies which are manifested in depression.

Adolescents may not recognize feelings of unhappiness in themselves. Signs of depression can go unnoticed "until matters erupt in some acute, overcrisis," according to Adele D. Hoffman, M.D. Even if depression is recognized, it can be difficult to help. Few resources exist where young people can seek guidance when they cannot confide in their parents. It is also difficult for teenagers to ask for help because they would be admitting to personal weaknesses or deficiencies.

Contributing factors to adolescent suicide include conflicts involving the family. As teenagers become more independent from their parents, they take on

more demanding responsibilities which they may not be able to cope with. Lack of communication leads to frustration because the teen has not voiced his opinion or has not been understood. Moreover, the loss of a family member, through death or even divorce, may also cause a great deal of hardship. The home may be an unhappy place altogether, and it may place burdens on the adolescent, leading to suicide.

Boredom also leads to suicide. The adolescent may be unhappy with his lifestyle especially when he cannot find ways to improve it. The youth must have a willingness to try new things, otherwise the boredom will lead to desperate and helpless feelings.

School places academic and social pressures on the troubled adolescent with which he may not be able to cope with. Since school is such an integral part of a teenager's life, the teenager must be able to face these pressures. Classmates cause problems for the adolescent, in and out of school. If a teen is turned on to drugs by his friends, his physical well-being will suffer for it. If the adolescent is involved in a relationship that breaks up, feelings of guilt and rejection will be hard to handle effectively. These mental pressures could lead to suicide.

In general, suicide is a very complex and important problem. The pressures caused by today's society have increased the number of teenage suicides. In order to correct this, people have to recognize the anguish of adolescents and try to understand them. In turn, adolescents need to be more open with their problems with the people who can help them.

3. Copy over the following sentences, correcting inappropriate punctuation and capitalization and providing appropriate punctuation and capitalization where necessary.

  1. I checked before I left to make sure I had everything I would need; books, paper, pencil, eraser.
  2. The winners are: Judy Brand from El Paso, Jeffery Phelan from Denver, Murray Mitchell from Atlanta.
  3. I asked her to go with me, but did not insist.
  4. The book is neither Fredericks' nor mine, could it be Charles'?
  5. William Carlos Williams, citizen of New Jersey, physician, poet, often referred to his native state and his profession in his poetry.
  6. How much activity about women's rights have we seen in the last few years?
  7. The woman was adamant in saying that the Smith's had been out of town that week.
  8. I plan to register for spring semester during the fall pre-registration period.
  9. I am a little wary of taking the history of renaissance england next term but I feel fairly confident that I will do well in second year german.
  10. Blake walked up to the soldier and said "What do you think you are doing in my garden?
  11. Do you agree that Dostoyevsky is the greatest Russian novelist.

Continued

12. Your insurance premium has been overdue for three months consequently we are forced to cancel your policy.
13. On May 22 1978 he wrote that threatening letter.
14. If you arrive after eight o'clock you will not be admitted.
15. The title of that book is the psychology of learning.
16. She kept staring into his blue slightly exophthalmic eyes as if mesmerized.
17. Walking down the street with Prof. Alden I told him of my plans for graduate school.
18. Norman Wood was born in Coventry England educated at King's College Cambridge and is now Professor of History at the University of Chicago.
19. Does the suspect own a gun is the crucial question.
20. Winning it seems is knowing when to quit losing is more a matter of overstaying your luck.
21. Nothing is to be gained by arguing with him the situation can only be worsened by doing so.
22. After listening to Ellen David June and I decided to vote for the proposition.
23. Easy come easy go.
24. When the truck hit Jeremy Martin shouted at the driver.
25. 13 is my lucky number.

WORKS CITED

Addison, Joseph. "Recreation." *The Spectator.* No. 115, 12 July 1711.

Bass, Paul B. *A Complete Critical Outline of Don Quixote.* Boston: Student Outlines, 1957. 32–33.

Bernstein, Theodore. *The Careful Writer.* New York: Atheneum, 1965.

Blair, Hugh. *Lectures on Rhetoric and Belle Lettres:* Brooklyn: Thomas Kirk, 1812.

Boulton, Marjorie. *The Anatomy of Prose.* London: Routledge and Kegan Paul, 1954.

Burke, Kenneth. *A Grammar of Motives and a Rhetoric of Motives.* Cleveland: World, 1962.

Charlton, James, ed. *The Writer's Quotation Book: A Literary Companion.* New York: Penguin, 1981.

Christensen, Francis. "A Generative Rhetoric of the Sentence." *Notes Toward a New Rhetoric.* New York: Harper, 1967.

_____. "Symposium on the Paragraph." *College Composition and Communication,* 17 (1966): 60–88.

_____, and Bonniejean Christensen. *A New Rhetoric.* New York: Harper, 1976.

Davis, Robert Gorham. "Logic and Logical Fallacies." *Harvard Handbook for English.* Cambridge: Harvard University Press, 1947.

Elbow, Peter. *Writing Without Teachers.* New York: Oxford University Press, 1973.

Evans, Bergan and Cordellia. *Dictionary of Contemporary American Usage.* New York, 1957.

Francis, Nelson W. "Revolution in Grammar." *Quarterly Journal of Speech.* Oct. 1954.

Gardner, John. *Excellence.* New York: Harper, 1961.

Girdansky, Michael. *The Adventures of Language.* Rev. and ed. by Mario Pei. New York: Fawcett, 1967.

Gowers, Sir Ernest. *The Complete Plain Words.* Rev. Sir Bruce Fraser. London: Her Majesty's Stationery Office, 1973.

Gunther, John. *Inside Asia.* New York: Harper & Row, 1942.

Hall, Donald. *Writing Well.* Boston: Little, 1976.

Huppe, Bernard F. and Jack Kiminsky. *Logic and Language.* New York: Knopf, 1956.

Lask, Thomas. "Publishing." *New York Times.* 21 Dec. 1979.

Lobsenz, Norman. *Writing as a Career.* New York: Henry Z. Walck, 1963.

Lord, John. *The Paragraph: Structure and Style.* New York: Holt, 1964.

Lucas, F. L. *Style.* New York: Macmillan, 1962.

Moffett, James. "Writing, Inner Speech, and Meditation." *College English* 14, No. 3 (1982): 231.

Orwell, George. *Shooting an Elephant and Other Essays.* New York: Harcourt, 1950.

Partridge, Eric. *A Dictionary of Clichés.* New York: Dutton, 1963.

Podhoretz, Norman. *Making It.* New York: Random, 1968.

Potter, Stephen. *Our Language.* London: Books, Ltd., 1950.

Progoff, Ira. *Depth Psychology and Modern Man.* New York: Julian, 1959.

Read, Herbert. *English Prose Style.* Boston: Beacon, 1955.

_____. *Modern Prose Style.* Boston: Beacon, 1952.

Rico, Gabriele L. *Writing the Natural Way: Using Right-Brain Techniques to Release Your Expressive Powers.* Los Angeles: Tarcher, 1983.

Ruby, Lionel. *The Art of Making Sense.* Philadelphia: Lippincott, 1968.

Schulz, Charles M. "But a Comic Strip Has to Grow." *Saturday Review,* 12 April 1969: 73–74.

Strunk, William, Jr. and White, E. B. *The Elements of Style,* 3rd ed. New York: Macmillan, 1979.

Whately, Richard. *Elements of Rhetoric.* Boston and Cambridge: James Monroe, 1854.

Whitehall, Harold. *Structural Essentials of English.* New York: Harcourt, 1956.

Williams, Craig B. and Allan H. Stevenson. *A Research Manual.* New York: Harper, 1963.

Young, Richard E., Alton L. Becker, and Kenneth Pike. *Rhetoric: Discovery and Change.* New York: Harcourt, 1970.

PERMISSIONS

Jamaica Kincaid, "Coming to Antigua" from *A Small Place* by Jamaica Kincaid. Copyright © 1988 by Jamaica Kincaid. Reprinted by permission of Farrar, Straus & Giroux, Inc.

Martin Luther King, Jr., "Three Types of Resistance to Oppression" from *Stride Toward Freedom* by Martin Luther King, Jr. Copyright © 1958 by Martin Luther King, Jr. Copyright © 1986 by Coretta Scott King, Yolanda King, Dexter King, Martin Luther King, III, Bernice King. Reprinted by permission of Harper & Row, Publishers, Inc.

Martin Luther King, Jr. "Letter from Birmingham Jail" from *Why We Can't Wait* by Martin Luther King, Jr. Copyright © 1963, 1964 by Martin Luther King, Jr. Reprinted by permission of Harper & Row, Publishers, Inc.

Maxine Hong Kingston, "Uncle Bun" from *China Men* by Maxine Hong Kingston. Copyright © 1980 by Maxine Hong Kingston. Reprinted by permission of Alfred A. Knopf, Inc.

Francine Klagsbrun, "What Really Makes a Marriage Work" from *Married People: Staying Together in the Age of Divorce* by Francine Klagsbrun. Copyright © 1985 by Francine Klagsbrun. Used by permission of Bantam Books, a division of Bantam Doubleday Dell Publishing Group, Inc.

Jonathan Kozol. "The Equality of Innocence" from *Savage Inequalities* by Jonathan Kozol. Copyright © 1991 by Jonathan Kozol. Reprinted by permission of Crown Publishers, Inc.

Christopher Lee, "How I Learned a New Way to Write" from *Faking It* by Christopher Lee. Reprinted by permission of Christopher Lee & Rosemary Jackson: *Faking It: A Look Into the Mind of a Creative Learner* (Boynton/Cook Publishers Inc., Portsmouth, NH, 1992).

John Leonard, "Review of *A Weave of Women*" from *The New York Times,* July 25, 1978. Copyright © 1978 by The New York Times Company. Reprinted by permission.

Primo Levi, "A Small Cause" from *Moments of Reprieve,* trans. by Ruth Feldman. Translation copyright © 1979, 1981, 1982, 1983, 1986 by Summit Books, a division of Simon & Schuster, Inc. Copyright © 1981, 1985 by Giullo editore s.p.a. Reprinted by permission of Summit Books, a division of Simon & Schuster, Inc.

Paule Marshall, "The Poets in the Kitchen" from *New York Times Book Review,* Jan. 9, 1983.

Katinka Matson, "Sylvia Plath: A Short Life" from *Short Lives* by Katinka Matson. Published by William Morrow & Co.

Paul Monette, "Sifting Through the Evidence" from *Becoming A Man: Half A Life Story* by Paul Monette. Copyright © 1992 by Paul Monette, reprinted by permission of Harcourt Brace & Company.

Paul Monette, "Here" from *Love Alone: Eighteen Elegies for Rog.* © 1988.

Jan Morris, "The Latest Fashion in Travel." Reprinted by permission of The Julian Bach Literary Agency, Inc. Copyright © 1981 by Jan Morris.

Seth Mydans, "Giving Voice to Hurt and Betrayal" from *The New York Times,* May 2, 1993. Copyright © 1993 by The New York Times Company. Reprinted by permission.

Gloria Naylor, "A Question of Language" from *Multitude.* Reprinted by permission of Sterling Lord Literistic, Inc. Copyright © 1993 by Gloria Naylor.

Bill Neal, "Southern Fried Chicken with Country Gravy" from *Bill Neal's Southern Cooking,* Revised and Enlarged Edition, by Bill Neal. Copyright © 1989 by Bill Neal. Published by the University of North Carolina Press. Reprinted by permission.

Peggy Noonan, "Why We Dream About the Stars" from *Dial* Magazine, January 1987.

Merrill Pannitt, "Review: *Discover—The World of Science*" from *TV Guide,* November 5, 1988. Reprinted with permission from TV Guide® Magazine. Copyright © 1988 by News America Publications Inc.

Sylvia Plath, "Winter Trees" from *Winter Trees* by Sylvia Plath. Copyright 1963; 1972 by Ted Hughes. Reprinted by permission of Harper & Row, Publishers, Inc.

Anna Quindlen, "Erin Go Brawl" from *Thinking Out Loud* by Anna Quindlen. Copyright © 1993 by Anna Quindlen. Reprinted by permission of Random House, Inc.

Anna Quindlen, "The Great White Myth" from *Thinking Out Loud* by Anna Quindlen. Copyright © 1993 by Anna Quindlen. Reprinted by permission of Random House, Inc.

Terrence Rafferty, "Predators" (Review of *Jurassic Park*). Reprinted by permission; © 1993 Terrence Rafferty. Originally in *The New Yorker.* All rights reserved.

David Randolph, "Five Basic Elements of Music" from *This is Music* by David Randolph. Reprinted by permission of the author.

James Reston, "The Paradox of the Sixties" from *The New York Times,* Dec. 21, 1969. Copyright © 1969 by The New York Times Company. Reprinted by permission.

Matthew Rindfleisch, "Ireland: When Economic and Cultural Agendas Collide." Reprinted by permission of the author.

Richard Rodriguez, "Becoming an American" from *Days of Obligation: An Argument with My Mexican Father* by Richard Rodriguez. Copyright © 1992, Viking Penguin.

Carl Rogers, "Communication: Its Blocking and Its Facilitation." Reprinted from *Et Cetera,* Vol. IX, no. 2 by permission of the International Society for General Semantics.

Mike Rose, "The Skills of Liberal Learning" from *Lives on the Boundary: The Struggles and Achievements of America's Underprepared* by Mike Rose. Reprinted with the permission of The Free Press, a Division of Macmillan, Inc. Copyright © 1989 by Mike Rose.

A. M. Rosenthal, "No News From Auschwitz" from *The New York Times,* August 31, 1958. Copyright © 1958 by The New York Times Company. Reprinted by permission.

Bertrand Russell, "A Definition of Philosophy" from *A History of Western Philosophy*. Reprinted by permission of The Bertrand Russell Peace Foundation, Ltd.

David Schwartz, "Crazy About Weather Vanes: One Man's Breezy Obsession" from *Travel and Leisure,* April 1984.

Subhabrata Bapi Sen, "Village Home." Reprinted by permission of the author.

Ravi Shankar, "Studying Music in India" from *My Music, My Life* by Ravi Shankar. Copyright © 1968 Kinnara School of Indian Music, Inc. Reprinted with permission.

George B. Shaw, "On Experimenting with Animals" excerpted from Preface to *The Doctor's Dilemma* by George Bernard Shaw. Reprinted by permission of The Society of Authors Ltd.

Richard Shepard, "A Word for the New York Accent" from *The New York Times,* Nov. 5, 1966. Copyright © 1966 by The New York Times Company. Reprinted by permission.

John Simon, "Shakespeare's Most Riddling Creation— A Review of *Shylock: A Legend and its Legacy*" by John Simon. Originally published in *The Atlantic Monthly,* June 1993. Reprinted by permission of Atlantic Monthly.

Theodore Sorensen, "Writing and Rewriting the Inaugural Address" from *Kennedy* by Theodore Sorensen. Copyright © 1965 by Theodore Sorensen. Reprinted by permission of Harper & Row, Publishers, Inc.

Wole Soyinka, "The School at Ake" from *Ake: The Years of Childhood* by Wole Soyinka. Copyright © 1981 by Wole Soyinka. Reprinted by permission of Random House, Inc.

Jonathan Spence, "The Earthquake" from *The Death of Woman Wang* by Jonathan Spence. Reprinted by permission of the Peters Fraser & Dunlop Group Ltd.

Ann Squire, "Animal Research: An Unnecessary Evil?" by Ann Squire, in *ASPCA Report.* Fall/Winter 1986. Reprinted by permission of ASPCA Report.

George Stade, "Football—The Game of Aggression" from *Game Theory* by George Stade. Reprinted from *The Columbia Forum,* Fall 1966, Volume IX, Number 4. Copyright 1966 by The Trustees of Columbia University in the City of New York. Reprinted by permission.

R. W. Stallman, "An Interpretation of e. e. cummings's 'anyone lived in a pretty how town' " from *The Creative Reader,* Second Edition, by R. W. Stallman and R. T Watters. Copyright © 1962, The Ronald Press Company, New York. Reprinted by permission of John Wiley & Sons, Inc., and R. W. Stallman.

Hilary Stout, "Why College Students Should Take a 'Sabbatical' " from *The New York Times,* Nov. 14, 1982. Copyright © 1982 by The New York Times Company. Reprinted by permission.

Judy Syfers, "Why I Want a Wife." Reprinted from *Ms. Magazine* by permission of the author.

Dylan Thomas, "Do Not Go Gentle into That Good Night" from *Poems of Dylan Thomas* by Dylan Thomas. Copyright 1952 by Dylan Thomas. Reprinted by permission of New Directions Publishing Corporation.

Lewis Thomas, "The Tucson Zoo" from *The Medusa and the Snail* by Lewis Thomas. Copyright © 1977 by Lewis Thomas. All rights reserved. Reprinted by permission of Viking Penguin, a division of Penguin Books USA, Inc.

Lewis Thomas. "On Speaking of Speaking" from *Late Night Thoughts on Listening to Mahler's Ninth* by Lewis Thomas. Copyright © 1983 by Lewis Thomas. Used by permission of Viking Penguin, a division of Penguin Books USA Inc.

Alice Walker, "Remembering Mr. Sweet" from *Living By the Word.* Appeared in *New York Times Book Review,* May 8, 1988, Copyright © 1988 by The New York Times Company. Reprinted by permission.

Florence L. Wazl, "Interpretation of Joyce's 'Clay' " from *The Explicator,* February, 1962. Reprinted with permission of the Helen Dwight Reid Educational Foundation. Published by Heldref Publications, 1319 Eighteenth St., N.W., Washington, D.C., 20036-1802. Copyright © 1962.

Shirley Weissenborn, "How to Run for Office in a Very Small Town." Originally appeared in the Madison, NJ *Eagle.*

Cornel West, "Race Matters" from *Race Matters* by Cornel West. Copyright © 1993 by Cornel West. Reprinted by permission of Beacon Press.

Elizabeth M. Whelan and Frederick J. Stare, M. D., "Sweet Truths About Sugar" from *The One Hundred Percent Natural, Purely Organic, Cholesterol-Free, Megavitamin, Low-Carbohydrate Nutrition Hoax* by Elizabeth M. Whelan and Frederick J. Stare. Reprinted with the permission of Atheneum Publishers.

E. B. White, "Death of a Pig" from *Essays of E. B. White* by E. B. White. Copyright © 1956 by E. B. White. Reprinted by permission of Harper & Row, Publishers, Inc.

E. B. White, "Democracy" from *The Wild Flag* by E. B. White, published by Houghton Mifflin Company. © 1943, 1971 E. B. White. Originally published in *The New Yorker.*

INDEX

A

abbreviations, 663
absolutes, 628
abstracts, 518, 519
accurate word, the 609-612
active voice, 623
ad hominem argument, 444
Addison, Joseph, 324
adjectives, 624-625
Adler, Jerry, 340
"An Afternoon in Cleveland" (Kenan), 114-116
Agassiz, Louis, 19-20
Agee, James, 104
"All the Facts (Some True) About Gondolas" (Harris),
    203-208
almanacs, 515
American Psychological Association (APA), documenta-
    tion style, 538, 539, 541-542
analogy, 440-441
"Animal Research: An Unnecessary Evil?" (Squire),
    446-447
"Another School Year—What For?" (Ciardi), 231-234
"anyone lived in a pretty how town" (cummings),
    394-395
    interpretation of, 395-397
APA. *See* American Psychological Association
apostrophes, 659-660
argument
    checklist for, 461
    structure of, 433-434
Aristotle, xxxv, 5-6, 456
Asimov, Isaac, 215
"At the Dam" (Didion), 179-181
atlases, 516
Auden, W. H., 229
audience, 28-29
Auschwitz (death camp), 219, 293, 357-358
auxiliaries, 622

B

Baker, Russell, 150
Ballou, Sullivan, 183
Barton, Anne, 415
Berenbaum, Michael, 219
Bible, xxxiii
bibliography, 539
biographical sources, 513-514
Blair, Hugh, 585, 591, 592, 595-596, 599, 603-604
Boerner, Deborah A., 194
"Boy Meets Girl, Boy Loses Girl, Man Gets Woman"
    (Hamill), 117-119
brackets, 657
brainstorming, 15-16
Branagh, Kenneth, 415-423

Brandmayr, Ron, Jr., 216
Brautigan, Richard, 397
Broner, E. M., 405-407
Brown, Rita Mae, 281
Burke, Kenneth, xxix, 21
    "Pentad," 21-22

C

capitalization, 661-662
Capote, Truman, 116, 120
catalogs, card, 508-512
Catton, Bruce, 337
Chapman, R. L., 351
Chicago Manual of Style, Fourteenth Edition, 536
Christensen, Francis, 563, 565, 567, 569, 570,
    571, 573
Christian, Doug, 268
Ciardi, John, 67, 231
Cicero, 6
classification, 320, 321-322, 324
clauses, 628-629
"Clay" (Joyce), 388-392
    interpretation of, 392-394
clichés, 458-461, 589-590
Clinton, Bill, 458
clustering, 24-26
Cohen, I. Bernard, 486
Cole, Kenneth, 384
"College Lectures Are Obsolete" (Gilbert), 430-433
colons, 650-651
"Coming to Antigua" (Kincaid), 94-98
commas, 653-655
    paired, 656
    splices, 640
"Communication: Its Blocking and Its Facilitation"
    (Rogers), 469-473
Compaine, Benjamin, 309
"Composing a Ballet" (DeMille), 260-261
compound/complex sentences, 580-584, 630
"Computers and the New Literacy" (Compaine),
    309-312
computers, in research and writing, 41, 309-312, 507
concrete word, the, 609
conjunctions, 626-627
connectives, 625-627
    weak, 646
connotative word, the, 615-616
contractions, 663
coordinate sequence, 563-564
Coupland, Douglas, 247
"Crazy About Weather Vanes" (Schwartz), 182-183
"Creating an American" (Rodriguez), 262-265
Crichton, Michael, 413, 414
cummings, e. e., 394, 395

D
dashes, 651-652
    paired, 656
Davis, Mike, 314
deadwood words and expressions, 589-590
"Death Be Not Proud" (Donne), 350
"Death of a Pig" (E. B. White), 167-172
deduction, 436-439
"A Definition of Philosophy" (Russell), 212
DeMille, Agnes, 260
"Democracy" (E. B. White), 222
Dewey Decimal System (figure), 509
Diamond, Jared, 477
Dickens, Charles, 93
dictionaries, 514
Didion, Joan, 179
"Do Not Go Gentle into That Good Night" (Dylan
    Thomas), 350
Donne, John, 350
Dorsey, Thomas A., 340-344
"Dream Deferred" (Hughes), 329

E
"The Earthquake" (Spence), 100-101
editing, 66
editorial, newspaper, 455
Elbow, Peter, 10-11
The Elements of Style (Strunk and White), xxxiii
ellipses, 661
encyclopedias, 512-513
endnotes, 539
"Erin Go Brawl" (Quindlen), 185-186
essays
    factual, 193
    personal, 179
evaluating
    books, 404-411
    films, 412-423
    television shows, 424
Evans, Walker (photograph), 402. *See also* Agee, James
"Everything Has a Name" (Keller), 163-164
exclamation mark, 653
"The Expanding Universe" (Hawking), 199-201

F
feature story, 202
Feibleman, Peter, 347
"Fences" (Rooney), 37-38
Fielding, Henry, 92-93
figurative word, the, 613-615
"The First Girl at Second Base" (Jacoby), 359-361
"Five Basic Elements of Music" (Randolph), 254-255
Flaubert, Gustave, xxxii, 595
"Football—The Game of Aggression" (Stade), 382-383
Foote, Shelby, 124
footnotes, 539
Fordham, Freida, 320
Forster, E. M., 312
fragments, sentence, 639

Francis, W. Nelson, 214
Frederick, Jim, 230
freewriting, 11-13
fresh word, the, 612-613
fused sentences, 640-641

G
Geisel, Theodore. *See* Seuss, Dr.
"A Generation Under Curfew" (Davis), 314-318
"A Generation Without a Name" (Howe and Strauss),
    247-250
"Generation X," 247
Gibbon, Edward, xxxv
Gilbert, Allan H., 430
"Giving Voice to Hurt and Betrayal" (Mydans), 363-366
Gleick, James, 216
government publications, 519-520
"Grant and Lee: A Study in Contrasts" (Catton),
    337-340
"The Great White Myth" (Quindlen), 441-443
Greenberg, Douglas, 236
Gregory, Dick, 122
"The Gumbo Battle" (Feibleman), 347-349

H
Hall, Donald, 66
"Hallowed Be the Mall" (Cole), 384-388
Hamill, Pete, 117
Harris, MacDonald, 203
Harris, Nicole, 434
Harris, Sidney J., 220
Hawking, Stephen, 199
Henry, Patrick, xxxii
"Here" (Monette), 351-352
"Here Is the Jersey Tomato" (Boerner), 194-196
heuristics, 7
Holt, John, 325
"Honky-Tonking" (Ivins), 398-399
Hook, Sidney, 461
"How I Learned a New Way to Write" (Lee),
    265-267
"How to Lose Weight Sensibly and Successfully and
    Permanently" (Kaplan), 280-281
"How to Run for Office in a Very Small Town"
    (Weissenborn), 278-280
"how-to" writing, 276
Howe, Neil, 247
Hughes, Langston, 329
"A Humane and Scientific Necessity" (Robert White),
    449-454
Huxley, T. H., 269
hyphens, 652

I
In Cold Blood (Capote), 116, 120
"In Defense of Voluntary Euthanasia" (Hook),
    461-463
in-text notes, 538-539
Inaugural Address (Clinton), 458-461

Inaugural Address (Kennedy), 73-75
  about, 75-78
induction, 436-437, 440
"Inequalities in Education" (Kozol), 201-202
"Interpretation of e. e. cummings' 'anyone lived in a
      pretty how town'" (Stallman), 395-397
"Interpretation of James Joyce's 'Clay'" (Walzl), 392-394
"Ireland: When Economic and Cultural Agendas Clash"
      (Rindfleisch), 549-556
is and *ought* propositions, 429-430
"Isaac Newton" (Cohen), 486-490
italics, 662-663
Ivins, Molly, 397-398

J, K
Jacoby, Susan, 359
Jordan, Suzanne, 345
journal, as writing tool, 18
Joyce, James, 388, 392
"Jung's Psychological Types" (Fordham), 320-321
Jurassic Park, 412-415
"The Just: The Brave Christians Who Saved Jews from
      the Nazis" (Wiesel), 152-155
Kaplan, Norman, M.D., 280
Kazantzakis, Nikos, 112
Kazin, Alfred, 133
Keller, Helen, 161-163
  photograph, 162
Kenan, Randall, 114
Kennedy, John F., xxxiv, 72-78
Kincaid, Jamaica, 94
King, Martin Luther, Jr., 322-324, 490-502
  photograph, 332
"The Kingdom of Didd" (Seuss), 98
Kingston, Maxine Hong, 140
Klagsbrun, Francine, 251
Korean-Americans, 363-366
Kozol, Jonathan, 201

L
"The Latest Fashion in Travel" (Morris), 361-363
Lee, Christopher, 265
Leonard, John, 405
"Letter from Birmingham Jail" (King), 491-502
"Letter to Sarah" (Ballou), 183-184
Levi, Primo, 293
library use, in research, 507-512
"The Limitations of 'Holocaust'" (Berenbaum), 219
Lincoln, Abraham, xxxiv
linking verbs, 623
logical fallacies, 443-445

M
Marshall, Paule, 136
Marshall, Thurgood, 340-344
Matson, Katinka, 144
misplaced modifiers, 641-642
mixed construction, 642-643

mixed sequence, 568-571
MLA. *See* Modern Language Association
Modern Language Association, documentation style,
      538, 539-540, 543
"The Molly Maguire Movement" (Rammel), 543-547
"Mommy, What Does 'Nigger' Mean?" (Naylor),
      222-224
Monette, Paul, 173, 351
Mood, verb, 624
"Moonrise Over Monument Valley" (Young), 99-100
Morris, Jan, 361
Munch, Edvard (print), 305
"My Mother" (Kazin), 133-136
"My Wood" (Forster), 312-314
Mydans, Seth, 363

N
"National Holidays Unite Us" (Greenberg), 236-239
natural word, the, 608-609
Naylor, Gloria, 222
Neal, Bill, 276
"A Night in a Calabrian Village" (Kazantzakis), 112-114
"No News from Auschwitz" (Rosenthal), 357-358
non sequitur, 444-445
Noonan, Peggy, 299
"Not Poor, Just Broke" (Gregory), 122-124
notes, 527-528
numbers, 663-664

O, P
Oh, Angela, 363-366
omission period (dot), 661
"On Experimenting with Animals" (Shaw), 448-449
"On Speaking of Speaking" (Lewis Thomas), 290-293
online research, 508
order
  intuitive, 36-37
  logical, 35
  natural, 35
Orkin, Ruth (photograph), 367
Orwell, George, 51-52, 587, 608
Panitt, Merrill, 424
"The Paradox of the Sixties" (Reston), 378-380
paragraph, patterns in, 562-573
paraphrase, 528-529, 536
parentheses, 657
Parker, Dorothy, xxxi
"Pentad" (Burke), 21-22
periodical indexes and abstracts, 518-519
periods, 652
photocopying, 532
"Pickett's Charge" (Foote), 124-127
Podhoretz, Norman, 50
"Politics and the English Language" (Orwell), 608
plagiarism, 532-533
Plath, Sylvia, 144-150, 397
  photograph, 144
poetry, comparing and interpreting, 350-351, 394-397

"The Poets in the Kitchen" (Marshall), 137-140
"Predators" (Rafferty), 412-415
predicates, 622-627
preposition, 625-626
prepositional phrase, 627
pre-writing, xxxi
"The Prim Mr. Fleagle" (Baker), 150-152
pronoun-antecedent agreement, 632-634
pronoun case, 634-635
Publication Manual of the American Psychological Association, 538
punctuation, 649-661
    enclosing, 655-658
    linking, 650-652
    omissions, 659-661
    separating, 652-655
purpose, in writing, xxxvi

Q, R
"The Quality of Memory" (Wolfe), 160-161
question mark, 653
Quindlen, Anna, 185, 441
quotation marks, 657-658
quotation, direct, 528, 536-537. *See also* paraphrase
"Race Matters" (West), 370-374
Rafferty, Terrence, 412
Rammel, Melody, 543
Randolph, David, 254
Readers' Guide to Periodical Literature, 526
reader-writer relationship, 31-34
reference books
    general, 512-516
    subject-specific, 516-517
"Remembering Mr. Sweet" (Walker), 302-303
Research strategies, 520-525
Reston, James, 378
"Review of *A Weave of Women,* by E. M. Broner" (Leonard), 405-407
Review of *Discover: The World of Science* (Pannitt), 424-425
revising, guidelines for, 66-68
revision strategies, 68-72
"Rhetorical Stance of David Randolph in 'Five Basic Elements of Music,'" 256
Rindfleisch, Matthew, 549
Rodriguez, Richard, 262
Rogerian strategy, 456-458
Rogers, Carl, xxx, 456
Rooney, Andy, 37
Rose, Mike, 245
Rosenthal, A. M., 357
Russell, Bertrand, 212

S
"The School at Aké" (Soyinka), 101-103
Schulz, Charles, 506
Schwartz, David M., 181-182
The Scream (Munch), 305

semicolons, 650
Sen, Subhabrata Bapi, 164
sentence fragments, 649
sentence types, 629-630
Seuss, Dr., 98
"Shady Grove, Alabama, 1936" (Agee), 104-106
"Shakespeare in the Sun" (Barton), 415-423
"Shakespeare's Most Riddling Creation" (Simon), 407-412
"Shame on Ads that Use Culture to Sell Liquor" (Harris), 435-436
Shankar, Ravi, 44-45
Shaw, George Bernard, 447-448
Shepard, Richard, 455
shifts, unnecessary, 643-644
"Shootin' the Bull" (Christian), 268-269
Shylock: A Legend and Its Legacy (Gross), 407-414
"Sifting Through the Evidence" (Monette), 173-175
Simon, John, 407
"The Skills of Liberal Learning" (Rose), 245-247
"A Small Cause" (Levi), 293-295
Sorenson, Theodore, 75-78
sources, citing, 525-533, 536-537
"Southern Fried Chicken with Country Gravy" (Neal), 276-278
Soyinka, Wole, 101
"Speaking with a Single Tongue" (Diamond), 477-485
spelling, 664-665
Spence, Jonathan, 100
Spielberg, Steven, 412-414
splits, unnecessary, 645
Squire, Ann, 445-446
Stade, George, 382
Stallman, R. W., 395
Stare, Frederick J., M.D., 196
Stout, Hilary, 296
Strauss, Bill, 247
Strunk, William, Jr., xxxiii
"Studying Music in India" (Shankar), 44-45
subject, of sentence, 621
subject-verb agreement, 631
subordinate sequence, 565-568
summarizing
    events, 378
    ideas, 370, 536
    plots, 376-378
summary, 530-532, 536
"Sweet Truths About Sugar" (Whelan and Stare), 196-198
Syfers, Judy, 186
"Sylvia Plath: A Short Life" (Matson), 144-150

T
talking to self and others, as writing aid, 13-15
"That Lean and Hungry Look" (Jordan), 345-346
"Their Amazing Grace" (Adler), 340-344
"Thinking Scientifically" (Huxley), 269-270
Thomas, Dylan, 350

Thomas, Lewis, 234, 290
"Three Kinds of Discipline" (Holt), 325-327
"Three Meanings of Grammar" (Francis), 214-215
"Three Types of Resistance to Oppression" (King), 322-324
Thurber, James, xxxi
"Timor Mortis Conturbat Me" (Chapman), 351
topic sentence, 571
transitional devices, 561-562
"The Tucson Zoo" (Lewis Thomas), 234-236
twenty questions for the writer (list), by essay type, 8

U, V
"Uncle Bun" (Kingston), 140-144
"Universe and *University"* (Asimov), 215-216
verbal phrase, 628
verbs, 522-623
"Verbs, *or,* Put the Pedal to the Metal" (Brown), 282-284
"Village Home" (Sen), 165-166
voice, active and passive, 623

W
Walker, Alice, 302
Walzl, Florence L., 392
"We Are, Like, Poets" (Frederick), 230-231
Weissenborn, Shirley, 278
West, Cornel, 370, 374-376
"What Is Chaos?" (Gleick), 216-218

"What Is the Function of a Critic?" (Auden), 229-230
"What Makes a 'Jerk' a Jerk?" (Harris), 220-221
"What *Really* Makes a Marriage Work" (Klagsbrun), 251-254
"What the Word *Liberal* Used to Mean" (Brandmayr), 216
Whelan, Elizabeth, 196
"When You Gotta Go" (Capote), 120-121
White, E. B., xxxiii, 38, 52, 56, 67, 70, 166-167, 222
White, Robert J., 449
"Why College Students Take a Sabbatical" (Stout), 296-299
"Why I Want a Wife" (Syfers), 186-188
"Why We Dream About the Stars" (Noonan), 299-301
Wicker, Tom, 334, 336
Wiesel, Elie, 152
"Winter Trees" (Plath), 397
Wolfe, Thomas, 16, 160
"A Word for the New York Accent" (Shepard), 455-456
word processors. *See* computers
word selection, 607-616
"Writing and Rewriting the Inaugural Address" (Sorenson), 75-78

X, Y, Z
Yearbooks, 515
Young, John V., 99
"Your Departure versus the Hindenburg" (Brautigan), 397